# ORGANIZATIONAL PSYCHOLOGY

# Critical Concepts in Psychology
also available in this series

*Personality*

Edited with a new introduction by Cary L. Cooper and Lawrence A. Pervin
4 volume set

*Brain and Behaviour*

Edited with a new introduction by Jules Davidoff
4 volume set

*Psycholinguistics*

Edited with a new introduction by Gerry Altman
6 volume set

Forthcoming:

*Memory*

Edited with a new introduction by Jackie Andrade
4 volume set

*Social and Emotional Development*

Edited with a new introduction by William M. Bukowski, Brett Laursen and Kenneth Rubin
4 volume set

*Psychology of Ageing*

Edited with a new introduction by Patrick Rabbitt
4 volume set

# ORGANIZATIONAL PSYCHOLOGY

Critical concepts in psychology

*Edited by Jo Silvester*

**Volume I
The Meaning and Impact of Work**

Routledge
Taylor & Francis Group
LONDON AND NEW YORK

First published 2008
by Routledge
2 Park Square, Milton Park, Abingdon, Oxon, OX14 4RN, UK

Simultaneously published in the USA and Canada
by Routledge
270 Madison Avenue, New York, NY 10016

*Routledge is an imprint of the Taylor & Francis Group,
an informa business*

Editorial material and selection © 2008 Jo Silvester;
individual owners retain copyright in their own material

Typeset in Times New Roman by Keyword Group Ltd.
Printed and bound in Great Britain by
TJI Digital, Padstow, Cornwall

All rights reserved. No part of this book may be reprinted or reproduced or utilised in any form or by any electronic, mechanical, or other means, now known or hereafter invented, including photocopying and recording, or in any information storage or retrieval system, without permission in writing from the publishers.

*British Library Cataloguing in Publication Data*
A catalogue record for this book is available
from the British Library

*Library of Congress Cataloging in Publication Data*
A catalog record for this book has been requested

ISBN 10: 0-415-40008-2 (Set)
ISBN 10: 0-415-40009-0 (Volume I)

ISBN 13: 978-0-415-40008-4 (Set)
ISBN 13: 978-0-415-40009-1 (Volume I)

**Publisher's Note**

References within each chapter are as they appear in the original
complete work

# CONTENTS

**VOLUME I   THE MEANING AND IMPACT OF WORK**

*Acknowledgements*     xiii
*Chronological table of reprinted articles and chapters*     xvii

**Introduction**     1

**PART 1**
**How people become workers**     9

1  **The psychology of careers in organizations**     11
   JOHN ARNOLD

2  **The people make the place**     48
   BENJAMIN SCHNEIDER

3  **Police socialization: a longitudinal examination of job attitudes in an urban police department**     64
   JOHN VAN MAANEN

4  **Person-organization fit: an integrative review of its conceptualizations, measurement, and implications**     91
   AMY L. KRISTOF

5  **Are career jobs headed for extinction?**     137
   SANFORD M. JACOBY

6  **Violating the psychological contract: not the exception but the norm**     160
   SANDRA L. ROBINSON AND DENISE M. ROUSSEAU

## CONTENTS

7  Is the psychological contract worth taking seriously?  179
   DAVID E. GUEST

### PART 2
### Experiencing work and how work impacts on people  199

8  Organizational psychology and the pursuit of the
   happy/productive worker  201
   BARRY M. STAW

9  The job satisfaction–job performance relationship: a qualitative
   and quantitative review  215
   TIMOTHY A. JUDGE, CARL J. THORESEN, JOYCE E. BONO AND
   GREGORY K. PATTON

10 The measurement and antecedents of affective, continuance
   and normative commitment to the organization  285
   NATALIE J. ALLEN AND JOHN P. MEYER

11 When cashiers meet customers: an analysis of the role of
   supermarket cashiers  306
   ANAT RAFAELI

12 Experiencing work: values, attitudes, and moods  336
   JENNIFER M. GEORGE AND GARETH R. JONES

13 Emotion in the workplace: a reappraisal  358
   BLAKE E. ASHFORTH AND RONALD H. HUMPHREY

14 The measurement of well-being and other aspects of
   mental health  384
   PETER WARR

15 Well-being and occupational health in the 21st
   century workplace  404
   KATE SPARKS, BRIAN FARAGHER AND CARY L. COOPER

16 Working hours and health (Editorial)  427
   CARY L. COOPER

CONTENTS

17 Organizational justice: a fair assessment of the state of the literature 431
JASON A. COLQUITT AND JERALD GREENBERG

## VOLUME II   SELECTING AND DEVELOPING EMPLOYEES

*Acknowledgements* ix

Introduction 1

### PART 3
### How organizations attract, select and recruit employees 5

18 The validity and utility of selection methods in personnel psychology: practical and theoretical implications of 85 years of research findings 7
FRANK L. SCHMIDT AND JOHN E. HUNTER

19 The Big Five personality dimensions and job performance: a meta-analysis 35
MURRAY R. BARRICK AND MICHAEL K. MOUNT

20 Five reasons why the "Big Five" article has been frequently cited 59
MICHAEL K. MOUNT AND MURRAY R. BARRICK

21 The motivation to work: what we know 68
EDWIN A. LOCKE

22 Individual differences in work motivation: further explorations of a trait framework 104
RUTH KANFER AND PHILLIP L. ACKERMAN

23 General mental ability in the world of work: occupational attainment and job performance 117
FRANK L. SCHMIDT AND JOHN HUNTER

24 Why do assessment centers work? The puzzle of assessment center validity 142
RICHARD KLIMOSKI AND MARY BRICKNER

| | | |
|---|---|---|
| 25 | The perceived fairness of selection systems: an organizational justice perspective<br>STEPHEN W. GILLILAND | 159 |
| 26 | Applicants' perceptions of selection procedures and decisions: a critical review and agenda for the future<br>ANN MARIE RYAN AND ROBERT E. PLOYHART | 200 |

## PART 4
## Assessing and developing people at work 247

| | | |
|---|---|---|
| 27 | Performance evaluation in work settings<br>R. D. ARVEY AND K. R. MURPHY | 249 |
| 28 | Perspectives on models of job performance<br>CHOCKALINGAM VISWESVARAN AND DENIZ S. ONES | 277 |
| 29 | Organizational competencies: a valid approach for the future?<br>PAUL SPARROW | 295 |
| 30 | Think manager—think male: a global phenomenon?<br>VIRGINIA E. SCHEIN, RUEDIGER MUELLER, TERRI LITUCHY, AND JIANG LIU | 311 |
| 31 | The science of training: a decade of progress<br>EDUARDO SALAS AND JANIS A. CANNON-BOWERS | 322 |
| 32 | Kirkpatrick's levels of training criteria: thirty years later<br>GEORGE M. ALLIGER AND ELIZABETH A. JANAK | 352 |
| 33 | Transfer of training: a review and directions for future research<br>TIMOTHY T. BALDWIN AND J. KEVIN FORD | 363 |
| 34 | Application of cognitive, skill-based, and affective theories of learning outcomes to new methods of training evaluation<br>KURT KRAIGER, J. KEVIN FORD AND EDUARDO SALAS | 405 |

| 35 | Building a learning organization | 444 |

DAVID A. GARVIN

## VOLUME III  ENHANCING PERFORMANCE IN ORGANIZATIONS

| *Acknowledgements* | vii |
| *Introduction* | 1 |

### PART 5
### Individual and group performance          5

| 36 | Does the transactional–transformational leadership paradigm transcend organizational and national boundaries? | 7 |

BERNARD M. BASS

| 37 | The romance of leadership as a follower-centric theory: a social constructionist approach | 27 |

JAMES R. MEINDL

| 38 | The bases of social power | 40 |

JOHN R.P. FRENCH, JR. AND BERTRAM RAVEN

| 39 | Teams in organizations: recent research on performance and effectiveness | 56 |

RICHARD A. GUZZO AND MARCUS W. DICKSON

| 40 | Sparkling fountains or stagnant ponds: an integrative model of creativity and innovation implementation in work groups | 89 |

MICHAEL A. WEST

| 41 | Frontiers in group dynamics: concept, method and reality in social science; social equilibria and social change | 119 |

KURT LEWIN

| 42 | Cognition and corporate governance: understanding boards of directors as strategic decision-making groups | 161 |

DANIEL P. FORBES AND FRANCES J. MILLIKEN

CONTENTS

43 Social identity and self-categorization processes in
organizational contexts 187
MICHAEL A. HOGG AND DEBORAH J. TERRY

PART 6
**Organizational performance** 219

44 Principles of sociotechnical design revisited 221
ALBERT CHERNS

45 Motivation through the design of work:
test of a theory 230
J. RICHARD HACKMAN AND GREG R. OLDHAM

46 Work control and employee well-being:
a decade review 260
DEBORAH J. TERRY AND NERINA L. JIMMIESON

47 Organizational change and development 311
KARL E. WEICK AND ROBERT E. QUINN

48 Overcoming resistance to change 338
LESTER COCH AND JOHN R.P. FRENCH, JR.

49 Counterproductive behaviours at work 360
ADRIAN FURNHAM AND JOHN TAYLOR

50 What *is* the difference between organizational culture and
organizational climate? A native's point of view on a decade of
paradigm wars 411
DANIEL R. DENISON

VOLUME IV  LOOKING TO THE FUTURE: WORK AND
ORGANIZATIONAL PSYCHOLOGY

*Acknowledgements* ix

**Introduction** 1

# CONTENTS

## PART 7
## Globalization and new technology ... 5

**51 Cross-cultural, social and organizational psychology** ... 7
MICHAEL HARRIS BOND AND PETER B. SMITH

**52 Measuring organizational cultures: a qualitative and quantitative study across twenty cases** ... 39
GEERT HOFSTEDE, BRAM NEUIJEN, DENISE DAVAL OHAYV AND GEERT SANDERS

**53 Managerial competency modelling and the development of organizational psychology: a Chinese approach** ... 73
ZHONG-MING WANG

**54 Internet recruitment and selection: kissing frogs to find princes** ... 92
DAVE BARTRAM

**55 Research on Internet recruiting and testing: current status and future directions** ... 117
FILIP LIEVENS AND MICHAEL M. HARRIS

**56 Applicant and recruiter reactions to new technology in selection: a critical review and agenda for future research** ... 150
NEIL ANDERSON

**57 Call centres** ... 178
DAVID HOLMAN

**58 Managing a virtual workplace** ... 201
WAYNE F. CASCIO

## PART 8
## Next generation thinking ... 217

**59 Organizational behavior in the new organizational era** ... 219
DENISE M. ROUSSEAU

## CONTENTS

60 Organizations of the future: changes and challenges    252
LYNN R. OFFERMANN AND MARILYN K. GOWING

61 The Internet and industrial/organizational psychology: practice and research perspectives    281
MICHAEL M. HARRIS

62 Selecting for change: how will personnel and selection psychology survive?    294
PETER HERRIOT AND NEIL ANDERSON

63 Personnel selection: looking toward the future—remembering the past    329
LEAETTA M. HOUGH AND FREDERICK L. OSWALD

64 Epistemology and work psychology: new agendas    365
PHIL JOHNSON AND CATHERINE CASSELL

65 The practitioner–researcher divide in Industrial, Work and Organizational (IWO) psychology: where are we now, and where do we go from here?    386
NEIL ANDERSON, PETER HERRIOT AND GERARD P. HODGKINSON

66 Any nearer a "better" approach? A critical view    409
KAREN LEGGE

67 Whither industrial and organizational psychology in a changing world of work?    432
WAYNE F. CASCIO

*Index*    457

# ACKNOWLEDGEMENTS

The publishers would like to thank the following for permission to reprint their material:

John Wiley & Sons Ltd. for permission to reprint John M. Arnold, 'The psychology of careers in organizations', in C. L. Cooper and I. T. Robertson (eds), *International Review of Industrial and Organizational Psychology*, Vol. 12, 1997, pp. 1–37. Copyright © 1997 John Wiley & Sons Ltd.

Blackwell Publishing for permission to reprint Benjamin Schneider, 'The people make the place', *Personnel Psychology*, 40, 1987, pp. 437–453.

*Administrative Science Quarterly* for permission to reprint John Van Maanen, 'Police socialization: a longitudinal examination of job attitudes in an urban police department', *Administrative Science Quarterly*, 20, 1975, pp. 207–228. Copyright © 1975, all rights reserved.

Blackwell Publishing for permission to reprint Amy L. Kristof, 'Person-organization fit: an integrative review of its conceptualizations, measurement, and implications', *Personnel Psychology*, 49, 1996, pp. 1–49.

The Regents of the University of California for permission to reprint Sanford M. Jacoby, 'Are career jobs headed for extinction?', *California Management Review*, 42(1), 1999, pp. 123–145. Copyright © 1999, by the Regents of the University of California.

John Wiley & Sons Ltd. for permission to reprint Sandra L. Robinson and Denise M. Rousseau, 'Violating the psychological contract: not the exception, but the norm', *Journal of Organizational Behavior,* 15, 1994, pp. 245–259. Copyright © 1994 John Wiley & Sons Ltd.

John Wiley & Sons Ltd. for permission to reprint David Guest, 'Is the psychological contract worth taking seriously?', *Journal of Organizational Behavior*, 19, 1998, pp. 649–664. Copyright © 1998 John Wiley & Sons Ltd.

## ACKNOWLEDGEMENTS

The Regents of the University of California for permission to reprint Barry M. Staw, 'Organizational psychology and the pursuit of the happy/productive worker', *California Management Review*, 28(4), 1986, pp. 40–53. Copyright © 1986, by the Regents of the University of California.

The American Psychological Association for permission to reprint Timothy A. Judge, Carl J. Thoresen, Joyce E. Bono and Gregory K. Patton, 'The job satisfaction–job performance relationship: a qualitative and quantitative review', *Psychological Bulletin*, 127(3), 2001, pp. 376–407. Copyright © 2001 by the American Psychological Association.

*The Journal of Occupational Psychology* for permission to reprint Natalie J. Allen and John P. Meyer, 'The measurement and antecedents of affective, continuance, and normative commitment to the organization', *Journal of Occupational Psychology,* 63(1), 1990, pp. 1–18. © The British Psychological Society.

The Academy of Management (NY) in the format of Other Book via Copyright Clearance Center for permission to reprint Anat Rafaeli, 'When cashiers meet customers: an analysis of the role of supermarket cashiers', *Academy of Management Journal*, 32(2), 1989, pp. 245–273. Copyright © 1989 by Academy of Management (NY).

Sage Publications Ltd for permission to reprint Jennifer M. George and Gareth R. Jones, 'Experiencing work: values, attitudes, and moods', *Human Relations*, 50(4), 1997, pp. 393–415. Copyright © The Tavistock Institute, London, UK, 1997.

Sage Publications Ltd for permission to reprint Blake E. Ashforth and Ronald H. Humphrey, 'Emotion in the workplace: a reappraisal', *Human Relations*, 48(2), 1995, pp. 97–124. Copyright © The Tavistock Institute, London, UK, 1995.

*The Journal of Occupational Psychology* for permission to reprint Peter B. Warr, 'The measurement of well-being and other aspects of mental health', *Journal of Occupational Psychology*, 63, 1990, pp. 193–210. © The British Psychological Society.

*The Journal of Occupational and Organizational Psychology* for permission to reprint Kate Sparks, Brian Faragher and Cary L. Cooper, 'Well-being and occupational health in the 21st century workplace', *Journal of Occupational and Organizational Psychology*, 74(4), 2001, pp. 489–509. © The British Psychological Society.

Taylor & Francis for permission to reprint Cary L. Cooper, 'Working hours and health', *Work and Stress*, 10(1), 1996, pp. 1–4. www.tandf.co.uk/journals

Lawrence Erlbaum Associates, Inc. for permission to reprint Jason A. Colquitt and Jerald Greenberg, 'Organizational justice: a fair assessment of the state of the literature', in J. Greenberg (ed.), *Organizational Behavior: The State of the Science*, 2003, pp. 165–210.

## Disclaimer

The publishers have made every effort to contact authors/copyright holders of works reprinted in *Organizational Psychology: Critical Concepts in Psychology*. This has not been possible in every case, however, and we would welcome correspondence from those individuals/companies whom we have been unable to trace.

## Chronological table of reprinted articles and chapters

| Date | Author(s) | Title | Source | Vol. | Ch. |
|---|---|---|---|---|---|
| 1947 | Kurt Lewin | Frontiers in group dynamics | *Human Relations*, 1, 5–41 | III | 41 |
| 1948 | Lester Coch and John R. P. French, Jr. | Overcoming resistance to change | *Human Relations*, 1, 512–532 | III | 48 |
| 1959 | John R. P. French, Jr., and Bertram Raven | The bases of social power | D. Cartwright (ed.), *Studies in Social Power*, Ann Arbor, MI: Institute for Social Research, pp. 150–167 | III | 38 |
| 1975 | John Van Maanen | Police socialization: a longitudinal examination of job attitudes in an urban police department | *Administrative Science Quarterly*, 20, 207–227 | I | 3 |
| 1976 | J. Richard Hackman and Greg R. Oldham | Motivation through the design of work: test of a theory | *Organizational Behavior and Human Performance*, 16, 250–279 | III | 45 |
| 1986 | Barry M. Staw | Organizational psychology and the pursuit of the happy/productive worker | *California Management Review*, 28(4), 40–53 | I | 8 |
| 1987 | Albert Cherns | Principles of sociotechnical design revisited | *Human Relations*, 40(3), 153–161 | III | 44 |
| 1987 | Richard Klimoski and Mary Brickner | Why do assessment centers work? The puzzle of assessment center validity | *Personnel Psychology*, 40, 243–260 | II | 24 |
| 1987 | Benjamin Schneider | The people make the place | *Personnel Psychology*, 40, 437–453 | I | 2 |
| 1988 | Timothy T. Baldwin and J. Kevin Ford | Transfer of training: a review and directions for future research | *Personnel Psychology*, 41, 63–105 | II | 33 |

*Continued*

**Chronological table continued**

| Date | Author(s) | Title | Source | Vol. | Ch. |
|---|---|---|---|---|---|
| 1989 | George M. Alliger and Elizabeth A. Janak | Kirkpatrick's levels of training criteria: thirty years later | Personnel Psychology, 42, 331–342 | II | 32 |
| 1989 | Anat Rafaeli | When cashiers meet customers: an analysis of the role of supermarket cashiers | Academy of Management Journal, 32(2), 245–273 | I | 11 |
| 1990 | Natalie J. Allen and John P. Meyer | The measurement and antecedents of affective, continuance and normative commitment to the organization | Journal of Occupational Psychology, 63, 1–18 | I | 10 |
| 1990 | Geert Hofstede, Bram Neuijen, Denise D. Ohayv and Geert Sanders | Measuring organizational culture: a qualitative and quantitative study across twenty cases | Administrative Science Quarterly, 35, 286–316 | IV | 52 |
| 1990 | Lynn R. Offermann and Marilyn K. Gowing | Organizations of the future: changes and challenges | American Psychologist, 45(2), 95–108 | IV | 60 |
| 1990 | Peter Warr | The measurement of well-being and other aspects of mental health | Journal of Occupational Psychology, 63, 193–210 | I | 14 |
| 1991 | Murray R. Barrick and Michael K. Mount | The Big Five personality dimensions and job performance: a meta-analysis | Personnel Psychology, 44, 1–26 | II | 19 |
| 1993 | David A. Garvin | Building a learning organization | Harvard Business Review, 71 (July–Aug.), 78–91 | II | 35 |
| 1993 | Stephen W. Gilliland | The perceived fairness of selection systems: an organizational justice perspective | Academy of Management Review, 18(4), 694–734 | II | 25 |

| 1993 | Kurt Kraiger, J. Kevin Ford and Eduardo Salas | Application of cognitive, skill-based, and affective theories of learning outcomes to new methods of training evaluation | *Journal of Applied Psychology*, 78(2), 311–328 | II | 34 |
| 1994 | Sandra L. Robinson and Denise M. Rousseau | Violating the psychological contract: not the exception but the norm | *Journal of Organizational Behavior*, 15, 245–259 | I | 6 |
| 1995 | Blake E. Ashforth and Ronald H. Humphrey | Emotion in the workplace: a reappraisal | *Human Relations*, 48(2), 97–124 | I | 13 |
| 1995 | Wayne F. Cascio | Whither industrial and organizational psychology in a changing world of work? | *American Psychologist*, 50(11), 928–939 | IV | 67 |
| 1995 | James R. Meindl | The romance of leadership as a follower-centric theory: a social constructionist approach | *Leadership Quarterly*, 6(3), 329–341 | III | 37 |
| 1995 | Paul Sparrow | Organizational competencies: a valid approach for the future? | *International Journal of Selection and Assessment*, 3(3), 168–177 | II | 29 |
| 1996 | Michael H. Bond and Peter B. Smith | Cross-cultural social and organizational psychology | *Annual Review of Psychology*, 47, 205–235 | IV | 51 |
| 1996 | Cary L. Cooper | Working hours and health (Editorial) | *Work and Stress*, 10(1), 1–4 | I | 16 |
| 1996 | Daniel R. Denison | What *is* the difference between organizational culture and organizational climate? A native's point of view on a decade of paradigm wars | *Academy of Management Review*, 21(3), 619–654 | III | 50 |

*Continued*

**Chronological table continued**

| Date | Author(s) | Title | Source | Vol. | Ch. |
|---|---|---|---|---|---|
| 1996 | Richard A. Guzzo and Marcus W. Dickson | Teams in organizations: recent research on performance and effectiveness | *Annual Review of Psychology*, 47, 307–338 | III | 39 |
| 1996 | Amy L. Kristof | Person-organization fit: an integrative review of its conceptualizations, measurement, and implications | *Personnel Psychology*, 49, 1–49 | I | 4 |
| 1996 | Virginia E. Schein, Ruediger Mueller, Terri Lituchy and Jiang Liu | Think manager—think male: a global phenomenon? | *Journal of Organizational Behavior*, 17, 33–41 | II | 30 |
| 1997 | John Arnold | The psychology of careers in organizations | C.L. Cooper and I.T. Robertson (eds), *International Review of Industrial and Organizational Psychology*, Vol. 12, Chichester: John Wiley, pp. 1–37 | I | 1 |
| 1997 | Bernard M. Bass | Does the transactional–transformational leadership paradigm transcend organizational and national boundaries? | *American Psychologist*, 52(2), 130–139 | III | 36 |
| 1997 | Jennifer M. George and Gareth R. Jones | Experiencing work: values, attitudes, and moods | *Human Relations*, 50(4), 393–415 | I | 12 |

## CHRONOLOGICAL TABLE

| 1997 | Peter Herriot and Neil Anderson | Selecting for change: how will personnel and selection psychology survive? | N. Anderson and P. Herriot (eds), *International Handbook of Selection and Assessment*, Chichester: John Wiley, pp. 1–34 | IV | 62 |
| --- | --- | --- | --- | --- | --- |
| 1997 | Edwin A. Locke | The motivation to work: what we know | *Advances in Motivation and Achievement*, 10, 375–412 | II | 21 |
| 1997 | Denise M. Rousseau | Organizational behavior in the new organizational era | *Annual Review of Psychology*, 49, 515–546 | IV | 59 |
| 1998 | R. D. Arvey and K. R. Murphy | Performance evaluation in work settings | *Annual Review of Psychology*, 49, 141–168 | II | 27 |
| 1998 | David E. Guest | Is the psychological contract worth taking seriously? | *Journal of Organizational Behavior*, 19, 649–664 | I | 7 |
| 1998 | Michael K. Mount and Murray R. Barrick | Five reasons why the "Big Five" article has been frequently cited | *Personnel Psychology*, 51, 849–857 | II | 20 |
| 1998 | Frank L. Schmidt and John E. Hunter | The validity and utility of selection methods in personnel psychology: practical and theoretical implications of 85 years of research findings | *Psychological Bulletin*, 124(2), 262–274 | II | 18 |
| 1999 | Daniel P. Forbes and Frances J. Milliken | Cognition and corporate governance: understanding boards of directors as strategic decision-making groups | *Academy of Management Review*, 24(3), 489–505 | III | 42 |
| 1999 | Sanford M. Jacoby | Are career jobs headed for extinction? | *California Management Review*, 42(1), 123–145 | I | 5 |

*Continued*

**Chronological table continued**

| Date | Author(s) | Title | Source | Vol. | Ch. |
|---|---|---|---|---|---|
| 1999 | Deborah J. Terry and Nerina L. Jimmieson | Work control and employee well-being: a decade review | C.L. Cooper and I.T. Robertson (eds) *International Review of Industrial and Organizational Psychology*, Vol. 14, Chichester: John Wiley, pp. 95–148 | III | 46 |
| 1999 | Karl E. Weick and Robert E. Quinn | Organizational change and development | *Annual Review of Psychology*, 50, 361–386 | III | 47 |
| 2000 | Dave Bartram | Internet recruitment and selection: kissing frogs to find princes | *International Journal of Selection and Assessment*, 8(4), 261–274 | IV | 54 |
| 2000 | Wayne F. Cascio | Managing a virtual workplace | *Academy of Management Executive*, 14(3), 81–90 | IV | 58 |
| 2000 | Michael M. Harris | The Internet and industrial/organizational psychology: practice and research perspectives | *Journal of e-Commerce and Psychology*, 1(1), 8–24 | IV | 61 |
| 2000 | Michael A. Hogg and Deborah J. Terry | Social identity and self-categorization processes in organizational contexts | *Academy of Management Review*, 25(1), 121–140 | III | 43 |
| 2000 | Leaetta M. Hough and Frederick M. Oswald | Personnel selection: looking toward the future—remembering the past | *Annual Review of Psychology*, 51, 631–664 | IV | 63 |
| 2000 | Ruth Kanfer and Phillip L. Ackerman | Individual differences in work motivation: further explorations of a trait framework | *Applied Psychology: An International Review*, 49(3), 470–482 | II | 22 |

| | | | | | |
|---|---|---|---|---|---|
| 2000 | Ann Marie Ryan and Robert E. Ployhart | Applicants' perceptions of selection procedures and decisions: a critical review and agenda for the future | Journal of Management, 26(3), 565–606 | II | 26 |
| 2000 | Chockalingam Viswesvaran and Deniz S. Ones | Perspectives on models of job performance | International Journal of Selection and Assessment, 8(4), 216–226 | II | 28 |
| 2001 | Neil Anderson, Peter Herriot and Gerard P. Hodgkinson | The practitioner–researcher divide in Industrial, Work and Organizational (IWO) psychology: where are we now, and where do we go from here? | Journal of Occupational and Organizational Psychology, 74, 391–411 | IV | 65 |
| 2001 | Phil Johnson and Catherine Cassell | Epistemology and work psychology: new agendas | Journal of Occupational and Organizational Psychology, 74, 125–143 | IV | 64 |
| 2001 | Timothy A. Judge, Carl J. Thoresen, Joyce E. Bono and Gregory K. Patton | The job satisfaction–job performance relationship: a qualitative and quantitative review | Psychological Bulletin, 127(3), 376–407 | I | 9 |
| 2001 | Eduardo Salas and Janis A. Cannon-Bowers | The science of training: a decade of progress | Annual Review of Psychology, 52, 471–499 | II | 31 |
| 2001 | Kate Sparks, Brian Faragher and Cary L. Cooper | Well-being and occupational health in the 21st century workplace | Journal of Occupational and Organizational Psychology, 74, 489–509 | I | 15 |
| 2002 | Michael A. West | Sparkling fountains or stagnant ponds: an integrative model of creativity and innovation implementation in work groups | Applied Psychology: An International Review, 51(3), 355–387 | III | 40 |

*Continued*

**Chronological table continued**

| Date | Author(s) | Title | Source | Vol. | Ch. |
|---|---|---|---|---|---|
| 2003 | Neil Anderson | Applicant and recruiter reactions to new technology in selection: a critical review and agenda for future research | *International Journal of Selection and Assessment*, 11(2/3), 121–136 | IV | 56 |
| 2003 | Jason A. Colquitt and Jerald Greenberg | Organizational justice: a fair assessment of the state of the literature | J. Greenberg (ed.), *Organizational Behavior: The State of the Science*, Mahwah, NJ: Erlbaum, pp. 165–210 | I | 17 |
| 2003 | Filip Lievens and Michael M. Harris | Research on Internet recruiting and testing: current status and future directions | C.L. Cooper and I.T. Robertson (eds), *International Review of Industrial and Organizational Psychology*, Vol. 18, Chichester: John Wiley, pp. 131–165 | IV | 55 |
| 2003 | Zhong-Ming Wang | Managerial competency modelling and the development of organizational psychology: a Chinese approach | *International Journal of Psychology*, 38(5), 323–334 | IV | 53 |
| 2004 | Adrian Furnham and John Taylor | Counterproductive behaviours at work | A. Furnham and J. Taylor, *The Dark Side of Behaviour at Work: Understanding and Avoiding Employees Leaving, Thieving and Deceiving*, Basingstoke: Palgrave Macmillan, pp. 83–129 | III | 49 |

| 2004 | Frank L. Schmidt and John Hunter | General mental ability in the world of work: occupational attainment and job performance | *Journal of Personality and Social Psychology*, 86(1), 162–173 | II | 23 |
| 2005 | David Holman | Call centres | D. Holman, T.D. Wall, C.W. Clegg, P. Sparrow and A. Howard (eds), *The Essentials of the New Workplace: A Guide to the Human Impact of Modern Working Practices*, Chichester: John Wiley, pp. 115–134 | IV | 57 |
| 2005 | Karen Legge | Any nearer a 'better' approach? A critical view | D. Holman, T.D. Wall, C.W. Clegg, P. Sparrow and A. Howard (eds), *The Essentials of the New Workplace: A Guide to the Human Impact of Modern Working Practices*, Chichester: John Wiley, pp. 393–412 | IV | 66 |

# INTRODUCTION

> One of the symptoms of approaching nervous breakdown is the belief that one's work is terribly important. If I were a medical man, I should prescribe a holiday to any patient who considered his work important.
>
> Bertrand Russell

An invitation to edit a four-volume series of core readings that 'captures the field' of organizational psychology is both a great privilege and a daunting challenge. Organizational psychology as a discipline has gone from strength to strength since its early days in the immediate post-Second World War period. Those working in organizational psychology have had a tremendous impact on the workplace; producing innovations in work design and people strategies that have resulted in a substantially improved work experience for most employees (at least in the developed countries). Despite Russell's comment, as most adults of working age spend most of their waking hours in some form of paid occupation, work for them is undoubtedly important. Indeed, the consequences of work stretch from health and well-being to pay and status, and affect issues and lives well beyond the workplace. Yet the success of organizational psychologists in generating such a quantity of knowledge and research makes it very difficult to select what can only be a handful of key papers.

So, interpreting Russell as meaning that to take one's own work too seriously brings its own problems, I have taken an unashamedly eclectic approach to deciding which papers to include. No doubt some readers will question the omission of certain papers and the inclusion of others, and I apologize to all those authors whose excellent work I have overlooked. However, my principal aim in bringing this collection of papers together has been to produce a resource that celebrates the rich history and future potential of organizational psychology research and practice. Like many other people I wear several hats in my work life: I look after a postgraduate programme in organizational psychology, I conduct and publish research, and I run an organizational psychology consultancy. In each of these areas I have, at one time or another, been asked to point to an easily accessible resource that provides a one-stop shop for the best of academic thinking in the field.

INTRODUCTION

These four volumes are an attempt to respond to that need. University teachers should be able to recommend their students to this series and know that they will encounter core texts and learning. Similarly, practitioners (and no doubt some academics) who lack time or resources to access key texts will hopefully find this a useful source of learning and inspiration.

Organizational psychology is a broad discipline which has borders with a large number of other academic fields, such as: organizational sociology, business studies, human resource management, individual differences and management science, as well as social, cognitive and health psychology. Consequently it is worth me taking a little time to define the field as it relates to the papers included here. Organizational psychologists (who are variously referred to as occupational, work, or industrial/organizational [IO] psychologists) are 'concerned about the ethical use of psychological theories and techniques and their impact on the well-being and effectiveness of individuals, groups and organizations' (Arnold, Silvester, Patterson, Robertson, Cooper & Burnes, 2005, p. xvii). Organizational psychology is concerned with the way people think, feel and behave in relation to work and organizational contexts, and knowledge areas include: motivation and employee relations, selection and assessment of employees, training, and well-being at work, organizational development and change, appraisal and career development, work design and work safety. These four volumes attempt to capture core readings in these areas.

In general, decisions to include a paper or not have been guided by a number of factors, such as whether the paper has led to new thinking, or had an impact on subsequent research and practice. I have included papers that review important topic areas, and have tried not to rely too heavily on the most recently published research. Several of the papers are classic texts that, despite being nearly sixty years old, provide an important historical perspective on the development of the discipline. Other papers take a more critical or forward-looking perspective, and finally, there are papers that are simply enjoyable to read. My focus for the most part has been on readings that link research with practice and therefore describe studies conducted with people in organizations rather than laboratories.

One of the great opportunities afforded by a project like this is the opportunity to stand back and take a view of the field as a whole. Because organizational psychology has grown so large, most researchers and practitioners tend to focus on a relatively small area, be it selection and assessment or occupational health. Organizational psychology can be viewed as a relatively diverse collection of topic areas that draw on theoretical developments in other fields of psychology such as personality and individual differences. However, organizational psychologists have also been criticized, perhaps unfairly, for failing to develop theories unique to individuals and the workplace. Then again, perhaps organizational psychologists do not spend sufficient time reflecting on what has been achieved and how research and practice from organizational psychology has had an impact on other areas of psychology. These four volumes are an opportunity to revisit paradigms that have defined the field and celebrate the rich history of the field.

INTRODUCTION

A key difference between organizational psychology and other disciplines is that it applies psychological knowledge and theory to the work setting for the most part. Organizational psychologists adopt a scientific approach to identifying psychological constructs that impact reliably on work behaviour, and test theory in real-world settings. The emphasis is less on isolating variables than on understanding how they interact with environmental factors. Not surprisingly, the best research has not relied on undergraduate students in controlled experimental environments; it has involved researchers working in partnership with private, public and not-for-profit organizations to shape studies capable of accommodating the complexity of the workplace. Compared with laboratory research, good organizational psychology studies take more time and a much broader range of skills leading to persuade organizations to participate in research and develop partnerships. These involve being able to shared learning. Organizational psychologists face the challenge of demonstrating that their theories and research have an impact, not only on everyday work behaviour, but also on the effectiveness of organizations as a whole. Whilst this can make conducting good research more difficult, this also means that organizational psychologists have more opportunity than most other psychologists to demonstrate how their work can make a difference to the lives of large numbers of people.

Nevertheless, an opportunity to review the organizational psychology literature also provides a chance to consider what is not there. When I submitted the initial outline for this series I included several topics that have since proven more wishful thinking. Whilst organizational psychologists have been prolific in their output, certain topics have received very little attention: topics that should be studied if we are to consider this discipline a science of the workplace as a whole. Organizational psychology is overwhelmingly dominated by a white, Western, managerial and large organization focus—a discussion that is returned to in Bond and Smith's paper in Volume IV. There is considerably less research on small organizations, voluntary or part-time work and low-paid jobs. Other topics with comparatively little coverage include politics, union membership, and national topics such as worker migration and the impact of terrorism. In general there is very little consideration of work from any other perspective than that defined by and for senior managers. For example, most of the selection and assessment research depends on definitions of jobs and effective work performance provided by managers. I would have liked to include papers on the ethics of organizational psychology research and practice, and what organizational psychologists have to say in relation to child labour or work in developing countries, but there was little to be found. It seems that whilst organizational psychology has been extremely successful in introducing scientific methods and assumptions to the workplace, the time is right to reflect on whether it is a discipline devoted to work as a whole, or simply to a view of work that is important to managers in large corporations. Is it the case that topics such as pay, poverty and economic development should remain the preserve of sociologists and economists, or does organizational psychology have anything to offer?

INTRODUCTION

Hopefully these volumes will spark debate for what is not included, just as much as for what is.

The following are brief descriptions of each of the four volumes.

**Volume I: The Meaning and Impact of Work.** This volume considers how individuals experience work and the impact that it has on their lives more broadly. The first section considers how people become workers, employee socialization, career development and the psychological contract. The second section considers how work influences other areas of their lives. Topics include work–life balance, employee stress and well-being, whether happy or satisfied workers are productive workers, organizational commitment, and the experience of emotion at work.

**Volume II: Selecting and Developing Employees.** The second volume takes an employee-centric approach and concentrates on how organizational psychology has contributed to improvements in employee performance. The first section focuses on how organizations attract, select and recruit employees, and includes articles about the impact of individual differences (e.g. cognitive ability, personality, knowledge, skills and motivational traits) on work performance, and the design and effectiveness of different selection processes. The second section considers strategies for enhancing employee performance once they are in the job. It includes articles on training and development, defining and measuring work performance, and motivating people to perform.

**Volume III: Enhancing Performance in Organizations.** In contrast to the individual focus of the second volume, the third volume focuses on the design of organizational systems and processes capable of enhancing individual and group performance. The first section begins by considering leadership and followership, and the bases of power in organizations. It includes papers on the popularity of team-based work organization and how individuals define themselves in relation to work groups. This section provides a reminder of classic work on group dynamics that has helped to shape the discipline. The second section looks at how organizational environments, culture and the work itself can impact on motivation and worker well-being. It considers how organizations and employees change and the darker side of counterproductive behaviour at work.

**Volume IV: Looking to the Future: Work and Organizational Psychology.** The fourth volume takes a slightly different approach. Rather than focusing on an important area of organizational psychology, it considers how work has changed over the past 10–20 years and the implications for organizational psychology research and practice. The first section considers how developments in technology and communication have generated new ways of working, such as virtual organizations, e-relationships and call centres. There are also papers on globalization, cross-national working, global selection practices, expatriate working, ethical recruitment, and management of staff from different cultures. The second section takes a more critical perspective and includes papers that describe the opportunities afforded by these changes for the evolution of organizational psychology as a discipline.

INTRODUCTION

Before introducing the contents of the first volume I would like to thank all those people who have helped in putting these volumes together, particularly Julia Batova and Madeleine Dipper who have provided immeasurable support in collating materials. Finally, Simon Alexander from Routledge has provided the necessary motivation, and persuasion to enable me to bring this project to fruition. No doubt without him, it would still be in draft form. Thank you!

## Introduction to Volume I

Volume I is concerned with the meaning and impact of work. As such it includes papers that focus on the employee's perspective and how this can impact on organizations as a whole. It begins with a chapter by Arnold (1997) that asks 'What is a career?' and considers how recent changes in the structure of work will influence individuals seeking to navigate their own route through different work experiences. Arnold highlights changing assumptions regarding responsibility for careers. Whereas work and promotion were viewed historically as the preserve of paternalistic organizations, he discusses how individuals are now expected to take responsibility for managing their own careers. The next three papers consider the interaction between employees and the workplace. In a paper taken from his Presidential Address to the Society for Industrial and Organizational Psychology in 1985, Schneider (1987) describes how the kinds of people who work in an organization come to define how the place looks and feels. Schneider proposes an attraction–selection–attrition (ASA) model to explain why organizations are often populated by similar kinds of people. He argues that personality similarity drives the development of organizational culture and behavioural norms. Van Maanen (1975) provides one of only a few studies that combine qualitative and quantitative methodologies. By spending time in a US urban police department he provides a fascinating insight into how new police recruits are socialized to act. Van Maanen found that although recruits entered the training programme highly motivated and committed to the organization, their motivation swiftly decreased. However, police supervisors often perceived less motivated patrol officers as better policemen those who showed initiative were distrusted because they broke group norms. In a more recent paper, Kristof (1996) describes how the concept of person–organization fit can be used to explore how individuals are selected on the basis of compatible values and not simply whether they possess appropriate knowledge and skills. Suggesting that this may be key to retaining a flexible and committed workforce, Kristof draws a distinction between 'supplementary fit' (where an individual possesses similar characteristics to others in that environment) and 'complementary fit' (where an individual's characteristics 'make whole' or fill gaps in the characteristics held by others).

Jacoby's (1999) paper 'Are career jobs heading for extinction?' provides a relatively unusual perspective by including macro-level economic statistics from the US labour market to challenge some of the assumptions about new forms of career. He argues that it is a human tendency to believe that one lives in an exceptional era and draws on these statistics to show that productivity growth at the time the paper was published was actually slower than it was in the two decades after the Second World War. He suggests that we may be too quick to claim that technology developments are accelerating innovation and changes in organizational design and career structures. Jacoby cautions against faddish ways of thinking that may well be prompted by a desire to generate sales on the basis that old methods are redundant.

The next two papers discuss the psychological contract; a topic that has generated considerable interest among researchers and practitioners. Robinson and Rousseau (1994) study the consequences of perceived violations of the psychological contract and argue for an association with increased turnover, and reductions in trust, satisfaction and intention to remain with a company. Guest (1998) takes a more critical perspective and challenges researchers to examine whether the psychological contract stands up to critical scrutiny. He identifies several important challenges to the validity and utility of the psychological contract, but maintains that it is still worth taking seriously—in part because it has the potential to integrate a number of key organizational concepts such as trust and fairness.

The second section of this volume concentrates on papers concerned with how individuals experience work, and the positive and negative consequences that it can have on them. The section begins with a classic article by Staw (1986) which discuses organizational psychology and the pursuit of the happy/productive worker. In simple terms, Staw sets out to demonstrate why it is so difficult to make changes in both worker satisfaction and worker performance. With the aim of promoting a more reasoned and sustainable pursuit of the happy/productive worker, Staw explores the possibility that individuals may vary in their propensity to be satisfied. Importantly, he argues that some individuals are more likely to experience work satisfaction irrespective of situational work cues and challenge. However, Staw argues that despite stable dispositions there are still many ways in which organizations can create changes that can overwhelm job attitudes and performance. The next paper, by Judge, Thorensen, Bono and Patton (2001), published fifteen years later, provides a quantitative and qualitative review of current understanding of the job satisfaction–job performance relationship. They review seven models of job satisfaction and performance and argue for the need for future research to develop a more integrated model including moderators and mediators.

The next papers concentrate on different aspects of the affective work experience. Allen and Meyer (1990) identify and develop scales to measure three separate components of organizational commitment (affective, continuance and normative). They argue that researchers need to distinguish between these three components in order to build a more complete picture of factors that lead individuals to commit effort and energy to the organizations for which they work. Rafaeli's (1989) paper provides an excellent and somewhat unusual example of a researcher immersing herself in an organizational environment to better understand the feelings and emotions of customer service work. Whilst questionnaires provide a comparatively quick and standardized method of capturing information,

Rafaeli's study illustrates the rich diversity of information it is possible to obtain from participant observation. It provides a perfect context for the next two papers, that by George and Jones (1997) concerned specifically with how individuals experience work, and a paper by Ashworth and Ronald (1995) which examines the functional role played by emotions in organizational life.

Another important field of organizational psychology concerns the impact of work on employee health and well-being. Although there are clearly ethical and legal drivers to ensure that worker health does not suffer, there are also clear benefits of having healthy workers for organizations seeking to maximize productivity. Warr's (1990) paper is an important contribution for researchers and practitioners seeking to measure well-being and mental health at work. In their look ahead to well-being and occupational health in the twenty-first century, Sparks, Faragher and Cooper (2001) discuss the likely impact of workplace changes such as restructuring and an ageing workforce on employee well-being. They suggest that, to be effective, organizations will need to introduce changes, including more training, flexible working arrangements and access to health promotion schemes, and call for researchers to provide evidence to support these interventions. Cooper (1996) continues the discussion of organizational impact on worker well-being by considering the links between a long working hours culture and health outcomes such as heart disease.

The final paper in this volume by Colquitt and Greenberg (2003) takes a more broad perspective by considering employees' perceptions of organizational justice. Specifically, the extent to which employees think they are being treated by their organization can impact on worker experience and productivity. They review literature concerned with three types of organizational justice (distributive, procedural and interactional).

## Reference

Arnold, J.M., Silvester, J., Patterson, F., Robertson, I., Cooper, C.L. & Burnes, B. (2005). *Work Psychology: Understanding Human Behaviour in the Workplace, 4th edn*. London: Prentice Hall.

# Part 1

# HOW PEOPLE BECOME WORKERS

# 1

# THE PSYCHOLOGY OF CAREERS IN ORGANIZATIONS

*John Arnold*

Source: C.L. Cooper and I.T. Robertson (eds), *International Review of Industrial and Organizational Psychology*, Vol. 12, Chichester: John Wiley, 1997, pp. 1–37.

In one sense an exhaustive review of the literature on the psychology of careers is overdue—the last one in this series was provided by Michael Driver in 1988. But on the other hand there is no shortage of more recent reviews of career-related topics. In 1991, the *Journal of Vocational Behavior* commissioned a veritable blitz of reviews to mark its 20th anniversary (Borgen, 1991; Chartrand & Camp, 1991; Hackett, Lent & Greenhaus, 1991; London & Greller, 1991; Meier, 1991). Since then, its traditional annual reviews of the whole field of vocational behavior have been replaced by annual reviews of subareas of the field, each subarea appearing once every three years, usually right at the end of the year (Swanson, 1992; Blau, Linnehan, Brooks and Hoover, 1993; Fouad, 1994; Watkins & Subich, 1995). The *Career Development Quarterly* also publishes annual reviews, these mostly concerning the theory and practice of counseling (e.g. Salomone, 1993; Subich, 1994). Meanwhile, in the *Journal of Management*, Ornstein and Isabella (1993) produced a review of aspects of careers more exclusively orientated towards organizational issues. Feldman (1989) did a similar job four years earlier. Also, as we shall see shortly, some topics I would consider to be specific aspects of careers have been reviewed elsewhere, including in this present volume.

I want to use the existence of the generous supply of thorough reviews (albeit from a North American perspective) as an opportunity to take a different approach. Rather than seeking to mention briefly all research and theory produced in recent years in a kind of prose catalogue, I will present some observations and arguments about certain aspects of the psychology of careers in organizations. My primary purposes are to examine what careers are about in a changing world, to identify some topics which reflect current and future concerns, and to report and critically examine literature in those areas.

Ornstein and Isabella (1993, p. 244) commented that a review of the whole field of careers would be 'impossible and somewhat unnecessary' due to the large number of disciplinary approaches brought to bear upon it, and the variety of target audiences for different segments of it. Driver (1988) noted that other writers have characterized the study of careers as fragmented and unsatisfactory in important respects (see also Hall, 1991). Part of the reason for this may be that even amongst behaviorally-orientated writers there seems little consensus about what careers are, or rather what they are construed as being. An examination of some definitional differences will help us to clarify the many strands of career and begin to identify a framework for a structured examination.

## What is a career?

Some authors perhaps wisely do not attempt to define what a career is. Others have grasped the nettle. Below are some not very systematically chosen definitions of career, including some older ones because they have influenced or reflect subsequent work:

1. A sequence of positions occupied by a person during the course of a lifetime (Super & Hall, 1978).
2. A series of related job experiences that fit into some meaningful pattern. If you have a series of odd jobs all your working life, that is hardly a career (DuBrin, 1983).
3. A succession or an accumulation of role-related experiences over time (London & Mone, 1988).
4. A sequence of jobs occupied and performed throughout a person's working lifetime (Gray, Gault, Meyers & Walther, 1990).
5. Occupations that are characterized by interrelated training and work experiences, in which a person moves upward through a series of positions that require greater mastery and responsibility, and that provide increasing financial return (Perlmutter & Hall, 1992).
6. The sequence of negotiations and renegotiations of the psychological contract which the individual conducts with organizations during his or her work life (adapted from Herriot, 1992, referring to organizational careers).
7. The pattern of work-related experiences that span the course of a person's life (Greenhaus & Callanan, 1994).
8. Accumulations of information and knowledge embodied in skills, expertise, and relationship networks acquired through an evolving sequence of work experiences over time. In this context, work experiences constitute the primary mechanism by which careers occur though they are not in themselves a career (Bird, 1994).

Most academics familiar with careers literature agree that a career is NOT confined to upward and/or predictable movement within one kind of work. Yet this is the image conveyed in definition 2 (in a self-help 'how to be successful' guide), and definition 5 (a lifespan development text). Worse, it is not uncommon to see advertisements along the lines of 'Enrol at Salaryhike College if you want a career, not just a job'. The local newspaper in my current home town entitles its situations vacant section 'Jobs and Careers'. Readers can no doubt think of similar examples of this apparent dual labor market. Therefore, a continuing and pressing concern is that career *is* often thought of as something like definitions 2 and 5 by many people, including some who write about careers. Wider use of less restrictive implicit or explicit definitions of career would surely help social scientists to apply theories and concepts more effectively, enable popular writers to purvey more effective advice, and assist mere mortals to manage their careers better.

One fairly evident common feature of all these definitions is that they refer to *more than one* role, experience, or event. Words like series, sequence, succession, pattern and accumulation are used. This is a key point. The study of career involves study over time rather than taking snapshots of supposedly stable situations. Note also that although the above definitions agree on the 'more than one' aspect, what there is more than one of is in doubt. We are offered positions, related job experiences, role-related experiences, jobs occupied and performed, upward sequence of positions, negotiations, work-related experiences and skills, expertise and relationship networks. In other words, the studies of careers have variously focused on sequences of roles, experiences in those roles, behaviors in the roles, and personal attributes derived from the roles. No wonder it is a diverse field.

For present purposes, we can be said to be considering career if we are thinking about (i) potential or actual sequences of employment-related positions, roles, activities or experiences encountered by, or available to, one or more persons; (ii) their plans, decisions and attitudes concerning such sequences; (iii) their adjustment and development in new or changed employment-related positions, etc.; (iv) their preparation for future ones; and (v) their sense-making about past employment-related positions etc. in relation to their present ones. We are also in the realm of careers when we consider (vi) attempts made by focal individuals themselves or others to influence (normally facilitate or shape) any of the first five phenomena; and finally (vii) the interplay between personal and macro- or micro-situational variables and any of the preceding six phenomena.

## The context of careers

It is now well known that the context of employment in the Western world has changed and is still changing. Pressures brought about by globalization of economies and technological advance have led to some quite dramatic transformations in work organizations.

More than one *guru* has skillfully and eloquently described the new landscape. Bridges (1995) has argued that jobs and traditional employment are gone forever. Handy (1989, 1994) described various organizational forms that are emerging. They have in common a core of full-time employees who consider themselves members of the organization, and a periphery of casualized workers, some highly skilled carrying out specialized and limited-term projects and others semi- or unskilled working in contracted-out functions such as cleaning and catering. Some interesting questions revolve around managing the performance and commitment of these latter two groups (Pearce, 1993; Beard & Edwards, 1995). Along similar but more pessimistic lines, UK journalist Will Hutton (Hutton, 1995) has predicted the advent of a 30/30/40 society: 30% either unemployed or economically inactive, 30% in insecure and intermittent employment with few benefits, and 40% relatively privileged usually with marketable skills in relatively stable employment or self-employment. Particularly in countries which embraced the concept (and cost) of a welfare state after World War II, such scenarios have profound implications for social fabric and order, and for personal financial planning which in many countries has long been based on a norm of stable employment.

Perhaps mainly with Hutton's 40% in mind, some writers have referred to new kinds of career. This too has a rather longer history than might be first thought. Hall (1976) referred to the Protean career, where the individual is his or her own agent. More recently, people are urged to regard themselves as self-employed even if they have an employer (Bridges, 1995); to carry a portfolio of skills and experiences and make strategic moves which equip them for future employability (Handy, 1989; Kanter, 1989). Arthur (1994) has coined the term 'boundaryless career' to sum up the trend towards employment experiences which take individuals across employer boundaries. These boundaries are in any case blurred due to the proliferation of mergers and acquisitions (Cartwright & Cooper, 1992), wholly-owned subsidiaries, and autonomous business units. The boundaryless career may well also take a person across different types of work and it is validated and supported by networks such as professional groups.

Some further trends in employment, and in demography, add detail to this picture. The average age of the population in most Western countries is increasing due to increased longevity and historical patterns of birth rates. In the UK, out of a total labor force of about 30 million, an increase of 2.4 million in the number of 35 to 54 year olds and a drop of 1.6 million under 35s is expected between 1993 and 2006 (*Social Trends*, 1993). Increased participation by women in the labor market is occurring in many countries (Offermann & Gowing, 1990; Wheeler, 1990; Davidson, 1996), and an increasing proportion of the total jobs available are part-time (the two trends are not unconnected, since at present a greater proportion of women than men work part-time). Although somewhat vulnerable to the economic cycle, the proportion of people in self-employment has increased significantly in the UK and to a lesser extent in other European Union countries (Meager, Kaiser & Dietrich, 1992). The number and proportion of people working in small and medium enterprises (SMEs) has increased in many countries— a salutary reminder that analyses of organizational careers must not assume a large organization (in any case, as many have wryly observed, the sure-fire way to run a small business these days is to start with a large one).

So, with the earlier analysis of the nature of careers in mind, what issues arise from the trends described above that should interest psychologists? In no particular order, they seem to me to be those listed below. Having identified the issues, in each case I will then briefly examine recent literature in that area.

1. Job changes happen with increasing frequency (Inkson, 1995), and perhaps involve more radical change for individuals and less predictability than was once the case. Individuals and organizations are under pressure to perform quickly and creatively. Louis (1982) argued that career transitions had been neglected hitherto—has this been rectified in recent years? Psychological investigations of work-role transitions (Nicholson, 1989), relocation, newcomer information-seeking and socialization are all relevant here. So is the literature on commitment, but that is reviewed in Meyer's chapter in this volume. Hence it is not covered here. Also, tele-working, and the transition to it, have been covered recently in this series by Chapman, Sheehy, Heywood, Dooley and Collins (1995). Transitions involving unemployment received some attention from Winefield (1995), also in this series.

2. In some organizations individuals are explicitly told that it is up to them to manage their own careers—the organization as a corporate body will take no part and provide no support. In others, some responsibility is being taken for equipping individuals to manage their own career within a general framework that offers some signposts but fewer than was once the case. There is a strong case to be made that demographic changes and increasing competition mean that organizations need to utilize *all* their people better (Herriot & Pemberton, 1995b). What is the current contribution of the psychologically oriented literature concerning career interventions and their impact upon individuals and organizations?

3. Individuals are having to make and remake career decisions more frequently. They may experience periods of education and training scattered through their life, not just in their childhood and adolescence. The proportion of older people in the population of many countries is increasing. What can the psychological literatures on career, decision-making, aging and lifespan development contribute to an understanding of career?

These three issues seem to me to fall naturally out of the current context. That is not to say there are no others. In particular, I am aware of the need to include in each of the above three areas relevant literature on gender, ethnicity and internationalization in careers. Two other important issues arising from the current context but omitted here due to space constraints and coverage elsewhere are:

4. For many people working in organizations, the old understanding of their employment relationship has been disconfirmed by experiences over the last few years. What implications does this have for their interpretation of present experience relative to past and future? Recent literature on the psychological contract (e.g. Shore & Tetrick, 1994; Herriot & Pemberton, 1995a) and related issues has addressed this.

5   Delayering and downsizing have made promotions harder to obtain, and some organizations have shifted to project- or competency-bases (Lawler, 1994) where relatively constant job descriptions do not exist. For both reasons, externally verifiable career success is more difficult to obtain and to define. Indeed any sort of career map is hard to find. Within a managerial context, issues concerning career success are reviewed by Tharenou (this volume).

## Change and transition

### Incidence and types of change

One symptom of what Stephens (1994) has appropriately described as 'increasingly discontinuous and unstable work lives' is increased frequency of voluntary and involuntary work-role transitions. These include changes between jobs, substantial shifts in the requirements or opportunities inherent in an existing job or other employment situation, transitions into and out of employment, relocation of employment, and also changes in attitude to features of one's objective career. Regarding managers, Nicholson and West (1988) reported increasing frequency of job change in the UK. More recent work by Inkson (1995) and Cawsey and Inkson (1992) has reaffirmed this trend in the UK and New Zealand respectively, and noted that it has been relatively impervious to the economic cycle. Also, much of the increase in job changes for managers is accounted for by involuntary and/or sideways or downward status moves. Around half of managers' job changes involve a change of employer. Thus it is appropriate that no less than 12 of Hall's (1991) 'Twenty Questions: research needed to advance the field of careers' specifically refer to work-role transitions.

Potentially useful general typologies and models of work-role transitions were developed some time ago (e.g. Louis, 1980a, b; Nicholson, 1984, 1989) but have been used relatively little in subsequent research, though there are signs that this may be changing. Ashforth and Saks (1995) tested some predictions derived from Nicholson (1984) concerning whether business school graduates in the early months of employment would seek to change their roles (innovate) or be changed by them (personal change). Contrary to prediction, the amount of personal change was unrelated to the discretion and novelty of the new work role. However, as predicted, discretion was positively related to self-reported role innovation. Commenting upon the moderate level of support for their predictions, the authors noted that Nicholson's theory may be limited in that adjustment to new work roles is portrayed as a relatively asocial process. In line with this proposition, Major, Kozlowski, Chao and Gardner (1995) have recently reported that interactions with colleagues and supervisors in the early weeks of a new job can reduce the negative impact of unmet expectations.

In a review of some of the literature in this area, Stephens (1994) has integrated some concepts from the Nicholson (1984) model with others from lifelong approaches to career development. Stephens argued that the Nicholson model is more comprehensive than the perhaps better known Theory of Work Adjustment (Dawis & Lofquist, 1984). Certainly, to me, the Theory of Work Adjustment has a strangely dated appearance. Its prediction that satisfactoriness (of an employee's performance) and satisfaction (the extent to which the job meets the employees' needs) jointly determine job tenure seems to portray stability as the norm, disrupted only by unsatisfactory circumstances. This seems rather implausible these days. Returning to Stephens (1994), he also noted a dearth of research on the effects of work-role transitions on non-transitioners. This is a theme that has been mentioned in socialization literature and recently in job rotation literature but as yet rarely pursued.

Bruce and Scott (1994) adapted Louis' (1980a) typology of transitions to fit the context of the US Navy, where the structured career development system enabled them to test propositions in relatively controlled fashion. The five types of transition were entry events, promotion events, lateral moves, resignation, and retirement. The authors commented as follows upon their results (p. 26): 'In general, the career events studied were moderately high in magnitude and desirability, low in strain and role ambiguity, and seen as causing moderate adjustment difficulty. These events were seen as resulting in gains in both individuals' personal lives and their careers, and there was moderate eagerness toward all events'. Nicholson and West (1988) also noted that many work-role transitions are experienced quite positively, and questioned whether stress-based models were appropriate. Longitudinal work with degree-qualified samples by Newton and Keenan (1990) and Arnold (1994) supports the notion that job-changing produces either neutral or positive outcomes for psychological well-being, though this does not rule out the possibility that stress models may be useful in investigating the *process* of adjustment. The amount of stress experienced by a transitioner may depend partly upon the resources they bring to the transition. Heppner, Multon and Johnston (1994) reported the development and validation of the 40-item Career Transitions Inventory. Five subscales emerged. They did not precisely coincide with the theoretical constructs originally identified by the authors. The subscales are readiness, confidence, perceived support, control, and decision-independence. The Career Transitions Inventory may well prove to be a useful instrument in research and practice.

## *Relocation*

Relocation occurs when one or more employees of an organization move geographically whilst retaining the same employer. They may or may not be performing the same job in their new location as their old, and the move may or may not be of their own instigation. J. M. Brett, Stroh and Reilly (1992) reviewed the then-existing literature in volume 7 of this series. Their own work (Brett, Stroh & Reilly, 1993) with mobile managers in leading US corporations contradicted much earlier research by finding that sex, race and number of children at home were *not* related to willingness to relocate. Neither were work attitudes such as job satisfaction and company loyalty—as the authors point out, this is not surprising since the object of those attitudes is the job or company, not the relocation. The main factor predicting willingness to relocate was age. Older employees were less willing. These findings may be partly due to the sample, which consisted of managers who had relocated in the previous two years. Although not about relocation, a recent article by J. F. Brett, Cron and Slocum (1995) suggests a variable that has been neglected in relocation research. This is economic dependency on work. For some people, relocation is the only way of keeping a job, particularly in group moves.

Munton, Forster, Altman and Greenbury (1993) reported data from over 200 relocating employees and their families at relocation, and then three months and six months later. Respondents' worries focused mostly on extra-employment concerns such as property transactions and guilt at forcing children to move. Fisher and Shaw (1994) reported a study of 150 relocating military employees who provided data before and then three months after their move. Adjustment and attitudes toward the move were more strongly related to anticipated, and then actual, features of the new location than were demographic and pre-move location attributes. Past experience of moves was strongly negatively correlated with adjustment difficulty. However, this last point has not been the case in all research. Martin (1995) found some evidence, albeit in a small sample, that adjustment to relocation was most difficult for those with little experience of it and those with a great deal of experience. In the former case lack of know-how and disruption of community ties may have been the cause. In the latter group it may have been more a case of being worn down by yet another round of tedious and taxing tasks. Lawson and Angle (1994) found a more straightforward effect of prior experience of moving helping adjustment in their survey of 200 families involved in a company move. Overall, family and other extra-employment factors were better predictors of adjustment than were employment-related ones.

The concept of adjustment has come under rather closer scrutiny in the literature on international relocation. Brewster (1994) argues that it is most often construed by researchers as psychological comfort, but in the discussion of data researchers 'find themselves discussing the steps that the expatriate takes to bring his or her behavior into line with that of the host country' (p. 50). Brewster found that Swedish managers in the UK tended to adopt styles more characteristic of the UK than Sweden, and suggested that expatriates' behaviors may change more completely and quickly than is often realized. Janssens (1995) has pointed out that integration into a new environment should not necessarily be seen as a desirable outcome of work-role transitions. Sometimes (and particularly in international assignments) the employing organization's top managers may want the relocatee to retain a 'head office' perspective rather than 'go native'. She found that contact of international relocatees with members and the culture of the host country increased steadily as they spent longer there. This increase was still evident after 5 years and longer. Contrary to Brewster, then, some aspects of adjustment may be long drawn out.

There are of course individual differences in how international relocation is handled. Black and Gregersen (1992) distinguished two dimensions: maintenance of own cultural identity and contact with the host culture. This enabled a 2 × 2 classification: free agent (low, low); go native (low, high); heart at home (high, low); and dual citizen (high, high). Recent empirical work has reinforced earlier assertions that adjustment of family members is crucial to the work and general adjustment of the international relocatee him or herself. Nicholson and Imaizumi (1993, p. 130) have described this as '... a significant flow of adjustment from the domestic to the employment sphere'. W. Arthur and Bennett (1995) found that family situation was perceived as more important in determining success of international location than were job knowledge and motivation, relational skills, flexibility/adaptability and even extra-cultural openness. Furthermore, this finding from a sample of 338 international assignees in 45 multinational companies applied across different types of work and types of company. In an interesting analysis from a psychoanalytical perspective Schneider and Asakawa (1995) examined the role in international adjustment of dependency, separation and individualization, autonomy and control, and intimacy. They contrasted aspects of child-rearing in an attempt to identify differential adult adjustment patterns.

## *Experiencing work-role transitions*

Much research on work-role transitions has used samples of young people entering full-time employment for the first time. This is sometimes for good theoretical reasons, but often for convenience. Earlier work (see Arnold, 1990, for a review) tended to find that navigating the transition was not as difficult as previous theorizing had suggested it might be. That work tended to concentrate on adjustment to unfulfilling work for school-leavers, but utilization of skills and commitment in graduate samples. More recent work by Arnold and Nicholson (1991) and Fournier and Payne (1994) with graduates has examined the nature and extent of self-concept change in the early months and years of employment. There is significant qualitative change, though not necessarily towards potential role models in the organization.

There is perhaps good reason why the education to employment transition of young people has been going out of fashion. Trends towards higher unemployment, education interspersed throughout life, and work experience during education have made this transition less clearcut and uniform than it once was. Nevertheless, a special issue of the *Journal of Vocational Behavior* was recently devoted to the transition for non-college-educated youth. In the lead article, Feij, Whitely, Peiró and Taris (1995) reported a large-scale longitudinal study with cross-validation of young people in eight countries over the first 18 months of school to work transition. The sample was chosen on the basis of being employed in certain occupations. They formulated, tested and modified a model of the development of job content innovation and career enhancing strategies on the part of the young people. They proposed that supervisor relations, work centrality, work values and correspondence between individual and work were implicated in this. Findings supported the importance of relations with the supervisor in influencing the outcome variables.

A series of invited articles critiqued the Feij et al. paper. Hesketh (1995) examined the potential contribution of the Theory of Work Adjustment (Dawis & Lofquist, 1984) to the framing of the study and interpreting its findings. Blustein (1995) argued that it would have been strengthened by inclusion of theoretical constructs from career development and lifespan development theory, as well as more attention to the cultural contexts of the countries concerned. The most critical commentary was by Eldredge (1995), who highlighted Feij et al.'s inappropriate use of some existing literature and their failure to use concepts and measures of socialization and innovation.

One area Eldredge (1995) concentrated upon was the impact of socialization on the role orientation of newcomers. A recent reanalysis by Baker (1995) of data reported by Allen and Meyer (1990) has suggested that socialization tactics adopted by organizations with newcomers have their effect partly through the degree of role certainty as proposed by Allen and Meyer, but also partly through the degree of interaction with incumbents. Baker reiterated Jones' (1986) earlier conclusion that it is difficult to socialize newcomers in such a way that both commitment and innovation are fostered.

At the other end of employed life, there has been a little recent attention to retirement. This too is an increasingly ambiguous transition with respect to its timing, voluntariness, and suddenness. A model of psychological aspects of retirement has recently been presented in this series (McGoldrick, 1996), so coverage here is very brief. Feldman (1994) has called for more research linking decision to retire with subsequent adjustment. He drew on image theory (Beach & Mitchell, 1978) to identify sustaining a stable self-image, resolving approach-avoidance conflicts, and maintaining or regaining control over one's future as three themes that should be central to retirement research. No less than 14 hypotheses for future research were specified. Hanisch (1994) has reported research which made some links between reasons for retiring (work, personal, or health reasons) and subsequent attitudes and behaviors. Talaga and Beehr (1995) uncovered several factors (e.g. presence of dependents in the household) which had differential impacts on the retirement decisions of men relative to women.

## *Socialization and information-seeking*

The notion that individuals have inflated expectations of their new environment when starting work or making subsequent job changes has a long history (e.g. Vroom, 1966). It has subsequently been developed into unmet expectations—i.e. failure of the reality to live up to anticipation. Although recent research in this area is scant compared with the 1970s and 1980s, Wanous, Poland, Premack and Davis (1992) reported a meta-analysis of 31 studies which showed quite strong relationships between met expectations and job satisfaction, organizational commitment, and intention to leave, and a smaller but still significant one with actual job survival. Study design (experimental vs non-experimental) did not moderate these relationships. Wanous et al. acknowledged some conceptual and methodological limitations of met expectations.

One practical application of the met expectations literature has been realistic job previews—that is, attempts to portray the job to applicants 'warts and all' rather than in an entirely positive light. Again, published research in this area seems to have passed its peak, at least for the time being. However, Meglino, Denisi and Ravlin (1993) reported an investigation of a large sample of correctional officers. Surprisingly, a realistic job preview had significant effects on applicants who already had experience of the role, often in the opposite direction from those who did not have such experience. Findings were also different during the probationary period than subsequently. However, most of the effects were relatively small.

Researchers have devoted quite a lot of attention to learning and socialization in new jobs. Many studies in this area demonstrate a particularly painstaking and thorough approach on the part of their authors. For example, R. F. Morrison and Brantner (1992) investigated correlates of self-reported learning of departmental head jobs in a military setting. Reassuringly, increasing time in the job was positively correlated with learning, though a significant effect in regression analysis for time squared indicated a leveling off of learning towards the end of the 18-month assignments. Learning the job was also associated with low job challenge (presumably the benefits of simplicity more than offset any motivational problems caused by low challenge), and by high perceived importance to the real work of the organization. Self-efficacy (see also Saks, 1995) and role clarity were also positively correlated with learning. One interesting inhibitor of learning was prior experience of the role but in a different context and a subordinate position. The cross-sectional nature of this research inevitably leaves open the question of causality. Some of the correlates listed above could quite plausibly be outcomes of learning.

Chao, O'Leary-Kelly, Wolf, Klein and Gardner (1994) reported a large, impressive and informative study of organizational socialization. Construing organizational socialization as learning on the part of an individual who is adjusting to a new or changed role within an organization, they set out to examine content rather than process. They identified six areas of socialization: performance proficiency, people, politics, language, organizational goals and values, and history. A measure was developed, the factor structure of which reflected the theoretical concepts very well. The questions for four of the factors reflect learning 'about' or 'how to'. Those concerning people reflect social acceptance by others, whilst goals and values predominantly concerns personal acceptance or internalization of those goals and values. Longitudinal data showed that self-reported socialization had a positive impact on the career-related outcomes of career involvement, identity resolution and adaptability. People socialization however showed no relationships with outcomes, and history socialization showed negative ones!

Several studies have built upon earlier work (e.g. Ashford, 1986) concerning the information and feedback-seeking strategies of newcomers. This work is very much in the social-cognitive tradition. The newcomer is viewed as seeking to make sense of their new environment by acquiring and processing various forms of information in a social context. Miller and Jablin (1991) produced an exhaustive conceptual overview of types, sources and tactics of information-seeking as well as its potential costs and outcomes and individual differences. They specified a number of propositions for subsequent research. Some of these have subsequently been addressed (Ostroff & Koslowski, 1992; E. W. Morrison, 1993). Among Ostroff and Koslowski's findings were that newcomers focus primarily on acquiring information about task and role (as opposed to group and organization) and that acquisition of knowledge from supervisors and task knowledge was associated with positive changes in satisfaction, commitment and adjustment. Using somewhat different classifications of types and sources of information, E. W. Morrison (1993) also found cross-time relationships between certain aspects of information and adjustment outcomes.

Overall, the research on work-role transitions could benefit from a more consistent approach to what adjustment is. The term is used a lot, sometimes to mean integration or well-being, and sometimes to signal the individual's approach to their role. The same, only more so, applies to socialization. In spite of quite a rich and long-running literature in this area (see for example Brim, 1968), it is still conceptualized in many different ways. In keeping with the current dominance of social cognition in psychology, current work tends to construe it as learning various aspects of how to be an organizational member. Even so, distinctions are not always made between learning what to do, learning how to do it, and learning when to do it, let alone wanting to do it, believing it is the right thing to do, and viewing oneself as the kind of person who does it. In other words, socialization may cover cognitive learning, behavioral compliance, identification and internalization even though the first has had the vast majority of attention in recent research. The last of these in particular involves change in the self-concept, or at least the constellation of social selves (Schein, 1971). The methods used in most psychological research in this area also miss some of the richness of socialization and adjustment. Many writers have argued, for example, that socialization of women in male-dominated work environments presents women with a number of difficulties and dilemmas that may be qualitatively different from those experienced by men (Alvesson & Billing, 1992) and more acute the more the preponderance of males (Ely, 1994). These include how to respond to uncongenial value systems, whether or not to participate in organizational politics and adopt assertive behavior, with implications for self-concept and integrity. Marshall (1995) has reviewed much of this and other work, and has examined the dilemmas of advocating change whilst also speaking within academic conventions.

### *Commitment*

There is an extraordinarily large literature on organizational commitment, much of it quite recent, and relatively little challenging (as opposed to refining) the concept (for an exception, see Coopey & Hartley, 1991). The organizational commitment literature is reviewed in this volume by one of its leading contributors (Meyer, Chapter 5).

Commitment is not confined to organizations, however. For many years it has been recognized that for some people at work, commitments may be to other referents. Meyer, Allen and Smith (1993) have provided some tentative evidence that the three aspects of organizational commitment (normative, continuance and affective) are also observable in commitment to occupations. The related construct of career commitment has also been developed and measured in recent years. Building on the earlier work of Blau (e.g. 1985), Carson and Bedeian (1994) have recently developed the 12-item Career Commitment Measure (CCM), which incorporates the three dimensions of career identity, career planning and career resilience. The authors argued on the basis of their data that their measure exhibits good construct and content validity, whilst also avoiding some of the problems of Blau's (1985) measure. Carson and Bedeian went to some lengths to explain to people completing the CCM that career includes concepts like line of work, profession, occupation and vocation, but even so the measure clearly refers to quite a narrow concept of career. Another line of research in this area has concerned the compatibility or otherwise of commitment to organization and to occupation. Wallace (1993) reported a meta-analysis of 15 published studies which showed a positive correlation between the two types of commitment. This suggests that the two can go hand in hand. Whilst this is no doubt true in some workplaces, Herriot (1992) amongst others has presented an analysis which shows very clearly that it cannot be taken for granted.

## Career interventions in organizations

### *Overview*

As already noted, the state of flux in most organizations, and contraction in many, is widely held to have led to the abandonment of attempts to manage careers in organizations. This has been replaced by an emphasis on the need for employees to engage in self-development. This concept may be helpful. It has a history in the applied psychology and management literature, and at least some people seem to engage purposefully in it (McEnrue, 1989). However, it now seems to be accompanied by the message that the organization will not even give any clues about what skills and experiences it wants its people to have. So people are expected not only to look after their own development, but also to do so in the absence of any information (Hirsh, Jackson & Jackson, 1995).

Nevertheless, there is a strong case to be made that now more than ever it is advantageous for an organization to play a part in the management of careers. If career paths are necessarily ambiguous (Callanan & Greenhaus, 1992; Arnold & Mackenzie Davey, 1994) and if an organization's competitive advantage lies in its use of human resources (Lawler, 1994), then the organization's task is to provide a context where employees can learn to manage their own careers in conditions of change and uncertainty. This means providing a supportive context without actually doing the managing. It probably also means a shift from using the narrower definitions of career emphasizing advancement within one line of work to much broader definitions (Adams, 1991). Tensions often exist between employee and organizational interests, and it is often argued that successful interventions must reflect both (Gutteridge, Leibowirz & Shore, 1993). In workplaces with many outsourced contract workers, issues arise as to who should be eligible to participate in interventions (Pearce, 1993). Clarity is required about the purpose of any given intervention. Is it for assessment, identifying career options, action planning, skill development, vacancy filling, or some prioritized combination of these? (Hirsh, Jackson & Jackson, 1995). It is doubtful whether the Human Resource Management strategy of making line managers responsible for facilitating the career development of subordinates (Storey, 1992) will be effective. This doubt stems from many observations, not least gaps in perception, understanding and interest between line manager and subordinate (Arnold & Mackenzie Davey, 1992; Herriot, Pemberton & Pinder, 1994).

Career interventions in organizations can take a variety of forms (Russell, 1991). These include internal vacancy notification, career workbooks, career workshops, individual counseling (including outplacement), skills inventories, personal development plans, career pathing, educational opportunities, mentoring, development centers, succession planning, and developmental work experiences. In recognition of the less organizationally-based nature of careers, there are some initiatives to set up career centers for use by individuals but to some extent sponsored by employing organizations (Waterman, Waterman & Collard, 1994).

In spite of quite thorough analyses of how organizational career interventions might be evaluated (e.g. London & Stumpf, 1982, ch. 5), there is little good-quality research assessing the impact of these interventions, nor the necessary conditions for them to work well. As Herr and Cramer (1992, pp. 482–483) put it: 'In some ways the current state of the literature pertaining to career planning in organizations is reminiscent of the writing and research related to the condition of school counseling in the late 1950s and early 1960s—role studies, suggestions, reports of tentative programs, recommendations for practice, rudimentary attempts to link theory with practice, and very little empirical or evaluative research'. Of course it is understandable that evaluation is thin on the ground. It takes time to conduct, especially in a field like careers where any benefits will be medium rather than short term. Some organizations will not wish to go public about what they do and whether it works. The legitimate demands of journal editors for rigor are hard to meet in field settings, particularly over substantial time periods with (almost by definition) a potentially mobile population. Nevertheless, the correlation between use of certain HRM practices and organizational performance at least in some industries (Terpstra & Rozell, 1993; J. B. Arthur, 1994) does give some prospect of career interventions having a demonstrable impact on the bottom line.

## *Mentoring*

Mentoring is the intervention most often investigated in applied psychological research. To some extent this is justified by its apparent increasing popularity, although thorough information about the uptake of interventions is thin on the ground (Iles and Mabey, 1993). In turn, this popularity may be a function of the relatively small visible demands made by mentoring on a training budget and its resonance with preoccupations of baby-boomers reaching middle age. Mentoring can take a number of forms, but probably the most common one fits with the general definition provided by Kram (1985, p. 2): '... a relationship between a younger adult and an older, more experienced adult that helps the individual learn to navigate in the world of work'. The person in receipt of mentoring is often referred to as the protégé. A distinction is often made between informal mentoring (Levinson, Darrow, Klein, Levinson & McKee, 1978), where a relationship between mentor and protégé springs up spontaneously, and formal mentoring, where relationships are arranged and overseen by an employing or professional organization.

There is evidence that having had a mentoring relationship as opposed to not having had one is associated with indices of career success and/or socialization (e.g. Whitely, Dougherty & Dreher, 1991; Scandura, 1992; Ostroff & Kozlowski, 1993; Aryee & Chay, 1994), though see Chao, Walz and Gardner (1992) for more equivocal results. An interesting recent study (Pollock, 1995) has found that protégé benefits from mentoring seem to increase after the initial stages of the relationship, though this finding may be jeopardized by the method of asking respondents for retrospective accounts of their mentoring relationships, and leaving unspecified the time period associated with early, middle and late stages of the relationship. There are also data consistent with the idea that protégé individual differences such as socio-economic status (Whitely, Dougherty & Dreher, 1991) and personality (Turban & Dougherty, 1994) mediate and/or moderate the beneficial effects of mentoring for the protégé. Particular concern has been voiced about gender issues in mentoring. There is some feeling that women protégés may be at a disadvantage relative to male ones in obtaining a mentoring relationship and then profiting from it, especially if the mentor is male (e.g. Ragins & Cotton, 1991).

A number of writers seem willing on the basis of the above studies or their own experience and intuition to accept that mentoring normally produces benefits for mentor, protégé and employing organization, particularly the protégé (Clutterbuck, 1993). Attention therefore turns to how mentoring can be implemented effectively and pitfalls avoided. To be sure, those are vital issues, and the practicalities and politics of such interventions are often neglected by I/O psychologists (Johns, 1993). However, it really is necessary to point out a few important truths about the research cited above. Most of it did not distinguish between formal and informal mentoring. In the latter case, it may be that people who were clearly going to be successful were attractive to potential mentors, and that's why they received mentoring. Some experimental evidence in support of this conjecture has been provided by Olian, Carroll and Giannantonio (1993). With the exception of Chao, Walz and Gardner (1992) there were no comparable control groups of people who did not receive mentoring. The range of potentially confounding variables controlled for is rarely comprehensive, and certainly less comprehensive than in some of the related career success literature cited in Tharenou (this volume). Sometimes mentoring is defined as having someone the respondent calls their mentor, and sometimes as being in receipt of functions or benefits associated with mentoring, whatever the source. The research is very predominantly cross-sectional and/or retrospective. Interestingly, where an assessment is made of what immediate benefits of mentoring are experienced by the protégé, they have been fairly modest (Noe, 1988; Chao, Waltz & Gardner, 1992).

## *Succession*

There has been quite an extensive literature over the years on succession, particularly succession of Chief Executive Officers (CEOs). Unlike most other research on work-role transitions (see above) CEO succession literature focuses very little upon the experiences and adjustments of the incoming CEO. Instead, it concentrates on characteristics of the CEO and impact of his or her arrival upon organizational performance and employees. This is understandable given the supposed influence of CEOs, but it might be informative if more studies addressed how new CEOs are (for example) socialized. Even more to the point, research on other, 'ordinary' work-role transitions could place more emphasis upon the impact of the new arrival on those around them.

The literature on executive succession has recently been reviewed very thoroughly by Kesner and Sebora (1994), who noted that CEO succession happens relatively infrequently, with average CEO tenure of 14 years. They traced succession literature through from the 1950s and 1960s to the 1990s, identifying themes, ambiguities and progress along the way. Kesner and Sebora noted that one recurring theme was successor origin—particularly whether the incoming executive was an organizational insider or outsider. Research in this area has not drawn a clear conclusion about when each type of succession occurs, or whether one produces consistently better results than the other. The search is now on for moderator variables which may account for the variable findings. Cannella and Lubatkin (1993) for example found that in poor performing organizations, appointment of an outside CEO was likely only if there was no heir apparent and if the old CEO had little influence on the selection decision. Mabey and Iles (1993) have also made the point that succession is often a highly political process. Kesner and Dalton (1994) found that outsider CEOs induced more turnover in other upper management positions than outsider CEOs, but contrary to hypothesis, this latter turnover was unrelated to organizational performance. It should be noted, finally, that the outsider vs insider distinction is very broad. There is scope for greater use of more refined typologies of executive career path, such as that recently proposed by White, Smith and Barnett (1994).

## *Development centers*

There is increasing interest in using assessment center technology to identify developmental needs of existing employees, with a view to possible future job placement, training or promotion rather than immediate selection for a specific post. There is some evidence that candidates see assessment centers as relatively fair means of selecting people for jobs (Robertson, Iles, Gratton & Sharpley, 1991), so on the face of it one might expect those who experience a development center to act upon the feedback they obtain.

Jones and Whitmore (1995) conducted a 10-year follow-up of employees in an insurance company and found that acceptance of the feedback on the part of the assessees was quite high, and that (on the basis of self-report) 48% of developmental recommendations were implemented. This percentage was positively correlated with subsequent promotion, but close analysis showed that this was due to just two of the seven areas of developmental activity investigated. Engelbrecht and Fischer (1995) have also reported a study of insurance company employees. They compared experimental and control groups in an investigation of whether attendance at a development center was positively associated with work performance (supervisor ratings) relative to non-attendees three months later. It was, on nine of the eleven scales measured. However, there was no pre-test, and supervisors were aware of who had attended development centers so conclusions must be tentative.

## *Development through the job*

Various factors have provoked a recent career-oriented focus on how people can be developed for future work via present work. The most significant are probably the well-documented problems of transfer of learning in training courses to everyday work (see for example Baldwin & Padgett, 1993) and the increased pressure in organizations for development to interfere with immediate performance as little as possible.

Campion, Cheraskin and Stevens (1994) have reported an investigation of managerial job rotation amongst 255 employees in a large pharmaceutical company. They construed rotation as non-promotional job moves where the employee usually does not remain permanently in the new job but nor does he or she return to the old one. In their study, rotations occurred every one to five years. They found that self-reported knowledge and skill outcomes factored out into three areas: technical, administrative and business. What they termed career management outcomes of rotation included career affect, organizational integration, stimulating work and personal development, though only the last of these could be said directly to reflect on individuals' felt ability to manage their career. Potential costs of job rotation included workload and productivity and learning curve. On the whole, respondents gave numerically higher ratings to the benefits of rotation than to the costs, though they suggested an additional cost of lost motivation or commitment amongst those not rotating. Rate of job rotation was positively correlated with promotion and salary increases, being in early career, being highly educated, and perceived increase in skills. These findings are interesting, though there may well have been an element of self-fulfilling prophecy about some of them. Also, in some contexts job rotation is used to try to maintain the performance and motivation of plateaued staff (see for example Tremblay, Roger & Toulouse, 1995) so it may be of some concern that early career (presumably pre-plateau) employees were more interested in rotation than later career ones. The association between rotation and promotion may also not be replicated elsewhere. Campion and colleagues pointed out that further research could address generalizability issues and a finer analysis of which skills are most effectively developed through rotation as opposed to other means.

In another important line of work, McCauley and colleagues (e.g. McCauley, Ruderman, Ohlott & Morrow, 1994) have developed and validated the Development Challenge Profile, which is a self-report instrument for assessing the developmental opportunities inherent in managerially oriented jobs. They identified 15 developmental features of jobs, two of which concerned job transitions, nine task-related characteristics and four obstacles. Particularly in the last category, there were some features such as difficult boss that one presumably would not normally seek to build into a job. This leads to the question of what can truly be called developmental as opposed to just plain difficult, and the authors conceded that they underestimated the degree of stress associated with some of the developmental challenges. Ohlott, Ruderman and McCauley (1994) found that although there were no widespread differences between male and female managers in terms of the developmental challenges they experienced, women tended to experience more of the obstacles.

The contribution of on-the-job experiences to career is a fruitful area for further development, and one suspects that much more in this line will be done in the next few years.

### *Career counseling*

Most counseling occurs outside the person's work organization, but it is sometimes offered to employees as a stand-alone service or as part of a package such as outplacement or a career development workshop. A review of theory and research on career counseling theory, techniques and practice is outside the scope of this chapter, and is in any case provided elsewhere (e.g. Egan, 1990; Nathan & Hill, 1992; Sharf, 1992; see also Hermansson, 1993, for an interesting example of the application of some of Egan's ideas to counseling in organizations). Here I will confine comment to a few points about the evaluation of career counseling.

Most counselors do not seek to give advice. To use an old distinction, they help people to make decisions wisely, not wise (as judged by the counselor) decisions (Katz, 1969). This becomes ever more true as the pace of change increases and it is difficult to discern with confidence what a wise decision is. The need for ready access to counseling by adults throughout their career is increasingly evident (Watts, 1994) as non-normative events buffet us frequently (Vondracek & Schulenberg, 1992). Some of the earlier research evaluating careers counseling and guidance used stability in a job or occupation as a dependent variable, but this seems inappropriate as a goal of counseling now, and perhaps then too (Killeen, White & Watts, 1992). Given the number of other things happening in a person's life, it is difficult if not impossible to isolate the impact of a counseling intervention, which may in any case be additional to earlier interventions with the same person. The interconnections and continuities between different parts of a person's life at any one time also mean that any career counseling intervention must encompass, and may have an impact upon, leisure, personal relationships and so on (Krumboltz, 1993).

However, to the extent that it can be done, evaluation of career counseling work needs to be in terms of the client's cognitive processes (Kidd & Killeen, 1992) as well as outcomes such as job satisfaction. The latter are becoming more ephermeral and in any case are unlikely to be achieved without cognitive processes. These include reflecting on the past and present, monitoring and evaluating self, and exploration, as well as meta-cognitive skills such as knowing when to use these processes. This is touched on again in the next section.

## Career management and lifespan development of individuals

### *The nature of vocational personality*

John Holland's theory (e.g. Holland, 1985) remains the dominant one in the field of vocational personality measurement. Holland has proposed the existence of six 'pure types' of vocational personality, each of which any given individual or work environment can resemble to greater or lesser degrees. The types can be thought of as arranged at the vertices of a hexagon, with their positioning defining the relative similarity of the types. Holland's fundamental proposition concerning effective vocational choices is that a person whose personality is congruent with (i.e. similar to) their environment will, other things being equal, experience more satisfaction in it and perform better than a person not in congruent environment. Surprisingly perhaps, a recent meta-analytic review revealed little support for this prediction (Tranberg, Slane & Ekeberg, 1993).

If we assume that *some* kind of match between person and environment facilitates satisfaction and/or performance, the negative results reported by Tranberg, Slane and Ekeberg may indicate that Holland has not hit upon the optimal way of describing people and environments. One conclusion might be that something like Schein's (1993) career anchors might do a better job. There is no direct evidence for that, but Nordvik (1991) has shown that scores on career anchor measures are relatively independent of scores on Holland vocational personality measures. This leaves open the possibility that career anchors may tap aspects of personality more meaningful to congruence than Holland's. Tokar and Swanson (1995) have found that scores on Holland types correlate in interpretable ways with parts of the five-factor model of personality (McCrae & Costa, 1987), particularly Openness and Extroversion. This is encouraging for Holland's typology in that it should indeed link with other conceptualizations of personality, but discouraging in that large areas of the 'Big Five' do not seem well reflected in the Holland typology.

There have been recent debates concerning the structure of vocational personality. Gati (1991) argued for a hierarchical structure of vocational interests rather than a hexagonal or circular one. A stimulating series of articles in the *Journal of Vocational Behavior* (1992) debated Holland's hexagonal structure. Prediger and Vansickle (1992) advocated a two-dimensional model in which the axes (data-ideas and things-people) could be superimposed onto the hexagon, but with more utility and sensitivity than could be achieved by Holland type scores. Holland and Gottfredson (1992) presented a counterargument which focused on how some patterns of scores would not be adequately reflected by the Prediger and Vansickle reformulation, Dawis (1992) offered some perceptive further comments, including the observation that the choice of six clusters is arbitrary, and other formulations specify different numbers. Rounds and Tracey (1993) analyzed data from a large number of US studies in an attempt to identify which non-hierarchical structure, if any, best fitted the data. They concluded (p. 886) that '... a very simple circular-ordering structure can be validly used in thinking about RIASEC interests'. This means that the Prediger and Vansickle axes are not obviously any better or worse than any other pair of orthogonal axes, and that choosing different numbers and positions on the circle could lead to description of 'pure types' different from those of Holland, but equally valid. Rounds and Tracey also noted the presence of a general factor in response to vocational interest inventories: that is, a tendency to express (or not) interest in activities of all kinds. The interpretation of this factor was identified as an important issue for future research.

### *Decision processes and individual differences*

Holland's theory concerns the content of decisions more than the process of making decisions. Quite a lot of developmentally oriented theorizing some years ago attempted to map out how individuals clarify their sense of self and integrate this with vocational and other life choices (Super & Hall, 1990). Using concepts derived from this line of thinking, Blustein, Pauling, DeMania and Faye (1994) found that the extent to which students reported engaging in exploratory behavior was correlated with progress in vocational decision-making, whereas indices of congruence (see above) were not.

Recently a little attention has been paid to the detail of how individuals go about making and implementing decisions. The literature here concerns either on the one hand 'career' or 'vocation' (normally defined as an area of work) or on the other hand, job. Integration with work on decision-making from other areas of psychology is not particularly high, though for an exception see Gati, Fassa and

Houminer (1995). Use of concepts from social cognitive psychology is however more prevalent. Moss and Frieze (1993) found that students' preferences amongst job offers could be explained both by the extent to which offers matched students' desired job attributes and by the extent to which students' stereotypes of people working in the jobs offered matched their self-concept. The first of these explained more of the variance in preferences than the second. Gianakos (1995) extended an existing line of research applying sex-role self-concept to career variables. She found that androgynous individuals (i.e. those who described themselves in both stereotypically masculine and feminine terms) felt more able to tackle career decision-making tasks than others, and significantly more so than undifferentiated individuals (i.e. those who scored low on both traditionally feminine and masculine aspects of self-concept). However, in studies of this kind it is important to establish that a person's sex *per se* does not account for the variance in the dependent variable.

A recent monograph by Lent, Brown and Hackett (1994) has applied social cognitive theory to interests, choices and performance in employment and academic settings. The authors argued that existing work tended to view persons in overly static terms, with behavior being seen as a product of a person–situation interaction rather than an aspect of it. They continued: 'By contrast, social cognitive theory emphasizes the situation and domain-specific nature of behavior, relatively dynamic aspects of the self-system, and the means by which individuals exercise personal agency' (p. 82). With an emphasis on self-efficacy, outcome expectancies and personal goals, Lent, Brown and Hackett then built models of interests, choices and performance and specified many hypotheses, some of which they were able to test. This work may well succeed in doing what the authors hoped—to advance on the static trait-oriented views of decision-making and add specificity to the more learning-oriented but rather general development approaches.

The Lent, Brown and Hackett approach may be particularly well suited to a world where people need to make choices with a weather eye toward their future marketability in terms of skills and experiences as well as the congruence between present self and work requirements. Furthermore, individuals have fewer external markers of their progress (see above) and less opportunity to pursue a pre-defined sequence of jobs. All this places a greater emphasis on self-awareness and assessment, learning from experience and coping with uncertainty and setbacks. Some other recent work is also relevant here. Waterman, Waterman and Collard (1994) have referred to career-resilient workers, where career resilience is defined in terms of self-knowledge, long-term goals independent of an employing organization, knowledge of the market, flexibility, and willingness to move on when they no longer fit the organization. Although it was developed in the specific context of Silicon Valley in California, USA, and reflects economic rather than psychological imperatives, the concept of career resilience probably has wider applicability.

London (1993) has explored the concept of career motivation. He suggested that it has three components: career insight, career identity and career resilience. The last of these was defined (rather differently from Waterman, Waterman &

Collard) as the ability to adapt to changing circumstances. Career insight is the realism and clarity of the person's career goals and career identity is the extent to which a person defines him or herself in terms of work. The three constructs and their measurement are clearly important to the study of careers, but combining them and assigning the label motivation to the composite seems less than helpful despite London's attempt to equate them to the energizing, direction and persistence components of motivation. Carson, Carson and Bedeian (1995) have developed a self-report measure of career entrenchment, which is in some respects the opposite of career resilience. It has three components: career investments, emotional costs of changing careers, and limitedness of career alternatives.

Regarding self-assessment of attributes and/or performance, the earlier literature (e.g. Mabe & West, 1982) tended to concentrate on the degree of accuracy of self-assessment (or at least agreement with others' assessments), often with the assumption that accuracy would facilitate effective decision-making. More recent work has taken two rather different directions. First, it seems that agreement of self-ratings with those made by colleagues at work may reflect the possession of some social or self-insight skills which also contribute to a person's objective career success (Bass & Yammarino, 1991; Furnham & Stringfield, 1994). Second, self-efficacy theory suggests, with a little evidence to back the claim, that moderately over-optimistic self-estimates should enhance subsequent performance (Lent, Brown & Hackett, 1994).

### *Life-span development and aging*

The influence of development approaches was hinted at in the previous section. Led by the late Donald Super and others, developmental analyses of careers have emphasized the unfolding nature of cognition, emotion and behavior concerning careers. At first, these approaches tended to be confined purely to employment, and quite closely tied to normative age-related phenomena. But the developmental approaches themselves developed. They have increasingly considered roles other than employment and in some cases close links with age have been loosened (Super, 1990; see also Chi-Ching, 1995, for an empirical example).

As Super (1990, p. 194) put it: '... what I have contributed is not an integrated, comprehensive and testable theory, but rather ... a loosely unified set of theories dealing with specific aspects of career development taken from developmental, differential, social and phenomenological psychology and held together by self-concept or personal-construct psychology'. Developmental ideas, even more than most, require longitudinal examination. Thus it is perhaps not surprising that the use of developmental ideas in careers research and practice is common, but tests of theoretical propositions are rare. In the former category, Dix and Savickas (1995) have recently reported an interesting piece of work attempting to elicit from 50 successful male workers how they had tackled the six developmental tasks of the establishment stage of career. The authors pointed out that this helps to make explicit some of the tacit knowledge associated with successful career development. Through use of interviews, critical incident techniques, and content categorizing by expert judges, Dix and Savickas identified between three and eight coping behaviors for each of the six tasks. A similar exercise with female workers is planned, which is important given that this study focused on males, and that developmental approaches are often heavily criticized for working from male, middle-class perspectives.

One contribution often seen as particularly vulnerable on this last point is that of Levinson et al. (1978), (see also Levinson, 1986). On the basis of interviews with 40 men, they proposed a closely age-related developmental pattern which alternated between stable and transitional periods. The former is where a person pursues stable goals within a life structure, and the latter is where they question and perhaps change their goals and/or life structure. Smart and Peterson (1994) have tested these ideas in a cross-sectional analysis of 498 Australian professional women. There were 12 dependent variables, including for example professional commitment, intent to remain and need for achievement. They concluded that the pattern postulated by Levinson et al. was evident for only one of the dependent variables (pay satisfaction). However, it is not obvious to me why one would expect trends in the dependent variables consistent with Levinson et al. As Levinson et al. pointed out, stable periods are not necessarily experienced as stable or calm. A person may have stable goals, and these may include (for example) leaving their employer. During a transitional period they may be considering a different lifestyle, but still intend to build this around (for example) their current profession. Levinson's ideas can only really be tested using detailed case material, with all the practical and analytical problems that involves.

Recently Helms and Piper (1994) have lamented the small amount and simplistic nature of research on racial aspects of vocational behavior and development. Typically racial groups have been defined in nominal terms—that is, people are assigned to a category regardless of how they view themselves. But, '... unless one believes that vocational behavior is biogenetically determined and racial classification is a valid indicator of persons' biogenetic endowments, then there is no valid reason for explaining or anticipating consistent between-group differences on the basis of race *per se* on any of the commonly investigated vocational behavior'. In the same issue of the *Journal of Vocational Behavior*, Evans and Herr (1994) reported results which supported that assertion. Helms and Piper argued that use of racial identity theory (e.g. Helms, 1990) could further our understanding of the vocational development blacks and whites alike. The theory traces stages in the development of racial identity, and may have some parallels with other developmental approaches in careers and in adult cognitive development more generally (see e.g. Commons, Sinnott, Richards & Armon, 1989). Helms and Piper further suggested that racial identity should be seen as a dependent variable (i.e. an outcome of events and experiences) as well as an independent variable.

There is increasing recognition that the demographic trends described earlier require more attention to the psychology of aging and its integration with employment-related contexts (see Davies, Matthews & Wong, 1991 for a review).

Sterns and Miklos (1995) have provided a helpful recent review of some key areas here. They disaggregated the concept of aging into five different and not necessarily consistent aspects (chronological/legal, functional, psychosocial, organizational, and lifespan) and reviewed research related to each. Consistent with Neugarten's (1977) notion of 'fanning out' of members of a cohort as they progress through adulthood, Sterns and Miklos noted that 'Late careers are often more difficult to study than early careers because there is less consistency in the development tasks' (p. 259). In an article in the same edition of the *Journal of Vocational Behavior*, Hall and Mirvis (1995) have put forward some interesting propositions about the nature of career at midlife and beyond. They argued that the changing nature of the workplace holds both threats and opportunities for older workers. For example, older workers may be better able than younger ones to engage in 'relational' work such as helping and supporting others. This work is especially important when an organization is under pressure, but often goes unnoticed (or worse, it is seen as non-productive) and unrewarded. Hall and Mirvis also drew upon systems theory to suggest that an organization needs to contain at least as much complexity as is present in its environment. One form of complexity is diversity, and one form of diversity is age. 'Careers too are becoming more complex: we would argue that what we are seeing now, instead of one set of career stages spanning a lifespan (as the Super model posits), is a series of many shorter learning cycles over the span of a person's work life.... As a result, people's careers will become increasingly a succession of 'mini-stages' (or short-cycle learning stages) of exploration – trial – mastery – exit, as they move in and out of various product areas, technologies, functions, organizations, and other work environments.... Thus, the half-life of a career stage would be driven by the half-life of the competency field of that career work' (p. 277). Hall and Mirvis added that if older workers can be removed from various job and health insecurities, they are likely to be able to engage in the continuous learning (as opposed to isolated retraining) demanded by the labour market.

A number of studies have shown that stereotypes of older workers, whilst not wholly negative, are not particularly flattering. A comprehensive recent study in this area has been reported by Warr and Pennington (1994). In a study with 1140 personnel managers, they found that non-managerial jobs perceived as mainly for older workers were also perceived to make fewer cognitive demands, be slower paced and less demanding of energy than those for younger workers. Sterns and Miklos (1995) cited a study by Russell and Curtis (1992) which found that 63% of companies offered pre-retirement programs, but only 23% had programs to reduce obsolescence or plateauing. This is consistent with barriers to the effective development of older workers identified by Hall and Mirvis (1995), which included the perceptions that investment in the development of older workers is too costly, and that older workers are too inflexible and difficult to train.

These perceptions exist alongside research showing that there is little relationship between age and job performance (McEvoy & Cascio, 1989), except within early adulthood. Other work shows that, despite age-related decrements in some aspects of information-processing, the task performance of older people is often at least as good as that by younger people especially where tasks are of a relatively familiar kind and the use of learning strategies is encouraged (e.g. Salthouse, 1990). On the other hand the pace of change in the workplace more often requires learning *un*familiar tasks. Alwin (1994) has noted the existence of different patterns of stability in psychological constructs during adulthood. He suggested that the evidence on intelligence and personality traits indicated a pattern of persistently high stability from early adulthood to old age. Data on self-concepts and attitudes suggested a rather different pattern of low stability in early adulthood followed by stability in midlife and either further stability or more change thereafter. These findings might suggest another problem for older people—they really are less open to change than younger people. On the other hand, as Alwin and others have pointed out, it is wellnigh impossible to disentangle different influences on lifespan development. The pattern of findings may principally reflect typically low pressure in the past for people to change after early adulthood. Nowadays and in the future we may find that necessity is the mother of instability.

Future theory and practice in careers would do well to pay more attention to work on lifespan development, of which Alwin (1994) is just one example, though, an impressively far-sighted one. Warr and Conner (1992) presented another impressive contribution in their attempt to link research on intelligence, cognitive style and expertise with job competence, whilst Warr (1993) analyzed key differences between cognitive tasks and linked them to expected patterns of performance of people of different ages. Extension of this kind of work to the cognitive demands made by the self-management of careers offers an exciting and profitable way forward in helping all people, especially older ones, tackle the demands of contemporary life (Kegan, 1994). Another avenue here is the recent work on wisdom by Baltes and colleagues (e.g. Staudinger, Smith & Baltes, 1992). Although this might be criticized for taking a rather narrow and culture-specific view of what wisdom is (Assmann, 1994) it offers a measure of ways of thinking which may be very well suited to career management as we approach the millennium.

## Conclusions

The psychological literature on careers is appropriately diverse in content, though less so in method. Recent years have seen important advances in research in some areas, particularly (in my opinion) the psychological contract and work-role transitions and socialization. In some areas empirical research is relatively plentiful but over-arching theory rather thin. In others, especially developmental approaches to careers, the reverse is true.

A number of impressive contributions exhibiting at least two of methodological excellence, theory development, and practical application have been published in recent years. Most of these are either substantial longitudinal empirical studies or ground-breaking theoretical contributions which more often than not draw heavily upon work in other areas of psychology, particularly social cognition. Indeed, this last point is a real source of optimism—there are signs of increasing integration of career psychology with the rest of the discipline.

Of course, not all in the garden is rosy. A number of papers, including some mentioned in this review, have made at best a modest contribution to our understanding of careers (though in most cases I would have been proud enough to have produced them!). For the purposes of this review (including areas I have excluded from this chapter because of space limitations), I was most consistently impressed by the content of *Academy of Management Journal* and *Personnel Psychology*. Contributions in these journals seemed to me most often to combine rigor with a sensitive attempt to tackle issues of real importance in organizational life. *Journal of Applied Psychology* and *Journal of Vocational Behavior* carried many excellent articles but at times seemed in danger of over-emphasizing 'technical correctness' at the expense of contribution to understanding of issues of practical importance. The *Journal of Organizational Behavior* and *Human Relations* were also very valuable sources of good material, and the latter in particular published papers with diverse methods and varied theoretical orientations. But these two more than the other four journals mentioned also seemed to carry some of the modest contributions alluded to earlier. Often, but not always, cross-sectional and entirely self-report data were the limiting factor.

With large datasets and/or a longitudinal study design it is of course often appropriate for multiple papers to be published. Nevertheless, I felt there were some instances where researchers produced multiple articles from the same data even though a single bigger and more integrative contribution might have developed the field better. There is also a tendency (evident also in this article I suspect) for authors' to over-emphasize research conducted in their own country or continent even though they are writing on issues of international importance for international audiences.

The career literature is beginning to reorientate to take account of the changing world of employment. There is much still to be done in developing analyses of how individuals can and should manage their careers, achieve success against their own standards, and make appropriate decisions, but in many of the areas reviewed a start has been made. The Hall and Mirvis (1995) paper is a particularly good example of this.

One of several profitable lines of enquiry will be how people explain to themselves and others their past, present and future in a world with relatively few fixed points or signposts. This endeavor requires attention to discourse and narrative (e.g. Gergen, 1988) which would represent a useful addition to, and change from, the vast majority of existing careers research. It may depart from the positivist assumption that there is one 'truth' (albeit a complex one) waiting to be found. Interestingly, this assumption reflects quite a low level of development in models of cognitive development! But even if it is not really so novel, there is likely to be much value in placing somewhat more emphasis on people's accounts of their behavior and thinking (e.g. Dix & Savickas, 1995), and also more emphasis on direct observation of behavior and assessment of thinking strategies.

# References

Adams, J. (1991) Issues in the management of careers. In R. F. Morrison and J. Adams (eds), *Contemporary Career Development Issues*. Hillsdale, NJ: Erlbaum.

Allen, N. J. & Meyer, J. P. (1990) Organizational socialization tactics: A longitudinal analysis of links to newcomers' commitment and role orientation. *Academy of Management Journal*, **33**, 847–858.

Alvesson, M. & Billing, Y. D. (1992) Gender and organization: Towards a differentiated understanding. *Organization Studies*, **13**, 73–102.

Alwin, D. F. (1994) Aging, personality and social change: The stability of individual differences over the adult life span. In D. L. Featherman, R. M. Lerner & M. Perlmutter (eds), *Life-Span Development and Behavior*, Vol. 12. Hillsdale, NJ: Erlbaum.

Arnold, J. (1990) From education to labor markets. In S. Fisher and C. L. Cooper (eds), *On The Move*: *The Psychological Effects of Change and Transition*. Chichester: Wiley.

Arnold, J. (1994) Opportunity for skill use, job changing, and unemployment as predictors of psychological well-being amongst graduates in early career. *Journal of Occupational and Organizational Psychology*, **67**, 355–370.

Arnold, J. & Mackenzie Davey, K. (1992) Self-ratings and supervisor ratings of graduate employees' competences during early career. *Journal of Occupational and Organizational Psychology*, **65**, 235–250.

Arnold, J. & Mackenzie Davey, K. (1994) Graduate experiences of organizational career management. *International Journal of Career Management*, **6**, 14–18.

Arnold, J. & Nicholson, N. (1991) Construing of self and others at work in the early years of corporate careers. *Journal of Organizational Behavior*, **12**, 621–639.

Arthur, J. B. (1994) Effects of human resource systems on manufacturing performance and turnover. *Academy of Management Journal*, **37**, 670–687.

Arthur, M. B. (1994) The boundaryless career: A new perspective for organizational enquiry. *Journal of Organizational Behavior*, **15**, 295–306.

Arthur, W. & Bennett, W. (1995) The international assignee: The relative importance of factors perceived to contribute to success. *Personnel Psychology*, **48**, 99–114.

Aryee, S. & Chay, Y. W. (1994) An examination of the impact of career-oriented mentoring on work commitment attitudes and career satisfaction among professional and managerial employees. *British Journal of Management*, **5**, 241–249.

Ashford, S. J. (1986) Feedback-seeking in individual adaptation: A resource perspective. *Academy of Management Journal*, **29**, 465–487.

Ashforth, B. E. & Saks, A. M. (1995) Work-role transitions: A longitudinal examination of the Nicholson model. *Journal of Occupational and Organizational Psychology*, **68**, 157–175.

Assmann, A. (1994) Wholesome knowledge: Concepts of wisdom in a historical and cross-cultural perspective. In D. L. Feathermen, R. M. Lerner & M. Perlmutter (eds), *Life-Span Development and Behavior*, Vol. 12. Hillsdale, NJ: Erlbaum.

Baker, W. K. (1995) Allen and Meyer's (1990) longitudinal study: A reanalysis and reinterpretation using structural equation modeling. *Human Relations*, **48**, 169–186.

Baldwin, T. T. and Padgett, M. (1993) Management development. In C. L. Cooper and I. T. Robertson (eds), *International Review of Industrial and Organizational Psychology*, Vol. 8. Chichester: Wiley.

Bass, B. M. & Yammarino, F. J. (1991) Congruence of self and others' leadership ratings of naval officers for understanding successful performance. *Applied Psychology: An International Review*, **40**, 437–454.

Beach, L. R. & Mitchell, T. R. (1978) A contingency theory for the selection of decision strategies. *Academy of Management Review*, **3**, 439–449.

Beard, K. M. & Edwards, J. R. (1995) Employees at risk: Contingent work and the psychological experience of contingent workers. In C. L. Cooper and D. M. Rousseau (eds), *Trends in Organisational Behavior*, Vol. 2. Chichester: Wiley.

Bird, A. (1994) Careers as repositories of knowledge: A new perspective on boundaryless careers. *Journal of Organizational Behavior*, **15**, 325–344.

Black, J. S. & Gregersen, H. B. (1992) Serving two masters: Managing the dual allegiance of expatriate employees. *Sloan Management Review*, Summer, 61–71.

Blau, G. (1985) The measurement and prediction of career commitment. *Journal of Occupational Psychology*, **58**, 277–288.

Blau, G., Linnehan, F., Brooks, A. & Hoover, D. K. (1993) Vocational behavior 1990–1992: Personnel practices, organizational behavior, workplace justice, and industrial/organizational measurement issues. *Journal of Vocational Behavior*, **43**, 133–197.

Blustein, D. L. (1995) Toward a contextual perspective of the school-to-work transition: A reaction to Feij et al. *Journal of Vocational Behavior*, **47**, 257–265.

Blustein, D. L., Pauling, M. L., DeMania, M. E. & Faye, M. (1994) Relation between exploratory and choice factors and decisional progress. *Journal of Vocational Behavior*, **44**, 75–90.

Borgen, F. H. (1991) Megatrends and milestones in vocational behavior: A 20-year counseling psychology retrospective. *Journal of Vocational Behavior*, **39**, 263–290.

Brett, J. F., Cron, W. L. & Slocum, J. W. (1995) Economic dependency on work: A moderator of the relationship between organizational commitment and performance. *Academy of Management Journal*, **38**, 261–271.

Brett, J. M. (1992) Job transfer. In C. L. Cooper and I. T. Robertson (eds), *International Review of Industrial and Organizational Psychology*, Vol. 7. Chichester: Wiley.

Brett, J. M., Stroh, L. K. & Reilly, A. H. (1992) Job transfer. In C. L. Cooper and I. T. Robertson (eds), *International Review of Industrial and Organizational Psychology*, Vol. 7. Chichester: Wiley.

Brett, J. M., Stroh, L. K. & Reilly, A. H. (1993) Pulling up roots in the 1990s: Who's willing to relocate? *Journal of Organizational Behavior*, **14**, 49–60.

Brewster, C. (1994) The paradox of adjustment: UK and Swedish expatriates in Sweden and the UK. *Human Resource Management Journal*, **4**, 49–62.

Bridges, W. (1995) *Jobshift: How to Prosper in a Workplace Without Jobs*. London: Nicholas Brealey.

Brim, O. G. (1968) Adult socialization. In J. A. Clausen (ed.), *Socialization and Society*. Boston: Little, Brown.

Bruce, R. A. & Scott, S. G. (1994) Varieties and commonalities of career transitions: Louis' typology revisited. *Journal of Vocational Behavior*, **45**, 17–40.

Callanan, G. A. & Greenhaus, J. H. (1992) The career indecision of managers and professionals: An examination of multiple subtypes. *Journal of Vocational Behavior*, **41**, 212–231.

Campion, M. A., Cheraskin, L. & Stevens, M. J. (1994) Career-related antecedents and outcomes of job rotation. *Academy of Management Journal*, **37**, 1518–1542.

Cannella, A. A. & Lubatkin, M. (1993) Succession as a sociopolitical process: Internal impediments to outsider selection. *Academy of Management Journal*, **36**, 763–793.

Carson, K. D. & Bedeian, A. G. (1994) Career commitment: Construction of a measure and examination of its psychometric properties. *Journal of Vocational Behavior*, **44**, 237–262.

Carson, K. D., Carson, P. P. & Bedeian, A. G. (1995) Development and construct validation of a career entrenchment measure. *Journal of Occupational and Organizational Psychology*, **68**, 301–320.

Cartwright, S. & Cooper, C. L. (1992) *Mergers and Acquisitions: The Human Factor*. Oxford: Butterworth & Heinemann.

Cawsey, T. & Inkson, K. (1992) Patterns of managerial job change: A New Zealand study. *New Zealand Journal of Business*, **14**,14–25.

Chao, G. T., O'Leary-Kelly, A. M., Wolf, S., Klein, H. J. & Gardner, P. D. (1994) Organizational socialization: Its content and consequences. *Journal of Applied Psychology*, **79**, 730–743.

Chao, G. T., Walz, P. M. & Gardner, P. D. (1992) Formal and informal mentorships: A comparison on mentoring functions and contrast with nonmentored counterparts. *Personnel Psychology*, **45**, 619–636.

Chapman, A. J., Sheehy, N. P., Heywood, S., Dooley, B. & Collins, S. C. (1995) The organizational implications of teleworking. In C. L. Cooper and I. T. Robertson (eds), *International Review of Industrial and Organizational Psychology,* Vol. 10. Chichester: Wiley.

Chartrand, J. M. & Camp, C. C. (1991) Advances in the measurement of career development constructs: A twenty-year review. *Journal of Vocational Behavior*, **39**, 1–39.

Chi-Ching, Y. (1995) The effects of career salience and life-cycle variables on perceptions of work–family interfaces. *Human Relations*, **48**, 265–284.

Clutterbuck, D. (1993) *Everyone Needs a Mentor*, 2nd edn. London: Institute of Personnel Management.

Collin, A. & Watts, A. G. (1996) The death and transfiguration of career—and careers guidance? *British Journal of Guidance and Counselling*, in press.

Commons, M. L., Sinnott, J. D., Richards, F. F. & Armon, C. (eds) (1989) *Adult Development: Comparisons and Applications of Developmental Models*. New York: Praeger.

Coopey, J. & Hartley, J. (1991) Reconsidering the case for organizational commitment. *Human Resource Management Journal*, **1**, 18–32.

Davidson, M. J. (1996) Women and Employment. In P. B. Warr (ed.), *Psychology at Work*. Harmondsworth: Penguin.

Davies, D. R., Matthews, G. & Wong, C. S. K. (1991) Ageing and work. In C. L. Cooper and I. T. Robertson (eds), *International Review of Industrial and Organizational Psychology*, Vol. 6. Chichester: Wiley.

Dawis, R. V. (1992) The structure(s) of occupations: Beyond RIASEC. *Journal of Vocational Behavior*, **40**, 171–178.

Dawis, R. V. & Lofquist, L. H. (1984) *A Psychological Theory of Work Adjustment*. Minneapolis, MN: University of Minnesota Press.

Dix, J. E. & Savickas, M. L. (1995) Establishing a career: Developmental tasks and coping responses. *Journal of Vocational Behavior*, **46**, 93–107.

Driver, M. J. (1988) Careers: A review of personal and organizational research. In C. L. Cooper and I. T. Robertson (eds), *International Review of Industrial and Organizational Psychology*, Vol. 3. Chichester: Wiley.

DuBrin, A. J. (1983) *Human Relations for Career and Personal Success*. Reston, VA: Reston Publishing Co.

Egan, G. (1990) *The Skilled Helper* 4th edn. Pacific Grove: Brooks/Cole.

Eldredge, B. D. (1995) Some things not considered: Evaluation of a model of career enhancing strategic and content innovation with respect to organizational socialization. *Journal of Vocational Behavior*, **47**, 266–273.

Ely, R. J. (1994) The effects of organizational demographics and social identity on relationships among professional women. *Administrative Science Quarterly*, **39**, 203–238.

Engelbrecht, A. S. & Fischer, A. H. (1995) The managerial performance implications of a developmental assessment center process. *Human Relations*, **48**, 387–404.

Evans, K. M. & Herr, E. L. (1994) The influence of racial identity and the perception of discrimination on the career aspirations of African American men and women. *Journal of Vocational Behavior*, **44**, 173–184.

Feij, J. A., Whitely, W. T., Peiró, J. M. & Taris, T. W. (1995) The development of career-enhancing strategies and content innovation: A longitudinal study of new workers. *Journal of Vocational Behavior*, **47**, 231–256.

Feldman, D. C. (1989) Careers in organizations: Recent trends and future directions. *Journal of Management*, **15**, 135–156.

Feldman, D. C. (1994) The decision to retire early: A review and reconceptualization. *Academy of Management Review*, **19**, 285–311.

Fisher, C. D. & Shaw, J. B. (1994) Relocation attitudes and adjustment: A longitudinal study. *Journal of Organizational Behavior*, **15**, 209–224.

Fouad, N. A. (1994) Annual review 1991–1993: Vocational choice, decision-making, assessment, and intervention. *Journal of Vocational Behavior*, **45**, 125–176.

Fournier, V. & Payne, R. (1994) Change in self-construction during the transition from university to employment: A personal construct psychology approach. *Journal of Occupational and Organizational Psychology*, **67**, 297–314.

Furnham, A. & Stringfield, P. (1994) Congruence of self and subordinate ratings of managerial practices as a correlate of supervisor evaluation. *Journal of Occupational and Organizational Psychology*, **67**, 57–67.

Gati, I. (1991) The structure of vocational interests. *Psychological Bulletin*, **109**, 309–324.

Gati, I., Fassa, N. & Houminer, D. (1995) Applying decision theory to career counseling practice: The sequential elimination approach. *Career Development Quarterly*, **43**, 211–220.

Gergen, M. (1988) Narrative structures in social explanation. In C. Antaki (ed.), *Analyzing Everyday Explanation: A Casebook of Methods*. London: Sage.

Gianakos, I. (1995) The relation of sex-role identity to career decision-making self-efficacy. *Journal of Vocational Behavior*, **46**, 131–143.

Gray, D. A., Gault, F. M., Meyers, H. H. & Walther, J. E. (1990) Career planning. In J. C. Quick et al. (eds), *Career Stress in Changing Times*. New York: Haworth Press.

Greenhaus, J. H. & Callanan, G.A. (1994) *Career Management*, 2nd edn. London: Dryden Press.

Gutteridge, T. G., Leibowitz, Z. B. & Shore, J. E. (1993) *Organizational Career Development*. Reading, MA: Addison-Wesley.

Hackett, G., Lent, R.W. & Greenhaus, J. H. (1991) Advances in vocational theory and research: A twenty-year retrospective. *Journal of Vocational Behavior*, **38**, 3–38.

Hall, D. T. (1976) *Careers in Organizations*. Glenview, IL: Scott Foresman.

Hall, D. T. (1991) Twenty questions: Research needed to advance the field of careers. In R. F. Morrison and J. Adams (eds) *Contemporary Career Development Issues*. Hillsdale, NJ: Erlbaum.

Hall, D. T. & Mirvis, P. H. (1995) The new career contract: Developing the whole person at midlife and beyond. *Journal of Vocational Behavior*, **45**, 328–346.

Handy, C. (1989) *The Age of Unreason*. London: Business Books.

Handy, C. (1994) *The Empty Raincoat*. London: Hutchinson.

Hanisch, K. A. (1994) Reasons people retire and their relations to attitudinal and behavioral correlates in retirement. *Journal of Vocational Behavior*, **45**, 1–16.

Helms, J. E. (1990) *Black and White Racial Identity*. New York: Greenwood Press.

Helms, J. E. & Piper, R. E. (1994) Implications of racial identity theory for vocational psychology. *Journal of Vocational Behavior*, **44**, 124–138.

Heppner, M. J., Multon, K. D. & Johnston, J. A. (1994) Assessing psychological resources during career change: Development of the Career Transitions Inventory. *Journal of Vocational Behavior*, **44**, 55–74.

Hermansson, G. L. (1993) Counsellors and organizational change: Egan's systems model as a tool in organizational consulting. *British Journal of Guidance and Counselling*, **21**, 133–144.

Herr, E. L. & Cramer, S. H. (1992) *Career Guidance and Counseling through the Life Span*, 4th edn. New York: Harper Collins.

Herriot, P. (1992) *The Career Management Challenge*. London: Sage.

Herriot, P. & Pemberton, C. (1995a) *New Deals*. Chichester: Wiley.

Herriot, P. & Pemberton, C. (1995b) *Competitive Advantage Through Diversity*. London: Sage.

Herriot, P., Pemberton, C. & Pinder, R. (1994) Misperceptions by managers and their bosses of each other's preferences regarding the managers' careers: A case of the blind leading the blind? *Human Resource Management Journal*, **4**, 39–51.

Hesketh, B. (1995) Personality and adjustment styles: A Theory of Work Adjustment approach to career enhancing strategies. *Journal of Vocational Behavior*, **47**, 274–282.

Hirsh, W., Jackson, C. & Jackson, C. (1995) *Careers in Organisations: Issues for the Future*. Brighton: Institute for Employment Studies.

Holland, J. L. (1985) *Making Vocational Choices*, 2nd edn. Englewood Cliffs, NJ: Prentice-Hall.

Holland, J. L. & Gottfredson, G. D. (1992) Studies of the hexagonal model: An evaluation (or, the perils of stalking the perfect hexagon). *Journal of Vocational Behavior*, **40**, 158–170.

Hutton, W. (1995) *The State We're In*. London: Cape.

Iles, P. & Mabey, C. (1993) Managerial career development programmes: Effectiveness, availability and acceptability. *British Journal of Management*, **4**, 103–118.

Inkson, K. (1995) Effects of changing economic conditions on managerial job changes and careers. *British Journal of Management*, **6**, 183–194.

Janssens, M. (1995) Intercultural interaction: A burden on international managers? *Journal of Organisational Behavior*, **16**, 155–167.

Johns, G. (1993) Constraints on the adoption of psychology-based personnel practices: Lessons from organizational innovation. *Personnel Psychology*, **46**, 569–592.

Jones, G. R. (1986) Socialization tactics, self-efficacy, and newcomers' adjustments to organizations. *Academy of Management Journal*, **29**, 262–279.

Jones, R. G. & Whitmore, M. D. (1995) Evaluating developmental assessment centers as interventions. *Personnel Psychology*, **48**, 377–388.

Kanter, R. M, (1989) *When Giants Learn to Dance*. New York: Simon & Schuster.

Katz, M. R. (1969) Can computers make guidance decisions for students? *College Board Review*, No. 72, Summer.

Kegan, R. (1994) *In Over our Heads*: *The Mental Demands of Modern Life*. Cambridge, MA: Harvard University Press.

Kesner, I. F. & Dalton, D. R. (1994) Top management turnover and CEO succession: An investigation of the effects of turnover on performance. *Journal of Management Studies*, **31**, 701–713.

Kesner, I. F. & Sebora, T. C. (1994) Executive succession: Past, present and future. *Journal of Management*, **20**, 327–372.

Kidd, J. & Killeen, J. (1992) Are the effects of careers guidance worth having? *Journal of Occupational and Organizational Psychology*, **65**, 219–234.

Killeen, J., White, M. & Watts, A. G. (1992) *The Economic Value of Careers Guidance*. London: Policy Studies Institute.

Kram, K. E. (1985) *Mentoring at Work*. Lanham, MD: University Press of America.

Krumboltz, J. D. (1993) Integrating career and personal counseling. *Career Development Quarterly*, **42**, 143–148.

Kuhl, J. (1992) A theory of self-regulation: Action versus state orientation, self-discrimination, and some applications. *Applied Psychology*: *An International Review*, **41**, 97–129.

Lawler, E. (1994) From job-based to competency-based organizations. *Journal of Organizational Behavior*, **15**, 3–16.

Lawson, M. B. & Angle, H. (1994) When organizational relocation means family relocation: An emerging issue for strategic human resource management. *Human Resource Management*, **33**, 33–54.

Lent, R. W., Brown, S. D. & Hackett, G. (1994) Toward a unifying social cognitive theory of career and academic interest, choice and performance. *Journal of Vocational Behavior*, **45**, 79–122.

Levinson, D. J. (1986) A conception of adult development. *American Psychologist*, **41**, 3–13.

Levinson, D. J., Darrow, C. N., Klein, E. B., Levinson, M. H. & McKee, B. (1978) *Seasons of a Man's Life*. New York: Knopf.

London, M. (1993) Relationships between career motivation, empowerment and support for career development. *Journal of Occupational and Organizational Psychology*, **66**, 55–69.

London, M. & Greller, M. M. (1991) Demographic trends and vocational behavior: A twenty year retrospective and agenda for the 1990s. *Journal of Vocational Behavior*, **38**, 125–164.

London, M. & Mone, E. (1988) *Career Growth and Human Resources Strategies*. New York: Quorum Books.

London, M. & Stumpf, S. A. (1982) *Managing Careers*. Reading, MA: Addison-Wesley.

Louis, M. R. (1980a) Surprise and sense-making: What newcomers experience in entering unfamiliar organizational settings. *Administrative Science Quarterly*, **25**, 226–251.

Louis, M. R. (1980b) Career transitions: Varieties and commonalities. *Academy of Management Review*, **5**, 329–340.

Louis, M. R. (1982) Career transitions: A missing link in career development. *Organizational Dynamics*, **10**, 68–77.

Mabe, P. A. & West, S. G. (1982) Validity of self-evaluation of ability: A review and meta-analysis. *Journal of Applied Psychology*, **67**, 280–296.

Mabey, C. & Iles, P. (1993) The strategic integration of assessment and development practices: Succession planning and new manager development. *Human Resource Management Journal*, **3**, 16–34.

Major, D. A., Kozlowski, S. W. J., Chao, G. T. & Gardner, P. D. (1995) A longitudinal investigation of newcomer expectations, early socialization outcomes, and the moderating effects of role development factors. *Journal of Applied Psychology*, **80**, 418–431.

Marshall, J. (1995) Gender and management: A critical review of research. *British Journal of Management*, **6** (Special Issue), S53–S62.

Martin, R. (1995) The effects of prior job moves on job relocation stress. *Journal of Occupational and Organizational Psychology*, **68**, 49–56.

McCauley, C. D., Ruderman, M. N., Ohlott, P. J. & Morrow, J. E. (1994) Assessing the developmental components of managerial jobs. *Journal of Applied Psychology*, **79**, 544–560.

McCrae, R. R. & Costa, P. T. (1987) Validation of the five-factor model of personality across instruments and observers. *Journal of Personality and Social Psychology*, **56**, 586–595.

McEnrue, M. P. (1989) Self-development as a career management strategy. *Journal of Vocational Behavior*, **34**, 57–68.

McEvoy, G. M. & Cascio, W. F. (1989) Cumulative evidence of the relationship between employee age and job performance. *Journal of Applied Psychology*, **74**, 11–17.

McGoldrick, A. E. (1996) A psychological model of retirement decision and impact. In C. L. Cooper and I. T. Robertson (eds), *International Review of Industrial and Organizational Psychology*, Vol. 11. Chichester: Wiley.

Meager, N., Kaiser, M. & Dietrich, H. (1992) *Self-Employment in the UK and Germany*. London: Anglo-German Foundation for the Study of Industrial Society.

Meglino, B. M., Denisi, A. S. & Ravlin, E. C. (1993) Effects of previous job exposure and subsequent job status on the functioning of a realistic job preview. *Personnel Psychology*, **46**, 803–822.

Meier, S. T. (1991) Vocational behavior, 1988–1990: Vocational choice, decision-making, career development interventions, and assessment. *Journal of Vocational Behavior*, **39**, 131–181.

Meyer, J. P., Allen, N. J. & Smith, C. A. (1993) Commitment to organizations and occupations: Extension and test of a three-component conceptualization. *Journal of Applied Psychology*, **78**, 538–551.

Miller, V. D. & Jablin, F. M. (1991) Information seeking during organizational entry: Influences, tactics, and a model of the process. *Academy of Management Review*, **16**, 92–120.

Morrison, E. W. (1993) Newcomer information-seeking: Exploring types, modes, sources and outcomes. *Academy of Management Journal*, **36**, 557–589.

Morrison, R. F. & Brantner, T. M. (1992) What enhances or inhibits learning in a new job? A basic career issue. *Journal of Applied Psychology*, **77**, 926–940.

Moss, M. K. & Frieze, H. (1993) Job preferences in the anticipatory socialization phase: A comparison of two matching models. *Journal of Vocational Behavior*, **42**, 282–297.

Munton, A. G., Forster, N., Altman, Y. & Greenbury, L. (1993) *Job Relocation: Managing People on the Move*. Chichester: Wiley.

Nathan, R. & Hill, L. (1992) *Career Counselling*. London: Sage.

Neugarten, B. L. (1977) Personality and aging. In J. E. Birren and K. W. Schaie (eds), *Handbook of the Psychology of Aging*. New York: Van Nostrand Reinhold.

Newton, T. J. & Keenan, A. (1990) Consequences of changing employers amongst young engineers. *Journal of Occupational Psychology*, **63**, 113–127.

Nicholson, N. (1984) A theory of work-role transitions. *Administrative Science Quarterly*, **29**, 172–191.

Nicholson, N. & West, M. A. (1989) Transitions, work histories and careers. In M. B. Arthur, D. T. Hall and B. S. Lawrence (eds), *Handbook of Career Theory*. Cambridge: Cambridge University Press.

Nicholson, N. (1990) The transition cycle: Causes, outcomes, processes and forms. In S. Fisher and C. L. Cooper (eds), *On The Move: The Psychological Effects of Change and Transition*. Chichester: Wiley.

Nicholson, N. & Imaizumi, A. (1993) The adjustment of Japanese expatriates to living and working in Britain. *British Journal of Management*, **4**, 119–134.

Nicholson, N. & West, M. A. (1988) *Managerial Job Change: Men and Women in Transition*. Cambridge: Cambridge University Press.

Noe, R. A. (1988) An investigation of the determinants of successful assigned mentoring relationships. *Personnel Psychology*, **41**, 457–479.

Nordvik, H. (1991) Work activity and career goals in Holland's and Schein's theories of vocational personalities and career anchors. *Journal of Vocational Behavior*, **38**, 165–178.

Offermann, L. R. & Gowing, M. K. (1990) Organizations of the future. *American Psychologist*, **45**, 95–108.

Ohlott, P. J., Ruderman, M. N. & McCauley, C. D. (1994) Gender differences in managers' developmental job experiences. *Academy of Management Journal*, **37**, 46–67.

Olian, J. D., Carroll, S. J. & Giannantonio, C. M. (1993) Mentor reactions to protégés: An experiment with managers. *Journal of Vocational Behavior*, **43**, 266–278.

Ornstein, S. & Isabella, L. A. (1993) Making sense of careers: A review 1989–1992. *Journal of Management*, **19**, 243–267.

Ostroff, C. & Kozlowski, S. W. J. (1992) Organizational socialization as a learning process: The role of information acquisition. *Personnel Psychology*, **45**, 849–874.

Ostroff, C. & Kozlowski, S. W. J. (1993) The role of mentoring in the information gathering processes of newcomers during early organizational socialization. *Journal of Vocational Behavior*, **43**, 170–183.

Pearce, J. L. (1993) Toward an organizational behavior of contract laborers: Their psychological involvement and effects on employee coworkers. *Academy of Management Journal*, **36**, 1082–1096.

Perlmutter, M. & Hall, E. (1992) *Adult Development and Aging*. 2nd edn. Chichester: Wiley.

Pollock, R. (1995) A test of conceptual models depicting the developmental course of informal mentor-protégé relationships in the workplace. *Journal of Vocational Behavior*, **46**, 144–162.

Prediger, D. J. & Vansickle, T. R. (1992) Locating occupations on Holland's hexagon: Beyond RIASEC. *Journal of Vocational Behavior*, **40**, 111–128.

Quick, J. C, Hess, R. E., Hermalin, J. & Quick, J. D. (eds) (1990) *Career Stress in Changing Times*. New York: Haworth Press.

Ragins, B. R. & Cotton, J. L. (1991) Easier said than done: Gender differences in perceived barriers to gaining a mentor. *Academy of Management Journal*, **34**, 939–951.

Robertson, I. T., Iles, P. A., Gratton, L. & Sharpley, D. (1991) The impact of personnel selection and assessment mediods on candidates. *Human Relations*, **44**, 963–982.

Rounds, J. & Tracey, T. J. (1993) Prediger's dimensional representation of Holland's RIASEC circumplex. *Journal of Applied Psychology*, **78**, 875–890.

Russell, J. E. A. (1991) Career development interventions in organizations. *Journal of Vocational Behavior*, **38**, 237–287.

Russell, J. E. A. & Curtis, L. B. (1992) *Career development programs in the Fortune 500*. Paper presented at meeting of the Society for Industrial Organizational Psychology.

Saks, A. M. (1995) Longitudinal field investigation of the moderating and mediating effects of self-efficacy on the relationship between training and newcomer adjustment. *Journal of Applied Psychology*, **80**, 211–225.

Salomone, P. R. (1993) Annual review: Practice and research in career counseling and development, 1993. *Career Development Quarterly*, **42**, 99–128.

Salthouse, T. A. (1990) Cognitive competence and expertise in aging. In J. E. Birren and K. W. Schaie (eds), *Handbook of the Psychology of Aging*, 3rd edn. London: Academic Press.

Scandura, T. A. (1992) Mentorship and career mobility: An empirical investigation. *Journal of Organizational Behavior*, **13**, 169–174.

Scandura, T. A. & Ragins, B. R. (1993) The effects of sex and gender role orientation on mentorship in male-dominated occupations. *Journal of Vocational Behavior*, **43**, 251–265.

Schein, E. H. (1971) The individual, the organization, and the career: A conceptual scheme. *Journal of Applied Behavioral Science*, **7**, 401–426.

Schein, E. H. (1993) *Career Anchors: Discovering your Real Values*. Revised edn. London: Pfeiffer and Co.

Schneider, S. C. & Asakawa, K. (1995) American and Japanese expatriate adjustment: A psychoanalytic perspective. *Human Relations*, **48**, 1109–1127.

Sharf, R. F. (1992) *Applying Career Development Theory to Counseling*. Pacific Grove: Brooks/Cole.

Shore, L. & Tetrick, L. E. (1994) The psychological contract as an explanatory framework in the employment relationship. In C. L. Cooper and D. M. Rousseau (eds), *Trends in Organizational Behavior*, Vol. 1. Chichester: Wiley.

Smart, R. & Peterson, C. (1994) Stability versus transition in women's career development: A test of Levinson's theory. *Journal of Vocational Behavior*, **45**, 241–260.

*Social Trends*, (1993) No. 23. London: Central Statistical Office.

Staudinger, U. M., Smith, J. & Baltes, P. B. (1992) Wisdom-related knowledge in a life review task: Age differences and the role of professional specialization. *Psychology and Aging*, **7**, 271–281.

Stephens, G. K. (1994) Crossing internal career boundaries: The state of research on subjective career transitions. *Journal of Management*, **20**, 479–501.

Sterns, H. L. & Miklos, S. M, (1995) The aging worker in a changing environment: Organizational and individual issues. *Journal of Vocational Behavior*, **47**, 248–268.

Storey, J. (1992) *Developments in the Management of Human Resources*. Oxford: Blackwell.

Subich, L. M. (1994) Annual review: Practice and research in career counseling and development: 1993. *Career Development Quarterly*, **43**, 114–151.

Super, D. E. (1990) Career and life development. In D. Brown and L. Brooks (eds), *Career Choice and Development*, 2nd edn. San Francisco: Jossey-Bass.

Super, D. E. & Hall, D. T. (1978) Career development: Exploration and planning. *Annual Review of Psychology*, **29**, 257–293.

Super, D. E. & Hall, D. T. (1990) Career development: Exploration and planning. *Annual Review of Psychology*, **29**, 333–372.

Swanson, J. L. (1992) Vocational behavior, 1989–1991: Life-span career development and reciprocal interaction of work and nonwork. *Journal of Vocational Behavior*, **41**, 101–161.

Talaga, J. A. & Beehr, T. A. (1995) Are there gender differences in predicting retirement decisions? *Journal of Applied Psychology*, **80**, 16–28.

Terpstra, D. E. & Rozell, E. J. (1993) The relationship of staffing practices to organizational level measures of performance. *Personnel Psychology*, **46**, 27–48.

Tokar, D. M. & Swanson, J. L. (1995) Evaluation of the correspondence between Holland's vocational personality typology and the five-factor model of personality. *Journal of Vocational Behavior*, **46**, 89–108.

Tranberg, M., Slane, S. & Ekeberg, S. E. (1993) The relation between interest congruence and satisfaction: A meta-analysis. *Journal of Vocational Behavior*, **42**, 253–264.

Tremblay, M., Roger, A. & Toulouse, J.-M. (1995) Career plateau and work attitudes: An empirical study of managers. *Human Relations*, **48**, 221–237.

Turban, D. B. & Dougherty, T. W. (1994) Role of protégé personality in receipt of mentoring and career success. *Academy of Management Journal*, **37**, 688–702.

Vondracek, F. & Schulenberg, J. (1992) Counseling for normative and nonnormative influences on career development. *Career Development Quarterly*, **40**, 291–301.

Vroom, V. H. (1966) A study of pre- and post-decision processes. *Organizational Behavior and Human Performance*, **1**, 212–225.

Wallace, J. E. (1993) Professional and organizational commitment: Compatible or incompatible? *Journal of Vocational Behavior*, **42**, 333–349.

Wanous, J. P., Poland, T. D., Premack, S. L. & Davis, K. S. (1992) The effects of met expectations on newcomer attitudes and behaviors: A review and meta-analysis. *Journal of Applied Psychology*, **77**, 288–297.

Warr, P. B. (1993) Age and employment. In M. Dunnette, L. Hough and H. Triandis (eds), *Handbook of Industrial and Organizational Psychology*, Vol. 4. Palo Alto: Consulting Psychologists Press.

Warr, P. B. & Conner, M. (1992) Job competence and cognition. *Research in Organizational Behavior*, **14**, 91–127.

Warr, P. B. & Pennington, J. (1994) Occupational age-grading: Jobs for older and younger non-managerial employees. *Journal of Vocational Behavior*, **45**, 328–346.

Waterman, R., Waterman, J. & Collard, B. (1994) Toward a career resilient workforce. *Harvard Business Review*, July/August.

Watkins, C. E. & Subich, L. M. (1995) Annual review, 1992–1994: Career development, reciprocal work/non-work interaction, and women's workforce participation. *Journal of Vocational Behavior*, **47**, 109–163.

Watts, A. G. (1994) *Lifelong Career Development: Towards a National Strategy for Careers Education and Guidance*. Cambridge, UK: Careers Research and Advisory Centre.

Wheeler, K. G. (1990) Career experiences: Current and future themes. In J C. Quick et al. (eds), *Career Stress in Changing Times*. London: Haworth Press.

White, M. C., Smith, M. & Barnett, T. (1994) A typology of executive career specialization. *Human Relations*, **47**, 473–486.

Whitely, W., Dougherty, T. W. & Dreher, G. F. (1991) Relationship of career mentoring and socioeconomic origin to managers' and professionals' early career progress. *Academy of Management Journal*, **34**, 331–351.

Whitely, W., Dougherty, T.W. & Dreher, G. F. (1992) Correlates of career-oriented mentoring for early career managers and professionals. *Journal of Organizational Behavior*, **13**, 141–154.

# 2

# THE PEOPLE MAKE THE PLACE

*Benjamin Schneider*

Source: *Personnel Psychology* 40 (1987): 437–453.

## Abstract

A framework for understanding the etiology of organizational behavior is presented. The framework is based on theory and research from interactional psychology, vocational psychology, I/O psychology, and organizational theory. The framework proposes that organizations are functions of the kinds of people they contain and, further, that the people there are functions of an attraction-selection-attrition (ASA) cycle. The ASA cycle is proposed as an alternative model for understanding organizations and the causes of the structures, processes, and technology of organizations. First, the ASA framework is developed through a series of propositions. Then some implications of the model are outlined, including (1) the difficulty of bringing about change in organizations, (2) the utility of personality and interest measures for understanding organizational behavior, (3) the genesis of organizational climate and culture, (4) the importance of recruitment, and (5) the need for person-based theories of leadership and job attitudes. It is concluded that contemporary I/O psychology is overly dominated by situationist theories of the behavior of organizations and the people in them.

This talk is about people and places: about how the kinds of people in a place—a work organization, for example—come to define the way that place looks, feels, and behaves. My main thesis is that the attributes of people, not the nature of the external environment, or organizational technology, or organizational structure, are the fundamental determinants of organizational behavior. I will try to persuade you that we have been blind to the role of person effects as causes of organizational behavior because the fields of I/O psychology and organizational behavior have been seduced into the belief that situations determine behavior (see also Schneider, 1983a, 1983b, 1983c; Schneider & Reichers, 1983; Staw & Ross, 1985).

To convince you of the correctness of my thesis I need to draw on theories and findings from different areas of psychology, including personality theory, vocational psychology, and I/O psychology. From personality theory some recent debates over whether behavior is situationally, personally, or interactionally caused will be summarized. From vocational psychology, I will review some of the literature on vocational choice, including extensions of vocational choice theory and data for understanding organizational choice. Finally, from I/O psychology I will offer some new interpretations about the meaning of biodata prediction studies, the importance of research on turnover, and the importance of understanding the etiology of organizational goals for understanding organizational behavior.

In following the ideas I present, you will have to think about how whole organizations look, feel, and behave—your focus must shift from the individual to the organization as the unit of analysis. You must view organizations as situations containing patterned behaviors, as environments that are characterized by the coordinated activities of interdependent parts, including interdependent people (Barker, 1968; Schein, 1980). My basic thesis is that it is the people behaving in them that make organizations what they are. My thesis suggests that Kurt Lewin may have overstated the case when he hypothesized that behavior is a function of person and environment, that is, $B = f(P, E)$. My thesis is that environments are function of persons behaving in them, that is, $E = f(P, B)$.

## Interactional psychology

Interactional psychology, a subfield of contemporary personality theory, grew out of debates in the late 1960s and early 1970s between Mischel (e.g., 1968, 1973) and Bowers (e.g., 1973), among others (cf. Endler & Magnusson, 1976; Magnusson & Endler, 1977; Pervin & Lewis, 1978). In a sense, the debate was long overdue. For almost 100 years more individual- or trait-oriented psychologists—including such diverse people as Freud and Raymond Cattell—had pursued their person-based theories of behavior while the situationists, following in the traditions of Watson and Skinner, focused on environmental determinants of behavior. Each group established itself as a community of scholars, and each camp established ground rules about issues of importance and the kinds of problems appropriate for investigation.

Mischel (1968) opened the door to overt criticism of one group by the other when he published his book, *Personality and Assessment*. The book was a work of clarity and persuasion, supporting the situationist position. The problem for personologists was that the book cast great aspersions on their camp. Mischel's social behaviorist position argued, for example, that:

> Although it is evident that persons are the source from which human responses are evoked, it is situational stimuli that evoke them, and it is

changes in conditions that alter them. Since the assumption of massive behavioral similarity across diverse situations no longer is tenable, it becomes essential to study the difference in the behaviors of a given person as a function of the conditions in which they occur (1968, p. 295).

In other words, situations cause behavior.

Most of the criticisms of Mischel that followed were attacks on the extremeness of his social learning perspective. Some of the early critiques were neither as scholarly nor as persuasive as Mischel's book. The paucity of effective rebuttal was solved by Bowers (1973), who, in one of the most insightful papers of the 1970s, presented the interactionist perspective. My perspective, one influenced both by cognitive psychology and the developmental epistemology of Jean Piaget, argues for the inseparability of person and situation. While Bowers presented many sides of the interactionist perspective and many reasons why Mischel's conclusions were suspect, his most telling argument concerned the data base Mischel drew on for his conclusions. Bowers showed that Mischel's conclusion that situations dominate traits and cause behavior was based almost exclusively on experimental studies conducted in laboratory settings.

Bowers noted that one problem with laboratory experiments as a way of studying the relative contribution of traits and situations to behavior was that experimentalists play with experimental treatment conditions until the different conditions have their desired effects. To set up conditions to have an effect, and to then argue for the dominance of situations over traits, seemed to Bowers an unwarranted inferential leap. The problem here was that precisely when the laboratory study does what it should (i.e., demonstrates an effect) it presents enormous constraints on the display of individual differences, making it appear as if traits were irrelevant for understanding behavior.

A second problem with laboratory experiments that Bowers noted was that *the* major feature of the experiment, random assignment of participants to treatments, violates a basic reality in understanding real-time human behavior—humans, at least in Western societies, are not randomly assigned to settings. Humans select themselves into and out of settings.

Finally, Bowers presented some logic to suggest that persons cause human environments at least as much as environments cause persons. What he meant by this was that persons are inseparable from environments because environments only exist through the people behaving in them *knowing* them. In our own field, Weick (1979) has made a similar point.

This logic suggests that it is the kinds of persons in environments who determine the kinds of human environments they are. This point becomes critical in what follows because Bowers' and subsequent commentaries on the situationist position in personality research (cf. Aronoff & Wilson, 1985; Epstein & O'Brien, 1985) appear to be equally appropriate for questioning the overwhelming tendency in contemporary I/O psychology to assume that situational variables (groups, technology, structure, environment) determine organizational behavior.

By way of summary, I offer the following propositions for what research and theory in interactional psychology has shown:

*Proposition 1*: Experimental laboratories mask the display of individual differences. This method, then, is inappropriate for studying the relative contributions of traits and situations to understanding behavior.

*Proposition 2*: People are not randomly assigned to real organizations; people select themselves into and out of real organizations.

*Proposition 3*: People and human settings are inseparable; people *are* the setting because it is they who make the setting.

I want to build on these propositions to offer an alternative to the situationist perspective in I/O psychology. My perspective rests on the idea that people are not randomly assigned to settings. It argues that it is the people who are attracted to, are selected by, and remain in a setting that determine the setting. As I will show, it follows from what I call the attraction-selection-attrition, or ASA, framework for understanding organizations that technology, structure, and the larger environment of organizations are outcomes of, not the causes of, people and their behavior (Schneider, 1983b).

## The attraction-selection-attrition framework

The focus, or level of analysis, of what follows is on the organization as a location for human activity; it is not on the individual. Thus, the review of interactional psychology yielded the idea that environments and people are not separable and that the people in an environment make it what it is. We are, then, unconcerned with the individual differences *within* an organization; our gaze shifts to understanding the differences *between* organizations through a focus on the attributes of people.

I am going to show that it only *looks* like organizations determine behavior; it looks that way because we typically only study organizations after they have been in existence for a while (cf. Kimberly & Miles, 1980). When an organization has been in existence for a while it looks like the people there are behaving as they do because of its (seemingly) nonpersonal attributes. In reality the way it looks is a result of the people there behaving the way they do. They behave the way they do because they were attracted to that environment, selected by it, and stayed with it. Different kinds of organizations attract, select, and retain different kinds of people, and it is the outcome of the ASA cycle that determines why organizations look and feel different from each other.

These conclusions yield a fourth proposition:

*Proposition 4*: Attraction to an organization, selection by it, and attrition from it yield particular kinds of persons in an organization. These people determine organizational behavior.

### *Attraction*

One of the most consistent findings in psychology comes from vocational psychology. It concerns the fact that people are differentially attracted to careers as a function of their own interests and personality. The theoretical position that dominates the vocational psychology literature is one proposed by Holland (1985).

Holland's perspective is that careers are conveniently and empirically groupable into six major types: Intellectual, artistic, social, enterprising, conventional, and realistic. Literally hundreds of studies support Holland's classification, and the most recent version of the Strong-Campbell Interest Inventory (Campbell & Hansen, 1985) employs his scheme for grouping occupations. For present purposes Holland's most important contribution is his idea that not only can careers and career interests be grouped into six categories, but that career *environments* can also be so grouped. As Holland (1976) put it: "Vocational choice is assumed to be the result of a person's type, or patterning of types *and* the environment" (p. 533) and that "the character of an environment emanates from the types [of people] which dominate that environment" (p. 534). In brief, Holland showed that the career environments people join are similar to the people who join them.

There is also evidence in the organizational choice literature to support this match of person and environment. Tom (1971), for example, showed that people's most preferred environments are environments that have the same "personality" profile as they do. Vroom (1966) showed that people choose an organization in which to work that they believe will be most instrumental in obtaining their valued outcomes.

Theories like Holland's, findings like those of Vroom and Tom, and the abundant evidence that has accumulated about the utility of interest measures for predicting eventual occupational entry lead to the conclusion that similar kinds of people are likely to have similar kinds of personalities, are likely to choose to do similar kinds of things, and are likely to behave in similar kinds of ways.

Certainly the biodata research of Owens and his colleagues (cf. Neiner & Owens, 1985; Owens & Schoenfeldt, 1979) leads to this conclusion. In his programmatic research over the years Owens has shown that people can be clustered into types based on their profiles of personal characteristics. More importantly, he has shown that once the cluster to which persons belong is known, it is possible to make accurate predictions about what they will do. Indeed, predictions based on cluster membership are as accurate as those made by knowing a person's individual characteristics! More specifically, students' college majors, grade point averages, achievement imagery, memory capacity, leadership roles on campus, vocational interests, and even job choices are predictable; all by simply knowing the biodata cluster to which they belong. In fact, Owens (personal communication, June, 1985) is following up his samples of college students to see if the broad range of kinds of job and job environments to which they go is predictable by relating biodata cluster membership to PAQ (Position Analysis Questionnaire; McCormick, 1979) job clusters. It seems perfectly clear to me that Owens will be able to show that people who are of a similar type will be attracted, not only to jobs, but to organizations of a particular sort. It is this attraction of similar types to the same place that, I believe, begins to determine the place—but there is more to it than just attraction.

### *Attrition*

The opposite side of attraction is attrition. It is a dependent variable of great interest in I/O and OB as well as in vocational psychology (Staw, 1984). For our purposes, the important finding from turnover studies is that people who do not fit an environment well will tend to leave it (cf. Mobley, 1982). So, while people may be attracted to a place, they may make errors, and finding they do not fit, they will leave. This kind of logic is what Wanous and his colleagues (cf. Wanous, 1980) have used as a basis for their research on the realistic job preview (RJP). That work shows, as demonstrated quite convincingly in recent meta-analyses (Premack & Wanous, 1985), that the better the fit between individual expectations and the reality of organizational life, the higher the job satisfaction and the longer the tenure.

The importance of this finding for my thesis is that if people who do not fit leave, then the people who remain will be similar to each other. But the critical point is not just that they will be similar to each other, but that they will constitute a more homogeneous group than those who were initially attracted to the setting. The conclusion that particular kinds of people are attracted to particular settings, combined with the finding that those who do not fit leave, produces restriction in range—the range of variance in individual differences in a setting is much less than would be expected by chance—or by the random assignment of people to settings.

Recall that when laboratory studies artificially suppress variability in behavior, it looks like the situation determines behavior. I think the same kind of phenomenon exists in our field. That is, we look at organizations and the people behaving in them and see somewhat similar kinds of behavior from the individuals there. We conclude, quite erroneously I would argue, that this similarity in behavior is caused by situational influences. An alternative explanation is that because of attraction to organizations and attrition from them, similar people are there, and they behave similarly because they *are* similar not because of some external factors. This restriction in range yields people who not only are similar in kind but who will be similar in behavior, experiences, orientations, feelings, and reactions. This line of reasoning suggests a fifth proposition:

> *Proposition 5*: Attraction to an organization and attrition from it produce restriction in range in the kinds of people in an organization. This restriction in range of people yields similar kinds of behavior from the people there, making it appear as if the organization were a determinant of their behavior.

### *Goals*

To this point it is clear that thinking in interactional psychology contributes useful ideas for conceptualizing how people make a setting what it is and that theories and findings regarding attraction and attrition yield the conclusion that similar types of people are prone to end up in similar places. Here I introduce the idea that it is goals to which people are attracted, it is goals with which they interact, and if they don't fit, they leave.

Organizations are systems that are activated and directed by goals (Aldrich, 1979; Katz & Kahn, 1978). These goals are not actively chosen or consciously dictated goals. Rather, they emerge initially from the kind of person or persons who establish (found) the organization (Schein, 1985). As organizations evolve into maturity, it is the behavior of all of the people in them that defines organizational direction. But, more importantly for my present thesis, the behaviors of people in pursuit of organizational goals determine the processes and structures that evolve in organizations (Kimberly & Miles, 1980).

By this I mean that as an organization confronts both its larger environment and its internal environment, the processes and structures that are appropriate for survival will emerge and evolve. The processes and structures that emerge in a bank will differ from those in a YMCA—the environments they confront will be different because the people who formed them were different.

In any organization, then, structures and processes emerge out of day-to-day necessity, but the form and content of those structures and processes are ultimately traceable to the founder. This is true because the founder who starts a YMCA is different from one who founds a bank. As a consequence, the environments in which they operate will differ. The combination of differences in people and differences in environments produces differences in structures. Indeed, Miller and his colleagues (cf. Miller & Droge, 1986) have shown that, other things being equal, it is the founder's personality that determines organizational structure and strategy.

This line of thinking suggests a sixth proposition:

> *Proposition 6*: The goals, structures, and processes that attract people to organizations are determined by the founders' choices, that is, by his or her choices to found a particular kind of organization. The processes and

structures that emerge in an organization evolve from people meeting the daily demands associated with survival.

## *Selection*

Through formal and informal selection processes, the goals of organizations have another influence on the kinds of people there. When organizations exist in particular environments and have particular technologies, they need people with particular kinds of competencies (Aldrich, 1979). One thing we know about competencies is that different kinds of people tend to have different kinds of competencies (Campbell & Hansen, 1985). It follows that organizations further restrict the range of types of persons in them through the recruitment and hiring of people with the kinds of competencies needed for effectiveness.

But organizations require people with many different kinds of competencies if they are to survive. How can it be that organizations can be "typed" if people with many kinds of competencies are required? This is possible when people are conceptualized as profiles of personal attributes: people are not defined by a single characteristic, they are multidimensional (Owens & Schoenfeldt, 1979).

Organizations can be typed, then, by people sharing many common attributes and differing only with respect to specific competencies. Holland (1985), for example, types people by not only their dominant career interests, but by their secondary and tertiary interests as well. I hypothesize that through recruitment and selection procedures organizations actually end up choosing people who share many common personal attributes although they may not share common competencies. In other words accountants in YMCAs should share many personal attributes with YMCA social workers, while they share only some very specific competencies with accountants in banks.

The addition of selection to attraction and attrition as forces to restrict the range of types of people in an organization yields the following proposition:

> *Proposition 7*: As an outcome of the attraction, selection, and attrition cycle, organizations will have severely restricted the range of types of people in them.

## *Summary*

Figure 1 summarizes the theoretical framework. At the hub of the framework is goals. It is important to remember that goals here are in the head of the founder, becoming manifest through his or her behavior. Thus organizational goals become operationalized via behavior, and that behavior, in turn, yields structures and processes. These manifestations of goals determine the kinds of people who are attracted to, are selected by, and stay with a particular organization. Over time, persons attracted to, selected by, staying with, and behaving in organizations cause them to be what they are.

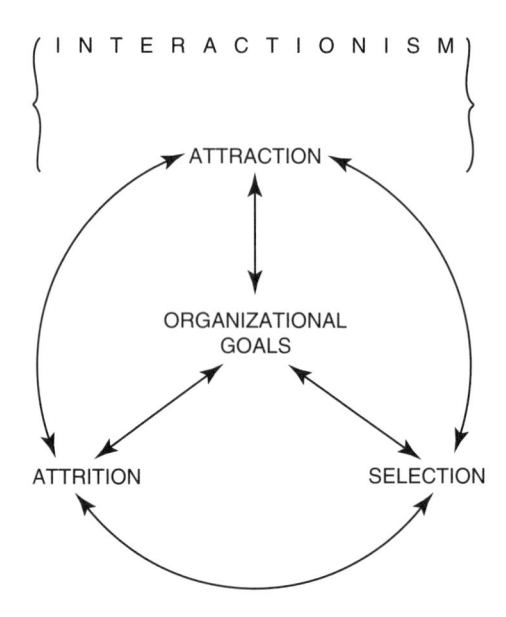

*Figure 1* The attraction-selection-attrition framework. (From "An interactionist perspective on organizational effectiveness" by B. Schneider in *Organizational Effectiveness*, edited by K. S. Cameron and D. S. Whetten, 1983, New York, Academic Press. Copyright 1983 by Academic Press. Reprinted by permission.)

Over time, in fact, an organization can become so ingrown in type that it begins to occupy an increasingly narrow ecological niche (Aldrich, 1979). When this happens, the organization can fail—its people, structures, and processes may become so appropriate for a particular segment of the environment that, when the environment changes, the kinds of people, processes, and structures are no longer viable. Organizations, may then experience what Argyris (1976) calls dry rot.

Organizations grow and die and usually do not have someone around to keep the environment from changing or, as in the Government's protection of Chrysler, to give them time to adapt to the environment. The ASA framework for understanding how people make the place suggests that the natural cycle portrayed in Figure 1 can be dangerous to long-term organizational health.

## Implications of the framework

### 1. Organizational survival and organization change

A first implication of the attraction-selection-attrition framework, then, concerns organizational survival. The framework indicates that unless organizations consciously fight restriction in the range of the kinds of people they contain, when the environment changes they will (1) not be aware that it has changed and (2) probably not be capable of changing.

In fact, the ASA framework is quite grim with respect to how organizations will cope with the requirement to change. They are likely to have great difficulty because they do not contain people with the appropriate inclinations. For example, suppose an organization that was basically a service business—the customer comes first—encounters an environmental change such that it needs to be more market- and profit-oriented. In this case the inclination towards good service can be self-defeating and the organization could fail. It could fail because, over time, it has attracted, selected, and retained persons with service inclinations.

A tendency in situations like this is to seek new "right types" (Argyris, 1957). This is a serious mistake if the new "right types" do not have secondary or tertiary inclinations that fit the old "right types." This is true because without some sharing of inclinations, ways of viewing the world, and so forth, the newcomers won't fit at all and the old-timers will force them out (Alderfer, 1971). So, the motto from the model is to be sure that newcomers brought in to turn around an organization (i.e., to change the old-timers' inclinations) share some attributes with those they are expected to change.

One last caution follows from the ASA framework regarding changing an organization: Changes in structure and process are not likely to be useful. This follows from the idea that structure and process are outcomes of the behavior of the kinds of people in the organization rather than the determinants of their behavior. Structures and processes will change when the behaviors of people change and the behaviors of people will change when different kinds of people are attracted to, selected by, and stay in an organization.

## *2. The use of personality and interest measures*

I have emphasized constructs variously labelled "personality," "interests," "type," "kind," "inclination," "profile of attributes," and so on. These terms are used here to connote a macro, organizational-level issue; they do not refer to individual differences within organizations. A second implication of the ASA framework is that I/O psychologists have erred in their use of personality and interest kinds of measures. We have erred in using them when the goal has been to only predict which of a number of persons being considered for a specific job in a particular company is more likely to succeed. Although this has been more successful than some have claimed (Schneider & Schmitt, 1986), the fact is that these kinds of measures were not designed to make fine-grained distinctions among people who are relatively similar to begin with.

Using typical personality or interest tests to make fine-grained distinctions among applicants for a particular job in a particular company is like employing a yardstick when a micrometer is required. These measures have typically either been designed to make gross distinctions between normals and non-normals or to cluster the population into relatively homogeneous subgroups. As such they should be useful for identifying the types of people who cluster in different organizations.

In fact, an early idea in climate research, that organizations have a personality, may have been closer to the truth than early theoreticians imagined (Gellerman, 1959). I believe that the use of measures of individual personality and interest to conduct research across organizations would be interesting from a scholarly point of view and practical from an organizational change standpoint.

We have lived too long now with the idea that organizations are what their structures and processes are and that the latest fad in structure and process change is best for all organizations. Somehow the early work by Lawrence and Lorsch (1967) showing that no one structure is best for all organizations has been forgotten. We live with the myth that people are infinitely adaptable and changeable, can work under any new structure or set of procedures, and that the one best system is the holy grail.

The ASA framework makes it very clear that we need to know much more about the kinds of people in whole organizations prior to reaching conclusions about a best structure. Good consultants try to figure out an organization's style (personality?) each time they enter a new setting; it is time for I/O psychology to document the data on which they focus. The ASA framework suggests that a useful set of data could be generated by the use of existing personality and interest measures administered to the members of entire organizations.

### 3. Organizational climate and organizational culture

Climate here refers to the ways by which organizations indicate to organizational participants what is important for organizational effectiveness. As I have indicated elsewhere (Schneider, 1975; Schneider & Reichers, 1983), by what they reward, support, and expect, organizations can indicate that customer service or safety or product quality is an organizational imperative (Schneider & Bowen, 1985).

Culture is an even more amorphous topic than is climate, and like Jello, it seems difficult to nail to the wall (I used to say the same thing about climate). Organizations are said to have certain cultures when the people there share a common set of assumptions, values, and beliefs. Culture is said to be transmitted through myths and stories, and when large groups within organizations share the meanings of these myths, a culture is said to exist (Schein, 1985; Schneider, 1985).

Obviously climate and culture are complimentary topics. Climate focuses on how the organization functions (what it rewards, supports, and expects), while culture addresses the assumptions and values attributed to why particular activities and behaviors are rewarded, supported, and expected. Culture focuses, then, on why thing's happen as they do, on the meaning or reasons for what happens.

The ASA framework provides a new vantage point from which one can understand the genesis of both climate and culture. As noted earlier, the processes and structures that emerge in organizations are functions of the kinds of people in them behaving in ways that facilitate the accomplishments of the goals of the founder. The attraction, selection, and retention of certain kinds of people yield people who are similar to each other and who will be interpersonally attracted to each other (Festinger, 1954). As a result of this interpersonal attraction, people will naturally share their views of why things occur the way they do. Given that the attribution of cause is a basic human tendency, when we share our attributions of cause with others they become the very stories and myths by which culture is transmitted (Bolman & Deal, 1984).

### *4. The importance of recruitment*

Compared to personnel selection, the research on personnel recruitment is relatively sparse (Rynes, in press). The ASA framework suggests that the major way organizations can actively determine the pool of candidates from which they will choose their members is through recruitment activities. Thus, if organizations are to make active choices to increase the range of the types of people they select, then it will be primarily through a focus on increasing the pool of candidates that this will happen. Haphazard recruitment and/or faith in the selection process, either self-selection or organizational selection, cannot be expected to yield the non-right types required for long-term viability.

### *Other implications of the ASA framework*

These four implications barely begin to scratch the surface of this person-based model for understanding why organizations look and feel the way they do. For example, the model has some interesting implications for research on leadership, motivation, job attitudes, and socialization to work, among others (Schneider, 1983a, 1983b). Here I only summarize some issues regarding leadership and job attitudes as my fifth and sixth implications of the ASA model.

With respect to leadership, for example, the ASA model predicts that different kinds of people are likely to be effective leaders in different kinds of organizations. This means that different dimensions or traits will be predictive of leadership effectiveness as a function of the kinds of people to be led. When Stogdill (1948), almost forty years ago, discovered that no single trait predicted leadership across settings, he drew the conclusion that personality measures would not be useful in the prediction of leadership at work.

Subsequent research on the prediction of leadership effectiveness, of course, substantiates the ASA prediction. For example, Miner's (cf., 1978) sentence completion measure seems to be effective in more bureaucratically structured organizations but not in the more free-floating world of high tech. Yukl (1981) interprets this finding in structural terms, but the ASA framework suggests that different kinds of people are attracted to, selected by, and stay with old-line manufacturing organizations, so the kinds of people who will be effective in leading them will be different. We desperately need some research on leader attributes.

This kind of research is needed because almost all of the current leadership theories are situational theories in the extreme; they tell a leader what to do, given a certain situation, and make the assumption that leaders are infinitely flexible and that followers from setting to setting are all the same.

From an ASA perspective, theory and research on job attitudes really are very depressing. The history of job attitude research leads us to believe implicitly that the attitudes of people at work are caused by the conditions of the work place. In the past ten years, this implicit belief has been made explicit through the social construction of reality perspective (Salancik & Pfeffer, 1978). In this perspective it is argued that people's job attitudes are really only social constructions of reality; that people's attitudes are a reflection of the social milieu in which they work.

The problem with this approach to job attitudes is that it assumes a group phenomenon wherein the group somehow or other takes over the minds of individuals and causes them to see things differently than they would if alone. Let us suppose that people in a setting *do* have the same job attitudes. The ASA model says they probably will, not because they are constructing a false reality, but because they are similar people experiencing similar conditions.

In other words, the sixth implication of the ASA model is that people in a setting *will* have the same job attitudes. In fact, the ASA model makes an even more interesting prediction. It predicts that the "same" organizational conditions will be differentially satisfying to people in different work environments and, conversely, that different work conditions can be equally satisfying to the people in different settings. So, the ASA framework predicts that a level of pay that may be very satisfying to community mental health center employees may be quite dissatisfying to stockbrokers. Or conversely, a considerate boss may have greater impact on a community mental health worker's attitudes than on a stockbroker's.

In other words, the ASA framework cautions against a situationist interpretation of what makes for positive job attitudes. It says that positive job attitudes for workers in an organization can be expected when the natural inclinations of the persons there are allowed to be reflected in their behaviors by the kinds of processes and structures that have evolved there. In fact, there is some evidence now that people's job attitudes may come with them to a setting (Pulakos & Schmitt, 1983; Staw, Bell & Clausen, 1986; Staw & Ross, 1985). These kinds of data indicate the need for an alternative to situationism in the study of job attitudes.

## Summary

The main thesis of the ASA perspective is that organizations are the people in them: that the people make the place. I have presented the idea that I/O psychologists have failed to incorporate people types into our theories of organizations. Failure to understand organizations as people has resulted in at least the following:

1  We have tried to change organizations by changing their structures and processes when it was the people that needed changing. With changes in people,

the necessary changes in structure and process will occur. We have also probably oversold the speed with which organizations can change; change will be slow.
2. We have assisted organizations in their inadvertent slide into decline by implementing selection systems that might further restrict the range of their adaptive capability.
3. We have accepted situationist interpretations of clearly psychological phenomena such as job attitudes, organizational climate, and leadership. In addition, we have implicitly accepted the idea that organizational forms and functions are determined by phenomena outside individuals' attributes; we have accepted environmental determinism.
4. We have erroneously accepted the idea that personality and interest measures are not useful; they can be tremendously useful in understanding organizations. But even in more micro studies, we have passively accepted criticisms of personality measures when, at least in leadership research, we have good evidence to show that different kinds of people are likely to be effective leaders in different kind of settings.

In short, we have been seduced into thinking that organizational processes and structures are the causes of the attitudes, feelings, experiences, meanings, and behaviors that we observe there. We attribute cause not to the people attracted to, selected by, and remaining with organizations, but to the *signs* of their existence in the organization: to structure, process, and technology.

Enough is enough. We are psychologists and behavioral scientists; let us seek explanation in people not in the results of their behavior. The people make the place.

## Acknowledgment

This is a slightly modified form of my Presidential Address to the Society for Industrial and Organizational Psychology, American Psychological Association Convention, Los Angeles, August, 1985.

## References

Aldrich HE. (1979). *Organizations and environments*. Englewood Cliffs, NJ: Prentice-Hall.

Alderfer CP. (1971). Effect of individual, group and intergroup relations on attitudes toward a management development program. *Journal of Applied Psychology*, 55, 302–311.

Argyris C. (1957). Some problems in conceptualizing organizational climate: A case study of a bank. *Administrative Science Quarterly*, 2, 501–520.

Argyris C. (1976). Problems and new directions for industrial psychology. In Dunnette MD (Ed.). *Handbook of industrial and organizational psychology* (pp. 151–184). Chicago: Rand, McNally.

Aronoff J, Wilson JP. (1985). *Personality in the social process*. Hillsdale, NJ: Erlbaum.

Barker RB. (1968). *Ecological psychology*. Stanford, CA: Stanford University Press.
Bolman LG, Deal TE. (1984). *Modern approaches to understanding and managing organizations*. San Francisco: Jossey-Bass.
Bowers KS. (1973). Situationism in psychology: An analysis and critique. *Psychological Review, 80*, 307–336.
Campbell DP, Hansen JC. (1985). *Manual for the SVIB-SCII*. Palo Alto, CA: Consulting Psychologists Press.
Endler NS, Magnusson D (Eds.). (1976). *Interactional psychology and personality*. New York: Hemisphere.
Epstein S, O'Brien EJ. (1985). The person-situation debate in historical and current perspective. *Psychological Bulletin, 98*, 513–537.
Festinger L. (1954). A theory of social comparison processes. *Human Relations, 7*, 117–140.
Gellerman SW. (1959). The company personality. *Management Review, 48*, 69–76.
Holland JL. (1976). Vocational preferences. In Dunnette MD (Ed.). *Handbook of industrial and organizational psychology* (pp. 521–570). Chicago: Rand, McNally.
Holland JL. (1985). *Making vocational choices: A theory of careers*. Englewood Cliffs, NJ: Prentice-Hall.
Katz D, Kahn RL. (1978). *The social psychology of organizations* (2nd ed.). New York: Wiley.
Kimberly JR, Miles RH (Eds.). (1980). *The organizational life cycle*. San Francisco: Jossey-Bass.
Lawrence PR, Lorsch JW. (1967). *Organizations and environments*. Boston: Division of Research, Harvard Business School.
Magnusson D, Endler NS (Eds.). (1977). *Personality at the crossroads: Current issues in interactional psychology*. Hillsdale, NJ: Erlbaum.
McCormick EJ. (1979). *Job analysis: Methods and application*. New York: Amacom.
Miller D, Droge C. (1986). Psychological and traditional determinants of structure. *Administrative Science Quarterly, 31*, 539–560.
Miner JB. (1978). Twenty years of research on role motivation theory of managerial effectiveness. *Personnel Psychology, 31*, 739–760.
Mischel W. (1968). *Personality and assessment*. New York: Wiley.
Mischel W. (1973). Toward a cognitive social learning reconceptualization of personality. *Psychological Review, 80*, 252–283.
Mobley WH. (1982). *Employee turnover in organizations*. Reading, MA: Addison-Wesley.
Neiner AG, Owens WA. (1985). Using biodata to predict job choice among college graduates. *Journal of Applied Psychology, 70*, 127–136.
Owens WA, Schoenfeldt LF. (1979). Toward a classification of persons. *Journal of Applied Psychology Monograph, 65*, 569–607.
Pervin LA, Lewis M (Eds.). (1978). *Perspectives in interactional psychology*. New York: Plenum.
Premack SL, Wanous JP. (1985). A meta-analysis of realistic job preview experiments. *Journal of Applied Psychology, 70*, 706–719.
Pulakos ED, Schmitt N. (1983). A longitudinal study of a valence model approach for the prediction of job satisfaction of new employees. *Journal of Applied Psychology, 68*, 307–312.
Rynes SL. (In press). Recruitment, organizational entry, and early work adjustment. In Dunnette MD (Ed.). *Handbook of industrial and organizational psychology* (2nd ed.).

Salancik GR, Pfeffer J. (1978). A social information processing approach to job attitudes and task design. *Administrative Science Quarterly, 23*, 224–252.

Schein EH. (1980). *Organizational psychology* (3rd ed.). Englewood Cliffs, NJ: Prentice-Hall.

Schein EH. (1985). *Organizational culture and leadership.* San Francisco: Jossey-Bass.

Schneider B. (1975). Organizational climates: An essay. *Personnel Psychology, 28*, 447–479.

Schneider B. (1983a). Interactional psychology and organizational behavior. In Cummings LL, Staw BM (Eds.), *Research in organizational behavior. Vol 5* (pp. 1–31). Greenwich, CT: JAI Press.

Schneider B. (1983b). An interactionist perspective on organizational effectiveness. In Cameron KS, Whetten DS (Eds.), *Organizational effectiveness: A comparison of multiple models* (pp. 27–54). New York: Academic Press.

Schneider B. (1983c). Work climates: An interactionist perspective. In Feimer NW, Geller ES (Eds.), *Environmental psychology: Directions and perspectives* (pp. 106–128). New York: Praeger.

Schneider B. (1985). Organizational behavior. *Annual Review of Psychology, 36*, 573–611.

Schneider B, Bowen DE. (1985). Employee and customer perceptions of service in banks: Replication and extension. *Journal of Applied Psychology, 70*, 423–433.

Schneider B, Reichers AE. (1983). On the etiology of climates. *Personnel Psychology, 36*, 19–40.

Schneider B, Schmitt N. (1986). *Staffing organizations* (2nd ed.). Glenview, IL: Scott, Foresman.

Staw BM. (1984). Organizational behavior: A review and reformulation of the field's outcome variables. *Annual Review of Psychology, 35*, 627–666.

Staw BM, Bell NE, Clausen JA. (1986). The dispositional approach to job attitudes: A lifetime longitudinal test. *Administrative Science Quarterly, 31*, 56–77.

Staw BM, Ross J. (1985). Stability in the midst of change: A dispositional approach to job attitudes. *Journal of Applied Psychology, 70*, 469–480.

Stogdill RM. (1948). Personal factors associated with leadership: A survey of the literature. *Journal of Psychology, 25*, 35–71.

Tom VR. (1971). The role of personality and organizational images in the recruiting process. *Organizational Behavior and Human Performance, 6*, 573–592.

Vroom VR. (1966). Organizational choice: A study of pre- and post-decision processes. *Organizational Behavior and Human Performance, 1*, 212–226.

Wanous JP. (1980). *Organizational entry: Recruitment, selection and socialization of newcomers.* Reading, MA: Addison-Wesley.

Weick KE. (1979). *The social psychology of organizing* (2nd ed.). Reading, MA: Addison-Wesley.

Yukl GA. (1981). *Leadership in organizations.* Englewood Cliffs, NJ: Prentice-Hall.

# 3

# POLICE SOCIALIZATION

A longitudinal examination of job attitudes in an urban police department

*John Van Maanen*

Source: *Administrative Science Quarterly* 20(1975): 207–227.

## Abstract

This article documents changes in the attitudes of police recruits moving through the series of experiences associated with their early careers. The data were obtained from questionnaires which were administered longitudinally to newcomers in a big-city department and cross-checked by the researcher who was a participant-observer in the police training program. The analysis concentrated upon the motivation, commitment, and need satisfaction of patrol officers. The findings indicated that recruits entered the department highly motivated and committed to their newly-adopted organization. However, their motivational attitudes declined swiftly. Evidence is presented which suggests the less motivated patrol officers are perceived by their relevant supervisors as better policemen than their more motivated peers. Commitment attitudes also dropped over time, although expressed commitment remained relatively high compared to several other occupational samples. A positive association was present between superior evaluations of performance and commitment attitudes. Need satisfaction remained fairly constant across time and a positive relationship was detected between evaluations of performance and reported satisfaction. These findings denote the speedy and powerful character of the police socialization process resulting in a final perspective which stresses a "lay low, don't make waves" approach to urban policing. The findings also suggest the beginning of a general theory of organizational socialization.[1]

## Introduction

The job attitudes of recruit police officers in a large, urban police department are examined longitudinally within the framework of what theorists have termed organizational socialization (Caplow, 1964; Berlew and Hall, 1966; Wheeler, 1966; Schein, 1968, 1971; Manning, 1970; Porter, Van Maanen and Crampon, 1972)—that is, the process by which an organizational member learns the required behaviors and supportive attitudes necessary to participate as a member of an organization.

Although organizational socialization occurs throughout all career stages, this analysis is directed primarily to the consideration of the person's entry into the organization. During this "breaking-in" period, the organization may be thought to be most persuasive for the individual has few, if any, guidelines to direct his behavior (Van Maanen, 1975). A wide range of studies indicate that early organizational learning is a major determinant of one's later organizationally-relevant attitudes and behaviors (Herzberg *et al*., 1957; Schein, 1965, 1971; Berlew and Hall, 1966; Denhart, 1968; Vroom and Deci, 1971).

This examination of the organizational socialization process focuses upon the attitudes of young men entering the police world. As others have noted, police organizations have been neglected by researchers interested in the relationships between individuals and their work (Neiderhoffer, 1967; President's Commission on Law Enforcement and the Administration of Justice, 1967; Bayley and Mendelson, 1969; Rubenstein, 1973). Most data regarding the police socialization process either examine certain hypothesized dimensions of the police personality—for example, cynicism, dogmatism, authoritarianism, and so forth—or survey opinions aimed at describing police attitudes toward certain audiences external to police departments—for example, minority groups, juveniles, judges, reporters, and so forth. As a result, little more than cross-sectional snapshots of the police socialization process exist. There are, however, two notable exceptions: Rubenstein's (1973) brilliant ethnology of the Philadelphia Police Department and Westley's (1951) classic account of the policeman's lot in a midwestern department. Several excellent observational reports, most concerned with rather specific aspects of police behavior—Skolnick (1966) on vice activities; Reiss (1971) on police-citizen encounters; Bittner (1967) and Cicourel (1967) on police interaction with skid-row alcoholics and juveniles, respectively—are also available. Yet, these studies are devoted mainly to the description of the more salient sociological features of the occupation and are concerned only peripherally with the subject of this paper, the learning process associated with a police career.

This study probes into police recruits' perceptions of three aspects of their relationship with the organization—motivation, commitment, and need satisfaction. These attitude areas can be seen to be distinct analytically if not empirically. The theoretical perspective combines an expectancy approach to work motivation (Fishbein, 1963; Vroom, 1964; and Porter and Lawler, 1968) with conceptions of organizational commitment (Kanter, 1968; Patchen, 1970; and Porter and

Table 1 Basic survey design

| Date* (1st adm.) | Group | Months in department |
|---|---|---|
| | | 0  1  2  3  4  5  6  7  8  9  10 ......30 |
| | | 1970                                            1973 |
| | | Administrative numbers |
| June 10 | I   |             1  2  3  4  5       — |
| June 10 | II  |       1  2  3  4  5             — |
| June 10 | III |    1  2  3  4  5                — |
| June 20 | IV  | 1  2  3  4  5                   6 |

*The date of first administration. The remaining questionnaires for each group were administered on the same date of the 4 following months.

Smith, 1970) and need satisfaction (Maslow, 1954; Porter, 1962; and Hall and Nougaim, 1968).

A substantial amount of descriptive data was obtained by attitude mapping via questionnaires administered over time to department initiates. Also, a major portion of this study was devoted to the observation of novice patrolmen *in situ*. The researcher became a fully participating member of the Police Academy recruit class (Recruit Group IV, Table 1). Following the training phase of the socialization process, the role of modified participant-observer was adopted and some time (approximately six months) was spent as an armed backseat observer in patrol units comprised of a member of the recruit class and his partner. This experiential technique proved extremely valuable and provided the background upon which much of this analysis is based. Yet the merging of the survey and observation approaches to field research was difficult. The two styles pulled one in opposite directions: one method being specific and the other general. In this particular case, the juxtaposition of the two methods created pressure on one hand to scrap the original aims of the study and tackle larger issues and on the other hand to ignore the richness of context and concentrate solely on the quantifiable aspects. Although in retrospect, the two methods provide an excellent—but arduous—check on one another—with the empirical aspects of the study acting as a limit upon the inferential and the observational portion of the study providing the fabric into which the survey results must be woven.

Finally, to suggest behavioral implications connected to the attitude landscape, independent judgments were collected on the recruits' job behavior. The two main concerns are listed below in the form of two research questions.

(1) What are job-related attitudes of police recruits when they first encounter the department and in what manner do these attitudes change as the recruits pass through their formal academy training and their experiences "on the street"?
(2) To what degree are the job-related attitudes of the police recruits associated with independent assessments of their behavior in the "field"?

## Contextual considerations

This study took place in "Union City," a large urban municipality, between April 1970 and February 1973.[2] The Union City Police Department is considered typical of most big-city departments and employs well over 1,500 uniformed personnel. Like all paramilitary organizations, the Union City Police Department is highly centralized with bureaucratic authority vested in formalized positions stressing the importance of the command structure for controlling subordinate behavior. In general, the organizational context values technical efficiency and pressures the officers to produce.

The police officer selection process in Union City is similar to that of most other large police departments in the country. The applicant must pass progressively the civil service examination, background investigation, medical examination, physical strength and agility test, oral interview and a psychiatric examination. If the applicant is successful, he is hired into the Department on the basis of authorized openings. Normally, a recruit's first assignment is with the Training Division. Here, the novice first encounters the police milieu as presented to him at the Police Academy.

In Union City, the formal training program for recruits apparently does not serve an additional screening function. Although recruits are told that they must achieve a minimum standard of competence, virtually all recruits graduate from the Academy despite their performance. Of the four recruit groups sampled in this study, only three men failed to graduate with their respective classes.

## Sample

Four regularly scheduled recruit classes were selected for the longitudinal portion of this study. All recruits ($N = 136$) in each of the classes received questionnaire packets on the first administration.

Each recruit group represented a different stage in the formal socialization process. Originally, the study was designed to approximate a modified version of Solomon's (1949) four-fold group design, but certain unpredictable circumstances intervened to prevent this more rigorous design. For example: training facilities became overcrowded and one group was prevented from following its planned sequence; maintenance of good will between the researcher and the Department required that certain changes be made in the study design; training policies were altered after the research was begun; and so on. However, the operational difficulties were of minor importance since the major research problem, access, had already been solved.[3]

The formal recruit training process consisted of a rigorous 18-week program. First, the newcomers attended a 12-week Basic Training School characterized by harsh discipline, didactic instruction, and detailed regimentation. Police academies across the country appear to be far more similar to one another than dissimilar. Most departments attempt to follow the guidelines established by the President's

Commission on Law Enforcement and the Administration of Justice (1967). The Union City department organized the material and daily routine of its academy—approximately 480 hours of training—according to a model training schedule developed and distributed by the International Association of Chiefs of Police (IACP). Correspondence with a number of police administrators indicated that the use of the IACP training plan is indeed quite common. For a microscopic descriptive treatment of a representative police academy, see Harris (1973). Following graduation from the Union City Police Academy, the recruits were introduced to the veritable complexities of policing by an experienced patrolman called the Field Training Officer (FTO). After completing this 6-week apprenticeship, most recruits were assigned permanent partners and considered to be real (albeit rookie) policemen.

Table 1 presents the basic survey design according to administration number (1 through 6) and according to the length of Departmental experience for each of the recruit groups (0 months through 30 months). The sixth administration occurred during January and February 1973. This follow-up study checked the accuracy—via observations, interviews, and questionnaires—of the original analysis as well as to discover what changes, if any, had taken place in the officers after two and one-half years of experience in the police world. Questionnaires were distributed however only to patrolmen who had been Group IV academy classmates in 1970 ($N = 38$) and were collected during a scheduled but relatively informal interview.

Each set of questionnaires was accompanied by a letter from the researcher requesting each person's cooperation in the study but making it clear that their participation was voluntary, that the information supplied would be held strictly confidential, that no one in the Department would ever see anyone's individual responses, and that the Department would not pressure them to cooperate.

As Table 2 indicates, the response rates were somewhat disappointing—notably from the group most advanced in the socialization process. The attrition was due

*Table 2* Response rates

| Group | Number of subjects | Administrative number |   |   |   |   |   |
|---|---|---|---|---|---|---|---|
|   |   | 1 | 2 | 3 | 4 | 5 | 6 |
|   |   | Response rates* |   |   |   |   |   |
| I | 41 | 73 | 60 | 56 | 33 | 31 | — |
| II | 16 | 100 | 94 | 69 | 75 | 63 | — |
| III | 39 | 93 | 80 | 100 | 88 | 76 |   |
| IV | 40 | 100 | 85 | 83 | 78 | 62 | 95 |
| Total number of subjects |   | 136 | 134 | 133 | 133 | 131 |   |
| Total returned (in percent) |   | 90 | 78 | 80 | 68 | 57 |   |

*Response rate in percent.

almost entirely to individuals leaving the study but remaining with the organization. Due to the low response rates, data collected during the eighth and ninth month of police experience have been deleted from the analysis.

From the reported recruit characteristics, a coarse profile of the typical Union City recruit can be constructed. The Union City "green pea" is male, about 24 years old, white, married, in excellent health and was raised in or around Union City.[4] There is a positive likelihood that he has attended college, although it is doubtful he has a degree. The recruit's family background is decidedly—and somewhat surprisingly—middle class. However, most of his work experience has been in occupations distinctly below the middle class level and required little in the way of supervisory duties. If he has performed leadership functions, it is probable that such experience resulted from his enlistment in one of the armed services. Without question, Union City recruits appear far more similar to police recruits from other departments than they are dissimilar—see Van Maanen (1972) for a more elaborate discussion. If anything, the Union City Police Department appears to be attracting slightly better young officers than other departments—from the perspective of the police professed professional ideal which stresses education and class background.

Finally, cross-sectional data were gathered from veteran officers with two but less than three years' experience. Questionnaire packets were mailed in December of 1970 to all officers graduating from the police academy in 1968 ($N = 58$). Of these experienced patrolmen, 72 percent returned completed questionnaires. The demographic characteristics of this group did not differ in any important way from those in the recruit sample.

## Attitude measures

The attitude questionnaires concentrated upon the police officers' perceptions and affective responses toward different features of their work situation. Each of the instruments focused upon one of three related, but conceptually different attitude areas. All measures were pretested in a small pilot study. Specifically, the respective questionnaire contained 88 items relevant to aspects of police officers' perceived organizational ecology.

### *Motivation*

The measurement of motivation is based upon expectancy theory. This theory assumes the strength of the tendency for an individual to behave in a particular manner is a function of: the degree to which the person expects certain outcomes to result from the particular behavior (expectancy); times the attractiveness to him of the expected result (valence). A number of studies have indicated the general usefulness of expectancy theory for understanding individual behavior in organizational settings (Georgopoulos, Mahoney, and Jones, 1957; Vroom, 1964;

Galbraith and Cummings, 1967; Porter and Lawler, 1968; Gurin and Gurin, 1970; and Mitchell and Biglan, 1971).

The specific work attitude data used to determine motivation were obtained by means of a 60-item questionnaire. The two-part questionnaire was developed by this researcher and modeled along the lines of an instrument constructed by Porter, Van Maanen and Crampon (1972).

### Part I: Expectancy beliefs

This part of the questionnaire was designed to measure the person's belief concerning the probability of effort leading to the obtainment of various job-related outcomes and contained 35 items. Each item asked the respondent to indicate on a seven-point Likert-type scale—ranging from "very true" (6) to "not true at all true" (0)—whether "working especially hard" on a particular activity would lead to one of five outcomes. The outcomes were: (1) receiving favorable responses from the community, (2) receiving favorable responses from the Department, (3) receiving favorable responses from the supervisor, (4) receiving favorable responses from peers, and (5) receiving greater personal satisfaction.

Seven activities were designated to represent the major areas of the total job-related activity space for patrol officers—field investigation, routine control, inspection, administrative, service, community relations and self-development activities. Each of these activities was defined fully in the questionnaire instructions, and, based on the results of the pilot study, meaningful to patrolmen.

### Part II: Values of outcomes

This part of the Motivational Force Questionnaire contained 25 items dealing with the value the individuals placed on the particular job-related outcomes. The respondents were asked to rate each outcome on a seven-point Likert-type scale ranging from "Like very much" (+3) to "Dislike very much" (−3). Five of the outcomes were identical to those listed in Part I and were the only ones used in the computation of motivational force.

### Motivational force

An overall measure of motivational force was determined by summing the belief strength times the outcome values across the 35 relevant pairs of items. The multiplicative motivational force score ranged from a −18 to a +18. Thus a higher belief times value score (MF) indicated greater motivational force. The summed force score was interpreted as the operational definition of motivation—the degree to which an individual wants to work especially hard to gain desired outcomes, that is, rewards.

Like most instruments used in organizational field studies, the underlying dimensionality of the motivation questionnaire is problematic. It is particularly troublesome in this case since the instrument was designed to tap a unique multidimensional psychological space differentiated by reward and activity categories as well as by time. In this context, traditional item-intercorrelation matrices have little meaning. However, the categories were developed after a careful reading of the police literature and extensive interviewing with knowledgeable working police officers. Furthermore, the motivation questionnaire has high face validity and based on feedback from study participants represents a reasonable approximation of the expansive task and outcome space associated with police work.

### *Organizational commitment*

The measurement of organizational commitment was accomplished through the use of a 15-item questionnaire developed by Porter and Smith (1970). This instrument focused on various components of overall commitment: that is, willingness to put forth extra effort to help the organization succeed, loyalty to the organization, concern about the fate of the organization, willingness to recommend the organization as a place to work, and so on. Each of the 15 items was phrased in terms of a statement to which the respondent was asked to rate his agreement on a seven-point Likert-type scale ranging from "strongly agree" (7) to "strongly disagree" (1). The individual's level of organizational commitment was computed by averaging across the items answered on the questionnaire—the higher the score, presumably the higher his commitment. The average interitem reliability correlation was +.73 (across six administration periods) indicating substantial internal consistency on the part of the respondents.

### *Need satisfaction*

Need satisfaction was measured by a 13-item questionnaire developed by Porter (1962) and based upon Maslow's (1954) hierarchy of needs. Each item contained a short statement describing a job characteristic (for example, security, opportunity to develop close friendships, feelings of worthwhile accomplishment, authority, and so forth), followed by questions concerning that particular characteristic.

The analysis of the data was based upon responses on two questions asked of each characteristic. The two questions asked the person to indicate on a seven point Likert-type scale ranging from "maximum" (7) to "minimum" (1):

(1) How much (of the characteristic) do you *now* have in your job?
(2) How much (of the characteristic) *should* you have in your job?

The difference between the response to the second question and the response to the first question was taken as a measurement of need dissatisfaction. Hence, the lower the difference score, the less dissatisfied the individual. On the other hand, if the differences between the "should be" and "is now" were high, the greater the person's dissatisfaction with the particular characteristic. The respondent's level of dissatisfaction was operationally defined as the mean difference score on either: (1) a cluster of characteristics representing one of the five Maslovian needs or (2) all need-related characteristics (total need dissatisfaction—13 items). A more detailed description of this much used instrument can be found in Porter and Lawler (1968) and more recently in Schneider and Alderfer (1973).

### *Job behavior measure*

A primary concern of this research was with the multifaceted aspects of a police officer's performance on the "street," hence, global ratings, as opposed to some summary index based on a number of specific behaviors, were used. Aside from convenience considerations, the choice of global ratings appeared appropriate since police organizations typically devote few resources toward either the subjective or objective evaluation of its members.

Rating forms were distributed for the first time in December 1970 to the immediate supervisors, the sergeants, of all participants in the study. Thus, each sergeant had an opportunity to observe a particular recruit for at least two months—92 percent of these forms were returned, in February 1973, rating forms were again distributed. However, only sergeants of the officers in Group IV (see Table 1) received rating forms—100 percent of these forms were returned.

The forms asked each sergeant to rate his subordinate on: how well the officer was performing on the job; and how much effort the officer was putting forth on the job. The ratings were made on an eight-point Likert-type scale ranging from "outstanding" (8) to "does not meet minimum requirements" (1). As with the attitude questionnaires, care was taken to assure each sergeant that his responses would be kept strictly confidential.

The Pearsonian correlation between effort and performance ratings was high—$+.87$ ($N = 118$) for the recruit sample and $+.78$ ($N = 38$) for the follow-up. Since these correlations were so high, the remainder of this article will be concerned with the performance ratings and ignore correlations between attitudes and effort ratings which, for all substantive purposes, were the same.

For purposes of analysis, the recruits were divided into two approximately equal groupings based on superior's performance ratings. The resulting division reflected the slightly skewed distribution of sergeants' evaluation—with the high group comprised of those recruits rated at five or above (54 percent) and the low group comprised of those recruits rated at four or below (46 percent).

All participants were also ranked according to their final standing in their respective academy training classes. These rankings were obtained from the Training Division and represent a summary index of the individual's performance in his respective Basic Training class. These rankings are based on the recruit's overall classroom or academic performance (test results). The obtained rankings were converted to standard scores for the purpose of data analysis.

# Findings

## *Data analysis*

The significance of differences in group means on the attitude questionnaires across time were determined by use of a simple analysis of variance. This technique provided a relatively clear-cut test regarding the likelihood of the change in group means over time. Thus, if the F-ratio was significant at the .05 level, the implication was that the between-time variation was greater than could be expected on the basis of chance.

To assess the degree of relationship among the numerous variables examined in this research, Pearsonian correlations were used and their significance tested by use of a t-statistic. However, in a study such as this where over time data provide the basis for analysis, the overall pattern of results rather than any one particular data point is most important. In other words, statistical significance must not be equated—or confused—with social significance. Therefore, the following sections are concerned primarily with the general trends plainly visible from the data.

## *Job attitudes*

The job attitudes of those recruits who quit the study were compared with those who remained in the study. The examination revealed very few significant differences between leavers and stayers. These differences furthermore were not consistent on any of the questionnaire measures across time periods, nor did they appear to have theoretical importance. Thus, no empirical basis separated the two groups. With respect to the available data, the job attitudes of those recruits who participated conscientiously in the study were indistinguishable from those recruits who did not, except of course when it came to returning questionnaires.[5]

In general, the correlations among the demographic characteristics and the job attitudes—motivation, commitment, and need satisfaction—indicated few significant associations. Those relationships which did appear significant occurred early in a recruit's career and were shortlived, playing an insignificant role in the subjects' attitude responses after the accumulation of several months of experience. For example, those with military experience tended to report more motivation, commitment and satisfaction at $t_0$ and $t_1$, than those without such experience but these relationships had vanished almost entirely by $t_2$. In fact, there were no significant correlations between attitude and demographic dimensions after $t_3$. Unlike several previous studies which postulated a strong compatibility between certain background characteristics and subsequent adaptation within the police milieu (Rokeach, Miller, and Snyder, 1971; Wolfe, 1970; Rapaport, 1949), this study found no evidence to assert that the recruits' demography was in any way related to their eventual profile. Consequently, the police culture can be viewed as molding the attitudes—with numbing regularity—of virtually all who enter.

THE MEANING AND IMPACT OF WORK

## *Motivational force*

The motivational force scores for the recruits and veteran officers are shown in Figure 1. As illustrated, overtime, the newcomers' motivational attitudes declined significantly. Furthermore, the motivation reported at $t_{30}$ was significantly lower than the level recorded at any other time period—although still positive relative to the construction of the index itself.

This overall decrease in motivation was primarily due to decreases in the expectancies. The attractiveness of all outcomes remained relatively constant for all the examined time periods. This would certainly seem to indicate a growing perception on the part of the recruits that "working especially hard" was linked to few, if any, of the system rewards.

In terms of the reward categories—rewards which presumably may result from "working especially hard"—four of the five fell rather sharply from their level on the first day—beliefs regarding favorable reactions from the department, the supervisor, the community, and fellow officers. Only recruit motivation associated with greater personal satisfaction failed to decline significantly. Similarly, six of the seven activity categories showed significant declines in motivational levels.

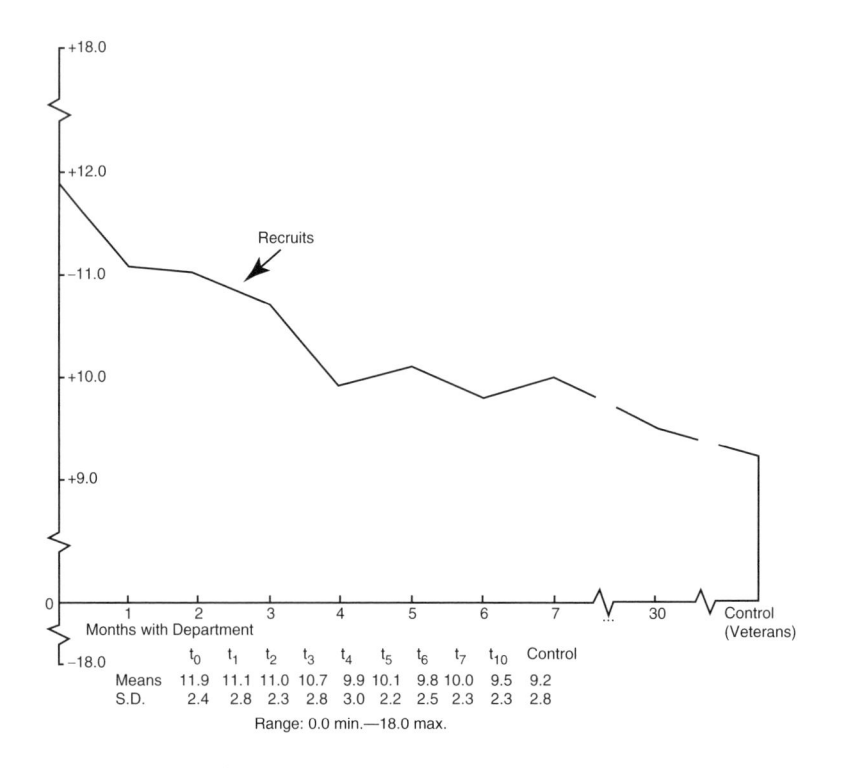

*Figure 1* Motivational force.

POLICE SOCIALIZATION

Only working especially hard on "field investigation activities" failed to drop appreciably.

The motivational force measure and the supervisors' evaluation of performance showed a rather interesting and surprising pattern of association across time. Table 3 shows that the positive association between motivation and the evaluation of field performance which was evident during the recruits' very early career stages ($t_0$ and $t_1$) vanished rapidly. In fact, by the sixth month, the relationship became inverted unmistakably, with those recruits having the least favorable—although possibly more realistic—attitudes being rated as better performers. The directionality of this association indicates that those police officers who cling to high expectations are least likely to be perceived as good performers in the field by their particular patrol sergeants.

The dramatic shift in attitude is readily apparent when the recruit sample is divided into the high and low rated groups, it appears that a work ethic involving high motivation does not characterize the "better" Union City patrolman, as judged by his patrol sergeant. (See Figure 2.)

The above trend is not observable when Academy rankings of performance are correlated with the motivation attitudes. Along this dimension, none of the

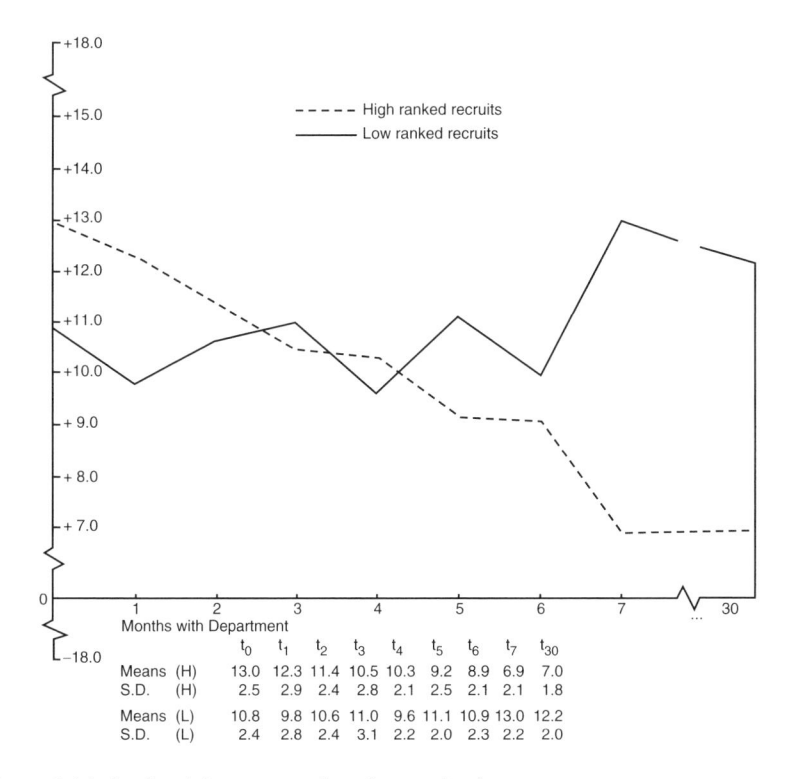

|  |  | $t_0$ | $t_1$ | $t_2$ | $t_3$ | $t_4$ | $t_5$ | $t_6$ | $t_7$ | $t_{30}$ |
|---|---|---|---|---|---|---|---|---|---|---|
| Means | (H) | 13.0 | 12.3 | 11.4 | 10.5 | 10.3 | 9.2 | 8.9 | 6.9 | 7.0 |
| S.D. | (H) | 2.5 | 2.9 | 2.4 | 2.8 | 2.1 | 2.5 | 2.1 | 2.1 | 1.8 |
| Means | (L) | 10.8 | 9.8 | 10.6 | 11.0 | 9.6 | 11.1 | 10.9 | 13.0 | 12.2 |
| S.D. | (L) | 2.4 | 2.8 | 2.4 | 3.1 | 2.2 | 2.0 | 2.3 | 2.2 | 2.0 |

*Figure 2* Motivational force comparison (across time).

Table 3  Relationships among job-behavior measures and job attitudes as a function of time in the organization

*Correlations between job attitudes and sergeants evaluation of job performance in the field*

|  | Months in the department |  |  |  |  |  |  |  | ... | Veterans |  |
|---|---|---|---|---|---|---|---|---|---|---|---|
|  | $t_0$ | $t_1$ | $t_2$ | $t_3$ | $t_4$ | $t_5$ | $t_6$ | $t_7$ |  | $t_{30}$ | Control |
| Motivational force | .36** | .21 | .17 | −.06 | .04 | −.09 | −.22* | −.41** |  | −.34** | −.10 |
| Commitment | .05 | .24 | .23** | .30* | .30** | .32** | .27** | .21 |  | .26* | .33** |
| Dissatisfaction | −.02 | −.19 | .13 | −.19* | −.25** | −.41** | −.33** | .56** |  | −.31** | −.23 |
| N = | 35 | 30 | 62 | 72 | 70 | 68 | 60 | 32 |  | 36 | 42 |

*Correlations between job attitudes and academy rankings of recruits' performance*

|  | $t_0$ | $t_1$ | $t_2$ | $t_3$ | $t_4$ | $t_5$ | $t_6$ | $t_7$ | ... | $t_{30}$ | Control |
|---|---|---|---|---|---|---|---|---|---|---|---|
| Motivational force | .01 | −.11 | .03 | .07 | .02 | −.12 | .01 | .01 |  | −.05 | −.17 |
| Commitment | −.24 | −.21 | −.21 | −.07 | −.09 | −.07 | −.10 | −.10 |  | .03 | −.12 |
| Dissatisfaction | −.01 | −.08 | .29** | .07 | .31** | −.19* | .07 | −.14 |  | −.07 | .19 |
| N = | 40 | 34 | 69 | 78 | 78 | 74 | 65 | 34 |  | 36 | 42 |

*Pearsonian correlation coefficient significant at .10 level.
**Pearsonian correlation coefficient significant at the .05 level.

POLICE SOCIALIZATION

correlations across time even approaches statistical significance; nor was there any directionality apparent.

## Organizational commitment

Figure 3 shows the significant decrease in the organizational commitment reported by the recruits across time. This decrease is relatively steady except for a small, nonsignificant increase to $t_5$. Yet, even with this declining trend, the absolute level of commitment remains relatively high vis-à-vis the seven-point index itself.

Some perspective on the absolute level of the reported commitment is provided by several other studies conducted with the same instrument (Dubin and Porter, 1972; Porter and Smith, 1970; Boulian and Porter, 1971). Results of these investigations reveal that the Union City recruits and veteran patrol officers responded with mean commitment scores significantly higher than five other occupational samples (first level managers ($N = 43$); public utility employees ($N = 600$); personnel managers ($N = 130$); hospital employees ($N = 142$); and bank employees ($N = 131$)—see Figure 3). While the inappropriateness of these norm groups is recognized, the comparison does suggest certain occupational characteristics noted in previous police-related research—for example, strong departmental loyalty, in-group solidarity, cohesiveness—may have an attitudinal analog in the form of the commitment variable examined here.

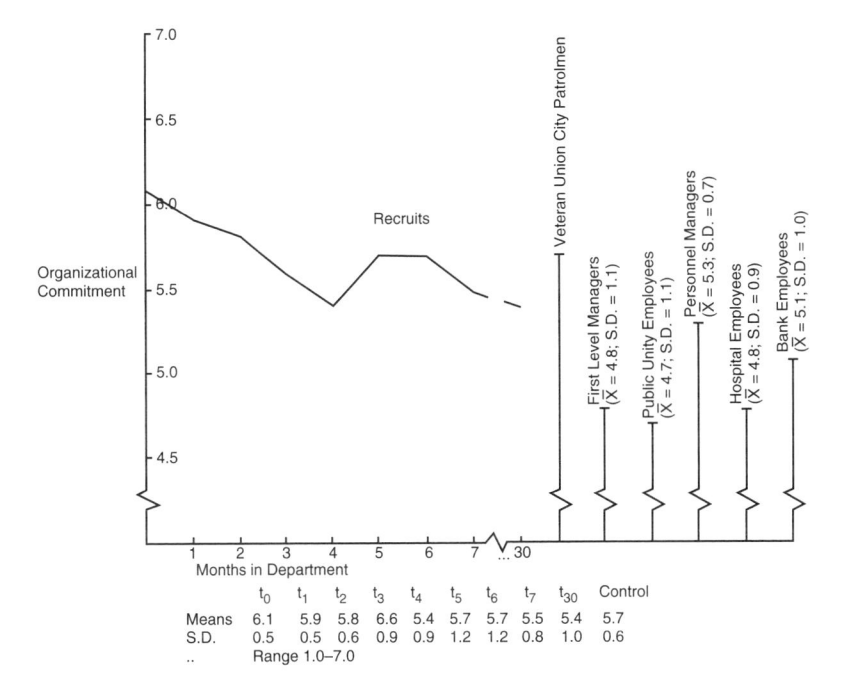

|  | $t_0$ | $t_1$ | $t_2$ | $t_3$ | $t_4$ | $t_5$ | $t_6$ | $t_7$ | $t_{30}$ | Control |
|---|---|---|---|---|---|---|---|---|---|---|
| Means | 6.1 | 5.9 | 5.8 | 6.6 | 5.4 | 5.7 | 5.7 | 5.5 | 5.4 | 5.7 |
| S.D. | 0.5 | 0.5 | 0.6 | 0.9 | 0.9 | 1.2 | 1.2 | 0.8 | 1.0 | 0.6 |
|  |  |  | Range 1.0–7.0 |  |  |  |  |  |  |  |

*Figure 3* Organizational commitment.

THE MEANING AND IMPACT OF WORK

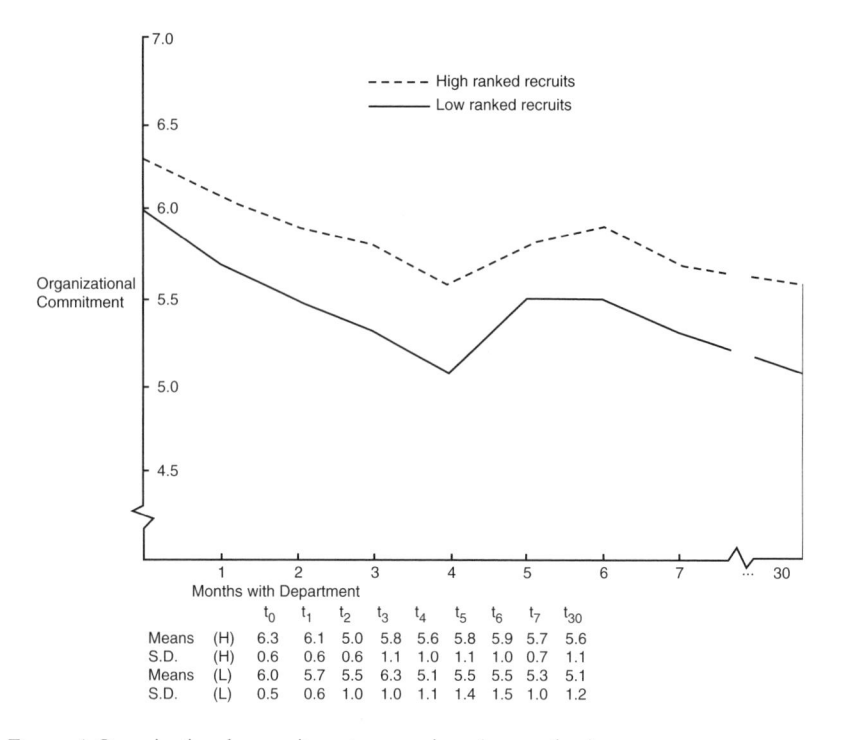

| | | $t_0$ | $t_1$ | $t_2$ | $t_3$ | $t_4$ | $t_5$ | $t_6$ | $t_7$ | $t_{30}$ |
|---|---|---|---|---|---|---|---|---|---|---|
| Means | (H) | 6.3 | 6.1 | 5.0 | 5.8 | 5.6 | 5.8 | 5.9 | 5.7 | 5.6 |
| S.D. | (H) | 0.6 | 0.6 | 0.6 | 1.1 | 1.0 | 1.1 | 1.0 | 0.7 | 1.1 |
| Means | (L) | 6.0 | 5.7 | 5.5 | 6.3 | 5.1 | 5.5 | 5.5 | 5.3 | 5.1 |
| S.D. | (L) | 0.5 | 0.6 | 1.0 | 1.0 | 1.1 | 1.4 | 1.5 | 1.0 | 1.2 |

*Figure 4* Organizational commitment comparison (across time).

Organizational commitment scores and patrol sergeants' evaluations of job performance in the field showed a strong positive relationship. As Table 3 points out, this relationship is relatively consistent and enduring. This association is depicted graphically in Figure 4 according to the mean scores over time of the high and low rated officers.

The relationship between Academy performance and organizational commitment did not reach significance at any of the particular time periods. However, the directionality between the two variables seems to suggest that, if anything, those recruits who do well academically are more likely to report lower commitment to the organization than those recruits who are doing less well.

Interestingly, the correlation between the individual's Academy rank and his sergeant's evaluation of field performance was +.02 (Spearman Rank Difference Coefficient). The lack of significant association between "street" performance and Academy rankings indicates the criteria on which the Training Division evaluates and rates police recruits do not correspond to the criteria used by the field sergeants.

Some light is shed on this engrossing lack of correlation by investigating the recruit demographic characteristics. The relationship between academy rank and educational level, in particular, is quite high ($r = .57$) as is academy rank and prior police experience ($r = .42$, biserial correlation). Such correlations should not be surprising in view of the construction of the academy index—based entirely upon the results of periodic examinations stressing the recall of lectures about federal, state, and local laws, traffic regulations, first aid, police procedures, and so on. Thus, those recruits with more education apparently had less difficulty absorbing and feeding back information than those with less education. Similarly, those officers with previous police experience had less difficulty in the classroom than those without such experience. However, these two demographic variables were not related significantly to the field evaluations at any point in the study.

### *Need satisfaction*

The expressed level of satisfaction associated with all five needs remained relatively constant across time. Upon examining the composition of this measure however a somewhat paradoxical situation was found. On the one hand, the level at which the recruits reported their needs fulfilled increased dramatically and significantly following their academy training. At the same time, the recruits also increased significantly their desired level of need fulfillment. As a result, the need satisfaction index remained relatively stable.

When the needs were examined individually, the self-actualization and social cluster were viewed generally as the most satisfied. Most dissatisfaction was indicated with the fulfillment of the officer's esteem, autonomy and security needs. In fact, security needs from $t_4$ on, were the least satisfied—significantly less than the degree to which the recruits' social or self-actualization needs were presumably satisfied.

A persistent association between need dissatisfaction and field evaluations is apparent in Table 3. This relationship is negative and indicates the higher-rated subjects were more satisfied than their lower-rated counterparts. The examination of the individual parts of the dissatisfaction index revealed that none of the five needs when analyzed separately were related significantly to the ratings—although most were negative. It was only when all needs were combined that the association was significant.

Dissatisfaction expressed by both recruits and experienced officers was related generally in a positive manner to the Academy rankings—although the correlations fluctuated widely. Again, needs taken separately showed no association with the Academy rankings.

### *Interrelations among attitudes*

hile the attitude measures used in this study can be shown to be associated with one another, they were by no means synonymous—that is, the intercorrelations among instruments ranged from .02 to .58 for the various administration periods. Some correlations among instruments was expected on purely a theoretical basis. For example, one would predict that those subjects who express more motivation would also report less need dissatisfaction (see Porter and Lawler, 1968). Yet, the attitude intercorrelations were relatively low—intercorrelations for officers more advanced in the socialization sequence were somewhat higher but by no means perfect. Consequently, there was enough variation among questionnaire responses to indicate that the variables were conceptually and, to some extent, empirically distinct.

## Discussion

Certain consistent themes appear throughout the combined results of the statistical and participant-observational analyses. Progress along the socialization continuum in the police world can be seen as the gradual development of an "in the same boat" collective consciousness stressing a "don't make waves" occupational philosophy. This process by which initiates acquire the motives, sentiments, and behavioral patterns of the occupational culture can be characterized as a four-stage socialization process: (1) entry; (2) introduction; (3) encounter; and (4) metamorphosis. While only analytically distinct, these phases serve as useful markers describing the socialization path of police recruits.[6]

### *Entry*

Although the available literature suggests that the police occupation is viewed by those who enter as simply one job among many and considered roughly along the same dimensions as any job choice—for example, security, salary, interesting work, and so forth (Sterling, 1972; President's Commission on Law Enforcement and the Administration of Justice, 1967; Neiderhoffer, 1967)—several qualifications of that position can be made which provide a greater understanding of the choice and entry process. First, the salary and security aspects have probably been overrated as inducement for persons choosing police careers. For instance, 46 percent of the recruit samples ($N = 125$) reported making more money per year before joining the department. Also the middle class bias of the Union City sample indicated that the popular conception which regards the choice of policing as a distinctly lower and working class phenomenon—as a sort of upward mobility assumption concerning the selection of police careers—does not hold across departments. In fact, the socioeconomic profile of Union City recruits is quite representative of the geographical area served—as described in the 1970 census. This would suggest that environmental qualifications must be made when discussing the calculus of police recruitment and selection.

Second, the protracted screening factor associated with police work is a most critical aspect of the socialization process. The nature of the long, arduous selection procedure (often taking up to a year or more)—representing the organizational or structural side of what Merton (1957) calls anticipatory socialization—assures that those who join the occupation will have strong positive attitudes concerning their new job. And the attitudes at day-one ($t_0$) support this.

Finally, as in most organizations, the police department presents its most favorable side to individuals who have yet to take the oath of office. A potential recruit is made to feel by virtue of the special attention paid him that he is important and valued by the organization. Furthermore, most recruitment occurs via generational and friendship networks involving on-line police officers and potential recruits—almost 80 percent of the recruits ($N = 121$) reported that they had a good friend or close relative working for the Union City Police Department before they joined. Hence, the individual receives personalized encouragement and support which helps sustain interest during the formidable screening process. Such social linkages most likely attract and bind the would-be recruit to the occupational culture long before he actually enters.

## *Introduction*

For police recruits, their first real contact with the occupational environment occurs at the police academy. The newcomer—surrounded by 30 to 40 contemporaries—is introduced to the often arbitrary discipline of the organization. A man soon learned that to be one minute late to class, to utter a careless word in formation, to relax in his seat or to be caught walking when one should be running may result in a "gig" or demerit costing him an extra day of work or the time it may take to write a long essay on, say, "the importance of keeping a neat appearance." Only the recruit's classmates aid in the struggle to avoid sanction from a punitively-oriented training staff and provide the recruit with the only rewards available. Yet, these rewards are contingent upon his internalization of the "no rat" rule which protects fellow-recruits and himself from departmental discipline.

The early stages of the person's police career are marked by some rather vivid attitude changes ($t_1$ through $t_3$). First, motivational attitudes drop considerably never to rise again. Only personal rewards remained associated with working hard. This seems to indicate a growing realization on the part of the recruits that a hard work ethic was not linked to most of the system rewards. Second, organizational commitment also fell sharply; yet, remained relatively high vis-à-vis several other occupations. Third, the recruits were somewhat dissatisfied—relative to later phases of the socialization process—with their experiences at the police Academy. The degrading nature of the recruits' role during the Academy's stress training serves to detach the newcomer from his old attitudes, resulting in a scaling down of high but unrealistic attitudes about the department. Hence, the Academy impresses upon the recruit that he must now identify with the new group—his fellow patrolmen. Furthermore, he learns that when the department notices his behavior, it is usually to administer a punishment, not a reward. The solution to this collective predicament is to "stay low and avoid trouble."

## *Encounter*

Following the classroom training period, a novice is introduced to the complexities of the "street" through his FTO. It is during this period of apprenticeship that the reality shock encompassing full recognition of being a police officer is likely to occur. Here he learns what attitudes and behaviors are appropriate and expected of a patrolman within the social setting. This traditional feature of police work—patrolmen training patrolmen—insures continuity from class to class of police officers regardless of the content of the Academy instruction. In large measure, the flow of influence from one generation to another accounts for the remarkable stability of the pattern of police behavior.

Importantly, those recruits who were least motivated to work hard tended to be ranked as better patrolmen. Clearly, while some zealousness may be tolerated early in one's career—maybe even expected—such attitudes must soon be altered if the recruit is to "make it" within the police milieu. Furthermore, the rookie discovers few connections between his efforts and the system rewards. In fact, he soon learns that the best solution to the labyrinth of hierarchy, the red tape and paperwork, the myriad of rules and regulations and the dirty work which characterize the occupation is to adopt the group norm stressing "staying out of trouble." And the best way to stay out of trouble is to minimize the set of activities he pursues. Those officers who persist in approaching their job from what police like to call a "gung-ho" perspective are distrusted and eyed cautiously by field supervisors. They may in fact be rated by their sergeants as less able policemen than their more prudent colleagues.

Inversely, sergeants tended to perceive those recruits who expressed more commitment to the department to be the better performing officers. This association was particularly apparent during and following the recruit's initial "street" experience ($t_3$ through $t_5$). This finding appears of major import since high commitment usually implies a relatively unquestioning belief and acceptance of the organizational system. The literature has speculated that loyalty and dedication—as behavioral correlates of a so-called "conformance to authority syndrome"—are the principal characteristics an initiate police officer must demonstrate if he is to be accepted within the system (Skolnick, 1966; Neiderhoffer, 1967; Ahern, 1972). Thus, this psychological dimension is empirically verified in this study and shown to have important consequences vis-à-vis one's organizational career.

As expected, the recruits did report slightly more need satisfaction once they began to actually act as policemen. This is not surprising in view of the limited opportunities to satisfy certain needs in the Academy. In general, the job satisfaction literature indicates that as one is accepted into the work group, satisfaction increases. However, the newcomers were still relatively deprived. Although the recruits reported more fulfillment, they concomitantly expressed a desire for higher levels of fulfillment. This may well be an indication of the "street learning" experience when the recruits are first exposed to actual police work.

### *Metamorphosis*

In this stage, recruits come to hold the characteristic attitudes regarding the back stage aspects of their careers—what Becker *et al.* (1961) labelled the final perspective. By the sixth month of police experience, the job-related attitudes of the recruits begin to approximate those of their more experienced colleagues. By becoming similar in attitude and behavior to his peers, the recruit avoids censure by the department, his supervisor, and, most importantly, his fellow patrolmen.

After only a short time on the job, the only activity in which patrolmen perceive any substantial likelihood of receiving valued rewards is through their "field investigation" activities—defined as "those activities which may result in an arrest." As others (Webster, 1970; Reiss, 1971) have pointed out, it is precisely these activities which account for the smallest amount of the patrolman's time. Service and administrative activities—which account for the largest amount of working time—were viewed in this final perspective as the areas in which effort was least likely to lead to favorable rewards.

A peculiar interdependent combination of several factors seems to account for this motivational pattern: (1) punishment centered and particularistic supervision concerned primarily with "mistakes" made by patrolmen; (2) institutionalized rewards having little to do with the everyday world of policing; (3) perceived public hostility of the police; (4) subcultural ethos emphasizing the "keep-a-low-profile" dictum; (5) an internalized and narrow perception of "real" police work consisting of only preventing crime and apprehending criminals; and (6) conflicting role demands placed on patrolmen in which successful or good performance is viewed differentially by the various audiences which witness police work.

Expressed organizational commitment, while declining somewhat steadily, still remains relatively high and is presumably an object of concern for both one's supervisor and his colleagues in the patrol division. Perhaps by committing one's self to the department, a recruit demonstrates his willingness to share the risks of police work, his attachment and concern for the welfare of his fellow officers, and his appreciation and involvement for the expressed goals of the organization. In a sense, the level of expressed commitment may indicate the presence of a pervasive moral order within the Union City Police Department which, in Weberian terms, serves to legitimize the bureaucratic structure as well as the police task itself. And as Figure 4 illustrates those who fail to strongly support this order are unlikely to be viewed as effective policemen.

Apparently, the police occupation offers one an excellent opportunity to satisfy social and self-actualizing needs—policing embodies intense social bonds and provides primarily personal satisfactions, involving subjective feelings of performing an important and worthwhile task. The fact that esteem needs are considerably unfulfilled would indicate that the patrol officers do not perceive others as recognizing the worth of their occupation.

On the surface, the dissatisfaction reported by the patrolmen with the degree to which their autonomy needs are fulfilled appears to contradict much of the literature which portrays the patrol task as requiring an inordinate amount of discretion in the field. However, most patrolmen feel "handcuffed" or constrained by a variety of audiences, including their own department. The independence the recruit feels would characterize the job soon becomes perceptually limited in too many ways.

The low degree to which the security needs are satisfied represents an interesting exception of Maslow's (1954) theory. To policemen, security needs represent a curious combination of both physiological and psychological factors. While the physiological aspects are well satisfied in terms of pay and job security, the psychological aspects—involving the danger characteristic intrinsic to the occupation—can never be guaranteed completely. Furthermore, the danger factor of the work setting is an important variable relating to the individual's evaluation of the challenge and importance associated with his role. While this does not question the general usefulness of Maslow's theory, the ordering of the needs may depend more upon situationally specific job features than upon underlying predispositions common to all individuals.

## Conclusion

Perhaps the thrust of this account of urban policing can most readily be appreciated via the inverse relationship discovered between sergeant's evaluation of field performance and the patrol's reported motivation. This finding seems to best capture the on-going reality and behavior norms involved in the occupation. Three interrelated aspects of police work provide a useful framework for viewing this disconcerting but quite illustrative relationship.

First, patrol work resembles a team-like activity. Officers in a squad—consisting of a sergeant and 15 to 25 patrolmen based territorially within the city geometry—back each other up on potentially dangerous calls, cover for one another on various assignments and generally share the work load of their particular district. Hence, those officers who actively seek out tasks to perform create more work—and perhaps more risk—for other squad members—an uninviting situation for experienced patrolmen.

Second, there are few institutionalized rewards involved in police work but many potential punishments. A whole canopy of departmental regulations exists to restrict a patrolman's discretion. Violations of these restrictions, if detected, can cost one his job or possibly his freedom. Since the rules and regulations are so numerous, no one can hope to obey all the canons of professional conduct. Thus those officers who engage in more activity than other members of a squad increase the visibility—and vulnerability—of the squad as a whole.

Finally, something akin to the "ratebuster" phenomenon seems to be at work in the Union City Police Department. Those patrolmen whose attitudes and actions conflict with a squad's projected definition of "normal" work threaten the intimate cooperation necessary among members of the team and create more uncertainty in an already uncertain environment.[7]

Overall, the model adjustment of novice patrolmen of the occupational culture is best epitomized by the "lay low, hang loose and don't expect too much" advice frequently heard within the Union City Police Department. Consequently, the following tip provided by a veteran Union City officer represents a very astute analysis of how to insure continuance in the police world. He suggested:

> There's only two things you gotta know around here. First, forget everything you've learned in the academy because the street's where you'll learn to be a cop; and second, being first around here don't mean shit. Take it easy, that's our motto.

## *Postscript: toward a theory of the middle-range*[8]

This account of recruit socialization emphasizes various situational and process features of the studied environment—but made no attempt to broaden the perspective beyond that of police organizations. Yet, a transituational framework can be constructed by reference to certain analytic properties common to most socialization settings. No effort is made here however to include all properties of such settings. Rather only those elements which seem to have a general importance across organizations and were important in this study are included.

Five interrelated but conceptually distinct characteristics can be expected to influence the outcomes of socialization attempts. First, the formality of the setting—that is, the degree to which the setting is segregated from the on-going work context—suggests the extent to which the organization is concerned with a novice's absorption of the appropriate demeanor and status associated with the target role. Hence, in very formal settings, the recruit's role is differentiated strictly from other organizational roles and the socialization focus is almost always upon the newcomer's internalization of a sort of organizational perspective. Paradoxically, the greater the separation of the newcomer from the work-a-day reality of the organization, the less the newcomer will be able to carry over or generalize any abilities or skills learned in the socialization setting. Therefore formal settings concentrate—implicitly, if not explicitly—more upon attitude than act. For example, police recruits commonly denounced their academy experiences as irrelevant, abstract, and dull. Yet, at the same time, they also expressed an attraction for components of the valued subcultural ethos such as autonomy, pragmatism, and personal independence.

Second, the degree to which new members are processed individually or collectively plays a related but somewhat different role influencing the results of the socialization process. As Becker *et al.* (1961) argued, collective settings nearly always provide the newcomer with understandings of the occupation that are shared by one's cohort group. Thus homogeneous results are promoted in collective settings through peer pressures brought to bear on the individual to conform to group standards. However, as with Union City police recruits, the correspondence between group standards and managerial objectives is always problematic—that is, the group is more likely to ignore or redefine the demands of the organization than the individual.

Third, the serial or disjunctive character of socialization settings also plays a significant part in the transition process. The serial mode in which experienced members groom newcomers about to assume similar roles in the organization is perhaps the best guarantee that the organization will not change over long periods of time. In the police world, this feature is virtually taken-for-granted and accounts in large measure for the remarkable intergenerational similarity of patrolmen views (see, Sterling, 1972; Bayley and Mendelsohn, 1969; and the President's Commission on Law Enforcement and the Administration of Justice, 1967). Innovation will be unlikely; stability will be maintained—sometimes in the face of a turbulent and changing environment.

Fourth, the length in which the newcomer must continue as a formally designated recruit is another powerful socialization mechanism. This temporal characteristic is associated—like the formality of the setting—with the amount of culture, tradition and everyday assumptions which must be absorbed by a newcomer before full participation in the organization will be granted. Furthermore, lengthy socialization often implies, as is apparent in the Union City Police Department, the existence of a trial or test period in which a newcomer is rigorously assessed as to his motivation, trustworthiness, ability, and loyalty. Therefore, the longer one is in the novice's shoes, the more demanding, degrading, and perhaps frustrating the process is likely to be. The endurance of such an ordeal promotes a strong fellowship among those who have traversed the same path to membership and, to a degree, isolates members from organizational outsiders.

Finally, the presence, distance and visibility of a "coach" (or coaches) to assist the newcomer through some or all of the socialization stages has an undoubtedly potent effect. For example, a one-on-one relationship such as the police apprenticeship situation leads generally to an intense, value oriented socialization program in which the outcome is dependent upon the affective bonds typifying the dyad. Thus the newcomer must be more concerned with satisfying the expectations of the coach than with satisfying the expectations of the organization—although such expectations are often congruent.

These setting properties provide a rough guide for evaluating the direction and impact of the organizational socialization process. Regardless whether the setting is designed consciously or unconsciously, the outcomes of the process depend upon the degree to which each feature is present or absent during the transition period. However, this is simply a beginning toward a general theory, for the properties described here are hardly exhaustive. But, if we are to ever fully understand the work perspectives of members of diverse organizations, the elemental structure of initial boundary passages must be classified in terms meaningful and comparative across settings.

## Notes

1 This research was supported in part by the Organizational Behavior Research Center at the University of California, Irvine and the Office of Naval Research (Contract No.

N00014-69-A-0200-9001 NR 151-315). I would like to gratefully acknowledge my academic colleagues, in particular Lyman W. Porter and Mason Haire for their insightful suggestions and assistance during various phases of this research.
2. "Union City" is a pseudonym for a sprawling metropolitan area populated by more than one million persons. The police department is considered to be professional, approaching the legalistic category postulated by Wilson (1968). In a survey conducted in 1968, Union City's police resources (per capita expenditures) were ranked in the upper third among similar sized cities. Furthermore, the starting salary for police officers ranked in the top quartile nationally—entering officers could expect to make over $11,000 during their first year on the force.
3. Over 20 urban police departments were approached before one of them agreed to this rather small scale and low profile study. In most cases, they refused without explanation.
4. All members of the various sample groups used in this were male.
5. Individuals were placed into either the "leaver" or "stayer" group on the basis of the number of administration periods in which they participated. A number of separate investigations were conducted which compared all possible combinations of groupings. For example, in one case the questionnaire responses of those who participated in one or two administrations were contrasted with those who participated in all five—that is, for time periods in which both "leavers" and "stayers" responded. In another case, the questionnaire responses of those who participated in one, two or three administrations were contrasted with the responses of those who participated in four or five administrations and so on.
6. This schematic device—a staged socialization model—glosses over much of the detailed and principled ambivalence a police recruit feels while undergoing passage. Furthermore, it suggests a sort of unilinear development of a career while overlooking the back and forth kinds of passages a recruit experiences—first viewing himself as a civilian, then as a professional, then as a unique person, and so forth. Davis (1968) suggests that socialization metaphorically represents a mirror one passes through to look at oneself from the other side. An insightful remark: but it is not a single passage through a mirror, but many. The characteristics of police socialization presented in this section are therefore a drastic condensation of a much more complex process and highlight only the more salient and irreversible elements involved in the outsider-to-insider passage. For a more detailed version of this process, see Van Maanen, 1973, 1974.
7. "Normal" as it is used here represents the taken-for-granted features of the work environment such as the rhythm, pace and everyday typifications used by organizational members in going about their tasks. For an excellent and organizationally relevant treatment of the sociological dimension of "normal," see Sudnow, 1965.
8. The Mertonian term of middle-range is used here to emphasize the fact that no theory of socialization will be complete unless the conditions which give rise to the use of various socialization techniques are understood. In the studied case of the urban police, the socialization methods that were utilized can be related, for example, to the: danger and uncertainty in the work environment (need for colleague support); frustration engendered on never knowing the worth of one's work (need for a narrow but consensual definition of police work in light of conflicting societal expectations and absence of performance criteria); and the territorial autonomy allowance inherent in the task (need for strong bonds linking the individual to the organization).

# References

Ahern, James F. (1972) *Police in Trouble*. New York: Hawthorne.
Bayley, David H., and Harold Mendelsohn (1969) *Minorities and the Police*. New York: Free Press.

Becker, Howard S., Blanche Greer, Everett C. Hughes, and Anslem Strauss (1961) *Boys in White: Student Culture in Medical School*. Chicago: University of Chicago Press.

Berlew, David E., and Douglas T. Hall (1966) "The socialization of managers: effects of expectations on performance." *Administrative Science Quarterly,* 11: 207–223.

Bittner, Egon (1967) "The police on skid row." *American Sociological Review,* 32: 699–715.

Boulian, Paul, and Lyman W. Porter (1971) Employee Attitudes in a State Mental Hospital. Unpublished paper, University of California, Irvine.

Caplow, Theodore (1964) *Principles of Organization*. New York: Harcourt, Brace and World.

Cicourel, Aaron V. (1967) *The Social Organization of Juvenile Justice*. New York: Wiley.

Davis, Fred (1968) "Professional socializational as subjective experience: the process of doctrinal conversion among student nurses." In Howard S. Becker, Blanche Greer, David Reisman, and Robert T. Weiss (eds.) *Institutions and the Person*: 185–192. Chicago: Aldine.

Denhart, Robert B. (1968) "Bureaucratic socialization and organizational accommodation." *Administrative Science Quarterly*, 13: 441–450.

Dubin, Robert, and Lyman W. Porter (1972) *Individual-Organizational Linkages* (Technical Reports 1–25), University of California, Irvine. Contact Nonr. N00014-69-A-0200-9001 NR151-315, Office of Naval Research.

Fishbein, Martin (1963) "An investigation of the relationships between beliefs about an object and the attitude toward that object." *Human Relations*, 16: 233–239.

Galbraith, Jay R., and L.L. Cummings (1967) "An empirical investigation of the motivational determinants of task performance: interactive effects between instrumentality-valence and motivation ability." *Organization Behavior and Human Performance*, 2: 237–257.

Georgopoulos, Basil S., Gerald M. Mahoney, and Nyle W. Jones (1957) "A path-goal approach to productivity." *Journal of Applied Psychology*, 41: 345–353.

Gurin, Gerald, and Patricia Gurin (1970) "Expectancy theory and the study of poverty." *Journal of Social Issues*, 26: 83–104.

Hackman, J. Richard, and Lyman W. Porter (1968) "Expectancy theory predictions of work effectiveness." *Organization Behavior and Human Performance*, 3: 417–426.

Hall, Douglas T., and Khalil E. Nougaim (1968) "An examination of Maslow's need hierarchy in an organizational setting." *Organization Behavior and Human Performance*, 3: 12–35.

Harris, Richard N. (1973) *The Police Academy: An Insider's View*. New York: Wiley.

Herzberg, Frederick, Bernard Mausner, R. Peterson, and Dora Capwell (1957) *Job Attitudes: Review of Research and Opinions*. Pittsburgh: Psychological Service of Pittsburgh.

Kanter, Roseabeth M. (1968) "Commitment mechanisms in Utopian communities." *American Sociological Review*, 33: 499–516.

Kolb, David A., Irwin M. Rubin, and James M. McIntyre (1971) *Organizational Psychology: An Experiential Approach*. Englewood Cliffs: Prentice-Hall.

Manning, Peter K. (1970) "Talking and becoming: a view of organizational socialization." In Jack D. Douglas (ed.) *Understanding Everyday Life*: 239–258. Chicago: Aldine.

Maslow, Abraham H. (1954) *Motivation and Personality*. New York: Harper and Row.

McNamara, John H. (1967) "Uncertainties in police work: the relevance of police recruits' backgrounds and training." in David J. Bordua (ed.) *The Police Six Sociological Essays*: 163–252. New York: Wiley.

Merton, Robert K. (1957) *Social Theory and Social Structure*. New York: Free Press.

Mitchell, Terence R., and Anthony Biglan (1971) "Instrumentality theories: current uses in psychology." *Psychological Bulletin*, 76: 432–454.

Neiderhoffer, Arthur (1967) *Behind the Shield*. New York: Doubleday.

Patchen, Milton (1970) *Participation, Achievement and Involvement on the Job*. Englewood Cliffs: Prentice-Hall.

Porter, Lyman W. (1962) "A study of perceived need satisfaction in bottom and middle management jobs." *Journal of Applied Psychology*, 45: 1–10.

Porter, Lyman W., and Edward E. Lawler (1968) *Managerial Attitude and Performance*. Homewood, Ill.: Richard D. Irwin.

Porter, Lyman W., and Frank E. Smith (1970) The Etiology of Organizational Commitment: A Longitudinal Study of the Initial Stages of Employee-Organization Reactions. Unpublished paper, University of California, Irvine.

Porter, Lyman W., John Van Maanen, and William J. Crampon (1972) *Continuous Monitoring of Employees' Motivational Attitudes during the Initial Employment Period*, University of California, Irvine. Contact Nonr. N00014-69-A-0200-9001 NR 151–315, Office of Naval Research.

President's Commission on Law Enforcement and the Administration of Justice (1967) *Task Force Report: The Police*. Washington, D.C.: United States Government Printing Office.

Rapaport, David (1949) *Diagnostic Psychological Testing*. Chicago: The Yearbook Publishers.

Reiss, Albert J. (1971) *The Police and the Public*. New Haven: Yale University Press.

Rokeach, Milton, Martin G. Miller, and John A. Snyder (1971) "The value gap between the police and the policed." *Journal of Social Issues*, 27: 155–171.

Rubenstein, Jonathan (1973) *City Police*. New York: Farrar, Straus and Giroux.

Schein, Edgar H. (1961) "Management development as a process of influence." *Industrial Management Review*, 2: 59–77.

——(1962) *Problems of the First Year of Work: Report on the First Panel Reunion*. Massachusetts Institute of Technology, Contact Nonr. 1841 (83), Office of Naval Research.

——(1965) *Organizational Psychology*. Englewood Cliffs: Prentice-Hall.

——(1968) "Organizational socialization." *Industrial Management Review*, 9, 37–45.

——(1971) "The individual, the organization and the career: a conceptual scheme." *Journal of Applied Behavioral Science*, 7: 401–426.

Schneider, Benjamin, and Clayton P. Alderfer (1973) "Three studies of need satisfaction in organizations." *Administrative Science Quarterly*, 18: 489–505.

Skolnick, Jerome (1966) *Justice without Trial: Law Enforcement in a Democratic Society*. New York: Wiley.

Solomon, Richard L. (1949) "Extension of control group design." *Psychological Bulletin*, 46: 137–150.

Sterling, James W. (1972) *Changes in Role Concepts of Police Officers*. Washington, D.C.: International Association of Chiefs of Police.

Sudnow, David (1965) "Normal crimes: sociological features of the penal code in a public defender's office." *Social Problems*, 12: 255–276.

Van Maanen, John (1972) Pledging the Police: A Study of Selected Aspects of Recruit Socialization in a Large, Urban Police Department. Doctoral Dissertation, University of California, Irvine.

——(1973) "Observations on the making of policemen." *Human Organizations*, 32, 407–418.

——(1974) "Working the street: a developmental view of police behavior." In Herbert Jacob (ed.) *The Potential for Reform of Criminal Justice*: 83–130. Beverly Hills, California: Sage.

——(1975) "Breaking-in: socialization to work." In Robert Dubin (ed.) *Handbook of Work, Organization and Society*: 32–103, Chicago: Rand-McNally,

Vroom, Victor H. (1964) *Work and Motivation*. New York: Wiley.

Vroom, Victor H., and Edward L. Deci (1971) "The stability of post-decisional dissonance: a follow-up study on the job attitudes of business school graduates." *Organization Behavior and Human Performance*, 6: 36–49.

Webster, J. A. (1970) "Police task and time study." *Journal of Criminal Law, Criminology and Police Science*, 61: 94–100.

Westley, William A. (1951) The Police: A Sociological Study of Law, Custom and Morality. Doctoral Dissertation, University of Chicago.

Wheeler, Stanton (1966) "The structure of formally organized socialization settings." In Orville G. Brim and Stanton Wheeler (eds.) *Socialization After Childhood: Two Essays*, 53–116. New York: Wiley.

Wilson, James Q. (1968) *Varieties of Police Behavior*. Cambridge, Mass.: Harvard University Press.

Wolfe, J. B. (1970) Some Psychological Characteristics of American Policemen: A Critical Review of the Literature. *Proceedings of the Annual Convention of the American Psychological Association*, Part 1: 453–464.

# 4

# PERSON-ORGANIZATION FIT

An integrative review of its conceptualizations, measurement, and implications

*Amy L. Kristof*

Source: *Personnel Psychology* 49 (1996): 1–49.

**Abstract**

This article presents a comprehensive definition and conceptual model of person-organization fit that incorporates supplementary as well as complementary perspectives on fit. To increase the precision of the construct's definition, it is also distinguished from other forms of environmental compatibility, such as person-group and person-vocation fit. Once defined, commensurate measurement as it relates to supplementary and complementary fit is discussed and recommendations are offered regarding the necessity of its use. A distinction is made between the direct measurement of perceived fit and the indirect measurement of actual person-organization fit, using both cross- and individual-level techniques, and the debate regarding differences scores is reviewed. These definitional and measurement issues frame a review of the existing literature, as well as provide the basis for specific research propositions and suggestions for managerial applications.

Person-organization (P-O) fit is a topic that has attracted the attention of both scholars and managers during recent years. In essence, research on P-O fit concerns the antecedents and consequences of compatibility between people and the organizations in which they work. As organizations confront downsizing, quality initiatives, and changes in or removal of job structures, the benefits of employing people who can be mobile within an organization have been widely recognized (e.g., Bowen, Ledford, & Nathan, 1991; Bridges, 1994; Dumaine, 1987; Howard, 1995). Achieving high levels of P-O fit through hiring and socialization is often touted as the key to retaining a workforce with the flexibility and organizational commitment necessary to meet these competitive challenges. Although the P-O fit literature has been reviewed (Judge & Ferris, 1992; Schneider, Goldstein, & Smith, 1995), there have been few attempts at integrating its various conceptualizations, operationalizations, or measurement strategies. Therefore, the present paper explores the domain, measurement issues, and contributions of this literature, while also suggesting research directions for future investigations of P-O fit.

The paper is organized around four specific objectives. The first objective is to clearly define the topic of interest. Rynes and Gerhart (1990) described P-O fit as "elusive" and as having an imprecise and inconsistent definition. Imprecision in a construct's definition can result in contradictory operationalizations, inadequate measures, and even conflicting results (Schwab, 1980). Therefore, this paper begins by describing P-O fit's multiple conceptualizations and distinguishing it from other forms of person-environment (P-E) fit.

Once a construct has been defined, it is critical that its measurement is aligned with that definition. Therefore, this paper's second objective is to clarify the measurement issues relevant to the operationalization and analysis of P-O fit. Commensurate measurement, direct assessments of perceived fit, indirect assessments of actual fit, and various fit indices are discussed in order to integrate the variety of measurement strategies that have been used to assess P-O fit. In addition, as sensitivity to levels of analysis issues is critical in establishing a construct's validity (Rousseau, 1985), recommendations regarding these issues as they pertain to measures of actual P-O fit are made.

The third objective is to propose a framework that highlights the antecedents and consequences of various conceptualizations of P-O fit. This framework is then used to organize a review of the existing P-O fit literature. Finally, the fourth objective is to suggest future research directions and practical implications. A discussion of general issues as well as specific propositions is offered as a guide for upcoming investigations. In addition, general conclusions are drawn to provide guidance for managers interested achieving and maximizing the benefits of P-O fit.

## Defining person-organization fit

The definition of P-O fit has been subject to confusion due to its multiple conceptualizations and operationalizations, as well as its limited distinction from other forms of P-E fit (Judge & Ferris, 1992; Rynes & Gerhart, 1990). When confusion exists regarding what falls under the rubric of P-O fit, research on the topic is necessarily open to misinterpretation and equivocal operationalizations.

The following section takes a two-step approach to defining P-O fit. First, various conceptualizations of P-O fit and their most common operationalizations are presented. The purpose of this first step is to describe clearly what *is* encompassed in the construct of P-O fit (Schwab, 1980). Second, a distinction is made between P-O fit and other types of P-E congruence to describe what *is not* included in the construct (Judge & Ferris, 1992; Schwab, 1980). Three additional categories of congruence are presented, each addressing the fit between a person and an aspect of the environment: the vocation, group, or job. Brief overviews of these other types of person-environment fit are presented to establish clear boundaries of the P-O fit constuct.

## *Multiple conceptualizations P-O fit*

Most researchers broadly define P-O fit as the compatibility between individuals and organizations. Compatibility, however, may be conceptualized in a variety of ways. Two distinctions have been raised that help clarify these multiple conceptualizations. The first distinction is between supplementary and complementary fit. *Supplementary fit* occurs when a person "supplements, embellishes, or possesses characteristics which are similar to other individuals" in an environment (Muchinsky & Monahan, 1987, p. 269). This congruence can be differentiated from *complementary fit*, which occurs when a person's characteristics "make whole" the environment or add to it what is missing (Muchinsky & Monahan, 1987, p. 271).

A second perspective on P-O fit is offered by the needs-supplies and demands-abilities distinction which is often raised in discussions of other forms of congruence (e.g., Caplan, 1987; Edwards, 1991). From the *needs-supplies* perspective, P-O fit occurs when an organization satisfies individuals' needs, desires, or preferences. In contrast, the *demands-abilities* perspective suggests that fit occurs when an individual has the abilities required to meet organizational demands.

Although these two distinctions have been discussed frequently by authors, they have rarely been integrated. For example, most empirical investigations have defined fit from only one perspective, while ignoring the existence of others (for exceptions see Bretz & Judge, 1994; Bretz, Rynes, & Gerhart, 1993). These multiple conceptualizations of fit reasonably explain the variety of operationalizations that have been used to examine P-O fit, yet to integrate the variety of P-O fit conceptualizations, a comprehensive definition is needed.

An illustrative figure may assist in generating this definition (see Figure 1). In this model, supplementary fit (arrow "a") is represented as the relationship between the fundamental characteristics of an organization and a person. For the organization these characteristics traditionally include the culture, climate, values, goals, and norms. On the person side of the model, the characteristics most often studied are values, goals, personality, and attitudes. When there is similarity between an organization and a person on these characteristics, supplementary fit is said to exist.

In addition to these underlying characteristics, organizations and individuals can also be described by what they supply and demand in employment agreements. These demands and supplies are likely to be influenced by the underlying characteristics of both entities (Hogan, 1991; Schein, 1992), as is indicated by the dotted arrows in Figure 1; however, they represent distinct dimensions on which fit or misfit may occur. More specifically, organizations supply financial, physical, and psychological resources as well as the task-related, interpersonal, and growth opportunities that are demanded by employees. When these organizational supplies

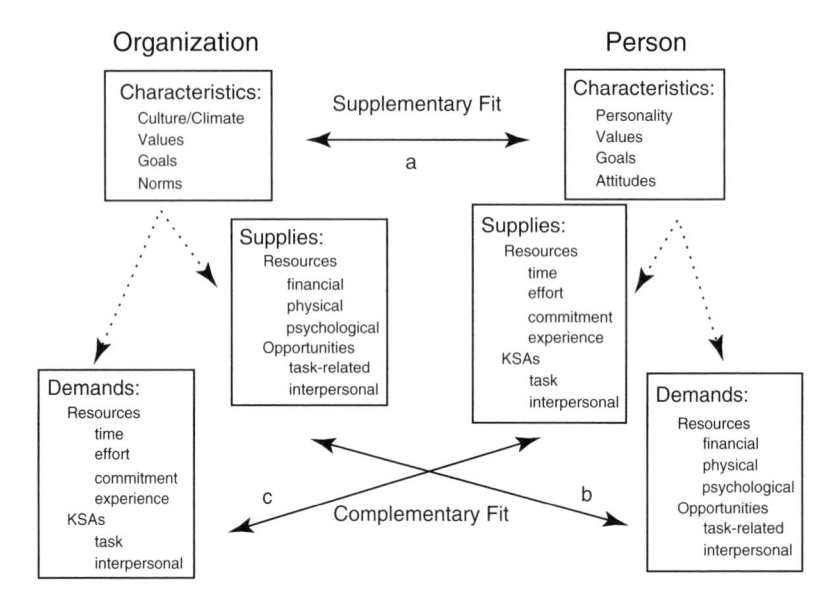

Figure 1 Various conceptualizations of person-organization fit.

meet employees' demands, needs-supplies fit is achieved (arrow "b" in Figure 1). Similarly, organizations demand contributions from their employees in terms of time, effort, commitment, knowledge, skills, and abilities. Demands-abilities fit is achieved when these employee supplies meet organizational demands (arrow "c" in Figure 1). Both of these demand-supply relationships can be described by expanding Muchinsky and Monahan's (1987) definition of complementary fit.

Based on the relationships described above and presented in Figure 1, in this paper P-O fit is defined as *the compatibility between people and organizations that occurs when: (a) at least one entity provides what the other needs, or (b) they share similar fundamental characteristics, or (c) both*. This definition recognizes the multiple conceptualizations of P-O fit and allows for both the supplementary and complementary perspectives to be considered concurrently.

## Operationalizations of P-O fit

The literature has focused primarily on four operationalizations of P-O fit. Two of these reflect supplementary fit and one stems from the needs-supplies conceptualization. The fourth operationalization may be interpreted with either of these two perspectives.

Investigations of supplementary fit have been concerned with measuring the similarity between fundamental characteristics of people and organizations. The most frequently used operationalization of this perspective on fit is the congruence between individual and organizational values (e.g., Boxx, Odom, & Dunn, 1991;

Chatman, 1989, 1991; Judge & Bretz, 1992; Posner, 1992). O'Reilly, Chatman, and Caldwell (1991) use the same description for person-culture fit. As they posited that "congruency between an individual's values and those of an organization may be at the crux of person-culture fit" (O'Reilly et al., 1991, p. 492), in this manuscript P-O and person-culture fit will be treated as equivalent terms. Value congruence is a significant form of fit because values are "fundamental and relatively enduring" (Chatman, 1991, p. 459) and are the components of organizational culture that guide employees' behaviors (Schein, 1992).

Guided by B. Schneider's (1987) attraction-selection-attrition (ASA) framework, several researchers have also used individuals' goal congruence with organizational leaders and peers to operationalize P-O fit (e.g., Vancouver, Millsap, & Peters, 1994; Vancouver & Schmitt, 1991; Witt & Nye, 1992; Witt & Silver, 1995). The ASA framework is based on the premise that similar people are attracted to and selected by organizations whose goals are similar to their own or will enable them to attain their individual goals (B. Schneider, 1987; Vroom, 1966). Thus, it uses P-O fit as an explanation for the increase of within-organization homogeneity over time.

The third common operationalization of fit reflects a strict needs-supplies perspective by defining fit as the match between individual preferences or needs and organizational systems and structures (e.g., Bretz, Ash, & Dreher, 1989; Cable & Judge, 1994; Turban & Keon, 1993). This operationalization has its roots in need-press theory in which environmental "presses" facilitate or hinder the meeting of people's physical and psychological needs (Murray, 1938). It can also be thought of in terms of the theory of work adjustment (Dawis & Lofquist, 1984). According to this theory, a person will be satisfied with work if his or her needs are fulfilled by the environment. Although the theory has most often been used to study person-vocation fit (e.g., Rounds, Dawis, & Lofquist, 1987), it has also been cited as an explanation for P-O fit (Bretz & Judge, 1994).

The fourth operationalization describes P-O fit as a match between the characteristics of individual personality and organizational climate—sometimes labeled organizational personality (e.g., Bowen et al., 1991; Burke & Deszca, 1982; Ivancevich & Matteson, 1984; Tom, 1971). Although this operationalization can be viewed as reflecting supplementary fit, because it describes congruence between the two entity's personalities (arrow a in Figure 1), its measurement often suggests a complementary needs-supplies perspective. This second interpretation is best explained by the acknowledgement that climate is frequently operationalized in terms of organizational supplies (such as reward systems or communication patterns) and individual personality is often construed in terms of needs. For example, an organization's collectivist climate may be operationalized as a team-based compensation system that may or may not meet an individual's need for achievement. Because few researchers specify their underlying conceptualization of fit, it is often difficult to determine whether the supplementary or complementary needs-supplies perspective is the basis for their models of personality based P-O fit.

Although the model in Figure 1 distinguishes between the various perspectives on fit, it is not meant to suggest that they are contradictory. In fact, quite the opposite is true. As was demonstrated in the operationalization of fit as the match between personality and organizational climate, often it is difficult to differentiate between fit perspectives. The definition presented above recognizes that the *optimum* P-O fit may be achieved when each entity's needs are fulfilled by the other *and* they share similar fundamental characteristics. Therefore, it is not contradictory with the definition posed in this paper that multiple perspectives on fit may be incorporated into one operationalization.

## *Other forms of person-environment fit*

The third step in defining P-O fit is to illustrate what lies outside this construct's domain by distinguishing it from other forms of P-E congruence. Although some authors have discussed the distinction between various types of P-E fit (e.g., Judge & Ferris, 1992), frequently the lines between these types are blurred (e.g., Blau, 1987; Edwards, 1991). Therefore, in this paper the differences between P-O fit and fit at three other levels of the environment—job, group, and vocation—are explicated. This paper does not include a discussion of fit between an individual and his or her supervisor, because this research has developed relatively independent of that of P-E fit—primarily in the literature on vertical dyadic linkage (e.g., Graen & Cashman, 1975; Pulakos & Wexley, 1983).

As suggested by B. Schneider et al. (1995), fit may be a viable construct at many levels of analysis. The "appropriate" level at which to examine fit is determined primarily by the a priori rationale for expecting fit to be relevent at that particular level. However, it is also important that the measurement strategies selected are appropriate to the level that is chosen.

### *Person-vocation (P-V) fit*

The broadest level of the work environment with which a person may fit is the vocational level. For example, Super's (1953) vocational development theory suggested that people choose an occupation based on its congruence with their self-concepts. Similarly, Holland (1985) suggested that both people and occupations have "personalities," which he characterized with the RIASEC typology (realistic, investigative, artistic, social, enterprising, and conventional personality types). Fit is determined by measures assessing the similarity between an individual's personality and that of a vocational environment (e.g., Holland, 1977).

Although these theories may predict vocational choice, they do not contribute to predictions of fit with particular organizations. Even in predominantly vocation-specific industries, such as law and accounting, the cultures of individual organizations may vary (e.g., Chatman, 1991; Deal & Kennedy, 1982; Schein, 1992). For example, biodata scores predicted specific accounting and law firms that people would join, even after vocation was held constant (J. Schneider, 1994).

Thus, there is some empirical support for the conceptual distinction between P-V and P-O fit.

## *Person-group (P-G) fit*

As work teams become more widely used in the corporate world, person-group fit becomes an increasingly relevant construct (e.g., Guzzo & Salas, 1995; Hoerr, 1989). Specifically, person-group (P-G) fit is defined as the compatibility between individuals and their work groups. The definition of work group, however, may range from a small group of immediate coworkers to any identifiable sub-unit of an organization, such as a functional department or geographic division. Few studies have examined antecedents or consequences of this type of fit, although there are several related research streams.

The literature most closely related to P-G fit is that of team composition. Although these literatures are distinct (composition is a group level variable, whereas P-G fit is most frequently considered for individuals), Klimoski and Jones (1995) suggested that achieving high levels of individual-team fit is the driving principle behind effective team composition. Studies of composition have shown that goal (e.g., Shaw, 1981; Weldon & Weingart, 1993), value (e.g., Haythorn, 1968; Klimoski & Jones, 1995), and sometimes personality (e.g., Driskell, Hogan, & Salas, 1987; Hackman & Morris, 1975) homogeneity influence behavioral and attitudinal outcomes for groups and their members. In line with a demands-abilities perspective on fit, other studies have shown that teams composed of members with heterogeneous knowledge, skills, and abilities (KSAs) are more effective than those with homogeneous KSAs (e.g., Haythorn, 1968; Laughlin, Branch, & Johnson, 1969; Shaw, 1981).

A related body of literature concerns group demography, or the composition of teams based on demographic, rather than psychological variables. Group demographic composition has been shown to influence behavioral patterns such as turnover (Jackson, Brett, Sessa, Cooper, Julin, & Peyronnin, 1991) and psychological patterns such as attachment to the group (Tsui, Egan, & O'Reilly, 1992).

This group composition research has suggested that the work group in which a person functions is a relevant and distinct type of P-E fit. Support for the distinction between P-G and P-O fit is found in the literature that suggests that sub-organizational units such as groups may have different norms and values than the organization in which they are contained (e.g., Louis, 1990; Patsfall & Feimer, 1985; Trice & Beyer, 1993). Thus, the degree of fit between an individual and group may differ radically from the fit between the person and the organization.

## *Person-job (P-J) fit*

One of the most well-studied types of P-E fit is the compatibility of individuals with specific jobs. Person-job (P-J) fit was defined by Edwards (1991) as the fit between the abilities of a person and the demands of a job (i.e., demands-abilities) or the desires of a person and the attributes of a job (needs-supplies). Unfortunately, "job" is a term that has been loosely equated to environment in some fit research (e.g., Blau, 1987), causing some confusion about its domain. In this paper, a job is defined as the tasks a person is expected to accomplish in exchange for employment, as well as the characteristics of those tasks. Using this definition, P-J fit should be judged relative to the tasks performed, not the organization in which the job exists.

Although it is likely that many job requirements will mirror characteristics of the organization, they are conceptually distinct elements of the work environment. For example, although organizational compensation policies establish guidelines, managers often have considerable flexibility in determining the reward structures for specific jobs (Bartol & Martin, 1988). Therefore, the reinforcement systems of the organization and the job should be considered as separate entities with which a person may or may not fit. Non-significant correlations between measures of P-O and P-J fit also support that, despite the potential overlap, individuals may experience varying degrees of fit at the job and the organization level (O'Reilly et al., 1991).

In summary, although various aspects of the environment may be interrelated, there is conceptual and empirical support for the distinction between P-O fit and other types of congruence. It is important that this distinction is made because of potential interactions between fit at the various environmental levels. Specific propositions regarding these interactions are suggested in the final portion of this paper. Although these other types of fit are equally interesting and viable determinants of various outcomes, in the present paper attention is focused on the distinct construct of P-O fit. Once P-O fit has been defined, both through an explanation of what it is and what it is not, the relevant measurement issues may be explored.

## Measuring person-organization fit

As with most constructs, the ideal P-O fit measurement procedures are a function of the research questions asked. This section begins with a description of the relevance and difficulties of commensurate measurement in the study of P-O fit. Following that discussion, direct measurement of perceived fit and two forms of indirect measurement of actual fit are presented, along with a description of the levels of analysis issues relevant to each. The section concludes with a description of indices of fit and of the recent debate between supporters of differences scores and polynomial regression.

### *Commensurate measurement*

Commensurate measurement—describing both person and organization with the same content dimensions—is often recommended for assessing fit because it ensures mutual relevance of the characteristics under investigation (e.g., Caplan, 1987; Edwards, 1991; French, Rogers, & Cobb, 1974). Patsfall and Feimer (1985), however, suggest that commensurate dimensions are not necessary because a priori hypotheses can be used to predict the level of fit of any individual characteristic in an organization. This ongoing debate is complicated further by the vagueness of the distinction between commensurate and non-commensurate measures. Although a construct may have similar characteristics at the individual and organizational levels, there will still be some inherent differences, resulting in non-identical measures. This leaves the interpretation of commensurate up to debate, as researchers strive to define how similar measures must be to meet the standard of "commensurability."

As noted, it is difficult to achieve perfectly commensurate measures. Keeping this limitation in mind, the position taken in this paper is that for supplementary fit, all attempts should be made to maximize the measures' commensurability. This ensures that high levels of fit imply similarity between an individual and an organization on specific characteristics, such as honesty values or social welfare goals. For complementary fit, however, the level of commensurability should depend on the breadth of the construct under investigation.

For narrowly defined, directly measured characteristics, such as pay level, fit can easily be assessed with commensurate questions such as "How much pay do you receive?" and "How much pay would you like to receive?" Fit on broader, latent characteristics, however, is not as amenable to commensurate measurement because of the characteristics' inherent multidimensionality. For example, there are many things that an organization can do to meet people's need for achievement, such as offering merit bonuses, commission-based pay, and formal recognition ceremonies. Because of the multiple ways for need for achievement to be satisfied, strictly commensurate measurement is not necessary. It is necessary, however, that researchers using non-commensurate measures precisely specify the constructs and dimensions they are investigating, as well as why the individual and organizational constructs are conceptually linked.

### Direct and indirect measures of fit

Once the individual and organizational characteristics have been selected for investigation, researchers have a variety of techniques at their disposal for assessing the extent of fit. Some authors have elected to use *direct* measurement, which involves asking people explicitly whether they believe that a good fit exists. Posner, Kouzes, and Schmidt's (1985) study is a good example of the use of direct measurement to assess value congruence. Managers directly rated how compatible their values were with those of their organizations and how often they had to compromise personal principles to meet organizational expectations. Those who evaluated their values as highly congruent with the organization reported a variety of positive effects such as greater feelings of personal success and higher organizational commitment than those reporting low value congruence.

Direct measures are beneficial if the construct under investigation is subjective or *perceived* fit, that is, if fit is conceptualized as the *judgment* that a person fits well in an organization (Cable & Judge, 1995; French et al., 1974). Using this conceptualization, good fit is said to exist as long as it is perceived to exist, regardless of whether or not the person has similar characteristics to, or complements/is complemented by, the organization. For example, perceived fit has been shown to influence the evaluation of job applicants, even when fit as calculated by a comparison of individual and organizational values showed no influence (Cable & Judge, 1995).

Although direct measures of perceived fit may show significant relationships with individual outcome variables, several criticisms have been leveled against their use. Edwards (1991) denounced direct measures primarily because they confound the constructs of the person and environment, thereby preventing estimation of their independent effects. Additionally, when the questions do not explicitly describe what values or other characteristics are to be considered in the respondents' answers, it is almost impossible to ensure that commensurate dimensions are being considered. Finally, when direct measures are used in conjunction with measures of other work-related attitudes, a consistency bias (i.e., "I think that I fit well, so I must be satisfied with my job.") could potentially influence the results (Salancik and Pfeffer, 1977).

In consideration of these drawbacks, some researchers rely on *indirect* measures to assess *actual* or objective fit (Cable & Judge, 1995; French et al., 1974). Whether interactions, difference scores, or polynomial regressions are used, indirect measures of fit involve an explicit comparison between separately rated individual and organizational characteristics. This type of measurement strategy is said to reflect actual fit because it allows a verifiable assessment of similarity or complementarity, without asking for implicit judgments of fit by those involved in the situation being analyzed. Whether actual and perceived P-O fit are the same constructs, simply measured differently, or whether they are two distinct constructs is an empirical question that deserves further investigation. Propositions regarding the distinction between these two conceptualizations are offered in the final section of this manuscript.

In addition to the distinction between direct and indirect measures of P-O fit, there are also different techniques for indirect measurement. Two of these techniques and their levels of analysis implications are discussed below.

*Indirect cross-levels measurement*

The cross-levels approach to indirect measurement is commonly used to assess both supplementary and complementary P-O fit. The cross-levels technique involves assessing the compatibility of individuals with verifiable organizational characteristics; therefore, it involves measuring characteristics at *two* levels of analysis. Research on level of analysis issues offers suggestions on appropriate procedures for this type of measurement (e.g., Klein, Dansereau, & Hall, 1994; Roberts, Hulin, & Rousseau, 1978; Rousseau, 1985).

Klein et al. (1994) suggested that specifying the level of one's theory is a critical step in addressing levels of analysis issues. In all theories of P-O fit individuals are hypothesized to have varying levels of compatibility with organizational characteristics. Individuals' characteristics are assumed to be independent, such that between-individual variation exists. Specifically, the values, goals, personality, or needs of one individual in an organization or applicant pool are assumed to be independent of these characteristics in others. Answering questions such as "What do you value?" each respondent describes him or herself. Because of their hypothesized independence, variability reflecting individual differences should exist in their responses.

Measurement of the organizational level variable, however, is more complicated. One type of organizational-level measure is "global data not divisible across individuals," such as organizational ownership or structure (Roberts et al., 1978, p. 85). This type of measure is not fundamentally perceptual in nature, as it can be verified by examining organizational charts or records. Measures of organizational variables that *are* perceptual, however, require the aggregation of data based on a composite of lower-level (individual) scores. In P-O fit research, the organizational constructs of interest are often values, goals, climate, or culture—variables that are most frequently measured by perceptions. Therefore, the aggregating of individual perceptions should be used in the measurement of actual P-O fit.

There is a controversy, however, as to whether a sufficient level of agreement should be shown before individual data can be aggregated to create an organizational level variable. The discourse between Glick (1985, 1988) and James (1982) and his colleagues (James, Joyce, & Slocum, 1988) is an example of this controversy. Glick (1985, 1988) suggested that agreement between individuals is unnecessary because variance between individuals can be considered error surrounding the one true score of the organizational variable. Alternatively, James and colleagues (1982, 1988) argued that when the organizational variable is perceptual in nature, one true organizational score may not exist. Their argument is based on the idea that variance between individuals' perceptions may not be simply error, but a representation of veridical differences within the organization regarding that variable. For example, if a mechanic does not perceive customer service as a value in an organization, but the CEO perceives it as one of the organization's primary values, then it may not be valid to assert that an organizational value for customer service exists at the organizational level. To use the mean of these two individuals' value ratings would mask the existence of different values for customer service in the two organizational sub-units (the mechanical division and the top management team).

Because of the perceptual nature of the organizational characteristics most often examined in studies of P-O fit, the position taken in this paper reflects that of James and his colleagues (1982, 1988). Specifically, it is suggested that agreement (although not perfect homogeneity) between individual responses to organizational level questions (i.e., "What does *your organization* value?") must be demonstrated to establish the organizational variable. It is important to note that individuals are not required to respond similarly to the individual-level question (e.g., "What do *you* value?"), only that they agree on the values of the organization as a whole. For example, Chatman (1989) describes organizational values as those that "are a group [organization] product; even though all members of the group would not have the same values, a majority of active members would agree on them and members of the group would be aware of the group's support for a given value" (p. 339).

This condition of sufficient agreement (the reader is referred to George and Bettenhausen, 1990, for an indication of what may be considered "sufficient") may appear to restrict the study of P-O fit to organizations in which one dominant culture exists. This is only partially true. If an organization does not have a culture that is agreed upon by its members, then it does not make sense to assess an individual's fit with that culture. It is more appropriate in this case, as in the customer service value example used above, to measure *P-G* fit with particular sub-units of that organization, rather than the organization as a whole. However, although there may not be organizational agreement on a particular aspect of culture, such as the value for customer service, there may be consensus on other aspects, such as a value for efficiency or cost-cutting. Therefore, P-O fit can meaningfully be investigated on those variables on which there is agreement, whereas P-G fit may be more meaningful on those where there is disagreement at the organizational level. It is important to remember, however, that agreement must then be shown at the group level to evaluate P-G fit.

The implication of this discussion is that verification of (a) variability on individual characteristics, *and* (b) sufficient agreement or consensus of responses for organizational characteristics is necessary for cross-level studies of actual P-O fit. In the P-O fit literature, Chatman (1991) provides one of the best examples of handling these levels of analysis issues by (a) using a large number of managers and partners, familiar with the organizational values, to create organizational culture profiles, (b) reporting indicators of the value structures' consistency over time (e.g., 0.78 median interrater correlation between time 1 and time 2), and (c) reporting coefficient alphas (0.84–0.90) and average interrater correlations to roughly estimate consensus on values within each organization.

Although Chatman builds some evidence for consensus on organizational values by using reliability indices, stronger evidence could have been demonstrated by the use of an agreement index such as $r_{wg}$ (James, Demaree, & Wolf, 1984). For a more thorough exploration of the differences between reliability indices (consistency estimates) and agreement indices (consensus estimates), the reader is referred to Kozlowski and Hattrup (1992).

### *Indirect individual-level measurement*

Although the very words "person-organization fit" seem to imply cross-levels research, this is not necessarily true. Whereas in cross-level studies organizational characteristics were assumed to be homogeneous (e.g., the organization as a whole is the unit of analysis), in individual-level investigations of actual fit, the organization construct is no longer verifiable organizational characteristics, but individuals' *perceptions* of those characteristics. Measures typically consist of each respondent answering parallel questions such as "What do *you* value?" and "What does your *company* value?" The similarity of the answers to these questions is then calculated, using either traditional difference scores or polynomial regression, resulting in an individual level measure of actual P-O fit. Regardless of the statistical analyses used to estimate fit, all measurement occurs at the individual level of analysis. Therefore, as in the case of other individual characteristics, peoples' perceptions of organizational characteristics are assumed to vary. This assumption could be (although rarely is) verified by showing a high level of variance or lack of agreement among individuals' perceptions.

Because many fit theories discuss congruence with organizational characteristics rather than with individuals' perceptions of them, why would researchers elect to use individual level measures? Similar to the rationale behind the importance of perceived fit, a primary reason is that people's perceptions of reality drive their cognitive appraisals of and reactions to specific situations (e.g., Nisbett & Ross, 1980). Therefore, the perception of organizational characteristics may have a stronger influence on individual outcome variables such as stress, satisfaction, or commitment than would fit with organization's actual characteristics. This may be particularly true for fit on characteristics that are difficult to verify, such as values or goals.

In summary, whether researchers use direct or indirect measures, it is important for them to recognize the link between those measures and the constructs they are investigating. Although both perceived and actual fit may be equally viable determinants of attitudinal and behavioral outcomes, care should be taken to interpret results in terms of which was the measured construct.

### *Indices of actual fit*

Whether cross-level or individual-level measurement is used, researchers have a variety of options available for assessing the actual fit of a person with an organization. Edwards (1991) described several ways that P-E fit can be measured, although two have been most used in the context of P-O fit. The first is the calculation of a product term that reflects the moderating effects of one of the entities (person or organization) on the relationship between the other entity and an outcome variable. This focus on the interaction between person and organization is used in a variety of studies (e.g., Chesney & Rosenman, 1980; Matteson & Ivancevich, 1982; Pritchard & Karasick, 1973), only a subset of which use commensurate dimensions to describe both entities.

A second popular method for assessing fit is the reduction of person and organization measures into a single index reflecting the degree of similarity between them. Researchers have typically used the bivariate congruence indices of algebraic $(X - Y)$, absolute $(|X - Y|)$, or squared differences $(X - Y)^2$. In the case of multiple predictors, profile similarity indices (PSIs) such as the sum of algebraic differences ($D^1$), the sum of absolute differences ($|D|$), the sum of the squared differences ($D^2$), the Euclidean distance ($D$), or the correlation between two profiles ($Q$) are used (Edwards, 1993; Edwards & Parry, 1993).

Much of the goal congruence literature has used the $D$ statistic (Cronbach & Gleser, 1953), choosing to ignore the direction of the difference between the person and organization variables (e.g., Vancouver & Schmitt, 1991; Witt & Nye, 1992). Value congruence, however, has more frequently been investigated with the use of Q-sort (Bem & Funder, 1978; Block 1978) based profile correlations such as the Organizational Culture Profile (OCP; O'Reilly et al., 1991) and the Organizational Fit Instrument (Ryan & Schmit, 1992).

Despite their wide-spread use in the fit literature, difference scores have been criticized repeatedly for a variety of problems (e.g., Cronbach, 1958; Edwards, 1993; Johns, 1981; Nunnally, 1962). One concern is with the *conceptual ambiguity* that results from difference scores concealing the individual contribution of each element to the overall score (Edwards, 1993; 1994). *Discarded information* is a second problem because the absolute level of the person and environment variables is lost (Edwards, 1993; 1994). This problem is compounded by a loss of information regarding the direction of the difference with "symmetric" indices (i.e., the absolute difference, squared difference, $D$, $D^2$, $|D|$, and $Q$). It is important to note that although Q-sort data may appear to give information on the direction of fit or misfit (i.e., fit could range from $-1.00$ to $+1.00$), it can only describe the similarity of profile shape. Specifically, parallel profiles yield correlations of $+1.00$, whereas "mirror-image" profiles yield correlations of $-1.00$ (Edwards, 1993). In the case of multiple predictors, PSIs are also *insensitive to the sources of profile differences* (Edwards, 1993; 1994). They do not reflect that a variety of elements may lead to differences between the two entities, while these elements may represent vastly different psychological experiences. Finally, *restrictive constraints* are placed on the sign and magnitude of the coefficients in difference score equations; constraints that are seldom substantiated by the data (e.g., Edwards & Parry, 1993; Edwards & Harrison, 1993).

In addition to these criticisms of difference scores in general, further concerns with profile correlations have been raised. Because profile correlations are ordinal and ipsative, Edwards (1993; 1994) strongly cautioned against their use because they cannot provide information regarding the magnitude of differences between the individual and the organization. This criticism is particularly relevant to, but difficult to overcome, in the value congruence literature (e.g., Chatman, 1991; O'Reilly et al., 1991). Much of the literature on values has indicated that they are arranged hierarchically and that Likert-type measures of values are prone to a social desirability bias. Therefore, Ravlin and Meglino (1987) support the use of ipsative measures because they are less prone to a social desirability response bias than Likert-type scales and they address the hierarchical arrangement of values. They do not, however, offer suggestions for how to overcome the problem of discarded information.

The alternative procedure suggested by Edwards (1993; 1994) is polynomial regression. The use of this procedure is based on the assumptions that: (a) The relationship between two entities and an outcome should be considered in three dimensions, (b) The analyses should use three-dimensional response surfaces to depict the joint relationship of the two entities (i.e., person and organization) with the outcome, and (c) The constraints implied by traditional fit indices should be considered as hypotheses that can be tested and supported to lend credibility to the proposed model.

The procedure begins with a researcher selecting the functional form of the conceptual model that should best underlie the data and identifying the corresponding constrained and unconstrained regression equations (Edwards & Parry, 1993). By testing the model with each of these equations, and comparing their results, the functional form corresponding to the conceptual model of interest may be directly tested, rather than assumed. Using this technique for a reanalysis of French, Caplan, and Harrison's (1982) study on P-E fit and stress revealed conceptually meaningful findings, concealed by the use of difference scores in the original study (Edwards & Harrison, 1993). In the process of reanalysis, the proportion of variance explained was more than doubled (Edwards & Parry, 1993).

Although Edwards' technique addresses some of the problems inherent in difference scores, it is not without limitations. One concern is with the multicollinearity that results from expanding the constrained to the unconstrained equations. For example, the algebraic difference $(P - O)^2$ for one set of person $(P)$ and organization $(O)$ variables is expanded to yield five terms: $P$, $O$, $P^2$, $O^2$, and $P \times O$ in the unconstrained equation. In this case, both of the quadratic terms and the interaction term have some multicollinearity with the initial $P$ and $O$ variables. A second concern is that Edwards' tests of constrained versus unconstrained models are highly dependent on sample size and power. Although this is a problem with any type of significance test, it is particularly relevant to Edwards' technique because of the high number of degrees of freedom used in each test. Additional difficulties with Edwards' technique are encountered when testing complex moderation models and in using dummy-coded variables. Interpreting a moderating relationship would involve the testing of interactions with quadratic expansion terms, and the polynomial expansion terms of dummy-coded variables are correlated perfectly with their original coding (e.g., for gender codes, $0^2 = 0$ and $1^2 = 1$).

Two final issues with the polynomial regression procedure reflect conceptual rather than statistical concerns. First, a concern has been voiced with the conceptual validity of the higher order terms that can be created using Edwards' technique (Bedeian & Day, 1994). Although these higher order terms may receive empirical support, unless they are theoretically relevant, they do not aid in conceptual understanding. It should be noted that Edwards (1994) acknowledges this argument and does not promote the use of his technique unless guided by theory. Finally, some researchers have argued that difference scores may represent something conceptually distinct from their components (Tisak & Smith, 1994). If this is true, then Edwards' technique of analyzing the component parts does not address the same construct as would analyzing a difference score. This assertion deserves empirical evaluation by contrasting the nomological nets of difference scores and their components.

Thus, the longstanding debate regarding the usefulness of difference scores to measure fit continues. In the future, research should be conducted that uses *both* the traditional methods of assessing fit and the polynomial regression technique recommended by Edwards. This will allow the strengths and weaknesses of each method to be explored, as well as add to our knowledge of the intricacies of congruence relationships. For example, as previously mentioned, much of the value congruence literature continues to be conducted with ipsative measures, such as the OCP (O'Reilly et al., 1991). In order to compare these methods with polynomial regression, researchers may try using Likert scales to assess values, rather than the currently supported measures. Using Likert scales with increased gradation at the upper end would allow respondents to discriminate more finely between positive responses, thereby reducing the social desirability effects indicated by Ravlin and Meglino (1987).

## Reviewing the person-organization fit literature

When researchers do not specify the type of P-O fit they are investigating (i.e., supplementary vs. complementary, perceived vs. actual), it is difficult to draw definitive conclusions regarding the construct. Therefore, in the previous two sections of this manuscript, relevant distinctions that can be used to describe the P-O fit literature were presented. In the following review, these distinctions are used to organize and integrate the existing literature on P-O fit and various aspects of the employment experience.

Theories regarding P-O fit have highlighted three aspects of the employment experience that affect or are affected by individual-organizational congruence. First, the ASA framework suggests that consideration of P-O fit during organizational entry is one of the primary influences in creating organizational homogeneity (B. Schneider, 1987). A recent review article by B. Schneider et al. (1995) reviews the role of P-O fit in determining individuals' job search and choice behaviors as well as organizations' selection decisions. Following organizational entry, individual and organizational socialization practices have been supported as a second contributor to P-O fit (Chatman, 1989). Finally, long-term outcomes attributed to P-O fit include turnover (e.g., B. Schneider, 1987), work attitudes (e.g., Dawis & Lofquist, 1984), pro-social behaviors (e.g., O'Reilly & Chatman, 1986), work performance (e.g., Tziner, 1987), and organizational outcomes (e.g., B. Schneider, Kristof, Goldstein, & Smith, in press).

These three aspects of the employment experience (organizational entry, socialization, and long-term outcomes) are used in conjunction with the supplementary and complementary fit distinction to provide a framework for the following literature review. Table 1 illustrates areas in this framework that have been well-explored, in addition to those that require future investigation. Because of the high

*Table 1* Empirical studies of P-O fit classified by conceptualization and field of research

| Field of research | Supplementary fit | Complementary fit |
|---|---|---|
| *Organizational entry* | | |
| Individual | | |
| Job search | | Rynes et al. (1991) |
| Job choice | Behling & Tolliver (1972) | Bretz et al. (1989) |
| | Burke & Deszca (1982) | Cable & Judge (1994) |
| | Judge & Bretz (1992) | Turban & Keon (1993) |
| | Keon et al. (1982) | |
| Organizational | | |
| Recruitment | | |
| Selection | Adkins et al. (1994) | Rynes & Gerhart (1990) |
| | Cable & Judge (1995) | |
| | Chatman (1991) | |
| | Rynes & Gerhart (1990) | |
| *Socialization* | | |
| Individual | Chatman (1991) | |
| Organizational | Chatman (1991) | |
| *Outcomes* | | |
| Individual | | |
| Work attitudes | Boxx et al. (1991) | Bretz & Judge (1994) |
| | Bretz & Judge (1994) | Downey et al. (1975) |
| | Chatman (1991) | Tziner (1987) |
| | O'Reilly et al. (1991) | |
| | Posner (1992) | |
| | Posner et al. (1985) | |
| | Vancouver et al. (1994) | |
| | Vancouver & Schmitt (1991) | |
| | Witt et al. (1993) | |
| | Witt & Nye (1992) | |
| | Witt & Silver (1995) | |
| | Witt & Voss (1995) | |
| Intention to | | |
| quit/attrition | Bretz & Judge (1994) | Bretz & Judge (1994) |
| | Chatman (1991) | |
| | O'Reilly et al. (1991) | |
| | Vancouver et al. (1994) | |
| | Vancouver & Schmitt (1991) | |
| Stress | | Chesney & Rosenman (1980) |
| | | Ivancevich & Matteson (1980) |
| | | Matteson & Ivancevich (1982) |
| Prosocial | | |
| behaviors | O'Reilly & Chatman (1986) | |
| | Posner (1992) | |
| | Posner et al. (1985) | |
| Work | | |
| performance | Bretz & Judge (1994) | Andrews (1967) |
| | | Bretz & Judge (1994) |
| | | Downey et al. (1975) |
| | | Pritchard & Karasick (1973) |
| | | Tziner (1987) |
| Organizational | | Livingstone & Nelson (1994) |

number of non-empirical research articles, as well as the limited number of studies utilizing different variables, it was not feasible to conduct a meta-analysis on the current body of P-O fit research. As more empirical research is conducted, however, future reviewers should consider using meta-analytic procedures (e.g., Hunter & Schmidt, 1990).

Two primary criteria were used in selecting studies to be included in this review. First, only articles that investigate the fit between people and organizations (rather than jobs, vocations, or groups) were reviewed. Theoretical and conceptual pieces, as well as empirical studies were included, because of their fundamental importance to the study of P-O fit. These studies were identified by an electronic search of the published management, I/O psychology, vocational psychology, and interactional psychology literature. In addition, unpublished papers from professional conferences were included if the authors provided them in response to a request for materials. Second, only those empirical studies using commensurate measurement or explicitly arguing for the conceptual link between the individual and organizational-level variables were included. As previously mentioned, the standards for consideration as commensurate measurement are often vague; therefore, the best judgment of the author was used when determining the inclusion or exclusion of a study.

## *Organizational entry*

### *Individual job search and choice*

Although job search and choice behaviors are conceptually distinct, they often have not been investigated as such (Bretz, Boudreau, & Judge, 1994). This is particularly true in the P-O fit literature, where individuals' preferences for organizations, rather than search behaviors or actual choice decisions have been the focus. Only one study concentrated specifically on job search behaviors as an antecedent of P-O fit. In this study, job applicants reported that they formed assessments of fit with companies at which they were interviewing based on interactions with both formal organizational representatives (i.e., recruiters) and informal contacts with others in the firm (Rynes, Bretz, & Gerhart, 1991). The specific influences on fit assessments were the firm's general reputation, attitude toward product/industry, status of particular functional areas within the firm, training and advancement opportunities, and geographic location (Rynes et al., 1991). With the exception of this study, the P-O fit literature has concentrated on the consequences, rather than the antecedents of individuals' assessments of P-O fit during organizational entry.

Much of the research on P-O fit and job choice has been conducted in laboratory settings; therefore, investigators have used organizational attractiveness ratings as a surrogate for job/organization choice. In particular, personality variables have been used to predict peoples' preferences for organizations with certain types of reward systems. Upper-level students with a high need for achievement have been reported to prefer hypothetical organizations characterized by encouragement and reward of competitive individual effort and accomplishment (Bretz et al., 1989; Turban & Keon, 1993). Other personality characteristics, such as materialism and self-efficacy, have significantly predicted individuals' preferences for organizations with pay systems involving specific characteristics such as high pay levels and individual-based pay (Cable & Judge, 1994). Corresponding results have been found for self-esteem and preferences for organizational centralization (Turban & Keon, 1993). These results indicate that needs-supplies fit between individual personality traits and organizational characteristics may significantly influence applicants' job choice decisions.

Supplementary P-O fit has also been found to predict organizational preferences. For example, Tom (1971) hypothesized that people prefer and choose to work for employers whose organizational images (knowledge, belief, and feeling structures) match their own personal self-concepts. Similar hypotheses have been supported by empirical studies operationalizing P-O fit as either (a) the match between individual personality and organizational climate, or (b) value congruence. For example, Type A and Type B personality (Friedman & Rosenman, 1974) students were found to prefer organizational climates reflecting commensurate characteristics (Burke & Deszca, 1982). Type A individuals—characterized by ambition, competitiveness, impatience, high needs for achievement, and hostility—preferred organizations exhibiting high performance standards, spontaneity, ambiguity, and toughness, labeled as Type A organizational behaviors. In terms of value congruence, graduate and professional students were more likely to accept job offers from hypothetical organizations whose value orientation matched their own than those that did not (Judge & Bretz, 1992). This relationship held true even when non-value information such as pay and promotion opportunities was also presented. Taken as a whole, these findings lend some support to the hypothesis that people are differentially attracted to organizations with which they anticipate a supplementary fit.

A few moderators of the relationship between supplementary fit and organizational attraction have also been investigated. Several studies have shown that the desire for self-organizational congruence is greater among students with positive versus negative self-images (Behling & Tolliver, 1972; Keon, Latack, & Wanous, 1982). Students with negative self-images were more likely to prefer organizations and graduate schools least like themselves (Behling & Tolliver, 1972; Keon et al., 1982). These findings support self-esteem or self-image strength as a moderator of the relationship between P-O fit and organizational choice.

*Organizational recruitment and selection*

Just as few studies have been conducted on individuals' job search behaviors and P-O fit, research is also lacking on the topic of P-O fit and organizational recruitment. Most research has focused on the importance of fit in selection decisions, rather than the recruitment process, and much of this research has been fairly recent. Prior to the late 1980s researchers of selection did not ignore the construct of

P-O fit (e.g., Argyris, 1957; Kanter, 1977; Wanous, 1980); however, their primary focus was on P-J fit rather than individual-organizational congruence. Even in the late 1980s when several practitioner-focused articles highlighted the benefits of hiring managers to fit with the strategies (Herbert & Deresky, 1987; Leontiades, 1982), life cycles (Kerr, 1982), or general business conditions of an organization (Gerstein & Reisman, 1983), the discussion centered on hiring those best able to meet job rather than organizational demands.

Bowen et al. (1991) made one of the first significant arguments for the desirability of P-O fit as a desired outcome of the hiring process. Whereas traditional models focused primarily on P-J fit, Bowen et al. (1991) suggested that individual-organizational fit becomes the critical factor when selecting employees for long-term employment and organizational flexibility. Selecting people whose personalities are compatible with the organizational culture creates a flexible workforce with employees who can be moved easily between jobs. As a guide for practitioners, Bowen et al. (1991) recommended a four step procedure that would help incorporate P-O fit at each step in the selection process. Despite the increased time and financial requirements for such a system, its adoption was predicted to improve employee attitudes, reduce absenteeism and turnover, and reinforce organizational design.

Several authors have argued that P-O fit criteria are *already* included in the selection process (Chatman, 1989; Ferris & Judge, 1991; Judge & Ferris, 1992). These researchers suggested that managers are reluctant to abandon the interview, despite its questionable reliability and validity (e.g., Harris, 1989), because it is the most effective way of selecting applicants who appear to fit well with the organization. This point is reinforced by Karren and Graves (1994), who found that the structured interview is one of the most effective ways to assess an applicant's fit with an organization. To more comprehensively describe how this assessment of fit coordinates with the traditional assessment of job-relevant criteria, Judge and Ferris (1992) proposed a descriptive model of selection that incorporates both P-J and P-O fit considerations.

Empirical support for the role of P-O fit in organizational selection decisions has been mixed. Some results suggest that interviewers desire firm-specific qualities in applicants, above and beyond general qualifications (Adkins, Russell, & Werbel, 1994; Rynes & Gerhart, 1990). Specifically, interviewers appear to be more stringent in their evaluation of firm-specific employability and show greater variability in firm-specific evaluations than in general employability assessments (Rynes & Gerhart, 1990). However, Cable and Judge (1995) found that only value congruence as *perceived* by the interviewers, rather than *actual*, value congruence, was predictive of interview outcomes. Similarly, Adkins et al. (1994) found no significant relationship between actual applicant-organization value congruence (as perceived by the recruiter) and the direct perceived fit assessments or judgments of general employability. Instead, they found that these assessments were significantly related to two other types of fit: (a) value congruence between the applicant and *recruiter* (idiosyncratic fit or what might be called a 'similar-to-me' bias); and (b) between the applicant and an "*ideal*" applicant (universal fit or what may be called a "similar-to-an-ideal" bias; Adkins et al., 1994).

Support for both idiosyncratic and universal fit has been found by several researchers; however, universal fit has been reported as the most influential on selection decisions (e.g., Bretz et al., 1993; Dalessio & Imada, 1984). When asked to directly rate applicants' P-O fit and then to list the reasons why those ratings were assigned, organizational representatives indicated that more emphasis was placed on job-specific and general fit (applicants with universally desirable traits) than on fit with their particular organizations during the early stages of hiring (Bretz et al., 1993). Thus, although P-O fit may play an important role in representatives' decision making, their assessments of fit may be influenced by universally desirable traits rather than firm-specific fit, at least during early stages of the selection process.

These results also demonstrate that perceived fit, as measured by direct assessments of organizational representatives, may not reflect actual levels of P-O fit. Further, although structured interviews may be an effective way to assess P-O fit, individual biases may influence the accuracy of these assessments (Karren & Graves, 1994). It has also been suggested that techniques such as personality measures, forced-choice scales, and Q-sort methodologies (e.g., individual and organizational profiles) could instead be used to assess fit, while negating the effects of interviewers' biases (Karren & Graves, 1994).

*Summary*

Substantial support has been shown for the positive relationship between all types of P-O fit and individuals' preferences for organizations. This relationship has also been supported for organizations' selection decisions; however, the relative importance of P-O fit, universal fit, and idiosyncratic fit have yet to be determined. It is also supported that perceived, rather than actual fit, is more influential during the selection process. This is understandable because of the short period of time that individuals and organizations have to express their value, goals, and personalities. It is also possible that P-O fit may play a larger role in organizations' decisions at later stages of the selection process, once overall qualifications have been established. This idea is explained further in the final section of this manuscript, along with specific suggestions for investigating the previously unresearched links between P-O fit, job search behaviors, and organizational recruitment practices.

**Socialization**

Because P-O fit is not the sole determinant of job choice or selection decisions, a range in the initial level of fit will most likely exist in an organization's new hires. Several studies have shown that simply as tenure increases, people learn and come to accept the goals and values of their employing organization (e.g., Hall,

Schneider, & Nygren, 1975; Hinrichs, 1964). In addition, Ostroff and Rothausen (1995) hypothesized that increased tenure leads to a better fit between individuals' personal orientations and organizational climate. Results from their study of secondary school teachers supported this hypothesis most strongly at the aggregate level, such that groups of teachers with longer tenure had higher levels of fit with their environments. Specific socialization activities are not discussed in these studies; however, it is evident that over time individuals come to assume characteristics of their organizations, resulting in higher levels of supplementary fit.

The purpose of socialization is to facilitate learning about various aspects of the organizational environment, including performance proficiency, people (the establishment of working relationships), politics, organization-specific language, organizational history, and organizational goals and values (Chao, O'Leary-Kelly, Wolf, Klein, & Gardner, 1994). This final dimension is the most common topic addressed in the socialization literature (Ostroff & Kozlowski, 1992), and appears particularly relevant to supplementary P-O fit. Recent research has focused on the importance of individual as well as organizational socialization practices, indicating that employees can take an active role in learning and increasing their level of P-O fit (Morrison, 1993a, 1993b).

Although researchers often offer increasing levels of P-O fit as an explanation of the positive effects of socialization (e.g., Chao et al., 1994; Hall et al., 1975), fit is rarely included as a variable in their studies. Chatman's (1991) investigation of accounting firms' new hires is an exception. In that study, supplementary fit on values and goals was proposed to mediate the relationship between socialization and outcomes such as job satisfaction and organizational commitment. Results indicated that socialization, particularly mentorship activities and attendance at firm-related social events, had positive effects on levels of P-O fit within one year of organizational entry. Furthermore, both initial and socialized levels of fit were found to predict turnover over the two and a half years of the study's duration (Chatman, 1991).

*Summary*

These results indicate that organizational tenure and socialization practices may lead to increased levels of supplementary P-O fit. The effects of these variables on complementary fit, however, has been relatively unexplored. Both organizational (mentorship) and individual socialization attempts (attendance at social activities) appear to increase fit, although only a small number of practices have been investigated. Remaining questions concerning socialization and P-O fit are posited in the final section of this manuscript.

### *Long-term consequences*

After devoting resources to attracting, selecting, and socializing employees for high levels of P-O fit, managers hope for positive results. Although researchers have examined the effects of fit on several outcomes, most studies center around positive outcomes for individuals, such as improved satisfaction and reduced intention to quit. However, several theorists have suggested that high levels of P-O fit produce negative outcomes at the organizational level (B. Schneider, 1987; B. Schneider, Kristof, Goldstein, & Smith, in press; B. Schneider, Smith, & Goldstein, 1994; Walsh, 1987). This section is organized around the various individual and organizational level outcomes of P-O fit.

## Work attitudes

Strong support has been found for the positive effects of P-O fit on individual work attitudes. In terms of supplementary fit, value congruence has been well supported as a determinant of job satisfaction and organizational commitment. This relationship has been documented for junior-level accountants (Chatman, 1991), executives in the public sector (Boxx et al., 1991), and MBA students, senior accountants, and middle-level managers (O'Reilly et al., 1991). Additional work attitudes affected by value congruence include motivation (Posner, 1992) and feelings of work group cohesion (Boxx et al., 1991), as well as feelings of personal success and greater concern for stakeholders by managers in large manufacturing firms (Posner et al., 1985).

Researchers have reported similar effects on work attitudes for supplementary fit operationalized as actual goal congruence. Vancouver and Schmitt (1991), in a study of teachers and principals from over 350 secondary schools, found that both superior-subordinate (teacher-principal) and member-constituency (teacher-other teachers) goal congruence were positively related to satisfaction and commitment. Of the two types of goal congruence, member-constituency congruence had the greatest impact on these work attitudes (Vancouver & Schmitt, 1991). Similar results were reported by Witt and his colleagues (e.g., Witt & Nye, 1992; Witt, Hilton, & Hellman, 1993; Witt & Voss, 1995); however, in one study they found supervisor-subordinate congruence to be most influential for non-supervisory employees.

In a follow-up to the Vancouver and Schmitt (1991) study, Vancouver et al. (1994) turned their attention to the group level of analysis. The focus in this study was on between-constituency (agreement of all teachers with the principal) and within constituency (overall level of agreement among teachers) goal congruence. Results indicated that both types of group level goal congruence had an effect on work attitudes after controlling for individual level congruence. Specifically, teachers in schools with high within-constituency congruence had more positive attitude scores than those with low within-constituency congruence. Contrary to their hypothesis, however, teachers in schools with high between-constituency congruence (i.e., most teachers' goals were congruent with the principal's) indicated lower attitude scores. These results, taken as a whole, indicate the strong impact of goal congruence, at both the individual and group levels of analysis, on the work attitudes of job satisfaction and organizational commitment.

Moderators and mediators of the relationship between goal congruence and work attitudes have also been explored. Exchange ideology, defined by Eisenberger, Huntington, Hutchinson, and Sowa (1986) as individuals' expectations for what should be given and received in an exchange relationship, has been shown to moderate the fit-satisfaction relationship (Witt et al., 1993). Their results indicated that fit is more strongly related to satisfaction for employees who have a strong exchange ideology (i.e., have high social exchange expectations) than for those with weaker ideologies (Witt et al., 1993). Additionally, workplace politics have been supported as a mediator of the relationship between goal congruence and work attitudes. Employees with high co-worker goal *in*congruence perceived higher levels of workplace politics, which in turn led to decreased focus on customers and reduced continuance commitment (Witt & Voss, 1995). Taking a different perspective, P-O fit has been supported as a moderator of the relationship between team politics and cohesion (Witt & Silver, 1995). Results indicate that high levels of goal congruence can mitigate the detrimental effects of politics on team cohesion (Witt & Silver, 1995).

Positive work attitudes have been shown to result from P-O fit conceptualized from a needs-supplies perspective as well as from these supplementary perspectives. High levels of fit between organizational climates and people's preferences for them (Tziner, 1987), as well as climates and personality characteristics (Downey, Hellriegel, & Slocum, 1975), have been found to predict high levels of satisfaction and organizational commitment. Industrial employees reporting low discrepancies between their organization's climate for achievement and their preferences for such a climate were more satisfied with their jobs and committed to their organizations than those reporting high discrepancies (Tziner, 1987). Similarly, individuals requiring social contact and interdependence with others were more satisfied in organizations with open and empathic climates than those with closed, bureaucratic, and impersonal climates (Downey et al., 1975). Further, individuals with high self-confidence were more satisfied in structured organizations versus all others in unstructured organizations (Downey et al., 1975).

One of the few studies to examine the effects of multiple conceptualizations of fit on work attitudes was conducted by Bretz and Judge (1994). They operationalized fit in four ways: (a) value congruence (supplementary), (b) individual personality and organizational image similarity (supplementary), (c) the degree to which organizational reinforcement systems met individuals' needs (needs-supplies), and (d) the extent to which individual KSAs met job requirements (more indicative of P-J than P-O fit). Their results showed powerful direct effects of P-O fit, when conceptualized in multiple ways, on organizational satisfaction.

*Intention to quit and turnover*

Not only do various conceptualizations of P-O fit significantly predict satisfaction and commitment, they are similarly predictive of intentions to quit. Specifically, high levels of supervisor-subordinate and peer goal congruence (individual level), as well as within-constituency congruence (group level), are negatively related to intentions to quit (Vancouver et al., 1994; Vancouver & Schmitt, 1991). Similarly, employees with lower levels of value congruence with their organizations are more likely to report an intention to leave their organizations than those with higher congruence levels (Chatman, 1991; O'Reilly et al., 1991).

Furthermore, several studies have shown that these intentions to quit are often realized. Survival analysis by O'Reilly et al. (1991) indicated that value congruence was a significant determinant of actual employee turnover within 2 years of the initial assessment of fit. Similarly, Chatman (1991) reported that levels of value congruence measured both at entry (initial) and after 1 year of employment and socialization (resulting) significantly predicted turnover. Utilizing multiple conceptualizations of P-O fit, Bretz and Judge (1994) also found that P-O fit had a strong direct effect on organizational tenure.

*Stress*

Lower levels of work-related stress have also been associated with high levels of P-O fit (Chesney & Rosenman, 1980; Ivancevich & Matteson, 1980; Matteson & Ivancevich, 1982). Researchers have typically used self-reports to characterize subjects and their organizations as either Type A or a Type B entities (Friedman & Rosenman, 1974). Results have shown that when individuals join matched-typed organizations (i.e., Type A individuals join Type A organizations and Type B individuals join Type B organizations) they experience lower levels of job stress, as indicated by self-reports and lower blood pressure, than do their "mismatched" counterparts.

*Prosocial behaviors*

Behavioral effects of P-O fit have included increased prosocial behaviors such as organizational citizenship behaviors (O'Reilly & Chatman, 1986), self-reported teamwork (Posner, 1992), and tendencies toward ethical behavior (Posner et al., 1985). Undergraduate students were more likely to report helping with orientation and school-related activities, and MBA students pledged more money to their schools, when high levels of value congruency existed (O'Reilly & Chatman, 1986). Similarly, congruence with an organization's core principles or values has been found to have significant positive effects on self-report ratings of teamwork (Posner, 1992) and tendencies toward ethical behavior (Posner et al., 1985). However, because most of these results are based on self-reports, future research should attempt to incorporate more objective behavioral measures, such as the pledges by MBA students (O'Reilly & Chatman, 1986).

*Work performance*

Self-reports have also been utilized to assess the effects of P-O fit on individuals' work performance. Industrial employees reporting low discrepancies between their organization's climate for achievement and their preferences for such a climate had higher self-appraised work performance than those reporting high discrepancies (Tziner, 1987). Other researchers have used more objective measures of work performance such as the number of promotions and percent salary increases for managers (Downey et al., 1975; Bretz & Judge, 1994). Downey et al. (1975) found that individuals with high need for social contact and interdependence with others performed better by these measures in organizations with humanitarian climates than did their less sociable counterparts. Bretz and Judge (1994) examined fit as a predictor of career success. Their results indicated indirect effects of P-O fit on job promotions and to a lesser extent salary level, in addition to direct effects on organizational tenure and satisfaction.

Andrews (1967) found an interaction between managers classified as achievement- or power-oriented and their organizations' values of achievement or power. Managerial performance composite scores, consisting of job status, number of promotions, and number of raises, were significantly higher for the managers in organizations "matching" their values. Pritchard and Karasick (1973) found support for similar hypotheses regarding managers with a high need for order in highly structured environment, and low level managers with a high need for dominance in low status polarization organizations.

*Organizational consequences*

As reviewed above, the majority of the P-O fit literature has focused on the positive outcomes for individuals. At the organizational level, however, the benefits of high levels of fit have been questioned. Argyris (1957) theorized that organizations with too many people of "the right type" would be in danger of stultification and lack of innovation. Others have begun to focus attention on this "dark side of good fit" that may result in myopic perspectives, an inability to adapt to a changing environment, and a lack of organizational innovation (B. Schneider, 1987; B. Schneider et al., in press). Walsh (1987) supported these propositions by suggesting that high levels of *poor* fit can stimulate organizational maturation and development. Thus, it appears that although fit may offer several benefits for individuals, these benefits may come at the expense of organizational effectiveness.

Some suggestions have been made, however, on how to help eleviate these negative organizational consequences. B. Schneider et al. (in press) propose that although high levels of fit may be desirable for lower level employees, managers at higher levels should be selected for heterogeneity. Further, Greenhalgh (1983) and B. Schneider and his colleagues suggested that "misfits" are particularly important during the later stages of an organization's maturation, when decline may be promoted by stagnation.

In contrast to these arguments, initial support has been found for a model of "creativity fit" that disputes the argument that high levels of fit necessarily lead to low levels of innovation (Livingstone & Nelson, 1994). Both demands-abilities and needs-supplies fit are incorporated in this model, to elucidate the positive consequences of matching creative people with creativity-rich organizations. More research concerning these ideas should be conducted to more accurately determine the long-term organizational consequences of P-O fit.

*Summary*

The empirical results supporting the positive consequences of P-O fit for job satisfaction, organizational commitment, extra-role behaviors, and retention rates are extensive. In addition, these benefits have been shown utilizing multiple conceptualizations of fit. However, the benefits of P-O fit for performance are still questionable. Studies employing objective measures of performance such as productivity, product quality, or cycle time would provide stronger tests of the fit-performance relationship for individuals. Also, although several authors suggested that high levels of P-O fit may have detrimental effects on organizations, this relationship has received little empirical examination.

## Recommending future research directions and implications of P-O fit

The demonstrated relevance of P-O fit in the hiring process and its subsequent effects on individual and organizational outcomes make it an important topic for continued research. As practitioners are encouraged to hire people for the organization, rather than for specific jobs, the importance of understanding the complexity of P-O fit becomes even more critical (Bowen et al., 1991; Bridges, 1994). One objective of the current paper was to integrate the existing theoretical and empirical research; however, this integration indicates that there are many issues that remain unaddressed. In this final section a variety of directions for future research are proposed, specific propositions to guide prospective investigations are offered, and recommendations for managers interested in the practical implications of P-O fit are made.

*Multiple conceptualizations of P-O fit*

One of this manuscript's major contributions is its specification and integration of multiple P-O fit conceptualizations. One benefit of recognizing these multiple perspectives is that by examining more than one in any single study, a more comprehensive picture of fit may be attained. The P-O fit definition presented earlier suggests that the benefits of fit may be maximized if both supplementary and complementary fit exist concurrently but on different characteristics. This suggests an additive effect of fit conceptualizations. However, it is also possible that once one type of fit is attained, the effects of other types might be constrained. For example, it may be proposed that supplementary fit on values produces such a high level of satisfaction that the complementarity of KSAs does little to add to this positive attitude. Only by investigating multiple conceptualizations of fit in a single study, can these two competing propositions be explored.

> *Proposition 1a:* Supplementary and complementary fit (on different characteristics) have additive effects on dependent variables, such that people who are high on both types of fit will have more positive work attitudes and lower turnover rates than will those who have only high supplementary or high complementary fit; or

> *Proposition 1b:* Supplementary and complementary fit (on different characteristics) have convergent effects on dependent variables, such that people who are high on one of these types of fit have similar attitudes and turnover rates as those who are high on both types.

Another possibility is that the various conceptualizations of fit may differentially predict particular dependent variables. Bretz and his colleagues (Bretz & Judge, 1994; Bretz et al., 1993) provide a good example of investigating multiple conceptualizations of fit, but this work could be extended to disentangle the effects of each type on the dependent variables. In particular, supplementary fit on values and goals may be predicted to have a strong effect on affective outcomes because they both involve attitudes, but a lesser effect on individual performance because they are distally removed from daily work behaviors. The opposite effect could be proposed for complementary fit on KSAs, such that this type of fit would strongly influence daily on-the-job performance.

> *Proposition 2:* Supplementary fit on values, goals, and personality will have a stronger effect on attitudinal outcomes than will complementary fit on KSAs; whereas, complementary fit on KSAs will have a stronger effect on individual performance.

The potential conflict that would result if fit existed on one conceptualization but not on others provides further opportunities for research. For example, if a person fits with an organization's reward system, but this system is incongruent with the organizational values and goals, job seekers and employees may have a difficult time assessing their fit with the company. Research on "paradoxical communication," described by Soldow (1981, p. 502) as that which "entails an obvious message that conflicts with an ambiguous and less obvious message...," has shown that these messages result in increased role confusion and job dissatisfaction. Therefore, such inconsistency may confuse or reduce employees' evaluations of perceived P-O fit. Therefore, the more internally consistent an organization's characteristics, the easier it should be for applicants and incumbents to evaluate their fit with the organization.

*Proposition 3:* Within-organization, cultural inconsistencies—such as conflicting values and reward systems—will reduce individuals' perceptions of their overall level of P-O fit.

Managers can benefit from recognizing the multiple conceptualizations of P-O fit. For example, organizations may receive optimal benefits from P-O fit if their employees have high levels of supplementary fit on goals but complementary fit on specific KSAs (B. Schneider et al., in press). This suggestion has received support in the group composition literature (e.g., Morgan & Lassiter, 1992), but has not yet been tested at the organizational level. By specifying what types of fit are most desired, managers can establish more precise guidelines for employee selection and develop training geared at improving particular types of fit.

### *Other types of P-E fit*

A second contribution of this manuscript is the expanded differentiation of P-O fit from other types of environmental compatibility (i.e., P-G or P-J fit), as suggested by previous researchers of P-O fit (e.g., Judge & Ferris, 1992). By distinguishing between these constructs, the fit or misfit of individuals with various aspects of their environment may be explored. The potential moderating, mediating, or even competing relationships between various types of fit raise questions regarding the relative importance of P-O fit. For instance, high levels of P-V or P-G fit may undermine organizational commitment.

Research has shown that organizational commitment may be displaced onto a group within that organization (e.g., Becker, 1992; Reichers, 1985; Zaccaro & Dobbins, 1989). Any organizational characteristic that would lead to the development of strong distinct group cultures—such as strong departmentalism, group-based reward systems, or merger-induced countercultures (Trice & Beyer, 1993)—is likely to reduce the influence of P-O fit, relative to P-G fit, on individual outcomes. For instance, organizational goals may be discarded for group goals, such as self-preservation or accumulation of scarce resources. Similarly, organizational values, such as innovation or creativity, may suffer as group values of precision and perfection take precedence.

*Proposition 4:* The relative influence of P-O fit on individual outcomes in organizations with multiple distinct subcultures or groups will be less than in organizations with one dominant culture.

Moreover, a distinction has been raised between people who identify most strongly with their vocations, and those who identify more closely with their specific employers (i.e., "cosmopolitans" and "locals," Gouldner, 1957). A recent study by B. Schneider, Hanges, Goldstein and Braverman (1994) showed support for the distinction of these two identification patterns, and found that each significantly predicted various types of performance. Because of their strong vocational ties, it is expected that cosmopolitans' performance and work attitudes would be more affected by P-V fit than P-O fit. Similarly, P-O fit should have more impact on locals' individual outcomes than would P-V fit.

> *Proposition 5:* The work attitudes of individuals who identify strongly with their vocations will be more influenced by fit with their vocation than by fit with any one particular organization.

Managers attempting to promote high levels of P-O congruence should consider these other environmental elements with which employees may desire good fit. To increase the relevance of fit with the organization, managers should promote a strong, consistent organizational culture by emphasizing corporate goals and values, reducing distinctions between organizational subunits, and publicizing the organization's unique contributions to employees' vocations.

## *Measurement of P-O fit*

Because of the variety of methods used to assess fit, a third important contribution of this manuscript was the elucidation of the link between measurement strategies and various P-O fit constructs. Currently, studies of P-O fit are discussed as investigations of the same construct, regardless of whether they employ (a) direct measurement of perceived fit, (b) indirect cross-levels measurement of actual fit, or (c) indirect individual-level measurement of actual fit. However, as mentioned previously, it is possible that each of these measurement strategies is assessing a distinct construct. This is a largely an empirical question that can be explored by investigating the nomological networks surrounding each construct. One way to begin to build evidence for the distinctiveness of these construct is to determine if each type leads to different outcomes.

When considering perceived fit, the construct closely resembles an attitude. As such, it can be predicted that other attitudes should be strongly affected by perceived fit. If a person perceives that he or she fits well in an organization, then it is likely that satisfaction, commitment, and low intent to leave will result (Posner et al., 1985). Similarly, if an interviewer perceives that a job applicant fits well with the company, then it is likely that the interviewer will have a positive reaction to the applicant and offer a favorable evaluation (Cable & Judge, 1995; Ferris & Judge, 1991).

Actual fit, however, may be predicted to have somewhat different effects. Cable and Judge (1995) explain that theories of similarity-attraction (e.g., Byrne, 1971) imply that even if congruence is not perceived to exist between a person and an organization, the actual congruence of these two entities could lead to positive outcomes because of facilitated communication. This argument can be extended to suggest that actual fit between people and organizations may result in improved *process* outcomes, such as communication, group functioning, or work coordination, even if the perception of fit does not exist. Thus, the following proposition is a first step toward differentiating between the constructs of perceived and actual fit.

> *Proposition 6:* Perceived fit should have more of an impact on individual attitudinal outcomes; whereas, actual fit should be more influential on process and performance outcomes.

Taking this discussion a step further, differential outcomes can also be predicted for actual fit depending on how it is measured. If researchers use individual-level measures of actual fit (i.e., an individual completes a self-evaluation of values and an evaluation of organizational values), then perceptions still play an important role in the construct. In this case it is the individual's perceptions of the organizational values, rather than a verified organizational level variable, on which fit is calculated. Therefore, similar to case of perceived fit, this measurement strategy may assess a more "socially constructed" judgment of fit than would cross-levels measurement. The question that is being answered is whether the person fits with the organization that he or she perceives to exist. Because of the similarities between this construct and directly measured perceived fit, it is likely that its effects will be more similar to those of perceived fit than actual fit as measured by cross-levels research.

> *Proposition 7:* Actual fit, measured only at the individual level, will have outcomes more similar to those of directly measured perceived fit than actual fit measured with a cross-levels technique.

Although researchers may debate the construct validity and relative importance of fit measured in these various manners, the relationship between the constructs offers a variety of exciting research opportunities. Although a variety of individual and environmental differences could influence their relationships, there have been few investigations into the correlation between perceived versus actual fit assessments, and none into the correlation between actual fit measured at multiple levels versus the individual level.

It could be predicted that when individuals first enter organizations they are not likely to have full information about their organizations' values, goals, or reward systems. The socialization process is a time during which individuals obtain information regarding these organizational characteristics (e.g., Ostroff & Kozlowski, 1992). Therefore, it is likely that individuals' direct assessments of perceived fit at organizational entry will show less correspondence to actual P-O fit than will those assessments made after socialization experiences. Similarly, after an organization undergoes a significant change, such as re-engineering, top management replacement, or downsizing, it may take time before new organizational values emerge and become consensually shared. Once again, perceived fit should become more similar to actual fit with the passage of time. These propositions are specified below:

*Proposition 8:* Levels of perceived P-O fit will be less aligned with actual levels immediately following organizational entry than after socialization experiences.

*Proposition 9:* After significant organizational change, levels of perceived and actual P-O fit will be highly divergent; this divergence will shrink as the organization's emergent values, goals, and culture become more apparent to employees.

Managers have a variety of available options for increasing the accuracy of employees' P-O fit assessments. Mentorship programs and extensive orientations conducted at the beginning of an employees' employment experience can provide early instruction on important organizational characteristics. Similarly, reorientation programs and question-and-answer sessions following organizational changes may be effective in helping to solidify emerging values and goals.

Because cross-levels measurement of actual fit is difficult in a field setting (i.e., the need to demonstrate consensus), many researchers have elected to use hypothetical organizational profiles, presented as scenarios in a laboratory setting, to create organizational variables. This avoids the extensive analyses required to support agreement on the organizational variable. This is a viable methodology for producing strong internal validity (Cook & Campbell, 1979); however, the practical applications are more limited than those of research conducted in actual organizations. In addition, because it is unclear to what extent real organizations are perceived in ways similar to the profiles used in these studies, further examination of the profiles' ecological validity is in order.

Pertaining to levels of analysis issues, Vancouver et al. (1994) and Ostroff and Rothausen (1995) have begun a new stream of research in the P-O fit domain. Their investigations of P-O fit at the aggregate level have illustrated a variety of similarities and differences with the individual level construct. For example, Ostroff and Rothausen found moderating effects of tenure on relationships between personal orientations and climate at the aggregate rather than the individual level. Similarly, differential relationships with outcome variables have been reported for aggregate and individual level goal congruence (Vancouver & Schmitt, 1991; Vancouver et al., 1994). Reasons for these differences include potential measurement error as well as substantively different processes operating at the individual and aggregate levels. For example, when examining between-constituency goal congruence (congruence between a group of teachers and the principal), Vancouver et al. (1994) found a *negative* relationship between fit and individual attitudes. This suggests that a person's level of P-O fit relative to others in the work environment may have a moderating effect on the relationship between that individual's absolute level of fit and work attitudes. Future research should continue to investigate potential group level moderation of other types of individual P-O fit relationships.

## *Antecedents of P-O fit*

A further contribution of this manuscript was the integration of empirical and conceptual literature regarding the antecedents and consequences of P-O fit. This section builds on the review of P-O fit's role in organizational entry and socialization, to make suggestions for future research as well as suggestions for practitioners interested in P-O fit. Because many of the research directions involve practical implications, they will be discussed concurrently.

Although studies indicate that fit influences individuals' organizational preferences and organizations' selection decisions, we still do not have a clear understanding of how specific recruitment practices and job search strategies affect levels of P-O fit. For instance, recruitment practices strive to present realistic organizational previews (e.g., site visits or meetings with potential coworkers), or target job candidates with particular characteristics (i.e., through specific recruitment sources such as professional outlets or personal references), may promote higher levels of fit than more general recruitment strategies such as newspaper advertisements (Rynes, 1991). Because it is difficult for applicants to assess organizational values during recruitment, a particular effort must be made to increase their salience to applicants.

> *Proposition 10:* Recruitment strategies, such as realistic organization previews or site visits, that illustrate firm-specific values and goals will increase the relevance of P-O fit to job applicants.

In addition to these organizational differences, there are individual differences between applicants that may predispose certain people to place more of an emphasis on fit during their job search and choice activities. For instance, individuals who display high levels of conscientiousness (Goldberg, 1992) are likely to thoroughly investigate potential employers. Therefore, they will have more information on which to assess P-O fit during their selection decisions than those who simply apply for all jobs for which they qualify. An individual's self-awareness is another individual difference that may affect the importance of P-O fit for job applicants. People who are more aware of their own values, goals, and personality are more likely to be attentive to those characteristics in organizations.

> *Proposition 11:* Conscientious and self-aware job seekers will weight anticipated P-O fit more heavily in their job/organization choice decisions than those who are less conscientious and self-aware.

Another relatively unexplored area regarding organizational entry and P-O fit is the accuracy of fit assessments made during recruitment and job/organization search.

Recruiters trained to convey important aspects of organizational culture may aid job seekers in more accurately determining levels of fit. Moreover, training recruiters to use individual value profiles, personality tests, and other means of assessing "non-job specific" qualifications may help them to recognize applicant qualities that reflect a good fit with the organization. Similar to realistic job previews (e.g., Rynes, 1991; Wanous, 1980), using these methods to increase the accuracy of early fit assessments can save individual and organizational resources by improving organizational screening mechanisms and individuals' self-selection out of particular firms.

*Proposition 12:* Training recruiters to present realistic organizational previews by understanding and communicating vital aspects of the organization's culture will increase the accuracy of both applicant and recruiter assessments of P-O fit.

It is likely, however, that differences in applicants will have an influence on the accuracy of fit judgments made by interviewers during the selection process. Ferris and Judge (1991) suggest that political influence tactics can be used to promote the perception of fit, and thus influence human resources decisions. For example, applicants who engage in high levels of self-monitoring (Snyder, 1987) and impression management (Tedeschi & Melberg, 1984) may be more capable of presenting the image that they fit with the company than those who do not engage in these self-presentation strategies. Because high self-monitors are capable of scanning the environment for social cues, they should be more able to attend to those cues and give an impression of good fit There is initial evidence that applicants who promote the image that they fit with a company will be evaluated favorably by recruiters and will be more likely to receive an offer for a site visit (Stevens & Kristof, 1995). However, because these self-presentation strategies may convey an unrealistic portrait of the applicant, the actual fit of these applicants to the organization should be lower than those who present their "true" selves during interviews.

*Proposition 13a:* Job applicants who engage in high levels of self-monitoring and assertive impression management will be more able to convince recruiters that they have a good fit with the company than those who do not engage in these self-presentation behaviors; and

*Proposition 13b:* Job applicants using these self-presentation strategies will have lower levels of actual P-O fit once hired than those who did not use these strategies.

Research on decision making offers additional suggestions for how P-O fit may be incorporated into organizational selection. Prospect theory (Kahneman & Tversky, 1979) suggests that people attempt to avoid losses during early stages of decision making. Image theory (e.g., Beach, 1990; Beach & Mitchell, 1987) would label this stage of decision making the *compatibility test*, in which applicants are judged to determine if they meet minimal job qualifications. During this stage it is likely that a demands-abilities perspective on P-J fit is being used, because applicants are screened based on the compatibility of their KSAs with job requirements. Once a subset of applicants pass the screening, however, *a profitability test* occurs in which the best remaining applicant is determined (Beach, 1990; Beach & Mitchell, 1987). Kahneman and Tversky (1979) would classify this stage as an attempt to assure a win in the gamble of selection. It is during this later stage that P-O fit is most likely to play a deciding role, as all applicants who passed the screening criteria are assured to meet the minimal job qualifications. It is important to remember, however, that because selection procedures are legally required to be job related, the reliance on P-O fit at the final stages of selection must also be justifiable as relevant to job performance. By incorporating both P-J and P-O fit into the selection process in this manner, managers can maximize the fit of new hires with both levels of the environment.

> *Proposition 14:* A demands-abilities perspective on P-J fit will influence an organization's early screening decisions; however, the final selection decision among the applicants deemed qualified by the screening process will be based primarily on P-O fit.

After organizational entry, both individual and organizational socialization practices continue to influence P-O fit. The mechanism for how these processes change P-O fit levels, however, has not been well-explored. One possible mechanism is the information acquisition process that newcomers undertake in order to assimilate into their organizations (Ostroff & Kozlowski, 1992). This acquisition is typically described as a learning process, with a focus on the attainment of cognitive knowledge. Although cognitive learning is a likely product of socialization, changes in P-O fit may be produced by other types of learning. For example, socialization leads to supplementary P-O fit through the process of newcomers' values and goals becoming more similar to those of the organization. This changing of goals, values, or attitudes implies affectively-based, rather than simply cognitive learning (Kraiger, Ford, & Salas, 1993). Socialization may also lead to complementary fit on KSAs by increasing employees' skill-based as well as cognitive learning (Kraiger et al., 1993).

> *Proposition 15:* Socialization processes lead to affectively-based and skill-based learning, which in turn lead to increases in supplementary and complementary P-O fit, respectively.

Behavioral modeling has been shown to be an effective means for promoting both affective- and skill-based learning (Kraiger et al., 1993); therefore, managers desiring to change employee values or goals may find this to be a particularly useful socialization technique. To maximize employees' affective- and skill-based change, managers should also encourage individuals' proactive socialization attempts by suggesting that they request information from peers, ask for feedback from supervisors, and read company literature.

Despite managers' best attempts at socializing for high levels of P-O fit, numerous individual differences are likely to affect the amount of socialization-induced learning. For example, the strength with which newcomers hold their values and goals should determine how likely they are to assimilate to those of the organization. The personality characteristic of openness to experience is another individual difference that may lead some newcomers to adopt organizational values or goals more easily than others (e.g., Goldberg, 1992).

> *Proposition 16:* Newcomers with strongly held values and goals and with low openness to experience will be less likely to experience affectively-based teaming and change their values and goals as a result of organizational socialization than will those with weakly held values and goals and high openness to experience.

## *Consequences of P-O fit*

Just as individual differences may affect the relationships between selection, socialization and P-O fit, they may also moderate the relationship between fit and outcomes. As was indicated in Figure 1, there are a variety of individual and organizational characteristics on which fit can be assessed. The relevance of fit on any one of these variables will be a function of how important that characteristic is to the individual and the organization. For example, if an individual has values congruent with those of the organization, but those values are irrelevant to everyday performance on the job, then a high level of fit on values is not likely to be a significant predictor of individual outcomes. Therefore, levels of P-O fit are most influential for the characteristics that are relevant to the individual and the organization.

> *Proposition 17:* The relationship between any specific form of P-O fit and an individual outcome variable will be moderated by the importance of the characteristics on which fit is assessed (e.g., achievement values or social welfare goals) to the individual.

Sheridan (1992) suggested that organizational differences may also moderate the relationship between fit and individual outcomes. He proposed that some situations may exert such extreme constraints that fit has little utility in determining employee reactions. His results showed that organizations with interpersonal orientations, as opposed to those with work task cultures, were characterized by lower turnover rates for *all* employees. Although individual values were not measured, which would have allowed stronger conclusions to be drawn regarding the role of P-O fit, his interpretation of the results suggested a situational moderator of the fit-outcome relationship.

*Proposition 18:* The strength of situations may moderate the relationship between levels of P-O fit and individual outcomes, such that strong situations eliminate fit-outcome relationships.

These propositions suggest that managers may be able to influence the strength of the relationship between P-O fit and individual outcomes. By emphasizing particular values and goals through memos from top management, monthly newsletters, and value-based reward systems, managers may be able to increase the importance of these values to employees. However, it is also possible that by maintaining a strong and consistent culture, managers will promote the attrition of those who do not fit well with the organization.

The discussion up to this point has been focused on what managers can do to promote higher levels of P-O fit, thereby creating positive outcomes for their employees. However, in the literature review it was noted that organizations employing people with high levels of fit become extremely homogeneous. This homogeneity, in turn, can create problems such as strategic myopia and inability to change. Therefore, B. Schneider, et al. (in press) offer a variety of recommendations for how to optimize the organizational benefits of P-O fit. They suggest that P-O fit should be a goal for employees at lower levels in the organization, but diversity of perspectives and competencies should be pursued for top managers. Moreover, value similarity at the top level may be useful if it signals a strong vision for the future, but steps should be taken to encourage diversity in strategic perspectives. Finally, it is suggested that high levels of fit should be pursued during the early stages of an organization's life cycle. During this time cohesiveness and cooperation are important, yet once the organization has achieved initial success, attempts to encourage innovative perspectives should be made. These attempts could include formal resocialization experiences, changes in an organization's recruitment strategy, or creativity training.

These recommendations by B. Schneider et al. (in press) suggest that managers can take particular steps to reduce the detrimental effects of homogeneity. However, it should be noted that like homogeneity, heterogeneity can also have detrimental side effects if employees have difficulty communicating or do not support common values. Therefore, the challenge for managers is to achieve an optimal level of various types of P-O fit in the organization.

Determining this optimal level, however, depends on several things. Primarily, it depends on the type of fit and the organizational outcome that is being considered. If the desired outcome is to reduce high levels of employee turnover, then pursuing a high level of supplementary fit on values and goals might be beneficial. If, however, the desired outcome is quick adaptation to environmental changes, a lower level of fit on these characteristics may be optimal.

Because of the many types of P-O fit and the large number of organizational outcomes, it is important to understand the functional form of the relationship between fit on a certain characteristic and a specific type of performance. For example, if this relationship has the form of an inverted-U, then performance will be harmed if fit levels fall below or exceed a particular level. This form may be expected for the relationship between fit on values and organizational responsiveness, with the optimal level of fit being high enough to facilitate communication but low enough to avoid groupthink and stagnation. This same dependent variable, however, may have a linear relationship with complementary fit on KSAs, such that higher levels of complementary fit will always improve the organization's ability to respond to change.

*Proposition 19:* Following an inverted-U relationship, both low and high levels of supplementary fit on values will harm an organization's flexibility in responding to environmental changes.

*Proposition 20:* Following a linear relationship, high levels of complementary fit on KSAs will be beneficial to an organization's responsiveness to the environment and high levels of supplementary fit on values will be beneficial to employee relations.

## Conclusion

As P-O fit becomes a more popular topic with both researchers and managers, increased attention must be paid to its multiple conceptualizations and measurement strategies. Only when these issues have been attended to can researchers draw convincing conclusions concerning the consequences of fit for individuals and organizations. Many of the questions raised in this paper can only be answered by further empirical research. Potential directions for this research are offered, so that by building on the frameworks proposed in this paper, future research can continue to specify and explore the domain of P-O fit.

## Acknowledgments

I wish to thank Cindy Stevens, Jeff Edwards, Ben Schneider, Katherine Klein, Stan Gully, Suzanne Masterson and especially Ken Brown for their substantive comments and moral support. Thanks also to three anonymous reviewers whose comments were as helpful as they were challenging.

## References

Adkins CL, Russell CJ, Werbel JD. (1994). Judgments of fit in the selection process: The role of work-value congruence. *Personnel Psychology, 47*, 605–623.

Andrews JDW. (1967). The achievement motive and advancement in two types of organizations. *Journal of Personality and Social Psychology, 6*, 163–168.

Argyris C. (1957). Some problems in conceptualizing organizational climate: A case study of a bank. *Administrative Science Quarterly*, 2, 501–520.

Bartol KM, Martin DC. (1988). Influences on managerial pay allocations: A dependency perspective. *Personnel Psychology*, 41, 361–378.

Beach LR. (1990). *Image theory: Decision making in personal and organizational contexts.* Chichester, UK: Wiley.

Beach LR, Mitchell TR. (1987). Image theory: Principles, goals, and plans in decision making. *Acta Psychologica*, 66, 201–220.

Becker TE. (1992). Foci and bases of commitment: Are they distinctions worth making. *Academy of Management Journal*, 35, 232–244.

Bedeian AG, Day DV. (1994). Point/counterpoint: Difference scores: Rationale, formulation, and interpretation. *Journal of Management*, 20, 673–698.

Behling O, Tolliver J. (1972). Self-concept moderated by self-esteem as a predictor of choice among potential employees. *Academy of Management Proceedings*, 32, 214–216.

Bem DJ, Funder DC. (1978). Predicting more of the people more of the time: Assessing the personality of situations. *Psychological Review*, 85, 485–501.

Blau GJ. (1987). Using a person-environment fit model to predict job involvement and organizational commitment. *Journal of Vocational Behavior*, 30, 240–257.

Block J. (1978). *The Q-sort method in personality assessment and psychiatric research.* Palo Alto, CA: Consulting Psychologist Press.

Bowen DE, Ledford GE Jr, Nathan BR. (1991). Hiring for the organization not the job. *Academy of Management Executive*, 5, 35–51.

Boxx WR, Odom RY, Dunn MG. (1991). Organizational values and value congruency and their impact on satisfaction, commitment, and cohesion. *Public Personnel Management*, 20, 195–205.

Bretz RD Jr, Ash RA, Dreher GF. (1989). Do people make the place? An examination of the attraction-selection-attrition hypothesis. *Personnel Psychology*, 42, 561–581.

Bretz RD Jr, Boudreau JW, Judge TA. (1994). Job search behavior of employed managers. *Personnel Psychology*, 47, 275–301.

Bretz RD Jr, Judge TA. (1994). Person-organization fit and the theory of work adjustment: Implications for satisfaction, tenure, and career success. *Journal of Vocational Behavior*, 44, 32–54.

Bretz RD Jr, Rynes SL, Gerhart B. (1993). Recruiter perceptions of applicant fit: Implications for individual career preparation and job search behavior. *Journal of Vocational Behavior*, 43, 310–327.

Bridges W. (1994, September 19). The end of the job. *Fortune*, 62–74.

Burke RJ, Deszca E. (1982). Preferred organizational climates of Type A individuals. *Journal of Vocational Behavior*, 21, 50–59.

Byrne DE. (1971). *The attraction paradigm*. New York: Academic Press.

Cable DM, Judge TA. (1994). Pay preferences and job search decisions: A person-organization fit perspective. *Personnel Psychology*, 47, 317–348.

Cable DM, Judge TA. (1995, August). *The role of person-organization fit in organizational selection decisions.* Paper presented at the Annual Meetings of the Academy of Management, Vancouver, BC.

Caplan RD. (1987). Person-environment fit theory and organizations: Commensurate dimensions, time perspectives, and mechanisms. *Journal of Vocational Behavior*, 31, 248–267.

Chao GT, O'Leary-Kelly AM, Wolf S, Klein HJ, Gardner PD. (1994). Organizational socialization: Its content and consequences. *Journal of Applied Psychology, 79*, 730–743.

Chatman J. (1989). Improving interactional organizational research: A model of person-organization fit. *Academy of Management Review, 14*, 333–349.

Chatman J. (1991). Matching people and organizations: Selection and socialization in public accounting firms. *Administrative Science Quarterly, 36*, 459–484.

Chesney MA, Rosenman RH. (1980). Type A behavior in the work setting. In Cooper CL, Payne R (Eds.), *Current concerns in occupational stress* (pp. 187–212). New York: Wiley.

Cook TD, Campbell DT. (1979). *Quasi-experimentation: Design and analysis issues for field settings.* Boston: Houghton Mifflin.

Cronbach LJ. (1958). Proposals leading to analytic treatment of social perception scores. In Tagiuri R, Petrullo L (Eds.), *Person perception and interpersonal behavior* (pp. 353–379). Stanford, CA: Stanford University Press.

Cronbach LJ, Gleser GC. (1953). Assessing similarity between profiles. *Psychological Bulletin, 50*, 456–473.

Dalessio A, Imada AS. (1984). Relationships between interview selection decisions and perceptions of applicant similarity to an ideal employee and self: A field study. *Human Relations, 37(1)*, 67–80.

Dawis RV, Lofquist LH. (1984). *A psychological theory of work adjustment.* Minneapolis, MN: University of Minnesota Press.

Deal TE, Kennedy AA. (1982). *Corporate cultures.* Reading, MA: Addison-Wesley.

Downey HK, Hellriegel D, Slocum JW Jr. (1975). Congruence between individual needs, organizational climate, job satisfaction and performance. *Academy of Management Journal, 18*, 149–155.

Driskell JE, Hogan R, Salas E. (1987). Personality and group performance. In Hendrick C (Ed.), *Review of personality and social psychology,* (Vol. 9, pp. 91–112). Beverly Hills: Sage.

Dumaine R. (1987, August 17). The new art of hiring smart. *Fortune,* 78–81.

Edwards JR. (1991). Person-job fit: A conceptual integration, literature review and methodological critique. *International Review of Industrial/Organizational Psychology,* (Vol. 6, pp. 283–357). London: Wiley.

Edwards JR. (1993). Problems with the use of profile similarity indices in the study of congruence in organizational research. *Personnel Psychology, 46*, 641–665.

Edwards JR. (1994). The study of congruence in organizational behavior research: Critique and a proposed alternative. *Organizational Behavior and Human Decision Processes, 58*, 51–100.

Edwards JR, Harrison RV. (1993). Job demands and worker health: Three-dimensional reexamination of the relationship between P-E fit and strain. *Journal of Applied Psychology, 78*, 628–648.

Edwards JR, Parry ME. (1993). On the use of polynomial regression equations as an alternative to difference scores in organizational research. *Academy of Management Journal, 36*, 1577–1613.

Eisenberger R, Huntington R, Hutchinson S, Sowa D. (1986). Perceived organizational support. *Journal of Applied Psychology, 71*, 500–507.

Ferris GR, Judge TA. (1991). Personnel/human resources management: A political influence perspective. *Journal of Management, 17(2)*, 447–488.

French JRP Jr, Caplan RD, Harrison RV. (1982). *The mechanisms of job stress and strain.* New York: Wiley.

French JRP Jr, Rogers W, Cobb S. (1974). Adjustment as person-environment fit. In Coelho GV, Hamburg DA, Adams JE (Eds.), *Coping and adaptation,* (pp. 316–333) New York: Basic Books.

Friedman M, Rosenman RH. (1974). *Type A behavior and your heart.* New York: Alfred Knopf.

George JM, Bettenhausen K. (1990). Understanding pro-social behavior, sales performance and turnover: A group level analysis in a service context. *Journal of Applied Psychology, 75,* 698–709.

Gerstein M, Reisman H. (1983). Strategic selection: Matching executives to business conditions. *Sloan Management Review, 24,* 33–49.

Glick WH. (1985). Conceptualizing and measuring organizational and psychological climate: Pitfalls in multi-level research. *Academy of Management Review, 10,* 601–616.

Glick WH. (1988). Response: Organizations are not central tendencies: Shadowboxing in the dark, Round 2. *Academy of Management Journal, 13,* 133–137.

Goldberg LR. (1992). The development of markers for the Big-Five factor structure, *Psychological Assessment, 4(1),* 26–42.

Gouldner AW. (1957). Cosmopolitans and locals: Toward an analysis of latent social roles. *Administrative Science Quarterly, 2,* 287–303.

Graen G, Cashman J. (1975). A rote making model of leadership in formal organizations: A developmental approach. In Hunt JG, Larson LL (Eds.), *Leadership frontiers* (pp. 143–165). Kent, OH: Kent State University Press.

Greenhalgh L. (1983). Organizational decline. In Bacharach S (Ed.), *Research in the sociology of organizations* (Vol. 2). Greenwich, CT: JAI Press.

Guzzo R, Salas E (Eds.). (1995). *Team effectiveness and decision making in organizations.* San Francisco: Jossey-Bass.

Hackman JR, Morris CG. (1975). Group tasks, group interaction process, and group performance effectiveness: A review and proposed integration. In Berkowitz L (Ed.), *Advances in experimental social psychology* (Vol. 8, pp. 45–99). New York: Academic Press.

Hall DT, Schneider B, Nygren HT. (1975). Personal factors in organizational identification. *Administrative Science Quarterly, 15,* 176–190.

Harris MM. (1989). Reconsidering the employment interview: A review of recent literature and suggestions for future research. *Personnel Psychology, 42,* 691–726.

Haythorn WW. (1968). The composition of groups: A review of the literature. *Acta Psychologica, 28,* 97–128.

Herbert TT, Deresky H. (1987). Should general managers match their business strategies? *Organizational Dynamics, 15(3),* 40–51.

Hinrichs JR. (1964). The attitudes of research chemists, *Journal of Applied Psychology, 48,* 287–293.

Hoerr J. (1989, July 10). The payoff from teamwork, *Business Week,* 56–62.

Hogan RT. (1991). Personality and personality measurement. In Dunnette MD, Hough LM (Eds.), *Handbook of industrial and organizational psychology* (Vol. 2, pp. 873–919). Palo Alto, CA: Consulting Psychologists' Press.

Holland JL. (1977). *The vocational preference inventory.* Palo Alto, CA: Consulting Psychologists Press.

Holland JL. (1985). *Making vocational choices: A theory of careers* (2nd ed.). Englewood Cliffs, NJ: Prentice-Hall.

Howard A (Ed.). (1995). *The changing nature of work.* San Francisco: Jossey-Bass.

Hunter JE, Schmidt FL. (1990). *Methods of meta-analysis: Correcting error and bias in research findings.* Newbury Park, CA: Sage.

lvancevich JM, Matteson MT. (1980). Nurses and stress: Time to examine the potential problem, *Supervisor Nurse*, *11*, 17–22.

lvancevich JM, Matteson MT. (1984). A Type A-B person-work environment interaction model for examining occupational stress and consequences. *Human Relations*, *37*, 491–513.

Jackson SE, Brett JF, Sessa VI, Cooper DM, Julin JA, Peyronnin K. (1991). Some differences make a difference: Individual dissimilarity and group heterogeneity as correlates of recruitment, promotions and turnover. *Journal of Applied Psychology*, *76*, 675–689.

James LR. (1982). Aggregation bias in estimates of perceptual agreement. *Journal of Applied Psychology*, *67*, 219–229.

James LR, Damaree RG, Wolf G. (1984). Estimating within group interrater reliability with and without response bias. *Journal of Applied Psychology*, *69*, 85–98.

James LR, Joyce WF, Slocum JW Jr. (1988). Comment: Organizations do not cognize. *Academy of Management Journal*, *13*, 129–132.

Johns G. (1981). Difference score measures of organizational behavior variables: A critique. *Organizational Behavior and Human Performance*, *27*, 443–463.

Judge TA, Bretz RD Jr. (1992). Effects of work values on job choice decisions. *Journal of Applied Psychology*, *77*, 261–271.

Judge TA, Ferris GR. (1992). The elusive criterion of fit in human resource staffing decisions. *Human Resource Planning*, *15(4)*, 47–67.

Kahneman D, Tversky A. (1979). Prospect theory: An analysis of decision under risk, *Econometrica*, *47*, 263–291.

Kanter R. (1977). *Men and women of the corporation.* New York: Basic Books.

Karren RJ, Graves LM. (1994). Assessing person-organization fit in personnel selection: Guidelines for future research. *International Journal of Selection and Assessment*, *2(3)*, 146–156.

Keon TL, Latack JC, Wanous JP. (1982). Image congruence and the treatment of difference scores in organizational choice research. *Human Relations*, *35*, 155–166.

Kerr J. (1982). Assigning managers on the basis of the life cycle. *Journal of Business Strategy*, *2*, 58–65.

Klein KJ, Dansereau F, Hall R. (1994). Levels issues in theory development, data collection and analysis. *Academy of Management Review*, *19*, 195–229.

Klimoski RJ, Jones RG. (1995). Staffing for effective group decision making: Key issues in matching people and teams? In Guzzo R, Salas E (Eds.), *Team effectiveness and decision making in organizations* (pp. 291–332). San Francisco: Jossey-Bass.

Kozlowski SWJ, Hattrup K. (1992). A disagreement about within-group agreement: Disentangling issues of consistency versus consensus. *Journal of Applied Psychology*, *77*, 161–167.

Kraiger K, Ford JK, Salas E. (1993). Application of cognitive, skill-based and affective theories of learning outcomes to new methods of training evaluation. *Journal of Applied Psychology*, *78*, 311–328.

Laughlin PR, Branch LG, Johnson HH. (1969). Individual versus triadic performance and unidimensional complementary task as a function of initial ability level. *Journal of Personality and Social Psychology, 12*, 144–150.

Leontiades M. (1982). Choosing the right manager to fit the strategy. *Journal of Business Strategy, 3*, 58–69.

Livingstone LP, Nelson DL. (1994, August). *Toward a person-environment fit perspective of creativity: The model of creativity fit.* Paper presented at the Annual Meetings of the Academy of Management, Dallas, TX.

Louis MR. (1990). Acculturation in the workplace: Newcomers as lay ethnographers. In Schneider B (Ed.), *Organizational culture and climate* (pp. 85–129). San Francisco: Jossey-Bass.

Matteson MT, Ivancevich JM. (1982). Type A and B behavior patterns and health symptoms: Examining individual and organizational fit. *Journal of Occupational Medicine, 24*, 585–589.

Morgan BB Jr, Lassiter DL. (1992). Team composition and staffing. In Swezey RW, Salas E (Eds.), *Teams: Their training and performance*, (pp. 75–100). Norwood, NJ: Ablex.

Morrison EW. (1993a). Newcomer information seeking: Exploring types, modes, sources and outcomes. *Academy of Management Journal, 36*, 557–589.

Morrison EW. (1993b). Longitudinal study of the effects of information seeking on newcomer socialization. *Journal of Applied Psychology, 78*, 173–183.

Muchinsky PM, Monahan CJ. (1987). What is person-environment congruence? Supplementary versus complementary models of fit. *Journal of Vocational Behavior, 31*, 268–277.

Murray HA. (1938). *Explorations in personality.* Boston, MA: Houghton Mifflin.

Nisbett RE, Ross L. (1980). *Human inference: Strategies and shortcomings of social judgment.* Englewood Cliffs, NJ: Prentice-Hall Inc.

Nunnally JC. (1962). The analysis of profile data. *Psychological Bulletin, 59*, 311–319.

O'Reilly CA III, Chatman J. (1986). Organization commitment and psychological attachment: The effects of compliance, identification and internalization on prosocial behavior. *Journal of Applied Psychology, 71*, 492–499.

O'Reilly CA III, Chatman J, Caldwell DF. (1991). People and organizational culture: A profile comparison approach to assessing person-organization fit. *Academy of Management Journal, 34*, 487–516.

Ostroff C, Kozlowski SWJ. (1992). Organizational socialization as a learning process: The role of information acquisition. *Personnel Psychology, 45*, 849–874.

Ostroff C, Rothausen TJ. (1995, May). *Tenure's role in fit: An individual and organizational level analysis.* Paper presented at the 10th Annual Conference of the Society for Industrial and Organizational Psychology, Orlando, FL.

Patsfall MR, Feimer NR. (1985). The role of person-environment fit in job performance and satisfaction. In Bernardin HJ, Bownas DA (Eds.), *Personality assessment in organizations* (pp. 53–81). New York: Praeger.

Posner BZ. (1992). Person-organization values congruence: No support for individual differences as a moderating influence. *Human Relations, 45*, 351–361.

Posner BZ, Kouzes JM, Schmidt WH. (1985). Shared values make a difference: An empirical test of corporate culture. *Human Resource Management, 24*, 293–309.

Pritchard RD, Karasick BW. (1973). The effects of organizational climate on managerial job performance and job satisfaction. *Organizational Behavior and Human Performance, 9*, 126–146.

Pulakos ED, Wexley KN. (1983). The relationship among perceptual similarity, sex and performance ratings in manager-subordinate dyads. *Academy of Management Journal*, *26*, 129–139.

Ravlin EC, Meglino BM. (1987). Effects of values on perception and decision making: A study of alternative work values measures. *Journal of Applied Psychology*, *72*, 666–673.

Reichers AE. (1985). A review and reconceptualization of organizational commitment. *Academy of Management Review*, 10, 465–476.

Roberts KH, Hulin CL, Rousseau DM. (1978). *Developing an interdisciplinary science of organizations.* San Francisco, CA: Jossey-Bass.

Rounds JB, Dawis RV, Lofquist LH. (1987). Measurement of person-environment fit and prediction of satisfaction in the theory of work adjustment. *Journal of Vocational Behavior*, *31*, 297–318.

Rousseau D. (1985). Issues of level in organizational research: Multilevel and cross-level perspectives. In Cummings LL, Staw BM (Eds.), *Research in organizational behavior* (Vol. 7, pp. 1–37). Greenwich, CT: JAI Press.

Ryan AM, Schmit MJ. (1992, July). *Validation of an organizational fit instrument.* Paper presented at the International Congress of Psychology. Brussels.

Rynes SL. (1991). Recruitment, job choice and post-hire consequences: A call for new research directions. In Dunnette MD, Hough LM (Eds.), *Handbook of industrial and organizational psychology* (2nd ed., pp. 399–444). Palo Alto, CA: Consulting Psychologists Press.

Rynes SL, Bretz RD, Gerhart B. (1991). The importance of recruitment in job choice: A different way of looking. *Personnel Psychology*, *44*, 487–521.

Rynes SL, Gerhart B. (1990). Interviewer assessments of applicant "fit:" An exploratory investigation. *Personnel Psychology*, *43*, 13–35.

Salancik GR, Pfeffer J. (1977). An examination of need-satisfaction models of job attitudes. *Administrative Science Quarterly*, *22*, 427–456.

Schein E. (1992). *Organizational culture and leadership.* San Francisco: Jossey-Bass.

Schneider B. (1987). The people make the place. *Personnel Psychology*, *40*, 437–453.

Schneider B, Hanges PJ, Goldstein HW, Braverman EP. (1994). Do customer service perceptions generalize? The case of student and chair ratings of faculty effectiveness. *Journal of Applied Psychology*, *79*, 685–690.

Schneider B, Goldstein HW, Smith DB. (1995). The ASA framework: An update, *Personnel Psychology*, *48*, 747–773.

Schneider B, Kristof AL, Goldstein HW, Smith DB. (in press). What is this thing called fit? In Anderson NR, Herriott P (Eds.), *Handbook of selection and appraisal* (2nd ed.). London: Wiley.

Schneider B, Smith DB, Goldstein HW. (1994, April). The *"dark side" of "good fit."* Paper presented at the Ninth Annual Conference of the Society of Industrial and Organizational Psychology, Nashville, TN.

Schneider J. (1994). *Biodata predictions of organizational membership: An organizational level interpretation of biodata.* Unpublished Ph.D. dissertation, Department of Psychology, University of Maryland, College Park.

Schwab DP. (1980). Construct validity in organizational behavior. In Cummings LL, Staw BM (Eds.), *Research in organizational behavior* (Vol. *2*, pp. 3–43). Greenwich, CT: JAI Press.

Shaw ME. (1981). *Group dynamics: The psychology of small group behavior* (3rd ed.). New York: McGraw-Hill.

Sheridan JE. (1992). Organizational culture and employee retention. *Academy of Management Journal, 35*, 1036–1056.

Snyder M. (1987). *Public appearances, private realities: The psychology of self-monitoring.* New York: Freeman.

Soldow GF. (1981). Change in the organization: The detriment and benefit of the double bind. *Group and Organization Studies, 6*, 500–513.

Stevens CK, Kristof AL. (1995). Making the right impression: A field study of applicant impression management during job interviews. *Journal of Applied Psychology, 80*, 587–606.

Super DE. (1953). A theory of vocational development. *American Psychologist, 8*, 185–190.

Tedeschi JT, Melburg V. (1984). Impression management and influence in the organization. In Bacharach SB, Lawler EJ (Eds.), *Research in the sociology of organizations* (Vol. 3, pp. 31–58). Greenwich, CT: JAI Press.

Tisak J, Smith CS. (1994). Rejoinder to Edwards's Comments. *Journal of Management, 20(3)*, 691–694.

Tom VR. (1971). The role of personality and organizational images in the recruiting process. *Organizational Behavior and Human Performance, 6*, 573–592.

Trice HM, Beyer JM. (1993). *The cultures of work organizations*. Englewood Cliffs, NJ: Prentice Hall.

Tsui AS, Egan TD, O'Reilly CA III. (1992). Being different: Relational demography and organizational attachment. *Administrative Science Quarterly, 37*, 549–579.

Turban DB, Keon TL. (1993). Organization attractiveness: An interactionist perspective. *Journal of Applied Psychology, 78*, 184–193.

Tziner A. (1987). Congruency issue retested using Fineman's achievement climate notion. *Journal of Social Behavior and Personality, 2*, 63–78.

Vancouver JB, Millsap RE, Peters PA. (1994). Multilevel analysis of organizational goal congruence. *Journal of Applied Psychology, 79*, 666–679.

Vancouver JB, Schmitt NW. (1991). An exploratory examination of person-organization fit: Organizational goal congruence. *Personnel Psychology, 44*, 333–352.

Vroom VR. (1966). Organizational choice: A study of pre-and post-decision processes. *Organizational Behavior and Human Performance, 1*, 212–226.

Walsh WB. (1987). Person-environment congruence: A response to the Moos perspective. *Journal of Vocational Behavior, 31*, 347–352.

Wanous JP. (1980). *Organizational entry: Recruitment, selection and socialization of newcomers*. Reading, MA: Addison-Wesley.

Weldon E, Weingart LR. (1993). Group goals and group performance. *British Journal of Social Psychology, 32*, 307–334.

Witt LA, Hilton TF, Hellman CM. (1993, March). *Person-organization fit and job satisfaction: A social exchange perspective*. Paper presented at the Annual Meeting of the Southwest Academy of Management, New Orleans, LA.

Witt LA, Nye LG. (1992, April). *Goal congruence and job attitudes revisited*. Paper presented at the Seventh Annual Conference of the Society for Industrial and Organizational Psychology, Montreal, Canada.

Witt LA, Silver NC. (1995, March). *Team politics and person-organization fit predicting team cohesiveness*. Paper presented at the annual meeting of the Southeastern Psychological Association, Savannah, GA.

Witt LA, Voss E. (1995, May). *Person-organization fit, customer focus and commitment*. Paper presented at the Tenth Annual meeting of the Society for Industrial and Organizational Psychology, Orlando, FL.

Zaccaro SJ, Dobbins GH. (1989). Contrasting group and organizational commitment: Evidence for differences among multilevel attachments. *Journal of Organizational Behavior, 10*, 267–273.

# 5

# ARE CAREER JOBS HEADED FOR EXTINCTION?

*Sanford M. Jacoby*

Source: *California Management Review* 42(1) (1999): 123–145.

Academics and journalists tell us that we are currently witnessing an historic event: the demise of career-type jobs. Richard Sennett, the sociologist, argues eloquently that the surge of corporate downsizing is the signal occurrence of our postmodern age, with ramifications far beyond the labor market. As careers condense, so do our time horizons and relationships. What Sennett calls "no long term" is a pervasive force eroding our moral strength. "No long term," he says, "disorients action over the long term, loosens bonds of trust and commitment, and divorces will from behavior."[1]

Despite the stock market rise and low unemployment, many Americans remain anxious about job security. The share of employees who say they are frequently concerned about layoffs has risen from 12 percent in 1981 to 37 percent this year.[2] Politicians are adept at tapping into these sentiments, as in the 1996 presidential campaign, when Patrick Buchanan excoriated executives for taking huge salaries while laying off thousands of workers. President Clinton responded predictably: He organized a conference, and invited employers to the White House to discuss corporate ethics and responsibilities.[3]

The notion that corporations have responsibilities to employees is hardly a new or radical idea. Its roots lie deep in the American past, dating back a century or more when companies first began systematically to provide for their employees' welfare. The movement was known as "welfare work" or "welfare capitalism." It was not unique to the United States, but its popularity in this country was uniquely American. Welfare capitalism shaped our nation's risk-sharing institutions—everything from "fringe" benefits to Social Security to career employment—the same institutions whose future is being questioned by Sennett and others.[4]

Yet institutional arrangements have changed much less than Sennett's "no long term" would suggest. Put bluntly, the welfare capitalist approach remains in place. Career-type employment practices—an amalgam that economists term "internal labor markets"—are still the norm in the labor market and employers continue to shoulder a variety of risks for employees. None of this is to deny the labor-market turbulence of the past fifteen years. The mixture of market and organizational principles that structures the employment relationship now gives more weight to market factors, especially in managerial positions. There also has been a change in risk sharing, with employers transferring more of the burden to employees. However, these are changes of degree, not of kind. They do not constitute a phase shift but rather a reallocation of responsibilities within a stable institutional structure. This article discusses the extent of change in recent years and analyzes the prospects for welfare capitalism's future.

## The crisis of welfare capitalism?

During the past twenty years, modern welfare capitalism has experienced its most critical test since the Great Depression. Starting in the 1980s, a series of shocks hit the economy. Heightened competition, rapid technological change, and corporate mergers led to layoffs throughout American industry. In the late 1970s and early 1980s, it was blue-collar industrial workers—often unionized—who bore the brunt of permanent job loss. Since the late 1980s, it has been white-collar, educated workers who have experienced the sharpest increases in permanent job loss. Less-educated workers still have the highest job loss rates, but their rates have fallen since the early 1980s. Hence the gap separating the job-loss rates of males with a high-school education and males with a college education narrowed by more than half between the early 1980s and the mid-1990s.[5] Companies that had never experienced a major layoff—firms like IBM, Kodak, and Digital Equipment—now jettisoned thousands of white-collar employees.

What is significant about these recent cuts is that they are occurring during a relatively tight labor market, unlike previous postwar layoffs that were keyed to the business cycle. Also, recent downsizing disproportionately affects educated professional and managerial employees, a group not previously targeted for layoff. The layoffs were—and are—a shock to those employees who believed themselves immune from job loss. Middle-level managers found that the elimination of their jobs was often the chief goal of industrial "restructuring." At large diversified companies, a combination of mergers, new information technology, and work reorganization reduced the need for headquarters staff. Fully 85 percent of large multinational corporations report that they have reorganized their headquarters since 1990.[6] Those who survive downsizing are being offered a different employment contract. Instead of employment security in exchange for loyalty, organizations are proffering a "new deal" that provides higher pay in return for broader skills and a tolerance of change.[7]

Meanwhile, there has been an expansion of nonstandard employment: jobs that are temporary, part-time, or contractual. In 1997, around 20 percent of all employees held nonstandard jobs. (The self-employed accounted for another 10 percent.)[8] There is a stratum of nonstandard workers (such as consultants working on contract) who are well paid. However, most of these workers are likely to be paid a low wage, and they are one-sixth as likely to receive health and pension benefits as those in standard full-time jobs. In fact, much of the decline in health insurance coverage since 1979 has been the result of cutbacks for temporary and other peripheral workers. Coverage has also declined for some of those holding standard jobs, notably less-educated males.[9]

Accompanying these changes has been a new ethos of market individualism, especially in places such as Wall Street and Silicon Valley where there is intense competition for skilled workers combined with a rapidly changing knowledge base. These workers—predominantly young and educated—have grown skeptical not only of welfare capitalism but of government, unions, and other large institutions. Believing that they must have a broad range of skills to succeed in today's labor market, these workers expect to spend no more than brief stints at any single firm. They ask only that the employer ensure their future employability by providing learning experiences that can be added to their resumes. Less concerned with job security than the generations who were touched by the Depression, they see themselves as masters of their own fates. They resemble nineteenth-century craft workers, who treasured their autonomy and hedged their labor-market risk with a diverse set of skills.

These changes have led to a widespread sense that the institutional structures erected over the course of the last century are tumbling down. It is hard not to feel that way when no less than the American Management Association issues a book entitled *Corporate Executions*, whose subtitle is: "How Corporate Greed Is Shattering Lives, Companies, and Communities."[10] But reports of welfare capitalism's demise are exaggerated. We are not moving to an economy made up only of short-term jobs, indifferent employers, and disloyal employees. Mid- to large-sized corporations continue to pursue employment practices that are sheltered from the momentary vicissitudes of the market. It would be a vast exaggeration to say that long-term employment is dead or that all jobs henceforth will be casual positions. "No long term" is hyperbole. "Less long term" is not as catchy but far more accurate.

It is a human tendency to believe that one lives in an exceptional era, fundamentally different from earlier periods. Many people today—including businessmen, academics, and government leaders—think that information technology is creating a "new economy" with accelerating innovation and productivity growth. However, economic statistics show that productivity growth today actually is slower than it was during the first two decades after the Second World War.[11]

Just as there is a certain amount of hype attached to rhetoric about the new economy, there is a tendency to exaggerate how much the labor market has changed in recent years. The big change, as mentioned, is the fact that companies are laying workers off during a prosperous period, with layoffs targeted at white-collar employees. Hence employees today bear more risk, including a greater risk of layoff. But there are still plenty of career-type jobs for educated workers, and employers still indemnify employees against many kinds of risk.

To understand the paradox of continuity amidst change, it is important to recall the distinction between stocks (our endowment of existing jobs) and flows (the jobs being created and destroyed in the current period). Just as in the distinction between the large national debt and the smaller annual deficit (or surplus), we sometimes forget that stocks tend to dwarf net flows. Moreover, another important fact is that net flows are composed of two enormous intersecting streams: job "deaths" (such as downsizing) and job "births" (new jobs).[12] Despite downsizing, the U.S. economy has been adept at maintaining a high birth rate of new jobs, many of which eventually will become long-term positions. In what follows, several types of evidence are marshaled in support of these claims, including data on employee tenure and mobility, new job creation and new job quality, cyclical factors, and on employee compensation.

## *Tenure and mobility*

Take, for example, the data on employee tenure, one indicator for gauging the prevalence of long-term or career employment. Tenure is not easy to measure. There are problems in controlling for the effect of the business cycle and in using cross-sectional as opposed to panel data. Also, there are biases that arise when individuals round off their self-estimates of tenure. Nevertheless, recent studies consistently find only a slight drop in the overall prevalence of long-term jobs. In the 1980s there was little change in aggregate job stability (job retention rates), while in the first half of the 1990s there was a modest decline in stability, particularly for long-tenure workers.[13]

For men ages 35-64, the share employed more than ten years with their current employer fell from 50 percent in 1979 to 40 percent in 1996. The sharpest tenure declines occurred in managerial and professional-technical occupations (although managers had and still have the highest probability of being in long-term employment relationships). However, during the same period there was an increase—albeit slight—in the share of those employed in long-term positions in service occupations and industries. Partly for this reason, female tenure has shown a different pattern: For women aged 35-64, the share employed in long-term positions rose moderately between 1979 and 1996.[14] While the rise in female tenure is partly due to changes in women's career patterns (they are less likely to quit for childbearing than in the past), it is important to remember that employers are responding to women's growing desire for stable, career-type positions by providing them with jobs of this kind.

The unadjusted data for the period 1983 to 1998 show similar trends. For males over 25, the percentage who worked for their current employer for ten years or more fell modestly from 38 to 33 percent; for women, the percentage increased from 25 percent to 28 percent, nearly canceling the drop in male tenure. In service and retail industries, median tenure rose slightly between 1983 and 1998; in manufacturing and transportation industries, median tenure declined slightly.[15]

What about data on employee separations (layoffs, dismissals, and quits)? Even if the amount of time people remain on their jobs has not changed much, it is possible that workers are experiencing less security. This could be due to higher levels of involuntary job loss as a cause of separations. Also, it could be reflected in lower levels of voluntary mobility. Unfortunately, there is no consensus on this issue; different data sets tell different stories. The Displaced Workers Survey focuses on involuntary job loss (job loss due to plant closings, position abolished, slack work, and other forms of layoff). The survey shows a slight increase in involuntary job loss in the 1990s compared to the 1980s, with most of the increase driven by job loss for "other" reasons, the nature of which is not clear.[16] Data from the Panel Study on Income Dynamics (PSID) paint a grimmer picture, with a steady weakening for male workers—but not female workers—of the negative effect of tenure on the probability of being dismissed. (That is, long-tenure male workers stood a greater chance of dismissal.)[17] However, another panel study, the Census Bureau's Survey of Income and Program Participation (SIPP), shows stability from the mid-1980s to the mid-1990s in aggregate layoff and discharge rates. The probability of permanent layoff declined for young (18–35) and middle-aged (41–55) workers, while rising sharply for workers in the 56–60 age bracket.[18]

The SIPP data on voluntary mobility (quits) exhibit little change since the 1980s, meaning that layoffs are neither inhibiting quits nor promoting them. Survey data show the same thing: Of those employed over 20 hours per week, there was no change between 1977 and 1997 in the proportion who say they will seeks new jobs with other employers in the coming year. Workers, in other words, are neither more nor less inclined to hop jobs than twenty years ago.[19]

Data on geographic mobility provide corroborating evidence. People who change their residence often change their jobs, especially when a move is out of state. Richard Sennett's protagonist, a high-tech venture capitalist; moved around the country four times in twelve years, leading Sennett to lament "the fugitive quality of friendship and local community" caused by new career patterns. In the suburbs where today's employees reside, "no one ... becomes a long-term witness to another person's life." But is it really the case that Americans are more mobile now than in the 1950s, the heyday of the Organization Man and the classic bedroom suburb? In fact, they are not. Cross-state geographic mobility rates actually are slightly lower in the 1990s than they were in the 1950s, when communities and workers allegedly were more stable.[20]

In short, the data indicate a very modest decline in aggregate job stability in the 1990s, with much of the effect concentrated among long-tenure males in managerial and professional occupations. The underlying stock of jobs, however, is still heavily composed of career-type positions. Indeed, as the population continues to age, it is likely that job tenure levels will rise across the labor market. Focusing on net flows over the past fifteen years, we see a drop of 1 to 8 percentage points in the proportion employed over 10 years with the same employer; focusing on stocks, we see that nearly one-third of the adult labor force in 1998 was employed in long-term jobs, rising to one-half for men aged 45–64. "Long-term employment relationships" says economist Henry Farber, "remain an important feature of the U.S. labor market."[21]

## *Deaths and births*

If one identifies the U.S. companies with the largest absolute net job losses since 1990, the list contains many familiar names. Near the top are Sears (down 166,000 since 1990), AT&T (down 155,000), and IBM (down 113,000). Other major losers include General Motors, General Dynamics, Digital Equipment (DEC), Kodak, Mobil, and Xerox.[22] Job losses at these blue-ribbon companies send a message that absolute job security no longer exists. Nevertheless, not all jobs are in peril, nor is modern welfare capitalism a relic of the past. Despite laying off thousands of workers, many of these companies continue to offer career employment and, in some instances, have been rehiring employees almost as quickly as shedding them. AT&T, which took a major public relations hit three years ago when it announced plans to eliminate 40,000 jobs, has had a net reduction of 20,000 jobs since then because of its new hires.[23]

Much of this is common knowledge. What is less well known is the extent to which employment has been reshuffled in recent years, either within industries (from unprofitable companies to rapidly growing ones) or between industries (from mature to expanding sectors). There has been a slew of companies whose headcount grew steadily in the 1990s. European and other critics of the U.S. employment "miracle" scoff at this new job creation, arguing that it is concentrated in sectors offering low-quality jobs.[24] In fact, several of the companies with the largest absolute employment growth since 1990 either offer relatively low-quality jobs—such as Marriott (up 194,000) and McDonald's (up 91,000)—or they are purveyors of temporary workers, like Kelly Services (up 172,000) and Robert Half (up 117,000).

However, the gainers also include companies offering stable, career-type positions. Those situated in expanding sectors tend to be newer companies that have not yet become household names. For example, the following companies each created at least 40,000 jobs since 1990: in financial services, Morgan Stanley and Norwest; in health care, Genesis Health Ventures and Sun Healthcare; and in entertainment, Disney and Viacom. Some of the better-quality job gainers come from the same industries as those on the losers list. Thus while Sears shrank, its competitors—like Dayton-Hudson, Home Depot, Lowe's, and Wal-Mart—added over 700,000 jobs. In the communications industry, AT&T contracted but SBC, MCI, Worldcom, and Motorola added many more jobs than AT&T cut. Gains by EDS, Intel, and Seagate surpassed losses at DEC and IBM, while even some chemical companies—unlike Kodak—managed to add considerable numbers of new jobs, including Praxair, Merck, and Eastman Chemical (once a division of Kodak).

These successful companies put enormous effort into transforming new recruits into company men and women, both in the way they think and the skills that they possess. While the new jobs do not provide the kind of iron-clad security that some employees, especially managers, once could expect, nevertheless these jobs are far from being short-term positions. Take, for example, Lowe's, a chain of home improvement stores. Lowe's is very similar to what Sears Roebuck was like in its heyday. The company has grown rapidly, adding 43,000 jobs and hundreds of new stores since 1990. Twice listed as one of the country's top 100 employers, it offers career jobs and a stock purchase plan for all of its employees, who own twenty-five percent of the company. Lowe's competitors—including Home Depot and Wal-Mart—similarly pride themselves on their low employee turnover rates. Wal-Mart, currently on the top 100 list, promotes from within and invests heavily in employee training, as does Home Depot. With new jobs like these, median tenure levels will rise in years to come.[25]

To find a parallel to the labor market of the 1990s, one has to go back seventy years. During the 1920s, the unemployment rate was low and new jobs were rapidly being created. However, the health of the aggregate labor market masked some painful shifts. One factor fostering job displacement in the 1920s was a high rate of investment in labor-saving plant and equipment, which gave rise to a new phrase, "technological unemployment." Another factor was sectoral dislocation. Employment was shifting from blue-collar to white-collar jobs; from manufacturing to services; and within manufacturing from older industries likes steel, shoes, cotton textiles, and railroad equipment to newer industries like electrical goods, chemicals, and food processing. The rate at which workers left the industry in which they had been employed more than doubled in the 1920s over the rate that had existed between 1899 and 1914.[26] During the Great Depression, contraction of these newer industries was less severe and recovery more rapid than average; they ultimately were the industries on which the postwar economy was based.[27] However, the 1920s were, despite the sectoral shifts, a decade of growing, if unevenly distributed, prosperity. All of this should sound eerily familiar—absent, one hopes, the stock-market crash that brought the decade to a close.

## *Job quality*

What about the quality of today's new jobs? We can assess job quality using proxy measures such as real wage growth and full-time status. One study finds that in the early 1980s there was a slight deterioration of real wages on new jobs relative to old jobs. Since then, however, relative real wages have been stable. While the less educated suffered sizeable real wage declines, that pattern occurred in both old and new jobs. Moreover, new jobs of the mid-1990s fell into the overall wage distribution in much the same way as in earlier years.[28] Thus the evidence is not consistent with the claim that the new jobs being produced by the U.S. economy are predominantly low-wage. Wage inequality is pervasive and not the result of inferior new jobs.[29]

Whether a job is permanent or full-time is another dimension of job quality. Temporary jobs have experienced rapid growth in recent years, faster than other jobs. However, while growth has been rapid, it started from a small base. Currently less than 2 percent of the workforce is employed on a contract basis or works for temporary help agencies. One reason for the growth in temporary positions is employer reluctance to hire probationary employees who might have to be dismissed if unsatisfactory. With dismissal costs rising, employers prefer to use temporary help agencies to screen persons suitable for career-type positions. (Temp agencies rarely fire unsatisfactory workers; they simply stop calling them.) That is, the growth in temporary positions is, at least in part, a complement to, not a substitute for, standard full-time employment.[30]

As for part-timers, some 21 percent of workers are employed part-time. That figure is the same as in the early 1970s. Moreover, for the period since 1980, there is no evidence that new jobs are more likely to be part-time than old jobs. Bear in mind that around 80 percent of part-timers are in those positions voluntarily—they are not seeking full-time jobs—and some have a significant stake in the companies they work for.[31]

Growth of nonstandard jobs has leveled off recently. As a share of the labor force, such employment actually declined slightly since 1995. One explanation for this is the recent tightening of labor markets. For those whose nonstandard employment is involuntary—as is the case for many temporary workers—such jobs are viewed as an inferior alternative to regular full-time positions. With the labor market heating up since the mid-1990s, fewer workers are finding themselves having to take these transitional jobs. To put this another way, labor shortages are forcing employers to assume greater risk when filling positions.[32]

## *Cyclical factors*

Labor markets are affected not only by structural and secular changes, but also by cyclical factors, such as the unemployment rate. Cyclical and secular components were difficult to disentangle when labor markets were stagnant, as was the case for much of the period since the mid-1970s. However, the recent drop in unemployment has revealed the limits of a purely structural perspective. Unemployment rates are lower now than at any time since 1973, when the monetary authorities first became obsessed with fighting inflation. In the future, we may well look back at the downsizing of the 1980s and 1990s and see more clearly its relationship to cyclical factors.

Low unemployment has two effects. Directly, it fosters the internalization of labor markets, as employers seek to retain scarce labor. Indirectly, as economist Michal Kalecki first observed fifty years ago, low unemployment enhances the bargaining power of employees and their ability to get employers to shoulder risks for them.[33] When labor markets are slack, power is on the employer's side; when unemployment rates are low, the tables are turned and employers are more inclined to accommodate worker demands. Indeed, it is revealing that Kalecki published his essay during the Second World War, a time when labor was scarce and unions strong. During the hundred-year span from 1870 to 1970, career employment practices did not grow steadily. Rather, they widened and deepened most rapidly in periods when unemployment was relatively low, such as the late 1880s, early 1900s, and the four major wars of this century. Conversely, there were reversions to more market-oriented employment relationships during slack periods like the 1890s and 1930s. What happened from the late 1970s through the early 1990s, then, was the confluence of relatively slow growth, a loose labor market, and structural shocks arising from deregulation, globalization, and sectoral shifts. Historical evidence suggests that any tightening of U.S. labor markets will—both directly (to retain scarce labor) and indirectly (via bargaining power)—shift employment practices back in the direction of insulation from market forces. We can call this the Kalecki effect.[34]

Presently, we again are witnessing the Kalecki effect, as unemployment plummets. Tight labor markets force employers to shed labor more carefully and make it easier for workers to find new jobs. That is one reason why there has been so little outcry over recent layoffs. Over two-thirds of workers permanently displaced from full-time jobs between 1995 and 1997 have found re-employment in full-time jobs. An additional 15 percent are working part-time or at home, and 15 percent left the labor market. The total re-employment rate has risen since the mid-1990s, while wage prospects have improved. Workers who were laid off in the last two years are much less likely to be suffering earnings declines than workers laid off in the early 1990s: Thirty-eight percent experienced earnings declines in the past two years, versus 55 percent five years ago. However, for some workers—especially the less educated—job loss was and still is the source of large and persistent earnings losses.[35]

Managers and skilled workers are experiencing especially high re-employment rates. One headhunting agency recently reported that managers at companies announcing layoff plans often find themselves with several job offers in hand before the layoffs occur. Hence while organizations today are somewhat flatter than before, they still have an enormous appetite for managers and management remains a growth occupation. The proportion of managers in the workforce actually increased over the course of the 1990s, as new employment growth exceeded the volume lost to downsizing.[36]

As companies scramble for help, they are luring new recruits with offers of traditional career opportunities. As a recent article put it, "employers are going to great lengths to persuade employees that they want them to stay for years."[37] Employers are dusting off and reintroducing old-style employee development and training programs intended to reassure managers and professionals of their prospects. Citibank, for example, despite recent layoffs, expects its workforce to grow in coming years. So it recently established a formal career development program for 10,000 managers. The company's vice president for human resources said, "We want to make people feel that they have a long-term career with us."[38]

The response to tighter labor markets suggests a swinging pendulum. Employers today want careers to be less "boundaryless" and more organization-centered.

The problem, of course, is that this runs directly counter to what today's educated young workers think is the route to career success: regular changing of employers to gain experience and to signal ambition. Recently, I spoke to the vice president for human resources of a *Fortune 500* company, who was lamenting the difficulty of attracting and retaining young managers and professionals. I reminded him that people in their 20s and early 30s were simply responding to the mantra they have heard employers chanting for the last ten years: that everyone should expect to regularly change jobs, and perhaps even careers, throughout their working lives. "Yes, we've been our own worst enemy," he said to me. "And now we've got to put a new message out."

## *Benefits and wages*

What about fringe benefits, a tangible sign of an employer's commitment to employees? In health insurance, there has been almost no change since 1979 in the proportion of private-sector employers offering health benefits. What has changed are the eligibility rules, which have become more stringent for short-term and part-time workers, and the take-up rate, which has declined for full-time "core" employees due to spousal coverage. Thus the evidence suggests that "employers are continuing to make health insurance available to their core long-term full-time employees but are restricting access ... by their peripheral employees."[39]

Pension coverage is a different story. In the 1980s, pension coverage fell sharply for younger, less educated men—the type of workers who once were employed in unionized manufacturing jobs. For mature workers and for college graduates, however, the coverage decline was modest; for women there was a slight increase in coverage. The situation stabilized in the 1990s. Between 1991 and 1997, the proportion of workers in mid- to large-sized establishments who were covered by a retirement plan rose slightly.[40] The big change, however, has been the shift from defined benefit to defined contribution plans, which is discussed below.

Again, it is important to recall the distinction between stocks and flows. Despite modest shifts in coverage, employers remain key elements in our health and pension systems. Two-thirds of all private-sector workers receive employer-provided health insurance, rising to 76 percent for those employed in medium to large establishments.[41] As for pensions, 63 percent of full-time workers and 21 percent of regular part-time workers are covered by employer-provided retirement plans, with coverage rising to 79 percent in mid- to large-sized establishments. Even as some employers are discontinuing particular programs, others are adopting new ones such as preventive medical care, day care, and other benefits targeted at employees with dependents. Recently, a group of twenty major corporations pledged to invest millions of dollars to make child and elder care more available. The companies included such paragons of modern welfare capitalism as Hewlett-Packard, IBM, Mobil, and Texas Instruments.[42]

Another way of assessing where an employer sits on the continuum between market- and organization-oriented policies is to examine the extent to which actual pay rates diverge from market rates. Companies that insulate employment relationships from market forces will be more likely to engage in wage-smoothing over the course of a long-term employment relationship; at any point in time, wages will be less sensitive to market conditions than in spot markets. Such companies also are more likely to pay a wage premium that deviates from market averages. There could be any number of reasons for this policy, such as turnover minimization (workers are less likely to quit high-pay employers) or productivity enhancement (workers are more diligent when the cost of termination—here, a fall back to market rates—is high). There is one recent study which finds that wages have become more sensitive to unemployment rates, although the study uses industry data and is limited to manufacturing industries adversely affected by foreign competition in the 1980s. On the other hand, another recent study uses a unique data set covering white- and blue-collar occupations in two hundred large firms over the last forty years. It finds no evidence of a decline in the magnitude or persistence of employer wage premia for individual occupations and groups of occupations. This suggests a high degree of stability in the way employers base their long-term wage strategies on organizational rather than market considerations.[43]

## Explaining the paradox

To summarize, a variety of sources have been examined to assess the degree of change in career-type employment practices. Blue-collar workers in the early 1980s and white-collar workers in the early 1990s experienced higher levels of permanent job loss. As a result, aggregate job tenure rates have declined modestly since the late 1970s. On the other hand, the majority of workers continue to hold career-type jobs that offer fringe benefits, training, and prospects of continuity. For women and for those in service occupations and industries, long-tenure employment has become more prevalent over the last twenty years. Also, the economy is creating new jobs that are predominantly neither low-wage nor part-time. Hence the majority of displaced workers are finding reemployment in career-type positions. The recent decline in unemployment rates has boosted prospects for displaced workers and strengthened employer reliance on career-type practices.

Taken as a whole, the evidence does not show a radical slide to the market pole of the organizational-market continuum. Organizational considerations still trump market logic for the bulk of the economy's jobs, and the majority of employers continue to shoulder income and employment risks for employees. How, then, does one explain the disparity between the perception of "no long term" and the fact that stability remains widespread in the labor market? There is no simple answer to this question, but explanatory elements can be found in cognitive psychology and the politics of punditry.

## *Perceptual biases*

A stream of research in cognitive psychology documents the pervasiveness of loss aversion: People weigh losses—like layoffs—more heavily than gains.[44] The job losses of the past ten years have weighed heavily on the nation's middle-classes because they involve educated, professionals and managers—people like us, people with whom we can identify. The downsizings and plant closures of the early 1980s did not generate nearly the same amount of angst or media coverage even though the displacement rate then was higher than in the 1990s.

Recent job cuts also rankled the middle-class because they were widely perceived as unfair: the violation of an implicit contract to provide security until senior management's own jobs were in peril, that is, until the company was close to closure. One former IBM employee said, "In January I was told my job was the safest in the nation. In February we were told half the jobs would be gone."[45] Fueling the sense of unfairness was the belief that layoffs resulted not from a search for efficiency but from a greed-driven change in corporate governance that favored owners over employees. Repeatedly in the late 1980s and early 1990s, there were reports of profitable companies laying workers off and then enjoying stock-price increases that benefited senior management and other major shareholders, as at General Dynamics or in the more egregious case of Al Dunlap, former CEO of Sunbeam.[46]

## *Fallacy of discontinuity*

Another reason for the discrepancy between the rhetoric and reality of change in employment relations is what might be called, following historian David Hackett Fischer, the fallacy of discontinuity—an erroneous belief that the present is fundamentally different from the periods that preceded it. Not only fashion designers but journalists, management consultants, and academics build their careers around this conceit. Consultants are particularly prone to a faddish way of thinking, since it helps to generate sales of new systems premised on the assumption that the world has changed so drastically as to render worthless existing ways of doing business. Academics have similar proclivities. Enthusiasts for change dramatically pronounce "the demise of organizational careers" and their replacement by something radically different: the "boundaryless career."[47]

The media, in particular, seized upon the layoffs of the early 1990s as evidence that the American workplace had become, as the *New York Times* put it, "new and unnerving." The *Times*' 1996 multi-part series and subsequent book on the "Downsizing of America" took two dozen people more than seven months to produce. It was the longest piece of journalism published by the *Times* since the Pentagon Papers in 1971.[48] Yet while the series was chock full of painful personal stories, it was virtually devoid of economic statistics for gauging the severity, extent, and consequences of layoff.

Then there is the Challenger, Gray data series, compiled by a Chicago-based company that specializes in outplacement services. They tabulate corporate announcements of intended, not actual, layoffs. Since the series began in the early 1990s, the media has regularly reported Challenger's monthly figures. But the number of workers actually laid off is often much lower than the job-elimination plans reported in the news releases. Companies announce the highest cutback totals they can justify to impress investors that they are getting lean and mean, and then pursue cuts through mechanisms other than layoff. Sudden mass departures do occur, but reductions also are handled through normal turnover, through transfers, through early retirements, or simply by leaving vacancies unfilled. That is, because the layoffs take place by mechanisms other than layoff and the process occurs over a lengthy period, a portion of the announced layoff never actually occurs.[49]

## Risk shifting: practices and prospects

None of this is intended to deny the fact that there has been a rise in job loss, especially for those employees thought to be most immune to it. While the direct effect has been overstated, the indirect effect surely has been to expose incumbent employees to a greater risk of job loss. Employers have in other respects been shifting more of the risk burden onto employees. That is the logic of managed care and of larger deductibles for health insurance, both of which have grown steadily since 1991.[50] It is also the rationale behind the change from defined benefit pension plans to defined contribution plans. Employers also are incorporating more variability into employee pay packages via discretionary bonuses, group incentives, profit sharing, and stock options. In economists' parlance, more pay is "at risk."[51]

The reallocation of risk—not the decline of career-type jobs—is the central dynamic driving today's internal labor markets. Employers are still protecting employees from the hazards of unemployment, sickness, and old-age. However, companies today operate in a turbulent environment of heightened competition, mergers, and rapid technological change. It is a riskier world, and employers are less willing to shoulder as much risk for employees as they did in the past.[52]

Some employees are adapting to this risk—especially younger, more educated workers with "hot" skills—while others are having a tough time of it. These workers still look to their employers as the first line of defense. As that line is pushed back, they question the fairness of today's risk-sharing arrangements. While most of these workers are not about to lose their jobs, they are left feeling more insecure. Forty-five percent of employees in 1977 thought it was not at all likely they would lose their jobs, but the figure has fallen to thirty percent today. Every layoff announcement affects the perceived probability of job loss and causes survivors to work harder and worry more. Thus layoffs can have ripple effects far beyond their direct labor cost saving.[53]

Does this mean, then, that eventually we can expect to see the risk burden completely shifted to employees, such that employers no longer will offer fringe benefits, career jobs, fixed salaries, and so on? The short answer is no.

Assuming that current trends will continue without limit is a *reductio ad absurdum*, just as it would have been equally absurd to predict in the 1880s that all jobs would become career positions carrying generous fringe benefits. There are economic, demographic, and political limits to the risk reallocation process. These limits ensure that the corporation likely will remain a central risk-bearing institution in American society.

One such limit has to do with the organizational realities of managing a workforce. For most employers, the net economic benefits of welfare capitalism remain positive. Employee loyalty and commitment still matter, especially in the burgeoning service sector where it is often difficult to directly supervise employees.[54] New workers have to be trained, which makes employee turnover costly. Employee skills are, if anything, more important today than in the past, especially in fast-changing situations where little is codified and knowledge is tacit. New systems of work organization—such as self-managed teams—are less prevalent than is commonly supposed but nevertheless have grown markedly in recent years. These systems are accompanied by higher levels of training and tend to be associated with career-type jobs, since job stability preserves the interpersonal relationships that make teams effective. Hence, to the extent these systems continue to proliferate, they create employer incentives to stabilize employment.[55]

For these reasons, companies like 3M, Intel, and Motorola have—despite layoffs—preserved career-type jobs, albeit lacking guarantees of permanence. There is plenty of evidence that the practices associated with career job policies—such as training, profit sharing, and participatory work systems—are positively related to corporate performance. Other companies that have downsized in recent years are discovering that outsourcing and temporary employees—while cheaper in the short-run—do not provide the levels of service and quality that are necessary for customer satisfaction.[56] A recent study of companies that have implemented "employability" contracts—offering learning experiences in return for heightened employee responsibilities—concludes that the most successful employers are those who retain "a sense of responsibility to protect the jobs of their people."[57]

Some argue that companies in dynamic sectors like Silicon Valley, Hollywood, and Wall Street operate according to a different, more market-oriented, logic. Here, workers tend to be relatively young and educated, and they can move easily from job to job. Employers do not penalize such mobility because it helps them to keep abreast of competitors and stay on the cutting edge. In Silicon Valley, for example, there is pervasive interfirm mobility. Workers are well paid and can afford their own health benefits and 401(k) plans. However, these workers are an atypical elite, just as footloose craft workers were an atypical but essential elite in American industry ninety years ago. Most workers do not have skills that are either as scarce or as critical to business performance as the technologists in the Valley.[58]

Also, the employers of this elite are dissimilar in important respects from the bulk of the companies that constitute our economy. Today, most U.S. companies are service providers whose success depends less on technological breakthroughs than on customer attraction and retention. One key to customer loyalty is employee loyalty: Experienced and satisfied employees are much better at finding and keeping customers than fresh recruits. In industries such as financial services, the fastest-growing occupations are those that require interpersonal skills, which, unlike accounting positions, are difficult to replace with computerized information systems. These interpersonal skills are relatively less important in high-technology industries that are mistakenly touted as exemplars of the future.[59]

Even high-technology companies are beginning to recognize that rapid turnover and short employment stints can be detrimental. Take, for example, SAS, a software company based in North Carolina. The company sounds like a throwback to the heyday of welfare capitalism. It offers a 35-hour workweek, on-site child care, a lavish exercise facility, and subsidized cafes with live piano music. To make sure employees are healthy, the company maintains its own medical facility with five nurse practitioners, two family practice doctors, a massage therapist, and a mental health nurse. To retain potentially mobile knowledge workers, it tries to accommodate people's changing careers within the company, not by losing them to competitors. (Turnover at SAS is only one-tenth the Silicon Valley norm.) The company's HR manager said, "At 5 P.M., 95 percent of our assets walk out the door. We have to have an environment that makes them want to walk back in the door the next morning." Past history suggests that as some companies accelerate the internalization process, others will follow suit as a defensive necessity.[60]

Second, there are demographic limits to restructuring. Many workers laid off during the past decade came from the relatively small pre-1945 generation that preceded the baby boomers. At one bank, for example, the director said "the machine guns started firing on day one [after a recent merger], with anyone over 50 in the front rank." Because older workers are paid more, they are targeted for layoff and are likely to experience subsequent earnings declines; younger displaced workers recently have been experiencing gains in their median weekly earnings.[61] Employer animus toward older workers reveals an important fact: Despite all the talk about delayering, corporations remain pyramidal organizations in which seniority and pay are positively related; hence you can cut labor costs by targeting senior workers for layoff.[62] It was feasible to conduct layoffs in the late 1980s and early 1990s because replacement workers from the baby boom generation were plentiful. However, the cohort behind the boomers—Generation X—is relatively small. Current estimates are that the number of 35 to 44 year olds will decline by 15 percent between 2000 and 2015.[63] There is little in sight to relieve the demographic pressure on employers. The long-term rise in female labor force participation is leveling off, while white-collar productivity gains are flat. In short, current employer concerns with labor scarcity and retention are likely to persist into the next century, putting a brake on future risk shifting.

Finally, there are political limits to the amount of risk shifting that American employers can or would want to pursue. Currently, the United States has lower unionization rates than any other advanced industrial country. Our government spends less on social insurance per worker than other advanced industrial countries. Corporate managers know—or may discover—that if they let welfare capitalism wither, there will be popular pressure for government and perhaps even for unions to fill the gap. That is precisely why Buchanan's candidacy caused such a stir in 1996 and may do so again in the 2000 campaign.

The only aspect of risk shifting that knows no limits is a belief in its inevitability, a habit of mind that Albert O. Hirschman associates with the "rhetoric of futility."[64] The futility argument proceeds by identifying deep forces—economic logic or human nature—that cannot be altered. Attempts to change them are hopeless and will perversely result in the reassertion of those forces. In economics, the doctrine of rational expectations—that activist fiscal policy is useless in permanently lowering the unemployment rate—is one such example. A similar rhetoric infuses assertions that market individualism has triumphed in the economy. Even when shown to be empirically implausible, those claims nevertheless have real consequences. They encourage the belief that alternative institutions are destined for extinction. Hence to retain those institutions—whether welfare capitalism or the welfare state—is an exercise in futility. Better to hasten the future by dismantling bureaucracies, dissociating from organizations, and taking care of "numero uno"—after all, no one else can or will.

However, as Hirschman goes on to point out, the rhetoric of futility is often proclaimed prematurely; it is a form of wishful thinking. Similarly, it is wishful thinking to believe that market individualism is rampant and that we are living in a world of tenuous associations and arm's-length relationships, the system idealized by nineteenth-century contract law.[65] In fact, we still inhabit a society where markets—including labor markets—co-exist and co-evolve with regulations, social norms, and other institutions. Economic historian Karl Polanyi was the first to identify this "double movement" of two great organizing principles: the expansion of the market and the simultaneous expansion of market regulation. If one studies closely the economic deregulation that has occurred in various sectors over the last twenty years, what one finds is not a move to pure laissez-faire but instead a redefinition of government responsibilities, a process that one political scientist calls "reregulation." As for social regulation, keep in mind that the Reagan administration had little luck in rolling back either Social Security or environmental and consumer protection. Meanwhile, the volume of such regulation has steadily grown in the 1990s, in the labor market and elsewhere.[66] This suggests a simple conclusion: While we cannot change the level of risk in today's economy, we can change the rules that govern how risk is shared among the participants to the economic game.

For example, the SEC could require companies to include statements on their balance sheets of how much they have invested in their employees. That would be a first step to getting managers and investors to accurately recognize the value of a firm's human capital. Second, we can reform our labor laws. Employer unfair labor practices have skyrocketed in recent years, and the law is failing to protect legitimate union organizing attempts. Third, we can change the incentives faced by investors. Today, institutional investors own two-thirds of the total equity in the stock market. Institutional investors are fickle creatures who move their capital with breath-taking rapidity. Pension funds should pay capital gains taxes on the stock they churn around. Also, mutual funds could do more to penalize short-term traders for the costs that they incur, such as raising transactions fees and contributing them to the purchased company or mutual fund to benefit long-term returns.[67]

## Conclusions

The labor market is in flux, but it would be a mistake to project the future out of recent trends. Career jobs are less expansive, but they have not melted into air. While people are unhappy with the risk they are being asked to shoulder, they still look to employers to share much of the burden. According to pollsters, today's middle-class Americans think that corporations "should balance their self-interest with the need to consider what benefits the larger society."[68] Those who ask that corporations be responsible are not asking for anything outside the welfare capitalist framework established by corporations themselves. There remains widespread support for the notion that corporations are—or should be—the keystone of economic security in American society. That is the path we have been on for the last one hundred years, and we remain on that trajectory.

The risk shifting experienced by workers in the economy's core is a serious problem. However, we must not let it overshadow the more critical situation facing less-educated and less-skilled workers. Those workers are steadily falling behind as a result of technological change and globalization as well as factors specific to the United States such as high immigration, weak minimum wage laws, and the decline of unionism. Since 1980, earnings inequality has grown more rapidly in the United States than other advanced countries. Low-wage U.S. workers are both relatively and absolutely poorer than their European or Japanese counterparts.[69]

The problem of inequality should not be confused with the rising risk of job loss. True, when less-educated workers lose their jobs, they are more likely than educated workers to experience a permanent reduction in earnings. However, a similar earnings disparity also exists for those who never lose their jobs. When we examine the stock of continuing jobs, we find that long-term employment relationships (over twenty years) currently are as prevalent for those with twelve or fewer years of education as they are for those with baccalaureate and advanced degrees.[70] In short, the primary cause of inequality is not downsizing but rising returns to education accompanied by the waning of wage-setting institutions in the low-wage labor market (e.g., the shrinkage of unions and of real minimum wages). Middle-class workers are entitled to a better deal, but their predicament—and our own anxieties—should not overshadow the plight of low-wage workers.

## Acknowledgments

This article was originally presented as the Kenneth M. Piper Memorial Lecture at Chicago-Kent Law School in April 1999. The author would like to thank Christopher Erickson, Matthew Finkin, and Martin Malin for helpful comments.

## Notes

1 Richard Sennett, *The Corrosion of Character*: *The Personal Consequences of Work in the New Capitalism* (New York, NY: Norton, 1998).
2 "Greenspan Says Job Insecurity Still High," *Daily Labor Report*, 31, February 17, 1999, p. AA-1.
3 Michael J. Mandel, "Economic Anxiety," *Business Week*, March 11, 1996, pp. 50–56; Alison Mitchell, "Clinton Prods Executives to Do the Right Thing," *New York Times*, May 17, 1996, p. C-2.
4 Sanford M. Jacoby, *Modern Manors*: *Welfare Capitalism since the New Deal* (Princeton, NJ: Princeton University Press, 1997).
5 In manufacturing, job loss rates in the mid-1990s were half the level observed in the early 1980s. Henry S. Farber, "The Changing Face of Job Loss in the United States, 1981–1995," Industrial Relations Section, Princeton University, working paper 382, June 1997; Lori Kletzer, "Job Displacement," *Journal of Economic Perspectives*, 12 (Winter 1998): 115–136, at 119.
6 The Conference Board, "Organizing the Corporate HQ: An HR Perspective," *HR Executive Review*, 6 (1998).
7 Peter Herriot and Carole Pemberton, *New Deals*: *The Revolution in Managerial Careers* (New York, NY: John Wiley & Sons, 1995); Peter Cappelli, *The New Deal at Work* (Boston, MA: Harvard Business School Press, 1999).
8 Arne Kalleberg, Edith Rasell, Naomi Cassirer, Barbara Reskin, Ken Hudson, David Webster, Eileen Applebaum, and Roberta Spalter-Roth, *Nonstandard Work, Substandard Jobs*: *Flexible Work Arrangements in the U.S.* (Washington, D.C.: Economic Policy Institute, 1997), p. 9.
9 Henry S. Farber and Helen Levy, "Recent Trends in Employer-Sponsored Health Insurance Coverage: Are Bad Jobs Getting Worse?" NBER working paper 6709 (August 1998); Kalleberg et al., op. cit., pp. 30–31; Henry S. Farber, "Job Creation in the United States: Good Jobs or Bad?" Industrial Relations Section, Princeton University, working paper 385, July 1997.
10 Alan Downs, *Corporate Executions*: *The Ugly Truth About Layoffs—How Corporate Greed is Shattering Lives, Companies, and Communities* (New York, NY: AMACOM, 1995).
11 Joel Kurtzman, "An Interview with Paul Krugman," *Strategy & Business*, 13/4 (1998): 87–96, at 88.
12 Steven J. Davis and John Haltiwanger, "Gross Job Creation, Gross Job Destruction, and Employment Reallocation," *Quarterly Journal of Economics*, 107 (August 1992): 819–863.
13 Francis X. Diebold, David Neumark, and Daniel Polsky, "Job Stability in the United States, *Journal of Labor Economics*, 15 (1997): 206–233; David Neumark, Daniel Polsky, and Daniel Hansen, "Has Job Stability Declined Yet? New Evidence for the 1990s," paper presented at the Russell Sage Foundation Conference on Changes in Job Stability and Job Security, February 1998.
14 Henry S. Farber, "Trends in Long-Term Employment in the United States, 1979–96," Industrial Relations Section, Princeton University, working paper no. 384, July 1997.

15 U.S. Bureau of Labor Statistics, "Employee Tenure in 1998," report 98–387, Washington D.C., 1998. If the analysis is limited to large firms, the evidence of job stability is even more striking. For 51 large companies that were clients of Watson Wyatt, a consulting firm, average tenure increased in the 1990s, as did the percentage of employees with ten years (and twenty years) of service or more. Even in firms with shrinking employment, the odds that a worker would be with the employer five years later were higher than the same odds for the labor market as a whole. Steven G. Allen, Robert L. Clark, and Sylvester J. Schieber, "Has Job Security Vanished in Large Corporations?" NBER working paper no. 6966, 1999.
16 Farber, "Changing Face of Job Loss," op. cit.
17 Robert G. Valletta, "Declining Job Security," working paper, Federal Reserve Bank of San Francisco, San Francisco, CA, November 1997.
18 Cynthia Bansak and Steven Raphael, "Have Employment Relationships in the U.S. Become Less Stable?" working paper, Department of Economics, U.C. San Diego, August 1998. Note, however, that when one focuses on tenure rather than separations, older workers do not show larger tenure declines than younger workers. One explanation could be that older workers who have suffered permanent layoff are more inclined to leave the labor market. See Neumark, Polsky, and Hansen, op. cit.
19 James T. Bond, Ellen Galinksy, and Jennifer E. Swanberg, *The 1997 National Study of the Changing Workforce*, Families and Work Institute, New York, NY, 1998, p. 115; Bansak and Raphael, op. cit.
20 U.S. Bureau of the Census, "Annual Geographic Mobility Rates," July 1998, at www.census.gov/population/socdemo/migration
21 U.S. Bureau of Labor Statistics, op. cit.; Farber, "Trends in Long-Term Employment," op. cit., p. 26.
22 These data are drawn from Compustat listings for U.S.-based companies for the period 1990–1997. Companies whose employment was affected by merger or liquidation were not included in the sample. MCI and Worldcom merged late in 1998.
23 Stuart Silverstein and Davan Maharaj, "Company Layoff Projections Often Don't Add Up," *Los Angeles Times*, January 17, 1999, p. D-1.
24 Richard B. Freeman, "War of the Models: Which Labour Market Institutions for the 21st Century?" *Labour Economics*, 5 (1998): 1–24.
25 R.S. Johnson, "Lowe's Borrows the Blueprint," *Fortune*, November 23, 1998, p. 212+; Sandra Vance and Roy Scott, *Wal-Mart: A History of Sam Walton's Retail Phenomenon* (New York, NY: Twayne Publishers, 1997); Chris Roush, *Inside Home Depot* (New York, NY: McGraw-Hill, 1999). One reason companies no longer tout explicit no-layoff policies is the spate of dismissal suits in recent years. Plaintiffs sometimes won by claiming breach of an implied promise to provide continuous employment, such as were found in employee handbooks and other personnel policies. Henry Perritt, *Employee Dismissal: Law and Practice* (New York, NY: Wiley Law Publications, 1998).
26 Sanford M. Jacoby, *Employing Bureaucracy: Managers, Unions, and the Transformation of Work in American Industry, 1900–1945* (New York, NY: Columbia University Press, 1985), pp. 167–170.
27 Michael Bernstein, *The Great Depression: Delayed Recovery and Economic Change in America, 1929–39* (Cambridge: Cambridge University Press, 1987).
28 Farber, "Job Creation in the U.S.," op. cit.
29 Sanford M. Jacoby and Peter Goldschmidt, "Education, Skill, and Wage Inequality: The Situation in California," *Challenge*, 41 (November/December 1998): 88–120.
30 David Autor, "Why Do Temporary Help Firms Provide Free General Skills Training," working paper, Kennedy School of Government, Harvard University, January 1999.

31 Kalleberg, op. cit., p. 9; Lewis M. Segal and Daniel G. Sullivan, "The Growth of Temporary Services Work," *Journal of Economic Perspectives*, 11 (Spring 1997): 117–136; Gillian Lester, "Careers and Contingency," *Stanford Law Review*, 51 (November 1998): 73–145.
32 U.S. Bureau of Labor Statistics, "Contingent and Alternative Employment Arrangements, February 1997," bulletin 97–422, Washington, D.C., 1997; Henry S. Farber, "Alternative Employment Arrangements as a Response to Job Loss," Industrial Relations Section, Princeton University, working paper 391, October 1997.
33 Michal Kalecki, "Political Aspects of Full Employment," in Michal Kalecki, ed., *Selected Essays on the Dynamics of the Capitalist Economy, 1933–1970* (Cambridge: Cambridge University Press, 1971), pp. 138–145.
34 Alexander Keyssar, *Out of Work: The First Century of Unemployment in Massachusetts* (Cambridge: Cambridge University Press, 1986). The idea of a market-organization continuum is nicely developed in Ronald Dore, "Where Are We Now? Musings of an Evolutionist," *Work, Employment, & Society*, 3 (1989): 425–446.
35 U.S. Bureau of Labor Statistics, "Worker Displacement, 1995–1997," report no. 98–347, August 1998; Gene Koretz, "Downsizing's Impact on Job Losers," *Business Week*, December 28, 1998, p. 30; Bruce Fallick, "A Review of the Recent Empirical Literature on Displaced Workers," *Industrial & Labor Relations Review*, 50 (1996): 5–16; Louis Jacobson, Robert LaLonde, and Daniel Sullivan, *The Costs of Worker Dislocation* (Kalamazoo, MI: W.E. Upjohn Institute of Employment Research, 1993). Over the past two years, the share of workers worried about losing their jobs fell from 44 percent to 37 percent. Charles Manski and John Straub, "Workers Perceptions of Job Insecurity in the Mid-1990s," NBER working paper no. 6908, 1999.
36 David M. Gordon, *Fat and Mean: The Corporate Squeeze of Working Americans and the Myth of Managerial "Downsizing"* (New York, NY: Martin Kessler Books, 1996), pp. 54–55.
37 "We Want You to Stay. Really," *Business Week*, June 22, 1998, p. 67.
38 Ibid., p. 70; "Employers Find that Tight Economy Requires Use of Creative Recruiting," *Daily Labor Report*, no. 237, December 10, 1998, pp. C1–C7.
39 Farber and Levy, op. cit., p. 25. Another reason for the decline in the take-up rate (the rate at which employees take benefits offered to them) is the recent rapid growth in tailored benefit plans permitting employees to pick and choose benefits. In 1988, thirteen percent of big companies gave employees this option; now over half do. "Unto Those that Have Shall Be Given," *Economist*, December 21, 1996, pp. 91–92.
40 David E. Bloom and Richard Freeman, "The Fall in Private Pension Coverage in the U.S.," *American Economic Review*, 82 (May 1992): 539–545; John Woods, "Pension Coverage Among the Baby Boomers," *Social Security Bulletin*, 57 (Fall 1994): 12–25; William Even and David MacPherson, "Why Did Male Pension Coverage Decline in the 1980s?" *Industrial & Labor Relations Review*, 47 (April 1994): 439–453; "Pension Plan Coverage Now Rising," *Employee Benefit Plan Review*, 48 (April 1994): 41–42; U.S. Bureau of Labor Statistics, "Employee Benefits in Medium and Large Private Establishments," report 99–02, Washington, D.C., 1999, table 11. If employers, in fact, move radically away from provision of retirement benefits, employees would likely respond by saving at higher rates. But despite the recrudescence of market individualism, the U.S. private savings rate has steadily trended down since the early 1980s.
41 Farber and Levy, op. cit.; U.S. Bureau of Labor Statistics, "Benefits in Private Establishments," op. cit., tables 5 and 6.
42 Ibid., table 11; Kalleberg et al., op. cit., p. 31; "Companies Pledge to Invest $100 Million for Dependent Care," *Daily Labor Report*, October 4, 1995, p. A–5.
43 Marianne Bertrand, "From the Invisible Handshake to the Invisible Hand? How Import Competition Changes the Employment Relationship," NBER working paper

no. 6900, 1999; Erica L. Groshen and David I. Levine, "The Rise and Decline (?) of U.S. Internal Labor Markets," Federal Reserve Bank of New York, research paper no. 9819, New York, NY, 1998.
44. Howard C. Kunreuther, "Limited Knowledge and Insurance Protection," *Public Policy*, 24 (1976): 227–261; Daniel Kahneman and Amos Tversky, "Prospect Theory: An Analysis of Decision Under Risk," *Econometrica*, 47 (1979): 263–291.
45. Anthony Sampson, *Company Man: The Rise and Fall of Corporate Life* (New York, NY: Times Business, Random House, 1995), p. 225.
46. Sanford M. Jacoby, "'Chainsaw Al' Gets His Due," *Los Angeles Times*, June 18, 1998, p. B–5. Note, however, that the evidence does not support the popular belief that downsizing boosts stock prices and CEO pay. After controlling for factors like firm size, the effect of layoffs on CEO pay is nil and there is a small negative share price reaction to layoff announcements. Kevin Hallock, "Layoffs, Top Executive Pay, and Firm Performance," *American Economic Review*, 88 (September 1998): 711–723.
47. David Hackett Fischer, *Historians' Fallacies: Toward a Logic of Historical Thought* (New York, NY: Harper & Row, 1970); Frederick Hilmer and Lex Donaldson, *Management Redeemed: Debunking the Fads that Undermine Our Corporations* (New York, NY: Free Press, 1996); Michael B. Arthur and Denise M. Rousseau, "The Boundaryless Career as a New Employment Principle," in Michael B. Arthur and Denise M. Rousseau, eds., *The Boundaryless Career: A New Employment Principle for a New Organizational Era* (New York, NY: Oxford University Press, 1996), p. 5.
48. John Cassidy, "All Worked Up: Is Downsizing Really News or Is It Business as Usual?" *The New Yorker*, April 22, 1996, pp. 51–56.
49. Silverstein and Maharaj, op. cit.; Patterson, op. cit.
50. U.S. Bureau of Labor Statistics, "Benefits in Private Establishments," op. cit., table 7.
51. In medium to large establishments, the proportion of employees with defined-benefit plans fell from 59 to 50 percent between 1991 and 1997; the proportion with defined-contribution plans rose from 48 to 57 percent. Note, however, that some employees are covered by both types of plans and that some of the shifting occurred across rather than within firms due to rapid job growth in smaller, nonunion companies that are less likely to offer defined benefit plans. U.S. Bureau of Labor Statistics, "Benefits in Private Establishments," op. cit., table 11. Also, see Richard Ippolito, "Toward Explaining the Growth of Defined Contribution Plans," *Industrial Relations*, 34 (1995): 1–20; Ellen Benoit, "Penny Wise, Pound Foolish," *Treasury and Risk Management*, 6 (July/August 1996): 18–27.
52. The head of human resources at IBM, Gerald Czarnecki, characterizes his company's new approach as a "readjustment which needs a new balancing act ... I never thought it was good for a corporation to take over the role of the family unit, which is more dependable for society. Now the pendulum will swing back, to give a larger role to the family. But there's still a role for all three—family, business, and government." Sampson, op. cit., p. 229.
53. Bond, Galinsky, and Swanberg, op. cit., pp. 76–79; Delorese Ambrose, *Healing the Downsized Organization* (New York, NY: Harmony Books, 1996). Efficiency wage models relate the probability of job loss to employee effort levels. These models are a microeconomic version of the Kalecki effect. Valletta, op. cit.; Daniel Aaronson and Daniel G. Sullivan, The Decline of Job Security in the 1990s: Displacement, Anxiety, and their Effect on Wage Growth," *Federal Reserve Bank of Chicago, Economic Perspectives*, 22/1 (1998): 17–43.
54. Stephen Herzenberg, John Alic, and Howard Wial, *New Rules for a New Economy: Employment and Opportunity in Postindustrial America* (Ithaca, NY: ILR Press, 1998).
55. Finding and training a replacement typically costs about 55 percent of a departing employee's annual salary. "Can America's Workforce Grow Old Gracefully?"

*Economist*, July 25, 1998, pp. 59–60. For establishments with over fifty employees, 30 percent use self-directed work teams, with a coverage rate (percent of employees affected) of around 12 percent. Christopher Erickson and Sanford Jacoby, "Training and Work Organization Practices of Private Employers in California," California Policy Seminar Report, Berkeley, CA, 1998; Maury Gittleman, Michael Horrigan, and Mary Joyce, "Flexible Workplace Practices: Evidence from a Nationally Representative Survey," *Industrial & Labor Relations Review*, 52 (October 1998): 99–115.

56 David I. Levine, *Reinventing the Workplace: How Employees and Business Can Both Win* (Washington, D.C.: Brookings Institution, 1995); U.S. Department of Labor, "Report on High Performance Work Practices and Firm Performance," July 26, 1993, reprinted in *Daily Labor Report*, no. 143, July 28, 1993, p. F1–F12; James Rebitzer, "Job Safety and Contract Workers in the U.S. Petrochemical Industry," *Industrial Relations*, 34 (January 1995): 40–57; Jeffrey Pfeffer, *The Human Equation: Building Profits by Putting People First* (Boston, MA: Harvard Business School Press, 1998). For some contrary evidence on the profitability of a low-road approach, see Thomas Bailey and Annette Bernhardt, "In Search of the High Road in a Low-Wage Industry," *Politics and Society*, 25 (June 1997): 179–201.

57 Christopher A. Bartlett and Sumantra Ghoshal, *The Individualized Corporation: A Fundamentally New Approach to Management* (New York, NY: Harper Business, 1997).

58 Candace Jones, "Careers in Project Networks: The Case of the Film Industry," in Michael B. Arthur and Denise M. Rousseau, eds., *The Boundaryless Career: A New Employment Principle for a New Organizational Era* (New York, NY: Oxford University Press, 1996), pp. 58–78; Annalee Saxenian, *Regional Advantage: Culture and Competition in Silicon Valley and Route 128* (Cambridge, MA: Harvard University Press, 1996). In fact, most of the employment growth in California is concentrated in jobs that do not require a college education. Within Silicon Valley during the boom of 1991–1997, real incomes for the poorest 20 percent of the Valley's households fell by 8 percent. Jacoby and Goldschmidt, op. cit.; David Friedman, "The Dark Side of the High-Tech Religion," *Los Angeles Times*, January 31, 1999, p. M–1.

59 Frances Frei, Patrick Harker, and Larry Hunter, "Performance in Consumer Financial Services Organizations," working paper 95–03, Wharton Financial Institutions Center, University of Pennsylvania, Philadelphia, 1995. For a similar argument by the head of Bain & Company, see Frederick F. Reichheld, *The Loyalty Effect: The Hidden Force Behind Growth, Profits, and Lasting Value* (Boston, MA: Harvard Business School Press, 1996). Although he does not remark upon it, Reichheld's case studies come from service industries that are the employment-growth sectors of the U.S. economy: financial services, retail sales, insurance, and eating establishments.

60 Martha Groves, "In Tight Job Market, Software Firm Develops Programs to Keep Employees," *Los Angeles Times*, June 14, 1998, p. D-5; "Overworked and Overpaid," *Economist*, January 30, 1999, pp. 55–56.

61 "Can America's Workforce Grow Old Gracefully?" *Economist*, July 25, 1998, 59–60; U.S. Bureau of Labor Statistics, "Worker Displacement, 1995–1997," op. cit.

62 A study of managerial downsizing in British companies reaches similar conclusions. It finds "no evidence of the kind of transformational change associated with the introduction of a new model. Instead, we find that the traditional model of managerial employment has been eroded rather than replaced." Patrick McGovern, Veronica Hope-Hailey, and Philip Stiles, "The Managerial Career After Downsizing: Case Studies from the 'Leading Edge,'" *Work, Employment, & Society*, 13 (September 1998): 457.

63 Elizabeth Chambers, Mark Foulon, Helen Handfield-Jones, Steven Hankin, and Edward Michaels, "The War for Talent," *McKinsey Quarterly*, 3 (1998): 44–57.

64 Albert O. Hirschman, *The Rhetoric of Reaction* (Cambridge, MA: Belknap Press, 1991).

65 Morton Horwitz, *The Transformation of American Law, 1780–1860* (Cambridge, MA: Harvard University Press, 1979).
66 Steven K. Vogel, *Freer Markets, More Rules: Regulatory Reform in Advanced Industrial Countries* (Ithaca, NY: Cornell University Press, 1996).
67 Paul C. Weiler, *Governing the Workplace: The Future of Labor and Employment Law* (Cambridge, MA: Harvard University Press, 1990); Reicheld, op. cit., p. 182.
68 Alan Wolfe, *One Nation, After All* (New York, NY: Viking, 1998), p. 237.
69 Lawrence Mishel, Jared Bernstein, and John Schmitt, *The State of Working America, 1998–99* (Ithaca, NY: ILS Press, 1999), pp. 367–373.
70 Fallick, op. cit.; David R. Howell, "Institutional Failure and the American Worker: The Collapse of Low-Skill Wages," Jerome Levy Economics Institute, Bard College, Public Policy Brief no. 29, 1997. Cutting the tenure data at over ten, rather than over twenty years, does give college graduates an edge over high-school dropouts in the percentage holding long-term jobs. But this advantage also existed twenty years ago, before wage inequality had grown wide. Farber, "Trends in Long-Term Employment," op. cit., p. 29; Diebold, Neumark, and Polsky, op. cit., p. 223.

# 6

# VIOLATING THE PSYCHOLOGICAL CONTRACT

## Not the exception but the norm

*Sandra L. Robinson and Denise M. Rousseau*

Source: *Journal of Organizational Behavior* 15 (1994): 245–259.

## Summary

The occurrence and impact of psychological contract violations were studied among graduate management alumni ($N = 128$) who were surveyed twice, once at graduation (immediately following recruitment) and then two years later. Psychological contracts, reciprocal obligations in employment developed during and after recruitment, were reported by a majority of respondents (54.8 per cent) as having been violated by their employers. The impacts of violations are examined using both quantitative and qualitative data. Occurrence of violations correlated positively with turnover and negatively with trust, satisfaction and intentions to remain.

## Introduction

Contemporary employment relationships are in transition. The demise of employee loyalty and the need for employees to take care of themselves are touted as a sign of the times (Hirsch, 1989). A major issue in employment relationships is the psychological contracts which permeate them (Rousseau, 1989). As beliefs in reciprocal and promised obligations between employee and employer, psychological contracts can, when violated, generate distrust, dissatisfaction, and possibly the dissolution of the relationship itself (Argyris, 1960; Rousseau, 1989). Using both quantitative and qualitative data, this study explores such violations within work relationships and investigates the impact of violations on employee trust, satisfaction and retention.

## Psychological contracts

Contracts, defined as a set of promises committing one to future action (Farnsworth, 1982), are a necessary component of employment relationships. Without the promise of future exchange, neither party has incentive to contribute anything to the other and the relationship may not endure. Promises in and of themselves do not a contract make. Paid-for-promises made in exchange for some consideration are what typically constitute the contract. Considerations such as hard work, accepting training or transfers can be offered in exchange for promise, either implied or stated, of pay, promotion, growth or advancement. Together, the promise and the consideration exchanged for it form the contract.

Rousseau (1989) defines the psychological contract as an individual's belief regarding the terms and conditions of a reciprocal exchange agreement between that focal person and another party. A psychological contract emerges when one party believes that a promise of future return has been made (e.g. pay for performance), a contribution has been given (e.g. some form of exchange) and thus, an obligation has been created to provide future benefits.

Lest psychological contracts be construed as a boundless bundle of obligations subjectively held, we define the psychological contract as beliefs in paid-for-promises or reciprocal obligations. It is comprised of a belief that some form of a promise has been made and that the terms and conditions of the contract have been accepted by both parties.

Note that these are *beliefs or perceptions* regarding promises and acceptance. Each party believes that both parties have made promises and that both parties have accepted the same contract terms. However, this does not necessarily mean that both parties share a common *understanding* of all contract terms. Each party only believes that they share the same interpretation of the contract.

Psychological contracts are subjective, residing in the 'eyes of the beholder'. Although beliefs in mutual obligations comprise a contract, two parties need not agree for each to believe a contract exists. As described by one recent MBA, 'Commissions earned on clients were retroactively cut. When I complained, the company partially re-instated the commission and paid me for those in the first half of '89 ... I still think that is unfair. The company and I aren't playing by the same pay-out rules'.

Parties are thus likely to possess somewhat different and possibly unique beliefs about what each owes the other. These beliefs can arise from overt promises (e.g. bonus systems discussed in the recruitment process), interpretations of patterns of past exchange, vicarious learning (e.g. witnessing other employees' experiences) as well as through various factors that each party may take for granted (e.g. good faith or fairness, MacNeil, 1985).

The psychological contract is distinct from expectations. Expectations refer simply to what the employee expects to receive from his or her employer (Wanous, 1977). The psychological contract, on the other hand, refers to the perceived *mutual obligations* that characterize the employee's relationship with his/her employer. The psychological contract, unlike expectations, entails a belief in what the employer is obliged to provide, based on perceived promises of reciprocal exchange.

The psychological contract, unlike formal employment contracts, is not made once but rather it is revised throughout the employee's tenure in the organization (Rousseau and Parks, 1993). The longer the relationship endures and/or the more the two parties interact with repeated cycles of contribution and reciprocity, the broader the array of contributions and inducements that might be included in the contract (Rousseau, 1989). Events in the form of new job assignments, relocations, and organizational restructuring may overlay new terms upon old ones.

Empirical research on psychological contracts is recent. Using policy capturing methodologies, Rousseau and Anton (1988, 1991) examined the factors underlying beliefs in implicit employment contracts in samples of managers and human resource specialists. They found that employment itself is perceived as a promise (i.e. the implied contract of continued future employment) and that an employee's performance is perceived as a consideration (a way of paying for the promise).

Rousseau (1990), examining the emergence of psychological contracts in a survey of newly recruited MBAs, found that employees developed psychological contracts during the recruitment process. The content of that contract was related to what type of relationship the employee sought with the employer. Employees using their current job as a stepping stone to another emphasized as their contract short-term monetizable benefits in exchange for hard work. Those seeking a long-term relationship with their employer felt party to a contract exchanging job security for their loyalty.

Robinson, Kraatz and Rousseau (in press) examined how psychological contracts change over time. They found that during the first two years of employment, employees came to perceive that they owed less to their employer while their employers in turn owed them more.

If psychological contracts are widespread in employment, how often are these contracts violated? What happens when they are? The present study will attempt to provide answers using both quantitative and qualitative data. Although both employers and employees can experience a contract violation by the other party in the employment relationship, this study will focus only upon the employee's perception of psychological contract violation.

## Psychological contract violation and its impact

A violation occurs when one party in a relationship perceives another to have failed to fulfil promised obligation(s). Since contracts emerge under assumptions of good faith and fair dealing (MacNeil, 1985) and involve reliance by parties on the promises of the other, violations can lead to serious consequences for the parties involved.

Violation of the psychological contract is distinct from unmet expectations and perceptions of inequity. Employees initially hold unrealistic expectations and when these expectations go unmet, employees may become less satisfied, perform less well, and become more likely to leave their employer (see Wanous, Poland, Premack and Davis (1992) for a review). When a psychological contract is violated, the responses are likely to be more intense than in the case of 'unfulfilled expectations'. The intensity of the reaction is attributable not only to unmet expectations of specific rewards or benefits, but also to more general beliefs about respect for persons, codes of conduct, and other patterns of behavior associated with relationships (Rousseau, 1989). For example, a person may expect to be paid market wages in exchange for hard work and feel disappointed when not. A person *promised* market wages in exchange for hard work who *does not receive* them feels wronged. Broken promises produce anger and erode trust in the relationship and thus, are expected to have more significant repercussions than unmet expectations.

Expectancies are the perceived probabilities of outcomes resulting from employee behavior (e.g. the likelihood of reward (Mitchell, 1974). Beliefs in the equity or inequity of exchanges between an employee and employer need not involve promise though they do assume reciprocity and fairness (Pritchard, Dunnette and Jorgenson, 1972). When experience does not match expectancies or equity beliefs, employees are disappointed or dissatisfied (e.g. Mitchell, 1974; Pritchard *et al.*, 1972). But again, the experience of psychological contract violation, involving a breach of promise and trust, goes beyond disappointment and produces feelings of betrayal.

Violation of the psychological contract is related to procedural and distributive injustice (Sheppard, Lewicki and Minion, 1992). Justice researchers (e.g. Greenberg, 1990) differentiate between fair outcomes and fair processes. Unfulfilled promises deprive employees of desired outcomes, an issue of distributive or outcome fairness, often associated with perceptions of inequity. Violations also involve issues of procedural fairness, reflecting the quality of treatment employees experience (e.g. unbiased, consistent, honest). Failure to honor a contract creates a sense of wrongdoing, deception and betrayal with pervasive implications for the employment relationship (Rousseau, 1989).

Procedural justice can offset some of the consequences associated with otherwise negative or undesirable outcomes such as job loss or lower pay. Rousseau and Aquino (1993) have found that certain procedural justice mechanisms can reduce the sense of unfairness associated with terminating employees, such as giving advance notice of job loss. But these processes appear not to offset the employer's obligation to the employee unless they also provide some sort of remedy for the lost job (e.g. substantial severance). While justice researchers often report high intercorrelations between perceptions of processes and outcomes (Sheppard *et al.*, 1992), contracts research suggests that outcomes associated with an obligation or promise are not easily offset by just procedures.

Violations decrease trust. When rules of friendship are violated, trust and respect decline (Davis and Todd, 1985). Similarly, when an employer breaks a basic rule in work relationships, such as good faith and fair dealing, trust declines.

Gabarro and Athos (1976) identified a number of bases of trust within business relationships: beliefs regarding the other's integrity, motives and intentions, behavioral consistency, openness and discreteness. Each of these bases can be undermined through psychological contract violation. If the employer reneges on a promise, that employer's integrity is questioned. Trust may be also lost in the employer's motives because a violation signals that the employer's original motives to build and maintain a mutually beneficial relationship have changed or were false to begin with. Violations may also reduce the predictability of the employer's future actions. Hence, we hypothesize:

> H1: Psychological contract violation by the employer will be negatively associated with the employee's trust in the employer.

When employees encounter a contract violations, their satisfaction with both the job and the organization itself can decline for a variety of reasons. First, there is the discrepancy between what was expected and what was received — a major source dissatisfaction (e.g. Wanous, 1973). Second, what the employer promised but failed to provide may often be those aspects of one's work which are important sources for work satisfaction. It may become very difficult for an employee to be motivated to perform, and obtain satisfaction from, doing the job when the employee can no longer rely on the promised inducement (Porter and Lawler, 1968). As such, the following hypothesis is proposed:

> H2: Psychological contract violations by the employer will be negatively associated with both job satisfaction and organizational satisfaction.

Violation of a psychological contract undermines the very factors (e.g. trust) that led to emergence of a relationship. In the words of two recent recruits: 'After I talked to my boss on several occasions and told him I was frustrated that I was working long hours and not doing what had been promised, I began contemplating leaving this job' and 'I only stayed 3 months and quit. I had no respect for my boss or the organizations after they lied to me'.

The psychological contract binds the employee and employer — a form of guarantee that if each does his or her part, the relationship will be mutually beneficial. Hence, violations weaken the bond. The violated party loses faith in the benefits of staying in the relationship and is therefore, more likely to leave.

> H3a: Psychological contract violations by the employer will be negatively associated with the employee's intent to remain with the employer.
> H3b: Psychological contract violations by the employer will be positively associated with actual employee turnover.

Career planning is the process through which individuals identify and implement steps to attain career goals (Milkovich and Boudreau, 1988). The individual's career orientation reflects both the nature of his or her goals and the strategies used to attain them (Schein, 1978). At the outset of their post-graduate career, the management school graduates involved in this study are postulated to vary in terms or their intentions to pursue employment in a variety of organizations. Employees taking the view that carrer advancement will occur outside the current organization have goals different from those focusing upon careers within a firm and pursue different career strategies. We label this orientation 'careerism'.[1]

Psychological contract violations may have a different impact upon employees whose career motives differ. More specifically, employees who place greater emphasis on the employment relationship itself will be more negatively influenced by the violation than those who do not. Rousseau (1990) identified careerism as an important factor in determining a desired employment relationship. Individuals high on careerism perceive their current employer as an instrumental stepping-stone up the interorganizational career ladder and are likely to adopt a more 'transactional' employment relationship with their employer. This relationship is not intended to be long term and what is exchanged has a short term focus: what the employee values are the more immediate rewards of the relationship such as pay, training, and credentials to obtain a better job in another organization. This motivational pattern is frequently ascribed to MBAs and other young professionals (*Business Week*, 1988). In contrast, those low on careerism scale have a more 'relational orientation'. They believe their career path to be through a long-term relationship with their employer and value not only that which they gain from their employer in the short run but, also, the relationship itself.

Careerist individuals are expected to react to violations differently than those lower on this orientation. Careerists, who place less value on the relationship itself, should experience less loss from psychological contract violation than do those low on careerism.

> H4: Careerism will moderate the associations between violations and trust, satisfaction, intentions to remain and turnover. The more careerist the employee, the weaker will be the relationships between violations and trust in employer, satisfaction, intentions to remain and turnover.

## Method

### *Subjects*

This research extends upon an earlier study investigating psychological contracts formed during recruitment (Rousseau, 1990). The present study follows up the same population: the 1987 alumni of an MBA program in a midwestern U.S. management school. This group was comprised of 35 per cent females. Nine per cent of the sample were minorities. Ten per cent of the sample were foreign nationals. Their average age at graduation was 28. Ninety-two per cent of the sample had at least two years of work experience before entering graduate school. Upon graduation, the chosen industries of this class included: investment banking (17 per cent), food/beverage/tobacco (14 per cent), commercial banking (14 per cent), consulting (8 per cent), consumer products (8 per cent), accounting (6 per cent), computers (4 per cent), real estate (4 per cent), health (4 per cent), advertising (4 per cent), and other (17 per cent). The functional areas in which they were placed were as follows: investment banking (22 per cent), brand management (21 per cent), consulting (15 per cent), financial analysis (6 per cent), financial services (5 per cent), accounting executives (4 per cent), lending (3 per cent), and other (24 per cent). Their starting salaries, in 1987, ranged from $24 000 to $90 000 with a median of $43 500.

The 1987 questionnaire was distributed to 260 of the total 480 students in this class just three weeks prior to graduation. This subsample represented students who had, at the time, already accepted an offer of employment. A total of 224, or 86 per cent of those eligible to participate, responded to the first questionnaire.

In 1989, a second questionnaire was mailed to 448 of the total alumni class (those for whom the school alumni office had a contact address). A total of 215 (48 per cent) returned the completed questionnaire. Of those who had responded to the first questionnaire, 128 (59.5 per cent) responded to the second questionnaire.

Given the longitudinal nature of this study, only those subjects who completed both the first survey and the second survey were used in the quantitative analyses. Hence, the sample size was 128. There are two exceptions to this sample size. First, for analyses involving intentions to remain with one's employer (at time 2), only those employees who filled out both questionnaires, and who were still with their first employer ($n = 96$) were included. Second, for the qualitative analyses of the nature of psychological contract violations, responses of all employees who answered the relevant questions on the second questionnaire ($n = 209$) were used.

## *Instruments*

Both questionnaires assessed respondents' perceptions of their employer, the employment relationship and the mutual obligations they and their employer had to one another. The 1987 questionnaire assessed employees' perceptions that developed *during recruitment* whereas the later questionnaire examined perceptions *after two years on the job*. For the sake of consistency and common frame of reference, the second questionnaire asked respondents to answer with regard to their *first* employer (some could be expected to have changed employers since graduation). Each of the following scales was developed for this study. Items on each scale were randomly ordered through the questionnaire. Scales were subjected to a principal factor analysis with varimax rotation which supported the independence of the factors underlying these scales. Factor analyses, available from the authors, provided evidence of the unidimensionality of each scale based upon examination of the factor loadings and eigenvalues. The means, standard deviations and reliabilities (Cronbach alphas) of these scales are presented in Table 1.

Table 1 Descriptive statistics and intercorrelations of all variables

|  | Mean | S.D. | Reliability* | 1. | 2. | 3. | 4. | 5. | 6. | 7. | 8. |
|---|---|---|---|---|---|---|---|---|---|---|---|
| 1. Violations (cont.) | 2.62 | 1.08 | n/a |  |  |  |  |  |  |  |  |
| 2. Violations (dich.) | n/a | n/a | n/a | 0.53†,‡ |  |  |  |  |  |  |  |
| 3. Trust | 27.03 | 7.40 | 0.93 | −0.79‡ | −0.42‡ |  |  |  |  |  |  |
| 4. Satisfaction | 10.90 | 3.82 | 0.92 | −0.76‡ | −0.46‡ | 0.69‡ |  |  |  |  |  |
| 5. Intentions (T1) | 3.81 | 1.24 | n/a | −0.13 | −0.12 | 0.23‡ | 0.22§ |  |  |  |  |
| 6. Intentions (T2) | 3.72 | 3.02 | n/a | −0.42‡ | −0.30‡ | 0.39‡ | 0.43‡ | 0.25§ |  |  |  |
| 7. Careerism (T1) | 15.56 | 3.92 | 0.78 | 0.12 | −0.01 | −0.23‡ | −0.20‡ | −0.58‡ | −0.32‡ |  |  |
| 8. Careerism (T2) | 15.59 | 4.07 | 0.78 | 0.17 | 0.10 | −0.24‡ | −0.31‡ | −0.39‡ | −0.60‡ | 0.52‡ |  |
| 9. Turnover | n/a | n/a | n/a | 0.32‡ | 0.24‡ | −0.18§ | −0.41‡ | −0.13 | n/a | 0.08 | 0.06 |

*Reliability entries represent Cronbach Alpha coefficients.
†Entries in matrix represent Pearson product moment correlations.
‡$p < 0.01$
§$p < 0.05$;
$N = 128$ ($n = 96$ for correlations involving intent T2).

### Careerism orientation

Measured both at recruitment and two years later, this scale assesses an employee's orientation toward his or her employer as an instrumental stepping stone up the career path. A 1 to 5 scale was used where 1 = strongly disagree and 5 = strongly agree. Responses were coded such that a high score would indicate high careerism.

> I took this job as a stepping stone to a better job with another organization.
> I expect to work for a variety of different organizations in my career.
> I do not expect to change organizations often during my career (reverse score).
> There are many career opportunities, I expect to explore after I leave my present employer.
> I am really looking for an organization to spend my entire career with (reverse score).

### Trust

Measured after the respondent joined the firm, this scale assessed the employee's degree of trust in his or her employer. A 1 to 5 scale was used, where 1 = strongly disagree, and 5 = strongly agree. Responses were coded such that a high score would indicate a high degree of trust in one's employer. The items were derived from the bases of trust identified by Gabarro and Athos (1976).

> I am not sure I fully trust my employer (reverse score).
> My employer is open and upfront with me.
> I believe my employer has high integrity.
> In general, I believe my employer's motives and intentions are good.
> My employer is not always honest and truthful (reverse score).
> I don't think my employer treats me fairly (reverse score).
> I can expect my employer to treat me in consistent and predictable fashion.

### Satisfaction

Employee satisfaction, with both work and organization, was assessed on the second questionnaire with the following items. Again, a 1 to 5 was used, where 1 = strongly disagree, and 5 = strongly agree. Items included:

> Working for this organization is very satisfying to me.
> I am satisfied with my job.

Also, to assess satisfaction with one's work situation, the GM Faces Scale was used (Kunin, 1955). Due to high intercorrelations these items were combined, yielding an internal consistency reliability of 0.92.

## Psychological contract violation

Violation of psychological contracts were assessed in two ways at time 2. The first was a continuous variable assessing contract fulfilment. Respondents were given a 5-point scale where 1 = 'very poorly fulfilled' and 5 = 'very well fulfilled' and the following instructions 'Using the scale below, please indicate how well, overall, your *first* employer has fulfilled the promised obligations that they *owed you*: (circle one number)'. This variable was reverse scored to provide a measure of contract violation. The test retest reliability of this measure, across a two-week period, is 0.78, suggesting moderate stability over time.

The second measure of violation was a dichotomous measure. Respondents were asked to answer yes of no to the question. 'Has or had your employer ever failed to meet the obligation(s) that were promised to you?' This measure was dummy coded (0 = experienced no violation; 1 = experienced violation). Respondents were then asked 'If yes, please explain ...' This gave respondents an opportunity to describe in detail what part of the contract was violated and how it occurred.

Use of the fulfilment/violation continuum permits us to examine the scope of contract completion while the violation dichotomy obtains the respondent's point of view as to whether the contract was actually violated. Though the measures are moderately intercorrelated ($r = 0.53$, $p \leqslant 0.01$), considering them separately improves our understanding of how contract violation is construed and where violation thresholds may be crossed in the employment relationship. Measures were cross-tabulated. Of those employees who reported that no violation bad occurred on the dichotomous measure of contract violation, 28.2 per cent reported being only 'somewhat fulfilled' on the fulfilment continuum. This suggests that degrees of fulfilment exist even when a contract is not considered broken. Moreover, of those employees who reported that their employer had violated their contract on the dichotomous measure, 22 per cent reported their employer had at least 'somewhat fulfilled' the terms of the agreement. In other words, some people with violated contracts reported a significant degree (moderate to high) of fulfilment. Perhaps quick resolution of a specific violation of the contract leads employees to perceive overall fulfilment despite an isolated violation.

## Remaining with one's employer

*Intentions to remain with one's employer* and actual *turnover* were both measured. On the first and second questionnaire, respondents were asked 'How long do you intend to remain with your current employer?' (in terms of years). On the second questionnaire, this intentions question was analyzed using only those subjects who had not yet left their first employer.

Actual turnover was also measured on the second questionnaire by asking respondents how many employers they had worked for since graduation. This information was dummy coded (0 = still with employer; 1 = had left first employer).

Of the 128 respondents, 32 (25 per cent) reported that they had left their first employer.

## Results

A majority of respondents (54.8 per cent), reported that their employer had, at some time, violated their psychological contract. The continuous measure of violation yielded a mean response score of 2.62 with a standard deviation of 1.08, indicating that the average employee reported some failure in contract fulfilment.

As predicted by hypothesis 1, employee trust was negatively related to the continuous measure of violation ($r = -0.79, p < 0.01$) as well as the dichotomous measure of violations ($r = -0.42, p < 0.01$). Hence, hypothesis 1 was supported (see Table 1 for zero-order correlations). Employee satisfaction was also found to be negatively related to both the continuous and dichotomous measure of violations ($r = -0.76, p < 0.01; r = -0.46, p < 0.01$). This supports hypothesis 2.

To test hypotheses 3 to 5, a series of hierarchical regressions were performed (Table 2). Hypothesis 3a predicted that violations would be negatively related to intentions to remain with one's employer. When intention to remain with one's employer (time 2) was regressed on contract violations by the employer (continuous measure) and initial intention to remain with one's employer (time 1), hypothesis 3a was supported. Controlling for *initial* intentions, contract violations significantly profile current intentions to remain with one's employer [$beta = -0.41, p < 0.01; F(2, 87) = 12.76, p < 0.01$; adjusted $R^2 = 0.21$], explaining approximately 16 per cent of the unique variance.

Hypothesis 3b predicted that violations would be positively related to actual turnover. To test the relationship between turnover and employer violations, a logistic regression was performed. When turnover was regressed on violations (continuous measure) and initial intentions to remain with one's employer, violations were found to be positively associated with turnover (beta $0.36, p < 0.01$). Furthermore, a $t$-test indicated that those who left had initially intended to remain with their employer (mean $= 3.62$) for as long as those who had not left (mean $= 3.93, r = -1.22$, n.s.). However, those who had actually left their employer had experienced a greater degree of contract violation by their employer (continuous measure) (mean $= 3.21$), than those who had not left their employer (mean $= 2.40, t = 4.99, p < 0.01$). Hence, hypothesis 3b is supported.

Similarly, when the dichotomous violation measure was cross-tabulated with the turnover measure, it was found that 48 per cent of those who remained with their employer had experienced violation whereas 76 per cent of those who had left their employer had experienced a violation. Although there is a relationship as predicted between violation and turnover, it is interesting to note that cases do occur 'off quadrant' (24 per cent of leavers had not experienced violation and 52 per cent of stayers had experienced violation). Most significant is the latter percentage suggesting that employment relations may be eroded without an obvious impact on attrition.

Table 2 Regressions of predictors on violation and careerism

|  |  | Beta | Adjusted $R^2$ | F |
|---|---|---|---|---|
| H3a: predicting intentions(T2) |  |  |  |  |
| Step 1: | Intentions (T1) | 0.22*,† (0.22*)‡ | 0.05 | 6.02¶ |
| Step 2: | Violations§ | −0.41¶ | 0.21 | 12.76¶ |
| H3b: predicting turnover (logistic regression) |  |  |  |  |
|  |  |  | Coeff/S.E. |  |
| Step 1: | Intentions T1 | −0.10 (−0.08) | −1.19 (−0.90) |  |
| Step 2: | Violations | 0.36¶ | 3.26 |  |
| H4: predicting careerisms as moderator of violation outcome relationships |  |  |  |  |
| Predictor: trust |  |  | Adjusted $R^2$ |  |
| Step 1: | Careerism T1 | −0.10 (−0.09) | 0.63 | 70.01§ |
|  | Careerism T2 | −0.05 (−0.04) |  |  |
|  | Violations | −0.76§(−0.79§) |  |  |
| Step 2: | Car T1 × Viol | 0.11* | 0.64 | 54.67§ |
| Predictors; satisfaction |  |  |  |  |
| Step 1: | Careerism T1 | 0.00 (0.00) | 0.60 | 63.08§ |
|  | Careerism T2 | −0.18¶(0.18‡) |  |  |
|  | Violations | −0.73¶(−0.74‡) |  |  |
| Step 2: | Car T1 × Viol | 0.07 | 0.60 | 47.82‡ |
| Predictor: intentions |  |  |  |  |
| Step 1: | Careerism T1 | −0.03 (−0.01) | 0.40 | 21.39§ |
|  | Careerism T2 | −0.50¶(−0.48*) |  |  |
|  | Violations | −0.29¶(−0.30†) |  |  |
| Step 2: | Car T1 × Viol | 0.10 | 0.41 | 16.43§ |

*$p < 0.05$.
†Entries represent standardized beta coefficients.
‡Entries in parentheses represent standardized beta coefficients in step 2.
§The continuous violations measure was used in all of the regression equations.
¶$p < 0.01$.

Hypothesis 4 predicted that careerism would moderate the relationship between violations and trust, satisfaction, intentions to remain with the employer and turnover. To test this hypothesis, a series of hierarchical regressions were performed, one for each predictor. In the first steps, violations (the continuous measure), careerism at time 1 and careerism at time 2 were regressed on the predictor. In the second steps, the interaction term (violation × careerism) was added to the equation. To reduce the common problem of multicollinearity in moderated regression equations, all of the independent variables were centered prior to entering them into the equation (Aiken and West, 1991). Hypothesis 4 was only partially supported. In the moderated regression equation of trust on violation, the interaction term was significant (beta $= 0.11, p < 0.05$), suggesting that the more careerist the employee, the stronger the negative relationship between contract violation and trust in one's employer [$F(4, 119) = 54.67$, $p < 0.01$. Adjusted $R^2 = 0.64$]. However, careerism did not moderate the relationship between contract violations and the other variables (although in all cases it was in the predicted direction).

### *Qualitative responses*

Responses to the open-ended questions suggest some ways in which psychological contract violations are experienced by employees. A total of 209 out of 215 employees who participated in the second questionnaire answered the following question: 'Has or had your employer ever failed to meet the obligation(s) that were promised you?' One hundred and twenty-three responded affirmatively and when asked to explain, most respondents described an experience (often several) of violation by their employer. Two coders categorized the response into categories. The first coder grouped them such that representative categories developed. Using the category names and definitions developed by the first coder, second coder also coded the responses. The interrater reliability was very high, with kappas ranging from 95 per cent to 100 per cent for each category. This coding scheme yielded 10 distinct categories of violations. Among the more frequently mentioned of these were training and compensation. These categories of violations and their degree of frequency are outlined in Table 3.

The qualitative data reveal that violations occur in almost every area related to human resource management with training, development, compensation, and promotion being the most frequently mentioned. The examples respondents provided evince general terms in which promises are often expressed and/or encoded. Terms such as 'good chance of promotion' and 'greater responsibility' suggest that promises may be subjectively expressed as well as subjectively interpreted. Mutuality may be inferred where it did not exist.

Analysis of open-ended responses also indicated that many of the individuals reporting a violation also took steps to remedy the situation. *Post hoc* analyses of remediated violations indicates that recruits who successfully challenged the violation (usually by bringing it to a boss's attention) were more likely to report higher levels of contract fulfilment than did those whose violations went unremediated.

## Discussion

Psychological contracts are frequently violated. Many recently recruited alumni could provide a detailed account of a particularly significant incident of violation. One could argue that for MBA alumni the frequency of violation may be unusually high. Upon graduation (in 1987), these management school graduates were in great demand and heavily recruited. Employers may have been inclined to make promises that they later could not keep, to lure these graduates into the firm. The motivation of recruiters to provide accurate information is quite low in general (Porter, Lawler and Hackman, 1975) and hence, this group was especially unlikely

*Table 3* Types of violations

| Violation type | Definition | Freq | Examples |
| --- | --- | --- | --- |
| Training/ development | Absence of training or training experience not as promised | 65 | 'Sales training was promised as an integral part of marketing training. It never materialized' |
| Compensation | Discrepancies between promised and realized pay, benefits, bonuses | 61 | 'Specific compensation benefits were promised and were either not given to me, or I had to fight for them' |
| Promotion | Promotion or advancement schedule not as promised | 59 | 'I perceived a promise that I had a good chance of promotion to manager in one year. While I received excellent performance ratings, I was not promoted in my first year' |
| Nature of job | Employer perceived as having misrepresented the nature of the department or the job | 40 | '(My) employer promised I would be working on venture capital projects. I was mainly writing speeches for the CEO' |
| Job security | Promises regarding degree of job security one could expect were not met | 37 | 'The company promised that no one would be fired out of the training program—that all of us were "safe" until placement (in return for this security we accepted lower pay). The company subsequently fired four people from the training program' |
| Feedback | Feedback and reviews inadequate compared to what was promised | 35 | '... (I did) not receive performance reviews as promised' |
| Management of change | Employees not asked for input or given notice of changes as they were promised | 29 | I was promised more knowledge and control over my future' |
| Responsibility | Employees given less responsibility and/or challenge than promised | 27 | '(I was) promised greater responsibility. More strategic thinking/ decision making'. |
| People | Employer perceived as having misrepresented the type of people at the firm, in terms of things such as their expertise, work style or reputation | 25 | 'I was promised as dynamic and as having challenging environment ... rubbing elbows with some of the brightest people in the business ... a big lie. The true picture started to come out ... after the initial hype ... of working at one of the best 100 companies in the US had worn off' |
| Other | Perceived promises not fulfilled by the employer not fit into above categories | 26 | Original representations of the company's financial and market that do strength became clearly fraudulent' |

to receive 'realistic job previews' (Wanous, 1977) during recruitment. Overselling a job's features can be compounded with subjective interpretation of what the promised 'great' job actually entails.

Psychological contract violations were negatively associated with satisfaction, trust and employees' intentions to remain with their employer and positively associated with actual turnover. Even after controlling for the amount of time the employee had originally intended to stay, violations accounted for approximately 16 per cent of the variance in the length of time an employee intended to stay with the employer at time 2. Violations were also positively associated with actual turnover.

The strong relationship found between violations and trust is particularly significant given that trust is crucial to organizational effectiveness (Golembiewski and McConkie, 1975). Trust has a 'spiral reinforcement' quality such that a decline in trust often leads to further decline in trust. A lack of trust associated with a decrease in the quantity and quality of communication (O'Reilly and Roberts, 1976), and cooperation (Deutsch, 1973), which in turn, may reduce subsequent trust. A lack of trust has also been associated with a decline in effective problem solving (Boss, 1978) and performance (Zand, 1972).

The fact that careerism moderated the relationship between violations and trust suggests that the employees whose trust was most affected by violation were those planning to build a career with their employer; employees whose trust the firm should value most. This interaction effect is consistent with a phenomenon reported by Brockner, Tyler and Cooper-Schneider (1992): people with higher than average faith in the judicial system had *far more* negative reactions to losing in court than those with lower expectations. Brockner *et al.* labelled this phenomenon 'the higher they are, the harder they fall'.

Although careerism moderated the relationship between violations and trust, it did not make a difference for the relationships between violations and satisfaction, intentions to remain with one's employer or actual turnover. These findings suggest that the experience of violation may have the same strong, negative impact on both employees who plan a long-term relationship with their employer and those who see their employer as a mere stepping stone.

Violations and unmet expectations, though conceptually related, function differently. Reported relationships between violation and reactions are much stronger than those typically found between unmet expectations and similar outcomes. Wanous *et al.* (1992), in their meta-analysis of the effect of met expectations on newcomer attitudes and behavior, concluded the correlations (and confidence intervals) between unmet expectations and job dissatisfaction, intentions to leave and turnover to be 0.39 (−0.05 − 0.60), 0.29 (0.07 − 0.40) and 0.13 (−0.03 − 0.27), respectively. By comparison, we report correlations between violations and satisfaction, intentions to stay (the inverse of intentions to leave), and turnover to be 0.76, −0.49 and 0.29. These comparisons suggest that violations, in comparison to unmet expectations, more strongly impact satisfaction, intentions to quit and turnover.

Out focus upon psychological contracts as beliefs in the existence of 'paid-for-promises' is predicated on the distinction between such beliefs and other types of expectations that employees hold regarding the conditions of their employment (*cf.* Wanous, 1977). Psychological contracts clearly are expectations, although ones originating from the individual's belief in a promise, stated or implied, that he or she has been offered in exchange for his or her contributions to the organizations. As a paid-for-promise, a psychological contract differs substantially from other expectations. Most expectations when unmet lead to a sense of disappointment. Employees whose contracts are violated feel wronged (Rousseau, 1989; Rousseau and Parks, 1993). The present study adds to the literature on employment expectations by assessing beliefs that are promissory, reciprocal, and operate in a context which can for some be more a relationship than a transaction.

This study focused solely on MBA graduates and hence, care must be taken when generalizing these results to other employee populations. As noted above, MBA graduates may experience more violation because of the overzealous efforts of recruiters. Second, MBA graduates' reactions to violations may be different from other employees. Given their marketability and relatively short tenure with their employer, these MBA graduates may be more likely to resign after experiencing violation than their less mobile counterparts. Nevertheless, we would expect that most employees, not only MBA graduates, would experience similar feelings of dissatisfaction, distrust and desire to quit following violations by their employer.

Several other limitations of this study should be noted. First, given the design of our study, those 32 respondents who had left their first employer had to rely on recall data for the measure of violation, trust and satisfaction. Recall data is subject to error and hence, it may have somewhat confounded our results. Second, this study would have benefited from better measures of contract violations. Our violations measures did not explicitly incorporate the notion of reciprocity which is central to our definition of psychological contracts. Further, our use of single-item measures to assess violations, as well as intentions to remain with one's employer, is potentially problematic. While our test–retest analysis demonstrated temporal stability of the continuous violation measure, we could not assess the internal reliability of any of our single-item measures. Multiple-item measures tend to be both more valid and reliable (Rushton, Brainerd and Pressley, 1983) and hence, would have been more likely to produce stronger results than those reported here.

Given the design of this study, we cannot confirm the direction of causality. For example, it is unreasonable to assume that the relationship between violations and trust is nonrecursive; that is, violation reduces trust but a decline in trust also increases the likelihood of perceiving violation. Future research on violations should incorporate designs which can better address this issue of causality. Nevertheless, the vividness of the violations reported suggests their salience to employees and potential impact on employment relations.

This study suggests a number of potential avenues for future research on psychological contracts. While this study has focused solely on employer violation of the employment contract, future research should also attend to employee violation of the contract. While considerable research has addressed employee behavior that goes beyond the contract, in terms of 'extra-role' behavior and organizational citizenship behavior (e.g. Organ, 1988, 1990), more attention should be given to employee breaches of contract behavior (Robinson and Bennett, 1993). Another direction for future research is to examine how both employees and employers seek to remedy or resolve violations to their pyschological contracts. Research that has explored employees' reactions to dissatisfaction—such as exit, voice and loyalty—might be a useful starting point for addressing this question (Hirschman, 1970; Robinson, 1993).

Although this study focused or breach of the psychological contract, it also says something about successful employment relationships. First, firms do tend to retain recruits who feel fairly treated. Moreover, the qualitative data suggests that managers who promote open two-way communication may be able to nip in the bud discrepancies in employer commitments and employee experiences. Further, recruits who expect a more transactional employment relationship (e.g. short-run, monetizable) have a less averse reaction to violations. Managing expectations more explicitly (and realistically) could lead to a more trusting employee–employer relationship. A challenge for contemporary management, facing economic and organizational changes, is to keep changes in employment conditions from becoming violations.

## Acknowledgments

We thank Jenny Chatman, Maggie Neale, and Pri Pradhan for their helpful comments on earlier drafts of this paper. This research was supported by a Kellogg Graduate School of Management research grant.

## Note

1 Careerism is distinct from Gouldner's (1958) 'cosmopolitans versus locals' typology. The cosmopolitan/local typology refers to latent social identities; how others perceive and classify organizational members in terms of their orientation to either the organization or a profession.

## References

Aiken, L. S. and West, S. G. (1991). *Multiple Regression: Testing and Interpreting Interactions*, Sage, Newbury Park, CA.

Argyris, C. (1960). *Understanding organizational Behavior*. Dorsey, Homewood, IL.

Boss, R. W. (1978). 'The effect of leader absence on a confrontation-team building design', *Journal of Applied Behavioral Science*, **14**(4), 469–478.

Brockner, J., Tyler, T. R. and Cooper-Schneider, R. (1992). 'The influence of prior commitment to an institution on reaction to perceived unfairness: The higher they are the harder they fall', *Administrative Science Quarterly*, **37**, 241–261.

Davis, K. and Todd, M. (1985). 'Friendship and love', In K. E. Davis and T. O. Mitchell (Eds) *Advances in Descriptive Psychology*, Vol. 2, JAI Press.

Deutsch, M. (1973). *The Resolution of Conflict*. Yale University Press, New Haven, Conn.

Farnsworth, E. A. (1982). *Contracts*, Little Brown, Boston.

Gabarro, J. J. and Athos, J. (1976). *Interpersonal Relations and Communications*, Prentice Hall, New York.

Golembiewski, R. T. and McConkie, M. L. (1975). 'The centrality of interpersonal trust in group processes'. In: Cooper, C. L. (Ed.) *Theories of Group Processes*, John Wiley, New York.

Gouldner, A. W. (1958). 'Cosmopolitans and locals: Toward an analysis of latent social roles — 1', *Administrative Science Quarterly*, **2**, 281–306.

Greenberg, J. (1990). 'Looking fair versus being fair: Managing impressions of organizational justice'. In: Staw, B. M. and Cummings, L. L. (Eds) *Research in Organizational Behavior*, Vol. 12, JAI Press, Greenwich, CT, pp. 111–157.

Hirsch, P. (1989). *Pack Your Own Parachute*, Addison-Wesley, Boston.

Hirschman, A. (1970). *Exit, Voice and Loyalty*, Harvard University Press, Cambridge, MA.

Kunin, T. (1955). 'The construction of a new type of attitude measure', *Personnel Psychology*, **8**, 65–78.

MacNeil, L. R. (1985). 'Relational contract: What we do and do not know', *Wisconsin Law Review*, 483–525.

Milkovich, G. T. and Boudreau, J. W. (1988). *Personnel–Human Resource Management*, BPI, Plano, TX.

Mitchell, T. R. (1974). 'Expectancy models of job satisfaction, occupational preferences and effort: A theoretical, methodological and empirical appraisal', *Psychological Bulletin*, **81**, 1053–1077.

Organ, D. W. (1988). *Organizational Citizenship Behavior*, Lexington, Lexington, MA.

Organ, D. W. (1990). 'The motivational basis of organizational citizenship behavior', B. M. Staw and L. L. Cummings (Eds) *Research in Organizational Behavior*, **12**, JAI Press, Greenwich, CT, 43–72.

O'Reilly, C. and Roberts, K. (1976). 'Relationships among components of credibility and communication behaviors in work units', *Journal of Applied Psychology*, **61**, 99–102.

Porter, L. W. and Lawler, E. E. (1968). *Managerial Attitudes and Performance*, Irwin, Homewood, IL.

Porter, L. W., Lawler, E. E. and Hackman, J. R. (1975). *Behavior in Organizations*, McGraw-Hill, New York.

Pritchard, R. D., Dunnette, M. D. and Jorgenson, D. O. (1972). 'Effects of perceptions of equity and inequity on worker performance and satisfaction', *Journal of Applied Psychology*, **56**, 75–94.

Robinson, S. L. (1993). 'Retreat, voice, silence and destruction: A typology of employees' behavioral responses to dissatisfaction'. Proceedings of the Annual Meeting of the Administrative Science Association of Canada, Lake Louise, Alberta.

Robison, S. L. and Bennett, R. J. (1993). 'The four P's of destruction: A multi-dimensional scaling study of deviance in the workplace'. Presented at the Academy of Management Meeting, Atlanta.

Robison, S. L., Kraatz, M. S. and Rousseau, D. M. (in press). 'Changing obligations and the psychological contract: A longitudinal study', *Academy of management Journal*.

Rousseau, D. M. (1989). 'Psychological and implied contracts in organizations', *Employee Responsibilities and Rights Journal*, **2**, 121–139.

Rousseau, D. M. (1990). 'New hire perceptions of their own and their employer's obligations: A study of psychological contracts', *Journal of Organizational Behavior*, **11**, 389–400.

Rousseau, D. M. and Anton, R. J. (1988). 'Fairness and implied contract obligations in termination: A policy capturing study', *Human Performance*, **1**, 273–289.

Rousseau, D. M. and Anton, R. J. (1991). 'Fairness and implied contract obligations in job terminations: The role of contributions, promises and performance', *Journal of Organizational Behavior*, **12**, 287–299.

Rousseau, D. M. and Aquino, K. (1993). 'Fairness and implied contract obligations in job terminations: The role of remedies, social accounts, and procedural justice', *Human Performance*, **6**, 135–149.

Rousseau, D. M. and Parks, J. M. (1993). 'The contracts of individuals and organizations'. In: Cummings, L. L. and Staw, B. M. (Eds) *Research in Organizational Behavior*, Vol 15. JAI Press, Greenwich, CT, pp. 1–43.

Rushton, J. P., Brainerd, C. J. and Pressley, M. (1983). 'Behavioral development and construct validity: The principle of aggregation', *Psychological Bulletin*, **94**, 18–38.

Schein, E. H. (1978). *Career Dynamics: Matching Individuals and Organizational Needs*, Addison-Wesley, Reading, Mass.

Sheppard, B. H., Lewicki, R. J. and Minton, J. W. (1992). *Organizational Justice*, Lexington, New York.

Wanous, J. P. (1973). 'Effects of a realistic job preview on job acceptance, job attitudes, and job survival', *Journal of Applied Psychology*, **58**, 327–332.

Wanous J. P. (1977). 'Organizational entry: Newcomers moving from outside to inside', *Psychological Bulletin*, **84**, 601–618.

Wanous, J. P., Poland, T. D., Premack, S. L. and Davis, K. S. (1992). 'The effects of met expectations on newcomer attitudes and behaviors: A review and meta-analysis', *Journal of Applied Psychology*, **77**, 288–297.

Zand, D. (1972). 'Trust and managerial problem solving', *Administrative Science Quarterly*, **17**, 229–239.

# 7

# IS THE PSYCHOLOGICAL CONTRACT WORTH TAKING SERIOUSLY?

*David E. Guest*

Source: *Journal of Organizational Behavior* 19 (1998): 649–664.

### Summary

Although the psychological contract has become the focus for a body of research, it retains a number of conceptual and empirical problems and challenges. This paper reviews some of the main problems associated with the construct and with the way in which it has been studied. It also considers critically the 'problem' of the psychological contract, namely that organizations are either no longer able to promise the traditional organizational career and job security or they violate their promises, and suggests that the novelty of this problem has been overstated. Finally, it sets out a case for retaining the psychological contract as a focus for policy and research and presents an embryonic theory built around the causes, content and consequences of the psychological contract which implies a rather different research agenda to that which has dominated the debates so far.

### Introduction

In a world of rapid organizational change and loss of confidence in some of the traditional certainties of organizational life, the psychological contract appears to provide a useful integrative concept around which to focus an emerging set of concerns. Indeed, in what has been described as an emerging 'contract culture', the psychological contract neatly captures the spirit of the times. Although the term was first used by Argyris in 1960 and then, rather differently, by Levinson in 1962, it is only in the past ten years that it has emerged as a serious topic for conceptual and empirical analysis. Its appeal in this respect is reflected in the growing body of research and writing, of which the papers in this special issue are just one illustration. At the same time, in capturing the popular imagination, and emerging into common usage, the concept risks becoming diffuse, losing analytic rigour and being devalued as a powerful explanatory concept. The aim of this paper therefore is to put the concept under the spotlight, to determine how well it stands up to critical scrutiny and to outline some of the steps that might be taken to ensure that it retains its value.

## How should we evaluate the psychological contract?

The psychological contract fits somewhat awkwardly within conventional psychological analysis. It is not a theory; nor is it a measure. Rather it is a hypothetical construct, drawn, probably inappropriately, from a legal metaphor. If we wish to develop the construct to the point where it can be systematically researched and evaluated, there appear to be three main choices. The first is to build a theory about the psychological contract; the second is to focus on what could be viewed as a sub-component of theory-building by constructing precise descriptive operationalizations and appropriate measures; and the third is to accept that it is a middle-level construct, a framework around which to focus policy and practice as well as broader research questions on topics such as careers and job insecurity, and to assess its utility in this light. Of course, these choices are not mutually exclusive, but they can be considered as preferred emphases.

This problem is not a new one in organizational psychology. Concepts such as commitment and job satisfaction have a somewhat similar status. However these are clearly perceptual and can be accessed through individual subjective perceptions. In psychology more generally, concepts such as intelligence, personality and motivation can be developed at a theoretical level, operationalized in terms of measures and judged for utility in terms of their explanatory and operational value. The psychological contract is of a different order. It is concerned with the interaction between one specific and another nebulous party. The contract resides in the interaction rather than in the individual or the organization. In this respect it possibly parallels concepts such as communication, flexibility and quality in that it cannot be found exclusively either in the subject or the object of the interaction. This difficulty with respect to quality was the one explored so memorably by Pirsig in *Zen and the Art of Motor Cycle Maintenance*. Yet the psychological contract is even more complex, given that there are at least two parties, each of whom may have their own agenda and each of whom may not be aware of the agenda of the other party. The result is an analytic nightmare.

How then are we to proceed to evaluate the concept? At present there is no more than embryonic theory about the psychological contract although there is emerging theory about the contracting process (Herriot and Pemberton, 1996). We will therefore start by examining the existing conceptualizations and operationalizations of the concept. First we look at definitions of the psychological contract and the issues these raise. Secondly we treat it *as if* it were theory and apply some of the conventional tests of validity, parsimony, independence and testability. We then move on to consider the utility of the construct by examining how far it is able to provide distinctive new insights into the 'problem' of the psychological contract. Emerging from this will be a broader view of the utility of the concept and an agenda for seeking to ensure its utility in the future.

## Conceptual and operational concerns about the psychological contract

### What is the psychological contract?

We run into problems as soon as we start to examine definitions of the psychological contract. This is illustrated by comparing some of the better-known definitions.

> 'A set of *unwritten reciprocal expectations* between an individual employee and the organization' (Schein, 1978).

> 'An *implicit* contract between an individual and his organization which specifies what each *expect* to give and receive from each other in their relationship' (Kotter, 1973).

> 'The *perceptions* of both parties to the employment relationship, organization and individual, of the *obligations* implied in the relationship. Psychological contracting is the process whereby these perceptions are arrived at' (Herriot and Pemberton, 1995).

> 'An individual's *belief* regarding the terms and conditions of a reciprocal exchange agreement between the focal person and another party. A psychological contract emerges when one party believes that a *promise* of future returns has been made, a contribution has been given and thus, an *obligation* has been created to provide future benefits' (Rousseau, 1989).

The first problem that emerges from a comparison of these definitions, focusing on the words that are emphasized, is that the psychological contract may be about perceptions, expectations, beliefs, promises and obligations. As Conway (1996) has observed, more particularly in comparing expectations, promises and obligations, these imply different levels of psychological engagement. Failure to meet expectations is of a rather different order than failure to meet obligations. It is therefore important to be clear about which is contained within the psychological contract. One response might be to claim that it includes all of them; but then we run into problems of parsimony. Rousseau, as her definition implies, is quite clear that the psychological contract is concerned with the 'stronger' promises and obligations rather than expectations. However, it is likely that promises lead to related and therefore relevant expectations. Furthermore, as Conway (1996) notes, in a contractual context it is only exchange-based promises that are relevant and, given their often implicit nature, the relevant promises may be hard to identify. If we follow Rousseau (1989, 1995) in seeking to distinguish promissory from implied contracts, then the promissory contract, which for Rousseau is the psychological contract, may get very close to the conventional employment contract, particularly for newcomers to an organization, and far removed from the spirit of the earlier definitions. We are therefore left with something of a conceptual muddle about whether to accept this restricted definition and an operational problem of how to distinguish promissory from implied contracts.

### *Who has a psychological contract and when does it develop?*

Arnold (1996) raises the question of whether everyone in employment has a psychological contract. As we know, all employment contracts have gaps in them. The socialization process for any newcomer to the organization and the social information processing that occurs, results in assumptions about appropriate behaviour and expectations about the consequences of conforming or transgressing which go beyond the content of the formal employment contract. Is this a psychological contract? And if so, does it embrace any perceptions and beliefs drawn from the informal social system and interaction between the employee and anyone in a position of authority? If so, it is surely too broad to be useful. To return to Arnold's point, must there be an awareness of promises?

While it is possible to acknowledge that with longer service the psychological contract is likely to become broader and deeper, there remains the conceptual problem of establishing at what point in a relationship between an individual and an organization a psychological contract can be said to exist. The literature on organizational identification even raises the question of whether, at least from an individual perspective, a formal employment relationship is necessary (Mael and Ashforth, 1995). Individuals can report a strong emotional bond to an organization without any formal stake in it. Perhaps the most obvious example is the enthusiastic armchair supporter of a sports team but a similar attachment can develop towards some more conventional industrial organizations once they have acquired a certain status and reputation. This can become reflected in consumer behaviour and implies that the psychological contract might transcend the employment relationship.

### *Is the legal metaphor appropriate?*

As Conway (1996) and others have noted, the psychological contract is a legal metaphor (Macneil, 1985). There are serious questions about whether it is an appropriate metaphor. A contract implies mutuality. While this is embedded in the first three definitions listed above, it has disappeared from Rousseau's definition. Conway cites Cheshire on contract law where 'an agreement, or at least the outward appearance of an agreement is an essential ingredient of a contract' (Cheshire, 1991). Since the psychological contract is largely in the 'eye of the beholder' the embedded subjectivity seems likely to undermine the central concept of an agreement. Where the implicit encounters the implicit, the result may be two strangers passing blindfold and in the dark, disappointed at their failure to meet. Or to put it another way, both may have drawn up contracts in the hope that the other has drawn up exactly the same contract. But since both contracts are locked away—in the mind rather than in the safe—there is no way of checking. Only the transactional contract will have the two signatures at the bottom suggesting both have read and agreed the same contract document. It is worth noting in passing that to agree such a document does not mean you have to like it. A contract between employer and employee may have legal force but it is rarely a document between equals. A possibly more important problem with the parallel is that while a legal contract between two parties can usually only be changed with the consent of both parties, the psychological contract can be arbitrarily and secretly changed by either party.

### *The agency problem*

The employment contract will be signed between the employee and an agent of the organization. The psychological contract faces the often-cited difficulty of defining what is meant by the organization. Rousseau (1995) devotes some space to analysis of 'agents' but fails to get round the problem, simply because there are multiple agents for the organization and they may be 'offering' different and sometimes competing contracts. Given the range of those creating expectations and making promises and those able to deliver on them, it is not surprising that there is evidence that the psychological contract has been violated.

The solution to the problem of 'agents' adopted by Rousseau and other contemporary U.S. researchers, is to note the dangers of anthropomorphizing 'the organization' by turning it into 'an individual' and therefore to redefine the psychological contract solely in terms of employee perceptions. However, in overcoming one problem and at the same time rejecting the traditional definition of the psychological contract offered by Argyris and Schein, most contemporary U.S. researchers who accept Rousseau's redefinition may be moving too far away from the concept of a contract, at the heart of which lies a two-way reciprocal agreement. Arguably they have identified a fruitful stream of research but in so doing have lost some of the richness behind the concept of contract, while perhaps inappropriately retaining the language of contract.

### *What are the key dimensions of the psychological contract?*

One of the directions of research on the psychological contract has been to identify and attempt to operationalize the key dimensions along which it can be distinguished from the conventional employment contract. Rousseau and McLean Parks (1993), for example, list five dimensions which they label stability, scope, tangibility, focus and time-frame. Providing a set of dimensions in this way is potentially useful, but raises a number of questions. The first is that the list seems to be intuitive rather than theoretically derived. This raises the question of whether the list is complete. Rousseau (1995), for example, gives some weight to a dimension concerned with performance requirements. It is also feasible to consider the dimension of agency which may range from individual to collective. The possibility and indeed the temptation of adding to the list in this way raises questions of parsimony. A second, and linked concern, is whether each dimension is equally important. Rousseau and others have given particular emphasis to the dimension of 'focus', reflected in the distinction between transactional and relational contracts. The relational dimension refers to contracts emphasizing social exchange and interdependence. In contrast, transactions emphasize the concrete content of the contract—what is agreed. In the conventional employment contract this might include the terms and conditions of employment, such as payment arrangements, sick pay and holiday arrangements and periods of notice on either side. However the boundary may be blurred. Where does a formal mentoring scheme or a graduate development programme, with its promise to provide a job on completion, fit?

Herriot and Pemberton (1995) have strongly advocated that one solution to the 'problem' of the psychological contract is to make all psychological contracts more transparent. But if psychological contracts are defined as being unwritten and implicit, do they then automatically cease to be psychological contracts upon being made open and explicit? Is what is left after the issues of key concern have been addressed in this way so insubstantial as not to merit the label of 'contract'? This points to the third problem resulting from the emphasis on dimensions—are those contracts at the concrete, explicit, public and transactional ends of the continua still usefully described as psychological contracts? Finally, it is worth noting that the concern for dimensions emphasizes the descriptive approach embedded in the concept of the psychological contract. The primary focus is on classification rather than theory. Nor is there any evaluation embedded in the concept. This has to be addressed separately.

### *What is the content of the psychological contract?*

Although the psychological contract has typically been operationalized in terms of descriptive dimensions, for many policy-makers and practitioners, it is the changing content of the psychological contract that is of particular interest. Contrasting the old, the new and potential future contracts is a popular and potentially useful exercise (Herriot and Pemberton, 1997). For example Guzzo, Noonan and Elroy (1994) explored the specific issue of support for expatriate managers, although interestingly they focused on what managers thought they *should* receive rather than any promise of support. Shore and Tetrick (1994), adopting a wider perspective, suggest that the key outcomes for workers are fair pay, good working conditions and job security, though these items seem to be derived from expectations rather than any sense of contractual obligation and exchange. In the U.K., studies by, for example, Herriot, Manning and Kidd (1996), Herriot, Pemberton and Hawtin (1996) and Sparrow (1996) highlight diversity of priorities and preferences.

In one of the most careful U.K. studies of the content of psychological contracts, which unusually explored both employee and employer perspectives among a cross-section of the working population using critical incidents, Herriot *et al.* (1996) found that employees most frequently mentioned aspects of the environment of work, pay and fairness. Job security was among three items in the next cluster while career issues did not figure prominently except indirectly through aspects of fairness. This suggests that we should be cautious in assuming that career concerns are particularly salient, a point we develop in the next section.

### *Constructing the 'problem' of the psychological contract*

An important stimulus to the increasing prominence of the psychological contract as a focus of study has been a widespread belief that the nature of the employment relationship is changing and also a view that organizational changes have resulted in a breakdown of traditional relationships. In seeking to understand and explore these changes the concept of the psychological contract can claim to have utility as an analytic construct. But it also holds a resonance among policy-makers concerned to manage change as well as among those affected by it. By providing a language with which to understand concerns about the employment relationship, both the concept of the psychological contract and the problems it seeks to address risk taking on a life of their own. It is easy to slip from noting a possible problem to claiming a major problem in the changing employment relationship that underpins the interest in the psychological contract; the rhetoric then out-runs the reality, overstating the problem. Abrahamson (1996), in his work on management fashions and fads, has emphasized, among other things, the need to understand the substance behind the claims that propel fashions to prominence. While much of his work has dealt with substantive techniques such as quality circles, job enrichment and process re-engineering, the psychological contract is in a powerful position to operate as a fashion partly because it is concerned primarily with perceptual issues rather than reality. It is therefore important to check out as far as possible the substantive claims behind both the behavioural and the perceptual assumptions that underpin the rise in interest.

The popular view is that the traditional promise of either a secure job and a fair day's pay for a fair day's work or a career in the organization in return for loyalty and hard, high quality work is no longer tenable. This raises a number of research questions. The first is whether we can show that the content of the psychological contract, in terms of what employees seek and what employers offer, has changed. The key focus, given the nature of current debates, might be on whether the career and job security are both central concerns in the psychological contract and at the same time becoming increasingly untenable, resulting in the 'problem' of contract violation when promises and expectations collide with reality. Secondly, if there is any questioning, by managers and professional workers in particular, of their commitment to an organizational career, either because of general changes in orientation or because of the experience of contract violation, and especially violation of the 'career promise', is this a new phenomenon? Perhaps because research on the psychological contract is relatively new, there is little long-term evidence about the change in the content of psychological contracts. However we can explore the question indirectly though qualitative and quantitative evidence collected over the years to explore aspects of career commitment. On the basis of such evidence, at least for the U.K., an argument can be constructed to show that there has been less change than many believed. In making this assertion, it is acknowledged that there is a considerable body of writing that supports the belief that the 'old' psychological contract is dead in both the U.S.A. (Capelli, 1997; Hirsch, 1987) and in the U.K. (Handy, 1989; Herriot, 1992; and Hutton, 1996).

In the U.K., researchers such as Herriot *et al*. (1996) and Sparrow (1996), both working in the financial sector, which has been particularly hard hit by job cutbacks, have shown that managers have a range of career preferences or orientations. While some retain the desire for a traditional career, moving onwards and upwards, others express a preference to stay in their present post or to devote more time and energy to non-work activities. In America, there has been some interest in the concept of 'downshifting', the deliberate choice to reduce input to work and a career and seek a more balanced life-style. In all cases, there is an implicit assumption that this is a new phenomenon in response to a changing organizational context, and that the damage to the psychological contract is likely to result in reduced commitment to the organization. It is worth recalling that one of the reasons for the initial interest in the concept of organizational commitment was the concern in the 1970s that organizations were failing to attract and retain high quality executives, suggesting that the 'problem' of the psychological contract is not a new one. In the 1980s, Scase and Goffee (1989) noted a desire on the part of many managers in the U.K. to reduce or at least control their engagement in organizational life; and in so doing, they echoed a phenomenon noted in the late 1960s (Sofer, 1970; Williams and Guest, 1971). From a slightly different perspective, the idea of varying career preferences matches the range of career anchors noted by Schein and the more sociological concept of the varying orientations to work identified first by Goldthorpe, Lockwood, Bechhofer and Platt (1968), and then explored in more detail for blue collar (Blackburn and Mann, 1979) and white collar workers (Prandy, Stewart and Blackburn, 1982). In other words, it is quite plausible to argue that each generation of post-war managers, perhaps for slightly different reasons, has expressed a diversity of career preferences and has questioned whether the traditional organizational career provides the fulfilment they seek.

Turning to the second part of the issue, the U.K. data indicate no dramatic increase in the past two decades in executive redundancies or in job loss and job movement (Robinson, 1997). Time spent in organizations and in jobs has reduced only marginally, if at all, in the past 20 years, although this does mask some reductions in male tenure compensated for by a rise in female tenure. Both a U.K. national survey on this issue (Guest and Conway, 1997) and the authoritative British Social Trends (Spencer, 1996) reveal that relatively few executives have personal experience of job loss and few are worried about it for the future.

Nor is there much evidence from a recent extensive study of student aspirations to suggest that they have abandoned traditional career ambitions (Purcell and Pitcher, 1997).

With respect to job security, there has been a slow but steady growth in the U.K., over many years, in the proportion of the workforce engaged on contracts other than the traditional, full-time, permanent employment. But this in itself is not a 'problem' of a changing psychological contract since the great majority of those affected choose this form of employment (Beatson, 1995). As noted earlier, a key reason for treating the 'problem' of the psychological contract seriously is that it deals in perceptions rather than in the realities of the labour market. There seem to be abundant surveys highlighting a sense of employment insecurity. Close scrutiny reveals that few of these surveys are based on representative samples. In contrast, a representative 1997 survey of 1000 people in employment in the U.K. (Guest and Conway, 1997) found that 55 per cent believe that their organization has 'always' or 'to a large extent' kept their promises about careers and 70 per cent believe they have done so with respect to job security. Those who claim that their employer has definitely not kept their promise are only 5 per cent with respect to careers and 4 per cent with respect to job security. These data, more particularly for job security, tend to confirm the labour market evidence. It is, of course possible to argue that the organization promised no security and has kept that promise but a separate section of the survey reveals that 86 per cent feel 'very' or 'fairly' secure in their present job and only 4 per cent are 'very worried' about job security. For the U.K. at least, it is possible to challenge the basis on which the change in the psychological contract has been 'talked up' and has attracted attention.

This brief discussion of some of the U.K. evidence about perceptions relating to career and job security is illustrative rather than comprehensive but serves to raise serious questions about the 'talking up' of changes that underpin an important part of the interest in and debates about the psychological contract. There is a danger, perhaps encouraged by promoting the idea that the old psychological contract is dead, of being overly critical of the present and of covering the past in an idyllic but rather false glow. Put another way, it is possible to assemble evidence to suggest that at any point in the past 50 years a significant proportion of managers believed that their organization had failed to deliver its 'career promise', leading career and development issues to emerge time and again as the major source of executive dissatisfaction, and, by implication, violation of the psychological contract. One implication is that interest in the psychological contract both captures and reinforces a focus on what has been a long-term concern but which debates about down-sizing and related changes in organizations imbue with a distinctive contemporary focus. There is therefore an appealing rhetoric around the psychological contract which confers on it a policy significance that serves both to enhance the justification for pursuing it as an object of academic study but at the same time can distract attention from some of the inherent problems in the underlying conceptualization and the underlying evidence about the changes it seeks to address.

## Contract violation and the problem of concept redundancy

There is the implication in the general analysis of the changing psychological contract that contract violation is on the increase. Leaving aside the evidence considered in the previous section which casts some doubt on the claim, we need to consider a number of empirical and conceptual problems with the concept of contract violation. Robinson and Rousseau (1994), on the basis of a study of the first two years of employment of a cohort of MBA graduates, have claimed that contract violation is the norm rather than the exception. Of course, we do not know from this whether contract violation is on the increase; given the problem of multiple agents, it is likely that it has always been a feature of organizational life. Indeed, as Rousseau (1995) notes 'contract violation can run the gamut from subtle misperceptions to stark breaches of good faith ... Given the subjectivity of contract terms, a contract could hardly exist without some inadvertent violation' (Rousseau, 1995, pp. 111–112). Building on this, it is far from clear that violations of the psychological contract, defined as unmet obligations or promises, differ from unmet expectations and are therefore any different from job dissatisfaction. For example, it is possible that contract violation reflects strong dissatisfaction (broken promises) as opposed to moderate dissatisfaction (unmet expectations). Although contract violation fits well within the language of the psychological contract, its possible similarity to job dissatisfaction raises the question of concept redundancy. Robinson and Rousseau (1994) are able to show that their correlations are stronger than those obtained by Wanous *et al.* (1992) in a meta-analysis of the relationship between unmet expectations and labour turnover. However the correlation between contract violation and job dissatisfaction was a high 0.76 and we need to know more about their independence.

Morrison and Robinson (1997) have recognized the need for greater precision in addressing contract violation and offer a process model moving from an unmet expectation to a breach of contract to contract violation. Contract violation is defined as 'an affective and emotional experience of disappointment, frustration, anger, and resentment that may emanate from an employee's interpretation of a contract breach and its accompanying circumstances' (1997, p. 242). This model of the evolution of contract violation is helpful but by focusing on the affective, emotional dimension, it retains the risk of considerable overlap, albeit around contract issues, with job dissatisfaction.

The focus of relevant, mainly American research has been on perceptions by workers of violations. This ignores two key issues which merit research in the future. The first is contract violation by employees. The study by Herriot *et al.* (1997) using critical incidents from employer representatives, found that the key obligations on the part of employees were considered to be working the hours contracted, doing a good job in terms of quality and quantity, honesty in all dealings and then, some way behind, loyalty and flexibility. An interesting illustration of the potential of such an approach was recently provided in a U.K. survey of absence from work. This examined the reasons for absence given by employees and

*Table 1* Assumptions about sickness absence

| Employee/medical explanation for sickness absence | Management assumptions about causes of sickness absence |
| --- | --- |
| Colds/flu | Colds/flu |
| Stomach upsets | Stress/personal problems |
| Headaches | Sickness of family member/childcare |
| Back problems | Low morale/boring job |
| Stress/personal problems | Monday blues/stomach upset |

Source: Industrial Society (1997).

management interpretations of what they meant. Some of these interpretations are shown in Table 1. This reveals that white certain reasons for sickness absence are accepted as legitimate and taken at face value, and some are accepted as legitimate even though the explanation might be re-interpreted, others are seen as potentially illegitimate.

The second issue for further research concerns the possibility of violation as over-fulfilment of promises. What happens when the individual exceeds expectations, or goes beyond contract and engages in outstanding organizational citizenship; or conversely, when someone receives a promotion or pay rise that exceeds expectations? Is this an equally serious violation of the psychological contract? There are some obvious parallels with equity theory and the problems of over-reward. The laboratory evidence suggested that over-reward was soon discounted rather than compensated for by increased effort. However a question remains as to whether this form of violation places an unfair burden on the other party or whether it is one they are, on balance, happy to live with.

It is tempting to extend the parallels with equity theory (Cropanzano and Folger, 1996; Mowday, 1996). In both cases, we are dealing with an exchange process where there are ambiguities about how that process is construed. Similarly there are parallels between the problems of establishing what constitutes violation or inequity and the whole question of social comparisons and choice of reference group. Thirdly there are questions about what constitute inputs and outputs in equity theory and the question for the psychological contract, of what constitutes the content of the contract. Finally, there are questions for both about the consequences of either meeting or violating the conditions for equity or for the contract. Is the result perceptual and cognitive readjustment or a change in behaviour? It is tempting to see in these extensive parallels some scope for concept redundancy and concept integration. It is also sobering to recognize that equity theory has never quite succeeded in throwing off some of these problems.

Taking the issue of concept redundancy a step further, there is an urgent need for research to demonstrate that the contemporary one-sided perceptual focus of the psychological contract of the sort advocated by Rousseau and others can be distinguished from well-established constructs such as job satisfaction and organizational commitment. At a slightly different level of analysis, there are potential overlaps between social exchange theory and the exchanges in the psychological contract. Building on this analysis, there are potentially interesting questions about the role of the social construction of exchange relationships, the influence of organizational culture and climate and about Gouldner's concept of the 'norms of reciprocity'. Conway (1996) has drawn attention to the anthropological approaches to social exchange which highlight the 'myth of reciprocity' which permits inequity in a relationship to be maintained. In particular the notion of the relational contract, which is implicit and unstated, allows for inequity while saving face, something which would not be possible with a transactional contract where flagrant violations would require redress; and it throws into the open difficult questions of power inequality. In short, variations of social exchange theory have the potential to explain much of the same range of attitudes and behaviour as the psychological contract. Interestingly, it can explain why violation may be tolerated or even denied.

## Reviewing the status of the psychological contract

Returning to the approach outlined at the start, what does this brief analysis tell us about the status of the concept of the psychological contract? The analysis raises serious doubts about the validity and parsimony of the concept. The *content validity* is in doubt because of problems of establishing whether the psychological contract is concerned with expectations, promises or obligations, problems in specifying the precise content of these expectations, promises or obligations and doubts about the stability of content across or indeed within organizational populations. This also raises doubts about the parsimony of the concept if it potentially covers most views of most issues at work and beyond.

Secondly there are doubts about the *construct validity* of the concept. Firstly, it translates uneasily from the legal metaphor due to its neglect of the principle of agreement. Secondly, it is unclear who or what constitutes the organization party to the contract. This problem is reflected in the research which has largely ignored the organizational perspective on the psychological contract, rendering it very one-sided and again raising the issue, developed below, of concept redundancy. Thirdly, while some U.S. researchers have concentrated on dimensions of psychological contracts, they have not established a coherent and conclusive list of dimensions, risk loss of parsimony by adding to the list and have yet to establish the independence of the dimensions.

Thirdly, there are questions about the testability and applicability of the psychological contract as defined to date. It is not clear how the presence of a psychological contract is established; nor is it clear what steps are necessary to alter the contract. There has been rather too much emphasis in the mainstream U.S. research on explicit rather than implicit promises, perhaps because, despite their centrality in the underlying concept, the latter are hard to identify. Among the most interesting work in this respect is that of Herriot and Pemberton (1996, 1997) on the process of contracting, but their key recommendation is to make the contract explicit; in other words to make it transactional. Leaving aside the practicality of constant renegotiation and the still-unresolved problem of who acts as agent for the organization, the emphasis on the explicit, transactional contract raises questions about whether we are still dealing with a psychological contract and whether everyone has a psychological contract. This question extends to all those who fall at the 'non-psychological' extremes of the dimensions of the psychological contract. There is an urgent task of establishing the boundaries of the psychological contract.

This leads to a final critical concern. Those who coined the term the psychological contract were almost certainly viewing it as a useful heuristic device. They did not seek to elevate it to the status of a major analytic construct. Others, who have sought to give it this status are entering a crowded territory. There is a real problem of concept redundancy. The increasing primacy given to employee perceptions in research on the psychological contract raises questions about whether evaluation of the state of the psychological contract differs substantially from job satisfaction and organizational commitment. And there are broader conceptual overlaps with equity and social exchange theories.

Given all these concerns, is the psychological contract worth taking seriously? Is it worth saving?

## Why the psychological contract *is* worth taking seriously

Despite the many problems with the way in which the concept has been developed to date, there is a case for taking the psychological contact seriously. Three main reasons will be outlined, all at a level of policy rather than theory.

The first reason for taking it seriously relates to the analysis of why it has come to the fore in the past decade. As noted at the outset, it captures the spirit of the times. The first key respect in which it achieves this is as a reflection of the individualizing of the employment relationship. The market philosophy which has dominated economic policy and permeated organizational ideology over a number of years, views the employee as a rugged independent individual offering knowledge and skills through a series of transactions in the labour market. Building on the analysis of Williamson (1975), Ouchi (1980) and Kalleberg and Reve (1993) it reflects a shift back from 'hierarchy' and 'clans' to the 'market' as the basis for organizing. Contracting, in all its guises, suddenly becomes an important focus of study and the value of the psychological contract lies in drawing attention to the range and complexity of contracts in organizations.

Taking this first point a step further, we now live in an era of employment relations rather than industrial relations. An increasing proportion of people at work do not have the protection and representation of a trade union. While this has been the norm for managers for a number of years, they have tended to enjoy more secure employment and the ubiquitous organizational career. The new employment relationship is only poorly understood. While there has been evidence for some years that non-union firms can engage in highly progressive human resource practices

(Foulkes, 1980), there is also evidence that alongside the 'good' we must line up the 'bad' and the 'ugly' (Guest and Hoque, 1994). The psychological contract provides a potentially fruitful construct with which to make sense of and explore this new employment relationship.

A second reason for retaining the psychological contract is its ability to focus attention on the distribution of power. The more anthropological use of social exchange theory is perhaps particularly insightful in this respect. One of the often cited features of the move towards a market-driven economy is the growth of inequality in wealth. When this is coupled with the growing inequality in power in the relationship between the unrepresented individual and the sometimes monolithic organization, we have a set of issues, which can be constructed around the concept of the psychological contract, and which draw attention to the costs of power inequalities in the new employment relationship. This seems to be the main point behind Herriot and Pemberton's prescription of an emphasis on explicit, transactional contracts. It makes it more difficult for the organization to renege. In the U.K. at least, there appears to be a growing awareness in industry of these inequities and at the same time a willingness to enter into new collective agreements that publicly guarantee job security. While such contracts can still be broken, the 'public' guarantee makes it less likely that this will occur.

A third reason for 'saving' the psychological contract is that it has the potential, not yet realized, to integrate a number of key organizational concepts. For this to occur, more analytic and research work is required to determine how far the concept of the psychological contract can usefully embrace and subsume overlapping concepts and theories. We also need to switch the focus much more to the content of the psychological contract and to issues such as trust, fairness and exchange. Transaction cost economics, with its economic roots, is based on assumptions of self-interest and distrust. Much of the research on the psychological contract to date has reflected the underlying pessimism of this view of human interaction; in other words it has focused on the problems of the psychological contract and on violation. We need to learn much more about the causes and consequences of a positive psychological contract and to build a psychology of contract process, both relational and transactional, that can act as an alternative or at least as a complement to transaction cost economics. Such a model may be based on Ouchi's ideas about 'clans' and there is much to learn from the research of institutional economists on issues such as sub-contracting. The key integrative concept is likely to be trust, though it presents problems of its own (Kramer and Tyler, 1996).

## Research priorities for the psychological contract

The previous paragraphs began to outline a possible direction for theory building around the psychological contract. At a more operational level there is also a need to build a general theory of the psychological contract. To date, too much of the research has been descriptive or has focused on micro-processes. What is needed is

## Causes
- Organizational culture/climate
- HRM policy and practice
- Experience
- Expectations
- Alternatives

## Content
- Fairness
- Trust
- The delivery of the "deal"

## Consequences
- Job satisfaction
- Organizational commitment
- Sense of security
- Employment relations
- Motivation
- Organizational citizenship
- Absence
- Intention to quit

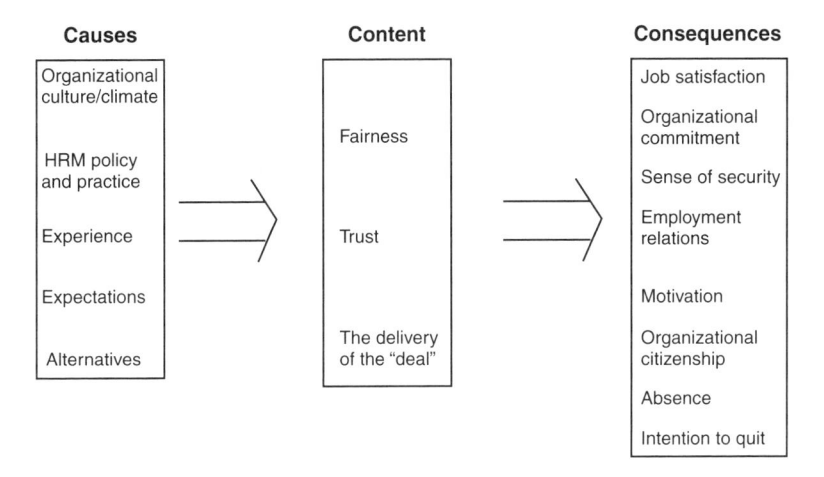

*Figure 1* A model of the psychological contract.

theory which cannot only describe but also evaluate the state of the psychological contract. At the very least we need to build theory around the causes, content and consequences of the psychological contract. One initial possibility is presented in Figure 1.

It should be emphasized that this is a first step towards a theory, but it raises several issues that would seem to be essential to the development of a coherent and actionable body of knowledge around the psychological contract. First, it seeks to go beyond the limited amount of work on how psychological contracts emerge (eg. Rousseau and Greller, 1994) to specify influences on the psychological contract. Broadly, these reside in the organization or in the individual, although both will be influenced by wider societal norms; and they include expectations. This is an important point to emphasize since it can be argued that much of the research to date has concentrated on expectations and obligations which can also be construed as inputs to the contract. In themselves they tell us little about the state of the psychological contract. Therefore a second key component is the focus on what is termed the 'state' of the psychological contract. This has three components which are constantly emphasized in the literature, namely trust, fairness and delivery of the deal. In particular, it takes us away from the descriptive focus on dimensions of the psychological contract. Without discounting the potential importance of contract violation, it also allows for the possibility that, more particularly in non-managerial jobs, many workers may have poor contracts, both formal employment contracts and psychological contracts, from the outset and it is the content of these rather than any violation of promises made at the outset that is the major source of dissatisfaction with the contract process. The final part of the theoretical model focuses on the consequences of the contract. Although some research, mainly that concerned with contract violation, has explored consequences, it has often been given insufficient weight. Clear theory about the range of possible consequences of the psychological contract and fuller testing of such theory is important if the concept is to have staying power since it is essential to demonstrate that it does have consequences for both individual and organization.

The theory outlined in Figure 1 presents an employee perspective. If this were its only perspective, then it would be limited. However, there is no reason why it cannot also be explored from an organizational perspective as well, although there is a risk that if this requires the perceptions of a range of potential agents, then it comes close to a measure of organizational climate. While this is no bad thing, it once again raises the spectre of concept redundancy.

An initial exploration of this framework, using a representative 1000 employee sample of the U.K. working population, and adopting an employee perspective, indicated that the model has some explanatory power (Guest and Conway, 1997). Based on simple stepwise regressions, and controlling for a range of organizational and individual background variables, the state of the psychological contract was explained by greater reported use of progressive human resource management practices, by the presence of an organizational climate that can be characterized as one of high involvement and partnership and by future expectations of employment security. The state of the psychological contract could be best summed up as 'moderately positive'. A positive psychological contract was associated with higher job satisfaction, higher organizational commitment, higher reported motivation and a positive evaluation of employment relations, as well as lower intention to quit. Two important provisos must be entered to these seemingly positive results. First, the measures of some of the variables were rather crude, an inevitable consequence of data collection through telephone interviews; secondly, we are dealing with cross-sectional data so no confident conclusions can be reached about cause and effect relationships. The important point to highlight is that theory building of this sort would appear to be an essential step in progressing the idea of the psychological contract as theory.

The second way in which research and thinking about the psychological contract might be advanced is through a more imaginative use of social exchange theory. Indeed there may be scope for some integration of social exchange and transaction cost economics to explore the interaction between transactional and relational contracts. If we were to go a step further and incorporate some of Deci's (1975) ideas about the non-additivity of intrinsic and extrinsic motives, we might be able to theorize about the appropriate combinations and additivity of what might be construed as extrinsic and intrinsic contracts.

A final area of potential development builds on the work of Herriot and Pemberton on deals but seeks to take it in a rather different direction. There is no doubt that an implicit, unwritten, vague promise is easy to break. So under what circumstances are psychological contracts more or less likely to be broken? One interesting line for positive theory development would be to explore conditions for contract conformity. Two lines of development could be considered.

As noted earlier, the psychological contract concept is broad, potentially too broad. One way of resolving this problem might be to try to classify the types of psychological and other contracts along what Rousseau and Parks (1993) term a 'contract continuum'. They were particularly interested in the transactional–relational dimension and, amending this key dimension only slightly, it is possible to identify at least four conceptually distinct steps in the continuum. The first is represented by the contract of employment. The second is found in the various handbooks and rule books that exist in most organizations. The third is contained within agreements, usually between manager and subordinate, that emerge from processes such as appraisal, performance reviews and goal setting. It is these elements or closely related ones that Herriot and Pemberton are eager to make more explicit. Finally, there will be those areas that remain implicit and unwritten such as understandings about career and reciprocal commitment. In the past, one of the aims of collective bargaining was to extend the 'frontier of control' to embrace more substantive issues, all of which would then be made subject to explicit, written agreements. In a country like Germany, the works councils have clearly defined rights of codetermination, consultation and communication. Recently in the U.K., as noted above, there have been signs of long-term, explicit collective deals on topics such as job security. The classification of the psychological contract simply makes this explicit at the individual level, although in many cases, it can still be backed by collective agreements and collective strength.

Taking Herriot and Pemberton's ideas a step further, behavioural commitment has been shown to have a powerful impact on behaviour. The main theoretical work on behavioural commitment was undertaken by Salancik (1977), building on the original ideas of Lewin. The principles are well established—if the agreement is public, specific, hard to revoke and based on an individual volunteering to pursue the agreement, then, rather like goal setting, it is more likely to be kept to. Of course, many relational agreements are not like this, and quite deliberately so. But a focus on these criteria, rather like Herriot's deals, would help the organization and its agents to be clearer about what they could and should or should not promise. Goal setting is often applied in a somewhat similar way to individuals. What is suggested here is a two-way agreement, that may emerge in the context of the appraisal process, and unions as much as management have a role to play in ensuring that such contracts are taken seriously and adhered to as far as possible.

The decline of collective arrangements at work and the consequent individualizing of the employment relationship and the related inequality in power relationships require a new language. The psychological contract provides a potentially useful framework around which to organize thinking and research. As the analysis in this paper suggests, the psychological contract is beset with conceptual problems and still has to establish itself as a useful and valid psychological construct. However it focuses on an area rich in potential for experts in organizational behaviour, particularly those with an interdisciplinary perspective and the issues it helps to address justify persevering further with it.

## References

Abrahamson, E. (1996). 'Management fashion', *Academy of Management Review*, **21**, 254–285.

Argyris, C. (1960). *Understanding Organizational Behavior*, Dorsey, Homewood, Ill.

Arnold, J. (1996). 'The psychological contract: a concept in need of closer scrutiny?', *European Journal of Work and Organizational Psychology*, **0**, 000–000.

Beatson, M. (1995). *Labour Market Flexibility*. Employment Department Research Series No 48, Dept of Employment, Sheffield.

Blackburn, R. M. and Mann, M. (1979). *The Working Class in the Labour Market*, Macmillan, London.

Capelli, P. (Ed.) (1997). *Change at Work*, Oxford University Press, Oxford.

Cheshire, G. C., Fifoot, C. H. S. and Furmston, M. P. (1991). *Laws of Contract*, 12th edition, Butterworths, London.

Conway, N. (1996). 'The psychological contract: a metaphor too far?', Paper presented to the British Academy of Management Conference, Bradford, September 1996.

Cropanzano, R. and Folger, R. (1996). 'Procedural justice and worker motivation', In: Steers R. M., Porter L. W. and Bigley G. A. (Eds), *Motivation and Leadership at Work*, 6th edition, McGraw-Hill, New York.

Deci, E. L. (1975). *Intrinsic Motivation*, Plenum Press, New York.

Guest, D. E. and Hoque, K. (1994). 'The good, the bad and the ugly: human resource management in new non-union establishments', *Human Resource Management Journal*, **5**(1), 1–14.

Guest, D. E. and Conway, N. (1997). *Motivation and The Psychological Contract*. Issues in People Management No. 21. London: IPD.

Guzzo, R. A., Noonan, K. A. and Elron, E. (1994). 'Expatriate managers and the psychological contract', *Journal of Applied Psychology*, **79**, 617–626.

Handy, C. (1989). *The Age of Unreason*, Hutchinson, London.

Herriot, P. (1992). *The Career Management Challenge*, Sage, London.

Herriot, P., Manning, W. E. G. and Kidd, J. M. (1997). 'The content of the psychological contract', *British Journal of Management*, **8**(2), 151–162.

Herriot, P. and Pemberton, C. (1995). *New Deals: The Revolution in Managerial Careers*, Wiley, Chichester.

Herriot, P. and Pemberton, C. (1996). 'Contracting careers'. *Human Relations*, **49**(6), 759–790.

Herriot, P. and Pemberton, C. (1997). 'Facilitating new deals', *Human Resource Management Journal*, **7**(1), 45–56.

Herriot, P., Pemberton, C. and Hawtin, E. (1996). 'The career attitudes and intentions of managers in the finance sector', *British Journal of Management*, **7**(2), 181–190.

Hirsch, P. M. (1987). *Pack Your Own Parachute*, Addison-Wesley, Reading, MA.

Hutton, W. (1996). *The State We're In*, Viking, London.

Industrial Society (1997). *Maximising Attendance*, Industrial Society, London.

Kalleberg, A. L. and Reve, T. (1993). 'Contracts and commitments: economic and sociological perspectives on employment relations', *Human Relations*, **46**(9), 1103–1132.

Kotter, J. P. (1973). 'The psychological contract', *California Management Review*, **15**, 91–99.
Kramer, R. M. and Tyler, T. R. (1996). *Trust in Organizations*, Sage, Thousand Oaks, CA.
Levinson, H. (1962). *Organizational Diagnosis*, Harvard Univ. Press, Cambridge, MA.
MacNeil, I. R. (1985). 'Relational contract: what we do and do not know', *Wisconsin Law Review*, **00**, 483–525.
Mael, F. A. and Ashforth, B. E. (1995). 'Loyal from day one: biodata, organizational identification, and turnover among newcomers', *Personnel Psychology*, **48**, 309–333.
Morrison, E. W. and Robinson, S. L. (1997). 'When employees feel betrayed: a model of how psychological contract violation develops', *Academy of Management Review*, **22**(1), 226–256.
Mowday, R. T. (1996). 'Equity theory predictions of behavior in organizations', In: Steers R. M., Porter L. W. and Bigley G. A. (Eds), *Motivation and Leadership at Work*, 6th edition, McGraw-Hill, New York.
Ouchi, W. G. (1980). 'Markets, hierarchies and clans', *Administrative Science Quarterly*, **23**, 293–317.
Prandy, K., Stewart, A. and Blackburn, R. M. (1982). *White-Collar Work*, Macmillan, London.
Robinson, P. (1997). 'Just How Far Has the UK Labour Market Changed? Flexible Employment and Labour Market Regulation'. Centre for Economic Performance Working Paper, LSE CEP, London.
Robinson, S. L. and Rousseau, D. M. (1994). Violating the psychological contract: not the exception but the norm', *Journal of Organizational Behavior*, **15**, 245–259.
Rousseau, D. M. (1989). 'Psychological and implied contracts in organizations', *Employee Responsibilities and Rights Journal*, **2**, 121–139.
Rousseau, D. M. (1995). *Psychological Contracts in Organizations*, Sage, Thousand Oaks, CA.
Rousseau, D. M. and Greller, M. M. (1994). 'Human resource practices: administrative contract makers', *Human Resource Management*, **33**(3), 385–401.
Rousseau, D. M. and MacLean Parks, J. (1993). 'The contracts of individuals and organizations', In: Cummings L. L. and Staw B. M. (Eds), *Research in Organizational Behavior*, Vol. 15, pp. 1–43, JAI Press, Greenwich, Conn.
Salancik, G. R. (1977). 'Commitment and the control of organizational behavior and belief', In: Staw B. M. and Salancik G. R. (Eds), *New Directions in Organizational Behavior*, pp. 1–54, St Clair Press, Chicago.
Scase, R. and Goffee, R. (1989). *Reluctant Managers: Their Work and Lifestyles*. Unwin Hyman, London.
Schein, E. H. (1978). *Career Dynamics: Matching Individuals and Organizational Needs*, Addison-Wesley, Reading, MA.
Shore, L. M. and Tetrick, L. E. (1994). 'The psychological contract as an explanatory framework in the employment relationship', In: Cooper C. L. and Rousseau D. M. (Eds), *Trends in Organizational Behavior*, pp. 91–103, Wiley, New York.
Sofer, C. (1970). *Men in Mid-Career*, Cambridge University Press, Cambridge.
Sparrow, P. R. (1996). 'The changing nature of psychological contracts in the U.K. banking sector: does it matter?', *Human Resource Management Journal*, **6**(4), 75–92.

Spencer, P. (1996). 'Reactions to a flexible labour market', In: Jowell R., Curtice J., Park A., Brook L. and Thomson K. (Eds), *British Social Attitudes: The 13th Report*, pp. 73–91, Aldershot, Dartmouth.

Wanous, J. P., Poland, T. D., Premack, S. L. and Davis, K. S. (1992). 'The effects of met expectations on newcomer attitudes and behaviors: a review and meta-analysis', *Journal of Applied Psychology*, **77**, 288–297.

Williams, A. R. T. and Guest, D. E. (1971). 'Are the middle classes becoming work-shy?', *New Society*, 457, July 1.

Williamson, O. E. (1975). *Markets and Hierarchies: Analysis and Anti-Trust Implications*, Free Press, New York.

# Part 2

# EXPERIENCING WORK AND HOW WORK IMPACTS ON PEOPLE

# 8

# ORGANIZATIONAL PSYCHOLOGY AND THE PURSUIT OF THE HAPPY/PRODUCTIVE WORKER

*Barry M. Staw*

Source: *California Management Review* 28(4) (1986): 40–53.

What I am going to talk about in this article is an old and overworked topic, but one that remains very much a source of confusion and controversy. It is also a topic that continues to attract the attention of managers and academic researchers alike, frequently being the focus of both popular books and scholarly articles. The issue is how to manage an organization so that employees can be both happy and productive—a situation where workers and managers are both satisfied with the outcomes.

 The pursuit of the happy/productive worker could be viewed as an impossible dream from the Marxist perspective of inevitable worker–management conflict. Such a goal could also be seen as too simple or naive from the traditional industrial relations view of outcomes being a product of necessary bargaining and compromise. Yet, from the psychological perspective, the pursuit of the happy/productive worker has seemed a worthwhile though difficult endeavor, one that might be achieved if we greatly increase our knowledge of work attitudes and behavior. In this article, I will examine this psychological perspective and try to provide a realistic appraisal of where we now stand in the search for satisfaction and productivity in work settings.

## Approaches to the happy/productive worker

One of the earliest pursuits of the happy/productive worker involved the search for a relationship between satisfaction and productivity. The idea was that the world might be neatly divided into situations where workers are either happy and productive or unhappy and unproductive. If this were true, then it would be a simple matter to specify the differences between management styles present in the two sets of organizations and to come up with a list of prescriptions for improvement. Unfortunately, research has never supported such a clear relationship between individual satisfaction and productivity. For over thirty years, starting with Brayfield and Crockett's classic review of the job satisfaction-performance literature,[1] and again with Vroom's discussion of satisfaction-performance research,[2] organizational psychologists have had to contend with the fact that happiness and productivity may not necessarily go together. As a result, most organizational psychologists have come to accept the argument that satisfaction and performance may relate to two entirely different individual decisions—decisions to participate and to produce.[3]

Though psychologists have acknowledged the fact that satisfaction and performance are not tightly linked, this has not stopped them from pursuing the happy/productive worker. In fact, over the last thirty years, an enormous variety of theories have attempted to show how managers can reach the promised land of high satisfaction and productivity. The theories shown in Table 1 constitute only an abbreviated list of recent attempts to reach this positive state.

None of the theories in Table 1 have inherited the happy/productive worker hypothesis in the simple sense of believing that job satisfaction and performance generally co-vary in the world *as it now exists*. But, these models all make either indirect or direct assumptions that *it is possible* to achieve a world where both satisfaction and performance will be present. Some of the theories focus on ways to increase job satisfaction, with the implicit assumption that performance will necessarily follow; some strive to directly increase performance, with the assumption that satisfaction will result; and some note that satisfaction and performance will be a joint product of implementing certain changes in the organization.

Without going into the specifics of each of these routes to the happy/productive worker, I think it is fair to say that most of the theories in Table 1 have been oversold. Historically, they each burst on the scene with glowing and almost messianic predictions, with proponents tending to simplify the process of change, making it seem like a few easy tricks will guarantee benefits to workers and management alike. The problem, of course, is that as results have come in from both academic research and from wider practical application, the benefits no longer have appeared so strong nor widespread. Typically, the broader the application and the more well-documented the study (with experimental controls and measures of expected costs

*Table 1* Paths to the happy/productive worker

| | |
|---|---|
| Worker participation | The pursuit of excellence |
| Supportive leadership | Socio–technical systems |
| 9–9 systems | Organizational commitment |
| Job enrichment | High performing systems |
| Behavior modification | Theory Z |
| Goal setting | Strong culture |

and benefits), the weaker have been the empirical results. Thus, in the end, both managers and researchers have often been left disillusioned, sceptical that any part of these theories are worth a damn and that behavioral science will ever make a contribution to management.

My goal with this article is to *lower our expectations*—to show why it is so difficult to make changes in both satisfaction and performance. My intention is not to paint such a pessimistic picture as to justify not making any changes at all, but to innoculate us against the frustrations of slow progress. My hope is to move us toward a reasoned but sustainable pursuit of the happy/productive worker—away from the alternating practice of fanfare and despair.

## Changing job attitudes

Although organizational psychologists have accepted the notion that job satisfaction and performance do not necessarily co-vary, they have still considered job attitudes as something quite permeable or subject to change. This "blank slate" approach to job attitudes comes from prevailing psychological views of the individual, where the person is seen as a creature who constantly appraises the work situation, evaluates the merits of the context, and formulates an attitude based on these conditions. As the work situation changes, individuals are thought to be sensitive to the shifts, adjusting their attitudes in a positive or negative direction. With such an approach to attitudes, it is easy to see why job satisfaction has been a common target of organizational change, and why attempts to redesign work have evolved as a principal mechanism for improving job satisfaction.

Currently, the major debate in the job design area concerns whether individuals are more sensitive to objective job conditions or social cues. In one camp are proponents of job redesign who propose that individuals are highly receptive to concrete efforts to improve working conditions. Hackman and Oldham, for example, argue that satisfaction can be increased by improving a job in terms of its variety (doing a wider number of things), identity (seeing how one's various tasks make a meaningful whole), responsibility (being in charge of one's own work and its quality), feedback (knowing when one has done a good job), and significance (the meaning or relative importance of one's contribution to the organization or society in general).[4] In the opposing camp are advocates of social information processing. These researchers argue that jobs are often ambiguous entities subject to multiple interpretations and perceptions.[5] Advocates of social information processing have noted that the positive or negative labeling of a task can greatly determine one's attitude toward the job, and that important determinants of this labeling are the opinions of co-workers who voice positive or negative views of the work. These researchers have shown that it may be as easy to persuade workers that their jobs are interesting by influencing the *perception* of a job as it is to make objective changes in the work role.

The debate between job design and social information processing has produced two recent shifts in the way we think about job attitudes. First, organizational psychology now places greater emphasis on the role of cognition and subjective evaluation in the way people respond to jobs. This is probably helpful, because even though we have generally measured job conditions with perceptual scales, we have tended to confuse these perceptions with objective job conditions. We need to be reminded that perceptions of job characteristics do not necessarily reflect reality, yet they can determine how we respond to that reality.

The second shift in thinking about job attitudes is a movement toward situationalism, stressing how even slight alterations in job context can influence one's perception of a job. It is now believed that people's job attitudes may be influenced not only by the objective properties of the work, but also by subtle cues given off by co-workers or supervisors that the job is dull or interesting. I think this new view is a mistake since it overstates the role of external influence in the determination of job attitudes. The reality may be that individuals are quite resistant to change efforts, with their attitudes coming more as a function of personal disposition than situational influence.

## The Consistency of job attitudes

Robert Kahn recently observed that, although our standard of living and working conditions have improved dramatically since World War II, reports of satisfaction on national surveys have not changed dramatically.[6] This implies that job satisfaction might be something of a "sticky variable," one that is not so easily changed by outside influence. Some research on the consistency of job attitudes leads to the same conclusion. Schneider and Dachler, for example, found very strong consistency in satisfaction scores over a 16-month longitudinal study (averaging .56 for managers and .58 for non-managers).[7] Pulakos and Schmitt also found that high school students' pre-employment expectations of satisfaction correlated significantly with ratings of their jobs several years later.[8] These findings, along with the fact that job satisfaction is generally intertwined with both life satisfaction and mental health, imply that there is some ongoing consistency in job attitudes, and that job satisfaction may be determined as much by dispositional properties of the individual as any changes in the situation.

A Berkeley colleague, Joseph Garbarino, has long captured this notion of a dispositional source of job attitudes with a humorous remark, "I always told my children at a young age that their most important decision in life would be whether they wanted to be happy or not; everything else is malleable enough to fit the answer to this question." What Garbarino implies is that job attitudes are fairly constant, and when reality changes for either the better or worse, we can easily distort that reality to fit our underlying disposition. Thus, individuals may think a great deal about the nature of their jobs, but satisfaction can result as much from the unique way a person views the world around him as from any social influence or objective job characteristics. That is, individuals predisposed to be happy may interpret their jobs in a much different way than those with more negative predispositions.

### The attitudinal consistency study

Recently, I have been involved with two studies attempting to test for dispositional sources of job attitudes. In the first study, Jerry Ross and I reanalyzed data from the National Longitudinal Survey, a study conducted by labor economists at Ohio State.[9] We used this survey to look at the stability of job attitudes over time and job situations. The survey's measures of attitudes were not very extensive but did provide one of the few available sources of data on objective job changes.

The National Longitudinal Survey data revealed an interesting pattern of results. We found that job satisfaction was fairly consistent over time, with significant relationships among job attitudes over three- and five-year time intervals. We also found that job satisfaction showed consistency *even when people changed jobs*. This later finding is especially important, since it directly contradicts the prevailing assumptions of job attitude research.

Most job design experiments and organizational interventions that strive to improve job attitudes change a small aspect of work, but look for major changes in job satisfaction. However, the National Longitudinal Survey data showed that when people changed their place of work (which would naturally include one's supervisor, working conditions, and procedures), there was still significant consistency in attitudes. One could, of course, argue that people leave one terrible job for another, and this is why such consistency in job attitudes arises. Therefore, we checked for consistency across occupational changes. The National Longitudinal Survey showed consistency not only across occupational changes, but also when people changed *both* their employers and their occupations. This evidence of consistency tells us that people may not be as malleable as we would like to think they are, and that there may be some underlying tendency toward equilibrium in job attitudes. If you are dissatisfied in one job context, you are also likely to be dissatisfied in another (perhaps better) environment.

### The dispositional study

The consistency data from the National Longitudinal Survey, while interesting, do not tell us what it is that may underlie a tendency to be satisfied or dissatisfied on the job. Therefore, Nancy Bell (a doctoral student at the Berkeley Business School), John Clausen (a developmental sociologist at Berkeley), and I undertook a study to find some of the dispositional sources of job satisfaction.[10] We sought to relate early personality characteristics to job attitudes later in life, using a very unusual longitudinal data source.

There are three longitudinal personality projects that have been running for over fifty years at Berkeley (the Berkeley Growth Study, the Oakland Growth Study, and the Guidance Study), and they have since been combined into what is now called the Intergenerational Study. Usually when psychologists speak of longitudinal studies, they mean data collected from one or two year intervals. These data span over 50 years. Usually, when psychologists refer to personality ratings, they mean self-reports derived from the administration of various questionnaires. Much of the Intergenerational Study data are clinical ratings derived from questionnaires, observation, and interview materials evaluated by a different set of raters for each period of the individual's life. Thus, these data are of unusual quality for psychological research.

Basically what we did with data from the Intergenerational Study was to construct an affective disposition scale that measured a very general positive–negative orientation of people. We then related this scale to measures of job attitudes at different periods in people's lives. The ratings used for our affective disposition scale included items such as "cheerful," "satisfied with self," and "irritable" (reverse coded), and we correlated this scale with measures of job and career satisfaction. The results were very provocative. We found that affective dispositions, from as early as the junior-high-school years, significantly predicted job attitudes during middle and late adulthood (ages 40–60). The magnitude of correlations was not enormous (in the .3 to .4 range). But, these results are about as strong as we usually see between two attitudes measured on the same questionnaire by the same person at the same time—yet, these data cut across different raters and over fifty years in time.

What are we to conclude from this personality research as well as our reanalyses of the National Longitudinal Survey? I think we can safely conclude that there is a fair amount of consistency in job attitudes and that there may be dispositional as well as situational sources of job satisfaction. Thus, it is possible that social information processing theorists have been on the right track in viewing jobs as ambiguous entities that necessitate interpretation by individuals. But, it is also likely that the interpretation of jobs (whether they are perceived as positive or negative) can come as much from internal, dispositional causes (e.g., happiness or depression) as external sources. Consequently, efforts to improve job satisfaction via changes in job conditions will need to contend with stable personal dispositions toward work—forces that may favor consistency or equilibrium in the way people view the world around them.

## The Intransigence of job performance

Although we have not conducted research on the consistency of performance or its resistance to change, I think there are some parallels between the problems of changing attitudes and performance. Just as job attitudes may be constrained by individual dispositions, there are many elements of both the individual and work situation that can make improvements in job performance difficult.[11]

Most of the prevailing theories of work performance are concerned with individual motivation. They prescribe various techniques intended to stimulate, reinforce, or lure people into working harder. Most of these theories have little to say about the individual's limits of task ability, predisposition for working hard, or the general energy or activity level of the person. Somewhat naively, our theories have maintained that performance is under the complete control of the individual.

Even though there are major individual differences affecting the quantity or quality of work produced, we have assumed that *if the employee really wants to perform better, his or her performance will naturally go up.*

There already exist some rather strong data that refute these implicit assumptions about performance. A number of studies[12] have shown that mental and physical abilities can be reliable predictors of job performance, and it is likely that other dispositions (e.g., personality characteristics) will eventually be found to be associated with effective performance of certain work roles. Thus, influencing work effort may not be enough to cause wide swings in performance, unless job performance is somewhat independent of ability (e.g., in a low skill job). Many work roles may be so dependent on ability (such as those of a professional athlete, musician, inventor) that increases in effort may simply not cause large changes in the end product.

In addition to ability, there may also be other individual factors that contribute to the consistency of performance. People who work hard in one situation are likely to be the ones who exert high effort in a second situation. If, for example, the person's energy level (including need for sleep) is relatively constant over time, we should not expect wide changes in available effort. And, if personality dimensions such as dependability and self-confidence can predict one's achievement level over the lifecourse,[13] then a similar set of personal attributes may well constitute limitations to possible improvements in performance. Already, assessment centers have capitalized on this notion by using personality measures to predict performance in many corporate settings.

Performance may not be restricted just because of the individual's level of ability and effort, however. Jobs may *themselves* be designed so that performance is not under the control of the individual, regardless of ability or effort. Certainly we are aware of the fact that an assembly line worker's output is more a product of the speed of the line than any personal preference. In administrative jobs too, what one does may be constrained by the work cycle or technical procedures. There may be many people with interlocking tasks so that an increase in the performance of one employee doesn't mean much if several tasks must be completed sequentially or simultaneously in order to improve productivity. Problems also arise in situations where doing one's job better may not be predicated upon a burst of energy or desire, but upon increases in materials, financial support, power, and resources. As noted by Kanter, the administrator must often negotiate, hoard, and form coalitions to get anything done on the job, since there are lots of actors vying for the attention and resources of the organization.[14] Thus, the nature of the organization, combined with the abilities and efforts of individuals to maneuver in the organization, may serve to constrain changes in individual performance.

## Assessing the damage

So far I have taken a somewhat dark or pessimistic view of the search for the happy/productive worker. I have noted that in terms of satisfaction and performance, it may not be easy to create perfect systems because both happiness and performance are constrained variables, affected by forces not easily altered by our most popular interventions and prescriptions for change. Should organizational psychologists therefore close up shop and go home? Should we move to a more descriptive study of behavior as opposed to searching for improvements in work attitudes and performance?

I think such conclusions are overly pessimistic. We need to interpret the stickiness of job attitudes and performance not as an invitation to complacency or defeat, but as a realistic assessment that it will take very strong treatments to move these entrenched variables. Guzzo, Jackson, and Katzell have recently made a similar point after a statistical examination (called meta-analysis) of organizational interventions designed to improve productivity.[15] They noted that the most effective changes are often *multiple treatments*, where several things are changed at once in a given organization. Thus, instead of idealistic and optimistic promises, we may literally need to throw the kitchen sink at the problem.

The problem of course is that we have more than one kitchen sink! As noted earlier, nearly every theory of organizational behavior has been devoted to predicting and potentially improving job attitudes and performance. And, simply aggregating these treatments is not likely to have the desired result, since many of these recommendations consist of conflicting prescriptions for change. Therefore, it would be wiser to look for compatible *systems* of variables that can possibly be manipulated in concert. Let us briefly consider three systems commonly used in organizational change efforts and then draw some conclusions about their alternative uses.

## Three systems of organizational change

### *The individually-oriented system*

The first alternative is to build a strong individually-oriented system, based on the kind of traditional good management that organizational psychologists have been advocating for years. This system would emphasize a number of venerable features of Western business organizations such as:

- Tying extrinsic rewards (such as pay) to performance.
- Setting realistic and challenging goals.
- Evaluating employee performance accurately and providing feedback on performance.
- Promoting on the basis of skill and performance rather than personal characteristics, power, or connections.
- Building the skill level of the workforce through training and development.
- Enlarging and enriching jobs through increases in responsibility, variety, and significance.

All of the above techniques associated with the individually-oriented system are designed to promote both satisfaction and productivity. The major principle underlying each of these features is to structure the work and/or reward system so that high performance is either intrinsically or extrinsically rewarding to the individual, thus creating a situation where high performance contributes to job satisfaction.

In practice, there can be numerous bugs in using an individually-oriented system to achieve satisfaction and performance. For example, just saying that rewards should be based on performance is easier than knowing what the proper relationship should be or whether there should be discontinuities at the high or low end of that relationship. Should we, for instance, lavish rewards on the few highest performers, deprive the lowest performers, or establish a constant linkage between pay and performance? In terms of goal-setting, should goals be set by management, workers, or joint decision making, and what should the proper baseline be for measuring improvements? In terms of job design, what is the proper combination of positive social cues and actual job enrichment that will improve motivation and satisfaction?

These questions are important and need to be answered in order to "fine-tune" or fully understand an individually-oriented system. Yet, even without answers to these questions, we already know that a well-run organization using an individually-oriented system *can* be effective. The problem is we usually don't implement such a system, either completely or very well, in most organizations. Instead, we often compare poorly managed corporations using individually-oriented systems (e.g., those with rigid bureaucratic structures) with more effectively run firms using another motivational system (e.g., Japanese organizations), concluding that the individual model is wrong. The truth may be that the individual model may be just as correct as other approaches, but we simply don't implement it as well.

### *The group-oriented system*

Individually-oriented systems are obviously not the only way to go. We can also have a group-oriented system, where satisfaction and performance are derived from group participation. In fact, much of organizational life could be designed around groups, if we wanted to capitalize fully on the power of groups to influence work attitudes and behavior.[16] The basic idea would be to make group participation so important that groups would be capable of controlling both satisfaction and performance. Some of the most common techniques would be:

- Organizing work around intact groups.
- Having groups charged with selection, training, and rewarding of members.
- Using groups to enforce strong norms for behavior, with group involvement in off-the-job as well as on-the-job behavior.

- Distributing resources on a group rather than individual basis.
- Allowing and perhaps even promoting intergroup rivalry so as to build within-group solidarity.

Group-oriented systems may be difficult for people at the top to control, but they can be very powerful and involving. We know from military research that soldiers can fight long and hard, not out of special patriotism, but from devotion and loyalty to their units. We know that participation in various high-tech project groups can be immensely involving, both in terms of one's attitudes and performance. We also know that people will serve long and hard hours to help build or preserve organizational divisions or departments, perhaps more out of loyalty and altruism than self-interest. Thus, because individuals will work to achieve group praise and adoration, a group-oriented system, effectively managed, can potentially contribute to high job performance and satisfaction.

### *The organizationally-oriented system*

A third way of organizing work might be an organizationally-oriented system, using the principles of Ouchi's Theory Z and Lawler's recommendations for developing high-performing systems.[17] The basic goal would be to arrange working conditions so that individuals gain satisfaction from contributing to the entire organization's welfare. If individuals were to identify closely with the organization as a whole, then organizational performance would be intrinsically rewarding to the individual. On a less altruistic basis, individuals might also gain extrinsic rewards from association with a high-performing organization, since successful organizations may provide greater personal opportunities in terms of salary and promotion. Common features of an organizationally-oriented system would be:

- Socialization into the organization as a whole to foster identification with the entire business and not just a particular subunit.
- Job rotation around the company so that loyalty is not limited to one subunit.
- Long training period with the development of skills that are specific to the company and not transferable to other firms in the industry or profession, thus committing people to the employing organization.
- Long-term or protected employment to gain organizational loyalty, with concern for survival and welfare of the firm.
- Decentralized operations, with few departments or subunits to compete for the allegiance of members.
- Few status distinctions between employees so that dissension and separatism are not fostered.
- Economic education and sharing of organizational information about products, financial condition, and strategies of the firm.
- Tying individual rewards (at all levels in the firm) to organizational performance through various forms of profit sharing, stock options, and bonuses.

The Japanese have obviously been the major proponents of organizationally-oriented systems, although some of the features listed here (such as profit sharing) are very American in origin. The odd thing is that Americans have consistently followed an organizationally-oriented system for middle and upper management and for members of professional organizations such as law and accounting firms. For these high-level employees, loyalty may be as valued as immediate performance, with the firm expecting the individual to defend the organization, even if there does not seem to be any obvious self-interest involved. Such loyalty is rarely demanded or expected from the lower levels of traditional Western organizations.

## Evaluating the three systems

I started this article by noting that it may be very difficult to change job performance and satisfaction. Then I noted that recognition of this difficulty should not resign us to the present situation, but spur us to stronger and more systemic actions—in a sense, throwing more variables at the problem. As a result, I have tried to characterize three syndromes of actions that might be effective routes toward the happy/productive worker.

One could build a logical case for the use of any of the three motivational systems. Each has the potential for arousing individuals, steering their behavior in desired ways, and building satisfaction as a consequence of high performance. Individually-oriented systems work by tapping the desires and goals of individuals and by taking advantage of our cultural affinity for independence. Group-oriented systems work by taking advantage of our more social selves, using group pressures and loyalty as the means of enforcing desired behavior and dispensing praise for accomplishments. Finally, organizationally-oriented systems function by building intense attraction to the goals of an institution, where individual pleasure is derived from serving the collective welfare.

If we have three logical and defensible routes toward achieving the happy/productive worker, which is the best path? The answer to this question will obviously depend on how the question is phrased. If "best" means appropriate from a cultural point of view, we will get one answer. As Americans, although we respect organizational loyalty, we often become suspicious of near total institutions where behavior is closely monitored and strongly policed—places like the company town and religious cult. If we define "best" as meaning the highest level of current performance, we might get a different answer, since many of the Japanese-run plants are now outperforming the American variety. Still, if we phrase the question in terms of *potential* effectiveness, we may get a third answer. Cross-cultural comparisons, as I mentioned, often pit poorly managed individually-oriented systems (especially those with non-contingent rewards and a bureaucratic promotion system) against more smoothly running group or organizationally-oriented systems. Thus, we really do not know which system, managed to its potential, will lead to the greatest performance.

## Mixing the systems

If we accept the fact that individual, group, and organizationally-oriented systems may each do *something* right, would it be possible to take advantage of all three? That is, can we either combine all three systems into some suprasystem or attempt to build a hybrid system by using the best features of each?

I have trepidations about combining the three approaches. Instead of a stronger treatment, we may end up with either a conflicted or confused environment. Because the individually-oriented system tends to foster competition among individual employees, it would not, for example, be easily merged with group-oriented systems that promote intragroup solidarity. Likewise, organizationally-oriented systems that emphasize how people can serve a common goal may not blend well with group-oriented systems that foster intergroup rivalry. Finally, the use of either a group- or organizationally-oriented reward system may diminish individual motivation, since it becomes more difficult for the person to associate his behavior with collective accomplishments and outcomes. Thus, by mixing the motivational approaches, we may end up with a watered-down treatment that does not fulfill the potential of *any* of the three systems.

In deciding which system to use, we need to face squarely the costs as well as benefits of the three approaches. For example, firms considering an individually-oriented system should assess not only the gains associated with increases in individual motivation, but also potential losses in collaboration that might result from interpersonal competition. Similarly, companies thinking of using a group-oriented system need to study the trade-offs of intergroup competition that can be a byproduct of increased intragroup solidarity. And, before thinking that an organizationally-oriented system will solve all the firm's problems, one needs to know whether motivation to achieve collective goals can be heightened to the point where it outweighs potential losses in motivation toward personal and group interests. These trade-offs are not trivial. They trigger considerations of human resource policy as well as more general philosophical issues of what the organization wants to be. They also involve technical problems for which current organizational research has few solutions, since scholars have tended to study treatments in isolation rather than the effect of larger systems of variables.

So far, all we can be sure of is that task structure plays a key role in formulating the proper motivational strategy. As an example, consider the following cases: a sales organization can be divided into discrete territories (where total performance is largely the sum of individual efforts), a research organization where several product groups are charged with making new developments (where aggregate performance is close to the sum of group efforts), and a high-technology company where success and failure is due to total collaboration and collective effort. In each of these three cases, the choice of the proper motivational system will be determined by whether one views individual, group, or collective effort as the most important element. Such a choice is also determined by the degree to which one is willing to sacrifice (or trade-off) a degree of performance from other elements of the system, be they the behavior of individuals, groups, or the collective whole. Thus, the major point is that each motivational system has its relative strengths and weaknesses—that despite the claims of many of our theories of management, there is no simple or conflict-free road to the happy/productive worker.

## Conclusion

Although this article started by noting that the search for the happy/productive worker has been a rather quixotic venture, I have tried to end the discussion with some guarded optimism. By using individual, group, and organizational systems, I have shown how it is *at least possible* to create changes that can overwhelm the forces for stability in both job attitudes and performance. None of these three approaches are a panacea that will solve all of an organization's problems, and no doubt some very hard choices must be made between them. Yet, caution need not preclude action. Therefore, rather than the usual academic's plea for further research or the consultant's claim for bountiful results, we need actions that are flexible enough to allow for mistakes and adjustments along the way.

## Acknowledgments

This article is based on an invited address delivered at the 1985 American Psychological Association, Los Angeles, California.

## References

1. A. H. Brayfield and W. H. Crockett, "Employee Attitudes and Employee Performance," *Psychological Bulletin*, 51 (1955): 396–424.
2. Victor H. Vroom, *Work and Motivation* (New York, NY: Wiley, 1969).
3. James G. March and Herbert A. Simon, *Organizations* (New York, NY: Wiley, 1958).
4. Richard J. Hackman and Greg R. Oldham, *Work Redesign* (Reading, MA: Addison-Wesley, 1980).
5. E.g., Gerald R. Salancik and Jeffrey Pfeffer, "A Social Information Processing Approach to Job Attitudes and Task Design," *Administrative Science Quarterly*, 23 (1978): 224–253.
6. Robert Kahn, (1985).
7. Benjamin Schneider and Peter Dachler, "A Note on the Stability of the Job Description Index," *Journal of Applied Psychology*, 63 (1978): 650–653.
8. Elaine D. Pulakos and Neal Schmitt, "A Longitudinal Study of a Valance Model Approach for the Prediction of Job Satisfaction of New Employees," *Journal of Applied Psychology*, 68 (1983): 307–312.
9. Barry M. Staw and Jerry Ross, "Stability in the Midst of Change: A Dispositional Approach to Job Attitudes," *Journal of Applied Phychology*, 70 (1985): 469–480.
10. Barry M. Staw, Nancy E. Bell, and John A. Clausen, "The Dispositional Approach to Job Attitudes: A Lifetime Longitudinal Test," *Administrative Science Quarterly* (March 1986).

11. See, Lawrence H. Peters, Edward J. O' Connor, and Joe R. Eulberg, "Situational Constraints: Sources, Consequences, and Future Considerations," in Kendreth M. Rowland and Gerald R. Ferris, eds., *Research in Personnel and Human Resources Management*, Vol. 3 (Greenwich, CT: JAI Press, 1985).
12. For a review, see Marvin D. Dunnette, "Aptitudes, Abilities, and Skills," in Marvin D. Dunnette, ed., *Handbook of Industrial and Organizational Psychology* (Chicago, IL: Rand McNally, 1976).
13. As found by John Clausen, personal communications, 1986.
14. Rosabeth M. Kanter, *The Change Masters* (New York, NY: Simon & Schuster, 1983).
15. Richard A. Guzzo, Susan E. Jackson, and Raymond A. Katzell, "Meta-analysis Analysis," in Barry M. Staw and Larry L. Cummings, eds., *Research in Organizational Behavior*, Volume 9 (Greenwich, CT: JAI Press, 1987).
16. See, Harold J. Leavitt, "Suppose We Took Groups Seriously," in E. L. Cass and F. G. Zimmer, eds., *Man and Work in Society* (New York, NY: Van Nostrand, 1975).
17. William Ouchi, *Theory Z: How American Business Can Meet the Japanese Challenge* (Reading, MA: Addison-Wesley, 1981); Edward E. Lawler, III, "Increasing Worker Involvement to Enhance Organizational Effectiveness," in Paul Goodman, ed., *Change in Organizations* (San Francisco, CA: Jossey-Bass, 1982).

# 9

# THE JOB SATISFACTION–JOB PERFORMANCE RELATIONSHIP

A qualitative and quantitative review

*Timothy A. Judge, Carl J. Thoresen, Joyce E. Bono and Gregory K. Patton*

Source: *Psychological Bulletin* 127(3) (2001): 376–407.

## Abstract

A qualitative and quantitative review of the relationship between job satisfaction and job performance is provided. The qualitative review is organized around 7 models that characterize past research on the relationship between job satisfaction and job performance. Although some models have received more support than have others, research has not provided conclusive confirmation or disconfirmation of any model, partly because of a lack of assimilation and integration in the literature. Research devoted to testing these models waned following 2 meta-analyses of the job satisfaction–job performance relationship. Because of limitations in these prior analyses and the misinterpretation of their findings, a new meta-analysis was conducted on 312 samples with a combined $N$ of 54.417. The mean true correlation between overall job satisfaction and job performance was estimated to be .30. In light of these results and the qualitative review, an agenda for future research on the satisfaction–performance relationship is provided.

The study of the relationship between job satisfaction and job performance is one of the most venerable research traditions in industrial–organizational psychology. This relationship has been described as the "Holy Grail" of industrial psychologists (Landy, 1989). Indeed, interest in the link between workplace attitudes and productivity goes back at least as far as the Hawthorne studies (Roethlisberger & Dickson, 1939), and the topic continues to be written about to this day. Although the area has not lacked for qualitative (Brayfield & Crockett, 1955; Herzberg, Mausner, Peterson, & Capwell, 1957; Locke, 1970; Schwab & Cummings, 1970) or quantitative (Iaffaldano & Muchinsky, 1985; Petty, Mc-Gee, & Cavender, 1984) reviews, these reviews deserve some scrutiny. Moreover, there have been many developments in the past several years that merit renewed discussion and integration of this literature.

Accordingly, the purpose of the present article is to reexamine the state of the literature concerning the relationship between job satisfaction and job performance. Given the breadth and complexity of the literature, as well as the nature of some of the issues that have arisen, we provide both a qualitative and a quantitative review of the literature. Thus, the article is organized into three major sections. First, we qualitatively review past research on the job satisfaction–job performance relationship. In this section, we briefly summarize previous reviews of the literature and then consider various conceptualizations of the satisfaction–performance relationship. Second, we report on the results of a meta-analysis that remedies limitations in past meta-analytic reviews and provides the most comprehensive evidence to date on the magnitude of the relationship between job satisfaction and job performance. Finally, in light of our qualitative and quantitative reviews, we provide suggestions for future research that could further understanding of the nature of the satisfaction–performance relationship.

## Past research on the job satisfaction–job performance relationship

The potential linkage between employee attitudes and performance was considered in earnest in the 1930s, coinciding with (and as a result of) the Hawthorne studies and the ensuing human relations movement. Although the Hawthorne studies are commonly credited with emphasizing a linkage between employee attitudes and performance, researchers were more circumspect in their conclusions than most assume (e.g., Roethlisberger, 1941). It is clear, however, that the human relations movement stimulated interest in the relationship. Following the human relations movement, the most influential narrative review of the job satisfaction–job performance relationship was published by Brayfield and Crockett (1955). In this article, the authors reviewed studies relating job satisfaction to job performance as well as to a number of other behavioral outcomes (accidents, absence, and turnover). Brayfield and Crockett concluded that there was not much of a relationship between job satisfaction and performance, labeling it as "minimal or no relationship" (p. 405). The Brayfield and Crockett review was limited by the very small number of published studies available for review at that time (only nine studies were reviewed that reported a correlation between individual job satisfaction and job performance) and the general subjectivity of qualitative reviews. In spite of these shortcomings, Brayfield and Crockett's article was perhaps the most frequently cited review in this area of research prior to 1985.

Since the Brayfield and Crockett (1955) review, several other influential narrative reviews have been published (Herzberg et al., 1957; Locke, 1970; Schwab & Cummings, 1970; Vroom, 1964). These reviews differed greatly in their orientation and, to some degree, in the optimism they expressed regarding the satisfaction–performance relationship, with Herzberg et al. being the most optimistic. The main gist of two of these reviews (Locke, 1970; Schwab & Cummings, 1970) was to issue a strong call for theory-driven investigations of the satisfaction–performance relationship. In response to these reviews, researchers began to consider more closely the nature of the relationship, giving particular consideration to factors that might moderate or mediate the relationship. Accordingly, in the next section of the article, we group these investigations into seven models of the satisfaction–performance relationship and review research that has been conducted on these functional forms.

## *Nature of the job satisfaction–job performance relationship*

There are at least seven different ways in which the satisfaction–performance relationship has been specified. A graphical depiction of the different functional forms is provided in Figure 1. These theoretical perspectives previously have not been reviewed together; accordingly, below we provide a review of each of these perspectives. Before each of these models is discussed, however, a brief discussion of the typical means through which studies investigating the satisfaction–performance relationship have been conducted is warranted. By far, the most dominant methodology has involved the concurrent investigation of these two variables. (However, as we note in discussing Model 6, the correlation between satisfaction and performance is not the focus of the vast majority of studies that have shown a correlation between the constructs.) In such studies, employees are asked about current satisfaction levels, and these responses are correlated with supervisory assessments of job performance, organizational performance records (e.g., sales, productivity), and the like. Some studies have made use of longitudinal, panel, or cross-lagged designs to investigate the satisfaction–performance relationship (e.g., Bagozzi, 1980; Sheridan & Slocum, 1975; Siegel & Bowen, 1971; Wanous, 1974), but such studies have been rare. Causal inferences based on cross-sectional data represent a contentious issue in nearly all areas of psychology (James, Mulaik, & Brett, 1982), and the legitimacy of drawing causal conclusions based on hypothesized models with cross-sectional data is directly dependent on the theoretical appropriateness of the model in question. Likewise, the use of longitudinal or panel designs does not ensure legitimate causal interpretations—one must control for (or at least rule out on logical grounds) any unmeasured variables that could spuriously influence the hypothesized relationship (Cook & Campbell, 1979). Thus, though the studies in Models 1–3 (reviewed below) are purportedly causal, rarely are the assumptions necessary to draw causal inferences satisfied.

Perhaps because of the logistical difficulties associated with conducting such studies in field settings, there also have been only a handful of quasi-experimental studies in the satisfaction–performance literature. Some of these studies have attempted to increase the satisfaction–performance correlation in a "real" work

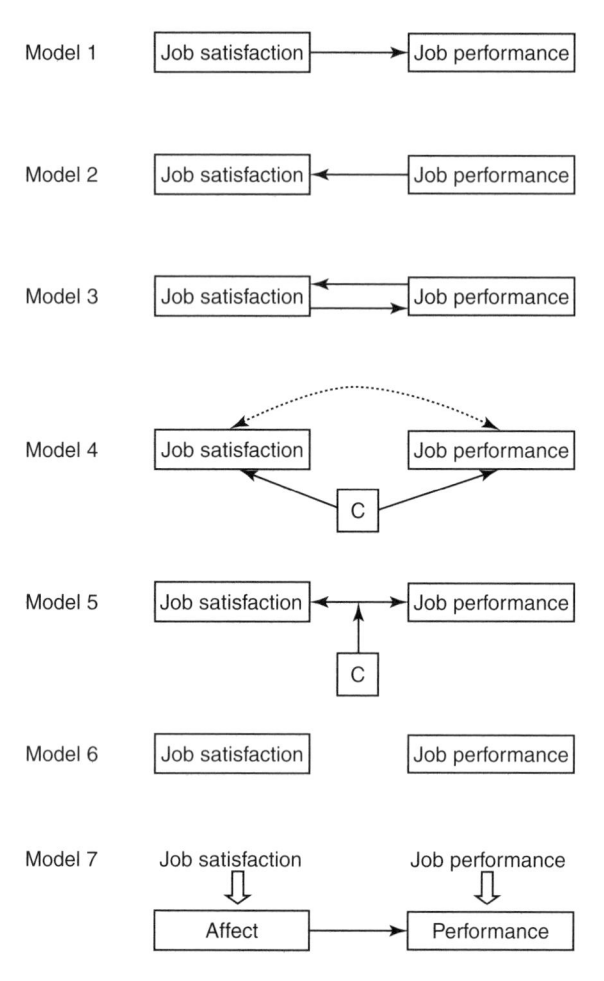

Figure 1  Models of the relationship between job satisfaction and job performance. (Note that in Models 4 and 5, C denotes a third variable.)

setting through some theoretically justified intervention, such as the use of contingent versus noncontingent reward schedules for performance (e.g., Orpen, 1981, 1982a). Other studies have investigated the effectiveness of organizational interventions on raising levels of both satisfaction and performance, although the magnitude of the relationship between these two variables was not the focus of these studies. For example, Oldham, Cummings, Mischel, Schmidtke, and Zhou (1995) examined the effects of having employees listen to music using personal stereo headsets on productivity, satisfaction, and a host of other work responses. It is unclear from these studies whether or not there were unmeasured factors that could have affected the selection of employees into experimental versus control groups (Cook & Campbell, 1979).

*Model 1: Job satisfaction causes job performance*

This model posits a causal effect of job satisfaction on job performance. This is probably the oldest specification of the relationship and is often attributed to the human relations movement. As G. Strauss (1968) commented, "Early human relationists viewed the morale–productivity relationship quite simply: higher morale would lead to improved productivity" (p. 264). This model is implicitly grounded in the broader attitudes literature in social psychology. The premise that attitudes lead to behavior is a prominent theme in the literature, and most attitude researchers assume that attitudes carry with them behavioral implications. Fishbein and Ajzen (1975), for example, defined an *attitude* as a "learned predisposition to respond in a consistently favorable or unfavorable manner with respect to a given object" (p. 6). Fishbein (1973) also noted that attitude measures "should be consistently related to the pattern of behaviors that the individual engages in with respect to the attitude object" (p. 22). More recently, Eagly and Chaiken (1993) concluded, "In general, people who evaluate an attitude object favorably tend to engage in behaviors that foster or support it, and people who evaluate an attitude object unfavorably tend to engage in behaviors that hinder or oppose it" (p. 12). Following this logic, attitudes toward the job should be related to behaviors on the job, the most central of which is performance on the job.

Surprisingly, however, outside of the causal studies that have investigated a reciprocal relationship between satisfaction and performance (Model 3—see below), we are aware of only two studies that have specifically stipulated a unidirectional causal effect of job satisfaction on job performance. Keaveney and Nelson (1993), in testing a complex model of the interrelationship among numerous attitudes (intrinsic motivation orientation, role conflict, role ambiguity, psychological withdrawal), found a job satisfaction → job performance path coefficient of .12 (*ns*) in a relatively saturated model involving these attitudes; a simpler model provided a much stronger (.29) but still nonsignificant coefficient. Shore and Martin (1989) found that when regressing supervisory ratings of job performance on job satisfaction and organizational commitment, job satisfaction explained more incremental variance in the performance of professionals ($\Delta R^2 = .07, p < .05$) and clerical workers ($\Delta R^2 = .06, p < .05$) than did commitment ($\Delta R^2 = .01$ in both samples, *ns*). Thus, few studies have posited a unidirectional effect of job satisfaction on job performance, and the findings of those studies are inconclusive.[1]

*Model 2: Job performance causes job satisfaction*

Though most attitude–behavior research in psychology has assumed that the link is from attitudes to behavior, this view has not gone unchallenged. Olson and Zanna

(1993) reviewed several theories in social psychology that argue attitudes follow behavior; these theories tend to be completely independent of the planned behavior models that dominate attitude → behavior research. Perhaps not surprisingly, then, the theoretical rationale for the performance → satisfaction relationship also is quite different from the basis for the opposite link. Although there are differences in these explanations, broadly construed the performance → satisfaction model is derived from the assumption that performance leads to valued outcomes that are satisfying to individuals.

Expectancy-based theories of motivation generally stipulate that satisfaction follows from the rewards produced by performance (Naylor, Pritchard, & Ilgen, 1980; Vroom, 1964). Lawler and Porter (1967), expectancy theorists themselves, argued that performance would lead to job satisfaction through the provision of intrinsic and extrinsic rewards. As these authors noted, "Briefly stated, good performance may lead to rewards, which in turn lead to satisfaction" (p. 23). Like expectancy theorists, Locke (1970) viewed satisfaction as resulting from performance, but in this case satisfaction was viewed as a function of goal-directed behavior and value attainment. Even advocates of intrinsic motivation would implicitly stipulate an effect of performance on satisfaction. Deci and Ryan's (1985) self-determination theory, for example, argues that satisfaction follows from the rewards that result from behavior (though they also argued that the motivations for the behavior are important to this process).

Compared with research stipulating a unidirectional effect of job satisfaction on job performance, more studies have posited a unidirectional effect of job performance on job satisfaction. We are aware of 10 studies that have investigated such a link. In 4 of the studies (S. P. Brown, Cron, & Leigh, 1993; Darden, Hampton, & Howell, 1989; MacKenzie, Podsakoff, & Ahearne, 1998; Stumpf & Hartman, 1984), job performance had a significant causal effect on job satisfaction. In 6 of the studies (Behrman & Perreault, 1984; Bimbaum & Somers, 1993; S. P. Brown & Peterson, 1994; Dubinsky & Hartley, 1986; Dubinsky & Skinner, 1984; Hampton, Dubinsky, & Skinner, 1986), there was no significant effect. Thus, as in the job satisfaction → job performance studies, results of studies testing the job performance → job satisfaction relationship are inconsistent. Several caveats are in order when interpreting these results. First, as before, though these studies are ostensibly causal, this does not mean that the associations are proven to be causally valid. Second, in the cases in which job performance did not have a unique effect on job satisfaction, one cannot conclude that no association exists. In fact, in many of these studies, there was a significant correlation between the two constructs, but the effect was reduced by the relative influence of other variables, or the effect was mediated through other constructs (e.g., in S. P. Brown & Peterson, 1994, a .31, $p < .01$, correlation became a .04, *ns*, performance → satisfaction path coefficient when effort and role conflict also were modeled to influence job satisfaction). Finally, and somewhat curiously, most (8 of 10) of these studies were published in marketing journals. Thus, the generalizability of the results is unclear.

## Model 3: Job satisfaction and job performance are reciprocally related

Models of the reciprocal relationship between job satisfaction and job performance have no distinct theoretical foundation. Rather, they are hybrid models of the previous two approaches, ostensibly accepted by those who believe that both theoretical explanations are plausible, that performance can be both satisfying and, in turn, caused by satisfaction. Although reciprocal models may well find unique justification in each literature, further theoretical grounding seems important. For example, if the relationship is reciprocal, how does the reciprocation work? A dynamic model seems necessary to firmly ground such an approach, yet we are aware of no dynamic models in the literature. Perhaps Schwab and Cummings (1970) came the closest to an elucidation of a dynamic model in their attempt to adapt March and Simon's (1958) model to the satisfaction–performance relationship.

Five studies have investigated the possibility of a reciprocal relationship between job satisfaction and job performance. In these studies, job satisfaction and job performance are related either in a cross-sectional nonrecursive causal model, or in a cross-lagged correlational model, where Time 2 job satisfaction is regressed on Time 1 job satisfaction and Time 1 job performance, and Time 2 job performance is regressed on Time 1 job performance and Time 1 job satisfaction. Two of these studies (Bagozzi, 1980; Siegel & Bowen, 1971) have suggested that job performance leads to job satisfaction but not the reverse. Two other studies provided some support for a reciprocal relationship (mutual causal effects between job satisfaction and job performance). Specifically, Sheridan and Slocum's (1975) study yielded partial support for a reciprocal relationship; Wanous (1974) found support for a reciprocal relationship, but it depended on the type of satisfaction—for extrinsic satisfaction, satisfaction → performance, whereas for intrinsic satisfaction, performance → satisfaction. Finally, Prestwich (1980) found no significant causal effect in either direction. Some of these studies were cross-sectional (e.g., Bagozzi, 1980), and some were longitudinal (e.g., Sheridan & Slocum, 1975; Siegel & Bowen, 1971). Although the results of these studies are somewhat inconsistent, four of the five studies suggest a causal effect of job performance on job satisfaction, and two of the five suggest a causal effect of job satisfaction on job performance.

## Model 4: The relationship between job satisfaction and job performance is spurious

A spurious correlation is observed when the relationship between two variables is due to the relation of these variables to a third, unmeasured variable (Cohen & Cohen, 1983). Although few studies have formally tested the hypothesis that the job satisfaction–job performance relationship is spurious, several studies support such an inference. S. P. Brown and Peterson (1993) found that a nonzero relationship between job satisfaction and job performance became nonsignificant when role ambiguity was allowed to influence both. Several studies have suggested that self-esteem might explain the association between job satisfaction and job performance. Pierce, Gardner, Cummings, and Dunham (1989) found that self-esteem was related to both job satisfaction and job performance. Further, Gardner and Pierce (1998) found that job satisfaction and job performance were significantly related ($r = .27, p < .01$), but once organization-based self-esteem was allowed to influence both, there was no significant relation between satisfaction and performance. Keller (1997) found that a significant satisfaction–performance correlation became nonsignificant once job involvement and organizational commitment were controlled. A significant satisfaction–performance correlation also has been rendered nonsignificant when controlling for trust in management (Rich, 1997) and participation in decision-making (Abdel-Halim, 1983).

Several caveats must be kept in mind when interpreting these results. First, the purpose of most of these studies was not to investigate the spuriousness of the job satisfaction–job performance relationship. Accordingly, other—more theoretically salient—variables not measured in the aforementioned studies may lend additional insight into the satisfaction–performance relationship. Second, the purported causal effects found in these studies may not be valid (i.e., failure to satisfy the assumptions required to make causal inferences may have rendered the conclusions invalid). Finally, a nonsignificant direct relationship between job satisfaction and job performance does not mean that there is not a meaningful relationship between job satisfaction and job performance—it might simply mean the relationship is mediated by other variables (we address this issue later in the article).

*Model 5: The relationship between job satisfaction and job performance is moderated by other variables*

By far the most common means of investigating the job satisfaction–job performance relationship has involved the use of moderator variables. Perhaps the most frequently investigated moderator is reward contingency. Numerous studies have hypothesized that job performance should affect job satisfaction only to the extent that people are compensated based on their performance. The logic of this argument is that, assuming pay is valued by employees, high performance should be satisfying (or low performance dissatisfying) to the extent that pay is linked to performance. Although this proposal generally was couched in terms of operant conditioning (Cherrington, Reitz, & Scott, 1971; Orpen, 1981, 1982a), this need not (and perhaps should not) be the case. Locke (1970) hypothesized that value attainment would moderate the performance–satisfaction relationship, such that performance is satisfying to the extent that it leads to important work values. Thus, a strong pay–performance contingency would make those who value pay satisfied because performance leads to valued rewards. Locke's (1970) hypothesis exposes another limitation of the pay-for-performance contingency hypothesis.

Pay is only one of many job rewards, and research indicates a weak correlation between pay and job satisfaction (Spector, 1997). Employees report that they value intrinsic rewards such as the nature of the work itself more than pay (Jurgensen, 1978). Furthermore, tests of the reward contingency hypothesis have ignored the possibility that performance itself may be intrinsically satisfying to individuals. Despite these limitations, in a review of this literature, Podsakoff and Williams (1986) found that the general satisfaction–job performance relationship was somewhat stronger in studies in which rewards were linked to performance (mean $r = .27$) than in studies where there was no performance–pay contingency (mean $r = .17$).

Another potential moderator of the job satisfaction–job performance relationship is job complexity or intrinsic job characteristics. This moderator is similar to the pay–performance contingency moderator in that both deal with work rewards. The distinction is that job complexity is intrinsic whereas pay is extrinsic; however, the direction of the effect should be the same. Namely, performing well in an interesting or stimulating job should be intrinsically satisfying, whereas performing well in a repetitive or boring job should be less rewarding (Baird, 1976). Only three studies have tested this proposition, and substantial differences in the nature of the studies make the results difficult to assimilate. One of the difficulties is that two of the studies (Ivancevich, 1978, 1979), in addition to testing the moderating role of job complexity, also investigated the causal directionality of the relationship. A study that posits joint causal effects, in the presence of a moderator variable, is a complicated proposition. Advances in causal modeling in the last 20 years might facilitate future tests of the relationship.

Beyond the pay–performance contingency, the most commonly investigated moderator of the satisfaction–performance relationship is self-esteem. Korman's (1970) self-consistency theory predicts that individuals will be most satisfied when engaging in those behaviors that are consistent with their self-image. Thus, the relationship between satisfaction and performance should depend on self-esteem, such that only for an individual with high self-esteem is performance satisfying (high performance would not necessarily be satisfying to individuals with low self-esteem because it is inconsistent with their self-perceived adequacy). Korman's theory has been reviewed by Dipboye (1977), who suggested that evidence provided "very weak" (p. 115) support for this aspect of the theory. Our reading of the literature since Dipboye's review suggests mixed support for the theory. Some studies appear to be supportive (Inkson, 1978; Jacobs & Solomon, 1977), others unsupportive (Kaldenberg & Becker, 1991; Tharenou & Harker, 1984), and still others partially supportive (Dipboye, Zultowski, Dewhirst, & Arvey, 1979; E. M. Lopez, 1982). It would not be fair to conclude that the theory is without support, nor would it be accurate to maintain that Korman's theory is wholly supported.

Myriad other moderators of the satisfaction–performance relationship have been proposed and/or tested, including attributions and organizational tenure (Norris & Niebuhr, 1984), cognitive ability (Varca & James-Valutis, 1993), need for achievement (Steers, 1975), career stage (Stumpf & Rabinowitz, 1981), pressure for performance (Ewen, 1973), time pressure (Bhagat, 1982), job fit (Carlson, 1969), occupational group (R. E. Doll & Gunderson, 1969), dyadic duration (Mossholder, Bedeian, Niebuhr, & Wesolowski, 1994), similarity in problem-solving styles (Goldsmith, McNeilly, & Ross, 1989), perceived appropriateness of supervisory task allocation decisions (Jabri, 1992), affective disposition (Hochwarter, Perrewé, Ferris, & Brymer, 1999), and situational constraints (Herman, 1973). A problem is that very few of these moderators have been tested in more than one study. This makes it difficult to assess their validity. Thus, though the large number of studies attests to the popularity of the moderator perspective, little assimilation has occurred.

### *Model 6: There is no relationship between job satisfaction and job performance*

Of all of the studies that report a correlation between job satisfaction and job performance, only a minority fall into the five models reviewed above (i.e., only a few posit any kind of a relationship between satisfaction and performance). Thus, most studies that include job satisfaction and job performance treat them as separate variables that have no direct relationship to one another. For example, Greenberger, Strasser, Cummings, and Dunham (1989) investigated the causal relationship between personal control and job satisfaction, and between personal control and job performance, but did not investigate the relationship between job satisfaction and job performance. Authors might ignore the satisfaction–performance relationship, while including the two constructs in their study, for different reasons. For example, authors might be convinced there is no relationship between job satisfaction and job performance, and/or they might believe that investigating the relationship between the constructs is beyond the scope of their study. Although either of these assumptions might be valid (we address the first assumption—no relationship between satisfaction and performance—shortly), studies operating from either of these assumptions are limited in what they can tell us about the nature of the relationship between job satisfaction and job performance.

### *Model 7: Alternative conceptualizations of job satisfaction and/or job performance*

The next three models of the relationship between job satisfaction and job performance are similar in that they argue that it makes little sense to consider job satisfaction as related to job performance in the traditional way. Rather, they argue that the general concept that attitudes lead to performance has merit, but only when attitudes and/or performance are reconceptualized. Collectively, these models are depicted as Model 7 in Figure 1.

RECONCEPTUALIZIING ATTITUDES

In response to the apparently low satisfaction–performance relationship, some researchers have recast the satisfaction–performance hypothesis in terms of the relationship between emotions and performance (George & Brief, 1996; Staw, Sutton, & Pelled, 1994). For example, Staw et al. demonstrated that positive emotions on the job led to favorable job outcomes. Why would positive emotions at work predict job performance where job satisfaction would not? Both theory (George & Brief, 1996) and empirical evidence (Isen & Baron, 1991) indicate that positive affect is related to employee motivation and other positive aspects of organizational membership. As reviewed by Wright and Staw (1999), employees with positive affect may be more motivated according to several theories of motivation, including expectancy theory, goal setting theory, and attribution theory. Research operationalizing positive emotions through a variety of methods and measures has demonstrated that positive emotions are related to job performance (Cropanzano, James, & Konovsky, 1993; George & Bettenhausen, 1990; Staw & Barsade, 1993; Staw et al., 1994; Wright, Bonett, & Sweeney, 1993; Wright & Staw, 1999).

Several researchers have gone so far as to argue that job satisfaction fails to predict job performance because extant job satisfaction measures reflect more cognitive evaluation than affective tone (Brief & Roberson, 1989; Organ & Near, 1985). Brief and Roberson concluded that three of the most widely used job satisfaction measures differed dramatically in the degree to which they captured affect. In support of this argument, Brief (1998) used this study to demonstrate that cognitions correlate more strongly (average $r = .70$) with job satisfaction than does affect (average $r = .43$). However, it seems likely that job beliefs (cognitions) are as influenced by affect as job satisfaction itself. Indeed, Brief and Roberson's results, as well as those of another study (Weiss, Nicholas, & Daus, 1999), demonstrate that both cognition and affect contribute to job satisfaction. Nevertheless, the hypothesis that positive emotions relate to performance has garnered considerable support in recent research (see Wright & Staw, 1999).

RECONCEPTUALIZING PERFORMANCE

Organ (1988) suggested that the failure to find a relationship between job satisfaction and performance is due to the narrow means often used to define job performance. Typically, researchers have equated job performance with performance of specific job tasks. However, some researchers (see Borman & Motowidlo, 1993) have broadened the performance domain to include citizenship behaviors. Borman, Motowidlo, Organ, and colleagues have argued that these behaviors, which include helping others with their jobs, volunteering for additional work, and supporting organizational objectives, shape the social and psychological context in which task performance takes place. Hence, Organ argued that when performance is conceptualized more broadly—to include both task performance and organizational citizenship behaviors—its correlation with job satisfaction will increase. Organ based his hypothesis on the argument that job satisfaction measures assess perceived fairness and, based on equity theory, fairness cognitions should correlate more strongly with citizenship behaviors than with typical measures of performance. Although support for the assumptions underlying Organ's proposition has not been directly examined, a recent meta-analysis supports the link between job satisfaction and citizenship finding nonzero correlations between job satisfaction and the two major dimensions of organizational citizenship behaviors—altruism ($\rho = .28$, $k = 28$, where $\rho$ is the estimated population true-score correlation, corrected for unreliability, and $k$ is the number of correlations) and compliance ($\rho = .28$, $k = 22$; Organ & Ryan, 1995).

ORGANIZATIONAL LEVEL OF ANALYSIS

Ostroff (1992) noted that one possible reason that the satisfaction–performance relationship has not been substantiated is that researchers have considered the relationship solely at the individual level of analysis. The individual level of analysis, Ostroff argued, may be too restrictive in the way that performance is measured because it fails to take into account the wide range of behaviors individuals may enact in response to (dis)satisfaction. This argument is similar to Organ's, though we are not aware of any studies that have related job satisfaction to organizational citizenship behaviors at the organizational level of analysis. Ostroff found significant correlations between average teacher job satisfaction in a school district and numerous indicators of school district effectiveness (student test scores, drop-out rate, vandalism costs, student satisfaction, teacher turnover). In several other studies, all of which were completed in the same educational context. Ostroff and colleagues have revealed reliable relations between job satisfaction and performance at the organizational level (Ostroff, 1993; Ostroff & Schmitt, 1993). Recently, Harter and Creglow (1998) linked overall satisfaction to various indicators (customer satisfaction, profitability, productivity, turnover) of the performance of a variety of business units.

## *Summary*

Among the seven general models of the job satisfaction–job performance relationship that have been reviewed herein, the results are inconsistent. Part of the confusion may be due to the piecemeal nature of the research—many models have been proposed, but, with a few exceptions, most have not been thoroughly or systematically tested. This has made assimilation and integration difficult. Some of the disarray can be attributed to disagreement over the nature of the satisfaction–performance relationship. If there is little relationship between job satisfaction and job performance, then there can be no direct causal effect of satisfaction on performance or performance on satisfaction (Models 1 and 2), nor can there be a reciprocal relationship (Model 3), nor would there be a correlation that could be spurious (Model 4). Thus, if there is an inconsequential relationship between satisfaction and performance, there is little to be gained by testing the validity of Models 1–4. On the other hand, Models 5–7 could be valid in the context of a zero or very weak correlation between individual satisfaction and performance. Thus, an important first step in determining the merits of models of the satisfaction–performance relationship is to determine the magnitude of the bivariate relationship. Accordingly, in the next section of the article, we review meta-analytic evidence of this relationship.

## *Meta-analytic reviews of the job satisfaction–job performance relationship*

There have been two meta-analyses of the job satisfaction–job performance relationship. Petty et al. (1984) provided a limited meta-analysis of the job satisfaction–job performance relationship. These authors confined their analyses to 16 studies that were published in five journals from 1964 to 1983 and that included a measure of overall job satisfaction. Correcting the correlations for unreliability in job satisfaction and job performance. Petty et al. reported a mean corrected correlation of .31 between the constructs. In interpreting their results, Petty et al. concluded, "The results of the present study indicate that the relationship between individual, overall job satisfaction and individual job performance is stronger and more consistent than that reported in previous reviews" (p. 719). Despite the fact that the results of this study reveal a stronger satisfaction–performance relationship than had been suggested by qualitative reviews, and perhaps because of the limited scope of the meta-analysis, this correlation is rarely cited by those currently investigating the satisfaction–performance relationship.

At about the same time as the Petty et al. (1984) review, Iaffaldano and Muchinsky (1985) conducted a more comprehensive meta-analysis of the job satisfaction–job performance literature. Meta-analyzing 217 correlations from 74 studies, they found a substantial range in satisfaction–performance correlations across the job satisfaction facets, ranging from a mean "true score" correlation of .06 for pay satisfaction to .29 for overall job satisfaction. For their primary analysis, Iaffaldano and Muchinsky averaged the facet-performance correlations and reported an average true score correlation of .17 between job satisfaction and job performance. In discussing their findings, the authors only made reference to the .17 correlation, concluding that job satisfaction and job performance were "only slightly related to each other" (p. 269).

Iaffaldano and Muchinsky (1985) also examined nine moderators of the satisfaction–performance relationship. With one exception (white-collar vs. blue-collar occupational type), the moderators pertained to the measures of job satisfaction (e.g., composite of satisfaction, global, unknown–unspecified) and job performance (e.g., quality vs. quantity, objective vs. subjective). The moderator analysis was not particularly successful—none of the moderators correlated .20 or greater with the satisfaction–performance correlation. However, when the moderators were broken down by satisfaction facet, some significant correlations were observed. Because all the moderators were dichotomous variables and many of their distributions were highly skewed, the lack of significant findings may have been due to the distributional problems with the moderators rather than truly insignificant moderator effects. Iaffaldano and Muchinsky concluded that the moderators were "of little consequence" (p. 267).

The Iaffaldano and Muchinsky (1985) study provided many advances. Most important, their quantitative review avoided the imprecision and subjectivity of earlier qualitative reviews and was more comprehensive than the Petty et al. (1984) meta-analysis. Despite these contributions, in retrospect several limitations of the study are apparent. Whereas some of these limitations may be of minor practical significance, others substantially impact the accuracy and interpretation of the results. First, the authors excluded unpublished studies (doctoral dissertations, working papers, unpublished data, and technical reports), leaving their results vulnerable to the possibility of publication bias (Rosenthal, 1995).

Second, because Iaffaldano and Muchinsky (1985) included in their study correlations between each satisfaction facet and job performance, they cumulated 217 correlations across only 74 studies. Their use of multiple correlations from a single study violates the independence assumption of meta-analysis and, thus, biases the results (Hunter & Schmidt, 1990). It is rare for contemporary meta-analyses to violate the independence assumption (include multiple correlations from the same sample). This is probably due to the fact that meta-analysis experts (Hunter & Schmidt, 1990; Rosenthal, 1995) have cautioned meta-analysts against including multiple correlations from the same sample in their analyses. In fairness, Iaffaldano and Muchinsky were aware of this problem. They noted, "The inclusion of several correlations from a single study does suggest a lack of independence in the data" (p. 255). They did so to avoid losing "considerable amounts of information" (p. 255). However, this does not make violation of the assumption any less serious of a problem. The violation is particularly problematic when the sources of the different correlations are related to each other (Hunter & Schmidt, 1990). Because the correlations among different facets of job satisfaction are so high that they represent a common construct (Parsons & Hulin, 1982), "there can be considerable distortion" (Hunter & Schmidt, 1990, p. 452).

Third, Iaffaldano and Muchinsky (1985) corrected for unreliability in ratings of job performance using internal consistency estimates of reliability. It is commonly accepted that internal consistency reliability overestimates the reliability of supervisory ratings of performance because it consigns variance idiosyncratic to raters to the true variance component of job performance ratings, resulting in downwardly biased corrected correlations (Schmidt & Hunter, 1996). For this reason, Viswesvaran, Ones, and Schmidt (1996) argued that researchers should use interrater reliability to correct job performance for measurement error. Indeed, all recent meta-analyses involving job performance have used this method (e.g., Ones, Viswesvaran, & Reiss, 1996; Roth, BeVier, Switzer, & Schippmann, 1996; Vinchur, Schippmann, Switzer, & Roth, 1998).

Fourth, and most important, in arriving at an overall estimate of the average correlation between job satisfaction and job performance, Iaffaldano and Muchinsky (1985) combined results from each specific facet measure of job satisfaction. In other words, the .17 correlation between satisfaction and performance reported by Iaffaldano and Muchinsky is actually the average of the correlation between pay satisfaction and job performance, coworker satisfaction and job performance, promotion satisfaction and job performance, and so forth. This approach is not an appropriate estimate of the relationship between overall job satisfaction and job performance. The average relationship involving job satisfaction facets is not the same as the relationship involving the overall construct any more than the validity of intelligence as a predictor of job performance can be estimated by the average correlation between responses to each item on an intelligence test and job performance. Job satisfaction facets define the construct of overall job satisfaction, so one must treat the facets as manifestations of the overall construct (i.e., one must create a composite of the facets or capture the shared variance among the facets, as opposed to correlating each facet with performance and then averaging these facet correlations). This point has been made specifically with reference to job satisfaction measurement (Hunter & Schmidt, 1990, p. 460). The averaging approach used by Iaffaldano and Muchinsky downwardly biases the mean correlation estimate. As Wanous, Sullivan, and Malinak (1989) concluded, "Facet satisfaction correlations will always be lower then [sic] overall satisfaction correlations, so combining them (as done by Iaffaldano & Muchinsky) lowers the effect size" (p. 261). Thus, the method Iaffaldano and Muchinsky used to combine the information from facet measures cannot be interpreted as an accurate estimate of the relationship between overall job satisfaction and job performance. In sum, there are a number of reasons to believe that .17 is not the best estimate of the true relationship between overall job satisfaction and job performance.

Though a number of reviews throughout the past 50 years have shaped researchers' views about the nature of the relationship between job satisfaction and performance, Iaffaldano and Muchinsky's (1985) review has had the most impact, as evidenced by the large number of citations the study has generated in the 15 years since it was published (a Social Sciences Citation Index search, conducted October 4, 2000, yielded 168 citations). Because Iaffaldano and Muchinsky concluded that there was no appreciable relationship between job satisfaction and job performance, researchers have accepted this conclusion, as evidenced by the following statements: "The seminal research on job satisfaction and job performance suggests that there exists only a modest correlation between these two constructs" (Côté, 1999, p. 65); "It is accepted among most researchers that there is not a substantial relationship between job satisfaction and productivity" (Judge, Hanisch, & Drankoski, 1995, p. 584); "Much evidence indicates that individual job satisfaction generally is not significantly related to individual task performance" (Brief, 1998, p. 3); and 'The magnitude of correlation between job performance and job satisfaction is unexpectedly low" (Spector, 1997, p. 56).

In light of these conclusions, it is probably safe to conclude that Models 1–4 are seen as archaic by most researchers. If there is little relationship between job satisfaction and job performance, researchers have concluded that either Model 5 (relationship is moderated by other variables) or Model 7 (alternative forms of the relationship) is valid. However, because of the limitations of previous reviews, it is also possible that we have erroneously accepted conclusions about the magnitude of the job satisfaction and job performance relationship. At the very least, given the importance of the topic, it seems appropriate to reexamine this relationship. Accordingly, in the next section of the article, we provide an updated, and more comprehensive, meta-analysis of the relationship between job satisfaction and job performance.

In the following meta-analysis, we focus on the relationship between overall job satisfaction and overall job performance. Theoretically, there are compelling reasons to focus on overall job satisfaction. As noted by Fishbein (1979), in order for attitudes to predict behaviors properly, the attitudes and behaviors must be congruent in terms of their generality or specificity. Because overall job performance is a general construct composed of more specific factors (Campbell, McCloy, Oppler, & Sager, 1993), in order to achieve construct correspondence with respect to the satisfaction–performance relationship, one must consider overall job satisfaction. As Hulin (1991) noted, failure to match constructs in terms of their generality leads to downwardly biased correlations when relating job satisfaction to other constructs. Fisher (1980) made this point specifically with reference to the satisfaction–performance relationship, noting, "Researchers interested in the job satisfaction/job performance relationship ... should be aware of the need to have an appropriate 'fit' between attitude measure specificity and behavioral criteria to obtain maximum predictability" (p. 611). Indeed, the limited empirical evidence that exists suggests that when job satisfaction is treated as a general construct, a stronger correlation with job performance emerges than suggested by Iaffaldano and Muchinsky's (1985) results. Accordingly, our focus here is on the relationship between overall job satisfaction and overall job performance.

## *Quantitative review of the job satisfaction–job performance relationship*

### *Rules for inclusion in the meta-analysis*

Consistent with the recommendations of meta-analytic researchers (Matt & Cook, 1994), we defined the population to which we wished to generalize a priori as consisting of the general population of employed adults. Hence, satisfaction and performance in original studies had to be measured at the individual (as opposed to group) level, and performance had to occur in a natural job setting (studies involving performance on laboratory tasks were excluded). Satisfaction was measured globally (general perceptions of one's job) or with reference to specific facets of the job situation (supervision, coworkers, opportunity for advancement, etc.), although in many cases the measure was not described in sufficient detail to determine its nature. Studies focusing on a single satisfaction facet were excluded in the overall analysis. However, we did include studies measuring at least two facets in the overall analysis as these facets could be combined to form a measure of overall job satisfaction. In addition, we were interested in analyzing studies focusing on job performance per se. Thus, we excluded studies correlating job satisfaction with absenteeism, turnover, job withdrawal, and the like.

*Identification of studies*

In order to locate studies containing relationships between individual job satisfaction and job performance, we first searched the PsycINFO electronic database (1967–1999).[2] Our primary focus was on locating published studies, unpublished doctoral dissertations, and cited but unpublished manuscripts and research reports from government agencies. We also reviewed the bibliographies from previous qualitative and quantitative reviews. Finally, in order to locate studies that might not have been referenced in these sources, we manually searched the 21 journals in which most of the satisfaction–performance correlations appeared from 1983 to the present.

*Results of searches*

From the computer-assisted searches, we were able to identify 1,008 references to studies concerning job satisfaction and performance. The abstracts of each of these studies were read to determine whether the study met the inclusion criteria. Although most of these references were to published reports, a significant number of unpublished studies were revealed by the search. To obtain the unpublished studies that met our inclusion criteria, we contacted libraries where doctoral dissertations and unpublished government reports were held in order to have access to these documents and were able to obtain 73 unpublished studies and dissertations (containing 88 independent samples) meeting the criteria for our meta-analysis. We do not specifically recall identifying any studies that simply reported a "nonsignificant" finding in our search. If such studies exist, failing to impute a value for these studies could be argued to lead to an upwardly biased estimate of the relationship (Rosenthal, 1995). However, imputation does introduce an element of subjectivity and imprecision into the analysis (Hunter & Schmidt, 1990). In any event, a sensitivity analysis revealed that even if there were 10 studies that simply reported a nonsignificant correlation, following Rosenthal (1995), assuming a correlation of .00 for these studies, it would change the overall results by only a trivial degree (.008 difference).

All told, 312 samples met our inclusion criteria. Our search resulted in a substantially larger sample of studies than that obtained by Iaffaldano and Muchinsky (1985) and Petty et al. (1984), who included only 24% and 4% of the independent samples included in this study, respectively. Our overall analysis of the relationships between satisfaction and performance was estimated from 312 independent samples contained in 254 studies (total $N = 54{,}417$). A summary of studies included in the meta-analysis is given in the Appendix.

## Meta-analytic procedures

We used the meta-analytic procedures of Hunter and Schmidt (1990) to correct observed correlations for sampling error and unreliability in measures of job satisfaction and job performance. Correlations were corrected individually. In terms of correcting job satisfaction measures for unreliability, when authors of original studies reported an overall internal consistency reliability for job satisfaction, we used this value to correct the observed correlation for attenuation. If correlations between multiple measures of job satisfaction were reported in original studies, we used these values to compute the reliability of an equally weighted composite of overall satisfaction using the Spearman–Brown prophecy formula (Hunter & Schmidt, 1990). Finally, for single-item measures of job satisfaction, we used meta-analytically derived estimates of the reliability of single-item measures of job satisfaction (Wanous, Reichers, & Hudy, 1997).

As is typical in meta-analyses involving supervisory ratings of job performance (e.g., Barrick & Mount, 1991), only a handful of studies in our database ($k = 4$) reported correlations among raters, making it impossible to form an accurate estimate of the reliability of performance ratings based on information contained in the articles. Accordingly, we took meta-analytic estimates of the reliability of various sources of performance information from the job performance literature. The most frequently used source of performance information in our sample of studies involved supervisory ratings of job performance. In fact, more than 80% of the total samples used supervisory ratings as the performance criterion. When supervisory or peer ratings of performance were used in original studies, we used Viswesvaran et al.'s (1996) estimate of the reliability of supervisory and peer performance ratings. In a number of studies, authors used objective measures (such as quality and quantity of output) to evaluate performance. When multiple objective measures were used, we estimated the composite reliability of these measures. In cases in which the reliability of objective indices of performance was not provided by authors, we estimated reliability of these measures with the mean reliability of all the studies in the given analysis. In a handful of studies (six samples in total), other sources of performance information were used for which meta-analytic reliability estimates were unavailable (ratings from subordinates, students, clients, customers). When these rating types were used, we estimated the reliability of these ratings with the distribution that was deemed most similar (e.g., Viswesvaran et al.'s estimate of the reliability of peer ratings was used as a reliability estimate in the one study using solely subordinate ratings).[3]

Often, studies reported performance information from multiple sources (e.g., peer and supervisory ratings, objective measures and supervisory ratings). In these samples, we estimated reliability using meta-analytic findings from the job performance literature pertaining to correlations between these sources (Bommer, Johnson, Rich, Podsakoff, & MacKenzie, 1995; Harris & Schaubroeck, 1988; Viswesvaran et al., 1996) and computed equally weighted composite correlations between satisfaction and performance. When sources for which no reliability information was available (listed previously) were used in conjunction with supervisory ratings of performance, we treated the former as peer ratings (Viswesvaran et al., 1996).

In cases in which multiple supervisors or multiple peers were used to generate ratings (and these ratings were not merely averaged), we substituted the meta-analytic reliability values into the Spearman–Brown prophecy formula to obtain an estimate of performance reliability for the given sample. Finally, a number of studies reported peer or supervisory ratings that had been averaged across multiple raters. Scullen (1997) demonstrated that this averaging process causes resulting correlations between these ratings and other variables of interest to be upwardly biased and provided a correction to eliminate this bias when the number of raters is known. Thus, we applied Scullen's correction to observed correlations to original studies in which ratings had been averaged and the number of raters was provided in the study. Across all samples, the average reliability of job satisfaction measures was .74 (square root = .86) and the average reliability for job performance was .52 (square root = .72).

We report several statistics that are used to explain heterogeneity in the correlations. First, we report the percentage of the variance in the correlations that is explained by statistical artifacts. We also report the $Q$ statistic (Hunter & Schmidt, 1990, p. 151), which tests for homogeneity in the true correlations across studies. The $Q$ statistic was recommended by Sagie and Koslowsky (1993), though it has all the limitations of a significance test (see Hunter & Schmidt, 1990, pp. 483–484). A low percentage of variance explained and a significant $Q$ statistic (which is approximately distributed as a chi-square) indicate the likelihood of moderators that explain variability in the correlations across studies.

Because it seemed unlikely that statistical artifacts would explain all of the variability in the correlations across studies, we investigated several study characteristics that may moderate the magnitude of the satisfaction–performance correlations. First, because meta-analyses are commonly criticized on the grounds that the correlations reported in the study are not representative of those in the population (see Rosenthal, 1998, pp. 377–378, for a review of this issue), we tested for differences in the satisfaction–performance correlation as a function of publication source. Second and third, because a heterogeneous set of measures was cumulated, we report the satisfaction correlations by measure of job performance (e.g., supervisory ratings of performance, "objective" measures) and by measure of job satisfaction (e.g., whether the measure of job satisfaction was a composite of the facets or a global measure). Fourth, because it might be expected that the satisfaction–performance correlation would vary according to the basic research design of the study, we investigated whether the correlation varies by longitudinal versus cross-sectional design. The fifth substantive moderator we examined was job complexity; it is frequently argued that the satisfaction–performance relationship should be higher in more complex, stimulating jobs (e.g., Baird, 1976; Ivancevich, 1979). Finally, it was of interest to determine the magnitude of the satisfaction–performance association in various occupational groups. Thus, we report estimates of the satisfaction–performance relationship for eight different occupational categories. To test for statistically significant differences as a function of dichotomous moderating conditions, we conducted pairwise comparisons using the Z test provided by Quiñones, Ford, and Teachout (1995). For this test, a significant test statistic indicates the presence of a moderator effect for this variable.

Coding of the moderator variables was straightforward as most of the moderators (measure of satisfaction and performance, research design, occupation) were clearly indicated in the studies. In two cases, however, coding of the study characteristics was more involved. We classified journal articles as top tier by quantitatively combining journal quality ratings from seven published articles rating journals in the areas of psychology, organizational behavior, and marketing (e.g., Starbuck & Mezias, 1996). We computed the reliability of ratings for these journals across these seven articles and found a substantial amount of agreement (standardized $\alpha = .97$). The journals ranked in the upper 20% of the distribution were designated top tier, the remaining 24 rated journals were categorized as other ranked, and the 23 journals for which no ratings were available were labeled unranked. Job complexity for studies that contained a single occupation was coded by matching job titles to substantive complexity scores using the ratings provided by Roos and Treiman (1980). Three of the authors independently assigned a complexity code to each job. There was a high level of agreement among the codes ($\alpha = .98$). Disagreements were resolved by consensus between two of the authors. After obtaining complexity scores where possible, we then split the sample of studies into a high-job-complexity group (more than 1 standard deviation above the mean complexity score), a medium-complexity group ($\pm 1$ standard deviation around the mean complexity score), and a low-complexity group (1 or more standard deviations below the mean complexity score). Trichotomizing job complexity in this way was necessary as we noted a nonlinear relationship between complexity and the satisfaction–performance relationship in our data.

## Results

### Overall analysis

Results of the overall meta-analysis of the relationship between job satisfaction and job performance are provided in Table 1. The sample size weighted mean correlation between overall job satisfaction and job performance, uncorrected for study artifacts or unreliability, was .18. The estimated population value of the correlation between overall job satisfaction and general job performance was .30 when the correlations were corrected for unreliability in satisfaction and performance

Table 1 Meta-analysis of relationship between job satisfaction and job performance

| k | N | Mean r | $SD_r$ | Mean $\rho$ | $SD_\rho$ | 80% CV | 95% CI | % variance | Q |
|---|---|---|---|---|---|---|---|---|---|
| 312 | 54,471 | .18 | .12 | .30 | .21 | .03–.57 | .27–.33 | 25.15 | 1,240.51* |

*Note.* $k$ = number of correlations; $N$ = total sample size for all studies combined; mean $r$ = average uncorrected correlation; $SD_r$ = standard deviation of uncorrected correlation; mean $\rho$ = average corrected correlation; $SD_\rho$ = standard deviation of corrected (true score) correlation; 80% CV = lower and upper limits of 80% credibility interval; 95% CI = lower and upper limits of 95% confidence interval; % variance = percentage of the variance in correlations explained by statistical artifacts; $Q$ = statistic used to test for homogeneity in the true correlations across studies.
*$p < .01$.

measures. For this estimate, the 95% confidence interval excluded zero, indicating that we can be confident that the average true correlation is nonzero and relatively invariable (.27 to .33). The 80% credibility interval also excluded zero, indicating that more than 90% of the individual corrected true score correlations are greater than zero (the other 10% of the correlations lie above the upper end of the interval, .57). Thus, these results indicate that the mean true correlation between job satisfaction and job performance is moderate in magnitude (.30) and distinguishable from zero.

### Comparison of present study findings to Iaffaldano and Muchinsky's (1985)

Because the results reported above stand in contrast to those of Iaffaldano and Muchinsky (1985), it is important to more directly compare our results to theirs and account for the differences. As was noted earlier, Iaffaldano and Muchinsky based their corrections on internal consistency estimates of reliability of performance ratings, as opposed to the corrections based on interrater reliability as used in this article. Because internal consistency estimates of reliability are generally higher than interrater estimates, this is one likely source of differences in the correlations. A second difference between our results and those of Iaffaldano and Muchinsky is based on how facets of job satisfaction are treated to arrive at an overall estimate of the satisfaction–performance relationship. Rather than treating each single facet as a measure of the overall job satisfaction construct, as Iaffaldano and Muchinsky implicitly did in their overall analysis, we created a composite measure of overall job satisfaction from the facet correlations reported in each study (in studies in which multiple facets were included). Accordingly, we reanalyzed both their and our data sets using measures of overall satisfaction and composite measures computed from job satisfaction facets. In our first comparative analysis, we used internal consistency estimates of reliability, relying on Viswesvaran et al.'s (1996) meta-analytic estimate of the internal consistency of performance ratings (.86).

In reanalyzing their data, we excluded several studies that did not meet our inclusion criteria (self-reports of performance, task performance in laboratory studies, studies that included only a single facet of job satisfaction).

The results of this comparative analysis are presented in Table 2. The first row simply provides Iaffaldano and Muchinsky's (1985) original estimates. The second row provides the results of our reanalysis of their data; as in their study, the estimates in row 2 correct performance measures for unreliability based on internal consistency reliability. Unlike Iaffaldano and Muchinsky, however, where a study reported correlations involving multiple job satisfaction facets, we combined

*Table 2* Direct comparison of present findings with those of Iaffaldano and Muchinsky (1985)

| Source | Mean r | Mean ρ | 80% CV | 95% CI |
|---|---|---|---|---|
| Comparisons including only those studies in Iaffaldano and Muchinsky (1985) ||||| 
| Original Iaffaldano and Muchinsky results | .15 | .17 | – | – |
| Job satisfaction facets combined with composite correlations and job performance corrections based on internal consistency reliability | .20 | .25 | .07–.43 | .21–.29 |
| Job satisfaction facets combined with composite correlations and job performance corrections based on interrater reliability | .20 | .33 | .09–.57 | .28–.38 |
| Comparisons including all studies |||||
| Job satisfaction facets combined with composite correlations and job performance corrections based on infernal consistency reliability | .18 | .25 | .01–.48 | .23–.27 |
| Job satisfaction facets combined with composite correlations and job performance corrections based on interrater reliability | .18 | .30 | .03–.57 | .27–.33 |

*Note.* Results in row 1 are taken from Iaffaldano and Muchinsky (1985) and include average correlations between single job satisfaction facets and job performance, where performance is corrected for unreliability based on internal consistency. Except for row 1, results for Iaffaldano and Muchinsky (rows 2 and 3) are based on the independent correlations that met our inclusion criteria ($k = 68$, where $k$ is the number of correlations, and $N = 9,397$). Calculations for all studies (rows 4 and 5) are based on $k = 312$ and $N = 54,471$. A dash indicates that data were not reported. Mean $r$ = average uncorrected correlation; mean $\rho$ = average corrected correlation; 80% CV = lower and upper limits of 80% credibility interval; 95% CI = lower and upper limits of 95% confidence interval.

these facets into a composite measure of overall job satisfaction. The uncorrected (.20) and corrected (.25) correlations are significantly higher than those originally reported by Iaffaldano and Muchinsky. This is due to the fact that row 2 represents an estimate of the relationship between overall job satisfaction (a composite of several facets) and job performance, as compared with Iaffaldano and Muchinsky's estimate of the relationship between job performance and an average of single facet measures. The third row provides results based on interrater estimates of reliability. The corrected correlation is higher still (.33).[4] Thus, results in row 2 demonstrate the effects of using a composite measure of job satisfaction and results in row 3 demonstrate the effects of correcting for interrater reliability. Finally, the fourth and fifth rows provide estimates from our data. Row 5, based on corrections due to interrater reliability, shows the results presented in Table 1. Row 4 is a reanalysis of those results using internal consistency estimates of reliability. This correlation (.25) is lower than estimates based on interrater reliability (.30), though still higher than Iaffaldano and Muchinsky's estimate.

Cumulatively, these results reveal two primary reasons why results of the present study differ from those of Iaffaldano and Muchinsky (1985). First, the difference of .08 between the corrected correlations in row 2 (.25) and row 3 (.33) reveals that a substantial reason for the difference is the way in which facet measures of job satisfaction were combined to form a measure of overall job satisfaction. We explain reasons for this difference in the Discussion and Future Research section. Second, the differences in the corrected correlations between estimates based on internal consistency versus interrater reliability estimates (row 2 vs. 3, and row 4 vs. 5), .08 and .05, respectively, reveal that much of the difference also is due to using interrater reliability (as opposed to internal consistency) estimates in correcting the correlations.

## *Moderator analyses*

Though the mean satisfaction–performance correlation in our study can be concluded to be nonzero, the credibility interval is relatively wide (from .03 to .57), indicating that there is substantial variation in the individual correlations across the 312 studies. Furthermore, the $Q$ statistic was significant, and sampling error and measurement error accounted for only 25% of this variability. This evidence suggests that there are moderators of the relationship at the study level. Results of the moderator analyses are provided in Table 3.

First, the satisfaction–performance correlation was stronger ($\rho = .33$) in top-tier journals (those ranked 1–6 in our analysis). The satisfaction–performance correlation was significantly smaller in other journals, including those ranked 7–30 in our analysis ($\rho = .26$), as well as unranked journals ($\rho = .25$). However, there did not appear to be a publication bias because the average satisfaction–performance correlation in unpublished studies or dissertations ($\rho = .31$) was quite similar to the overall estimate.

*Table 3* Results of moderator analyses

| Moderator | k | N | Mean r | Mean ρ | SD_ρ | Q | Significant difference |
|---|---|---|---|---|---|---|---|
| **Source of correlation** | | | | | | | |
| a. Top-tier journal article | 103 | 21,052 | .19 | .33[a,b] | .24 | 518.01* | b, c |
| b. Other ranked journal article | 76 | 11,653 | .17 | .26[a,b] | .20 | 269.67* | a |
| c. Unranked journal article | 41 | 5,953 | .16 | .25[a,b] | .18 | 113.76* | a |
| d. Unpublished study–dissertation | 92 | 15,813 | .19 | .31[a,b] | .18 | 299.65* | — |
| **Measure of job performance** | | | | | | | |
| a. Supervisory ratings | 242 | 44,518 | .18 | .30[a,b] | .19 | 913.52* | — |
| b. Objective records | 34 | 5,216 | .16 | .26[a,b] | .19 | 108.74* | — |
| c. Peer–subordinate ratings or other | 36 | 4,737 | .18 | .36[a] | .34 | 186.68* | — |
| **Measure of job satisfaction** | | | | | | | |
| a. Global measure | 44 | 5,561 | .22 | .35[a,b] | .27 | 214.01* | — |
| b. Facet composite | 176 | 34,707 | .18 | .30[a,b] | .22 | 786.42* | — |
| c. Unknown–not specified | 92 | 14,203 | .18 | .28[a,b] | .15 | 221.04* | — |
| **Research design** | | | | | | | |
| a. Cross-sectional | 291 | 51,484 | .18 | .31[a,b] | .21 | 1,201.04* | a |
| b. Longitudinal | 21 | 2,987 | .14 | .23[a,b] | .12 | 36.72 | b |
| **Job complexity** | | | | | | | |
| a. Low | 38 | 4,372 | .18 | .29[a] | .27 | 159.77* | c |
| b. Medium | 148 | 22,841 | .18 | .29[a,b] | .16 | 378.02* | c |
| c. High | 24 | 3,349 | .26 | .52[a,b] | .38 | 152.52* | a, b |
| **Occupation** | | | | | | | |
| a. Scientists–engineers | 18 | 2,344 | .19 | .45[a,b] | .34 | 80.98* | h |
| b. Salespersons | 22 | 4,384 | .19 | .28[a,b] | .10 | 39.82 | h |
| c. Teachers | 8 | 2,019 | .20 | .33[a,b] | .10 | 16.36 | h |
| d. Managers and supervisors | 34 | 4,422 | .21 | .34[a,b] | .19 | 97.67* | h |
| e. Accountants | 7 | 1,240 | .17 | .26[a,b] | .12 | 15.10 | — |
| f. Clerical workers–secretaries | 18 | 3,019 | .19 | .34[a,b] | .23 | 80.01* | h |
| g. Laborers (unskilled–semiskilled) | 27 | 3,389 | .16 | .26[a] | .29 | 140.81* | — |
| h. Nurses | 13 | 2,129 | .12 | .19[a,b] | .10 | 21.17 | a, b, c, d, f |
| i. Miscellaneous–mixed | 165 | 31,525 | .18 | .29[a,b] | .21 | 694.49* | — |

*Note.* k = number of correlations; N = total sample size for all studies combined; mean r = average uncorrected correlation; mean ρ = average corrected correlation; SD_ρ = standard deviation of corrected (true score) correlation; Q = statistic used to test for homogeneity in the true correlations across studies. Letters in the significant difference column correspond to row letters and denote means that are significantly different from one another at the .01 level (two-tailed). Dashes indicate no significant difference.
[a] The 95% confidence interval excluded zero. [b] The 80% credibility interval excluded zero.
*p < .01.

Second, the true score correlations did not vary significantly according to the measure of performance, although it should be noted that the vast majority of the studies measured job performance with supervisory ratings. Third, global measures had somewhat higher correlations with job performance than did composite facet measures, or unknown or unspecified measures (measures that were not described in sufficient detail in the studies to determine their nature). However, none of these differences were significant. We should note that in the relatively small number of studies ($k = 13$) in which 2–4 facets were used to assess job satisfaction, the average correlation ($\rho = .28$) was not significantly smaller than in those studies based on five or more job satisfaction facets ($\rho = .30$). Fourth, as might be expected, cross-sectional designs yielded significantly stronger satisfaction–performance correlations ($\rho = .31$) than did longitudinal designs ($\rho = .23$).

Fifth, consistent with research suggesting that job complexity moderates the satisfaction–performance relationship (Baird, 1976; Ivancevich, 1978, 1979), results indicate that the satisfaction–performance correlation is substantially stronger in high-complexity jobs than low-complexity jobs. Though job satisfaction and job performance were correlated for jobs with medium and low complexity ($\rho = .29$), these values were significantly lower than the average correlation for high complexity jobs ($\rho = .52$). Some differences in the satisfaction–performance relationship were observed across occupations. Although some of these differences appear to be due to job complexity (the strongest correlation was observed for scientists–engineers and one of the weakest for laborers), this is an incomplete explanation (the correlation was weaker for nurses and accountants than for clerical workers). A few of these differences were significant, all such that the correlation for nurses was significantly lower than for the comparison groups (scientists–engineers, salespersons, teachers, managers–supervisors, and clerical workers–secretaries).

We should note that for almost all of the moderator metaanalyses reported in Table 3, the $Q$ statistic was statistically significant at the .01 level. There were a few exceptions, namely, correlations involving longitudinal designs ($Q_{21} = 36.72$, $\rho = .02$) and a number of the occupation correlations—salespersons ($Q_{22} = 39.82$, $\rho = .011$), teachers ($Q_8 = 16.36$, $\rho = .04$), accountants ($Q_7 = 15.10$, $\rho = .03$), and nurses ($Q_{13} = 21.17$, $\rho = .07$). Thus, with the possible exception of within occupation, the within-moderator analyses failed to reduce the heterogeneity of the estimates to a nonsignificant level.

## Discussion and future research

Few topics in the history of industrial–organizational psychology have captured the attention of researchers more than the relationship between job satisfaction and job performance. Researchers have investigated the relationship operating from different assumptions and with different goals. We have grouped these investigations under the rubric of seven models. These models, positing different forms of relations between job satisfaction and job performance, have received differential support in the literature. In particular, the performance → satisfaction model, the moderator model with respect to pay-for-performance, and models with alternative conceptualizations of job satisfaction and job performance all have received considerable support. However, it is also safe to conclude that there are many inconsistencies in the results testing these models (and in the ways the models have been tested) and a lack of consensus regarding the validity of the models. It is our contention that one reason for the lack of assimilation and consensus is that many researchers have dismissed the relationship between employee satisfaction and job performance.

Indeed, beginning in 1955 and culminating in 1985, reviews of the literature suggested that the satisfaction–performance relationship was, as a general rule, not valid. In the most influential review, Iaffaldano and Muchinsky (1985) went so far as to describe the relationship as an "illusory correlation" (p. 270) that represented a "management fad" (p. 269), and, indeed, their results appeared to support this view. We have argued in this article that .17 is not an accurate estimate of the true relationship between overall job satisfaction and job performance. This is an important point, as researchers have used the .17 value to characterize the satisfaction–performance relationship. For example, Ostroff (1992) noted, "A recent meta-analytic study (Iaffaldano & Muchinsky, 1985) estimated the true population correlation between satisfaction and performance to be .17" (p. 963). Also relying on Iaffaldano and Muchinsky's estimate, the satisfaction–performance relationship has been described as "meager" (Brief, 1998, p. 42), "weak" (Côté, 1999, p. 65), "unexpectedly low" (Spector, 1997, p. 56), "modest ... at best" (Katzell, Thompson, & Guzzo, 1992, p. 210), "disappointing" (Wiley, 1996, p. 355), "negligible" (Weiss & Cropanzano, 1996, p. 51), and "bordering on the trivial" (Landy, 1989, p. 481). Recently, Ellingson, Gruys, and Sackett (1998) reported an uncorrected satisfaction–performance correlation of .30 (.32 if corrected for internal consistency or .44 if corrected for interrater reliability). Ellingson et al., relying on Iaffaldano and Muchinsky's .17 estimate (and their conclusions), were sufficiently skeptical about their .30 correlation that they collected additional performance data and then reestimated the satisfaction–performance correlation with the new data. Thus, the Iaffaldano and Muchinsky result, and its misinterpretation, continues to have a profound impact on researchers' beliefs about the satisfaction–performance relationship.

It is striking to note that Iaffaldano and Muchinsky's (1985) estimate of the correlation between job satisfaction and job performance, as well as their overall pessimism for the relationship, is remarkably similar to Wicker's (1969) influential characterization of the attitude–behavior relationship, a pessimism that subsequently has been concluded to be unfounded (see Eagly & Chaiken, 1993). Yet, although most social psychologists would argue that attitudes do predict corresponding behaviors, industrial–organizational psychologists continue to hold the view that the most focal attitude about the job (job satisfaction) is unrelated to the most focal behavior on the job (job performance). Eagly (1992) commented, "Understanding of attitudes both as causes and predictors of behavior has advanced very considerably since the 1960's claim that attitudes are unimportant causes and weak predictors" (p. 697).

Just as attitude researchers have reexamined the literature in light of Wicker's (1969) qualitative review, we believe Iaffaldano and Muchinsky's (1985) quantitative review deserves reexamination. As Wanous et al. (1989) noted with respect to meta-analysis, "The lure of a quantitative result and the potential for finding unequivocal conclusions may contribute to a less critical acceptance of the results produced" (p. 259). Indeed, when we critically examined the Iaffaldano and Muchinsky meta-analysis and sought to remedy the limitations, the results presented here suggest different conclusions about the true magnitude of the satisfaction–performance relationship. Although the estimated true correlation of .30 is considerably different from the oft-cited Iaffaldano and Muchinsky finding of .17, the overall correlation is not strong—a correlation of .30 would qualify as a "moderate" effect size using Cohen and Cohen's (1983) rule of thumb. However, it is important to evaluate the satisfaction–performance correlation in the context of other correlates of job performance. For example, the magnitude of the relationship between job satisfaction and performance found in the current study is similar to (within .07 of) four of the strongest and most consistent correlates of job performance: measures of Conscientiousness ($\rho = .23$; Barrick & Mount, 1991), biodata inventories ($\rho = .37$; Hunter & Hunter, 1984), structured interviews ($\rho = .31$ without range restriction corrections; McDaniel, Whetzel, Schmidt, & Maurer, 1994), and assessment centers ($\rho = .37$; Gaugler, Rosenthal, Thornton, & Bentson, 1987). Thus, the satisfaction–performance correlation compares favorably with other correlates of job performance. It does not appear to be a correlation that should be generally dismissed.

Although we can be confident that the true correlation is close to .30 and that the great majority (more than 90%) of the individual corrected correlations are greater than zero, most of the variability in the correlations was not explained by study artifacts. Though, consistent with Model 5, we found that the size of the satisfaction–performance correlation was related to job complexity (the satisfaction–performance correlation was stronger in high-complexity jobs), we were not able to explain most of the variability in the correlations across studies. One potential explanation for the moderating role of job complexity is that complex, autonomous jobs represent "weak situations." Research has shown that when there are fewer situational constraints and demands on behavior, correlations between individual characteristics and attitudes (e.g., job satisfaction) have a stronger potential to affect behaviors (e.g., job performance), resulting in higher attitude–behavior correlations (Barrick & Mount, 1993; Herman, 1973). Because incumbents in complex jobs are relatively free of such situational constraints on behaviors, these results provide some support for the situational constraints argument.

Why is the average correlation substantially higher in our re-analysis? The average uncorrected correlation is higher because Iaffaldano and Muchinsky (1985) analyzed correlations at the single satisfaction facet (vs. the overall job satisfaction construct) level (nearly all of the correlations in their overall estimate involved averaging correlations between a single job satisfaction facet and job performance).[5] This lack of correspondence in terms of generality—using a specific attitude to predict a general behavior—should result in a lower correlation (Wanous et al., 1989). We believe that the proper estimate of the overall relationship is between overall job satisfaction and overall job performance, which is why we took a composite average of the specific facets to arrive at a measure of overall job satisfaction. Hence, in the case of this study, composite correlations simply estimate the correlation between job satisfaction and job performance as if the facet satisfactions had been added together. As Hunter and Schmidt (1990) noted, if one wants an accurate estimate of the relationship of a variable to the job satisfaction construct, composite correlations must be used.[6]

The average corrected correlation also is higher because we used interrater reliability to correct the estimates. Here again, we believe the use of interrate, reliability is the most appropriate correction, and all contemporary meta-analyses involving job performance use this estimate. As Schmidt and Hunter (1996) noted,

> The problem with intrarater reliability is that it assigns specific error (unique to the individual rater) to true (construct) variance. ... Use of intrarater reliabilities to correct criterion-related validity coefficients for criterion reliability produces substantial downward biases in estimates of actual validity. (p. 209)

Furthermore, generalizability theory (Cronbach, Gleser, Nanda, & Rajaratnam, 1972) would suggest that corrections based on interrater reliability are more likely to reflect the context to which one seeks to generalize the relationship. Specifically, if one is generalizing to one supervisor's performance rating at one point in time, then one should only correct for unreliability in that one supervisor's rating (correction based on internal consistency). However, if one seeks to generalize across situations (i.e., if a different but equally knowledgeable rater evaluated the same employee), then one should correct for lack of reliability across raters (correction based on interrater reliability). Because in most circumstances one is interested in generalized performance across situations, corrections based on interrater reliability are more appropriate.

On average, global job satisfaction measures correlated somewhat more highly with job performance than did composite measures of job satisfaction facets, but the difference in the average correlations was not significant. The issue of whether global and faceted measures of job satisfaction are equivalent has been debated in the literature. Scarpello and Campbell (1983) went so far as to conclude, "The results of the present study argue against the common practice of using the sum of facet satisfaction as the measure of overall job satisfaction" (p. 595). Although our results cannot address this issue, at least as far as the satisfaction–performance relationship is concerned, it appears that global measures display somewhat higher correlations with job performance than do measures formed from a composite of job satisfaction facets. Future research should compare the predictive validity of these alternative measurement strategies.

## Future research

In light of the estimated job satisfaction–job performance correlation, it appears premature to dismiss the relationship. Thus, the model that assumes no relationship between the constructs (Model 6) can be ruled out, but what about the other models? In an effort to integrate the qualitative and quantitative portions of our review, we provide a model in Figure 2 that integrates Models 1–5. (We discuss Model 7 shortly.) We propose this integrative model because it is plausible that several of the models coexist and thus are best considered in a unified framework. For example, job satisfaction could exert a causal effect on job performance (Model 1 or 3), or performance on satisfaction (Model 2 or 3), and yet the relationship could be moderated by other variables (i.e., be stronger in some situations than others; Model 5). Similarly, there may be causal effects between satisfaction and performance (Models 1, 2, or 3) that are explained by psychological processes (Model 4). The integrative model posits a bidirectional relationship between job satisfaction and job performance and thus incorporates Models 1–3. However,

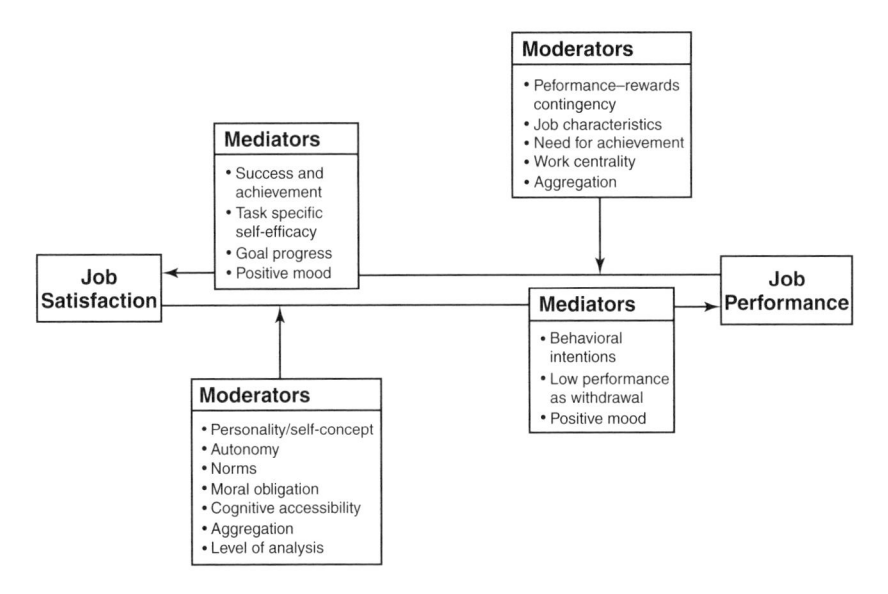

*Figure 2* Integrative model of the relationship between job satisfaction and job performance.

by including both mediating and moderating effects in both directions, it also incorporates Models 4 and 5. Below we discuss the linkages contained in the model and future research that is needed to test the various components of the model.

Tests of the causal nature of the satisfaction–performance relationship are fragmented and dated. Although there is some support for the performance → satisfaction relationship and the satisfaction → performance relationship, as well as for reciprocal relations, this literature is somewhat archaic; causal satisfaction–performance studies appeared only in the 1970s. If the relationship is an important one, as our results suggest, studies of causal influence should resume. Even if job satisfaction and job performance mutually influence each other, it appears quite possible that the relationship between satisfaction and performance is indirect, mediated by other variables. Though some research has indirectly supported mediating influences, direct tests are lacking. Such causal studies are particularly appropriate in light of advances in causal modeling techniques in the past 20 years. Further research also is needed in terms of moderators of the satisfaction–performance relationship. We are aware of 17 specific moderators of the satisfaction–performance relationship that have been proposed, yet few of these have been investigated in more than one study. Given the large variability in correlations across studies, future investigation into the conditions under which job satisfaction and performance are related is needed.

Within the general framework presented in Figure 2, there are many specific topics that are worthy of investigation. Table 4 provides a brief summary of areas for future research that we view as most promising, grouped according to the seven performance–satisfaction models discussed earlier. We discuss these areas in more detail below. In terms of moderating influences, various personality traits may affect the satisfaction → performance relationship. Mount, Harter, Barrick, and Colbert (2000) argued that job satisfaction would be more strongly related to job performance for less conscientious employees because conscientious employees would be less willing to respond to dissatisfaction with reduced performance levels. Mount et al. found support for this hypothesis across three independent samples. Other personality traits may exhibit moderating effects, such as a doer self-concept, which has been found to moderate attitude–behavior relationships in general (see Eagly, 1992), or affective disposition, which has been found to moderate job satisfaction–turnover relations in particular (Judge, 1993). Though not a trait, self-identity has been shown to be relevant in attitude–behavior relationships such that attitudes are more likely to lead to behaviors when the behavior is central to one's self-concept (Charng, Piliavin, & Callero, 1988). In this context, job satisfaction would be expected to lead to job performance when performing well on the job is central to an employee's identity. Finally, we encourage further research on the validity of self-esteem as a moderator. Dipboye (1977) proposed many refinements to Korman's (1970) theory that might advance research in this area, yet few of the propositions and suggestions in Dipboye's review have been investigated.

*Table 4* Topics for future research on the job satisfaction–job performance relationship

| Model | Topic |
|---|---|
| 3 | Is the satisfaction–performance relationship reciprocal when tested using contemporary causal modeling techniques? |
| 5 | Does personality moderate the job satisfaction–job performance relationship? |
| 1, 5 | Is job satisfaction more likely to result in performance when job performance is central to one's self-concept? |
| 1, 5 | Does autonomy moderate the satisfaction → performance relationship such that the effect of job satisfaction on performance is stronger for jobs high in autonomy? |
| 1, 5 | Do subjective norms moderate the satisfaction → performance relationship? |
| 1, 5 | Does moral obligation moderate the satisfaction → performance relationship such that the relationship is weaker for employees who feel an obligation to perform a job well irrespective of their attitudes toward it? |
| 1, 5 | It the satisfaction → performance relationship stronger for individuals whose job attitudes are easily accessed? |
| 1, 5 | How does temporal and behavioral aggregation affect the satisfaction–performanee relationship? |
| 7 | Is the satisfaction–performance relationship stronger at the group or organization (vs. individual) level of analysis? |
| 1 | What role do intentions play? Is the Fishbein–Ajzen model relevant to the satisfaction–performance relationship? |
| 1 | Do dissatisfied employees tend to use poor performance as a withdrawal or adaptive response? |
| 2, 5 | Does the performance–rewards contingency moderate the performance → satisfaction relationship? |
| 2, 5 | Is Locke's value model relevant to the job performance → job satisfaction relationship? |
| 2, 5 | Are high levels of job performance more satisfying to individuals high in need for achievement (achievement motivation)? |
| 2, 5 | Is the effect of performance on satisfaction stronger for individuals whose work is a central life interest? |
| 2, 4 | To what degree do success and achievement explain the job performance → job satisfaction relationship? |
| 2, 4 | Does task specific self-efficacy mediate the effect of job performance on job satisfaction? |
| 2, 4 | Does progression toward important goals explain the effect of performance on satisfaction? |
| 2, 4 | Does positive mood mediate the effect of performance on job satisfaction? |

Another potential moderating variable is autonomy. Because jobs with a high degree of autonomy provide greater opportunity for attitudes and motives to affect behavior, the satisfaction–performance relationship should be stronger in high-autonomy jobs. This is consistent with our results with respect to job complexity, as well as related arguments with respect to personality (Batrick & Mount, 1993). However, direct tests of this hypothesis are lacking. In addition, norms would be expected to influence the magnitude of the satisfaction → performance relationship. In Fishbein and Ajzen's (1975) theory of reasoned action, *subjective norms* are relevant others' attitudes about whether one should engage in an act. In the context of the satisfaction → performance relationship, subjective norms could be interpreted to represent a performance orientation. Where the norms indicate high performance standards, then dissatisfaction is less likely to result in reduced levels of performance because to respond in such a manner would violate the norms. A similar view with specific reference to the satisfaction–performance relationship lies in Triandis' (1959) conception of pressure for production. According to Triandis, job satisfaction should be less related to job performance when there is pressure for production because such pressure provides motivation to perform. Absent this pressure, motivation must come from elsewhere, in this case, from an intrinsic satisfaction with the job and the desire to perform it well. A similar standard might affect the satisfaction–performance relationship, but in this case a personal standard—moral obligation (Schwartz & Tessler, 1972). Just as others' views of acceptable responses to dissatisfaction may shape performance, one's personal views (the obligation to perform up to one's capabilities) may exhibit the same moderating effect.

Research by Fazio (e.g., Fazio, 1986) has shown that cognitive accessibility of an attitude affects its relationship with behavior, such that the attitude–behavior relationship is stronger for individuals whose attitudes about an object are easily accessed (measured in terms of response latency). Thus, one might hypothesize that individuals whose job satisfaction is accessible (fresh in their minds) are more likely to perform in ways consistent with their satisfaction (or dissatisfaction). Other potential moderating variables from the attitude literature are perceived relevance of the attitude (Snyder, 1982) and introspection about the attitude (see Eagly & Chaiken, 1993, pp. 212–215). Another potential moderating influence on the satisfaction → performance relationship is the degree to which satisfaction and/or performance are aggregated. Weigel and Newman (1976) showed that though general attitudes typically predicted specific behaviors (mean $r = .32$), their validity increased when the specific behaviors were grouped into categories of behaviors (mean $r = .42$) and became quite strong and significant when the behavioral categories were used to form a single behavioral index ($r = .62$). Finally, a prominent theme in alternative conceptualizations of the job satisfaction–job performance relationship is that the relationship will be stronger at the organizational level of analysis. However, the theoretical rationale for such an argument is somewhat murky, nor is it clear that the empirical data are consistent with this hypothesis. For example, the Ostroff (1992) and Harter and Creglow (1998) satisfaction–performance correlations at the organizational level of analysis are comparable to the individual-level correlations reported in this article. Thus, comparing the relative predictive power of job satisfaction at various levels (individual, group, organization) of analysis would be a worthwhile topic for future research, as would further theoretical development underlying expected differences.

In terms of mediators, both affective and cognitive processes underlie the satisfaction → performance relationship, yet there is a dearth of understanding of any such processes. In Fishbein and Ajzen's (1975) model of reasoned action, intentions mediate the effect of attitudes on behaviors. Does this general process, which has been shown across a wide array of behaviors, generalize to job performance? Specifically, do individuals use attitudes about their jobs in forming intentions regarding their prospective behaviors on the job (many of which are presumably performance related)? Hulin (1991) suggested that job dissatisfaction leads to a general withdrawal construct that is manifested in various behaviors such as absence, turnover, and the like. For some employees, reduced performance of job duties may be a manifestation of withdrawal. Finally, research has suggested that mood in the form of positive affect is related to both satisfaction (Brief, Butcher, & Roberson, 1995) and performance (Staw & Barsade, 1993). Thus, one reason why job satisfaction might lead to job performance is because individuals who like their jobs are more likely to be in good moods at work, which in turn facilitates job performance in various ways, including creative problem solving, motivation, and other processes (Isen & Baron, 1991).

Turning to the performance → satisfaction linkage, research has suggested that the contingency between pay and performance (Podsakoff & Williams, 1986) and intrinsic rewards (e.g., Ivancevich, 1979) moderate the performance–satisfaction relationship, such that jobs in which rewards are contingent on performance are more satisfying than jobs with a weaker performance–rewards contingency. It strikes us that many of these reward-oriented moderator variables proposed in past research would fruitfully be investigated under Locke's (1970) value theory. For example, job complexity may moderate the job performance–job satisfaction correlation because effective performance in complex jobs may satisfy many individuals' values for intrinsic fulfillment in their work. Locke's (1970) theory would further advance this hypothesis by proposing that the rewards that are produced will differentially satisfy individuals depending on their values. Thus, in addition to the positive general effect of the performance–rewards link on satisfaction, those rewards valued most by an individual will have the greatest potential to satisfy. Although direct tests of Locke's (1970) theory are lacking, it has enjoyed support in the studies that have tested it (Hochwarter et al., 1999; Nathanson & Becker, 1973). Research testing the validity of these moderators under Locke's (1970) theory would hold the promise of providing some needed integration to this area.

Research on achievement motivation reveals that individuals with high need for achievement (Nach) prefer moderately challenging tasks because tasks that are too challenging carry with them a higher risk for failure, which is unacceptable to high-Nach individuals (McClelland, 1985). It would then stand to reason that performing a job well is likely to be more satisfying (and performing a job poorly more dissatisfying) to high-Nach individuals because success is their primary motivation (McClelland & Franz, 1992). Indeed, some initial evidence supports this proposition (Steers, 1975). Similarly, for individuals for whom work is a central life interest (high scores on work centrality), performance should be more satisfying because their jobs are an important part of their identity. Finally, as with the satisfaction → performance relationship, aggregation is an important moderating influence. Job performance would be expected to best predict job satisfaction when the constructs correspond in terms of their generality and, beyond this, when both constructs are measured broadly. These issues of construct generality and correspondence have fundamental effects on the nature and magnitude of the relationships between attitudes and behaviors (see Eagly & Chaiken, 1993, for a review) but have rarely been considered in the satisfaction–performance literature (see Fisher, 1980).

In terms of mediators of the performance → satisfaction relationship, perhaps the most logical explanation of the effect of performance on satisfaction is that of success—performance is satisfying because it brings success in the form of valued rewards. Success and achievement are primary causes of life satisfaction (Argyle & Martin, 1991), and so should they be of job satisfaction. These rewards can be extrinsic (pay, recognition from others) as well as intrinsic (satisfaction with a job well done) but would have to be measured broadly. Despite the logic of this hypothesis, we are aware of only one empirical test (S. P. Brown et al., 1993). Within the realm of success, there are numerous ways success on the job (resulting from job performance) can affect job satisfaction. One of the sources of self-efficacy is past accomplishments. Bandura (1997) noted that "successes build a robust belief in one's personal efficacy" (p. 80). It seems plausible that individuals who believe in their abilities and competence to perform a job will be more satisfied in it. Under this explanation, self-efficacy should mediate the performance–satisfaction relationship.

Diener, Suh, Lucas, and Smith's (1999) review shows that progress toward one's goals is predictive of subjective well-being (though the type of goal and the reasons for pursuing it also matter). Thus, if effective job performance promotes achievement of major goals in work and life, individuals should be more satisfied with their jobs as a result. This explanation is related to, but distinct from, the success and achievement explanation as the latter may be satisfying irrespective of the explicit or conscious goals of the individual. In reality, achievement and goal progression are likely to be intertwined in that success will be most satisfying when it is tied to progress toward important personal goals (Locke, 1997).

Finally, although there is a great deal of research on the effect of mood on performance, it surprises us that research on the effects of performance on mood is lacking. Most individuals would rather do something well than poorly, and thus doing something well is likely to elevate mood. Mood, in turn, is related to job satisfaction (Weiss et al., 1999). Thus, in addition to mediating the satisfaction → performance relationship, positive mood also might mediate the performance → satisfaction relationship.

Although it was not possible to include Model 7 in the integrative model in Figure 2, this is not to suggest that the model is undeserving of future research. Research in the past decade has provided strong indications that investigations into the attitude–behavior relationship need not be confined to the satisfaction–performance relationship. It has been suggested that replacing job satisfaction with affect and performance with organizational citizenship behaviors will lead to stronger relationships (see George & Brief, 1992), though the relationship, noted earlier, of job satisfaction with citizenship behaviors ($\rho = .28$; Organ & Ryan, 1995) appears to be no stronger than the relationship with job performance reported here ($\rho = .30$). Despite the promise of this literature, more construct validity evidence is needed for both the affective constructs and the performance constructs. Specifically, a plethora of affective concepts have been proposed, including positive mood at work (George & Brief, 1992), positive and negative affectivity (Cropanzano et al., 1993), positive affect (Isen & Baron, 1991), well-being (Wright & Bonett, 1997), positive emotion (Staw & Barsade, 1993), and mental health (Wright et al., 1993). Similarly, within the broad realm of performance, various constructs have been promulgated, including prosocial organizational behaviors (Brief & Motowidlo, 1986), organizational citizenship behaviors (Organ, 1988), contextual performance (Motowidlo & Van Scotter, 1994), and organizational spontaneity (George & Brief, 1992). If some or all of these constructs are surrogates for one another, then collectively these investigations manifest the jangle fallacy (Block, 1995)—constructs carrying different labels but indicating the same core construct are investigated separately. Thus, further construct validity evidence is needed.

## *Conclusion*

The present study provided a review and reexamination of the relationship between job satisfaction and job performance. Though the potential linkage between satisfaction and performance is nearly as old as the field of industrial–organizational psychology, the relationship between employee satisfaction and job performance is no longer considered an important area of research. As Roznowski and Hulin (1992) commented,

> Job satisfaction ... has been around in scientific psychology for so long that it gets treated by some researchers as a comfortable "old shoe." one that is unfashionable and unworthy of continued research. Many organizational researchers seem to assume that we know all there is to know about job satisfaction; we lose sight of its usefulness because of its familiarity and past popularity, (p. 124)

Though Roznowski and Hulin were writing with reference to the whole body of job satisfaction research, this commentary may be particularly descriptive of the satisfaction–performance relationship. Of the number of studies that include job satisfaction and job performance in their key words, 25% fewer such studies were published in the 1990s compared with the 1980s. Thus, the rate of studies investigating the relationship appears to be declining. Given the substantial impact of the Iaffaldano and Muchinsky (1985) study, it seems plausible that the meta-analysis had a "chilling effect" on subsequent research. Although we endorse continued research involving recent reconceptualizations of both job satisfaction and job performance, we do not believe that research on the satisfaction–performance relationship should be abandoned. As Eagly and Wood (1994) noted,

> Although research synthesis can facilitate the development of under standing in a research area by channeling subsequent research to resolve the uncertainties that emerge, the impact of synthesis has not been uniformly beneficial. [Research syntheses] have sometimes distorted understanding of a phenomenon and discouraged further research. (p. 487)

Given the scope of the current review and the consistency of results across studies, we believe the time has come for researchers to reconsider the satisfaction–performance relationship. According to Rosenthal (1995), the overall goal of the discussion of a meta-analysis is to answer the question. "Where are we now that this meta-analysis has been conducted?" (p. 190). In light of the results presented herein, we believe we are at a quite different place, regarding the magnitude of the satisfaction–performance relationship, than most researchers believe.

## Acknowledgment

We thank Frank L. Schmidt for his comments that inspired this study.

## Notes

1 As noted by a reviewer, studies that measure performance subsequent to satisfaction implicitly assume Model 1, and studies that measure satisfaction after performance implicitly assume Model 2. However, as Siegel and Bowen (1971) documented 30 years ago and we reaffirm below, very few satisfaction–performance studies are longitudinal, and most of these do not explicitly model a causal relationship between satisfaction and performance.
2 We also partially searched Dissertation Abstracts International (DAI). However, early in our search, we discovered that all of the dissertations uncovered in DAI were also indexed in PsycINFO (PsycINFO, unlike PsycLIT, includes dissertations). Thus, we subsequently confined our search to PsycINFO.
3 Murphy and DeShon (2000) argued against the practice of correcting correlations based on current estimates of interrater reliability. They did so on the grounds that raters may disagree for reasons other than random error (e.g., rater effects—some of which may be shared and some of which may be idiosyncratic). Thus, according to Murphy and DeShon, treating correlations among raters as a measure of reliability is inappropriate because it assumes that all lack of agreement is due to random error. Schmidt, Viswesvaran, and Ones (2000), although not disagreeing that there are many potential influences on performance ratings, argued that such influences are an issue not of the

reliability of the ratings but rather of the theoretical nature (construct validity) of the ratings. Although a full airing of this debate is beyond the scope of this article, we note that our practice is consistent with all contemporary (post-1990) meta-analyses involving job performance.
4. The reestimated correlation of .33 based on the Iaffaldano and Muchinsky (1985) studies is somewhat higher than the .30 estimate for all studies combined for several reasons. Compared with all studies in the analysis ($k = 312$), Iaffaldano and Muchinsky's studies were more likely to be based on jobs of high complexity and to appear in top-tier journals.
5. We conducted a meta-analysis by the five facets in the Job Descriptive Index (Smith, Kendall, & Hulin, 1969) and found that the average corrected correlation was .18—a figure identical to Iaffaldano and Muchinsky's (1985) overall estimate. Thus, even with our updated meta-analysis, the facets substantially underestimate the relationship of overall job satisfaction to job performance.
6. Meta-analysis has been criticized on various fronts, which include general criticisms of the technique (see Rosenthal, 1998, for a review), as well as criticisms of the specific procedures (e.g., Hunter & Schmidt, 1990; Rosenthal, 1998) Many of the criticisms directed at the Hunter and Schmidt (1990) technique are on statistical grounds (e.g., Erez, Bloom, & Wells, 1996; James, Demaree, Mulaik, & Ladd, 1992; Johnson, Mullen, & Salas, 1995), and, of course, our results are only as valid as this technique. However, many of these criticisms have been addressed by Hunter, Schmidt and colleagues (e.g., Schmidt & Hunter, 1999). More generally, meta-analysis requires judgment calls that can affect the results. Wanous et al. (1989) advised authors to think carefully about the decisions they make and to conduct a narrative review in addition to a quantitative review. We have tried to follow these recommendations and to be explicit about the decisions that we have made and the implications of these decisions (as in the case of corrections for unreliability).

# References

References marked with an asterisk indicate studies included in the meta-analysis.

*Abdel-Halim, A. A. (1980). Effects of higher order need strength on the job performance–job satisfaction relationship. *Personnel Psychology, 33,* 335–347.

Abdel-Halim, A. A. (1983). Effects of task and personality characteristics on subordinate responses to participative decision making. *Academy of Management Journal, 26,* 477–484.

*Abramis, D. J. (1985). *Job stressors, strains, job performance, social support, and social conflict: Causal relationships in a four-wave longitudinal panel study.* Unpublished doctoral dissertation, University of Michigan, Ann Arbor.

*Abramis, D. J. (1994). Relationship of job stressors to job performance: Linear or an inverted-U? *Psychological Reports, 75,* 547–558.

*Adkins, C. L. (1995). Previous work experience and organizational socialization: A longitudinal examination. *Academy of Management Journal, 38,* 839–862.

*Adkins, C. L., Ravlin, E. C., & Meglino, B. M. (1996). Value congruence between co-workers and its relationship to work outcomes. *Group and Organization Management, 21,* 439–460.

*Alexander, E. R., Helms, M. M., & Wilkins, R. D. (1989). The relationship between supervisory communication and subordinate performance and satisfaction among professionals. *Public Personnel Management, 18,* 415–429.

*Allen, G. M. (1992). *Person-in-job characteristics and work outcomes of fit*. Unpublished doctoral dissertation. University of Illinois at Urbana-Champaign.

*Anand, U., & Sohal, T. S. (1981). Relationship between some personality traits, job satisfaction, and job performance of employees. *Indian Journal of Applied Psychology, 18*, 11–15.

*Anderson, J. C., & O'Reilly. C. A., III. (1981). Effects of an organizational control system on managerial satisfaction and performance. *Human Relations, 34*, 491–501.

*Apasu-Gbotsu, Y. (1982). *The role of personal values in the explanation of salespersons' performance, satisfaction and propensity to quit*. Unpublished doctoral dissertation, University of Southern California.

*Araghi, M. A. K. (1981). *The relationship between university faculty job satisfaction, role conflict, task clarity, and productivity*. Unpublished doctoral dissertation, University of Houston, Houston, Texas.

Argyle, M., & Martin, M. (1991). The psychological causes of happiness. In F. Strack, M. Argyle, & N. Schwarz (Eds.), *Subjective well-being* (pp. 77–100). Oxford, England: Pergamon Press.

*Ayman, R. (1983). *A study of leadership effectiveness in Mexican organizations*. Unpublished doctoral dissertation, University of Utah, Salt Lake City.

*Bagozzi, R. P. (1978). Salesforce performance and satisfaction as a function of individual difference, interpersonal, and situational factors. *Journal of Marketing Research, 15*, 517–531.

Bagozzi, R. P. (1980). Performance and satisfaction in an industrial sales force: An examination of their antecedents and simultaneity. *Journal of Marketing, 44*, 65–77.

*Baird, L. S. (1976). Relationship of performance to satisfaction on stimulating and non-stimulating jobs. *Journal of Applied Psychology, 61*, 721–727.

*Baklien, B. (1980). *Job performance and satisfaction as a function of job characteristics and organizational climate across eight Tanzanian organizations*. Unpublished doctoral dissertation. Michigan State University, East Lansing.

Bandura, A. (1997). *Self-efficacy: The exercise of control*. New York: Freeman.

Barrick, M. R., & Mount, M. K. (1991). The Big Five personality dimensions and job performance: A meta-analysis. *Personnel Psychology, 44*, 1–26.

Barrick, M. R., & Mount, M. K. (1993). Autonomy as a moderator of the relationship between the Big Five personality dimensions and job performance. *Journal of Applied Psychology, 78*, 111–118.

*Bateman, T. S. (1980). *A longitudinal investigation of role overload and its relationships with work behaviors and job satisfaction*. Unpublished doctoral dissertation. Indiana University, Bloomington.

*Bauer, T. N., & Green, S. G. (1998). Testing the combined effects of newcomer information seeking and manager behavior on socialization. *Journal of Applied Psychology, 83*, 72–83.

*Bedeian, A. G., Mossholder, K. W., & Armenakis, A. A. (1983). Role perception–outcome relationships: Moderating effects of situational variables. *Human Relations, 36*, 167–184.

Behrman, D. N., & Perreault, W. D. (1984). A role stress model of the performance and satisfaction of industrial salespersons. *Journal of Marketing, 48*, 9–21.

*Berger-Gross, V., & Kraut, I. (1984). "Great expectations:" A no-conflict explanation of role conflict. *Journal of Applied Psychology, 69*, 261–271.

*Bernardin, H. J. (1979). The predictability of discrepancy measures of role constructs. *Personnel Psychology, 32*, 139–153.

*Bhagat, R. S. (1982). Conditions under which stronger job performance–job satisfaction relationships may be observed: A closer look at two situational contingencies. *Academy of Management Journal, 25*, 772–789.

*Bhagat, R. S., & Allie, S. M. (1989). Organizational stress, personal life stress, and symptoms of life strains: An examination of the moderating role of sense of competence. *Journal of Vocational Behavior, 35*, 231–253.

*Birnbaum, D., & Somers, M. J. (1993). Fitting job performance into turnover model: An examination of the job performance–turnover relationship and a path model. *Journal of Management, 19*, 1–11.

*Bittle, M. L. (1991). *The moderating effect of task characteristics on disposition–work outcome relationships*. Unpublished doctoral dissertation. Virginia Polytechnic Institute and State University, Blacksburg.

*Bizot, E. B., & Goldman, S. H. (1993). Prediction of satisfactoriness and satisfaction: An 8-year follow up. *Journal of Vocational Behavior, 43*, 19–29.

*Blanchard, J. L. (1991). *Work attitudes and performance in human service workers*. Unpublished doctoral dissertation. University of Denver. Denver, Colorado.

Block, J. (1995). A contrarian view of the five-factor approach to personality description. *Psychological Bulletin, 117*, 187–215.

*Bluen, S. D., Barling, J., & Burns, W. (1990). Predicting sales performance, job satisfaction, and depression by using the achievement strivings and impatience–irritability dimensions of Type A behavior. *Journal of Applied Psychology, 75*, 212–216.

Bommer, W. H., Johnson, J., Rich, G. A., Podsakoff, P. M, & MacKenzie, S. B. (1995). On the interchangeability of objective and subjective measures of employee performance: A meta-analysis. *Personnel Psychology, 48*, 587–605.

Borman, W. C., & Motowidlo, S. J. (1993). Expanding the criterion domain to include elements of contextual performance. In N. Schmitt & W. C. Borman (Eds.), *Personnel selection in organizations* (pp. 71–98). San Francisco: Jossey-Bass.

*Boyles, R. B. (1968). *The interaction between certain personality variables and perceived supervisory styles and their relation to performance and satisfaction*. Unpublished doctoral dissertation, New York University, New York.

*Brass, D. J. (1981). Structural relationships, job characteristics, and worker satisfaction and performance. *Administrative Science Quarterly, 26*, 331–348.

Brayfield, A. H., & Crockett, W. H. (1955). Employee attitudes and employee performance. *Psychological Bulletin, 52*, 396–424.

*Brayfield, A. H., & Marsh, M. M. (1957). Aptitudes, interests, and personality characteristics of farmers. *Journal of Applied Psychology, 41*, 98–103.

*Breaugh, J. A. (1981). Relationships between recruiting sources and employee performance, absenteeism, and work attitudes. *Academy of Management Journal, 24*, 142–147.

Brief, A. P. (1998). *Attitudes in and around organizations*. Thousand Oaks, CA: Sage.

*Brief, A. P., & Aldag, R. J. (1976). Correlates of role indices. *Journal of Applied Psychology, 61*, 468–472.

Brief, A. P., Butcher, A., & Roberson, L. (1995). Cookies, disposition, and job attitudes: The effects of positive mood inducing events and negative affectivity on job satisfaction in a field experiment. *Organizational Behavior and Human Decision Processes, 62*, 55–62.

Brief, A. P., & Motowidlo, S. J. (1986). Prosocial organizational behaviors. *Academy of Management Review, II,* 710–725.

Brief, A. P., & Roberson, L. (1989). Job attitude organization: An exploratory study. *Journal of Applied Social Psychology, 19,* 717–727.

*Brody, M., (1945). *The relationship between efficiency and job satisfaction.* Unpublished master's thesis. New York University, New York.

*Brown, N. J. (1989). *The relative contribution of organizational climate, supervisory leadership, and peer leadership to job satisfaction, performance, and retention.* Unpublished doctoral dissertation, University of Denver.

*Brown, S. P., Cron, W. L., & Leigh, T. W. (1993). Do feelings of success mediate sales performance–work attitude relationships? *Journal of the Academy of Marketing Science, 21,* 91–99.

Brown, S. P., & Peterson, R. A. (1993). Antecedents and consequences of salesperson job satisfaction: Meta-analysis and assessment of causal effects. *Journal of Marketing Research, 30,* 63–77.

*Brown, S. P., & Peterson, R. A. (1994). Effect of effort on sales performance and job satisfaction. *Journal of Marketing, 58,* 70–80.

*Burns, B. A. (1977). *The role of control orientation in the perception and handling of job-related technological change.* Unpublished doctoral dissertation, George Washington University, Washington, DC.

Campbell, J. P., McCloy, R. A., Oppler, S. H., & Sager, C. E. (1993). A theory of performance. In N. Schmitt & W. C. Borman (Eds.), *Personnel selection in organizations* (pp. 35–70). San Francisco: Jossey-Bass.

*Carlson, R. E. (1969). Degree of job fit as a moderator of the relationship between job performance and job satisfaction. *Personnel Psychology, 22,* 159–170.

Charng, H., Piliavin, J. A., & Callero, P. L. (1988). Role identity and reasoned action in the prediction of repeated behavior. *Social Psychology Quarterly, 51,* 303–317.

Cherrington, D. J., Reitz, H. J., & Scott, W. E. (1971). Effects of contingent and noncontingent reward on the relationship between satisfaction and task performance. *Journal of Applied Psychology, 55,* 531–536.

*Clayton, S. H. (1981). *Moderators of the relationship between indvidual-task-structure congruencies and job satisfaction and performance.* Unpublished doctoral dissertation, University of Texas, Dallas.

*Cleveland, J. N., & Shore, L. M. (1992). Self- and supervisory perspectives on age and work attitudes and performance. *Journal of Applied Psychology, 77,* 469–484.

Cohen, J., & Cohen, P. (1983). *Applied multiple regression/correlation analysis for the behavioral sciences.* Hillsdale, NJ: Erlbaum.

*Colarelli, S. M., Dean, R. A., & Konstans, C. (1987). Comparative effects of personal and situational influences on job outcomes of new professionals. *Journal of Applied Psychology, 72,* 558–566.

Cook, T. D., & Campbell, D. T. (1979). *Quasi-experimentation: Design and analysis issues for field settings.* Boston: Houghton Mifflin.

Côté, S. (1999). Affect and performance in organizational settings. *Current Directions in Psychological Science, 8,* 65–68.

*Crisera, R. A. (1965). *A study of job satisfaction and its relationship to performance in the job situation.* Unpublished doctoral dissertation, Washington University, St. Louis, Missouri.

Cronbach, L. J., Gleser, G. C. Nanda, H., & Rajaratnam, N. (1972). *The dependability of behavioral measurements: Theory of generalizability for scores and profiles*. New York: Wiley.

*Cropanzano, R., James, K., & Konovsky, M. A. (1993). Dispositional affectivity as a predictor of work attitudes and job performance. *Journal of Organizational Behavior*, *14*, 595–606.

Darden, W. R., Hampton. R., & Howell, R. D. (1989). Career versus organizational commitment: Antecedents and consequences of retail salespeople's commitment. *Journal of Retailing*, *65*, 80–105.

*Dawis, R. V., & Ace, M. E. (1973). Dimensions of threshold work experience for high school graduates and dropouts: A factor analysis. *Journal of Vocational Behavior*, *3*, 221–231.

*Day, D. V., & Bedeian, A. G. (1995). Person similarity and work-related outcomes among African-American nursing personnel: A test of the supplementary model of person–environment congruence. *Journal of Vocational Behavior*, *46*, 55–70.

Deci, E. L., & Ryan, R. M. (1985). *Intrinsic motivation and self-determination in human behavior*. New York: Plenum.

*De Frain, J. H. (1979). *College teachers' work motivation, central life interests, and voluntarism as predictors of job satisfaction and job performance*. Unpublished doctoral dissertation, University of Kansas, Lawrence.

*Deis, D. L. (1982). *Trust and efficacy in organizations: The impact on satisfaction and performance*. Unpublished doctoral dissertation. University of Utah, Salt Lake City.

*Denton, R. T. (1976). *The effects of differing leadership behaviors on the job satisfaction and job performance of professional mental health workers*. Unpublished doctoral dissertation, Ohio State University, Columbus.

Diener, E., Suh, E. M., Lucas, R. E., & Smith, H. L. (1999). Subjective well-being: Three decades of progress. *Psychological Bulletin*, *125*, 276–302.

Dipboye, R. L. (1977). A critical review of Korman's self-consistency theory of work motivation and occupational choice. *Organizational Behavior and Human Decision Processes*, *18*, 108–126.

*Dipboye, R. L., Zultowski. W. H., Dewhirst, H. D., & Arvey, R. D. (1979). Self-esteem as a moderator of performance–satisfaction relationships. *Journal of Vocational Behavior*, *15*, 193–206.

*Doll, L. D. (1973). *A multidimensional study of job satisfaction and performance*. Unpublished doctoral dissertation, Washington University, St. Louis, Missouri.

*Doll, R. E., & Gunderson, E. K. E. (1969). Occupational group as a moderator of the job satisfaction–job performance relationship. *Journal of Applied Psychology*, *53*, 359–361.

*Dorfman, P. W., Stephan, W. G., & Loveland, J. (1986). Performance appraisal behaviors: Supervisor perceptions and subordinate reactions. *Personnel Psychology*, *39*, 579–597.

*Dougherty, T. W. (1981). *Role-based stressors: An investigation of relationships to personal and organizational outcomes*. Unpublished doctoral dissertation. University of Houston, Houston, Texas.

*Dreher, G. F. (1981). Predicting the salary satisfaction of exempt employees. *Personnel Psychology*, *34*, 579–589.

*Dubinsky, A. J., & Hartley, S. W. (1986). A path-analytic study of a model of salesperson performance. *Journal of the Academy of Marketing Science*, *14*, 36–46.

*Dubinsky, A. J., & Skinner, S. J. (1984). Impact of job characteristics on retail sales people's reactions to their jobs. *Journal of Retailing, 60*, 35–62.

Eagly, A. H. (1992). Uneven progress: Social psychology and the study of attitudes. *Journal of Personality and Social Psychology, 63*, 693–710.

Eagly, A. H., & Chaiken, S. (1993). *The psychology of attitudes.* Fort Worth, TX: Harcourt Brace Jovanovich.

Eagly, A. H., & Wood, W. (1994). Using research syntheses to plan future research. In H. Cooper & L. V. Hedges (Eds.), *The handbook of research synthesis* (pp. 485–500). New York: Russell Sage Foundation.

*Efraty, D., & Sirgy, M. J. (1990). The effects of quality of working life (QWL) on employee behavioral responses. *Social Indicators Research, 22*, 31–47.

*Efraty, D., & Wolfe, D. M. (1988). The effect of organizational identification on employee affective and performance responses. *Journal of Business and Psychology, 3*, 105–112.

*Ellingson, J. E., Gruys, M. L., & Sackett, P. R. (1998). Factors related to the satisfaction and performance of temporary employees. *Journal of Applied Psychology, 83*, 913–921.

*El-Safy, H. E. H. (1985). *Job satisfaction and job performance among the middle management personnel of the Sudanese public service.* Unpublished doctoral dissertation, University of Southern California, Los Angeles.

Erez, A., Bloom, M. C., & Wells, M. T. (1996). Using random rather than fixed effects models in meta-analysis: Implications for situational specificity and validity generalization. *Personnel Psychology, 49*, 275–306.

*Ettington, D. R. (1998). Successful career plateauing. *Journal of Vocational Behavior, 52*, 72–88.

Ewen, R. B. (1973). Pressure for production, task difficulty, and the correlation between job satisfaction and job performance. *Journal of Applied Psychology, 58*, 378–380.

Fazio, R. H. (1986). How do attitudes guide behavior? In R. M. Sorrentino & E. T. Higgins (Eds.), *Handbook of motivation and cognition: Foundations of social behavior* (pp. 204–243). New York: Guilford Press.

*Fiedler, A. M. (1993). *The effect of vision congruence on employee empowerment, commitment, satisfaction, and performance.* Unpublished doctoral dissertation, Florida International University, Miami.

Fishbein, M. (1973). The prediction of behaviors from attitudinal variables. In C. D. Mortensen & K. K. Sereno (Eds.), *Advances in communication research* (pp. 3–38). New York: Harper & Row.

Fishbein, M. (1979). A theory of reasoned action. In H. Howe & M. Page (Eds.), *Nebraska Symposium on Motivation* (pp. 65–118). Lincoln: University of Nebraska Press.

Fishbein, M., & Ajzen, I. (1975). *Belief, attitude, intention, and behavior: An introduction to theory and research*, Reading, MA: Addison-Wesley.

Fisher, C. D. (1980). On the dubious wisdom of expecting job satisfaction to correlate with performance. *Academy of Management Review, 5*, 607–612.

*Fox, M. L., Dwyer, D. J., & Ganster, D. C. (1993). Effects of stressful job demands and control on physiological and attitudinal outcomes in a hospital setting. *Academy of Management Journal, 36*, 289–318.

*Frey, J. R. (1977). *A study of employee satisfaction, satisfactoriness, and salaries of completers of Kansas-area vocational–technical school training programs for stereotypical male or female occupations.* Unpublished doctoral dissertation, Kansas State University, Manhattan.

*Funk, C. D. (1968). *The relationship between Dogmatism scores of county extension agents and measures of the job performance, job satisfaction, and job aspirations.* Unpublished doctoral dissertation, University of Wisconsin.

*Futrell, C. M., & Parasuraman, A. (1984). The relationship of satisfaction and performance to salesforce turnover. *Journal of Marketing, 48*, 33–40.

*Gadel, M. S., & Kriedt, P. H. (1952). Relationships of aptitude, interest, performance, and job satisfaction of IBM operators. *Personnel Psychology, 5*, 207–213.

*Gardner, D. G., Dunham, R. B., Cummings, L. L., & Pierce, J. L. (1987). Focus of attention at work and leader–follower relationships. *Journal of Occupational Behavior, 8*, 277–294.

*Gardner, D. G., & Pierce, J. L. (1998). Self-esteem and self-efficacy within the organizational context. *Group and Organization Management, 23*, 48–70.

Gaugler, B. B., Rosenthal, D. B., Thornton, G. C., III, & Bentson, C. (1987). Meta-analysis of assessment center validity. *Journal of Applied Psychology, 72*, 493–511.

*Gavin, J. F., & Ewen, R. B. (1974). Racial differences in job attitudes and performance: Some theoretical considerations and empirical findings. *Personnel Psychology, 27*, 455–464.

*Gellatly, I. R., Paunonen, S. V., Meyer, J. P., Jackson, D. N., & Goffin, R. D. (1991). Personality, vocational interest, and cognitive predictors of managerial job performance and satisfaction. *Personality and Individual Differences, 12*, 221–231.

George, J. M., & Bettenhausen, K. (1990). Understanding prosocial behavior, sales performance, and turnover: A group-level analysis in a service context. *Journal of Applied Psychology, 75*, 698–709.

George, J. M., & Brief, A. P. (1992). Feeling good–doing good: A conceptual analysis of the mood at work–organizational spontaneity relationship. *Psychological Bulletin, 112*, 310–329.

George, J. M., & Brief, A. P. (1996). Motivational agendas in the workplace: The effects of feelings on focus of attention and work motivation. *Research in Organizational Behavior, 18*, 75–109.

*Giovannini, P. C. (1974). *A study of the interaction between job satisfaction, job involvement, and job performance.* Unpublished doctoral dissertation. Columbia University, New York.

*Goldsmith, R. E., McNeilly, K. M., & Ross, F. A. (1989). Similarity of sales representatives' and supervisors' problem-solving styles and the satisfaction–performance relationship. *Psychological Reports, 64*, 827–832.

*Grady, T. L. (1984). *The relationship between job satisfaction and teacher performance of vocational agriculture teachers in Louisiana,* Unpublished doctoral dissertation, Louisiana State University.

*Graham, D. L. (1983). *The relationship of personality types of Arkansas Cooperative Extension Service faculty to job satisfaction and performance.* Unpublished doctoral dissertation, University of Maryland.

*Greenberger, D. B., Strasser, S., Cummings, L. L., & Dunham, R. B. (1989). The impact of personal control on performance and satisfaction. *Organizational Behavior and Human Decision Processes, 43*, 29–51.

*Greene, C. N. (1972). Relationships among role accuracy, compliance, performance evaluation, and satisfaction within managerial dyads. *Academy of Management Journal, 15*, 205–215.

*Greene, C. N. (1973). Causal connections among managers' merit pay, job satisfaction, and performance. *Journal of Applied Psychology, 58*, 95–100.

*Gregson, T. (1987). *An empirical investigation of the relationship between communication satisfaction, job satisfaction, turnover, and performance for public accountants.* Unpublished doctoral dissertation, University of Arkansas.

*Griffin, R. W. (1980). Relationships among individual, task design, and leader behavior variables. *Academy of Management Journal, 23*, 665–683.

*Griffin, R. W. (1991). Effects of work redesign on employee perceptions, attitudes, and behaviors: A long-term investigation. *Academy of Management Journal, 34*, 425–435.

*Griffiths, R. D. P. (1975). The accuracy and correlates of psychiatric patients' self-assessment of their work behaviour. *British Journal of Social and Clinical Psychology, 14*, 181–189.

*Gross, R. H. (1978). *Moderators of the job performance–job satisfaction relationship for research scientists.* Unpublished doctoral dissertation, University of Tennessee.

*Gustafson, S. B., & Mumford, M. D. (1995). Personal style and person–environment fit: A pattern approach. *Journal of Vocational Behavior, 46*, 163–188.

*Hackman, R. J., & Lawler, E. E., III. (1971). Employee reactions to job characteristics. *Journal of Applied Psychology, 55*, 259–286.

*Hamid Ud-Din, M. (1953). *The relationship between job satisfaction and job performance.* Unpublished doctoral dissertation, Columbia University, New York.

Hampton, R., Dubinsky, A. J., & Skinner, S. J. (1986). A model of sales supervisor leadership and retail salespeople's job-related outcomes. *Journal of the Academy of Marketing Science, 14*, 33–43.

*Harding, F. D., & Bottenberg, R. A. (1961). Effect of personal characteristics on relationships between attitudes and job performance. *Journal of Applied Psychology, 45*, 428–430.

Harris, M. M., & Schaubroeck, J. (1988). A meta-analysis of self–supervisor, self–peer, and peer–supervisor ratings. *Personnel Psychology, 41*, 43–62.

Harter, J. K., & Creglow, A. (1998). *A meta-analysis and utility analysis of the relationship between core GWA perceptions and business outcomes* (Working Paper 2.0). Lincoln, NE: Gallup Organization.

*Haywood, G. D. (1980). *The relationship of job satisfaction, job satisfactoriness and personal characteristics of secondary school teachers in Georgia.* Unpublished doctoral dissertation. University of Georgia, Athens.

*Heneman, R. L., Greenberger, D. B., & Strasser, S. (1988). The relationships between pay-for-performance perceptions and pay satisfaction. *Personnel Psychology, 41*, 745–759.

Herman, J. B. (1973). Are situational contingencies limiting job attitude–job performance relationships? *Organizational Behavior and Human Decision Processes, 10*, 208–224.

*Heron, A. (1954). Satisfaction and satisfactoriness: Complementary aspects of occupational adjustment. *Journal of Occupational Psychology, 28*, 140–153.

Herzberg, F., Mausner, B., Peterson, R. O., & Capwell, D. F. (1957). *Job attitudes: Review of research and opinion.* Pittsburgh, PA: Psychological Service of Pittsburgh.

*Hesketh, B., McLachan, K., & Gardner, D. (1992). Work adjustment theory: An empirical test using a fuzzy rating scale. *Journal of Vocational Behavior, 40*, 318–337.

*Hester, G. L. (1981). *A comparative analysis of job satisfaction and job satisfactoriness for two groups of clerical employees.* Unpublished doctoral dissertation, Wayne State University.

Hochwarter, W. A., Perrewé. P. L., Ferris, G. R., & Brymer, R. A. (1999). Job satisfaction and performance: The moderating effects of value attainment and affective disposition. *Journal of Vocational Behavior, 54*, 296–313.

*Holley, W. H., Jr., Feild, H. S., & Holley, B. B. (1978). Age and reactions to jobs: An empirical study of paraprofessional workers. *Age and Work, 1*, 33–40.

Hulin, C. L. (1991). Adaptation, persistence, and commitment in organizations. In M. D. Dunnette & L. M. Hough (Eds.), *Handbook of industrial and organizational psychology* (2nd ed. Vol. 2. pp. 445–505). Palo Alto. CA: Consulting Psychologists Press.

Hunter, J. E., & Hunter, R. F. (1984). Validity and utility of alternative predictors of job performance. *Psychological Bulletin, 96*, 72–98.

Hunter, J. E., & Schmidt, F. L. (1990). *Methods of meta-analysis*. Newbury Park, CA: Sage.

Iaffaldano, M. T., & Muchinsky, P. M. (1985). Job satisfaction and job performance: A meta-analysis. *Psychological Bulletin, 97*, 251–273.

*Im, Y. (1991). *Job satisfaction and its relationship with job performance among apparel specialty store managers*. Unpublished doctoral dissertation, Texas Woman's University, Denton.

*Inkson, J. H. K. (1978). Self-esteem as a moderator of the relationship between job performance and job satisfaction. *Journal of Applied Psychology, 63*, 243–247.

Isen, A. M., & Baron, R. A. (1991). Positive affect as a factor in organizational behavior. *Research in Organizational Behavior, 13*, 1–53.

*Ivancevich, J. M. (1974). Effects of the shorter workweek on selected satisfaction and performance measures. *Journal of Applied Psychology, 59*, 717–721.

*Ivancevich, J. M. (1978). The performance to satisfaction relationship: A causal analysis of stimulating and non-stimulating jobs. *Organizational Behavior and Human Performance, 22*, 350–365.

*Ivancevich, J. M. (1979). High and low task-stimulation jobs: A causal analysis of performance–satisfaction relationships. *Academy of Management Journal, 22*, 206–232.

*Ivancevich, J. M. (1980). A longitudinal study of behavioral expectation scales: Attitudes and performance. *Journal of Applied Psychology, 65*, 139–146.

*Ivancevich, J. M., & Donnelly. J. H., Jr. (1975). Relation of organizational structure to job satsifaction, anxiety–stress, and performance. *Administrative Science Quarterly, 20*, 272–280.

*Ivancevich, J. M., & McMahon, J. T. (1982). The effects of goal setting, external feedback, and self-generated feedback on outcome variables: A field experiment. *Academy of Management Journal, 25*, 359–372.

*Ivancevich, J. M., & Smith, S. V. (1981). Goal setting interview skill training: Simulated and on-the-job analyses. *Journal of Applied Psychology, 66*, 697–705.

*Jabri, M. M. (1992). Job satisfaction and job performance among R&D scientists: The moderating influence of perceived appropriateness of task allocation decisions. *Australian Journal of Psychology, 44*, 95–99.

*Jacobs, R., & Solomon, T. (1977). Strategies for enhancing the prediction of job performance from job satisfaction. *Journal of Applied Psychology, 62*, 417–421.

James, L. R., Demaree, R. G., Mulaik, S. A., & Ladd, R. T. (1992). Validity generalization in the context of situational models. *Journal of Applied Psychology, 77*, 3–14.

James, L. R., Mulaik. S. A., & Brett, J. M. (1982). *Causal analysis: Assumptions, models, and data*. Beverly Hills, CA: Sage.

*Jenkins, J. M. (1990). *Commitment in organizations: Integrating the construct.* Unpublished doctoral dissertation. University of Southern Mississippi, Hattiesburg.

Johnson, B. T., Mullen, B., & Salas, E. (1995). Comparison of three major meta-analytic approaches. *Journal of Applied Psychology, 80,* 94–106.

*Johnston, M. W., Futrell, C. M., Parasuraman, A., & Sager, J. (1988). Performance and job satisfaction effects on salesperson turnover: A replication and extension. *Journal of Business Research, 16,* 67–83.

*Joyce, W., Slocum, J. W., & Von Glinow, M. A. (1982). Person–situation interaction: Competing models of fit. *Journal of Occupational Behavior, 3,* 265–280.

Judge, T. A. (1993). Does affective disposition moderate the relationship between job satisfaction and voluntary turnover? *Journal of Applied Psychology, 78,* 395–401.

*Judge, T. A., & Bono, J. E. (2000). *Job attitudes of employees at Hawkeye Foodsystems.* Unpublished manuscript. University of Iowa, Iowa City.

Judge, T. A., Hanisch, K. A., & Drankoski, R. D. (1995). Human resources management and employee attitudes. In G. R. Ferris, S. D. Rosen, & D. T. Barnum (Eds.), *Handbook of human resources management* (pp. 574–596). Oxford, England: Blackwell.

*Judge, T. A., & Thoresen, C. J. (1996, April). *Demographic differences in pay satisfaction: A study of race and gender.* Symposium conducted at the Eleventh Annual Conference for Industrial and Organizational Psychology. San Diego, CA.

*Judge, T. A., Thoresen, C. J., Pucik, V., & Welbourne, T. M. (1999). Managerial coping with organizational change: A dispositional perspective. *Journal of Applied Psychology, 84,* 107–122.

Jurgensen, C. E. (1978). Job preferences (What makes a job good or bad?). *Journal of Applied Psychology, 50,* 479–487.

*Kaldenberg, D.O., & Becker, B. W. (1991). Test of the Korman hypothesis: Performance, self-esteem, and job satisfaction among dentists. *Psychological Reports, 69,* 201–202.

*Kantak, D. M. (1998). *The link between salesperson job satisfaction and customer satisfaction.* Unpublished doctoral dissertation. Texas A&M University, College Station.

Katzell, R. A., Thompson, D. E., & Guzzo, R. A. (1992). How job satisfaction and job performance are and are not linked. In C. J. Cranny, P. C. Smith, & E. F. Stone (Eds.), *Job satisfaction* (pp. 195–217). New York: Lexington Books.

Keaveney, S. M., & Nelson, J. E. (1993). Coping with organizational role stress: Intrinsic motivational orientation, perceived role benefits, and psychological withdrawal. *Journal of the Academy of Marketing Science, 21,* 113–124.

*Keller, R. T. (1984). The role of performance and absenteeism in the predicting of turnover. *Academy of Management Journal, 27,* 176–183.

*Keller, R. T. (1997). Job involvement and organizational commitment as longitudinal predictors of job performance: A study of scientists and engineers. *Journal of Applied Psychology, 82,* 539–545.

*Kesselman, G. A., Wood, M. T., & Hagen, E. L. (1974). Relationships between performance and satisfaction under contingent and noncontingent reward systems. *Journal of Applied Psychology, 59,* 374–376.

*Khaleque, A., Hossain, M. M., & Hoque, M. E. (1992). Job satisfaction. mental health, fatigue and performance of industrial workers. *Psychological Studies, 37,* 136–141.

*Kinicki, A. J., Lockwood, C. A., Hom, P. W., & Griffeth, R. W. (1990). Interviewer predictions of applicant qualifications and interviewer validity: Aggregate and individual analyses. *Journal of Applied Psychology, 75*, 477–486.

*Kirchner, W. K. (1965). Relationships between general and specific attitudes toward work and objective job performance for outdoor advertising salesmen. *Journal of Applied Psychology, 49*, 455–457.

*Kittrell, D. L. (1980). *The relationship among the interest score on six occupational themes and job satisfaction and performance of Ohio Cooperative Extension county agents*. Unpublished doctoral dissertation. Ohio State University, Columbus.

*Konovsky, M. A., & Cropanzano, R. (1991). Perceived fairness of employee drug testing as a predictor of employee attitudes and job performance. *Journal of Applied Psychology, 76*, 698–707.

Korman, A. K. (1970). Toward an hypothesis of work behavior. *Journal of Applied Psychology, 54*, 31–41.

*Kuhn, D. G., Slocum, J. W., Jr., & Chase, R. B. (1971). Does job performance affect employee satisfaction? *Personnel Journal, 50*, 455–459, 485.

*La Follette, W. R. (1973). *An empirical study of job satisfaction, organizational climate, organizational practices and job performance in a medical center*. Unpublished doctoral dissertation, Indiana University.

Landy, F. J. (1989). *Psychology of work behavior*. Pacific Grove. CA: Brooks/Cole.

*Lawler, E. E., III, & Porter, L. W. (1967). The effect of performance on job satisfaction. *Industrial Relations, 7*, 20–28.

*Leana, C. R. (1986). Predictors and consequences of delegation. *Academy of Management Journal, 29*, 754–774.

*Lee, C. Ashford, S. J. & Bobko, P. (1990). Interactive effects of "Type A" behavior and perceived control on worker performance, job satisfaction, and somatic complaints. *Academy of Management Journal, 32*, 870–881.

*Lee, T. W., & Mowday, R. T. (1987). Voluntarily leaving an organization: An empirical investigation of Steers and Mowday's model of turnover. *Academy of Management Journal, 30*, 721–743.

*Leveto, G. A. (J974). *Self-esteem as a moderator of the satisfaction/performance relationship: A multivariate approach*. Unpublished doctoral dissertation. Georgia State University, Atlanta.

*Levy, P. E., & Williams, J. R. (1998). The role of perceived system knowledge in predicting appraisal reactions, job satisfaction, and organizational commitment. *Journal of Organizational Behavior, 19*, 53–65.

*Lichtman, C. M. (1970). Some intrapersonal response correlates of organizational rank. *Journal of Applied Psychology, 54*, 77–80.

*Livingstone, L. P., Nelson, D. L., & Barr, S. H. (1997). Person-environment fit and creativity: An examination of supply-value and demand-ability versions of fit. *Journal of Management, 23*, 119–146.

Locke, E. A. (1970). Job satisfaction and job performance: A theoretical analysis. *Organizational Behavior and Human Performance, 5*, 484–500.

Locke, E. A. (1997). The motivation to work: What we know. *Advances in Motivation and Achievement, 10*, 375–412.

*London, M., & Klimoski, R. J. (1975). Self-esteem and job complexity as moderators of performance and satisfaction. *Journal of Vocational Behavior, 6*, 293–304.

*Lopez, E. M. (1982). A test of the self-consistency theory of the job performance–job satisfaction relationship. *Academy of Management Journal, 25*, 335–348.

*Lopez, F. M., Jr. (1962). *A psychological analysis of the relationship of role consensus and personality consensus to job satisfaction and job performance.* Unpublished doctoral dissertation, Columbia University, New York.

*Lucas, G. H. (1985). The relationship between job attitudes, personal characteristics, and job outcomes: A study of retail store managers. *Journal of Retailing, 61*, 35–62.

*Lucas, G. H., Babakus, E., & Ingram, T. N. (1990). An empirical test of the job satisfaction–turnover relationship: Assessing the role of job performance for retail managers. *Journal of the Academy of Marketing Science, 18*, 199–208.

*Lusch, R. F., & Serpkenci, R. R. (1990). Personal differences, job tension, job outcomes, and store performance: A study of retail store managers. *Journal of Marketing, 54*, 85–101.

*Macan, T. H. (1994). Time management: Test of a process model, *Journal of Applied Psychology, 79*, 381–391.

*MacKenzie, S. B., Podsakoff, P. M., & Ahearn, M. (1998). Some possible antecedents of in-role and extra-role salesperson performance. *Journal of Marketing, 62*, 87–98.

*Magee, M. C. (1976). *Job success as a moderator variable in the prediction of job satisfaction: A test of the theory of work adjustment.* Unpublished doctoral dissertation. Texas Tech University, Lubbock.

March, J. G., & Simon, H. A. (1958). *Organizations.* New York: Wiley.

*Marr, K. V. (1965). *The relationship of intrinsic and extrinsic job satisfaction to intern teacher performance.* Unpublished doctoral dissertation, Stanford University, Stanford, California.

*Marshall, A. A., & Stohl, C. (1993). Participating as participation: A network approach. *Communication Monographs, 60*, 137–157.

*Mathieu, J. E., & Farr, J. L. (1991). Further evidence for the discriminant validity of measures of organizational commitment, job involvement, and job satisfaction. *Journal of Applied Psychology, 76*, 127–133.

Matt, G. E., & Cook, T. D. (1994). Threats to the validity of research syntheses. In H. Cooper & L. V. Hedges (Eds.), *The handbook of research synthesis* (pp. 503–520). New York: Russell Sage Foundation.

*Matteson, M. T., Ivancevich. J. M., & Smith, S. V. (1984). Relation of Type A behavior to performance and satisfaction among sales personnel. *Journal of Vocational Behavior, 25*, 203–214.

McClelland, D. C. (1985). *Human motivation.* Glenview, IL: Scott, Foresman.

McClelland, D. C., & Franz, C. E. (1992). Motivational and other sources of work accomplishments in mid-life: A longitudinal study. *Journal of Personality, 60*, 679–707.

McDaniel, M. A., Whetzel, D. L., Schmidt, F. L., & Maurer, S. D. (1994). The validity of employment interviews: A comprehensive review and meta-analysis. *Journal of Applied Psychology, 79*, 599–616.

*McNeilly, K., & Goldsmith, R. E. (1991). The moderating effects of gender and performance on job satisfaction and intentions to leave in the sales force. *Journal of Business Research, 22*, 219–232.

*McPherson, T. (1974). *Job satisfaction and performance of elementary and secondary classroom teachers in Region IX service center area of Texas.* Unpublished doctoral dissertation. North Texas State University.

*Mekky, A. F. A. (1973). *Organizational climate as a moderator variable in the job satisfaction/job performance relationship.* Unpublished doctoral dissertation, University of Illinois.

*Meyer, J. P., Paunonen, S. V., Gellatly, I. R., Goffin, R. D., & Jackson, D. N. (1989). Organizational commitment and job performance: It's the nature of the commitment that counts. *Journal of Applied Psychology, 74,* 152–156.

*Miller, J. C. (1984). *Locus of control, job enrichment, demographic and situational variables as predictors of job performance and job satisfaction.* Unpublished doctoral dissertation, Boston University, Boston, Massachusetts.

*Misshauk, M. J. (1968). *An investigation into supervisory skill mix among heterogeneous operative employee groups and the effectiveness in determining satisfaction and productivity of employees.* Unpublished doctoral dissertation, Ohio State University, Columbus.

*Misshauk, M. J. (1970). Importance of environmental factors to scientist–engineers. *Personnel Journal, 49,* 319–323.

*Mossholder, K. W., Bedeian, A. G., & Armenakis, A. A. (1981). Role perceptions, satisfaction, and performance: Moderating effects of self-esteem and organizational level. *Organizational Behavior and Human Performance, 28,* 224–234.

*Mossholder, K. W., Bedeian, A. G., Niebuhr, R. E., & Wesolowski, M. A. (1994). Dyadic duration and the performance–satisfaction relationship: A contextual perspective. *Journal of Applied Social Psychology, 24,* 1251–1269.

*Mossholder, K. W., Bedeian, A. G., Norris, D. R., Giles, W. F., & Feild, H. S. (1988). Job performance and turnover decisions: Two field studies. *Journal of Management, 14,* 403–414.

*Mossin, A. C. (1949). *Selling performance and contentment in relation to school background* (Tech. Rep. No. 952). New York: Teachers College. Columbia University, Bureau of Publications.

Motowidlo, S. J., & Van Scotter, J. R. (1994). Evidence that task performance should be distinguished from contextual performance. *Journal of Applied Psychology, 79,* 475–480.

Mount, M. K., Harter, J. K., Barrick, M. R., & Colbert, A. (2000, August). *Does job satisfaction moderate the relationship between conscientiousness and job performance?* Paper presented at the meeting of the Academy of Management, Toronto, Ontario, Canada.

*Munoz, M. (1973). *Job satisfaction in policemen and its relation to locus of control, ego strength, and performance.* Unpublished doctoral dissertation, City University of New York, New York.

Murphy, K. R., & DeShon, R. (2000). Inter-rater correlations do not estimate the reliability of job performance ratings. *Personnel Psychology, 53,* 873–900.

*Nathan, B. R., Mohrman, A. M., Jr., & Millman, J. (1991). Interpersonal relations as a context for the effects of appraisal interviews on performance and satisfaction: A longitudinal study. *Academy of Management Journal, 34,* 352–369.

*Nathanson, C. A., & Becker, M. H. (1973). Job satisfaction and job performance: An empirical test of some theoretical propositions. *Organizational Behavior and Human Performance, 9,* 267–279.

Naylor, J. C., Pritchard, R. D., & Ilgen, D. R. (1980). *A theory of behavior in organizations.* New York: Academic Press.

*Nhundu, T. J. (1992). Job performance, role clarity, and satisfaction among teacher interns in the Edmonton public school system. *Alberta Journal of Educational Research, 38,* 335–354.

*Nice, D., Stephen, D. S., & Steele, T. P. (1988). *Determinants and outcomes of collective organizational climate among shipboard independent duty hospital corpsmen* (Report No. 88-47). San Diego, CA: Naval Health Research Center, Health Services Research Department.

*Norris, D. R., & Niebuhr, R. E. (1984). Organization tenure as a moderator of the job satisfaction–job performance relationship. *Journal of Vocational Behavior, 24,* 169–178.

*O'Connor, E. J., Peters, L. H., Pooyan, A., Weekley, J., Frank, B., & Erenkrantz, B. (1984). Situational constraint effects on performance, affective reactions, and turnover: A field replication and extension. *Journal of Applied Psychology, 69,* 663–672.

*Oldham, G. R., Cummings, A., Mischel, L. J., Schmidtke, J. M., & Zhou, J. (1995). Listen while you work? Quasi-experimental relations between personal-stereo headset use and employee work responses. *Journal of Applied Psychology, 80,* 547–564.

*Oldham, G. R., Hackman, J. R., & Pearce, J. L. (1976). Conditions under which employees respond positively to enriched work, *Journal of Applied Psychology, 61,* 395–403.

*Oldham, G. R., Kulik, C. T., Ambrose, M. L., Stepina, L. P., & Brand, J. F. (1986). Relations between job facet comparisons and employee reactions. *Organizational Behavior and Human Decision Processes, 38,* 28–47.

*Oldham, G. R., Kulik, C. T., & Stepina, L. P. (1991). Physical environments and employee reactions: Effects of stimulus-screening skills and job complexity. *Academy of Management Journal, 34,* 929–938.

Olson, J. M., & Zanna, M. P. (1993). Attitudes and attitude change. *Annual Review of Psychology, 44,* 117–154.

Ones, D. S., Viswesvaran, C., & Reiss, A. D. (1996). Role of social desirability in personality testing for personnel selection: The red herring. *Journal of Applied Psychology, 81,* 660–679.

*Oppenheimer, R. J. (1981). *Testing three-way interactions among leader behaviors, task structure and personal characteristics of subordinates as indicated by the path-goal theory of leadership*. Unpublished doctoral dissertation, University of Toronto, Toronto, Ontario, Canada.

*O'Reilly, C. A., III, & Roberts, K. H. (1978). Supervisor influence and subordinate mobility aspirations as moderators of consideration and structure. *Journal of Applied Psychology, 63,* 96–102.

Organ, D. W, (1988). A restatement of the satisfaction–performance hypothesis. *Journal of Management, 14,* 547–557.

Organ, D. W., & Near, J. P. (1985). Cognition vs. affect in measures of job satisfaction. *International Journal of Psychology, 20,* 241–253.

Organ, D. W., & Ryan, K. (1995). A meta-analytic review of attitudinal and dispositional predictors of organizational citizenship behavior. *Personnel Psychology, 48,* 775–802.

*Orpen, C. (1974). The effect of reward contingencies on the job satisfaction–task performance relationship: An industrial experiment. *Psychology, 11,* 9–14.

*Orpen, C. (1978). Relationship between job satisfaction and job performance among Western and tribal Black employees. *Journal of Applied Psychology, 63,* 263–265.

Orpen, C. (1981). The relationship between satisfaction and performance under contingent and noncontingent reward schedules. *Psychological Studies, 26,* 104–109.

*Orpen, C. (1982a). The effects of contingent and noncontingent rewards on employee satisfaction and performance. *Journal of Psychology, 110*, 145–150.

*Orpen, C. (1982b). The effects of social support on reactions to role ambiguity and conflict. *Journal of Cross Cultural Psychology, 13*, 375–384.

*Orpen, C. (1984). Managerial stress, relaxation and performance. *Journal of Management Development, 3*, 24–47.

*Orpen, C. (1985). The effects of need for achievement and need for independence on the relationship between perceived job attributes and managerial satisfaction and performance. *International Journal of Psychology, 20*, 207–219.

*Orpen, C. (1986). The effect of job performance on the relationship between job satisfaction and turnover. *Journal of Social Psychology, 126*, 277–278.

*Orpen, C, & Bernath, J. (1987). The effect of role conflict and role ambiguity on employee satisfaction and performance. *Psychological Studies, 32*, 25–28.

Ostroff, C. (1992). The relationship between satisfaction, attitudes, and performance: An organizational level analysis. *Journal of Applied Psychology, 77*, 963–974.

Ostroff, C. (1993). Comparing correlations based on individual-level and aggregated data. *Journal of Applied Psychology, 78*, 569–582.

Ostroff, C. & Schmitt, N. (1993). Configurations of organizational effectiveness and efficiency. *Academy of Management Journal, 36*, 1345–1361.

*Packard, J. S., & Motowidlo, S. J. (1987). Subjective stress, job satisfaction, and job performance of hospital nurses. *Research in Nursing and Health, 10*, 253–261.

*Papper, E. M. (1983). *Individual and organizational effects of perceived work load*. Unpublished doctoral dissertation, Bowling Green State University, Bowling Green, Ohio.

*Parasuraman, S., & Alutto, J. A. (1984). Sources and outcomes of stress in organizational settings: Toward the development of a structural model. *Academy of Management Journal, 27*, 330–350.

Parsons, C. K., & Hulin, C. L. (1982). An empirical investigation of item response theory and hierarchical factor analysis in applications to the measurement of job satisfaction. *Journal of Applied Psychology, 67*, 826–834.

*Pavia, E. S. (1985). *Differences between new and established industrial workers: An interactional model*. Unpublished doctoral dissertation. Texas Christian University.

*Pearson, J. M. (1981). *Organizational entry in a hospital setting: Tasks, problems, and outcomes*. Unpublished doctoral dissertation. University of Minnesota.

*Penley, L. E., & Hawkins, B. L. (1980). Organizational communication, performance, and job satisfaction as a function of ethnicity and sex. *Journal of Vocational Behavior, 16*, 368–384.

*Peris, H. J. (1984). *Predictors of job satisfaction and performance of principals*. Unpublished doctoral dissertation. University of Rochester, Rochester, New York.

*Peters, L. H., O'Connor, E. J., Eulberg, J. R., & Watson, T. W. (1988). An examination of situational constraints in Air Force work settings. *Human Performance, 1*, 133–144.

Petty, M. M., McGee, G. W., & Cavender, J. W. (1984). A meta-analysis of the relationships between individual job satisfaction and individual performance. *Academy of Management Review, 9*, 712–721.

*Pierce, J. L., Dunham, R. B., & Blackburn, R. S. (1979). Social systems structure, job design, and growth need strength: A test of a congruence model. *Academy of Management journal, 22*, 223–240.

*Pierce, J. L., Gardner, D. G., Cummings, L. L., & Dunham, R. B. (1989). Organization-based self-esteem: Construct definition, measurement, and validation. *Academy of Management Journal, 32*, 622–648.

*Podsakoff, P. M., Niehoff, B. P., Mackenzie, S. B., & Williams, M. L. (1993). Do substitutes for leadership really substitute for leadership? An empirical examination of Kerr and Jermier's situational leadership model. *Organizational Behavior and Human Decision Processes, 54*, 1–44.

*Podsakoff, P. M., Tudor, W. D., & Skov, R. (1982). Effects of leader contingent and noncontingent reward and punishment behaviors on subordinate performance and satisfaction. *Academy of Management Journal, 25*, 810–821.

Podsakoff, P. M., & Williams, L. J. (1986). The relationship between job performance and job satisfaction. In E. A. Locke (Ed.), *Generalizing from laboratory to field settings* (pp. 207–253). Lexington, MA: Lexington Press.

*Prestwich, T. L. (1980). *The causal relationship between job satisfaction and job performance*. Unpublished doctoral dissertation, University of North Carolina. Chapel Hill.

Quiñones, M. A., Ford, J. K., & Teachout, M. S. (1995) The relationship between work experience and job performance: A conceptual and meta-analytic review. *Personnel Psychology, 48*, 887–910.

*Ramser, C. D. (1972). Performance, satisfaction, effort. *Personnel Administration and Public Personnel Review, 1*, 4–8.

*Randall, M., & Scott, W. A. (1988). Burnout, job satisfaction, and job performance. *Australian Psychologist, 23*, 335–347.

*Randall, M. L., Cropanzano, R., Bormann, C. A., & Birjulin, A. (1999). Organizational politics and organizational support as predictors of work altitudes, job performance, and organizational citizenship behavior. *Journal of Organizational Behavior, 20*, 159–174.

*Randklev, B. S. (1984). *The relationships among performance ratings, job satisfaction perceptions, and preferred non-monetary rewards for elementary school teachers*. Unpublished doctoral dissertation. University of North Dakota, Grand Forks.

*Renn, R. W., & Prien, K. O. (1995). Employee responses to performance feedback from the task: A field study of the moderating effects of global self-esteem. *Group and Organization Management, 20*, 337–354.

*Rentsch, J. R., & Steel, R. P. (1992). Construct and concurrent validation of the Andrews and Withey job satisfaction questionnaire. *Educational and Psychological Measurement, 52*, 357–367.

*Rich, G. A. (1997). The sales manager as a role model: Effects on trust, job satisfaction, and performance of salespeople. *Journal of the Academy of Marketing Science, 25*, 319–328.

*Riggio, R. E., & Cole, E. J. (1992). Agreement between subordinate and superior ratings of supervisory performance and effects on self and subordinate job satisfaction. *Journal of Occupational and Organizational Psychology, 65*, 151–158.

*Roberts, H. E., & Foli, R. J. (1998). Evaluating the interaction between self-leadership and work structure in predicting job satisfaction. *Journal of Business and Psychology, 12*, 257–267.

Roethlisberger, F. J. (1941). *Management and morale*. Cambridge, MA: Harvard University Press.

Roethlisberger, F. J., & Dickson, W. J. (1939). *Management and the worker*, Cambridge. MA: Harvard University Press.

Roos, P. A., & Treiman, D. J. (1980). Worker functions and worker trails for the 1970 U.S. census classification. In A. R. Miller, D. J. Treiman, P. S. Cain, & P. A. Roos (Eds.), *Work, jobs, and occupations: A critical review of the Dictionary of Occupational Titles* (pp. 336–389). Washington, DC: National Academy Press.

Rosenthal, R. (1995). Writing meta-analytic reviews. *Psychological Bulletin, 118*, 183–192.

Rosenthal, R. (1998). Meta-analysis: Concepts, corollaries and controversies. In J. G. Adair, & D. Belanger (Eds.), *Advances in psychological science: Vol. 1. Social, personal, and cultural aspects* (pp. 371–384). Hove, England: Psychology Press/Erlbaum.

*Ross, L. E. (1991). *The impact of role stress on the sales performance of professional service providers*. Unpublished doctoral dissertation, Georgia State University. Atlanta.

*Rossano, E. (1985). *Factors associated with the turnover intentions of Ohio Cooperative Extension county agents*. Unpublished doctoral dissertation. Ohio State University, Columbus.

Roth, P. L., BeVier, C. A., Switzer, F. S., III, & Schippmann, J. S. (1996). Meta-analyzing the relationship between grades and job performance. *Journal of Applied Psychology, 81*, 548–556.

Roznowski, M., & Hulin, C. (1992). The scientific merit of valid measures of general constructs with special reference to job satisfaction and job withdrawal. In C. J. Cranny, P. C. Smith, & E. F. Stone (Eds.), *Job satisfaction* (pp. 123–163). New York: Lexington Books.

Sagie, A., & Koslowsky, M. (1993). Detecting moderators with metaanalysis: An evaluation and comparison of techniques. *Personnel Psychology, 46*, 629–640.

*Saks, A. M. (1995). Longitudinal field investigation of the moderating and mediating effects of self-efficacy on the relationship between training and newcomer adjustment. *Journal of Applied Psychology, 80*, 211–215.

*Saks, A. M., & Ashforth, B. E. (1996). Proactive socialization and behavioral self-management. *Journal of Vocational Behavior, 48*, 301–323.

*Sales, C. A. (1977). *Subordinate personality, nature of supervision and task complexity in leadership effectiveness*. Unpublished doctoral dissertation, University of Waterloo, Waterloo, Ontario, Canada.

*Sargent, L. D., & Terry, D. J. (1998). The effects of work control and job demands on employee adjustment and work performance. *Journal of Occupational and Organizational Psychology, 71*, 219–236.

Scarpello, V., & Campbell, J. P. (1983). Job satisfaction: Are all the parts there? *Personnel Psychology, 36*, 577–600.

*Schatz, A. E. (1980). *Personality and satisfaction characteristics as factors in predicting job performance of word processing secretaries and administrative secretaries*. Unpublished doctoral dissertation. Utah State University, Logan.

*Schau, E. J. (1974). *The development of forced-choice instruments to evaluate work performance of firefighters and paramedics, and an examination of correlates of those instruments*. Unpublished doctoral dissertation, University of Washington, Seattle.

*Schaubroeck, J., & Fink, L. S. (1998). Facilitating and inhibiting effects of job control and social support on stress outcomes and role behavior: A contingency model. *Journal of Organizational Behavior, 19*, 167–195.

Schmidt, F. L., & Huntet, J. E. (1996). Measurement error in psychological research: Lessons from 26 research scenarios. *Psychological Methods, 1*, 199–223.

Schmidt, F. L., & Hunter, J. E. (1999). Comparison of three meta-analysis methods revisited: An analysis of Johnson, Mullen, and Salas (1995). *Journal of Applied Psychology, 84,* 144–148.

Schmidt, F. L., Viswesvaran, C., & Ones, D. S. (2000). Reliability is not validity and validity is not reliability. *Personnel Psychology, 53,* 901–924.

*Schriesheim, C. A., Cogliser, C. C., & Neider, L. L. (1995). Is it "trustworthy"? A multiple-levels-of-analysis reexamination of an Ohio State leadership study, with implications for future research. *Leadership Quarterly, 6,* 111–145.

*Schriesheim, C. A., & Murphy, C. J. (1976). Relationships between leader behavior and subordinate satisfaction and performance: A test of some situational moderates. *Journal of Applied Psychology, 61,* 634–641.

*Schriesheim, C. A., Neider, L. L., Scandura, T. A., & Tepper, B. J. (1992). Development and preliminary validation of a new scale (LMX-6) to measure leader-member exchange in organizations. *Educational and Psychological Measurement, 52,* 135–147.

*Schuster, F. A. (1979). *An analysis of the effects that attitude toward work and job satisfaction have on the performance of Black mates employed as CETA custodial workers.* Unpublished doctoral dissertation, Northern Illinois University, De Kalb.

Schwab, D. P., & Cummings, L. L. (1970). Theories of performance and satisfaction: A review. *Industrial Relations, 9,* 408–430.

Schwartz, S. H., & Tessler. R. C. (1972). A test of a model for reducing measured attitude–behavior discrepancies. *Journal of Personality and Social Psychology, 24,* 225–236.

*Schwoerer, C. E., & May, D. R. (1996). Age and work outcomes: The moderating effects of self-efficacy and tool design effectiveness. *Journal of Organizational Behavior, 17,* 469–487.

Scullen, S. E. (1997). When ratings from one source have been averaged, but ratings from another source have not: Problems and solutions. *Journal of Applied Psychology, 82,* 880–888.

*Secrist, G. E. (1975). *Occupational performance and satisfaction.* Unpublished doctoral dissertation, University of Utah, Salt Lake City.

*Seers, A. (1989). Team-member exchange quality: A new construct for role-making research. *Organizational Behavior and Human Decision Processes, 43,* 118–135.

*Seers, A., & Graen, G. B. (1984). The dual attachment concept: A longitudinal investigation of the combination of task characteristics and leader–member exchange. *Organizational Behavior and Human Decision Processes, 33,* 283–306.

*Sheridan, J. E., & Slocum, J. W., Jr. (1975). The direction of the causal relationship between job satisfaction and work performance. *Organizational Behavior and Human Performance, 14,* 159–172.

*Shore, L. M., & Martin, H. J. (1989). Job satisfaction and organizational commitment in relation to work performance and turnover intentions. *Human Relations, 42,* 625–638.

Siegel, J. P., & Bowen, D. (1971). Satisfaction and performance: Causal relationships and moderating effects. *Journal of Vocational Behavior, 1,* 263–269.

*Simmons, P. R. (1986). *Organizational effects of several appraisal approaches.* Unpublished doctoral dissertation, University of South Florida, Tampa.

*Sirota, D. (1958). *Job performance as related to attitudes, motivation and understanding.* Unpublished manuscript. University of Michigan Institute for Social Research. Ann Arbor.

*Skotdal, N. M. (1971). *The relationship between job satisfaction, job dissatisfaction, and job performance of correctional workers.* Unpublished doctoral dissertation. University of Oregon, Eugene.

*Slocum, J. W., Jr. (1971). Motivation in managerial dyads: Relationship of need satisfaction to job performance. *Journal of Applied Psychology, 55,* 312–316.

*Slocum, J. W., Jr., Miller, J. D., & Misshauk, M. J. (1970). Needs, environmental work satisfaction and job performance. *Training and Development Journal, 24,* 12–15.

*Smith, B. L. (1989). *The effect of situational constraints on the job satisfaction/job performance relationship: Is there a choice?* Unpublished doctoral dissertation, University of Washington, Seattle.

Smith, P. C., Kendall, L. M., & Hulin, C. L. (1969). *The measurement of satisfaction in ivork and retirement.* Chicago: Rand McNally.

*Smith-Fraser, D. (1984). *Nurse aides in nursing homes: An exploratory study of factors affecting job satisfaction and performance.* Unpublished doctoral dissertation. Teachers College, Columbia University, New York.

Snyder, M. (1982). When believing means doing: Creating links between attitudes and behavior. In M. P. Zanna, E. T. Higgins, & C. P. Herman (Eds.), *Consistency in social behavior: The Ontario Symposium* (Vol. 2, pp. 105–130). Hillsdale, NJ: Erlbaum.

Spector, P. E. (1997). *Job satisfaction: Application, assessment, causes, and consequences.* Thousand Oaks. CA: Sage.

*Spector, P. E., Dwyer, D. J., & Jex, S. M. (1988). Relation of job stressors to affective, health, and performance outcomes: A comparison of multiple data sources. *Journal of Applied Psychology, 73,* 11–19.

*Spencer, D. G., & Steers, R. M. (1981). Performance as a moderator of the job satisfaction-turnover relationship. *Journal of Applied Psychology, 66,* 511–514.

Starbuck, B., & Mezias, J. (1996). Journal impact ratings. *The Industrial-Organizational Psychologist, 33,* 101–105.

Staw, B. M., & Barsade, S. G. (1993). Affect and managerial performance: A test of the sadder-but-wiser vs. happier-and-smarter hypotheses. *Administrative Science Quarterly, 38,* 304–331.

Staw, B. M., Sutton, R. I., & Pelled, L. H. (1994). Employee positive emotion and favorable outcomes at the workplace. *Organization Science, 5,* 51–71.

*Steel, R. P., & Lloyd, R. F. (1988). Cognitive, affective, and behavioral outcomes of participation in quality circles: Conceptual and empirical findings. *Journal of Applied Behavioral Science, 24,* 1–17.

*Steers, R. M. (1975). Effects of need for achievement on the job performance–job attitude relationship. *Journal of Applied Psychology, 60,* 678–682.

*Stepina, L. P., Perrewé, P. L., Hassell, B. L., Harris, J. L., & Mayfield, C. R. (1991). A comparative test of the independent effects of interpersonal, task, and reward domains on personal and organizational outcomes. *Journal of Social Behavior and Personality, 6,* 93–104.

Strauss, G. (1968). Human relations—1968 style. *Industrial Relations, 7,* 262–276.

*Strauss, P. S. (1966) Psychology of the scientist: XIX. Job satisfaction and productivity of engineers and scientists. *Perceptual and Motor Skills, 23,* 471–476.

Stumpf, S. A., & Hartman, K. (1984). Individual exploration to organizational commitment or withdrawal. *Academy of Management Journal, 27,* 308–329.

*Stumpf, S. A., & Rabinowitz, S. (1981). Career stage as a moderator of performance with facets of job satisfaction and role perceptions. *Journal of Vocational Behavior, 18*, 202–218.

*Summers, T. P., & Hendrix, W. H. (1991). Development of a turnover model that incorporates a matrix measure of valence–instrumentality–expectancy perceptions. *Journal of Business and Psychology, 6*, 227–245.

*Sundstrom, E., Burt, R. E., & Kamp, D. (1980). Privacy at work: Architectural correlates of job satisfaction and job performance. *Academy of Management Journal, 23*, 101–117.

*Sundstrom, E., Town, J. P., Rice, R. W., Osborn, D. P., & Brill, M. (1994). Office noise, satisfaction, and performance. *Environment and Behavior, 26*, 195–222.

*Sward, R. E. (1974). *The relationship of job satisfaction to performance rating and selected personal characteristics of Nebraska Cooperative Extension Service home agents.* Unpublished doctoral dissertation. University of Nebraska.

*Tharenou, P. (1993). A test of reciprocal causality for absenteeism. *Journal of Organizational Behavior, 14*, 269–290.

*Tharenou, P., & Harker, P. (1984). Moderating influence of self-esteem on relationships between job complexity, performance and satisfaction. *Journal of Applied Psychology, 69*, 623–632.

*Thoresen, C. J. (1999). [Job attitudes and performance of pharmaceutical sales representatives]. Unpublished raw data.

*Toner, J. A. (1980). *Instrument development: Attitudes toward working with older people.* Unpublished doctoral dissertation. Teachers College, Columbia University.

Triandis, H. C. (1959). A critique and experimental design for the study of the relationship between productivity and job satisfaction. *Psychological Bulletin, 56*, 309–312.

*Tseng, M. S. (1975). Job performance and satisfaction of successfully rehabilitated vocational rehabilitation clients. *Rehabilitation literature, 36*, 66–72.

*Turban, D. B., & Jones, A. P. (1988). Supervisor–subordinate similarity: Types, effects, and mechanisms. *Journal of Applied Psychology, 73*, 228–234.

*Varca, P. E., & James-Valutis, M. (1993). The relationship of ability and satisfaction to job performance. *Applied Psychology: An International Review, 42*, 265–275.

*Vecchio, R. P., & Gobdel, B. C. (1984). The vertical dyad linkage model of leadership: Problems and prospects. *Organizational Behavior and Human Performance, 34*, 5–20.

Vinchur, A. J., Schippmann, J. S., Switzer, F. S., & Roth, P. L. (1998). A meta-analytic review of predictors of job performance for salespeople. *Journal of Applied Psychology, 83*, 586–597.

Viswesvaran, C, Ones, D. S., & Schmidt, F. L. (1996). Comparative analysis of the reliability of job performance ratings. *Journal of Applied Psychology, 81*, 557–574.

*Vosburgh, R. M. (1979). *The effects of job involvement on the relationship between job characteristics, job satisfaction, and performance.* Unpublished doctoral dissertation. University of South Florida, Tampa.

*Vroom, V. H. (1960). *Some personality determinants of the effects of participation.* Englewood Cliffs, NJ: Prentice Hall.

Vroom, V. H. (1964). *Work and motivation.* New York: Wiley.

*Wanous, J. P. (1974). A causal–correlational analysis of the job satisfaction and performance relationship. *Journal of Applied Psychology, 59,* 139–144.

Wanous, J. P., Reichers, A. E., & Hudy, M. J. (1997). Overall job satisfaction: How good are single-item measures? *Journal of Applied Psychology, 82,* 247–252.

Wanous, J. P., Sullivan, S. E., & Malinak, J. (1989). The role of judgment calls in meta-analysis. *Journal of Applied Psychology, 74,* 259–264.

Weigel, R. H., & Newman, L. S. (1976). Increasing attitude–behavior correspondence by broadening the scope of the behavioral measure. *Journal of Personality and Social Psychology, 33,* 793–802.

*Weintraub, Z. (1981). Job satisfaction factors in the industry of electronic components and their relationships with work performance. *Revue Romaine des Sciences Sociales—Série de Psychologie, 25,* 13–20.

Weiss, H. M., & Cropanzano, R. (1996). Affective events theory. *Research in Organizational Behavior, 18,* 1–74.

Weiss, H. M., Nicholas, J. P., & Daus, C. S. (1999). An examination of the joint effects of affective experiences and job beliefs on job satisfaction and variations in affective experiences over time. *Organizational Behavior and Human Decision Processes, 78,* 1–24.

*Weslander, D. L. (1981). *Vocational interest patterns of social studies teachers and rated performance.* Unpublished doctoral dissertation, University of Delaware, Newark.

*Wexley, K. N., Alexander, R. A., Greenwalt, J. P., & Couch, M. A. (1980). Attitudinal congruence and similarity as related to interpersonal evaluations in manager–subordinate dyads. *Academy of Management Journal, 23,* 320–330.

Wicker, A. W. (1969). Attitude versus actions: The relationship of verbal and overt behavioral responses to attitude objects. *Journal of Social Issues, 25,* 41–78.

*Wiggins, J. D., & Moody, A. (1983). Identifying effective counselors through client–supervisor ratings and personality–environmental variables. *Vocational Guidance Quarterly, 31,* 259–269.

*Wiggins, J. D., & Weslander, D. L. (1979). Personality characteristics of counselors rated as effective or ineffective. *Journal of Vocational Behavior, 15,* 175–185.

*Wiggins, J. D., & Weslander, D. L. (1986). Effectiveness related to personality and demographic characteristics of secondary school counselors. *Counselor Education and Supervision, 26,* 26–35.

*Wilcox, K. E. (1979). *Motivation, central life interests, voluntarism, and demographic variables as predictors of job satisfaction and perceived performance of teachers.* Unpublished doctoral dissertation, University of Kansas, Lawrence.

Wiley, J. W. (1996). Linking survey results to customer satisfaction and business performance. In A. I. Kraut (Ed.), *Organizational surveys* (pp. 330–359). San Francisco: Jossey-Bass.

*Wilson, A. A. (1990). *Participating in a participative management system: The role of active participation, organizational knowledge, and individual motivation in employee satisfaction and performance.* Unpublished doctoral dissertation, Purdue University, West Lafayette, Indiana.

Wright, T. A., & Bonett, D. G. (1997). The role of pleasantness and activation-based well-being in performance prediction. *Journal of Occupational Health Psychology, 2,* 212–219.

Wright, T. A., Bonett, D. G., & Sweeney, D. A. (1993). Mental health and work performance: Results of a longitudinal field study. *Journal of Occupational and Organizational Psychology, 66,* 277–284.

*Wright, T. A., & Cropanzano, R. (1998). Emotional exhaustion as a predictor of job performance and voluntary turnover. *Journal of Applied Psychology, 83,* 486–493.

Wright, T. A., & Staw, B. M. (1999). Affect and favorable work outcomes: Two longitudinal tests of the happy–productive worker thesis. *Journal of Organizational Behavior, 20,* 1–23.

## Appendix

### Summary of studies included in meta-analyses

| Study | N | r | $r_{jp}$ | $r_{js}$ | ρ | Source | Measure JP | Measure JS | Design | Complexity | Occupation |
|---|---|---|---|---|---|---|---|---|---|---|---|
| Abdel-Halim (1980) | 123 | .22 | .52[a] | .75[b] | .35 | TT | SR | FC | CS | M | S |
| Abramis (1985) | 112 | .13 | .42[c] | .74[d] | .23 | U-D | P-S-O | U | CS | | M-M |
| Abramis (1994) | 281 | .10 | .52[e] | .74[d] | .16 | OR | P-S-O | U | L | | M-M |
| Adkins (1995) | 171 | .00 | .52[a] | .55 | .00 | TT | SR | FC | CS | | M-M |
| Adkins et al. (1996) | 89 | .10 | .52[a] | .56[b,f] | .19 | UR | SR | FC | L | L | L |
| Alexander et al. (1989) | 130 | .23 | .47[g] | .75 | .39 | OR | OR | FC | CS | H | M-M |
| Allen (1992) | 81 | .33 | .52[c] | .52[b] | .63 | U-D | OR | FC | CS | M | M-M |
| Anand & Sohal (1981) | 22 | .28 | .52[e] | .74[d] | .45 | UR | SR | U | CS | M | S-E |
| Anand & Sohal (1981) | 24 | .25 | .52[e] | .74[d] | .40 | UR | SR | U | CS | M | S-E |
| Anand & Sohal (1981) | 116 | .26 | .52[e] | .74[d] | .42 | UR | OR | U | CS | M | S-E |
| Anderson & O'Reilly (1981) | 66 | .11 | .52[e] | .56 | .20 | OR | OR | FC | CS | M | M-M |
| Apasu-Gbotsu (1982) | 135 | .26 | .52[a] | .63[b] | .45 | U-D | SR | U | CS | M | C |
| Araghi (1981) | 156 | .00 | .73[g] | .88 | .00 | U-D | OR | U | CS | H | M-M |
| Ayman (1983) | 81 | .28 | .52[a] | .74[b] | .45 | U-D | SR | FC | CS | M | M-S |
| Bagozzi (1978) | 38 | .45 | .52[c] | .78 | .71 | OR | OR | U | CS | M | S |
| Bagozzi (1978) | 123 | .30 | .52[c] | .77 | .47 | OR | OR | U | CS | M | S |
| Baird (1976) | 51 | .22 | .52[a] | .75[b] | .35 | TT | SR | FC | CS | M | M-M |
| Baird (1976) | 116 | .24 | .52[a] | .75[b] | .38 | TT | SR | FC | CS | M | M-M |
| Baklien (1980) | 336 | .14 | .52[a] | .74[d] | .23 | U-D | SR | U | CS | | M-M |
| Bateman (1980) | 74 | .41 | .52[a] | .74[d] | .66 | U-D | SR | FC | CS | | M-M |
| Bauer & Green (1998) | 205 | .53 | .52[a] | .92 | .77 | TT | SR | FC | CS | | M-M |
| Bedeian et al. (1983) | 193 | .05 | .52[a] | .68 | .08 | OR | SR | U | CS | M | N |
| Berger-Gross & Kraut (1984) | 887 | .22 | .52[a] | .75 | .35 | TT | SR | U | CS | M | M-S |

*(Continued)*

Appendix cont'd

| Study | N | r | $r_{jp}$ | $r_{js}$ | ρ | Source | Measure JP | Measure JS | Design | Complexity | Occupation |
|---|---|---|---|---|---|---|---|---|---|---|---|
| Bernardin (1979) | 53 | .29 | .62[b] | .58[b] | .48 | TT | SR, P-S-O | FC | CS | M | M-M |
| Bhagat (1982) | 104 | .35 | .52[a] | .94 | .50 | TT | SR | FC | CS | M | M-S |
| Bhagat & Allie (1989) | 137 | −.06 | .52[a] | .67[b] | −.10 | OR | SR | FC | CS | M | M-M |
| Bimbaum & Somers (1993) | 142 | −.03 | .52[a] | .85 | −.05 | OR | SR | G | CS | M | N |
| Bittle (1991) | 138 | .19 | .52[a] | .79[b] | .30 | U-D | SR | FC | CS | | M-M |
| Bizot & Goldman (1993) | 65 | .13 | .52[a] | .58[b] | .24 | OR | SR | FC | CS | | M-M |
| Blanchard (1991) | 349 | .20 | .52[a] | .93 | .29 | U-D | SR | FC | CS | | M-M |
| Bluen et al. (1990) | 110 | .20 | .52[e] | .88 | .30 | TT | OR | U | CS | | S |
| Boyles (1968) | 168 | .04 | .39[f] | .74[d] | .07 | U-D | SR, OR | U | CS | M | M-M |
| Brass (1981) | 140 | .40 | .52[a] | .72[b] | .65 | TT | SR | FC | CS | M | M-M |
| Brayfield & Marsh (1957) | 50 | .12 | .52[a] | .60 | .21 | TT | SR | G | CS | M | M-M |
| Breaugh (1981) | 112 | .16 | .52[a] | .72[b] | .26 | TT | SR | FC | CS | M | S-E |
| Brief & Aldag (1976) | 77 | .01 | .52[a] | .37[b] | .02 | TT | SR | FC | CS | L | M-M |
| Brody (1945) | 40 | .68 | .52[e] | .74[d] | 1.10[j] | U-D | OR | U | CS | L | L |
| N. J. Brown (1989) | 272 | .17 | .52[a] | .70[b] | .28 | U-D | SR | FC | CS | M | N |
| S. P. Brown et al. (1993) | 466 | .13 | .52[a] | .91[b] | .19 | UR | SR | FC | CS | M | S |
| S. P. Brown & Peterson (1994) | 380 | .31 | .52[a] | .68 | .52 | TT | SR | U | CS | M | S |
| Burns (1977) | 30 | .09 | .52[a] | .74[d] | .15 | U-D | SR | FC | CS | L | L |
| Burns (1977) | 181 | −.07 | .52[a] | .74[d] | −.11 | U-D | SR | FC | CS | L | L |
| Carlson (1969) | 252 | .13 | .52[a] | .74[d] | .21 | TT | SR | G | CS | | M-M |
| Carlson (1969) | 254 | .17 | .52[a] | .74[d] | .27 | TT | SR | G | CS | L | L |
| Clayton (1981) | 222 | .14 | .52[a] | .79[b] | .22 | U-D | SR | FC | CS | | M-M |
| Cleveland & Shore (1992) | 410 | −.12 | .52[a] | .68 | .20 | TT | SR | U | CS | | M-M |
| Colarelli et al. (1987) | 280 | .18 | .52[a] | .75 | .29 | TT | SR | FC | CS | M | A |
| Crisera (1965) | 57 | −.03 | .52[a] | .75[b] | −.05 | U-D | SR | FC | CS | | M-S |
| Crisera (1965) | 160 | .06 | .52[a] | .75[b] | .10 | U-D | SR | FC | CS | L | L |
| Cropanzano et al. (1993) | 198 | .18 | .52[a] | .85 | .27 | OR | SR | FC | CS | | M-M |

| | | | | | | | | |
|---|---|---|---|---|---|---|---|---|
| Dawis & Ace (1973) | 90 | −.12 | .52[a] | .74[d] | −.19 | OR | U | CS | | M-M |
| Dawis & Ace (1973) | 183 | .01 | .52[a] | .74[d] | .02 | OR | U | CS | | M-M |
| Day & Bedeian (1995) | 171 | .08 | .52[a] | .75 | .13 | OR | U | CS | | N |
| De Frain (1979) | 131 | .34 | .52[a] | .74[d] | .55 | U-D | U | CS | M | M-M |
| Deis (1982) | 470 | .16 | .52[a] | .60[b] | .29 | U-D | FC | CS | H | M-M |
| Denton (1976) | 73 | −.01 | .52[a] | .74[d] | −.02 | U-D | FC | CS | | M-M |
| Dipboye et al. (1979) | 73 | .30 | .52[a] | .74[d] | .48 | OR | FC | CS | M | M-M |
| Dipboye et al. (1979) | 264 | .32 | .52[a] | .74[d] | .52 | OR | FC | CS | M | C |
| L. D. Doll (1973) | 16 | .36 | .52[a] | .74[d] | .58 | U-D | G | CS | M | M-S |
| L. D. Doll (1973) | 70 | .39 | .52[a] | .74[d] | .63 | U-D | G | CS | L | L |
| R. E. Doll & Gunderson (1969) | 66 | .44 | .62[h] | .74[d] | .65 | TT | U | CS | H | S-E |
| R. E. Doll & Gunderson (1969) | 129 | .04 | .62[h] | .74[d] | .06 | TT | U | CS | | M-M |
| Dorfman et al. (1986) | 121 | .41 | .52[a] | .83 | .62 | TT | U | CS | | M-M |
| Dougherty (1981) | 85 | .48 | .52[a] | .95 | .68 | U-D | FC | CS | | M-M |
| Dreher (1981) | 692 | .19 | .52[a] | .72 | .31 | TT | U | CS | H | M-M |
| Dubinski & Hartley (1986) | 120 | .17 | .52[e] | .73 | .28 | UR | FC | CS | M | S |
| Dubinski & Skinner (1984) | 116 | .00 | .52[e] | .74[d] | .00 | OR | FC | CS | M | S |
| Efraty & Sirgy (1990) | 219 | .09 | .52[a] | .78 | .14 | UR | FC | CS | | M-M |
| Efraty & Wolfe (1988) | 215 | −.09 | .52[a] | .78[h] | −.14 | UR | FC | CS | | M-M |
| Ellingson et al. (1998) | 163 | .30 | .52[a] | .91 | .44 | TT | U | CS | | M-M |
| El-Safy (1985) | 100 | .17 | .52[a] | .74[d] | .27 | U-D | FC | CS | M | M-S |
| Ettington (1998) | 373 | .16 | .52[a] | .82 | .25 | OR | U | CS | M | M-M |
| Fiedler (1993) | 213 | .07 | .52[a] | .69 | .12 | U-D | FC | CS | L | M-M |
| Fox et al. (1993) | 136 | .06 | .52[a] | .66 | .10 | TT | G | CS | M | N |
| Frey (1977) | 113 | .19 | .52[a] | .74[d] | .31 | U-D | FC | CS | | M-M |
| Funk (1968) | 486 | .19 | .52[a] | .74[d] | .31 | U-D | U | CS | M | M-M |
| Futrell & Parasuraman (1984) | 263 | .13 | .52[a] | .77[b] | .21 | TT | FC | CS | M | S |
| Gadel & Kriedt (1952) | 193 | .08 | .52[a] | .74[d] | .13 | TT | U | CS | L | M-M |

*(Continued)*

Appendix cont'd

| Study | N | r | $r_{jp}$ | $r_{js}$ | ρ | Source | Measure JP | Measure JS | Design | Complexity | Occupation |
|---|---|---|---|---|---|---|---|---|---|---|---|
| Gardner et al. (1987) | 430 | .14 | .52[a] | .85 | .21 | OR | SR | FC | CS | | M-M |
| Gardner et al. (1987) | 476 | .15 | .52[a] | .91 | .22 | OR | SR | FC | CS | M | M-M |
| Gardner et al. (1987) | 492 | .07 | .52[a] | .83 | .11 | OR | SR | FC | CS | | C |
| Gardner & Pierce (1998) | 145 | .21 | .52[a] | .88 | .31 | UR | SR | FC | CS | M | M-M |
| Gavin & Ewen (1974) | 81 | .28 | .52[a] | .75 | .45 | TT | SR | FC | CS | | M-M |
| Gavin & Ewen (1974) | 390 | .30 | .52[a] | .75 | .48 | TT | SR | FC | CS | | M-M |
| Gellatly et al. (1991) | 59 | .06 | .52[a] | .89 | .09 | UR | SR | FC | CS | | M-S |
| Giovannini (1974) | 145 | .34 | .52[a] | .85[h] | .51 | U-D | SR | FC | CS | M | M-M |
| Giovannini (1974) | 152 | .27 | .52[a] | .86[b] | .40 | U-D | SR | FC | CS | H | S-E |
| Goldsmith et al. (1989) | 34 | .43 | .52[a] | .70[b] | .71 | OR | SR | FC | CS | M | S |
| Grady (1984) | 49 | .25 | .52[a] | .74[d] | .40 | U-D | SR | FC | CS | M | T |
| Graham (1983) | 136 | −.17 | .42[a] | .74[d] | −.30 | U-D | P-S-O | U | CS | H | M-M |
| Greenberger et al. (1989) | 196 | .40 | .52[a] | .85 | .60 | TT | SR | FC | CS | | M-M |
| Greenberger et al. (1989) | 272 | .16 | .52[a] | .90 | .23 | TT | SR | FC | CS | M | C |
| Greene (1972) | 62 | .27 | .59[k] | .74[d] | .41 | TT | P-S-O | U | L | M | M-S |
| Greene (1973) | 142 | .58 | .52[a] | .74[d] | .93 | TT | SR | FC | CS | M | M-S |
| Gregson (1987) | 311 | .24 | .52[a] | .78 | .38 | U-D | SR | U | CS | M | A |
| Griffin (1980) | 107 | −.18 | .52[a] | .72[h] | −.29 | TT | OR | U | CS | L | L |
| Griffin (1991) | 526 | .06 | .52[a] | .85[h] | .09 | TT | SR | FC | L | M | M-M |
| Griffiths (1975) | 22 | .11 | .52[a] | .86 | .16 | OR | SR | G | CS | | M-M |
| Gross (1978) | 65 | .24 | .39[a] | .74[d] | .45 | U-D | SR, OR, P-S-O | FC | CS | | M-M |
| Gustafson & Mumford (1995) | 367 | .16 | .52[a] | .90 | .23 | OR | SR | FC | CS | M | M-M |
| Hackman & Lawler (1971) | 272 | .16 | .52[a] | .76 | .25 | TT | SR | U | CS | | M-M |
| Hamid Ud-Din (1953) | 552 | .28 | .39[a] | .45[b] | .67 | U-D | SR, OR | FC | CS | | C |
| Harding & Bottenberg (1961) | 376 | .26 | .52[a] | .74[d] | .42 | TT | SR | U | CS | M | M-M |
| Haywood (1980) | 292 | .35 | .52[a] | .63[b] | .61 | U-D | SR | FC | CS | M | T |
| Heneman et al. (1988) | 104 | .26 | .52[a] | .91 | .38 | TT | SR | FC | CS | | M-M |
| Heron (1954) | 144 | .35 | .52[a] | .74[a] | .56 | OR | SR | U | CS | L | M-M |

| Study | N | r1 | r2 | r3 | Design1 | Design2 | Design3 | Design4 | Design5 | Type |
|---|---|---|---|---|---|---|---|---|---|---|
| Hesketh et al. (1992) | 159 | .31 | .52[a] | .82 | .47 | OR | SR | U | CS | | M-M |
| Hester (1981) | 22 | .37 | .52[a] | .74[d] | .60 | U-D | SR | FC | CS | M | C |
| Hester (1981) | 61 | .28 | .52[a] | .74[d] | .45 | U-D | SR | FC | CS | M | C |
| Holley et al. (1978) | 119 | −.12 | .52[a] | .74[d] | −.19 | UR | SR | FC | CS | M | M-M |
| Holley et al. (1978) | 121 | .08 | .52[a] | .74[d] | .13 | UR | SR | FC | CS | M | M-M |
| Im (1991) | 117 | .68 | .52[a] | .74[d] | 10.10[j] | U-D | SR | FC | CS | M | M-S |
| Inkson (1978) | 93 | .38 | .52[a] | .75[b] | .61 | TT | SR | FC | CS | L | L |
| Ivancevich (1974) | 104 | .20 | .52[a] | .74[d] | .32 | TT | SR | U | L | | L |
| Ivancevich (1974) | 106 | .08 | .52[a] | .74[d] | .13 | TT | SR | U | L | | L |
| Ivancevich (1978) | 62 | .33 | .39[i] | .70[b] | .63 | TT | SR, OR | FC | L | M | M-M |
| Ivancevich (1978) | 108 | .39 | .39[i] | .70[b] | .75 | TT | SR, OR | FC | L | M | M-M |
| Ivancevich (1979) | 42 | .32 | .39[i] | .77[b] | .58 | TT | SR, OR | FC | L | H | S-E |
| Ivancevich (1979) | 48 | .32 | .39[i] | .77[b] | .58 | TT | SR, OR | FC | L | H | S-E |
| Ivancevich (1980) | 249 | .24 | .23[g] | .39[b] | .80 | TT | OR | FC | CS | H | S-E |
| Ivancevich & Donnelly (1975) | 77 | .21 | .52[e] | .74[d] | .34 | TT | OR | U | CS | M | S |
| Ivancevich & Donnelly (1975) | 100 | .16 | .52[e] | .74[d] | .26 | TT | OR | U | CS | M | S |
| Ivancevich & Donnelly (1975) | 118 | .10 | .52[e] | .74[d] | .16 | TT | OR | U | CS | M | S |
| Ivancevich & McMahon (1982) | 209 | .38 | .39[i] | .18[b] | 1.43[j] | TT | SR, P-S-O | FC | CS | H | S-E |
| Ivancevich & Smith (1981) | 150 | .15 | .17[g] | .29[h] | .68 | TT | SR, OR | FC | CS | H | S-E |
| Jabri (1992) | 98 | .28 | .52[a] | .67[h] | .47 | OR | SR | FC | CS | M | S-E |
| Jacobs & Solomon (1977) | 251 | .16 | .52[a] | .72[b] | .26 | TT | SR | FC | CS | | M-M |
| Jenkins (1990) | 120 | .14 | .52[a] | .75[b] | .22 | U-D | SR | FC | CS | | M-M |
| Jenkins (1990) | 233 | .25 | .52[a] | .75[b] | .40 | U-D | SR | FC | CS | | M-M |
| Johnston et al. (1988) | 102 | .18 | .52[a] | .70[b] | .30 | OR | SR | FC | CS | M | S |
| Joyce et al. (1982) | 193 | .08 | .52[a] | .87 | .12 | OR | SR | FC | CS | M | M-S |
| Judge & Bono (2000) | 246 | .31 | .52[a] | .82 | .47 | U-D | SR | G | CS | | M-M |
| Judge & Thoresen (1996) | 500 | .36 | .52[a] | .88 | .53 | U-D | SR | FC | CS | | M-M |

*(Continued)*

Appendix cont'd

| Study | N | r | $r_{jp}$ | $r_{js}$ | ρ | Source | Measure JP | Measure JS | Design | Complexity | Occupation |
|---|---|---|---|---|---|---|---|---|---|---|---|
| Judge et al. (1999) | 31 | −.13 | .42[c] | .60[b] | −.26 | U-D | P-S-O | G | CS | M | M-S |
| Judge et al. (1999) | 91 | .18 | .42[c] | .89[b] | .29 | U-D | P-S-O | G | CS | M | M-S |
| Judge et al. (1999) | 392 | .13 | .52[a] | .75[b] | .21 | U-D | SR | G | CS | M | M-S |
| Kaldenberg & Becker (1991) | 147 | .16 | .52[e] | .82 | .25 | OR | OR | U | CS | H | M-M |
| Kaldenberg & Becker (1991) | 166 | .16 | .52[e] | .82 | .25 | OR | OR | U | CS | H | M-M |
| Kantak (1998) | 516 | .19 | .52[e] | .93 | .27 | U-D | OR | FC | CS | M | S |
| Keller (1984) | 532 | .07 | .39[l] | .88 | .12 | TT | SR, OR | FC | CS |  | S-E |
| Keller (1997) | 190 | .08 | .52[a] | .87 | .12 | TT | SR | FC | CS |  | M-M |
| Kesselman et al. (1974) | 76 | .54 | .52[a] | .75[b] | .86 | TT | SR | FC | CS |  | M-M |
| Khaleque et al. (1992) | 100 | .59 | .52[a] | .74[d] | .95 | UR | SR | G | CS | L | L |
| Kinicki et al. (1990) | 312 | .12 | .52[a] | .94 | .17 | TT | SR | U | CS | M | N |
| Kirchner (1965) | 72 | .67 | .92[g] | .83[b] | .77 | TT | OR | U | CS | M | S |
| Kittrell (1980) | 212 | .14 | .52[a] | .74[d] | .23 | U-D | SR | G | CS | M | M-M |
| Konovsky & Cropanzano (1991) | 195 | .18 | .52[a] | .85 | .27 | TT | SR | FC | CS | M | M-M |
| Kuhn et al. (1971) | 184 | .11 | .52[c] | .74[d] | .18 | OR | OR | U | CS | L | L |
| La Follette (1973) | 768 | .27 | .52[a] | .75[h] | .43 | U-D | SR | FC | CS |  | M-M |
| Lawler & Porter (1967) | 148 | .31 | .62[h] | .74[d] | .46 | OR | SR, P-S-O | U | CS | M | M-M |
| Leana (1986) | 198 | −.02 | .39[i] | .68[b] | −.04 | TT | SR, OR | FC | CS | M | M-M |
| C. Lee et al. (1990) | 91 | −.15 | .52[a] | .81 | −.23 | TT | SR | U | CS |  | M-M |
| T. W. Lee & Mowday (1987) | 445 | −.11 | .52[a] | .74[d] | −.18 | TT | SR | FC | CS |  | M-M |
| Leveto (1974) | 43 | .00 | .52[a] | .74[d] | .00 | U-D | SR | U | CS |  | A |
| Levy & Williams (1998) | 46 | −.06 | .52[a] | .72 | −.10 | OR | SR | FC | CS | M | M-M |
| Lichtman (1970) | 95 | .21 | .52[a] | .74[d] | .34 | TT | SR | U | CS |  | M-M |
| Livingstone et al. (1997) | 143 | .31 | .52[a] | .78 | .49 | OR | SR | U | CS |  | M-M |
| Livingstone et al. (1997) | 143 | .31 | .52[a] | .78 | .49 | OR | SR | FC | CS |  | M-M |
| London & Klimoski (1975) | 34 | −.07 | .62[h] | .60[b] | −.11 | OR | SR, P-S-O | FC | CS | M | N |
| London & Klimoski (1975) | 40 | .51 | .62[h] | .60[b] | .84 | OR | SR, P-S-O | FC | CS | M | N |

| | | | | | | | | | |
|---|---|---|---|---|---|---|---|---|---|
| London & Klimoski (1975) | 79 | −.05 | .62[h] | .60[b] | −.08 | OR | SR, P-S-O | FC | CS | | N |
| E. M. Lopez (1982) | 579 | .60 | .52[a] | .75[b] | .96 | TT | SR | FC | CS | M | M-M |
| F. M. Lopez (1962) | 124 | .11 | .52[a] | .86[b] | .16 | U-D | SR | U | CS | | M-M |
| Lucas (1985) | 213 | .13 | .52[a] | .37[b] | .30 | UR | SR | FC | CS | M | M-S |
| Lucas et al. (1990) | 213 | .16 | .52[a] | .56[b,f] | .30 | UR | SR | U | L | M | M-S |
| Lusch & Serpkenci (1990) | 182 | .06 | .52[a] | .81[b] | .09 | TT | SR | FC | CS | M | M-S |
| Macan (1994) | 353 | .13 | .52[a] | .57 | .24 | TT | SR | FC | CS | | M-M |
| MacKenzie et al. (1998) | 672 | .19 | .52[c] | .87 | .28 | TT | OR | FC | CS | M | S |
| Magee (1976) | 190 | .30 | .52[a] | .74[d] | .48 | U-D | SR | FC | CS | | M-M |
| Marr (1965) | 82 | .21 | .52[e] | .66[h] | .35 | U-D | SR | U | CS | M | T |
| Marshall & Stohl (1993) | 143 | .10 | .52[a] | .72[b] | .16 | UR | SR | FC | CS | L | L |
| Mathieu & Farr (1991) | 311 | .08 | .52[a] | .91[b] | .12 | TT | SR | FC | CS | H | S-E |
| Matteson et al. (1984) | 355 | .18 | .90[g] | .85 | .21 | OR | OR | FC | CS | M | S |
| McNeilly & Goldsmith (1991) | 138 | .13 | .52[a] | .75[b] | .21 | OR | SR | FC | CS | M | S |
| McPherson (1974) | 1,272 | .18 | .52[a] | .75[b] | .29 | U-D | SR | FC | CS | M | T |
| Mekky (1973) | 213 | −.05 | .52[a] | .74[d] | −.08 | U-D | SR | FC | CS | | M-M |
| Meyer et al. (1989) | 61 | −.07 | .52[a] | .89 | −.10 | TT | SR | FC | CS | M | M-S |
| Miller (1984) | 183 | .13 | .52[a] | .74[d] | .21 | U-D | SR | FC | CS | | M-M |
| Misshauk (1968) | 24 | .77 | .52[a] | .73[b] | 1.25[j] | U-D | SR | FC | CS | L | L |
| Misshauk (1968) | 24 | .63 | .52[a] | .97[b] | .89 | U-D | SR | FC | CS | M | M-M |
| Misshauk (1968) | 24 | .49 | .52[a] | .77[b] | .77 | U-D | SR | FC | CS | H | S-E |
| Misshauk (1970) | 37 | −.02 | .52[a] | .69[h] | −.03 | U-D | SR | FC | CS | | S-E |
| Mossholder et al. (1981) | 161 | .11 | .52[a] | .73 | .18 | TT | SR | U | CS | M | N |
| Mossholder et al. (1984) | 102 | .02 | .52[a] | .70[h] | .03 | OR | SR | FC | CS | | M-M |
| Mossholder et al. (1988) | 220 | .05 | .52[a] | .83[h] | .08 | OR | SR | FC | CS | | L |
| Mossholder et al. (1988) | 365 | .05 | .52[a] | .88 | .07 | OR | SR | FC | CS | | M-M |
| Mossin (1949) | 94 | −.03 | .52[a] | .74[d] | −.05 | U-D | SR | U | CS | M | S |

*(Continued)*

Appendix cont'd

| Study | N | r | $r_{jp}$ | $r_{js}$ | ρ | Source | Measure JP | Measure JS | Design | Complexity | Occupation |
|---|---|---|---|---|---|---|---|---|---|---|---|
| Munoz (1973) | 120 | −.02 | .52[a] | .74[d] | −.03 | U-D | SR | FC | CS | M | M-M |
| Nathan et al. (1991) | 360 | .12 | .52[e] | .74[b] | .19 | TT | OR | FC | L | | M-M |
| Nathanson & Becker (1973) | 21 | .44 | .42[e] | .72 | .80 | TT | P-S-O | U | CS | H | M-M |
| Nathanson & Becker (1973) | 36 | .23 | .42[e] | .72 | .42 | TT | SR | U | CS | H | M-M |
| Nhundu (1992) | 80 | .23 | .52[e] | .74[d] | .37 | UR | P-S-O | FC | CS | M | T |
| Nice et al. (1988) | 356 | .20 | .52[a] | .78[b] | .31 | UR | SR | FC | CS | H | M-M |
| Norris & Niebuhr (1984) | 116 | .09 | .52[a] | .70[b] | .15 | OR | SR | FC | CS | M | M-M |
| O'Connor et al. (1984) | 1,450 | .22 | .52[a] | .29[h] | .57 | TT | SR | FC | CS | | M-M |
| Oldham et al. (1995) | 298 | .14 | .52[a] | .88 | .21 | TT | SR | FC | CS | | M-M |
| Oldham et al. (1976) | 256 | .08 | .77[l] | .79 | .10 | TT | SR | FC | L | M | C |
| Oldham et al. (1986) | 201 | −.09 | .52[c] | .74[b] | −.15 | TT | OR | FC | CS | M | C |
| Oldham et al. (1991) | 207 | .12 | .52[a] | .69[b] | .20 | TT | SR | FC | CS | | M-M |
| Oppenheimer (1981) | 231 | .20 | .52[a] | .62[b] | .35 | U-D | SR | G | CS | | M-M |
| O'Reilly & Roberts (1978) | 301 | .16 | .52[a] | .63[b] | .28 | TT | SR | FC | CS | | M-M |
| Orpen (1974) | 75 | .69 | .52[a] | .74[d] | 1.11[j] | OR | SR | G | CS | L | L |
| Orpen (1974) | 75 | .30 | .52[a] | .74[d] | .48 | OR | SR | G | CS | L | L |
| Orpen (1974) | 75 | .02 | .52[a] | .74[d] | .03 | OR | SR | G | CS | L | L |
| Orpen (1978) | 47 | .45 | .52[a] | .68 | .76 | TT | SR | G | CS | M | M-S |
| Orpen (1978) | 54 | .02 | .52[a] | .71 | .03 | TT | SR | G | CS | M | M-M |
| Orpen (1982a) | 21 | .70 | .52[e] | .74[d] | 1.13[i] | OR | OR | G | CS | L | L |
| Orpen (1982a) | 21 | .39 | .52[e] | .74[d] | .63 | OR | OR | G | CS | L | L |
| Orpen (1982a) | 21 | .01 | .52[e] | .74[d] | .02 | OR | OR | G | CS | L | L |
| Orpen (1982b) | 90 | .24 | .52[a] | .74[d] | .39 | OR | SR | G | CS | M | C |
| Orpen (1982b) | 93 | .25 | .52[a] | .74[d] | .40 | OR | SR | G | CS | M | C |
| Orpen (1984) | 18 | .16 | .52[a] | .74[d] | .26 | UR | SR | U | CS | M | M-S |
| Orpen (1984) | 18 | .12 | .52[a] | .74[d] | .19 | UR | SR | U | CS | M | M-S |
| Orpen (1985) | 346 | .23 | .52[a] | .74[d] | .37 | UR | SR | FC | CS | M | M-S |

| | | | | | | | | | |
|---|---|---|---|---|---|---|---|---|---|
| Orpen (1986) | 98 | .13 | .52[a] | .74[d] | .21 | OR | SR | U | CS | | M-M |
| Orpen & Bernath (1987) | 80 | .03 | .52[a] | .74 | .05 | UR | SR | U | CS | M | M-S |
| Packard & Motowidlo (1987) | 206 | .24 | .52[c] | .86 | .35 | TT | P-S-O | U | CS | M | N |
| Papper (1983) | 217 | .13 | .52[a] | .91 | .19 | UR | SR | FC | CS | | M-M |
| Parasuraman & Alutto (1984) | 102 | .24 | .52[a] | .74 | .39 | U-D | SR | FC | CS | M | M-S |
| Pavia (1985) | 72 | .20 | .52[a] | .86 | .30 | U-D | SR | U | CS | | M-M |
| Pavia (1985) | 148 | −.01 | .52[a] | .85 | −.02 | U-D | SR | U | CS | | M-M |
| Pearson (1981) | 64 | .23 | .52[a] | .74[d] | .37 | U-D | SR | G | CS | | M-M |
| Penley & Hawkins (1980) | 264 | .00 | .52[a] | .96[b] | .01 | OR | SR | FC | CS | | M-M |
| Peris (1984) | 92 | .12 | .52[a] | .68 | .20 | U-D | SR | U | CS | M | M-M |
| Peters et al. (1988) | 720 | .12 | .52[a] | .78[b] | .19 | UR | SR | FC | CS | | M-M |
| Pierce et at. (1979) | 398 | .14 | .52[a] | .74[d] | .23 | TT | SR | FC | CS | | M-M |
| Pierce et al. (1989) | 96 | .06 | .52[a] | .83 | .09 | TT | SR | FC | CS | | M-M |
| Pierce et al. (1989) | 116 | .07 | .52[c] | .83 | .11 | TT | OR | FC | CS | M | C |
| Podsakoff et al. (1993) | 612 | .28 | .52[a] | .90[b] | .41 | TT | SR | FC | CS | | M-M |
| Podsakoff et al. (1982) | 72 | .18 | .52[a] | .68 | .30 | TT | SR | FC | CS | | M-M |
| Prestwich (1980) | 33 | −.02 | .52[a] | .71[b] | −.03 | U-D | SR | FC | L | M | M-M |
| Prestwich (1980) | 36 | .61 | .52[a] | .86[b] | .91 | U-D | SR | FC | L | M | M-M |
| Ramser (1972) | 54 | .41 | .52[a] | .74[d] | .66 | OR | SR | U | CS | M | M-S |
| Ramser (1972) | 104 | .04 | .52[a] | .74[d] | .06 | OR | SR | U | CS | | M-M |
| Randall et al (1999) | 128 | .21 | .52[a] | .74[d] | .34 | OR | SR | FC | CS | | M-M |
| Randall & Scott (1988) | 99 | .14 | .52[a] | .72 | .23 | UR | SR | U | CS | L | C |
| Randall & Scott (1988) | 163 | .25 | .52[a] | .72 | .41 | UR | SR | U | CS | M | N |
| Randklev (1984) | 85 | −.04 | .52[a] | .75[b] | −.06 | U-D | SR | FC | CS | M | T |
| Renn & Prien (1995) | 33 | .24 | .52[a] | .71 | .39 | UR | OR | FC | CS | M | M-M |
| Rentsch & Steel (1992) | 119 | .00 | .52[a] | .74[d] | .00 | OR | SR | G | CS | | M-M |
| Rentsch & Steel (1992) | 557 | .12 | .52[a] | .74[d] | .19 | OR | SR | G | CS | | L |
| Rich (1997) | 183 | .10 | .52[a] | .82 | .15 | UR | SR | G | CS | M | S |

*(Continued)*

Appendix cont'd

| Study | N | r | $r_{jp}$ | $r_{js}$ | $\rho$ | Source | Measure JP | Measure JS | Design | Complexity | Occupation |
|---|---|---|---|---|---|---|---|---|---|---|---|
| Riggio & Cole (1992) | 71 | .25 | $.62^h$ | $.75^b$ | .37 | OR | SR, P-S-O | FC | CS | M | M-M |
| Riggio & Cole (1992) | 173 | .22 | $.62^h$ | $.75^b$ | .32 | OR | SR, P-S-O | FC | CS | | M-M |
| Roberts & Foti (1998) | 76 | .42 | $.52^a$ | .88 | .62 | UR | SR | FC | CS | M | M-M |
| Ross (1991) | 172 | .00 | $.71^g$ | .92 | .00 | U-D | OR | U | CS | M | A |
| Ross (1991) | 205 | .09 | $.71^g$ | .92 | .11 | U-D | OR | U | CS | M | A |
| Rossano (1985) | 218 | .10 | $.52^a$ | $.65^h$ | .17 | U-D | SR | FC | CS | M | M-M |
| Saks (1995) | 76 | .29 | $.52^a$ | .72 | .47 | TT | SR | U | CS | M | A |
| Saks & Ashforth (1996) | 153 | .28 | $.52^a$ | .72 | .46 | OR | SR | U | CS | M | A |
| Sales (1977) | 380 | .10 | $.52^a$ | .74 | .16 | U-D | SR | FC | CS | | M-M |
| Sargent & Terry (1998) | 62 | .28 | $.52^a$ | $.90^b$ | .41 | OR | SR | U | L | M | M-M |
| Schatz (1980) | 50 | .49 | $.52^a$ | $.74^d$ | .79 | U-D | SR | FC | CS | M | C |
| Schatz (1980) | 50 | .45 | $.52^a$ | $.74^d$ | .73 | U-D | SR | FC | CS | L | C |
| Schau (1974) | 27 | .07 | $.52^a$ | $.61^b$ | .12 | U-D | SR | FC | CS | M | M-M |
| Schaubroeck & Fink (1998) | 184 | .19 | $.52^a$ | $.61^b$ | .34 | OR | SR | FC | CS | M | S |
| Schriesheim et al. (1995) | 48 | −.08 | $.52^a$ | $.74^d$ | −.13 | UR | SR | FC | CS | M | M-S |
| Schriesheim & Murphy (1976) | 54 | −.09 | $.52^a$ | $.74^d$ | −.15 | TT | SR | FC | CS | M | M-M |
| Schriesheim et al. (1992) | 115 | .39 | $.52^a$ | $.74^d$ | .63 | OR | SR | FC | CS | L | M-M |
| Schuster (1979) | 136 | .35 | $.52^e$ | $.74^d$ | .56 | U-D | SR | G | CS | L | L |
| Schwoerer & May (1996) | 311 | −.05 | $.42^e$ | .73 | −.09 | OR | P-S-O | FC | CS | L | L |
| Secrist (1975) | 123 | .23 | $.62^b$ | $.74^d$ | .34 | U-D | SR, P-S-O | U | CS | | S-E |
| Seers (1989) | 123 | .46 | $.52^a$ | $.75^d$ | .74 | TT | SR | U | CS | L | L |
| Seers & Graen (1984) | 101 | .21 | $.52^a$ | $.76^b$ | .33 | TT | SR | U | CS | L | M-M |
| Sheridan & Slocum (1975) | 35 | .31 | $.52^a$ | $.68^{b,f}$ | .52 | TT | SR | FC | L | M | M-S |
| Sheridan & Slocum (1975) | 59 | −.04 | $.52^a$ | $.45^{b,f}$ | −.08 | TT | SR | FC | L | L | M-M |
| Shore & Martin (1989) | 71 | .24 | $.52^a$ | .68 | .40 | OR | SR | U | CS | | M-M |
| Shore & Martin (1989) | 72 | .26 | $.52^a$ | .68 | .44 | OR | SR | U | CS | | M-M |
| Simmons (1986) | 51 | .19 | $.52^a$ | $.74^d$ | .31 | U-D | SR | FC | CS | M | C |

| | | | | | | | | | |
|---|---|---|---|---|---|---|---|---|---|
| Sirota (1958) | 377 | .11 | .52[a] | .74[d] | .18 | U-D | SR | U | CS | | M-M |
| Skotdal (1971) | 167 | .34 | .52[a] | .79[b] | .53 | U-D | SR | FC | CS | L | M-M |
| Skotdal (1971) | 199 | .14 | .52[a] | .76[b] | .22 | U-D | SR | FC | CS | L | M-M |
| Slocum (1971) | 87 | .19 | .52[a] | .74[d] | .31 | TT | SR | U | CS | M | M-S |
| Slocum (1971) | 132 | .26 | .52[a] | .74[d] | .42 | TT | SR | U | CS | M | M-S |
| Slocum et al. (1970) | 62 | .54 | .52[a] | .74[d] | .87 | OR | SR | U | CS | M | M-S |
| Smith (1989) | 69 | .22 | .52[a] | .74[d] | .35 | U-D | SR | FC | CS | | L |
| Smith-Fraser (1984) | 60 | .18 | .52[a] | .74[d] | .29 | U-D | SR | G | CS | L | M-M |
| Spector et al. (1988) | 148 | .42 | .52[a] | .90 | .61 | TT | SR | G | CS | M | C |
| Spencer & Steers (1981) | 295 | .17 | .52[a] | .71 | .28 | TT | SR | FC | CS | | M-M |
| Steel & Lloyd (1988) | 225 | .14 | .52[a] | .74[d] | .23 | OR | SR | G | L | L | M-M |
| Steers (1975) | 133 | .26 | .52[a] | .74[d] | .42 | TT | SR | FC | CS | M | M-S |
| Stepina et al. (1991) | 81 | .15 | .52[a] | .84[b] | .23 | UR | SR | FC | CS | | M-M |
| P. S. Strauss (1966) | 20 | .36 | .62[b] | .74[d] | .53 | OR | SR, P-S-O | G | CS | M | M-S |
| P. S. Strauss (1966) | 29 | .09 | .62[b] | .74[d] | .13 | OR | SR, P-S-O | G | CS | H | S-E |
| Stumpf & Rabinowitz (1981) | 102 | .19 | .39[i] | .52b | .42 | OR | SR, OR | FC | CS | H | M-M |
| Summers & Hendrix (1991) | 143 | .14 | .52[e] | .80 | .22 | UR | OR | FC | CS | M | M-S |
| Sundstrom et al. (1980) | 67 | .12 | .52[a] | .68 | .20 | TT | SR | G | CS | M | C |
| Sundstrom et al. (1994) | 96 | .10 | .52[a] | .61 | .18 | UR | SR | G | CS | | M-M |
| Sundstrom et al. (1994) | 132 | .23 | .52[a] | .87 | .34 | UR | SR | G | CS | | M-M |
| Sundstrom et al. (1994) | 137 | −.12 | .52[a] | .88 | −.18 | UR | SR | G | CS | | M-M |
| Sward (1974) | 47 | −.24 | .52[a] | .74[d] | −.39 | U-D | SR | U | CS | M | M-M |
| Tharenou (1993) | 200 | .13 | .52[a] | .65[b,f] | .22 | OR | SR | FC | L | M | M-M |
| Tharenou & Harker (1984) | 166 | .11 | .52[a] | .74 | .18 | TT | SR | FC | CS | M | M-M |
| Thoresen (1999) | 119 | .34 | .52[a] | .81 | .52 | U-D | SR | G | CS | | M-M |
| Toner (1980) | 193 | .15 | .52[a] | .72 | .25 | U-D | SR | U | CS | L | M-M |
| Tseng (1975) | 49 | .17 | .52[a] | .74[d] | .27 | UR | SR | G | CS | | M-M |
| Turban & Jones (1988) | 155 | .22 | .52[a] | .74 | .35 | TT | SR | U | CS | | M-M |
| Varca & James-Valutis (1993) | 95 | .14 | .52[a] | .74[d] | .23 | OR | SR | FC | CS | M | M-M |
| Vecchio & Gobdel (1984) | 45 | .05 | .39[i] | .51[b] | .11 | TT | SR, OR | FC | CS | M | M-M |

*(Continued)*

Appendix cont'd

| Study | N | r | $r_{jp}$ | $r_{js}$ | ρ | Source | Measure JP | Measure JS | Design | Complexity | Occupation |
|---|---|---|---|---|---|---|---|---|---|---|---|
| Vosburgh (1979) | 220 | .13 | .52[a] | .74[d] | .21 | U-D | SR | FC | CS | M | N |
| Vroom (1960) | 96 | .21 | .52[a] | .74[d] | .34 | UR | SR | U | CS | M | M-S |
| Wanous (1974) | 80 | .18 | .52[a] | .84[b] | .27 | TT | SR | FC | L | L | M-M |
| Weintraub (1981) | 64 | .08 | .52[e] | .75[b] | .13 | UR | OR | FC | CS | L | M-M |
| Weintraub (1981) | 69 | .38 | .52[a] | .74[d] | .61 | UR | SR | FC | CS | M | M-M |
| Weslander (1981) | 57 | .22 | .52[a] | .74[d] | .35 | U-D | SR | U | CS | M | T |
| Wexley et al. (1980) | 194 | .13 | .52[a] | .86[b] | .19 | TT | SR | FC | CS | | M-M |
| Wiggins & Moody (1983) | 160 | .65 | .62[b] | .74[d] | .96 | UR | SR, P-S-O | G | CS | H | M-M |
| Wiggins & Weslander (1979) | 123 | .86 | .52[a] | .74[d] | 1.39[j] | OR | SR | G | CS | H | M-M |
| Wiggins & Weslander (1986) | 320 | .39 | .52[a] | .74[d] | .63 | OR | SR | G | CS | H | M-M |
| Wilcox (1979) | 102 | .13 | .52[a] | .79 | .20 | U-D | SR | U | CS | M | T |
| Wilson (1990) | 138 | .10 | .52[a] | .72[b] | .16 | U-D | SR | FC | CS | | M-M |
| Wright & Cropanzano (1998) | 52 | .11 | .52[a] | .75 | .18 | TT | SR | U | CS | M | M-M |

*Note.* N = sample size; r = uncorrected correlation (includes composites of multiple measures); $r_{js}$ = reliability of job satisfaction (includes composite reliability estimates); $r_{jp}$ = reliability of job performance (includes composite reliability measures); ρ = corrected correlation; Source = source of correlation (TT = top-tier journal, OR = other ranked journal, UR = unranked journal, U-D = unpublished study–dissertation); Measure JP = measure of job performance (SR = supervisory ratings, OR = objective records, P-S-O = peer–subordinate ratings or other); Measure JS = measure of job satisfaction (G = global measure, FC = facet composite measure, U = unknown–not specified); Design = research design (CS = cross-sectional, L = longitudinal); Complexity = job complexity (L = low, M = medium, H = high; blank in case of multiple jobs); Occupation = occupation of sample (S-E = scientists–engineers, S = sales, T = teachers, M-S = managers and supervisors, A = accountants, C = clerical workers–secretaries, L = unskilled and semiskilled laborers, N = nurses, M-M = miscellaneous–mixed). [a] Meta-analytic estimate for the reliability of ratings from one supervisor taken from Viswesvaran et al. (1996). [b] A composite reliability estimate for job satisfaction involving multiple measures or multiple facets computed for the given study. [c] Meta-analytic estimate for the reliability of ratings from one peer taken from Viswesvaran et al. (1996). [d] A substituted reliability value for job satisfaction based on all other studies providing this information in the meta-analysis. [e] A substituted reliability value for job performance based on all other studies providing this information in the meta-analysis. [f] A longitudinal composite reliability estimate for job satisfaction. [g] A composite reliability estimate for objective measures of job performance involving multiple measures computed for the given study. [h] An estimate of composite reliability for studies involving both supervisory and peer ratings of job performance based on the meta-analyzed correlation of these measures taken from Harris and Schaubroeck (1988). [i] An estimate of composite reliability for studies involving both supervisory ratings of job performance and objective records of performance based on the meta-analyzed correlation of these measures taken from Sommer et al. (1995). [j] For a discussion of individually corrected estimates of ρ ≥ 1 in meta-analysis, see Hunter and Schmidt (1990). [k] A meta-analyzed Spearman–Brown reliability estimate for ratings of two peers taken from Viswesvaran et al. (19%). [l] A meta-analyzed Spearman–Brown reliability estimate for ratings of two supervisors taken from Viswesvaran et al. (1996).

# 10

# THE MEASUREMENT AND ANTECEDENTS OF AFFECTIVE, CONTINUANCE AND NORMATIVE COMMITMENT TO THE ORGANIZATION

*Natalie J. Allen and John P. Meyer*

Source: *Journal of Occupational Psychology* 63 (1990): 1–18.

## Abstract

Organizational commitment has been conceptualized and measured in various ways. The two studies reported here were conducted to test aspects of a three-component model of commitment which integrates these various conceptualizations. The *affective* component of organizational commitment, proposed by the model, refers to employees' emotional attachment to, identification with, and involvement in, the organization. The *continuance* component refers to commitment based on the costs that employees associate with leaving the organization. Finally, the *normative* component refers to employees' feelings of obligation to remain with the organization. In Study 1, scales were developed to measure these components. Relationships among the components of commitment and with variables considered their antecedents were examined in Study 2. Results of a canonical correlation analysis suggested that, as predicted by the model, the affective and continuance components of organizational commitment are empirically distinguishable constructs with different correlates. The affective and normative components, although distinguishable, appear to be somewhat related. The importance of differentiating the components of commitment, both in research and practice, is discussed.

A great deal of attention has been given recently to the study of commitment to the organization (Mowday, Porter & Steers, 1982). Like many constructs in organizational psychology, however, commitment has been conceptualized and measured in various ways. Common to all the conceptualizations of commitment found in the literature is a link with turnover; employees who are strongly committed are those who are least likely to leave the organization. Perhaps more important than this similarity, however, are the differences between the various conceptualizations of commitment. These differences involve the psychological state reflected in commitment, the antecedent conditions leading to its development, and the behaviours (other than remaining) that are expected to result from commitment.

Not surprisingly, confusion surrounding the conceptual distinctions is reflected in attempts to measure the construct. Indeed, relatively little attention has been given to the development of measures of commitment that conform closely to the researcher's particular conceptualization of the commitment construct. Our intention here, therefore, is threefold: (1) to delineate the distinctions between three of the more common conceptualizations of 'attitudinal' commitment,[1] (2) to develop measures of each, and (3) to demonstrate that these measures are differentially linked to variables identified in the literature as antecedents of commitment. The third aim serves the dual purpose of providing evidence for the convergent and discriminant validity of the new measures and of providing a preliminary test of hypotheses concerning the development of commitment.

## The conceptualization and measurement of attitudinal commitment

Although several conceptualizations of attitudinal commitment have appeared in the literature, each reflects one of three general themes: affective attachment, perceived costs and obligation (Meyer & Allen, 1987a).

### *Affective attachment*

The most prevalent approach to organizational commitment in the literature is one in which commitment is considered an affective or emotional attachment to the organization such that the strongly committed individual identifies with, is involved in, and enjoys membership in, the organization. This view was taken by Kanter (1968) who described 'cohesion commitment' as 'the attachment of an individual's fund of affectivity and emotion to the group' (p. 507) and by Buchanan (1974) who conceptualized commitment as a 'partisan, affective attachment to the goals and values of the organization, to one's role in relation to the goals and values, and to the organization for its own sake, apart from its purely instrumental worth' (p. 533). The affective attachment approach is perhaps best represented, however, by the work of Porter and his colleagues (Mowday, Steers & Porter, 1979; Porter, Crampon & Smith, 1976; Porter, Steers, Mowday & Boulian, 1974) who defined organizational commitment as 'the relative strength of an individual's identification with and involvement in a particular organization' (Mowday *et al.*, 1979, p. 226).

Porter and his colleagues developed the Organizational Commitment Questionnaire (OCQ) to measure the commitment construct (Mowday *et al.*, 1979). This 15-item scale has been used extensively in research and has acceptable psychometric properties. A parallel measure developed in Great Britain for use with blue-collar workers has also been shown to be 'psychometrically adequate and stable' (Cook & Wall, 1980, p. 39). Although other measures of affective attachment have been developed for use in specific studies, they typically have not been subjected to rigorous psychometric evaluation.

## *Perceived costs*

For other authors, affect plays a minimal role in the conceptualization of commitment. Instead, commitment is viewed as a tendency to 'engage in consistent lines of activity' (Becker, 1960, p. 33) based on the individual's recognition of the 'costs' (or lost side-bets) associated with discontinuing the activity (Becker, 1960; Farrell & Rusbult, 1981; Rusbult & Farrell, 1983). Kanter (1968), for example, defined 'cognitive–continuance commitment' as that which occurs when there is a 'profit associated with continued participation and a "cost" associated with leaving' (p. 504). For Stebbins (1970), continuance commitment is the 'awareness of the impossibility of choosing a different social identity ... because of the immense penalties in making the switch' (p. 527).

Cost-induced commitment has typically been assessed using a measure developed by Ritzer & Trice (1969), and modified by Hrebiniak & Alutto (1972), that requires respondents to indicate the likelihood that they will leave the organization given various inducements to do so (e.g. increases in pay, status, freedom, promotional opportunity). It is doubtful, however, that this measure actually reflects cost-based commitment (Meyer & Allen, 1984; Stebbins, 1970). Indeed, the fact that high scores on the scale reflect an unwillingness to leave the organization, in spite of attractive inducements to do so, suggests that it may measure affective attachment rather than, or in addition to, cost-induced commitment (Meyer & Allen, 1984).

## *Obligation*

Finally, a less common but equally viable approach has been to view commitment as a belief about one's responsibility to the organization. Wiener (1982, p. 471) defined commitment as the 'totality of internalized normative pressures to act in a way which meets organizational goals and interests', and suggests that individuals exhibit behaviours solely because 'they believe it is the "right" and moral thing to do' (p. 421). Although they do not refer to it as commitment, other authors (e.g. Prestholdt, Lane & Mathews, 1987; Schwartz, 1973; Schwartz & Tessler, 1972) have identified personal norms (defined as internalized moral obligation) as important contributors to behaviour, including terminating employment with an organization (Prestholdt *et al.*, 1987).

The only measure of this obligation-based commitment in the literature is the three-item scale used by Wiener & Vardi (1980). Respondents are asked the extent to which they feel 'a person *should* be loyal to his organization, *should* make sacrifices on its behalf, and *should* not criticize it' (Wiener & Vardi, 1980, p. 86, italics added). Other than internal consistency, the psychometric properties of the scale are not reported.

## A three-component conceptualization of organizational commitment

In a model of commitment developed recently by Meyer & Allen (1987*a*), the three approaches outlined above were labelled 'affective', 'continuance' and 'normative' commitment, respectively. Although common to these approaches is a *link* between the employee and organization that decreases the likelihood of turnover, it is clear that the nature of that link differs. Employees with strong affective commitment remain because they *want* to, those with strong continuance commitment because they *need* to, and those with strong normative commitment because they feel they *ought* to do so.

Affective, continuance and normative commitment are best viewed as distinguishable *components*, rather than *types*, of attitudinal commitment; that is, employees can experience each of these psychological states to varying degrees. Some employees, for example, might feel both a strong need and a strong obligation to remain, but no desire to do so; others might feel neither a need nor obligation but a strong desire, and so on. The 'net sum' of a person's commitment to the organization, therefore, reflects each of these separable psychological states.

Given their conceptual differences, it seems reasonable to suggest that each of the three components of commitment develop somewhat independently of the others as a function of different antecedents. It has been suggested (Mowday *et al.*, 1982) that the antecedents of affective attachment to the organization fall into four categories: personal characteristics, job characteristics, work experiences and structural characteristics. As Meyer & Allen (1987*a*) pointed out, however, the strongest evidence has been provided for work experience antecedents, most notably those experiences that fulfil employees' psychological needs to feel comfortable within the organization and competent in the work-role.

It is proposed that the *continuance* component of organizational commitment will also develop on the basis of two factors: the magnitude and/or number of investments (or side-bets) individuals make and a perceived lack of alternatives. These predictions derive from the theoretical work of Becker (1960) and Farrell & Rusbult (1981; Rusbult & Farrell, 1983). According to Becker, individuals make side-bets when they take an action that increases the costs associated with discontinuing another, related, action. Consider, for example, employees who invest considerable time and energy mastering a job skill that cannot be transferred easily to other organizations. In essence, they are 'betting' that the time and energy invested will pay off. Winning the bet, however, requires continued employment in the organization. According to Becker, the likelihood that employees will stay with the organization will be positively related to the magnitude and number of side-bets they recognize.[2]

Like investments, the lack of employment alternatives also increases the perceived costs associated with leaving the organization (Farrell & Rusbult, 1981; Rusbult & Farrell, 1983). Therefore, the fewer viable alternatives employees believe are available, the stronger will be their continuance commitment to their current employer.

Finally, it is proposed that the *normative* component of organizational commitment will be influenced by the individual's experiences both prior to (familial/cultural socialization) and following (organizational socialization) entry into the organization (Wiener, 1982). With respect to the former, we might expect, for example, that an employee would have strong normative commitment to the organization if significant others (e.g. parents) have been long-term employees of an organization and/or have stressed the importance of organizational loyalty. With respect to organizational socialization, it is proposed that those employees who have been led to believe – via various organizational practices – that the organization *expects* their loyalty would be most likely to have strong normative commitment to it.

## RESEARCH OVERVIEW

If the three components of commitment reflect distinct psychological states, it should be possible to develop independent measures of these states. This was the purpose of Study 1. Moreover, if the three components of commitment develop as described above, these measures should correlate with measures of those work experiences predicted to be their antecedents, but not with those predicted to be antecedent to the other components. This hypothesis was tested in Study 2. Because there has been less of a research tradition to guide the identification and measurement of predictors of normative commitment compared to affective and continuance commitment, the focus of Study 2 was on the latter two components. Normative commitment was included because, by examining the pattern of its relations with predicted antecedents of the affective and continuance components, its relation to these components can be better understood.

### Study 1: Development of measures

#### *Method*

*Subjects and data collection procedures*

Data were collected from full-time, non-unionized employees in three organizations: two manufacturing firms and a university. Approximately 500 questionnaires were distributed to employees in clerical, supervisory and managerial positions at these organizations; of these, 256 (52 per cent) were completed and returned. Females comprised 57 per cent of this sample. Forty-two per cent were under 30 years of age; 39 per cent were between 30 and 40 years of age; the remaining 19 per cent were above 40 years of age.

Questionnaires were distributed to employees by a member of the personnel department in the participating organization. Accompanying each questionnaire was a letter explaining the general purpose of the study and a stamped envelope addressed to one of the authors. Participation in the study was entirely voluntary.

*Measures*

A pool of 51 items was generated for purposes of scale construction. Some of these items were modified versions of those used in other scales; others were written by the authors. Each item was worded in accordance with one of the conceptualizations of commitment described above. Included along with these 51 items was the 15-item OCQ (Mowday *et al.*, 1979). With the exception of the OCQ items, which were presented first, the order of items on the questionnaire was random. Responses to all 66 items were made on seven-point scales ('strongly disagree' to 'strongly agree').

### Results and discussion

*Scale development*

Selection of items for inclusion on the final scales was based on a series of decision rules concerning item endorsement proportions, item–total correlations (with both keyed and non-keyed scales), direction of keying and content redundancy. Specifically, items were eliminated if (*a*) the endorsement proportion was greater than .75,[3] (*b*) the item correlated less with its keyed scale than with one or both of the other scales, and (*c*) the content of the item was redundant with respect to other items on the scale. An attempt was made to select both positively and negatively keyed items. Finally, the number of items selected for each scale was set equal to that for the scale with the minimum number of items surviving the aforementioned exclusion criteria. Although it was not of primary concern, equality of scale length was considered desirable when it became apparent that few items would be lost as a result. Following the application of these rules, eight items were selected for inclusion in each of the Affective Commitment Scale (ACS), Continuance Commitment Scale (CCS) and Normative Commitment Scale (NCS). The reliability for each scale (i.e. coefficient alpha) was as follows: ACS, .87; CCS, .75; NCS, .79. The 24 items comprising these scales were subjected to a factor analysis (principal factor method). Three factors, accounting for 58.8, 25.8 and 15.4 per cent of the total variance, respectively, were extracted and rotated to a varimax criterion. The items and their factor loadings are reported in Table 1. In all cases, the items loaded

Table 1 Varimax rotated factor matrix based on correlations among the items of the affective, continuance and normative commitment scales

|  | Factor 1 | Factor 2 | Factor 3 |
|---|---|---|---|
| *Affective Commitment Scale items* | | | |
| 1. I would be very happy to spend the rest of my career with this organization | 55 | 47 | −07 |
| 2. I enjoy discussing my organization with people outside it | 56 | 10 | −07 |
| 3. I really feel as if this organization's problems are my own | 52 | 39 | −06 |
| 4. I think that I could easily become as attached to another organization as I am to this one (R) | 45 | 21 | 18 |
| 5. I do not feel like 'part of the family' at my organization (R) | 63 | 15 | −04 |
| 6. I do not feel 'emotionally attached' to this organization (R) | 81 | 23 | 03 |
| 7. This organization has a great deal of personal meaning for me | 79 | 19 | 02 |
| 8. I do not feel a strong sense of belonging to my organization (R) | 82 | 18 | −05 |
| *Continuance Commitment Scale items* | | | |
| 1. I am not afraid of what might happen if I quit my job without having another one lined up (R) | −10 | 02 | 39 |
| 2. It would be very hard for me to leave my organization right now, even if I wanted to | 22 | 14 | 58 |
| 3. Too much in my life would be disrupted if I decided I wanted to leave my organization now | 33 | 27 | 44 |
| 4. It wouldn't be too costly for me to leave my organization now (R) | 18 | 12 | 46 |
| 5. Right now, staying with my organization is a matter of necessity as much as desire | −24 | −01 | 59 |
| 6. I feel that I have too few options to consider leaving this organization | −14 | 00 | 67 |
| 7. One of the few serious consequences of leaving this organization would be the scarcity of available alternatives | −17 | −07 | 60 |
| 8. One of the major reasons I continue to work for this organization is that leaving would require considerable personal sacrifice—another organization may not match the overall benefits I have here | 15 | −01 | 50 |
| *Normative Commitment Scale items* | | | |
| 1. I think that people these days move from company to company too often | 14 | 67 | −06 |
| 2. I do not believe that a person must always be loyal to his or her organization (R) | 29 | 43 | 00 |

*(continued)*

Table 1 (Cont'd)

|  | | Factor 1 | Factor 2 | Factor 3 |
|---|---|---|---|---|
| 3. | Jumping from organization to organization does not seem at all unethical to me (R) | 07 | <u>63</u> | 01 |
| 4. | One of the major reasons I continue to work for this organization is that I believe that loyalty is important and therefore feel a sense of moral obligation to remain | 17 | <u>59</u> | 07 |
| 5. | If I got another offer for a better job elsewhere I would not feel it was right to leave my organization | 17 | <u>49</u> | 09 |
| 6. | I was taught to believe in the value of remaining loyal to one organization | 15 | <u>49</u> | 10 |
| 7. | Things were better in the days when people stayed with one organization for most of their careers | 05 | <u>56</u> | 11 |
| 8. | I do not think that wanting to be a 'company man' or 'company woman' is sensible anymore (R) | 17 | 47 | −03 |
| % of variance accounted for | | 58.8 | 25.8 | 15.4 |

*Note.* The following items were adapted from items used in previous research: ACS items 1 and 3 from Buchanan (1974) and CCS items 1 and 2 from Quinn & Staines (1979). Factor loadings greater than 0.40 ate underlined; decimal points have been omitted. R = reverse keyed items.

Table 2 Means, standard deviations and intercorrelations of commitment measures

| Scale | $\overline{X}$ | SD | ACS | CCS | NCS | OCQ |
|---|---|---|---|---|---|---|
| ACS | 4.63 | 1.33 | — | | | |
| CCS | 4.51 | 1.16 | .06 | — | | |
| NCS | 3.77 | 1.13 | .51* | .14 | — | |
| OCQ | 5.32 | 1.07 | .83* | −.02 | .51* | — |

*Key.* *$P < 0.001$. ACS = Affective Commitment Scale; CCS = Continuance Commitment Scale; NCS = Normative Commitment Scale; OCQ = Organization Commitment Questionnaire.

highest on the factor representing the appropriate construct. Shown in Table 2 are the means and standard deviations for the three new commitment scales and the OCQ.

*Relationships among the commitment scales*

Also shown in Table 2 are the correlations among the new scales and the OCQ. As can be seen, the CCS is relatively independent of both the ACS and NCS. The OCQ correlated significantly with the ACS but not with the CCS, thus providing evidence for the convergent validity of the former and for the discriminant validity of the latter. The correlation between the OCQ and the NCS is consistent with the correlation between the ACS and NCS noted above.

Taken together, the results of the present study suggest that each of the psychological states identified in the literature as 'commitment' to the organization can be reliably measured. The independence of CCS scores from scores on the other two measures was expected. Not expected, however, was the significant relationship between the ASC and the NCS. This was observed despite efforts to include items that correlated only with others on the same scale, suggesting that feelings of obligation to maintain membership in the organization, although not identical to feelings of desire, may be meaningfully linked. The purpose of Study 2 was to examine the generalizability of these findings and to test the hypothesis that the three components of commitment would be related to variables assumed to be their antecedents.

## Study 2: Antecedents of commitment

### Method

### Subjects and data collection procedures

Following the same procedure used in Study 1, data were collected from full-time, non-unionized employees in three organizations: a retail department store, a hospital and a university library. In total, 634 questionnaires were distributed to employees in clerical, supervisory, management and technical positions within these organizations. Of these, 337 (53.2 per cent) were completed and returned. Females comprised 80.2 per cent of this sample. The mean age of participants was 38 years.

### Measures

The commitment and antecedent measures used were as follows.

ORGANIZATIONAL COMMITMENT MEASURES

The Affective, Continuance and Normative Commitment Scales, developed in Study 1, were included on the questionnaire.

PROPOSED ANTECEDENTS OF THE AFFECTIVE COMPONENT

Also included on the questionnaire were 11 two-item measures assessing various work experiences. The work experience variables selected for inclusion were those found in previous research to correlate with affective commitment. Specifically, we assessed employees' perceptions of the extent to which their jobs were challenging (job challenge), roles (role clarity) and goals (goal clarity) were clearly defined, goals were difficult (goal difficulty), management was receptive to employee suggestions (management receptiveness), employees were cohesive (peer cohesion), the organization was dependable (organizational dependability), employees were treated equitably (equity), employees were made to feel that they were important to the organization (personal importance), feedback concerning their work performance was provided (feedback), and they were allowed to participate in decisions regarding their own work (participation). As noted earlier, work experience variables contributing to affective commitment can be grouped into those that satisfy employees' needs to feel comfortable in their relationship with the organization and to feel competent in the work-role. Although experiences may contribute to the satisfaction of both needs, it might be argued that the comfort need would be best served by organizational dependability, management receptiveness, equity, peer cohesion, role clarity and goal clarity, whereas feelings of competence would be enhanced most by job challenge, goal difficulty, personal importance, feedback and participation.

Some of the work experience measures used were modifications of those used in Buchanan's (1974) study of managers; others were developed by the authors. Each scale item had a seven-point response format ('strongly disagree' to 'strongly agree'). Sample items are presented in the Appendix.

PROPOSED ANTECEDENTS OF THE CONTINUANCE COMPONENT

Several single-item measures were used to assess the magnitude of the organization-relevant investments respondents had made. These included questions about the transferability of both organization-based skills (skills) and formal education (education) to other organizations, the likelihood that employees would have to move to another geographical area if they were to leave the organization (relocate), the extent to which employees felt they 'themselves' had invested (i.e. time and energy 'learning the ropes') in the organization (self-investment), and the extent to which their pension fund would be reduced if they left the organization (pension). Responses to these questions were made on seven-point scales. Also included—as an index of 'investments in the community'—was the proportion of employees' life during which they had resided locally (community). It was predicted that each of these variables, with the exceptions of skills and education, would be positively correlated with continuance commitment; the relationships involving skills and education were expected to be negative.

The perceived availability of alternatives was assessed by asking employees to indicate, on a seven-point response scale, how easy they felt it would be to obtain comparable or better employment in another organization (alternatives). Scores on this measure were expected to correlate negatively with CCS scores.

PROPOSED ANTECEDENT OF THE NORMATIVE COMPONENT

Although normative commitment was included in this study primarily for exploratory purposes, one variable, the two-item Organizational Commitment Norm Scale (Buchanan, 1974), was included as a potential predictor of this component of commitment. Scores on this scale, which reflect the extent to which employees feel that the organization *expects* their loyalty, were expected to correlate positively with NCS scores.

## Data analysis

The relationships among the three commitment measures and those variables hypothesized to be their antecedents were examined using canonical correlation analysis. The aim of canonical correlation analysis is to derive a linear combination from each of two sets of variables (commitment measures and antecedent measures, in this case) in such a way that the correlation between them is maximized. As such, this analysis is particularly appropriate for the present data. If the affective, continuance and normative commitment measures represent separable components, we would expect them to define distinct canonical variates. In addition, the linear combination of antecedent variables that corresponds to a particular commitment measure should weight most heavily those variables predicted to be antecedent to that commitment component.

## **Results and discussion**

### *Relationships among the commitment and antecedent measures*

To handle missing data, a list-wise deletion procedure was used; this reduced the sample to 250 individuals who responded to every item on the questionnaire. Means, standard deviations, reliabilities and intercorrelations of all measures appear in Table 3.[4] As in Study 1, the reliabilities for each of the newly developed commitment measures were acceptably high; the same is true of the two-item antecedent measures. Once again, the correlation between the ACS and the CCS was negligible ($r = .01$), and that between the ACS and the NCS was significant ($r = .48, P < .001$). Although the relationship between the CCS and the NCS was also significant ($r = .16, P < .01$), the magnitude of the correlation suggests that the two scales share little variance. In general, the pattern of correlations between the antecedent and commitment measures provides support for the hypothesis outlined above. This was examined further using canonical correlation analysis.

### *Antecedents of commitment: canonical correlation analyis*

The results of the canonical correlation analysis are summarized in Table 4. As can be seen, three significant canonical roots were produced; the correlations associated

Table 3 Means, standard deviations, reliabilities and intercorrelations of commitment and antecedent measures

| Variable | $\overline{X}$ | SD | 1 | 2 | 3 | 4 | 5 | 6 | 7 | 8 | 9 | 10 | 11 | 12 | 13 | 14 | 15 | 16 | 17 | 18 | 19 | 20 | 21 | 22 |
|---|---|---|---|---|---|---|---|---|---|---|---|---|---|---|---|---|---|---|---|---|---|---|---|---|
| 1 ACS | 4.36 | 1.38 | (86) | 01 | 48 | 63 | 53 | 35 | 56 | 48 | 51 | 61 | 55 | 68 | 36 | 51 | 25 | -15 | 06 | 13 | 20 | -12 | -13 | 39 |
| 2 CCS | 4.49 | 1.35 | - | (82) | 16 | -14 | -11 | -04 | -17 | -16 | -05 | -04 | -02 | -18 | -18 | -12 | -20 | -16 | 06 | 06 | 17 | 14 | -43 | -12 |
| 3 NCS | 3.80 | 1.08 | - | - | (73) | 29 | 39 | 31 | 25 | 20 | 24 | 38 | 26 | 34 | 21 | 27 | 19 | -15 | -10 | 00 | 22 | 14 | -08 | 24 |
| 4 Job challenge | 4.75 | 1.86 | - | - | - | (89) | 42 | 31 | 78 | 44 | 40 | 48 | 40 | 66 | 37 | 48 | 37 | -11 | 06 | 25 | 21 | -20 | -06 | 51 |
| 5 Role clarity | 4.55 | 1.59 | - | - | - | - | (74) | 65 | 36 | 58 | 31 | 66 | 48 | 63 | 44 | 48 | 25 | -04 | 00 | -12 | 10 | -12 | -02 | 27 |
| 6 Goal clarity | 4.91 | 1.56 | - | - | - | - | - | (76) | 25 | 41 | 18 | 52 | 37 | 36 | 32 | 40 | 21 | 02 | -02 | -06 | 07 | -06 | -02 | 15 |
| 7 Goal diff'y | 4.74 | 1.76 | - | - | - | - | - | - | (73) | 36 | 39 | 32 | 36 | 57 | 48 | 36 | 35 | -08 | 06 | 30 | 23 | -18 | 01 | 48 |
| 8 Mgmt recept. | 3.98 | 1.75 | - | - | - | - | - | - | - | (78) | 44 | 55 | 53 | 63 | 42 | 59 | 22 | -08 | 12 | 00 | 02 | -20 | -09 | 33 |
| 9 Peer cohesion | 4.32 | 1.52 | - | - | - | - | - | - | - | - | (44) | 35 | 40 | 48 | 31 | 40 | 22 | -09 | 06 | -07 | 05 | -03 | -08 | 37 |
| 10 Org. depend'y | 4.61 | 1.75 | - | - | - | - | - | - | - | - | - | (73) | 51 | 54 | 37 | 51 | 18 | -11 | -05 | -12 | 14 | -16 | -11 | 25 |
| 11 Equity | 3.62 | 1.49 | - | - | - | - | - | - | - | - | - | - | (61) | 52 | 30 | 47 | 18 | -06 | 10 | 05 | 05 | -16 | -14 | 21 |
| 12 Pers. import. | 4.61 | 1.79 | - | - | - | - | - | - | - | - | - | - | - | (78) | 46 | 57 | 35 | -12 | 07 | 09 | 14 | -18 | -01 | 45 |
| 13 Feedback | 3.97 | 1.86 | - | - | - | - | - | - | - | - | - | - | - | - | (81) | 48 | 20 | 01 | 04 | 06 | 06 | -08 | -01 | 19 |
| 14 Participation | 4.46 | 1.60 | - | - | - | - | - | - | - | - | - | - | - | - | - | (61) | 25 | -10 | 13 | 02 | 10 | -17 | -08 | 23 |
| 15 Skills | 5.77 | 1.59 | - | - | - | - | - | - | - | - | - | - | - | - | - | - | - | -09 | 14 | 04 | 04 | -18 | 14 | 28 |
| 16 Education | 5.04 | 2.07 | - | - | - | - | - | - | - | - | - | - | - | - | - | - | - | - | -11 | -02 | -08 | -04 | 09 | -11 |
| 17 Relocate | 3.10 | 2.29 | - | - | - | - | - | - | - | - | - | - | - | - | - | - | - | - | - | 14 | 02 | -27 | -10 | 14 |
| 18 Self-invest. | 4.51 | 1.90 | - | - | - | - | - | - | - | - | - | - | - | - | - | - | - | - | - | - | 10 | -07 | -06 | 23 |
| 19 Pension | 3.02 | 2.32 | - | - | - | - | - | - | - | - | - | - | - | - | - | - | - | - | - | - | - | 03 | -10 | 27 |
| 20 Community | 0.47 | 0.32 | - | - | - | - | - | - | - | - | - | - | - | - | - | - | - | - | - | - | - | - | 05 | -14 |
| 21 Alternatives | 3.78 | 1.88 | - | - | - | - | - | - | - | - | - | - | - | - | - | - | - | - | - | - | - | - | - | 02 |
| 22 Commit. norm | 4.64 | 1.43 | - | - | - | - | - | - | - | - | - | - | - | - | - | - | - | - | - | - | - | - | - | (67) |

*Note.* Decimals have been omitted from correlation coefficients.
For correlations > .12, $p < .05$. Reliabilities appear in the diagonal.

*Table 4* Results of canonical correlation analysis of the relationships of affective, continuance and normative commitment and their hypothesized antecedents

| Canonical root | $R_c$ | $R_c^2$ | Wilks' lambda | F | $R_{dx}$ | $R_{dy}$ |
|---|---|---|---|---|---|---|
| 1 | .81 | .65 | .20 | 8.43** | .28 | .29 |
| 2 | .56 | .32 | .59 | 3.89** | .11 | .06 |
| 3 | .38 | .14 | .86 | 2.25* | .03 | .06 |

<table>
<thead>
<tr><th rowspan="3">Variables</th><th colspan="6">Canonical variates</th></tr>
<tr><th colspan="2">1</th><th colspan="2">2</th><th colspan="2">3</th></tr>
<tr><th>Struc. coeff.</th><th>Stand. coeff.</th><th>Struc. coeff.</th><th>Stand. coeff.</th><th>Struc. coeff.</th><th>Stand. coeff.</th></tr>
</thead>
<tbody>
<tr><td>Commitment variables</td><td></td><td></td><td></td><td></td><td></td><td></td></tr>
<tr><td>Affective</td><td>98</td><td>93</td><td>17</td><td>14</td><td>−10</td><td>−65</td></tr>
<tr><td>Continuance</td><td>−15</td><td>−19</td><td>99</td><td>98</td><td>−01</td><td>−19</td></tr>
<tr><td>Normative</td><td>53</td><td>11</td><td>26</td><td>03</td><td>81</td><td>116</td></tr>
<tr><td>Antecedent variables</td><td></td><td></td><td></td><td></td><td></td><td></td></tr>
<tr><td>Job challenge</td><td>80</td><td>19</td><td>−08</td><td>−05</td><td>−12</td><td>−25</td></tr>
<tr><td>Role clarity</td><td>69</td><td>12</td><td>−04</td><td>05</td><td>32</td><td>41</td></tr>
<tr><td>Goal clarity</td><td>46</td><td>−04</td><td>03</td><td>14</td><td>35</td><td>22</td></tr>
<tr><td>Goal difficulty</td><td>71</td><td>09</td><td>−15</td><td>−17</td><td>−12</td><td>−07</td></tr>
<tr><td>Mgmt. receptiveness</td><td>62</td><td>−11</td><td>−15</td><td>−27</td><td>−14</td><td>−24</td></tr>
<tr><td>Peer cohesion</td><td>63</td><td>20</td><td>05</td><td>19</td><td>−13</td><td>−21</td></tr>
<tr><td>Org. dependability</td><td>77</td><td>31</td><td>09</td><td>12</td><td>14</td><td>−02</td></tr>
<tr><td>Equity</td><td>67</td><td>13</td><td>12</td><td>12</td><td>−14</td><td>−09</td></tr>
<tr><td>Personal importance</td><td>87</td><td>31</td><td>−12</td><td>05</td><td>−06</td><td>23</td></tr>
<tr><td>Feedback</td><td>49</td><td>00</td><td>−22</td><td>−20</td><td>10</td><td>11</td></tr>
<tr><td>Participation</td><td>65</td><td>07</td><td>−07</td><td>−06</td><td>01</td><td>14</td></tr>
<tr><td>Skills</td><td>36</td><td>01</td><td>−28</td><td>−13</td><td>25</td><td>37</td></tr>
<tr><td>Education</td><td>−16</td><td>−02</td><td>−32</td><td>−23</td><td>−13</td><td>−16</td></tr>
<tr><td>Relocate</td><td>04</td><td>−01</td><td>13</td><td>13</td><td>−45</td><td>−35</td></tr>
<tr><td>Self-investment</td><td>14</td><td>09</td><td>13</td><td>19</td><td>−25</td><td>−14</td></tr>
<tr><td>Pension</td><td>22</td><td>02</td><td>35</td><td>29</td><td>24</td><td>18</td></tr>
<tr><td>Community</td><td>−15</td><td>03</td><td>22</td><td>18</td><td>56</td><td>48</td></tr>
<tr><td>Alternatives</td><td>−06</td><td>03</td><td>−79</td><td>−69</td><td>19</td><td>06</td></tr>
<tr><td>Commitment norm</td><td>50</td><td>01</td><td>−09</td><td>−11</td><td>11</td><td>33</td></tr>
</tbody>
</table>

*$p < .01$; **$p < .001$.
*Note.* $R_c$ = canonical correlation; $R_{dx}$ = redundancy of antecedent variables given the canonical variate for commitment variables; $R_{dy}$ = redundancy of commitment variables given the canonical variate for the antecedent variables; Struc. coeff. = structure coefficients; Stand. coeff. = standardized coefficients. Decimals have been omitted from coefficients.

with these were .81; .56 and .38, respectively. For each of the three canonical variates, both the structure coefficients and standardized coefficients associated with each variable are shown. The standardized coefficients are the weights used in the computation of the commitment and antecedent canonical variates whereas the structure coefficients are the correlations of these linear combinations with each variable. Because structure coefficients tend to be more stable (Cooley & Lohnes, 1971), these were used for the purpose of interpretation. Following Pedhazur's (1982) recommendation, interpretation was based on variables correlating .30 or greater with the canonical variate.

Within the commitment set, both affective and normative commitment correlate strongly with the first canonical variate. A comparison of the two correlations (.98 vs. .53) suggests, however, that the first variate represents affective commitment. The fact that this variate also correlates with normative commitment reflects the overlapping variance between the two scales. Within the antecedent set, the largest correlations are associated with those variables hypothesized to be antecedents of affective commitment; these range from .46 to .87. Only two variables in the antecedent set (skills and commitment norm) which were *not* identified as affective antecedents correlated above .30 with the first canonical variate.

The second canonical variate was clearly defined, within the commitment set, by continuance commitment ($r = .99$) and, within the antecedent set, by education, pension and alternatives, all of which were hypothesized to be antecedent to continuance commitment. The correlation with skills, also predicted as an antecedent of continuance commitment, fell just below the cut-off ($r = -.28$).

Finally, the third canonical variate was defined, within the commitment set, by normative commitment and, within the antecedent set, by goal clarity, role clarity, relocate and community. Organizational commitment norm, the only variable within the set which was predicted to be an antecedent of normative commitment, did not correlate significantly with the third canonical variate.

This pattern of results provides partial support for the predictions made about the three components of commitment and their antecedents. At this stage in the development of the three-component view of commitment, it is particularly encouraging that the three commitment measures defined the three canonical variates as distinctly as they did. The fact that normative commitment correlated with both the first and third variates suggests that, although the desire to remain with an organization is not synonymous with the feeling of obligation to do so, there is a tendency for these feelings to co-occur. It is not clear at this point whether there is a causal ordering in the development of these two attitudes or, if so, what that ordering might be. One might speculate that as moral obligations are internalized to form personal norms, they influence individuals' feelings about what they *want* to do. Alternatively, to justify behaving in accord with their desires, individuals may come to accept that their actions are morally right.

With respect to the antecedent variables, the evidence seems strongest for our predictions about affective commitment. Each of the affective antecedent variables correlated significantly with the first canonical variate. Thus, employees who felt comfortable in their roles and who felt competent in the job, expressed greater affective attachment to the organization.

The relationships between the 'continuance antecedents' and the second canonical variate suggest that, in general, the strength of employees' need to remain with an organization is related to their perceptions regarding the availability of alternatives and the magnitude of particular investments they have made. It will be noted, however, that these relationships are not as strong as were those for the antecedents of affective commitment. This may be explained, at least in part, by the fact that, because respondents were employed at different levels in different organizations, it was necessary to restrict the assessment of investments to categories that would be relevant to employees in general (e.g. time and energy). The costs associated with leaving an organization, however, may be quite specific to an individual (e.g. losing a day-care benefit; moving from the home one has built) and not easily translated into these more general categories. It may be possible to account for more variance in continuance commitment using measures that permit employees to generate (and perhaps weigh the importance of) specific investments they have made. This would be analogous to the improvements in prediction obtained in expectancy theory research when outcomes were generated by subjects rather than the experimenters (Matsui & Ikeda, 1976).

The failure of the organizational commitment norm to correlate with the third canonical variate (defined by normative commitment) also may be attributed, in part, to its very general nature. Unfortunately, the diversity (e.g. organization, position, tenure) within the sample used in this study made it difficult to obtain more specific information about the various channels (e.g. recruitment, selection, socialization) through which the organization's expectations regarding commitment (or norms) are communicated.

## General discussion

The purpose of this research was to provide preliminary evidence that the affective, continuance and normative components of attitudinal commitment are conceptually and empirically separable. It was argued that each component corresponds closely to one of three major conceptualizations of commitment found in the literature and represents a somewhat distinct link between employees and an organization that develops as the result of different experiences. It was found in Study 1 that the three components of commitment can be measured reliably and that, although there was some overlap between affective and normative commitment, both were relatively independent of continuance commitment. The results of Study 2 revealed a pattern of relationships between the commitment measures, particularly affective and continuance commitment, and the antecedent variables which was, for the most part, consistent with prediction.

Although the results of Study 2 are generally consistent with the hypothesis that the components of commitment develop as a function of different work experiences, it was not our intention at this preliminary stage in the research to address issues of causality. The dangers of causal inference in research of this nature have been described elsewhere (e.g. Clegg, 1983; James, Mulaik & Brett, 1982) and need not be elaborated here. The present results, therefore, should be seen as having set the stage for the kind of longitudinal study of commitment antecedents carried out recently by Bateman & Strasser (1984) and Meyer & Allen (1987*b*, 1988) using the OCQ.

Finally, it is clear from the results of Study 2 that further attention should be given to the development of the normative component of commitment. The inclusion of a single general antecedent measure in this study was not intended to suggest that this component is any less important than the other two. Unfortunately, there is little in the literature upon which to base predictions regarding the antecedents of normative commitment. Wiener (1982) suggested that such commitment may develop as the result of socialization prior to and following entry into the organization, but it is unclear how such influences, particularly those occurring prior to entry, might be measured. One potential source of pre-entry socialization is the example set by parents or significant others in an employee's life. The impact of this modelled behaviour is extremely complex, however, as illustrated in the following comment from one of the subjects in Study 2.

> I was brought up in a house where we were taught that loyalty was very important to the company you worked for. My father gave that kind of loyalty [to his employer] for 30 years. He is now on strike pay receiving $65 per week ... and really doesn't know if he will have a job tomorrow. So although I was taught to believe in the value of loyalty, my attitude has changed.

The focus of the present research was on post-entry socialization. Even here, however, because of diversity in the sample tested, the measurement was restricted to a very general assessment of perceived organizational expectations of commitment. It would be useful in future research to examine the impact of specific socialization practices such as those identified by Van Maanen & Schein (1979).

### *Implications*

The research reported here ties together what has, to date, been three separate streams of commitment research. The use of the term 'commitment' to describe very different constructs has led to considerable confusion in the literature. Indeed, some may argue that the term commitment cannot, or should not, be used to describe such distinct constructs. We retain the term, however, in recognition of the literature on which this research was based, and because it reflects the common denominator believed to underlie each of the three conceptualizations. In each case, commitment refers to a psychological state that binds the individual to the organization (i.e. makes turnover less likely). However, this may be where the similarity ends. Nonetheless, it should be recognized that the three approaches provide valuable insight into the employee–organization link, and that a more comprehensive understanding of this link is achieved when all three are considered simultaneously. By attaching the labels affective commitment, continuance commitment and normative commitment to the three constructs, both the similarity (i.e. link to turnover) and differences among them are acknowledged.

Another contribution of this research was the development of reliable measures of the three components of commitment. With the exception of the OCQ, relatively little attention has so far been given to the development and psychometric evaluation of commitment measures. The fact that the Affective and Continuance Commitment Scales generally correlate as predicted with the proposed antecedent variables provides preliminary evidence that they are valid measures of commitment, as conceptualized here, and may be useful tools in future research. More evidence is required before the Normative Commitment Scale can be used with as much confidence. The Affective Commitment Scale is shorter than the OCQ[5] and has the advantage that its items were written to assess only affective orientation towards the organization and not employees' behaviour or behavioural intentions (e.g. intention to exert effort or leave the organization). Thus, it can be used to test hypotheses concerning the consequences of affective commitment without concern that the relationships obtained merely reflect overlap in the content of the commitment and behaviour measures. This problem has been identified in studies that have used the OCQ (e.g. Hom, Katerberg & Hulin, 1979). To date, the Continuance Commitment Scale has no counterpart in the research literature. Although the commitment scale developed by Ritzer & Trice (1969), and revised by Hrebiniak & Alutto (1972), was purported to measure Becker's (1960) 'side-bet' commitment, this interpretation has been challenged both conceptually (Stebbins, 1970) and empirically (Meyer & Allen, 1984).

Finally, the conceptual framework provided here suggests an important consideration for the future study of the *consequences* of commitment. As noted above, in all three approaches to organizational commitment, commitment is seen as a negative indicator of turnover. A logical conclusion to be drawn from this is that one form of commitment is as useful as another. What is not recognized in such logic, however, is the fact that what employees *do* on the job is as important, or more important, than whether they remain. Dalton and his associates have acknowledged this by making a distinction between functional and dysfunctional turnover (Dalton, Krackhardt & Porter, 1981; see also Staw, 1980). It is important to consider, therefore, that the link between commitment and on-the-job behaviour may vary as a function of the strength of the three components. There is some evidence that this is the case. Specifically, Meyer, Paunonen, Gellatly, Goffin & Jackson (1989) found that supervisors' ratings of the overall job performance and the promotability of their subordinates correlated positively with those subordinates' affective commitment scores and negatively with their continuance commitment scores. Allen & Smith (1987) reported a positive relationship between affective commitment and a self-report measure of employee innovativeness; this measure was negatively correlated with continuance commitment scores. In the same study, affective and normative commitment scores, but not continuance commitment scores, were positively related to self-report measures of employees' consideration for co-workers and their efficient use of time.

In future research, it may be possible to identify 'commitment profiles' that differentiate employees who are likely to remain with the organization and to contribute positively to its effectiveness from those who are likely to remain but contribute little. If so, it should be possible for organizations to use the results of research examining antecedents (e.g. Study 2) to better manage the experiences of their employees so as to foster the development of the desired profile.

## Acknowledgements

This research was supported by a grant from the Social Sciences and Humanities Research Council of Canada (No. 410-87-1235).

## Notes

1 A distinction is made in the commitment literature between attitudinal commitment and behavioural commitment (Mowday *et al.*, 1982; Staw, 1977). The focus of the present research is on attitudinal commitment, conceptualized as a psychological state that reflects employees' relationship to the organization.
2 In the past, Becker's (1960) side-bet theory has often been discussed in the context of behavioural commitment. Like Kiesler (1971) and Salancik (1977), Becker defines commitment as the tendency to persist in a course of action. Unlike Kiesler and Salancik, however, Becker emphasizes the importance of *recognizing* the cost associated with discontinuing an action. Recognition of the costs associated with leaving an organization can be viewed as a psychological state reflecting the employee's relationship to the organization and is, therefore, included here as a component of attitudinal commitment.
3 To calculate endorsement proportions for ratings made on seven-point scales, responses were divided into three categories: 1, 2 and 3 (strongly, moderately and slightly disagree); 4 (neither agree nor disagree); and 5, 6 and 7 (slightly, moderately, or strongly agree).
4 The factor structure of the 24 commitment items administered in Study 2 closely resembled that of Study 1. Although not included here, it is available from the authors.
5 Although a nine-item version of the OCQ has been used in the literature, Mowday *et al.* (1979) caution that this version includes only positively keyed items and may, therefore, increase the tendency towards acquiescent responding. Furthermore, they point out that some of the negatively keyed items excluded from the nine-item version 'were more highly correlated with the total score than several of the positively phrased items' (p. 244).

## References

Allen, N. J. & Smith, J. (1987). An investigation of 'extra-role' behaviours within organizations. Paper presented at the annual meeting of the Canadian Psychological Association, Vancouver, British Columbia, June.

Bateman, T. S. & Strasser, S. (1984). A longitudinal analysis of the antecedents of organizational commitment. *Academy of Management Journal*, **27**, 95–112.

Becker, H. S. (1960). Notes on the concept of commitment. *American Journal of Sociology*, **66**, 32–42.

Buchanan, B. (1974). Building organizational commitment: The socialization of managers in work organizations. *Administrative Science Quarterly*, **19**, 533–546.

Clegg, C. (1983). Psychology of employee lateness, absence, and turnover: A methodological critique and an empirical study. *Journal of Applied Psychology*, **68**, 88–101.

Cook, J. & Wall, T. (1980). New work attitude measures of trust, organizational commitment and personal need non-fulfilment. *Journal of Occupational Psychology*, **53**, 39–52.

Cooley, W. W. & Lohnes, P. R. (1971). *Multivariate Data Analysis*. New York: Wiley.

Dalton, D. R., Krackhardt, D. M. & Porter, L. W. (1981). Functional turnover: An empirical assessment. *Journal of Applied Psychology*, **66**, 716–721.

Farrell, D. & Rusbult, C. E. (1981). Exchange variables as predictors of job satisfaction, job commitment, and turnover: The impact of rewards, costs, alternatives, and investments. *Organizational Behavior and Human Performance*, **27**, 78–95.

Hom, P. W., Katerberg, R. & Hulin, C. L. (1979). Comparative examination of three approaches to the prediction of turnover. *Journal of Applied Psychology*, **64**, 280–290.

Hrebiniak, L. G. & Alutto, J. A. (1972). Personal and role-related factors in the development of organizational commitment. *Administrative Science Quarterly*, **17**, 555–573.

James, L. R., Mulaik, S. A. & Brett, J. M. (1982). *Causal Analysis*. Beverly Hills, CA: Sage.

Kanter, R. M. (1968). Commitment and social organization: A study of commitment mechanisms in Utopian communities. *American Sociological Review*, **33**, 499–517.

Kiesler, C. A. (1971). *The Psychology of Commitment*. New York: Academic Press.

Matsui, T. & Ikeda, H. (1976). Effectiveness of self-generated outcomes for improving predictions in expectancy theory research. *Organizational Behavior and Human Performance*, **17**, 289–298.

Meyer, J. P. & Allen, N. J. (1984). Testing the 'side-bet theory' of organizational commitment: Some methodological considerations. *Journal of Applied Psychology*, **69**, 372–378.

Meyer, J. P. & Allen, N. J. (1987a). Organizational commitment: Toward a three-component model, Research Bulletin No. 660. The University of Western Ontario, Department of Psychology, London.

Meyer, J. P. & Allen, N. J. (1987b). A longitudinal analysis of the early development and consequences of organizational commitment. *Canadian Journal of Behavioural Science*, **19**, 199–215.

Meyer, J. P. & Allen, N. J. (1988). Links between work experiences and organizational commitment during the first year of employment: A longitudinal analysis. *Journal of Occupational Psychology*, **61**, 195–210.

Meyer, J. P., Paunonen, S. V., Gellatly, I. R., Goffin, R. D. & Jackson, D. N. (1989). Organizational commitment and job performance: It's the nature of the commitment that counts. *Journal of Applied Psychology*, **74**, 152–156.

Mowday, R. T., Porter, L. W. & Steers, R. M. (1982). *Employee–Organization Linkages: The Psychology of Commitment, Absenteeism and Turnover*. New York: Academic Press.

Mowday, R. T., Steers, R. M. & Porter, L. W. (1979). The measurement of organizational commitment. *Journal of Vocational Behavior*, **14**, 224–247.

Pedhazur, E. J. (1982). *Multiple Regression in Behavioral Research*, 2nd ed. New York: Holt, Rinehart & Winston.

Porter, L. W., Crampon, W. J. & Smith, F. J. (1976). Organizational commitment and managerial turnover. *Organizational Behavior and Human Performance*, **15**, 87–98.

Porter, L. W., Steers, R. M., Mowday, R. T. & Boulian, P. V. (1974). Organizational commitment, job satisfaction, and turnover among psychiatric technicians. *Journal of Applied Psychology*, **59**, 603–609.

Prestholdt, P. H., Lane, I. M. & Mathews, R. C. (1987). Nurse turnover as reasoned action: Development of a process model. *Journal of Applied Psychology*, **72**, 221–228.

Quinn, R. P. & Staines, G. L. (1979). *The 1977 Quality of Employment Survey*. Ann Arbor, MI: Institute for Social Research.

Rifzer, G. & Trice, H. M. (1969). An empirical study of Howard Becker's side-bet theory. *Social Forces*, **47**, 475–479.

Rusbult, C. E. & Farrell, D. (1983). A longitudinal test of the investment model: The impact on job satisfaction, job commitment, and turnover of variations in rewards, costs, alternatives, and investments. *Journal of Applied Psychology*, **68**, 429–438.

Salancik, G. R. (1977). Commitment and the control of organizational behavior and belief. In B. M. Staw & G. R. Salancik (Eds), *New Directions in Organizational Behavior*. Chicago: St Clair Press.

Schwartz, S. H. (1973). Normative explanations of helping behavior: A critique, proposal, and empirical test. *Journal of Experimental Social Psychology*, **9**, 349–364.

Schwartz, S. H. & Tessler, R. C. (1972). A test of a model for reducing measured attitude–behavior discrepancies. *Journal of Personality and Social Psychology*, **24**, 225–236.

Staw, B. M. (1977). Two sides of commitment. Paper presented at the annual meeting of the Academy of Management, Orlando, FL, August.

Staw, B. M. (1980). The consequences of turnover. *Journal of Occupational Behavior*, **1**, 253–273.

Stebbins, R. A. (1970). On misunderstanding the concept of commitment: A theoretical clarification. *Social Forces*, **48**, 526–529.

Van Maanen, J. & Schein, E. H. (1979). Towards a theory of organizational socialization. In B. M. Staw (Ed.), *Research in Organizational Behavior*. Greenwich, CT: JAI Press.

Wiener, Y. (1982). Commitment in organizations: A normative view. *Academy of Management Review*, **7**, 418–428.

Wiener, Y. & Vardi, Y. (1980). Relationships between job, organization, and career commitments and work outcomes: An integrative approach. *Organizational Behavior and Human Performance*, **26**, 81–96.

# Appendix

## Sample items: proposed antecedents of organizational commitment

*Antecedents of affective commitment*

Job challenge: In general, the work I am given to do at my organization is challenging and exciting

Role clarity: This organization always makes clear what is expected of me

Goal clarity: In my organization, I often find myself working on assignments without a clear understanding of what it is I am supposed to be doing (R)

Goal difficulty: The requirements of my job are not particularly demanding (R)

Management receptiveness: The top management people in my organization pay attention to ideas brought to them by other employees

Peer cohesion: Among the people in this organization there are few close relationships (R)

Organizational dependability: I feel I can trust this organization to do what it says it will do

Equity: There are people in this organization who are getting much more than they deserve and others who are getting much less (R)

Personal importance: In this organization you are encouraged to feel that the work you do makes important contributions to the larger aims of the organization

Feedback: I am rarely given feedback concerning my performance on the job (R)

Participation: In my organization, I am allowed to participate in decisions regarding my workload and performance standards

*Antecedents of continuance commitment*

Skills: To what extent do you think the skills and experiences you have obtained at your current organization would be useful at other organizations? That is, how many of these skills/experiences would 'transfer' from one organization to another?

Education: My formal education would not be very useful if I was working anywhere but at this or a very similar organization (R)

Relocate: If you were to leave your organization, do you think you would have to move to a different location?

Self-investment: I have had to invest a great deal of time and effort in this organization ('learning the ropes', etc.)

Pension: If you were to leave your current organization now, would you lose any of the retirement funds you would have received if you stayed with the organization?

Community: Approximately how long have you resided in the local area? (Response to this item was divided by the respondent's age.)

Alternatives: If I were to leave this organization, I would have little difficulty finding a comparable or better job elsewhere

*Antecedent of normative commitment*

Organizational commitment norm: Employees in this organization are expected to have a strong sense of personal commitment to the organization

*Note.* Reverse keyed items are indicated by (R). With the exception of the community variable, all items had seven-point response scales.

# 11
# WHEN CASHIERS MEET CUSTOMERS
## An analysis of the role of supermarket cashiers

*Anat Rafaeli*

Source: *Academy of Management Journal* 32(2) (1989): 245–273.

### Abstract

In a qualitative investigation of the role of supermarket cashiers, the influence of management, co-workers, and customers over cashiers was analyzed. Customers had immediate influence over cashiers at the time of job performance; management influence was more legitimate but more remote. The analysis further revealed that cashiers and customers held different views on who had the right to control service encounters and that cashiers employed various strategies to maintain their control of those encounters.

The customer is paying for the merchandise. But he is not paying my salary. Why does he think he can tell me what to do?
—a supermarket cashier

Service organizations and "service encounters" (Czepiel, Solomon, & Surprenant, 1985) are an inevitable part of modern life. We can hardly get through a day without engaging in a service transaction—with a bank, a grocery store, or the phone company. In view of this social trend, management theoreticians and practitioners are also trying to understand, and improve, the context of service (Albrecht & Zemke, 1985; Czepiel et al., 1985; Desatnick, 1987; Hochschild, 1983).

Key participants in any service transaction are service employees. It is they whom customers meet on entering a department store or boarding an aircraft. Thus, a single employee may tint a customer's image of a service enterprise. Indeed, research has documented that service employees can be important to promoting organizational goals. Schneider, Parkington, and Buxton (1980), for example, reported that bank employees' perceptions of the organization they work for are closely related to customers' perceptions of the quality of service that the organization provides. Moreover, Sutton and Rafaeli (1988) found a complex relationship between the behavior of clerks in convenience stores and organizational sales.

Some evidence has also suggested that organizational strategies can manipulate the external facade that service employees convey. In particular, Hochschild (1983) reported that the gracious behavior of flight attendants and the aggressiveness of bill collectors is largely attributable to the man-dates of their management. Rafaeli and Sutton (1987) extended Hochschild's (1983) work and illustrated how service organizations attempt to shape their organizational image by monitoring and controlling the emotions that their employees convey.

Nonetheless, a host of issues about service contexts and service employees remain unexamined. There is a consensus that service is bad (Russel, 1987), but there isn't much agreement about how it can be improved.

One critical question concerns the relationship between employee-customer dynamics and the attainment of organizational goals. Marketing experts have long acknowledged the influence of this relationship over consumer behavior and resultant organizational profits. In *Personal Selling*, for example, Jacoby and Craig addressed the question, "How can the salesperson influence the customer to buy?" (1984: 1). Jacoby and Craig discussed strategies that salespeople use for persuasion and influence and contended that interpersonal attraction affects selling effectiveness.

There is also initial evidence that, because service occupations are boundary spanning (Adams, 1976; Bowen & Schneider, 1985), interactions with customers hold special qualities for service employees. Lombard (1955) reported how salespeople took a customer's rejection of merchandise as a personal rejection of themselves. Similarly, Whyte (1948) related the personal aggravation, sometimes to the point of crying, that waitresses felt when customers did not leave a tip.

Whyte (1948) and later Mars and Nicod (1984) argued that the relationship between waiters or waitresses and their customers is especially complex because of the conflict between servers' interest in controlling service encounters and their desire that customers feel good about the service and leave large tips. In his famous restaurant study, Whyte referred to the waitresses' struggle to "get the jump" on the customers (1948: 132–133). Butler and Snizek (1976) documented how this struggle can affect a waitress's tip. Mars and Nicod later generalized the notion to a discussion of "the politics of service" (1984: 65).

Whyte (1948), Butler and Snizek (1976), and Mars and Nicod (1984) examined only restaurant employees. Nonetheless, their reasoning suggests that other service organizations may benefit from considering the special complexities of transactions with customers. The present study extended that notion. My goal was to place another stone on the path toward improved service by offering a close examination of the role of service employees and their interaction with customers. Understanding the role of service employees should promote the development of knowledge and theory about service operations.

The initial goal of the study was to understand the relationship between service employees and various members of their organizations.[1] For the sake of simplicity, I chose a very mundane service context—that of supermarket checkout clerks. Relationships between cashiers and customers were initially perceived as one part of a web of relationships involving various other parties, including management and co-workers. As the study evolved, however, customers emerged as having a unique role in shaping cashiers' "role set" (Biddle, 1979; Katz & Kahn, 1978: 188–192; Merton, 1957). Customers were found to have a great degree of immediate influence while cashiers are on the job; management's influence on the other hand, was legitimate, but remote. The work of Marks and Mirvis (1981) and Trist (1977) would suggest that customers constitute the transactional environment of supermarket employees and therefore affect behavior at the time of task execution. In contrast, management authority only sets the general tone of the environment and affects extreme behaviors of service employees, notably those governed by rules.

Unraveling the reasons for the immediate cashier-customer relationship was therefore an objective. Observations of the cashiers studied suggested that the immediacy of the clerk-customer relationship creates a certain tautness. Closer scrutiny revealed a tension about who was in control. Thus, as in the findings of Whyte (1948) and of Mars and Nicod (1984), the struggle for control between cashiers and customers seemed to strain the checkout process. Cashiers and customers had very different perceptions of who had the right to control this process. And cashiers, who considered the checkout process a part of their job, were observed to develop strategies to maintain control of their encounters with customers.

The study described was inductive (Glaser & Strauss, 1967). My goal was to conduct an in-depth investigation of a set of people employed in a service job, in the interest of advancing the development of theory on the service encounter. Because of the logic of inductive research (Glaser & Strauss, 1967), the methodology employed is first described; the insights and theory that emerged from the analysis of the data then follow.

## Methods

A qualitative study was conducted in a chain of supermarkets in Jerusalem, Israel, during the winter and spring of 1986. The individuals studied were cashiers and customers in six stores that were randomly selected from all the chain's stores in Jerusalem.

### *The research context: supermarkets in Israel*

Supermarket technology in Israel is similar to that in the United States: a multibrand product assortment of foods and nonfoods, a large physical scale, a large sales volume, and self-service are typical features of supermarkets (Goldman, 1981;

Rachman, 1975). After loading their carts with desired items, customers wait in line until a cashier processes the purchases and accepts payment. Cash registers are automated; cashiers type in the code of an item and the register rings up the price. Electronic scanners are still rare in Israel; only one of the stores included in the study had them. Pay for cashiers is low, usually around the minimum wage.

Four distinct attributes of Israeli supermarkets should be noted. First, Israeli customers pack their own purchases. Customers are expected to bring their own shopping bags and to pack each item right after a cashier has processed it as counters by the cash registers are usually small. Second, Israeli supermarkets offer a home delivery service, usually for a nominal fee. When this service is requested, it is the cashier's responsibility to pack the merchandise in a large plastic crate. Third, in Israel, going to a farmers' market is the prevalent alternative to supermarket shopping; such shopping is considered cheaper but less convenient. Fourth, consumer rights and the concept of service are not as developed in Israel as they are elsewhere in the West. Cashiers and other service employees are often argumentative, and rudeness is common.

Jerusalem is a large, cosmopolitan city. Most supermarket shoppers are permanent residents, although there are also tourists and students. The city has rich and poor neighborhoods, but the diversity is not extreme. Supermarkets and shoppers in Jerusalem are representative of Israel as a whole.

All the observed supermarkets employed a store manager, a head cashier, and 8–15 cashiers. All the store managers studied were men and all the head cashiers and cashiers were women.[2] Personnel files indicated that this was representative of the organization. Store managers were the official supervisors of all store employees and were also responsible for other aspects of store performance, including ordering merchandise and dealing with vendors. Thus, managers were the top authority for cashiers. Managers did, on occasion, order cashiers back to their registers or discuss work schedules with them; such monitoring was, however, the direct responsibility of head cashiers.

Head cashiers, the direct supervisors of line cashiers, were usually senior cashiers who had been promoted. Head cashiers were also responsible for collecting and counting the money from the various registers. Head cashiers usually sat in the manager's office, answered the phone, went over work schedules, and did other administrative chores; only rarely (once or twice during the day) would a head cashier walk "down" to the registers.[3]

## *Data collection and analysis*

Data collection included unstructured observations of cashiers and customers, participant observation as a cashier, interviews with cashiers, and interviews with customers. I conducted the observations and interviews in Hebrew but took notes and developed thoughts and theory throughout the study in English. Research notes did not name individuals; when it was necessary—where repeated references to a particular cashier were desired—specific cashiers were coded by a letter or a set of letters to ensure confidentiality of the data.

I did most of the data collection and analysis, employing research assistants as needed in various portions of the study. One assistant made unstructured observations. Two other assistants helped in the process of data analysis by working with me on categorizing incidents and phenomena and participating in brainstorming sessions.

*Unstructured observations* were conducted in all six stores. Observation times were predetermined to ensure appropriate time sampling. Store hours in Israel are 7:30 a.m.—1:00 p.m. and 3:30 p.m.—7:00 p.m.; observations were planned so that each store was visited once during early morning, once during late morning, once during early afternoon, and once during late afternoon. Additional visits were conducted, one in each store, after the initial round of observations was completed. These visits were randomly spaced throughout the day.

Observations were conducted in a nonobtrusive manner, and each lasted 30–45 minutes; the exact duration of an observation could not be predetermined because the observers did not want to evoke suspicion. After entering the store, an observer usually walked around the aisles for a few minutes and then stopped at the magazine rack or the chocolate rack as if searching for an item; these racks are usually close to the checkout area and offer a good vantage point for observation of cashiers and customers. After selecting an item, the observer stood in one of the lines and continued to observe the cashier and the customers. If the lines were short, the observer acted as if she had forgotten to buy something and walked out of the line and back into the store.[4] After a few minutes she again began to stand in line. After her order had been processed, the observer stood behind the cash register area, as if waiting for someone. Because of the size of the stores and the heavy influx of customers, this process did not seem to evoke suspicion.

The management of the corporation was advised that such observations would possibly be conducted; store managers, however, were not informed about specific store visits. Considering the public nature of the behaviors observed, it does not seem that there is an ethical question about such observations (Mintzberg, 1979; Salancik, 1979; Webb, Campbell, Schwartz, Sechrest, & Grove, 1981).

A second form of data collection involved *participant observation*. I went through the process of applying, training, and working as a cashier.[5] The participant observation consisted of three months of part-time employment for about 18 hours a week. My part-time, short-term status was not unusual; about 60 percent of the cashiers in this chain are employed part-time, and turnover among cashiers is high, up to 50 percent a year. Detailed field notes, in English, were taken after each shift of participant observation.

*Semistructured interviews* with cashiers were the third means of data collection. I conducted interviews with a random sample of 30 cashiers employed in stores other than the one in which the participant observation was conducted. The sample was stratified by age and tenure. The interview included general questions about the work as well as questions probing perceptions of customers and customer behavior. The interview also asked about two critical incidents (Flanagan, 1954) involving customer attempts to influence cashiers. Cashiers were asked how they would react to the following two incidents that had been observed during the unstructured observation phase of the data collection: 1) A customer said to a cashier, "How can you wear three earrings on one ear. That is ridiculous." 2) A customer said to a cashier, "Will you stop talking and start working! You're wasting everyone's time." The Appendix gives the complete interview schedule.

Interviews, which were conducted on store premises during the employee's shift hours, each lasted 45–90 minutes; the motivation and participation levels of the interviewee determined the exact length. All interviews were conducted in one session, in Hebrew, and were tape-recorded. I summarized notes from these interviews in English. I also interviewed store managers and head cashiers, using an adapted version of the cashier's interview schedule.

Semistructured interviews with customers were also conducted. I interviewed 30 men and women who had shopped in one of the stores, 5 from each store. I approached customers after they had finished their shopping and asked them if they were willing to participate in the study, telling them that they would be asked to discuss their shopping experience. Customers who agreed to be interviewed (about 60 percent of those who were approached) were invited for a cup of coffee at a nearby coffee shop. Of the customers interviewed, 21 (70%) were women. The interviewees' ages ranged from 32 to 65. The Appendix also presents the schedule for the interviews with customers.

*Data analysis* began with unstructured brainstorming sessions among members of the research team and proceeded following Miles's proposals for qualitative data analysis (Miles, 1983; Miles & Huberman, 1984). Miles did not offer a structured sequence of steps to guide such analyses. Rather, he suggested continuous conceptual development throughout projects. Specifically, he discussed a process of "intertwining of analysis and data collection, in an attempt to formulate classes of phenomena, and to identify themes in the data" (1983: 126). Three specific rules of thumb proposed by Miles guided the present analysis: examining whether any particular generalization held true for different people or occasions, testing all possible implications of any one proposition, and examining closely any extreme bias cases (Miles, 1983: 127).

The analysis started with a rough working framework: understanding the relationship between the observed service employees (cashiers) and various members of their role set. We went back and forth between the emerging theory and the data and mostly attempted to let ideas stimulated by the sites and the data revise and reshape the general framework. This process revealed the set of relations that a cashier encounters.

An attempt to understand the qualitative difference between customers, managers, and co-workers followed. This phase included repeated references to the notes from the various data sources. I followed an iterative process of systematically going back and forth between theoretical insights and data. The goal of the process, which followed the recommendations of Glaser and Strauss (1967), was to verify support of theoretical developments and search for inconsistencies between new insights and the data.

This iterative process suggested that, compared to their relationships with their managers and co-workers, cashiers spent more time with customers, were physically closer to customers, and got more feedback and information from customers. Cashiers also viewed customers as more crucial than managers or co-workers. In short, customers appeared to have immediate influence over cashiers, and management's influence, although perceived as legitimate, was remote.

During the iterative process, the importance of control for both cashiers and customers began to emerge. In light of previous writings on the importance of control, which I encountered in a preliminary literature review, I pursued a closer focus on the dynamics of control over the observed service encounters. This focus suggested interesting and important differences between cashiers' and customers' perceptions of the right to control the encounters. Thus, another round of data-scanning was necessary to search for support and inconsistencies between theoretical insights on the struggle for control and the data. During the process of refining the theoretical implications of the data, I also drew on feedback from colleagues and organizational contacts.

To familiarize the reader with the socialization of supermarket cashiers, a brief overview of the process of becoming a cashier follows. Next, the set of relations a cashier encounters on the job is presented. The differences between the influence role of customers and that of management, and cashiers' and customers' perceptions of control of service encounters are then examined. Finally, I present a typology of strategies employed by cashiers to gain control of interactions with customers.

## Findings

### *The process of becoming a cashier*

Learning how to be a cashier was, in my experience, an extremely informal process. Table 1 summarizes the various stages of the socialization process through the end of my first day of participant observation. As can be seen, I spent less than a half hour with the various members of the organizational hierarchy, other than peers or customers.

The formal socialization began with a brief meeting with the personnel manager of the corporation about two weeks before the participant observation started. The meeting consisted of a few personal questions and assignment to a store. After the meeting a secretary asked me to take a short screening test, which mostly concerned knowledge of arithmetic, and had me sign a form labeled "Basic Rules of Cashier Behavior." This form included ten rules of behavior; I later learned that,

*Table 1* Cashier socialization process up to the end of the first day of the participant observation

| Stage | Approximate duration |
|---|---|
| Telephone call to head office | 2 minutes |
| Meeting with personnel manager | 13 minutes |
| Meeting with store manager | 2 minutes |
| Waiting | 7 minutes |
| Meeting with head cashier | 5 minutes |
| Session with training cashier and customers | 3¾ hours |
| Time spent with other cashiers and employees | 20 minutes |

among cashiers, the form is nicknamed the "Ten Commandments." The Appendix displays these rules.

The encounter with the formal organization also included a two-minute meeting with the store manager who basically said "See the head cashier," and a five minute talk with the head cashier, who gave me a general introduction to the store including information on store hours, instructions on how to punch the time clock, and about where to put my coat and purse, and a very brief and informal introduction to my "trainer," an older woman with 16 years of experience on the job. The shortness of my interaction with members of the formal hierarchy contrasted sharply with the three and three-quarter hours I spent with customers on the very first day. These hours were spent standing behind the cashier who had been designated as my trainer. She explained that she was often selected as a trainer for new cashiers because she "enjoyed it and also knew the work really well." Nonetheless, it was quite quickly evident that she had little structured, formal training to offer. After a few minutes of "This is the register," "See, there are special keys for produce, drinks, meats," and "You need to learn the codes for the various items," she said "OK, now you can watch me work"; she then went on to "pass customers through,"[6] expecting me to continue watching.

During the training period, the trainer occasionally reentered her training role. For instance, pulling a large notebook from her drawer, she said "Here are all the codes for the different items. Take it home and you can learn the codes in the evening." Yet structured training was a rare event, for me and for other trainees who were observed throughout the study; most of the time trainers passed customers through while trainees sat or stood behind them and watched.

In short, in the process of becoming a cashier, there was little structured, formal interaction with the trainer or with management. Because of the store's open-space design, however, there was a lot of unmediated exposure and close physical proximity to customers. Such exposure is an integral part of a cashier's job from the very beginning. It was also the first clue to the differences between the various role senders, that is, the various holders of expectations about the cashiers' role (Katz & Kahn, 1978: 190).

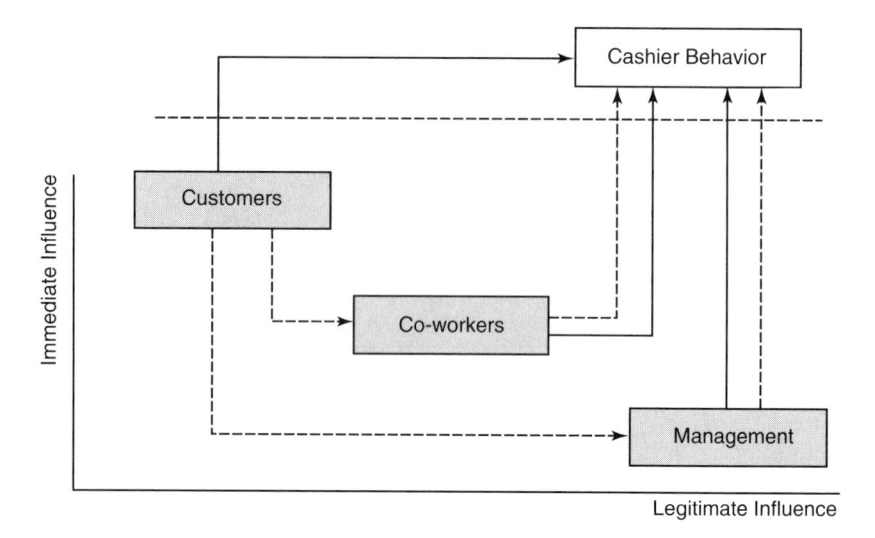

*Figure 1* Parties and dynamics driving cashiers' behavior: customer, co-worker, and management influence.

## *The set of relations that cashiers encounter*

Figure 1 summarizes several aspects of the relationship of customers, co-workers, and management to cashiers. Cashiers were placed outside the figure because the intent is to summarize the relationships of the various other parties to cashiers. Furthermore, the figure displays only relations to cashiers. The solid arrows in Figure 1 imply direct influence. Thus, customers have direct influence over cashiers, as do co-workers and management. The broken lines in Figure 1 indicate indirect influence; customers also have indirect influence over cashiers through other employees and through management.

Figure 1 includes two axes that facilitate the understanding of cashiers' role set. The horizontal axis refers to legitimate influence. The person with formal authority over a cashier—her manager—has the strongest legitimate right to influence the cashier's behavior. The vertical axis in Figure 1 suggests the dimension of immediate influence. The results of this study suggest that customers hold more immediate influence at the time of job performance than either co-workers or management. The immediacy of customer influence is due to the physical proximity between cashiers and customers, the extent of time they spend together, customers' opportunity for supplying direct feedback and other information, and the immediate importance that cashiers attribute to customers.

### *Management power*

The horizontal axis of Figure 1 refers to legitimate influence. In the cashiers' formal organization (Katz & Kahn, 1978), management holds the greatest amount of legitimate influence because it represents the employing organization and has the power to reward (French & Raven, 1960).

Legitimate power belongs to management by definition, and cashiers are well aware of this. Cashiers usually accentuated behavior according to the rules (the Ten Commandments) whenever the manager or assistant manager walked around the register area. Similarly, during my training I was explicitly told, "Sure you can keep a cup at the register. Just be sure he [the manager] doesn't see it." Moreover, implied consent of the manager or the head cashier allowed the breaking of organizational rules. To illustrate, when a cashier wanted to get a pastry from the bakery across the street, she usually asked the manager or the head cashier if he or she would also like something (PO).[7] Because of insurance liability, cashiers were not allowed to leave the store during work hours (PO). But the unwritten rule seemed to be that if a member of management was a party to such activity, "It was OK to do it" (PO).

Management's legitimate influence (Figure 1) is also due to the store manager's apparent control over formal rewards; the manager handed out monthly pay checks and holiday bonuses (PO). Management's reward power is not as strong as it could be since wages in the chain are centrally determined and are not linked to performance. Moreover, the store managers have very little leverage when it comes to personnel policies. However, a manager can fire a cashier, especially if she is caught disobeying rules, and can have an effect on promotions. Thus, cashiers refused to be tape-recorded when they talked about eating or smoking at the register because the Ten Commandments prohibited such activities. As one cashier said, "They could immediately fire me if they knew" (I). Similarly, when one cashier was called to the manager because a customer had reported that she pocketed some money, the other cashiers immediately began to sympathize: "Poor D., now he will fire her" (PO).

As Figure 1 further indicates, customers have no legitimate influence. Co-workers—other cashiers—were, however, occasionally observed to exert a moderate amount of legitimate power. This was rare, but it occurred, for example, when as a newly hired cashier, I felt that my trainer was an authority. Trainers had the authority to decide how well a trainee was doing and when she could begin working alone (PO, I). I also heard a senior cashier urge a younger co-worker to "work more quickly, stop talking to your friends, can't you see that there is a long line waiting?" (PO). The younger cashier clearly reacted to this comment by focusing more directly on her register and discontinuing her conversation with her friend; she also said to her friend (casually, but in a very soft voice), "She [the more senior cashier] is almost like the manager around here" (UO).

Occasionally, customers might also attempt to influence cashiers' rewards. But such attempts have to operate through co-workers or management, as implied by the broken arrows in Figure 1. In order to punish a cashier who pocketed money, a customer had to report the incident to the manager (PO); the cashier in this event was ultimately fired. Similarly, when customers wanted to reward cashiers for desirable behavior, they commented about it to the manager or to other cashiers.

To illustrate, several customers said to me while I was in training: "You really have a very good trainer; she is the best one around." This was always said when my trainer was around, and in a loud enough voice so that she could hear. Thus, it was a form of indirectly complementing the trainer. Along similar lines, one customer was heard saying to a manager who happened to be standing by a cash register, "You should really do something for her; give her a bonus or something; she does such a good job" (UO).

### Customer power

The vertical axis of Figure 1 suggests that customers, and therefore customer influence, are much more immediate than management and management influence. Co-workers, in turn, have more immediate influence over cashiers than management, but less than customers. Five factors cause this immediacy: physical proximity, the amount of time customers and cashiers spend together, the amount of feedback customers give, the amount of information they provide, and the crucial role cashiers attribute to customers. The following examines each of these factors in detail.

Cashiers are physically much closer to their customers than to anyone else. About 25 inches separate a cashier and her customer, as opposed to the 80 inches or more separating two cashiers. Management is very remote, usually many yards away. The physical structure of supermarkets means that cashiers have little opportunity to interact with each other or with management without an audience of customers.

Moreover, cashiers usually view other cashiers either from the back (during training) or from the side. They view management from below (see Note 3), or from far away. In contrast, there is constant frontal contact with customers. To gain the physical proximity that people enjoy, a cashier has to leave her work station and walk over to whomever she wishes to meet. That is, she must stop her work. Customers resent such breaks, as does management (I, CI). Thus, because of the physical structure of the supermarkets, cashiers can easily and continuously get verbal and nonverbal messages from customers. Communication with co-workers and with management is more difficult than it is with customers, and it is much less intimate since it is usually in front of an audience.

In short, the physical layout of supermarket work constrains interpersonal relationships among cashiers and makes customers the most immediate source of communication. Throughout the study I observed that the physical layout makes for little informal interaction among cashiers and that the informal network of relations among cashiers was very weak. To illustrate, approximately two hours of my first participant observation shift had passed before any of the other cashiers asked my name. By the end of the participant observation, I had not managed to collect much information about the other cashiers. I barely knew the names of all the other cashiers. I knew little about their personal lives. Likewise, they knew very little about me.

Several cashiers specifically mentioned that the physical distance between cashiers, combined with the noise and hustle in the store, usually do not allow interaction among cashiers or between cashiers and management (PO, I). Indeed, during the participant observation, it was often impossible to talk to cashiers while they were working. One cashier said,

> You need to talk to someone. And the only one you can talk to is customers. But if you talk to them too much you can make mistakes (I).

A second reason for the greater immediacy of customer influence is the amount of time cashiers spend with customers, compared to the amount of time they spend with any of the other members of their role set. This was first evident from the extremely brief formal socialization procedure encountered in the process of becoming a cashier (see Table 1).

Observations of cashiers during their routine work revealed a pattern similar to that encountered on my first day and reported in Table 1. Approximately 78 percent of cashiers' time was spent interacting with customers; only 13 percent of their time was spent interacting with management, including task-related interactions, such as verifying a price or getting change. The constant interaction with others was an attractive job attribute for many cashiers:

> I looked for a job where I would be with people. I couldn't see myself in an office job (I).
> I liked the fact that there would be a lot of people around me. Otherwise I would get bored (I).

Nonetheless, once she has started working, a cashier may find it burdensome that the customers are constantly there.

Cashiers spend most of their time with customers because that is the way their work is structured. They are instructed to work independently; what one cashier does is usually relevant only to customers, and a cashier is expected to be equipped to deal with most customer needs. Certain events do require a cashier to interact with management or co-workers (e.g., verifying a price, getting check approval, asking for a break), but walking over to a fellow employee for a friendly chat is clearly a waste of time that interferes with the work.

Events that include interacting with co-workers or with management require time. Such use of time is often unpleasant to the cashiers because customers view it as a waste of time (UO, CI). One cashier summarized this feeling well: "What do I care how I pass my eight hours, but the customers get really angry when things move really slowly or if I have to leave the register" (UO). Thus, cashiers try to avoid "wasting" their time dealing with management or other store employees. To illustrate, cashiers expressed annoyance when customers changed their mind about purchases, and the head cashier had to be called for a cancellation (PO, UO). Many cashiers were aggravated when their registers seemed stuck for some reason and they had to call for help (UO, PO). Likewise, upon encountering an unmarked item, many cashiers relied on the price that the customer reported, rather than asking a co-worker or the manager (UO). Several cashiers specifically mentioned that they encouraged customers to pay cash to avoid spending the time to get checks approved:

> For checks I have to get approval and it wastes time; but I can get in trouble if I don't get approval. So I like cash, only cash (I).

A third reason for the greater immediacy of customer influence is the amount and immediacy of the feedback that customers provide. The physical proximity between cashiers and customers increases the degree of verbal and nonverbal communication between them. The great amount of time that cashiers spend with customers also increases the probability of such communication. Thus, customers have the opportunity to provide cashiers with immediate positive or negative feedback.

Comments like "Oh, that is really nice of you" (PO) and "You work so fast" (UO) constitute positive feedback; "Your check-out is slower than all the other ones, you know" (UO) and "Why can't you be more polite" (PO) are examples of immediate negative feedback from customers. In contrast, management gives inconsistent, delayed, partial feedback that previous research has shown to have less powerful effects than immediate feedback (Hilgard & Bowers, 1975).

Customers' attempts to discourage cashiers from interacting with other cashiers or with management are another form of feedback. Customers make such attempts because they resent the "time wasted" (UO, I). They often try to persuade cashiers that it is unnecessary to take this time, saying "It is OK, the check is OK, you don't have to waste time getting approval" (UO) or "Why do you have to keep running back and forth to the office? It is such a waste of time" (UO).

Customers may also offer information that a cashier wants but cannot get elsewhere on her job. Since cashiers attend to customers in order to get this information, the stage is set for immediate customer influence. Customers offer three types of information: work-related information, general knowledge, and information about their status that may help cashiers elevate their self-attributed status.

First, customers may offer information that helps a cashier continue her work, such as information about the price or code of an item. Although such information is available elsewhere, obtaining it through the manager or through a co-worker would cause an unwelcome delay.

Second, customers may offer general knowledge that is not work-related. To illustrate, a cashier asked a regular customer[8] who was the owner of a local furniture store how much a rocking chair cost, explaining that she wanted to buy someone a rocking chair as a present (PO). Along similar lines, a cashier asked a customer, "What do you do with this? Do you boil it?" (UO). One cashier presented the opportunity to obtain such information as a positive attribute of the job. She tried to encourage me to feel that the job was not as boring as it seemed:

> After a while, after you learn how to work the cash register, it gets to be fun. You can talk to the customers and you can learn from them how to cook different things. You'll see (PO).

Third, customers may offer information that helps cashiers elevate their self-perceived status. Goodsell (1976) documented that service employees clearly observe customer status cues. There were several indications here that cashiers derived status from the status of their customers. The head cashier's introduction to the store in which I conducted the participant observation was very brief (see Table 1), but it included the comment "You know, this is an important store, and very important people shop here, including people from [the local] TV [network]" (PO). Similary, an interviewed cashier said, "We have some really famous customers here, and some of them buy on credit, without even paying, like the prime minister's house and the president's house."

Moreover, when asked "Who are your favorite customers," several cashiers responded by referring to a high-status person: "this professor who shops here with his wife" (I) or "the president's house" (I). Another cashier gave a more general response:

> ... people that have style. Some people just look classy. You know, they are dressed well and they know how to behave. I like them. It is respectable to work with them (I).

It is as if the status of the client raises the status of the clerk.

Finally, the immediacy of customer influence is enhanced because cashiers view customers as crucial. Cashiers summarized this notion:

> We should always try to keep the customers happy. Sometimes I even sing to them. And if I see a customer leave a full cart by my register and prepare to leave the store I call him and try to convince him to stay. Because if the customers leave us, where will we be? They make the store. They make my salary (I).
>
> Without the customers the store would never exist. Without the cashiers it might be hard. Without the manager—we get along, and you can always find a replacement for cashiers or managers. But not without the customers. They make the money (I).

In sum, although management's legitimate influence allows it to have a certain degree of remote control over cashiers, several factors set the customers apart as having the potential for immediate influence over cashiers. Management plans and rules may set the stage for the interaction between a cashier and her customer, but because of their physical proximity, the amount of time spent together, the flow of feedback and information, and the crucial role cashiers attribute to customers, it is the cashier and the customer who determine how this interaction unfolds.

## *The struggle for control between cashiers and customers*

As mentioned above, the interaction with customers was an attractive job attribute for many cashiers. The constant exposure to customers, however, may be more than was bargained for. Specifically, customers' perspective on the interaction with cashiers appears to be qualitatively different from cashiers' perceptions of the same interaction. As one cashier said, "He is one of the customers and I have to pass him through and take money from him" (I). In contrast, customers said "I am paying, so I should get service" (CI) and "Since it is my time, don't I have a right to try and avoid wasting it?" (CI). What emerges is a struggle for control of the interaction.

### *Service encounters: customers' perspective*

The data suggested two key resources that guide customers' perceptions of service encounters in the supermarket: money and time. Customers who have given or are about to give money expect to get something in return. Customers may enjoy spending time selecting merchandise, but they resent time spent waiting for a cashier.

As far as customers are concerned, they are paying not only for merchandise but also for service:

> When I go to the market all I want is good, cheap stuff. But a supermarket is supposed to offer something more. You pay more. So you should at least get a pleasant shopping experience (CI).
> Why can't you be more polite? I am paying! And *you* are serving *me* you know! (UO).

Moreover, customers often view cashiers as liaisons between the retail organization and themselves: "She works for the organization, doesn't she?" (CI) and "She's the only one from the store that I get to talk to" (CI). Since they pay the organization, customers expect to have some say about how it functions. Thus, customers may comment to a cashier about things that are obviously not part of her job: "Why are shopping bags so expensive here?" (PO) or "Why don't they get those imported sardines anymore?" (UO). This is the only opportunity that customers see to influence the organization. Since customers are paying, they believe that the organization and its representatives—the cashiers—should deliver (CI).

From a customer's point of view, cashiers also determine how much money the customer must part with. Because money is very important, customers see themselves as having a right to monitor and control its expenditure. Customers were often suspicious that they were being cheated, as these comments from my interviews with them show:

> Cashiers always steal.
>
> You always have to watch over them carefully.
>
> It's real easy for them to overcharge. You never have time to watch when they type the stuff. And every time I check the slip I find some error.

I also observed customers saying:

> Please slow down. Last time they cheated me so I want to see what you type (PO).
>
> Can't you wait so I can watch what you do? (UO).

It was hard, if not impossible, to assess the extent to which cashiers actually engaged in cheating (Mars, 1984). Over 80 percent of the incidents noted in the present study in which customers asked to check a price or a sales slip indicated no fault on the cashier's part. Nonetheless, the point is that since the customers are paying, they feel they have a right to monitor and control how much is paid, which implies monitoring and controlling the cashiers' behavior.

As with money, the desire to save time also drives customers to monitor the cashiers. The checking out process often causes bottlenecks in the store. Customers are forced to stand, wait, and do nothing while a cashier processes orders. Such waiting is a nuisance (Maister, 1985). Indeed, customers waiting in line were often annoyed, angry, and helpless; the aggressive reactions mentioned in Seligman's (1975) discussion of helplessness were frequently evident. To illustrate:

> I can't stand it. Why can't they open another register? [very aggressive tone of voice] (UO).
>
> I don't believe it [to a cashier who didn't know a code]. You sit here all day and you don't know the code for potatoes? As if this is something unusual! (UO).

Exhibiting behavior that is consistent with Maister's (1985) observations on the psychology of waiting in line, customers seek means to shorten their objective or subjective waits. They may do this by suggesting to cashiers various mechanisms for saving time. They also try to do things instead of letting the cashiers do them. I saw customers packing delivery crates (the cashiers' job), going to the shelves to check a price or a code, placing fruit and vegetables on the scale to be weighed, or placing items so the codes were easily visible (UO, PO). One customer tried to create group support, saying to other people waiting in line "Come on, let's help her, if we help her maybe things will move along a little bit more quickly" (UO). The following incident, which occurred during the participant observation, is also illustrative:

> One customer could not find her checkbook, and seemed to be "wasting everybody's time" looking for it. Customers waiting in line put pressure on the cashier to start processing their orders; they glared at the cashier and glared at the customer. They offered suggestions about where the checkbook might be or sugested that maybe she could pay with a credit card. Then they began requesting that the cashier process the next customer's order while this woman was looking for her checkbook. One customer attempted to explain to the cashier that such a move would be logical. He said, "Since she is paying with a check, when she finds her checkbook you can take it from her."

In sum, because of the time and money involved, customers seek, and see themselves as having a right, to control their encounter with a cashier.

### Service encounters: cashiers' perspective

Customers' intense involvement in the service encounters studied creates resistance and resentment among cashiers. As suggested by the quote at the beginning of this article, cashiers realize that customers want to control them, but they are not willing to relinquish control of the encounters. Cashiers seek control of service encounters because they feel they need and have a right to this control in order to do their job.

Cashiers perceive their main responsibilities to be to "pass customers through" (I) and "take money and give change" (I), functions requiring a fair amount of concentration. A cashier needs to recall the codes or prices of many unmarked items, to verify that she has entered the correct information into the register, to count the money she receives, and to count the change she gives out. At the same time, she needs to keep track of which items she has entered and to guard against customer theft. These tasks entail a responsibility, and errors may be personally costly to the cashier since cash differences can be deducted from her salary. Cashiers seek to maintain control over the checkout process in order to avoid errors.

Customers' attempts to control an encounter can also be offensive to cashiers. The consensus among cashiers is that they know best how to do the job, even though customers sometimes try to tell them otherwise:

> It is my job. I know best how to do it (I).

> He thinks that because he shops here he can run things. But I am here every day. It's my job. I know how to do it. And it drives me nuts when he tells me what to do (I).

Thus, when customers attempt to monitor cashiers' behavior and to tell them what to do, cashiers seek ways to establish who is in control.

There is also a strong theoretical rationale behind cashiers' struggle for control. Extensive research has discussed the psychological importance of personal control (Langer, 1983; Seligman, 1975; Sutton & Kahn, 1986). Goffman (1959) argued that control over an individual's immediate environment is especially important, explaining that "we seek control over the people in our environment with whom we interact, particularly individuals who are likely to react to us" (1959: 3). Since cashiers constantly interact with customers, it is clear why they struggle to control them. What is intriguing is the way in which this struggle is conducted.

*Strategies in cashiers' struggle for control*

The existing literature on service employee's fight for control (Bigus, 1972; Butler & Snizek, 1976; Mars & Nicod, 1984; Whyte, 1948) was used as a point of departure for developing a typology of the strategies employed by cashiers for reclaiming control of service encounters. The data suggested four such strategies: ignoring customers, rejecting customers' right to control, reacting to customers' attempt at control, and engaging customers so that they don't try to seek control. Table 2 presents examples of the use of each of these strategies. The strategies presented in Table 2 can be viewed as a continuum of actions by cashiers ranging from passive, through reactive, to proactive. Ignoring a customer means taking no action. Rejecting is somewhat more active; it reflects some active thought on the cashier's part about why the customer does not have a right of control. Reacting entails an overt response to a customer's behavior, a response that makes the customer aware that the cashier is annoyed. Finally, engaging is a proactive strategy in which a customer is occupied and thus too busy to demand control.

Ignoring is the most passive strategy. Cashiers can ignore a customer, and frequently do so, by avoiding eye contact. Less than half the cashiers observed during the unstructured observation phase made some form of eye contact with customers. In another study, which included structured observations, 61 percent of the cashiers observed made no eye contact with customers, and an additional 32.8 percent made eye contact only once, for less than one minute (Rafaeli, 1989).

Cashiers may also ignore customers' comments or their attempts to take charge. To illustrate, when customers commented that a cashier should "speed things up" (UO) or "stop talking to your friend" (UO), many cashiers simply continued what they were doing and ignored the comment.

The terminology that cashiers have developed to refer to their interaction with customers is in itself a form of ignoring. As noted earlier, cashiers refer to "passing customers through," an impersonal term that does not acknowledge any individual differences among customers and suggests that a customer is another item to be processed. In actuality, it is the merchandise that cashiers "pass through"; considering a customer as of one the items that is being passed through allows ignoring the customer as a social partner and promotes perceived control of the encounter.

Table 2  Cashiers' strategies in the struggle for control

| Strategies | Source of data | | |
|---|---|---|---|
| | Unstructured observations | Participant observation | Interviews |
| Ignoring | Cashiers focus their eyes on the cash register, avoid eye contact with customers if they can. | Trainer told observer: "Sometimes they say really nasty things about how you should do your work. I think you should ignore them because there is no end to such comments." | "When they tell me what to do, like how many earrings to wear, and I don't want to do it, I simply ignore them and don't listen." |
| Rejecting | No evidence noted. | Cashiers label customers who request continuous monitoring of prices entered "pests" and "naggers." | "He is paying for the merchandise. He is not paying my salary. Why does he think he can tell me what to do?" |
| Reacting | Customer was angry that cashier had to "waste" time looking for a code, started yelling. Cashier tried to calm him down by saying, "Why do you have to yell? Why do you have to talk like that?" | A customer said, "In America, all the cashiers smile." Cashier replied: "So go to America. What do you want from me?" | "After a customer has rushed me through his purchases I love to sit back, cross my arms, watch him, and let everyone see how he is wasting everyone's time now." |
| Engaging | Cashier to customer: "Now if you smile, everything will be OK." Cashiers ask customers to put produce on scale. | Cashier keeps customers busy by telling them what to do: "You can take the bread, now pack the oranges, I typed the coffee." | "If I see that they are upset I might sing. I don't sing that well but it makes them laugh and forget they were angry." |

Ignoring is sometimes a necessary strategy for survival; it enables cashiers to concentrate on their work:

> I feel really stressed at the register, because I don't really know all the codes yet. And then customers come and tell me what to do and I get into even more stress. The only way I can keep going is by ignoring them and going my own way (I).

Cashiers who ignore customers may justify this behavior to themselves by being slightly more active and rejecting the customers' right of control. This strategy entails the internal justification that "the customer has no business telling me what to do" (I). The transition from ignoring to rejecting is not always obvious and may be known only to the cashier herself. Conceptually, the difference is important, however, both because cashiers make the distinction (e.g., "Before I ignore her, I make sure I am right" [I]) and because rejecting implies a more active and involved employee.

Reacting is a yet more active strategy; a cashier not only thinks that a customer has no right of control but also finds a way to convey that to the customer. The reaction may be verbal but emphasized with blatant nonverbal gestures.

A reaction may simply convey rejection; that was the strategy adopted by the following cashier:

> You need to let the customer know that this is how you work and if he doesn't like it he has a problem. If he complains about how I work I don't even bother replying to what he asks. I just say "My name is _____ and you can tell the manager if you don't like me or my work" (I).

It might be noted that this cashier provided legitimacy for her reaction by implying that management will support her behavior.

A reaction may also attempt to convince customers that they are wrong or to dissuade them from an attempt at control. When a customer got upset and started scolding a cashier about not knowing the code for a certain item, she replied,

> Why do you have to yell? Why do you have to talk like that? You think I do it on purpose? You think it will help that you yell? It only slows things down and makes them worse! (UO).

Furthermore, a reply may attempt to calm the customer by expressing agreement. To illustrate, during the participant observation one customer got annoyed that the codes on several items were wrong. The cashier replied,

> Ok. Yes, you are right. They put codes on the items and don't bother to check. But why are you yelling at me? I didn't put the codes on. I am just trying to help you (PO).

Nonverbal components of a reaction may include sitting with folded arms, glaring, and purposefully dropping merchandise. The first was a favorite strategy of a young and very efficient cashier. When asked how she dealt with difficult customers she replied,

> What I love is to finish my work, announce out loud his total, then twiddle my thumbs. It can really embarrass him because everyone can see who is waiting for whom (I).

Reactions may get extreme and may entail raised voices:

> I can't stand the customers who bullshit. It must be something about me, maybe because I have all these personal problems and I got divorced. Maybe it is my personality. But I like working fast. And when they move slowly and they try to slow me down it drives me nuts. And I let them know it in the way I do things, like packing their stuff or giving them change. One time I even yelled at a customer.

Engaging is the most proactive strategy a cashier can adopt. It entails keeping customers busy so that they don't bother her. A cashier may engage customers by telling jokes, making small talk, or asking them to do certain things, such as put their vegetables on the scale to be weighed. Engaging the customers requires extensive experience because a cashier needs to do it while she continues with her routine tasks. Engaging is therefore more frequently evident among senior cashiers, as was apparent from observing and talking to both new and experienced cashiers:

> My mother is also a cashier, so I am lucky. I learned from her how to handle the job and how to handle customers. But still, I feel I need more experience to really know what to do (cashier with four months tenure, PO).
>
> I always keep the customer busy, it helps me with my work and they are happy. I have been on the job for 16 years. I know it really well (I).

One cashier developed an engaging strategy that appeared very sophisticated. She focused her eyes on the register and only glanced at the strip with the items on it, calling out the items she had entered on the register. She constantly told the customer which items to pack while she worked the register. Her communication with the customer mostly included comments such as "You can take the bread" and "OK, I got the coffee." Occasionally, however, she would remind the customer that she was in control by saying "No, wait, I haven't entered the ice cream yet" (PO). The last statement reinforced her control because it verified that she was monitoring the customer's behavior; that is, she was the one in charge.

## Discussion

The goal of this study was to examine closely the role of service employees. This close examination called for a qualitative, in-depth investigation of one group of employees. Previous research has revealed that organizations invest in efforts to monitor the image set by such employees (Hochschild, 1983; Rafaeli & Sutton, 1987), that organizational sales bear a complex relationship to the behavior of these employees (Sutton & Rafaeli, 1988), and that such employees hold a special relationship to their customers (Adams, 1976; McCallum & Harrison, 1985; Mars & Nicod, 1984; Whyte, 1948). The present study placed in focus a central component of the work of service employees—service encounters (Czepiel et al., 1985).

The study suggests four notions relevant to the research and management of service employees. First, the tight interdependence between cashiers and customers suggests that it is important to focus additional research effort on their encounters, rather than on the participants—clerks or customers—singly. Second, the complexity of the role-sending process that cashiers face suggests that a high degree of tension and strain accompany their service encounters. Third, the contrast between the data collected and other research findings on service suggests several paradoxes about service encounters. And fourth, the dynamics that customers inspire in service encounters suggest several threats to service employees and to service organizations.

Customer influence was instantaneous, continuous, and simultaneous with job performance. Moreover, customer influence stimulates cashiers to react in certain ways. Thus, customers form the transactional environment of these service employees (Marks & Mirvis, 1981; Trist, 1977). In contrast, management, which holds legitimate influence, creates the organizational environment and sets the stage for employee's performance. Management is ultimately responsible for setting up service encounters and also bears responsibility for extreme behaviors. For example, management must get involved if rules are broken or money is stolen. But routine service transactions are affected most by an interplay between service employees and their customers. Their interdependence implies the impropriety of studying service employees independently of their customers.

Other authors have written about interdependence in service encounters (McCallum & Harrison, 1984). What emerged here, however, was that such encounters cannot be understood without a full view of both participants and an emphasis on the interaction between them. Thus, the encounters themselves are important units of analysis in the study of service. Most previous writings have emphasized either employees (cf. Hochschild, 1984) or customers (Desatnick, 1987; Peters & Waterman, 1982).

The findings about interdependence suggest a new research question: How much interpersonal interaction is beneficial and motivating? Job design theoreticians (e.g., Sims, Szilagyi, & Keller, 1976) have argued that the opportunity for interacting with others is a positive job attribute. Indeed, employees may enjoy constant exposure to, and interaction with, clients. As discussed above, however, constant exposure can also be a burden. It is unclear to what extent dealing with others is desirable when the others pose a threat and introduce strain. Too much interaction may not be highly positive and may be a source of frustration.

A second question raised by the findings on interdependence is how customers fit into organizational theory. Customers' role as active participants reinforces the notion that there is room to study the management of customers (Bowen, 1988) because they are actually "partial employees" (Mills & Morris, 1986: 726). Bowen (1988: 2) suggested applying Vroom's (1964) model of employee performance to the assessment of customer performance and noted some questions that such an application raises: Do customers understand how they are expected to perform? Are they able to perform as expected? And are there valued rewards for performing as expected?

The present study also suggests various constraints that introduce tension into service encounters and put a strain on service employees. Four such constraints come to mind: employee's inability to develop a strong social network with co-workers, the limited and constrained nature of relations with customers, the role conflict and ambiguity resulting from a multiply defined role, and the constant struggle for control with customers.

Social frustration was not the focus of the present study. Nonetheless, customers were observed to hinder the development of an informal network among cashiers. Thus, it is likely that cashier's social needs remain frustrated because it is difficult to imagine that the weak set of interpersonal relations evident among the cashiers studied could fulfill social needs.

A second source of strain is the constrained nature of interactions with customers. Cashiers themselves may desire interaction with customers to experience some form of social interaction. (Recall the cashier who said "The only one you can talk to is the customer.") In this case, however, strain may arise as the result of the very short, superficial interactions with a long line of only vaguely familiar people, circumstances that hardly constitute a social network.

Informal interactions between cashiers and customers can create a stressful service encounter if they detract from the cashiers' ability to concentrate on the monetary components of the job, and cause errors. Perhaps customers' suspiciousness about theft is attributable to such swaying of the cashiers' attention. Furthermore, informal interaction with customers may also generate customers' resistance if they view it as a waste of time (Sutton & Rafaeli, 1988).

Service employees may also suffer strain because of the role ambiguity and role conflict associated with multiple role senders (Kahn, Wolfe, Quinn, & Snoek, 1981; Miles & Perreault, 1976; Parkington, 1979; Shamir, 1980). Customer expectations and comments were sometimes found to run counter to management rules (e.g., there is no need to get a check approved), setting the stage for role conflict. Similarly, there is a fair extent of ambiguity about customer service. The Ten Commandments, the organization's rules for cashiers, did not mention good-quality service, yet customers felt they were paying for good service and conveyed to cashiers that they expected it. The difference in the quality of management's and customers' influence likely exacerbates the strain of the conflict between role senders. It is as if a cashier needs to choose between the immediate, current demands of customers and the formal, but, remote influence of management.

The disagreement about control is also a source of tension in the service encounters observed at the supermarkets. Customers feel they have a right to control these encounters, but cashiers view the encounters as part of their job and engage in a struggle to destroy customer control. In short, the presence of customers constrains the cashiers' interaction with other people and is itself accompanied by a struggle, all of which provides fertile ground for tension and strain.

The tight interdependence between cashiers and customers and the tension inherent in the observed service encounters also suggest several paradoxes about the concept of service. First, it is paradoxical that service employees, who face customer demands all day, actually have very little autonomy to deal with those demands. Second, from the customers' point of view it is paradoxical that the only representative of the organization with whom they interact has so little leeway; the cashiers take the customers' money but can do little more than take money.

Third, from the cashiers' perspective, it is paradoxical that their interpersonal relations at work are so weak and superficial, in spite of their constant exposure to, and interaction with, other people. Of course, the fact that the constant interaction consists of many short interactions with hurried customers who do not view themselves as cashiers' social partners accounts for the paradox; nonetheless, it sheds light on the complexities of service encounters.

Fourth, the strategies developed by cashiers to establish their control of service encounters also pose a paradox. Many of the cashiers observed reinforced a consensus that exists among career counselors, that people who go into service occupations seek and enjoy interpersonal interactions (cf. Osipow, 1973). At the same time, this group of service employees was busy developing strategies to unnerve the people with whom they interacted.

Finally, it is paradoxical that although popular authors concerned with organizational management recommend that organizations, and in particular, service employees, keep "close to the customer" (Peters & Waterman, 1982: 156), in reality, employees often must tune out customer communication in order to pay close attention to the financial details of their work. Worse yet, some service employees intentionally engage their customers in behavior that conforms with their own needs rather than customer needs.

Customers may actually pose a threat to service employees and organizations. Errors and losses may occur when customers divert attention from a cash register or when they try to sway cashiers from complying with organizational rules. Furthermore, cashiers may perceive customers as a threat because they claim to have the right to control the cashiers' work and sometimes use indirect channels to punish cashiers (recall the cashier who was fired because a customer reported that she put money in her purse).

Organizations may also incur indirect costs because of the struggle for control. Obviously, cashiers ignoring customers or reacting unpleasantly to customer demands in order to establish who is in control may have a negative influence on customer satisfaction and on the likelihood that they will return, that is, on "encore gains" (Rafaeli & Sutton, 1987: 32). Similarly, the strains cashiers endure may result in mental and physical health costs to an organization (Beehr & Newman, 1978; Kasl, 1978) as well as turnover and absenteeism costs. It is not unlikely, for example, that the high turnover rate reported in this study is related to the strain that the employees have to endure.

In closing, it is important to note the limitations of the present study. The encounters examined may differ from other service encounters. Supermarket service encounters are relatively short; they do not require the customers' active involvement (customers have to tell waiters what food to bring and cab drivers where to go); they usually do not involve direct monetary payment to a cashier from the customer (no tips); and they aren't that important to the customer.

Moreover, some of the special attributes of supermarket shopping in Israel may have tinted the results. Since customers in Israel usually bag their own groceries, customer involvement may be more active and their influence more immediate than is true in other countries. The lenient attitude in Israel about rudeness, and the poorly developed service concept, may allow cashiers greater freedom in their struggle for control than might be evident elsewhere. Nonetheless, the present study offers a point of departure for further research and theory development on service employees and service encounters.

Finally, the qualitative nature of the present study offers a rich and deep picture of the nature of interactions between clerks and customers in one setting. Such investigations are useful for theory building (Glaser & Strauss, 1967; Mintzberg, 1979). However, more qualitative and quantitative data on supermarkets and on other service settings are essential before researchers will really understand service encounters.

## Acknowledgments

I would like to thank two anonymous reviewers for their detailed and thoughtful comments that significantly improved this paper. I would also like to thank Bob Sutton, Eyal Ben-Arie, and Boaz Shamir for their comments on earlier versions of the paper. The study was supported by a grant to the author from the Mutual Fund of the Hebrew University of Jerusalem.

## Notes

1 Several authors have recently referred to customers as "partial employees" (cf. Mills & Morris, 1986: 726). The term is used to suggest that customers are actually temporary members or participants of service organizations because their participation is crucial to service production.

2 Since all the cashiers observed and interviewed in the study were women, I use the feminine pronoun hereafter in reference to cashiers for the sake of convenience.
3 Employees used the term "down" in all of the stores included in the study when referring to the register area; cashiers referred to the office as "up there" and to the cash register area as "down." The usage may reflect the physical structure of these stores, since the office is usually situated a few steps higher than the registers. It may also reflect the hierarchical relations in the stores.
4 All the research assistants who acted as observers were women.
5 The corporate personnel manager chose the site of my participant observation according to store needs for a cashier. Senior management and the store manager were aware that I was conducting a study about supermarket cashiers. I informally told individual cashiers about the study whenever they asked or whenever it seemed appropriate. At the end of the study, all the cashiers were briefed about the study.
6 The term used by the cashiers to describe a transaction was "pass through." Thus, a cashier might say, "I passed [the customer] through and then went to get change," or "Let me just pass her through and then I'll help you." This terminology is especially interesting because in reality it is merchandise that is being passed through, not customers.
7 For the sake of simplicity, where it is not evident from the text the following codes are used to denote the source of quotations: I = an interview with a cashier, UO = unstructured observation, PO = participant observation, and CI = an interview with a customer.
8 Cashiers frequently referred to "regular" or "permanent" customers. These were customers who shopped in the store regularly. Such customers often selected a favorite cashier, and cashiers frequently knew the names and addresses of these customers from taking checks or delivery orders.

# References

Adams, J. S. 1976. The structure and dynamics of behavior in organization boundary roles. In M. D. Dunnette (Ed.), *Handbook of industrial and organizational psychology.* 1175–1200. Chicago: Rand McNally College Publishing.

Albrecht, K., & Zemke, R. 1985. *Service America! Doing business in the new economy.* Homewood, Ill.: Dow Jones-Irwin.

Beehr, T. A., & Newman, J. E. 1978. Job stress, employee health, and organizational effectiveness: A facet analysis, model, and literature review. *Personnel Psychology,* 31: 665–699.

Biddle, B. J. 1979. *Role theory: Expectations, identities, and behaviors.* New York: Academic Press.

Bigus, O. E. 1972. The milkman and his customer: A cultivated relationship. *Urban Life and Culture,* 1: 131–165.

Bowen, D. E. 1988. *Managing the on-site customer in service organizations: A human re source management perspective.* Paper presented at the annual meeting of the Academy of Management, Anaheim, Calif.

Bowen, D., & Schneider, B. 1985. Boundary-spanning-role employees and the service encounter: Some guidelines for management and research. In J. A. Czepiel, M. R. Solomon, & C. E. Surprenant (Eds.), *The service encounter*: 127–148. Lexington, Mass.: Lexington Books.

Butler, S. R., & Snizek, W. E. 1976. The waitress-diner relationship: A multimethod approach to the study of subordinate influence. *Sociology of Work and Occupations,* 3: 2209–2223.

Czepiel, J. A., Solomon, M. R., & Surprenant, C. F. 1985. *The service encounter*. Lexington, Mass.: Lexington Books.

Desatnick, R. L. 1987. *Managing to keep the customer*. San Francisco: Jossey-Bass.

Flanagan, J. C. 1954. The critical incident technique. *Psychological Bulletin*, 51: 327–358.

French, J. R. P., & Raven, B. H. 1960. The bases of social power. In D. Cartwright & A. Zander (Eds.), *Group dynamics*: 607–623. New York: Harper & Row.

Glaser, B., & Strauss, A. 1967. *The discovery of grounded theory: Strategies for qualitative research*. London: Widenfeld & Nicholson.

Goffman, E. 1959. *The presentation of self in everyday life*. Garden City, N.Y.: Doubleday.

Goldman, A. 1981. Transfer of a retailing technology into the less developed countries: The supermarket case. *Journal of Retailing*, 57(2): 5–29.

Goodsell, C. T. 1976. Cross-cultural comparisons of behavior of postal clerks toward clients. *Administrative Science Quarterly*, 21: 140–150.

Hilgard, E. R., & Bowers, G. H. 1975. *Theories of learning*. Englewood Cliffs, N.J.: Prentice-Hall.

Hochschild, A. R. 1983. *The managed heart*. Berkeley: University of California Press.

Jacoby, J., & Craig, C. S. 1984. *Personal selling*. Lexington, Mass.: Lexington Books.

Kahn, R. L., Wolfe, D. M., Quinn, R. P., & Snoek, J. D. 1981. *Organizational stress: Studies in role conflict and ambiguity*. Malabar, Fla.: Krieger Publishing.

Kasl, S. V. 1978. Epidemiological contributions to the study of work stress. In C. L. Cooper & P. Payne (Eds.), *Stress at work*: 3–48. New York: Wiley.

Katz, D., & Kahn, R. L. 1978. *The social psychology of organizing*. New York: Wiley.

Langer, E. J. 1983. *The psychology of control*. Beverly Hills: Sage Publications.

Lombard, G. F. 1955. *Behavior in a selling group*. Boston: Harvard University Press.

McCallum, J. R., & Harrison, W. 1985. Interdependence in the service encounter. In J. A. Czepiel, M. R. Solomon, & C. E. Surprenant (Eds.), *The service encounter*: 35–48. Lexington, Mass.: Lexington Books.

Marks, M., & Mirvis, P. 1981. Environmental influences on the performance of a professional baseball team. *Human Organization*, 40: 355–360.

Maister, D. H. 1985. The psychology of waiting lines. In J. A. Czepiel, M. P. Solomon, & C. F. Surprenant (Eds.), *The service encounter*: 113–124. Lexington, Mass.: Lexington Books.

Mars, G. 1984. *Cheats at work: An anthropology of workplace crime*. Winchester, Mass.: Allen & Unwin Inc.

Mars, G., & Nicod, M. 1984. *The world of waiters*. Boston: George Allen.

Merton, R. K. 1957. *Social theory and social structure*. New York: Free Press.

Miles, M. E. 1983. Qualitative data as an attractive nuisance. In J. Van Maanen (Ed.), *Qualitative methodology*: 117–134. Beverly Hills: Sage Publications.

Miles, M. B., & Huberman, A. M. 1984. *Qualitative data analysis*. Beverly Hills: Sage Publications.

Miles, R. H., & Perreault, W. O. D. 1976. Organizational role conflict: Its antecedents and consequences. *Organizational Behavior and Human Performance*, 17: 19–44.

Mills, P. K., & Morris, J. H. 1986. Clients as partial employees of service organizations: Role development in client participation. *Academy of Management Review*, 11: 726–736.

Mintzberg, H. 1979. An emerging strategy of "direct" research. *Administrative Science Quarterly*, 24: 580–589.

Osipow, S. H. 1973. *Theories of career development.* Englewood Cliffs, N.J.: Prentice-Hall.

Parkington, J. J. 1979. Some correlates of experienced job stress: A boundary role study. *Academy of Management Journal,* 22: 270–281.

Peters, T. J., & Waterman, R. H., Jr. 1982. *In search of excellence.* San Francisco: Harper & Row.

Rachman, D. J. 1975. *Retail strategy and structure.* Englewood Cliffs, N.J.: Prentice-Hall.

Rafaeli, A. 1989. *Service employees' emotional behavior: Cause or effect?* Paper in progress, Hebrew University of Jerusalem, Israel.

Rafaeli, A., & Sutton, R. I. 1987. The expression of emotion as part of the work role. *Academy of Management Review,* 12: 23–37.

Russel, G. 1987. Pul-eeze! Will somebody help me. *Time,* February 2: 28–34.

Salancik, G. R. 1979. Field stimulations for organizational behavior research. *Administrative Science Quarterly,* 24: 638–649.

Schneider, B., Parkington, J. J., & Buxton, V. M. 1980. Employee and customer perceptions of service in banks. *Administrative Science Quarterly,* 25: 252–267.

Seligman, M. E. P. 1975. *Helplessness: On depression, development and death.* San Francisco: Freeman.

Shamir, B. 1980. Between service and servility: Role conflict in subordinate service roles. *Human Relations,* 33: 741–756.

Sims, H. P., Szilagyi, A. D., & Keller, R. T. 1976. The measurement of job characteristics. *Academy of Management Journal,* 19: 195–212.

Sutton, R. I., & Kahn, B. 1986. Prediction, understanding, and control as antidotes to occupational stress. In J. Lorsch (Ed.), *Handbook of organizational behavior*: 272–285. Englewood Cliffs, N.J.: Prentice-Hall.

Sutton, R. I., & Rafaeli, A. 1988. Untangling the relationship between displayed emotions and organizational sales: The case of convenience stores. *Academy of Management Journal,* 31: 461–487.

Trist, E. 1977. Collaboration in work settings: A personal perspective. *Journal of Applied Behavioral Science,* 13: 268–278.

Vroom, V. H. 1964. *Work and motivation.* New York: Wiley.

Webb, E. J., Campbell, D. T., Schwartz, D. S., Sechrest, L., & Grove, G. B. 1981. *Nonreactive measures in the social sciences.* Boston: Houghton Mifflin Co.

Whyte, W. 1948. *Human relations in the restaurant industry.* New York: McGraw-Hill Book Co.

# Appendix

*Semistructured interview with cashiers*

How long have you been working as a cashier? At this store?
How did you get to be a cashier?
Who do you talk to while at work? About what? Why?
Do you know the other cashiers who work with you? What can you tell me about them?
Do you meet other cashiers or other employees after work? Why?
Which customers do you like most? Why? How do you deal with them?
Which customers do you like least? Why? How do you deal with them?
Can you describe to me an interaction with an "especially good customer?"
Can you describe to me an interaction with an "especially bad customer?"

How did you learn how to do your job? How to deal with customers?
How would you react to the following situations?

1. Customer who said to cashier: "How can you wear three earrings on one ear. That is ridiculous."
2. Customer who said to cashier, "Will you stop talking and start working! You're wasting everyone's time,"

What else do you have to tell me about the job? About your manager? About the other cashiers? About customers? About anything else?

*Semistructured interview with customers*

How long have you been shopping at this store?
Why do you shop here? Do you enjoy it? Why?
Do you feel you know any of the cashiers? Do you like them?
What are your perceptions of the cashiers? What do you think about the way they work?
What would you like to see different in the way they work?
Can you recall specific examples where you felt especially *content* about a cashier's work?
Can you recall specific examples where you were especially *annoyed* with a cashier?
Would you like to tell me anything else about cashiers or about the store?
How old are you?

*Basic rules of cashier behavior* [a,b] *("The Ten Commandments")*

1. Each cashier should wear a smock and a name tag while at work.
2. It is forbidden while at work to hold by the cash register and/or on the body—money, a wallet, or a personal handbag.
3. It is forbidden to have merchandise in the area of the cash registers and/or to eat and/or drink and/or to smoke and/or to chew gum while on the job.
4. Upon receiving money from a customer, and after giving out change, it is mandatory to immediately put the money or the checks that were received into the register drawer. It is forbidden to receive money from a client before the price of the merchandise has been entered into the register.
   IT IS DEFINITELY PROHIBITED to work while the register drawer is open.
5. It is mandatory to ask every person and an employee while he is a customer to display the merchandise he purchased on the table for payment.
6. It is forbidden to let a relative pay for merchandise that he purchased at the register that you are working. Family members will pay for their purchases at a register where the cashier is not a relative.
7. In the case of an error or a return you write a PAY OUT slip (withdraw from the register). The merchandise and the sales slip on which the returned sum appears should be immediately shown to the head cashier and/or the assistant manager and/or the manager in order to get their signed approval.
   At the registers where the VOID operates the note should be attached to the PAY OUT slip.

8. PERSONAL SHOPPING IS DONE ONLY AFTER YOU HAVE FINISHED WORKING.
9. It is strictly forbidden for the cashiers to enter their own merchandise.
10. (a) Keeping the area clean is the cashier's responsibility.
    (b) Also, when leaving the register for a break or at the end of your work you should remove the key from the register and lock the path (to your register) with a chain.

[a] In translating this set of instructions from Hebrew into English, I kept the style as close to the original as possible. Thus, problems of clarity or style reflect the originally convoluted presentation of the various rules.

[b] As Hebrew is a gender-specific language, these rules are all phrased as addressing only woman cashiers.

# 12

# EXPERIENCING WORK

## Values, attitudes, and moods

*Jennifer M. George and Gareth R. Jones*

Source: *Human Relations* 50(4) (1997) 393–415.

### Abstract

This paper describes a model (the VAM model) which integrates three of the most significant dimensions of the work experience, work values, attitudes, and moods, into one overarching framework. The VAM model proposes that a rich and more complete understanding of the experience of work necessitates the simultaneous consideration of work values, attitudes, and moods. After describing how work values, attitudes, and moods, each capture key aspects of experiencing work, we discuss three important dimensions along which they vary: time, dynamism, and focus. These dimensions underscore the need for the simultaneous consideration of values, attitudes, and moods for a fuller understanding of the work experience. We then describe now work values, attitudes, and moods have the potential to influence each other. Finally, we discuss the implications of the VAM model for understanding important organizational outcomes including extra-role behavior, job performance, social loafing, absenteeism, and turnover.

### Introduction

For decades, organizational theorists and researchers have been intrigued by the nature of the work experience and how it affects organizations and their members. Hundreds of studies have examined specific dimensions of the work experience such as job satisfaction or work values, and hundreds more have focused on the relationship between an aspect of the work experience such as job satisfaction and an outcome such as job performance or turnover. Much of this research is disjointed, however, and the component studies do not fit together in such a way as to give us a rich understanding of the way different factors such as work values, job satisfaction, and performance interact to affect one another. For example, meta-analyses have told us that the relationship between performance and job satisfaction is consistently small and positive (about .146; Iaffaldano & Muchinsky, 1985) but knowing that does not tell us why, and we still do not know how other aspects of the work experience such as work values or work moods fit into the picture.

In this paper, we discuss a model of the work experience (the VAM model) that integrates three of the most significant dimensions of the work experience, work values, attitudes, and moods, into one overarching framework. This model describes how people experience work and the psychological processes through which they define and structure their circumstances and give meaning to them. The VAM model proposes that there are three key dimensions along which work values, attitudes, and moods vary. These dimensions underscore why values, attitudes, and moods are each fundamental contributors to the experience of work and also why they need to be considered simultaneously.

Additionally, we use the VAM model to examine and reinterpret several ongoing debates in the literature. For example, we use it to suggest reasons why the performance–satisfaction relationship is so low and why social loafing occurs in some work situations and not in others. Our goal here is to show the utility of the model as a way to invigorate research into the work experience and its effects on organizations and their members.

## The experience of work: values, attitudes, and moods

At a most general level, the experience of work refers to the feelings, thoughts, and beliefs people have about work in general and their jobs and organizations in particular. These feelings, thoughts, and beliefs which describe how people experience work have been studied vis-à-vis the constructs of work values, attitudes, and moods. While progress has been made in terms of understanding the nature, antecedents, and consequences of work values, attitudes, and moods, we still do not have an adequate understanding of how, together, they encapsulate the experience of work and the consequences of this experience for the behavior of individuals in organizations.

A principle premise underlying our model is that the experience of work is multidimensional and includes work values, attitudes, and moods and their interactions. While each of these constructs represents an important aspect of the work experience, considering them in isolation from each other, as has been customary in the past, provides an incomplete and inadequate perspective on the work experience.

The joint or simultaneous consideration of work values, attitudes, and moods necessarily requires an appreciation of how these aspects of the work experience are similar to each other, differ from each other, and how they are interrelated or affect each other. To explore the relationships between work values, attitudes, and moods, we first describe theory and research on these three constructs. Our intent, however, is not to provide exhaustive reviews of the extensive literatures on these

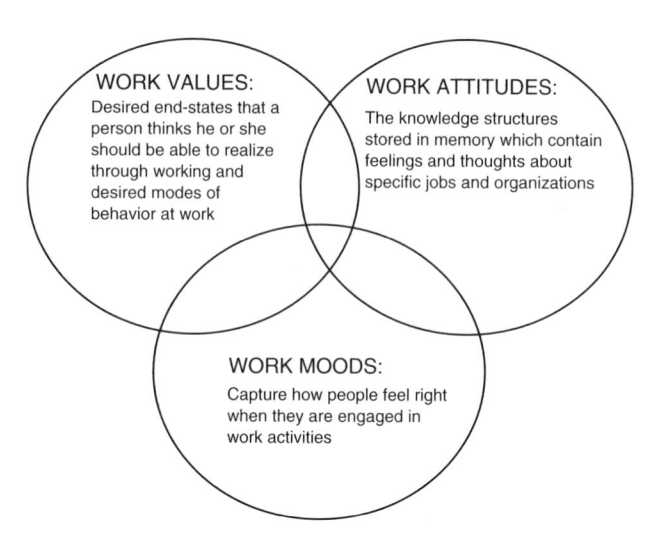

*Figure 1* Ways of experiencing work.

constructs but rather to describe them as aspects of the work experience along with some representative theory and research (Fig. 1).

## *Work values*

Theory and research on work values has preceded largely from the premise that work values are derived from people's basic value systems that help them navigate through the multiple spheres of their lives (e.g., work and family). A value system is a generalized knowledge structure or framework about what is good or desirable which develops over time through an individual's involvement in the world. A value system guides behavior by providing criteria that an individual can use to evaluate and define actions and events in the world surrounding him or her. An individual's personal set of values determine which types of actions and events are desirable or undesirable. Unlike goals, however, values are never fully attained but rather are more permanent guides for experience. An individual does not fully "reach" or achieve a value such as the value of fairness, for example, fairness "guides" the evaluation of prospective actions and events and allows an individual to define and give meaning to work experiences (Lewin, 1951). Values are generalized and relatively abstract superseding evaluative standards that define desirable ends and ways to achieve them (Olson & Zanna, 1993; Rokeach, 1973).

### *Models of values*

One of the most prominent and influential writers on values and value systems is Rokeach (1973, p. 5) who defines a value as "an enduring belief that a specific mode of conduct or end-state of existence is personally or socially preferable to an opposite or converse mode of conduct or end-state of existence" and a value system as "an enduring organization of beliefs concerning preferable modes of conduct or end-states of existence along a continuum of relative importance." Central to these definitions is the fact that values and value systems are thought of in relative terms; values in terms of preferences for behaviors or end-states relative to their converses and value systems in terms of the relative importance of any given value relative to others in the system.

Rokeach called beliefs about preferable modes of conduct *instrumental values* and beliefs about preferable end-states *terminal values*. Based on his research, he identified 18 instrumental values and 18 terminal values, which when rank ordered in terms of importance as guiding principles in one's life, represent a person's value system or the interpretive structure individuals use to define actions and events. Many of these values can be seen as guiding principles for people's lives in the world of work such as the instrumental values of being ambitious, broadminded, courageous, helpful, honest, intellectual, and imaginative and the terminal values of a comfortable life, a sense of accomplishment, family security, freedom, self-respect, and social recognition.

Nord, Brief, Atieh, and Doherty (1990) suggest that it is useful to view work values as desired end-states that a person thinks he or she should be able to realize through working and thus, which guide a person's choice of and reaction to specific jobs or work activities. They suggest that work values can be classified as intrinsic or extrinsic. Intrinsic work values refer to end-states that occur through work or in the course of people engaging in work activities such as a sense of accomplishment and are dependent on the content of work. Intrinsic work values can be illustrated by a quote from a librarian in which the value of freedom at work is emphasized, "I feel free as a bird ... I'm the boss. I buy what I like. I initiate things. I can experiment with all kinds of things the kids might be interested in. Nobody interferes. For me it's no chore to go to work. I'm fortunate" (Terkel, 1974, p. 543). Extrinsic work values refer to end states that occur as a consequence of work, regardless or independent of the content of work per se such as family security. Extrinsic work values are illustrated by a quote from an advertising executive in which the work value of earning money is emphasized, "I came into advertising because I was looking for a way to make money ... You have to remain calm ... When you're doing administrative work, you should think about it as little as possible" (Terkel, 1974, pp. 73–76).

Alternatively, the research of Meglino, Ravlin, and their colleagues suggests that it is useful to view work values as desired modes of behavior. In their research, seven categories of desired behaviors or types of work values were identified (achievement, concern for others, honesty, working hard, positive outlook, helping others, and fairness; Cornelius, Ullman, Meglino, Czajka, & McNeely, 1985). In subsequent studies, they collapsed these types of values into the four categories of achievement, helping and concern for others, honesty, and fairness (Meglino, Ravlin, & Adkins, 1989; Ravlin & Meglino, 1987). How work values such as these shape the experience of work is exemplified by a quote from an installment dealer whose value of helping and concern for others caused him to hate a major aspect of his job, collecting money, and to despise himself for doing it, "I hate to collect. Collecting is a terrible, horrible thing ... Another week, I sit down and make deadbeat calls. It's a miserable thing ... I could wind up throwing the phone against the wall. It's very, very discouraging." (Terkel, 1974, p. 91). These are some examples of representative conceptions of work values and other perspectives have been offered as well (e.g., England, 1967). (For a recent review of theory and research on work values, see, for example, Dawis, 1991.)

Work values are central aspects of the experience of work because they determine the meaning that work, jobs, and organizational experiences have for people (James & James, 1989). People try to make sense of their work experiences by judging how these experiences stack up against their work values (James & James, 1989; Jones & Gerard, 1967; Mandler, 1982). Work values are the evaluative standards that people use to interpret their work experiences. The meaning that a work environment stressing individual, zero-sum competition has for a person, for example, is likely to depend upon the relative strengths of the person's "achievement," "concern for others," and "helping others" values. As another example, the meaning that a job redesign effort to enrich jobs has for people whose jobs are changed is likely to depend upon their work values. For people whose intrinsic work values (a) stress the importance of a sense of accomplishment and achievement, and (b) are more important as guiding principles than their extrinsic work values, enrichment is likely to be seen as a positive change that contributes to their well-being. Conversely, for people whose extrinsic work values (a) stress the importance of a comfortable life and family security, and (b) are more important as guiding principles than their intrinsic work values, enrichment may be more likely to be viewed as a neutral event or even negatively to the extent that the redesigned jobs are more demanding and tiring.

Obviously, whether these conjectures are reasonable or not is an empirical question. The key point, however, is that people's work values determine the meaning that work, jobs, organizations, and specific events and conditions have for them (James & James, 1989). It is for this reason that work values need to be considered in developing an integrated model of the work experience.

## *Work attitudes*

Work attitudes are a second key aspect of the work experience and have received extensive research attention in the organizational literature as well as in the fields of psychology and sociology. Three of the most widely studied work attitudes are job satisfaction, job involvement, and organizational commitment. While these three attitudes are interrelated, they represent distinct and different aspects of the work experience (Brooke, Russell, & Price, 1988; Mathieu & Farr, 1991). As mentioned above, the literature on these and other work attitudes is vast and our intent is not to provide a comprehensive review here (for a recent review, see, for example Hulin, 1991). True to the focus of our paper, we will instead discuss work attitudes vis-à-vis their role in experiencing work.

While there is disagreement among theorists and researchers on the exact definition of an attitude, some general conclusions can be drawn on the nature of this construct (Olson & Zanna, 1993). First, an attitude pertains to a specific or particular target or attitude object (such as a job, an organization, a supervisor, or an action). Second, an attitude includes affect toward the object (e.g., liking for a job) (e.g., Greenwald, 1989). Third, an attitude includes cognitions about the object which tend to be evaluative in nature (e.g., is a job interesting or boring? is an organization concerned about the well-being of its members?) (e.g., Eagly & Chaiken, 1992; Kruglanski, 1989). Fourth, an attitude includes predispositions to behave in certain ways with respect to the object (Olson & Zanna, 1993; Triandis, 1991).

Given disagreements over the precise definition of an attitude, it is not surprising that different researchers emphasize one or another of these theorized aspects of an attitude. For example, some researchers maintain that attitudes are most usefully viewed in terms of affective evaluations of an object (e.g., Fishbein, 1966), others that attitudes are best viewed in terms of affect toward and cognitions about an object (e.g., Bagozzi & Burnkrant, 1979, 1985), and still others that attitudes are composed of affect, cognitions, and behavioral intentions (e.g., Allport, 1935; Rosenberg & Hovland, 1960; for the history of this view, see Isen & Hastorf, 1982).

As a key dimension of the work experience, work attitudes are (a) the knowledge structures containing the specific feelings and thoughts people have about their jobs and organizations, and (b) are the means by which people express themselves as workers, that is, the means through which they define and structure their specific work experiences. (For an in-depth discussion of the structure and function of job attitudes, see Pratkanis & Turner, 1994.)

*Attitudes as knowledge structures*

As people perform their jobs and participate in organizational life, they accumulate an array of feelings and thoughts about their jobs and organizations. Work attitudes can be seen as the knowledge structures stored in memory which contain and organize these feelings and thoughts (Anderson & Armstrong, 1989; Kruglanski, 1989; Olson & Zanna, 1993). As knowledge structures, work attitudes can be evoked, for example, to aid in the perception and evaluation of work-related stimuli, in making decisions, and in choosing how to act. Work attitudes organize and summarize how people feel and think about their jobs and organizations which, in turn, affects their subsequent experiences. The positive work attitudes of a glue factory worker in the following quote demonstrate how people think and feel about their jobs, as the negative work attitudes of the steel worker also encapsulate his thoughts and feelings about his work: "You speak of my working life? I like what I'm doing.

I never have been laid off in thirty-six years. I look forward to going to work. I'd be lost if I wasn't working ... I still think it's a wonderful thing to be employed" (a worker in a rendering and glue factory; Terkel, 1974, p. 112). "My attitude is that I don't get excited about my job ... The day I get excited is the day I go to a head shrinker ... Strictly muscle work ... pick it up, put it down ... It's dying ... You can't take pride anymore" (a steel worker, Terkel, 1974, p. xxxii–xxxii).

*Attitudes as self-expressions*

Work attitudes also can be seen as the means through which people express themselves as workers (Olson & Zanna, 1993). Attitudes can serve self-expressive functions both internally and externally (Eagly & Chaiken, 1992; Shavitt, 1989). Internally, work attitudes can be seen as one lens through which people think about themselves. For example, a person might think of him or herself as a worker dissatisfied with a dead-end job, satisfied with a fulfilling and meaningful job, or the quintessential organizational man or woman who is highly committed to an employing organization. The steel worker quoted earlier, for example, sees himself as the type of person who would never get excited about the kind of work he does nor develop a positive attitude towards it. Externally, work attitudes are means through which people express themselves to others vis-à-vis work. For example, work attitudes are one way in which people can express their work values to others (Olson & Zanna, 1993). By serving as knowledge structures stored in memory and as a means of self-expression, work attitudes are fundamental aspects of experiencing work.

## Work moods

The third aspect of the work experience, work moods, capture how people feel at work and when they are performing their jobs (George, 1989). Work moods are pervasive and generalized affective states that are not explicitly linked to particular events or circumstances which may have originally induced the mood (Morris, 1989). Moods are "low-intensity, diffuse and relatively enduring affective states without a salient antecedent cause" (Forgas, 1992, p. 230). A relatively minor event such as a pleasant chat with a co-worker or a somewhat more significant event such as receiving recognition for a job well done may result in a positive mood being experienced. This positive mood, however, comes to be divorced from the event that triggered it and has pervasive effects on cognitive processes and behaviors unrelated to the mood-inducing event (Forgas, 1995; Morris, 1989; Thayer, 1989). Moods provide people with information about their general state of being (Jacobsen, 1957; Morris, 1989; Nowlis, 1970; Pribram, 1970).

As affective states, moods are often distinguished from emotions which "are more intense, short-lived and usually have a definite cause and clear cognitive content" (Forgas, 1992, p. 230). Emotions demand attention and interrupt ongoing cognitive processes and behaviors (Morris, 1989; Simon, 1982). The relatively fleeting nature of emotions means that people normally do not feel, for example, intensely elated or intensely angry, for extended periods of time. When emotions do have more long-lasting effects, often times this occurs because the emotion, once it has been cognitively and/or behaviorally dealt with, feeds into a more enduring affective state or a mood.

Given our concern with the work experience as a whole and not with intense and transitory affective experiences, in the VAM model we focus on work moods rather than emotions to capture how people feel while performing their jobs. While not denying the relevance or importance of emotions in the workplace, work moods capture more of the day-to-day feelings people experience on the job and are a prime indicator of the experience of work in an affective sense (Clark & Isen, 1982; George, 1989; George & Brief, 1992). Furthermore, as mentioned above, when emotions do have more enduring effects, it is often because they feed into less transient mood states which, while originally triggered by the emotion and whatever induced it, come to exist without a salient connection to their original cause (Forgas, 1995).

## Positive and negative affect

While there are many different types of moods that people experience in general and at work in particular, one way of categorizing moods is in terms of the extent to which they entail positive affect or negative affect. Work moods entailing high levels of positive affect can be described by adjectives such as excited, enthusiastic, active, strong, or peppy while work moods entailing low levels of positive affect can be described by adjectives such as drowsy, dull, or sluggish (Watson & Tellegen, 1985). Work moods entailing high levels of negative affect can be described by adjectives such as distressed, fearful, scornful, hostile, jittery, or nervous while work moods entailing low levels of negative affect can be described by adjectives such as calm, placid, or relaxed (Watson & Tellegen, 1985). Positive and negative emotions also can be described by these adjectives; it is the intensity of the affective state that distinguishes between moods and emotions (George, 1996). The following quotes from a press agent and a stone cutter exemplify how work moods capture the ongoing experience of work in an affective sense: "I can't relax" (a press agent, Terkel, 1974, p. 85); "I feel good and enjoy myself" (a stone cutter, Terkel, 1974, p. 544).

Positive and negative moods are not the result of a reflective or interpretive process through which an individual steps back and "brackets" actions and events to understand and define what is being experienced and give it meaning. Work moods have little explicit cognitive content (Forgas, 1995), are the direct expression of an individual in the "here and now," and encapsulate the feeling of what is being experienced (Schutz, 1972). Work moods are "on-line feelings" rather than reflections, sensations rather than contemplations, which clue people into their general state of being (Morris, 1989).

## Dimensions of experiencing work

In order to gain a theoretical understanding of the way in which work values, attitudes, and moods interact to determine an individual's work experience, it is necessary to identify the dimensions that both differentiate between and integrate across them. We propose that three dimensions capture how work values, attitudes, and moods illuminate different aspects of the work experience and also why they need to be considered simultaneously to penetrate the experience of work. The dimensions we propose are first, a time dimension which differentiates between the way individuals experience work retrospectively, contemporaneously, and prospectively; second, a dynamism dimension which captures the stability or change associated with the experience of work over time; and third, a focus dimension that differentiates between experiencing work at a general and a specific level (Fig. 2).

### *Time: experiencing work retrospectively, contemporaneously, and prospectively*

The role of time in the experience of work has only received limited attention in the research literature. We propose that an adequate explanation of the work experience requires simultaneous consideration of the retrospective, contemporaneous, and prospective work experience of individuals over time (Schutz, 1972).

The work experience is retrospective in that people make sense of job and organizational events and conditions by reflecting on and evaluating these events and conditions after they have occurred. The work experience is contemporaneous in that work takes place on a "real-time" basis; work is experienced directly from

| DIMENSIONS OF EXPERIENCING WORK | WAYS OF EXPERIENCING WORK | | |
|---|---|---|---|
| | VALUES | ATTITUDES | MOODS |
| TIME | Prospective | Retrospective | Contemporaneous |
| DYNAMISM | Stable | Evolving | Fluctuating |
| FOCUS | General | Specific | General |

*Figure 2* Three dimensions of work values, attitudes, and moods.

hour to hour, day to day, and week to week. The work experience is prospective in that how people experience work is rooted in their ideas about what work should be like (i.e., what behaviors it should entail and what end states it should lead to). In other words, how people experience work is affected by their expectations about what prospective jobs or organizations should be like.

### *Experiencing work retrospectively*

Earlier we described how work attitudes can be viewed as knowledge structures which contain people's feelings and thoughts about their jobs and organizations. Moreover, regardless of which definition of an attitude is adopted, researchers agree that a key aspect of work attitudes is that they are inherently evaluative in nature. Consistent with this reasoning, research suggests that work attitudes like job satisfaction are postcognitive and formed after the perception and interpretation of job events and conditions (James & Tetrick, 1986). Thus, work attitudes are retrospective, they are formed after events and conditions are experienced at work. More specifically, in the VAM model, work attitudes are proposed to capture the retrospective experience of work. This assertion does not mitigate against the fact that work attitudes can be formed about a future task to be performed, a future job, or while a person is engaged in a task. However, in these cases a fundamental underpinning of attitude formation is a person's accumulated experiences and knowledge base.

### *Experiencing work contemporaneously*

While part of the experience of work is the result of retrospective sense-making that results in the formation of work attitudes, work also is experienced on an ongoing basis as people perform their job activities and participate in organizational life. The contemporaneous experience of work deals not with how people come to interpret and evaluate aspects of their jobs and organizations but rather with how people feel *as* they perform their jobs and behave in organizations or work moods. Regardless of the content of work activities, how people experience work is dependent upon how they feel contemporaneously, that is, while actually engaging in work. In the VAM model, work moods are proposed to capture the contemporaneous experience of work.

### *Experiencing work prospectively*

In addition to thinking back over past experiences and experiencing work in the present, experiencing work also includes a prospective element. Work is an important part of life and many people in modern society think about what work should be like from an early age. Such prospective beliefs might start out in the form of preferences for certain kinds of jobs and occupations. At some point in their lives, people develop beliefs about desired end states that should be attained through working and desired ways of behaving at work. As we mentioned above, these beliefs can be thought of as work values. Thus, work values are prospective in that they describe what people are striving to be or what they are hoping to attain through work. Work values guide people in their choice of jobs or organizations to work for and define the desirability of different prospective work outcomes and behaviors. Using work values as their guide, individuals are able to think about certain prospective jobs or organizations as if they had *already* been experienced. Work values affect the choices an individual makes about how to perform on the job or even what job to select. In the VAM model, work values are proposed to capture the prospective experience of work.

As this discussion suggests and as emphasized in the VAM model, work is being experienced by individuals in all three ways *simultaneously*. At any one moment, an individual may be in a retrospective, contemporaneous, or prospective mode of experiencing work, but in any time period, individuals are constantly switching back and forth between these modes (at times, instantaneously). People directly and contemporaneously experience work through their moods. They process information about work retrospectively, give meaning to it, and express their evaluations of it through their attitudes. Finally, values are the prospective guides used to approach and interpret various aspects of work. Thus, work values guide the kinds of work choices that people make in and for the future, work attitudes help people assess the result of those choices, and moods provide direct feedback about how these choices are experienced.

## *Dynamism: stability and change in experiencing work*

The second dimension in the VAM model that differentiates between work values, attitudes, and moods concerns the degree to which they are stable or change over time. The work experience is dynamic and changing yet with an important undercurrent of stability.

In the last decade, there has been mounting evidence that people's work experiences are partially determined by personality. Research suggests that there are dispositional underpinnings of work values, attitudes, and moods (e.g., Arvey, Bouchard, Segal, & Abraham, 1989; George, 1989; Keller, Bouchard, Arvey, Segal, & Dawis, 1992; Staw, Bell, & Clausen, 1986; Williams, Suls, Alliger, Learner, & Wan, 1991). These dispositional underpinnings imply that there is an element of stability in each of the three aspects of the work experience because each of them is affected by an individual's personality (Staw & Ross, 1985). Thus, in general, we would expect values, attitudes, and moods to exhibit some stability.

The experience of work also is affected by the situation, however, broadly defined to include actions and events encountered in everyday life as well as a wide variety of contextual factors such as social influence from culture, groups, and co-workers. Environmental events and conditions also can affect the work experience including the hierarchical structuring of a society (e.g., in terms of social class), dominant political ideologies, the state of the economy, and social norms and customs. Importantly, it is the interaction of person *and* situation factors which determine how work is experienced so that even though values, attitudes, and moods may be relatively stable, we would still expect them to change. In general, the VAM model proposes that values, attitudes, and moods differ in their *dynamism*, that is, the rate at which they are likely to change.

Work values, as conceptions of what work should be, transcend the particular jobs a person may have and the different organizations a person may be a member of. While values can certainly change over time (for example, in times of major societal upheavals), they are not rooted to specific experiences and people take their values with them from job to job and organization to organization. As standards that guide the interpretation of actions and events, and as standards that have been developed and refined by a person through the result of his or her exposure to many different types of situations, we might expect values to be the most stable aspect of the work experience.

Work attitudes, on the other hand, are object-specific and are organized around specific jobs and organizations. Because of the effects of dispositions, there is stability in work attitudes even when individuals change jobs and organizations (Staw & Ross, 1985). However, there is also instability because there has been a change in the attitude object (Newton & Keenan, 1991). Moreover, even when jobs and organizations remain the same, attitudes can change over time because the situation or people's evaluations of the situation may change. For example, as people become more enlightened about how they are treated relative to other classes of workers, their evaluations of their jobs and organizations or their work attitudes may change. Thus, work attitudes, as knowledge structures, should exhibit a certain degree of stability, but not as much stability as values because one of the functions of attitudes is to help the individual adjust to changing conditions over time and stay attuned to the social context.

While dispositions also affect work moods, moods can and do fluctuate over hours, days, and weeks as a result of the interaction of situational factors and personality (e.g., Williams et al., 1991). For example, work moods have been linked to major and minor work and nonwork events and conditions, group characteristics, and contextual or environmental conditions, in addition to disposition or personality (George & Brief, 1992). Moods are the most immediate aspect of the experience of work and vary as that experience unfolds. Thus, of all three aspects of the work experience we propose that moods change most rapidly in response to the changing realities of the work situation. Hence, the VAM model suggests that work values are more stable than work attitudes and work attitudes are more stable than work moods.

We propose that the different rates of change of the three aspects of the work experience provide individuals with an effective way to adapt to work situations. The relative stability provided by work values provides the platform on which individuals can approach work situations, make stable interpretations of them, and define their experience. Moods, and particularly changes in moods, provide direct sensory input that allows individuals to continually test their interpretations and to discover whether or not they "enjoy" their work experiences. Attitudes provide a basis for an evolving perspective on how particular jobs and organizations are experienced.

### *Focus: experiencing work at general and specific levels*

We noted above that work values are general modes of experiencing work which transcend specific jobs and organizations. Work attitudes, on the other hand, are object-specific and based on particular jobs and organizations. For this reason, as Rokeach points out, while a person typically has only about 36 basic values that are standards used to evaluate all kinds of objects, events, or behaviors, an individual is likely to have hundreds of attitudes because attitudes are specific to attitude objects.

On the other hand, work moods are aspects of the work experience that are not necessarily tied to any specific job or organization. The same kind of moods can be experienced in a wide variety of jobs and organizations and as a result of a wide range of potential interactions between dispositions and situational factors. Indeed, moods are not necessarily tied to specific stimuli (Clark & Isen, 1982), may be affected by a wide variety of work and nonwork-related factors, and people may be unaware of the exact origins of the positive and negative moods they experience. Even though a work event may trigger a given mood, the mood itself is not specific to the event and will be experienced again, at different points in time, and in response to different circumstances and events. For all practical purposes this means that, as with values, moods are a general aspect of the work experience; they are not specific to any action, event, or social context. Thus, work is experienced at a general level through work values and moods and at a specific level through work attitudes.

## Relationships between ways of experiencing work

The components in the VAM model, values, attitudes, and moods, are three distinct ways in which people experience work. Even though these are distinct ways of experiencing work, however, they are interrelated and can affect one another.

Values, the most long-lasting ways of experiencing work, can affect both work attitudes and work moods. Work attitudes are evaluative in nature and values are a key determinant of how people come to evaluate their jobs and organizations and form their work attitudes. In fact, some definitions of work attitudes like job satisfaction incorporate the fact that attitudes are formed by comparing current conditions to one's values (e.g., Locke, 1976). The librarian who appeared to be so satisfied with her job in our earlier quote, for example, evaluated her job so positively because it was consistent with her work values of autonomy and independence. Work values also can affect work moods such as when negative feelings result from engaging in work activities which are inconsistent with one's values.

While work attitudes are less stable than work values, there is still the potential for attitudes to affect values, especially in the long run. Being very dissatisfied with one's job for an extended period of time might start to change a person's beliefs about what work should be so that rather than being seen as a source of fulfillment, work comes to be viewed as a way to make a living and little more. Conversely, a person whose work values stressed the importance of the extrinsic outcomes of work (namely, pay and job security) might experience a shift in values when high levels of job satisfaction are experienced for an extended period of time because work is perceived to be very meaningful, significant, and important. Work attitudes also can affect work moods. As knowledge structures, work attitudes can affect how people feel while they are performing their jobs. Being highly dissatisfied with a job, for example, may result in a person rarely experiencing positive moods at work.

Finally, while work moods are the most transitory of the three ways of experiencing work, when a certain kind of work mood is experienced more or less consistently for an extended period of time, values and attitudes might be affected. A person who experiences a negative work mood on and off for several months might eventually start thinking that his or her job and organization are not so great after all which causes work attitudes to become more negative. Similarly, work values might eventually change as beliefs about what work should be like are altered. Conversely, being in a positive mood at work for an extended period of time might cause a person's attitudes to become more positive and even cause work values to change such that work is now seen as a part of life that should be enjoyable.

Some preliminary evidence is consistent with these conjectures. For example, Brief, Burke, George, Robinson, and Webster (1988) found that job satisfaction was negatively related to negative mood at work in a sample of professional and managerial personnel in an insurance company. As another example, George (1995) found job involvement and job satisfaction to both be positively associated with positive mood in a sample of managers in a retail setting.

Based upon these ideas, we propose that work values, attitudes, and moods each have the potential to affect one another. Importantly, while work values, attitudes, and moods each are part of the work experience and can affect each other, they are distinct constructs both conceptually and empirically (e.g., George, 1989; George & Brief, 1992; Olson & Zanna, 1993; Rokeach, 1973).

By now it should be clear that to gain a true understanding of the nature of the work experience and its consequences for individuals and organizations, work values, attitudes, and moods must be considered simultaneously rather than in isolation from each other. Each is a different way of experiencing work, each captures different dimensions of experiencing work, and each has the potential to affect the other two ways work is experienced. Hence, we propose that the simultaneous consideration of work values, work attitudes, and work moods will not only enable us to better understand the work experience, but also will lead to a better understanding of the consequences of the work experience for organizations and their members.

## Implications of the VAM model

The VAM model suggests that considering the interactive effects of values, attitudes, and moods is likely to enhance our understanding of work-related behaviors and outcomes. While the specific forms of these interactions are likely to vary depending upon the behavior in question, studying these interactions is likely to provide a richer account of the consequences of the work experience for organizations and their members. At a minimum, researchers exploring the effects of one or more of the ways of experiencing work on a particular class of behaviors or outcomes would be well advised to take into account all three ways of experiencing work and their potential interactions in their theory development and study design efforts. This recommendation follows directly from the VAM model which also provides researchers with a theoretical guide to the three ways of experiencing work and the dimensions along which they vary. By understanding how values, attitudes, and moods each contribute to the experience of work, researchers are likely to be in a better position to more fully and richly explore the consequences of the experience of work.

Since we know of no research which has simultaneously considered the effects of work values, attitudes, and moods, perhaps the easiest way to describe why we think simultaneous consideration is so important is to consider the implications of the VAM model for some important research issues.

### *VAM and extra-role behavior*

Extra-role behaviors are receiving increasing attention in the literature and include various behaviors that are not normally required of organizational members (e.g., Brief & Motowidlo, 1986; George & Brief, 1992; Organ, 1988). Regardless of the precise definition and name adopted for these behaviors (e.g., organizational citizenship behavior, prosocial behavior, or organizational spontaneity), it is clear that extra-role behaviors help organizations remain viable and attain their goals while also having the potential to benefit their individual members.

Extra-role behaviors have been explicitly linked to different aspects of the work experience. Relationships have been theorized and found between extra-role behaviors and work attitudes (e.g., Moorman, 1993; Organ & Konovsky, 1989), work values (e.g., McNeely & Meglino, 1994), and work moods (e.g., George, 1991). While relationships have been documented between these aspects of the work experience and extra-role behavior, they have not been especially strong. Moreover, researchers have not explored how the varied and complex interactions between values, attitudes, and moods might affect individuals' propensities to perform these behaviors and their actual occurrence in an organization. Simultaneous consideration of attitudes, values, and moods may help unlock the extra-role behavior puzzle. Individuals with value systems stressing the importance of, for example, concern for others, helping, and having a positive outlook, may be likely to perform extra-role behaviors even if their attitudes or moods are not positive.

Conversely, individuals who value fairness might only go above and beyond the call of duty when they think they are being treated fairly and thus, have positive attitudes toward their jobs or organizations. Similarly, moods might play a stronger or weaker role in determining the extent to which people perform extra-role behaviors depending upon their values and attitudes.

It is likely that varied and perhaps complex interactions between work values, attitudes, and moods culminate in at least certain forms of extra-role behavior. A key challenge for researchers is to theoretically consider how all three aspects of the work experience, simultaneously, may help account for the occurrence of, or lack of, extra-role behaviors in organizations.

### *VAM and job performance*

Why might two salespeople with similar work values and work attitudes perform customer service behaviors at different levels such that one is polite and obliging while the other is not? One potential explanation for the differences in their performance levels lies in an often neglected aspect of the work experience: work moods. If one person has been experiencing positive moods on the job pretty regularly and the other has not, this might account for their differing performance levels when their values and attitudes are similar because positive moods foster helping behaviors like customer service.

Why might one middle manager be energized and motivated by a major restructuring that increases her level of responsibility, autonomy, and the number of subordinates who report to her while another middle manager whose job was similarly expanded and who had similar work attitudes and work moods before the change becomes demotivated and paralyzed? An answer to this question might be found in the work values of the managers and the relative emphasis placed on achievement vs. concern for others in the managers' value systems. The manager who was motivated by the change may greatly value achievement, and because her expanded job provides more opportunities for achievement, her motivation and performance increase. Alternatively, the manager who was demotivated and paralyzed by the change may place great value on concern for others, and because she had to lay off subordinates as well as see co-workers being laid off as part of the restructuring, she experiences dysfunctionally high levels of stress which impair her motivation and performance. Hence, even though the managers' attitudes and moods were similar prior to the change, value differences may help explain their differing reactions.

Why might two secretaries with similar work values and work moods differ in the extent to which they are willing to take on additional responsibilities? An answer to this question might be found in the differing attitudes the secretaries have about their jobs and organizations which cause them to behave differently even though their values and moods are similar.

While all three of these examples are overly simplistic, hopefully they demonstrate why we think simultaneous consideration of work values, attitudes, and moods is so important. The VAM model has the potential to explain such well-documented research findings as job satisfaction being, at best, weakly related to job performance. The weak relationship between job satisfaction and performance has surprised researchers and may cause them to wonder if how work is experienced really matters (from an organization's perspective). However, if the full VAM model is taken into account, the weak relationship between job satisfaction and performance is not surprising and does not imply that the experience of work per se is unimportant for understanding performance. Rather, in exploring how the experience of work affects performance, researchers need to consider not just attitudes like job satisfaction but also work values and moods and the interactive effects of these three ways of experiencing work on performance. In a more fully specified model of the work experience-job performance relationship, that is, one which includes values, attitudes, and moods and their interactions, we might hypothesize that a stronger set of predictive relationships would be found.

### *VAM and social loafing*

When individual contributions to group performance are difficult to identify because of such factors as large group size or high task interdependence, there is a well-documented tendency for individuals to engage in social loafing or put forth less effort than they would have if they were working individually. However, social loafing does not always occur in groups and some people are more prone to social loafing than others. While explanations for some of these findings have been provided (e.g., Earley, 1989; Jones, 1984; Williams, Harkin, & Latane, 1981), the VAM model promises to shed additional light on social loafing.

The importance of considering the simultaneous effects of work values, attitudes, and moods on social loafing is illustrated by the following example. Suppose an individual has extremely negative attitudes toward his or her job and thinks that the work is boring. Other things being equal, we might expect such a person to take advantage of opportunities to engage in social loafing (George, 1992). However, suppose that individual also has a set of work values about fairness or about a "fair day's work for a fair day's pay." That individual might resist the temptation to loaf even when the situation presents itself (he or she is a member of a work group in which it is impossible to identify individual contributions). We propose that the desire to loaf or to perform at a high level is the result of the interaction of all three aspects of the work experience.

### *VAM, turnover, and absenteeism*

In several models of turnover (e.g., Mobley, 1977; Hom, Caranikas-Walker, Prussia, & Griffeth, 1992), attitudes like job satisfaction are seen as triggering the turnover process, ultimately leading to intentions to quit, and final quit or stay decisions. While the link between job satisfaction and turnover has been established, it too is weak, and it may be the case that work values, moods, and their interactions with attitudes also play a role in turnover. For example, being in a positive mood or possessing strong work values of loyalty may prevent a person from quitting even though job satisfaction is low.

Similar considerations apply to absenteeism. Empirically, weak relationships between absence and attitudes (Farrell & Stamm, 1988) and absence and moods (George, 1989) have been found. What is the combined effects of both of these aspects of the work experience on absence and under what conditions is excessive absence most likely to occur? Similarly, what is the role of values in this equation and, once again, will certain work values moderate these relationships? Once again only empirical research guided by theory which simultaneously considers the effects of values, attitudes, and moods on absence behaviors will help untangle these relationships and provide insight into how the experience of work influences decisions to attend or be absent.

### *Implications for research*

The VAM model provides a number of interesting avenues for future theorizing and research, both in terms of the basic tenets of the model and in terms of its implications and logical extensions. Rather than advocate a particular type of research methodology, we feel that research in this area may be most enlightening if researchers adopt a variety of approaches and engage in collaborative triangulation. Qualitative methodologies may, for example, contribute to our understanding of the three ways of experiencing work, the dimensions that distinguish between them, and how they affect each other. As another example, quantitative methodologies may help us to explore how values, attitudes, and moods interact to influence a behavior such as extra-role behavior. For instance, work values, attitudes, and moods could be measured with existing survey instruments which have evidence supporting their reliability and validity. A behavior such as extra-role behavior could be measured via direct observation, co-worker reports, supervisor reports, or through information obtained from multiple sources. Hypotheses concerning the interactive effects of work values, attitudes, and moods on behavior could then be tested. Once again, rather than advocate a particular research approach, we think that it will be most fruitful if researchers adopt a diversity of approaches.

## Conclusions

Work values, attitudes, and moods are each remarkably complex concepts. Because of the complexity of each of these concepts, and the wide range of their potential determinants and consequences, it is not surprising that, with a few exceptions, they have tended to be studied in isolation from one another. However, work values, attitudes, and moods each capture important ways of experiencing work. Grasping the experience of work necessitates simultaneous consideration of each of these ways of experiencing work as does gaining a better understanding of the consequences of the work experience for both individuals and organizations.

## References

Allport, G. W. Attitudes. In C. Murchison (Ed.), *A handbook of social psychology*. Worcester, MA: Clark University Press, 1935.

Anderson, N. H., & Armstrong, N. A. Cognitive theory and methodology for studying marital interaction. In D. Brindberg and D. Jaccard (Eds.), *Dyadic decision making*. New York: Springer-Verlag, 1989, pp. 3–49.

Arvey, R. D., Bouchard, T. J., Segal, N. L., & Abraham, L. M. Job satisfaction: Environmental and genetic components. *Journal of Applied Psychology*, 1989, *74*, 187–192.

Bagozzi, R. R., & Burnkrant, R. E. Attitude organization and the attitude–behavior relationship. *Journal of Personality and Social Psychology*, 1979, *37*, 913–929.

Bagozzi, R. R., & Burnkrant, R. E. Attitude organization and the attitude–behavior relation: A reply to Dillon and Kumar. *Journal of Personality and Social Psychology*, 1985, *49*, 47–57.

Brief, A. P., Burke, M. J., George, J. M., Robinson, B. S., & Webster, J. Should negative affectivity remain an unmeasured variable in the study of job stress? *Journal of Applied Psychology*, 1988, *73*, 193–198.

Brief, A. P., & Motowidlo, S. Prosocial organizational behaviors. *Academy of Management Review*, 1986, *11*, 710–725.

Brooke, P. P., Russell, D. W., & Price, J. L. Discriminant validation of measures of job satisfaction, job involvement, and organizational commitment. *Journal of Applied Psychology*, 1988, *73*, 139–145.

Clark, M. S., & Isen, A. M. Toward understanding the relationship between feelings states and social behavior. In A. H. Hastorf and A. M. Isen (Eds.), *Cognitive social psychology*. New York: Elsevier, 1982, pp. 73–108.

Cornelius, E. T., Ullman, J. C., Meglino, B. M., Czajka, J., & McNeely, B. A New Approach to the Study of Worker Values and Some Preliminary Results. Paper presented at the Meeting of the Southern Management Association, Orlando, FL, 1985.

Dawis, R. V. Vocational interests, values, and preferences. In M. D. Dunnette and L. M. Hough (Eds), *Handbook of industrial and organizational psychology* (2nd ed., Vol. 2). Palo Alto, CA: Consulting Psychologists Press, 1991, pp. 833–871.

Eagly, A. H., & Chaiken, S. *The psychology of attitudes*. San Diego, CA: Harcourt Brace Janovich, 1992.

Earley, P. C. Social loafing and collectivism: A comparison of the United States and the People's Republic of China. *Administrative Science Quarterly*, 1989, *34*, 565–581.

England, G. W. Personal value systems of American managers. *Academy of Management Journal*, 1967, *10*, 53–68.

Farrell, D., & Stamm, C. L. Meta-analysis of the correlates of employee absence. *Human Relations*, 1988, 41, 211–227.

Fishbein, M. The relationship between beliefs, attitudes, and behavior. In S. Feldman (Ed.), *Cognitive consistency: Beliefs, attitudes, and behavior*. New York: Academic Press, 1966.

Forgas, J. P. Affect in social judgments and decisions: A multi-process model. In M. Zanna (Ed.), *Advances in experimental social psychology* (Vol. 25). San Diego, CA: Academic Press, 1992, pp. 227–275.

Forgas, J. P. Mood and judgment: The affect infusion model (AIM). *Psychological Bulletin*, 1995, *117*, 39–66.

George, J. M. Mood and absence. *Journal of Applied Psychology*, 1989, *74*, 317–324.

George, J. M. State or trait: The effects of positive mood on prosocial behaviors at work. *Journal of Applied Psychology*, 1991, *76*, 299–307.

George, J. M. Extrinsic and intrinsic origins of perceived social loafing in organizations. *Academy of Management Journal*, 1992, *35*, 191–202.

George, J. M. Leader positive mood and group performance: The case of customer service. *Journal of Applied Social Psychology*, 1995, *25*, 778–794.

George, J. M. Trait and state affect. In K. Murphy (Ed.), *Individual differences and behavior in organizations*. San Francisco: Jossey-Bass, 1996, pp. 145–171.

George, J. M., & Brief, A. P. Feeling good-doing good: A conceptual analysis of the mood at work-organizational spontaneity relationship. *Psychological Bulletin*, 1992, *112*, 310–329.

Greenwald, A. G. Why attitudes are important. Defining attitude and attitude theory 20 years later. In A. R. Pratkanis, S. J. Breckler, and A. G. Greenwald (Eds.), *Attitude structure and function*. Hillsdale, NJ: Erlbaum, 1989, pp. 429–440.

Hom, P. W., Caranikas-Walker, F., Prussia, G. E., & Griffeth, R. W. A metaanalytical structural equations analysis of a model of employee turnover. *Journal of Applied Psychology*, 1992, *77*, 890–909.

Hulin, C. Adaptation, persistence, and commitment in organizations. In M. D. Dunnette and L. M. Hough (Eds.), *Handbook of industrial and organizational psychology* (2nd ed., Vol. 2). Palo Alto, CA: Consulting Psychologists Press, 1991, pp. 445–505.

Isen, A. M., & Hastorf, A. H. Some perspectives on cognitive social psychology. In A. H. Hastorf and A. M. Isen (Eds.), *Cognitive social psychology*. New York: Elsevier, 1982.

James, L. A., & James, L. R. Integrating work environment perceptions: Explorations into the measurement of meaning. *Journal of Applied Psychology*, 1989, *74*, 739–751.

James, L. R., & Tetrick, L. E. Confirmatory analytic tests of three causal models relating job perceptions to job satisfaction. *Journal of Applied Psychology*, 1986, *71*, 77–82.

Jones, G. R. Task visibility, free riding, and shirking: Explaining the effect of structure and technology on employee behavior. *Academy of Management Review*, 1984, *9*, 684–695.

Jones, E. E., & Gerard, H. B. *Foundations of social psychology*. New York: Wiley, 1967.

Keller, L. M., Bouchard, T. J., Arvey, R. D., Segal, N. L., & Dawis, R. V. Work values: Genetic and environmental influences. *Journal of Applied Psychology*, 1992, *77*, 79–88.

Kruglanski, A. W. *Lay epistemics and human knowledge: Cognitive and motivational bases*. New York: Plenum, 1989.

Lewin, K. *Field theory in social science*. New York: Harper, 1951.

Locke, E. A. The nature and causes of job satisfaction. In M. D. Dunnette (Ed.), *Handbook of industrial and organizational psychology*. Chicago: Rand McNally, 1976, pp. 1297–1349.

Iaffaldano, M., & Muchinsky, P. Job satisfaction and job performance: A meta-analysis. *Psychological Bulletin*, 1985, *97*, 251–273.

Jacobsen, E. Normal and pathological moods: Their nature and functions. In R. S. Eisler, A. F. Freud, H. Hartman, and E. Kris (Eds.), *The psychoanalytic study of the child.* New York: International University Press, 1957, pp. 73–113.

Mandler, G. The structure of value: Accounting for taste. In M. S. Clarke and S. T. Fiske (Eds.), *Affect and cognition.* Hillsdale, NJ: Erlbaum, 1982, pp. 3–36.

Mathieu, J. R., &. Farr, J. L. Further evidence for the discriminant validity of measures of organizational commitment, job involvement, and job satisfaction. *Journal of Applied Psychology,* 1991, *76,* 127–133.

McNeely, B. L., & Meglino, B. M. The role of dispositional and situational antecedents in prosocial organizational behavior: An examination of the intended beneficiaries of prosocial behavior. *Journal of Applied Psychology,* 1994, *79,* 836–844.

Meglino, B. M., Ravlin, E. C., & Adkins, C. L. A work values approach to corporate culture: A field test of the value congruence process and its relationship to individual outcomes. *Journal of Applied Psychology,* 1989, *74,* 424–432.

Moorman, R. H. The influence of cognitive and affective based job satisfaction measures on the relationship between satisfaction and organizational citizenship behavior. *Human Relations,* 1993, *46,* 759–776.

Morris, W. N. *Mood: The frame of mind.* New York: Springer-Verlag, 1989.

Newton, T., & Keenan, T. Further analyses of the dispositional argument in organizational behavior. *Journal of Applied Psychology,* 1991, *76,* 781–787.

Nord, W. R., Brief, A. P., Atieh, J. M., & Doherty, E. M. Studying meanings of work: The case of work values. In A. P. Brief and W. R. Nord (Eds.), *Meanings of occupational work.* Lexington, MA: Lexington Books, 1990, pp. 21–64.

Nowlis, V. Mood: Behavior and experience. In M. Arnold (Ed.), *Feelings and emotions.* New York: Academic Press, 1970, pp. 261–277.

Olson, J. M., & Zanna, M. P. Attitudes and attitude change. *Annual Review of Psychology,* 1993, *44,* 117–154.

Organ, D. W. *Organizational citizenship behavior: The good soldier syndrome.* Lexington, MA: Lexington Books, 1988.

Organ, D. W., & Konovsky, M. A. Cognitive versus affective determinants of organizational citizenship behavior. *Journal of Applied Psychology,* 1989, *74,* 157–164.

Pratkanis, A. R., & Turner, M. E. Of what value is a job attitude? A socio-cognitive analysis. *Human Relations,* 1994, *47,* 1545–1576.

Pribram, K. H. Feelings as monitors. In M. Arnold (Ed.), *Feelings and emotions.* New York: Academic Press, 1970, pp. 41–53.

Ravlin, E. C., & Meglino, B. M. Effect of values on perception and decision making: A study of alternative work values methods. *Journal of Applied Psychology,* 1987, *72,* 666–673.

Rokeach, M. *The nature of human values.* New York: The Free Press, 1973.

Rosenberg, M. J., & Hovland, C. I. Cognitive, affective, and behavioral components of attitudes. In M. J. Rosenberg and C. I. Hovland (Eds.), *Attitude organization and change.* New Haven, CT: Yale University Press, 1960.

Schutz, A. *The phenomenology of the social world.* London: Heinemann, 1972.

Shavitt, S. Operationalizing functional theories of attitudes. In A. R. Pratkanis, S. J. Breckler, and A. G. Greenwald (Eds.), *Attitude structure and junction.* Hillsdale, NJ: Erlbaum, 1989, pp. 311–337.

Simon, H. A. Comments. In M. S. Clark and S. T. Fiske (Eds.), *Affect and cognition.* Hillsdale, NJ: Erlbaum, 1982, pp. 333–342.

Staw, B. M., Bell, N. E., & Clausen, J. A. The dispositional approach to job attitudes: A lifetime longitudinal test. *Administrative Science Quarterly*, 1986, *31*, 56–77.

Staw, B. M., & Ross, J. Stability in the midst of change: A dispositional approach to job attitudes. *Journal of Applied Psychology*, 1985, *70*, 469–480.

Terkel, S. *Working: People talk about what they do all day and how they feel about what they do*. New York: Pantheon Books, 1974.

Thayer, R. E. *The biopsychology of mood and arousal*. New York: Oxford University Press, 1989.

Triandis, H. C. Attitude and attitude change. *Encyclopaedia of Human Biology* (Vol. 1). San Diego, CA: Academic Press, 1991, pp. 485–496.

Watson, D., & Tellegen, A. Toward a consensual structure of mood. *Psychological Bulletin*, 1985, *98*, 219–235.

Williams, K., Harkins, S., & Latane, B. Identifiability as a deterrent to social loafing: Two cheering experiments. *Journal of Personality and Social Psychology*, 1981, *40*, 303–311.

Williams, K. J., Suls, J., Alliger, G. M., Learner, S. M., & Wan, C. K. Multiple role juggling and dairy mood states in working mothers: An experience sampling study. *Journal of Applied Psychology*, 1991, *76*, 664–674.

# 13

# EMOTION IN THE WORKPLACE
## A reappraisal

*Blake E. Ashforth and Ronald H. Humphrey*

Source: *Human Relations* 48(2) (1995) 97–124.

## Abstract

Although the experience of work is saturated with emotion, research has generally neglected the impact of everyday emotions on organizational life. Further, organizational scholars and practitioners frequently appear to assume that emotionality is the antithesis of rationality and, thus, frequently hold a pejorative view of emotion. This has led to four institutionalized mechanisms for regulating the experience and expression of emotion in the workplace: (1) neutralising, (2) buffering, (3) prescribing, and (4) normalizing emotion. In contrast to this perspective, we argue that emotionality and rationality are interpenetrated, emotions are an integral and inseparable part of organizational life, and emotions are often functional for the organization. This argument is illustrated by applications to motivation, leadership, and group dynamics.

## Introduction

Plas and Hoover-Dempsey (1988, pp. 26–27) describe a meeting in a law firm where a senior partner critiqued the way an attorney had handled a case:

> During the twenty-five minutes that the focus remained on his case, Jake said nothing. He reported that at first he was sure he had turned "beet red" from embarrassment. Pretty quickly, though, the embarrassment turned to another emotion as he found himself with clenched fists at his sides. He then (literally) bit his lip in order to hold back a sharp retort or a sarcastic comment. In telling the story, he remarked that he would have "decked the guy" if he had been a senior partner.

Terkel (1975, pp. 392–393) quotes a waitress discussing her work:

> I'd get intoxicated with giving service. People would ask for me and I didn't have enough tables. Some of the girls are standing and don't have customers. There is resentment. I feel self-conscious. I feel a sense of guilt. It cramps my style. I would like to say to the customer, "Go to so-and-so." But you can't do that, because you feel a sense of loyalty.

As these examples illustrate, emotions are an integral and inseparable part of everyday organizational life. From moments of frustration or joy, grief or fear, to an enduring sense of dissatisfaction or commitment, the *experience* of work is saturated with feeling. This is readily apparent in even a cursory examination of ethnographic accounts of work (e.g., Garson, 1977; Terkel, 1975; Wall, 1986).

Despite the prevalence of emotion in the workplace, research has generally been confined to: (1) a limited set of relatively generalized and stable affective states, principally satisfaction, stress, mood, and certain aspects of commitment, and (2) the role of emotions in discrete, critical events, such as organizational change, role transitions, and intergroup conflict.[1] The relative neglect of the role of everyday emotion in mundane organizational life is surprising because this role has been a more or less implicit feature of research since the dawn of the human relations perspective (e.g., Likert, 1967; Mayo, 1945; Roethlisberger & Dickson, 1943). Indeed, it could be argued that everyday emotion helped fuel the initial interest in informal organizational processes, group dynamics, leadership, and so on.

Further, it appears that—at least until recently—the potential dysfunctions of everyday emotion have generally been more salient to management researchers and practitioners than the potential functions. Argyris (1985, p. 51), for example, argues that "the great paradox of managerial behavior" is the conflict between the rational approach to accomplishing tasks and the emotional barriers to rationality. To be sure, examples abound of how strong emotions have undermined seemingly rational enterprises: Brenner (1988) describes how emotional strife tore apart a family-run conglomerate, Burrough and Helyar (1990) discuss how greed and hubris fomented the most expensive leveraged buyout in history, that of RJR Nabisco, and Mainiero (1986) describes the disruptive effects that office romances may have on work group effectiveness. The variety and ubiquity of such examples appears to have helped foster a belief that emotion is the antithesis of rationality. This belief, in turn, may have contributed to a somewhat pejorative view of emotion and to frequent attempts to control the experience and expression of emotion in organizations.

However, we contend that this belief is simplistic and that the pejorative view of emotion has blinded many scholars and practitioners to the value and importance of emotions. We argue that emotionality and rationality are interpenetrated and that a "dialectic of emotionality and rationality" (Mumby & Putnam, 1992, p. 480) will suggest how the qualities are dependent upon each other. Further, we contend that emotions are a natural and inseparable concomitant of task activity (Matsumoto & Sanders, 1988; Sandelands, 1988) and that we need a more holistic conception of the experience of work.

The discussion proceeds as follows. First, we offer an interpretive approach to the nature of emotional experience in organizations. Second, the association between rationality and emotionality is discussed. We argue that a historical focus on rationality emerged partly as a defense against the perceived dysfunctions of emotion. Third, we describe four means by which the experience and expression of emotions are regulated in many organizations. Finally, we argue that—the focus on rationality notwithstanding—emotion is inextricably enmeshed in workplace activity, and that organizational effectiveness may at times be improved by celebrating rather than attempting to suppress emotion. The importance of everyday emotion is illustrated by applications to motivation, leadership, and group dynamics.

## An interpretive approach to the experience of emotion

Over 100 years ago, William James (1884) asked "What is an emotion?" Given the tremendous variety of perspectives on the nature and genesis of emotion, and on the components and classification of emotions, it should not be surprising that there is no widely agreed upon definition of emotion. We wish to capture what appears to be the central feature of this variety of perspectives without unduly or arbitrarily excluding certain perspectives. Accordingly, we define emotion in fairly broad and inclusive terms as simply a subjective feeling state. This definition includes the so-called basic emotions (e.g., joy, love, anger) and social emotions (e.g., shame, guilt, jealousy), as well as such related constructs as affect, sentiments, and moods.[2] Feeling states vary widely in terms of their intensity, duration, consistency, and valence. We focus on feeling states that occur frequently in the workplace and are not the result of a psychiatric disorder.

The literature on how emotions are experienced is generally divided between two major poles: (1) the social constructionist and the symbolic interactionist, and (2) the naturalistic and positivist perspectives (Ratner, 1989; Thoits, 1989). The first pole holds that the experience depends primarily on how a given situation is defined. Through social or symbolic interaction, individuals interpret the situation and label it as a certain kind of emotional experience. Social constructionists and symbolic interactionists disagree, however, on the extent to which emotions are socially constructed: symbolic interactionists are more willing to recognize the role of physiological arousal or change in prompting certain interpretations.

The naturalistic/positivist perspective holds that specific situational stimuli elicit specific emotions. All emotions are reducible to a few basic, universal emotions such as fear, joy, and anger. These emotions are hardwired, as each has its own "physiological determining mechanism" (Ratner, 1989, p. 215). The two poles disagree, then, over the extent to which emotions are cognitively and socially mediated. While the naturalistic/positivist pole holds that a given stimulus elicits the *same* emotion in a more or less automatic, biologically determined manner, the social constructionist/symbolic interactionist pole holds that a given stimulus may elicit *various* emotions depending on how it is interpreted.

The reconciliation of this division is beyond the scope of this paper (see Kemper, 1987, for one attempt). We instead take a middle-ground, "interpretive" approach to the experience of emotion. We assume that stimuli may elicit physiological arousal or change and that the precise cause and meaning will *at times* be ambiguous. At such times, interpretation may indeed be socially constructed. For example, one work group may interpret a shared sense of generalized arousal as shame at the group's failure to attain its performance standards, while another group interprets it as resentment against management for setting unrealistically high standards (cf. social information processing theory; Salancik & Pfeffer, 1978). The important point is that *neither* interpretation has greater intrinsic merit: the equivocality is resolved after-the-fact by a more or less arbitrary label. It should be emphasized that we are not assuming that every experience of emotion is cognitively and/or socially mediated.

The interpretation of physiological arousal or change is subject to cultural norms and individual differences. Cultures—whether societal, organizational, occupational, departmental, etc.—provide beliefs about emotional states, a vocabulary for discussing them, and a set of socially acceptable attributions for the states (cf. Gerhards, 1989; Gordon, 1990). The *breadth* of emotional states (e.g., fear, love, hate) and the *depth* of the states (i.e., the number of nuances) that are included often differ across cultures. A frequently cited example is Levy's (1973) observation that Tahitians have few words for sadness and attribute the experience of sadness to bodily distress. Individual differences in traits, beliefs, values, goals, and so on, also influence how an event is interpreted. Plas and Hoover-Dempsey (1988) provide organizational examples of how men and women differed in their attributions for events and in their subsequent emotions.

The strength, then, of this middle-ground approach is that: (1) it underscores the importance of one's *interpretation* in the experiencing of emotions in many situations, whether the interpretation is relatively automatic (e.g., experiencing anger at a direct insult) or studied (e.g., experiencing anger after reflecting on a manager's words), and (2) it underscores the importance of the *context* in inducing and/or interpreting arousal or change; yet, it does not require one to argue that the locus of emotional experience resides exclusively in either the person (physiology) or the situation (social context). As such, this treatment is consistent with the increasing prevalence of interactionist models in organizational behavior (Chatman, 1989).

## Emotion and the norms of rationality

The division of rationality and emotionality in work is, historically speaking, relatively recent. Sandelands and Buckner (1989) document the fusion of "the aesthetic and the practical" from primitive times to the Renaissance. The dawn of the Industrial Revolution and the widespread emergence of large organizations precipitated the rise of rationality as an administrative paradigm. Max Weber (1968), who articulated the principles of "rational-legal bureaucracy," stated that bureaucracy progresses

> ... the more it is "dehumanized," the more completely it succeeds in eliminating from official business love, hatred, and all purely personal, irrational, and emotional elements which escape calculation (p. 975).

Indeed, as this quote suggests, rationality emerged as an administrative paradigm partly as a defense against the perceived dysfunctions and pejorative connotations of emotion. Stearns and Stearns (1986), for example, argue that American organizations have waged a campaign throughout the twentieth century to control workplace emotions, principally anger.

Following Shrivastava and Schneider (1984), the current organizational "frame of reference" includes a coherent set of ends, instrumental means, and (intendedly) rational cognitive maps which connect the means and ends in a predictable and reliable manner. These maps are ostensibly constructed from objective and technical data and are subjected to scientific and empirical reality testing. More generally, Table 1 lists a variety of ways in which the notion of rationality as an administrative paradigm or frame of reference has tended to differ from what may be loosely termed "emotionality." These differences span the micro (intrapersonal), meso (interpersonal), and macro (organizational) levels of analysis. It is important to note that: (1) these tendencies are deliberately described in very broad and inclusive or "thick" terms (Geertz, 1973), (2) these tendencies—and differences in tendencies between rationality and emotionality—represent "fuzzy sets" (Yager, 1982) rather than mutually exclusive categories, and (3) the differences in tendencies are *not* meant to imply that emotionality is the opposite of rationality. As noted, emotionality is often implicitly viewed as the antithesis or absence of rationality, and this has contributed to the negative perception of emotion. We view rationality and emotionality as interpenetrated and, by retrieving the marginalized elements of emotionality, we seek to illustrate how they may help to reinvigorate conventional management topics.

The ascent of rationality as the dominant administrative paradigm has led to what Morgan (1986) terms an "overrationalized" conception of organizational life. Indeed, the emphasis on rationality has become institutionalized in the form of "norms of rationality" (Thompson, 1967) such that organizations must at least publicly conform to these norms to be perceived as legitimate (Ashforth & Gibbs, 1990). Manifestations abound of this overrationalization. Phenomena associated with processes, noninstrumentality, qualitativeness, spontaneity, or subjectivity are often viewed pejoratively—as "irrational" or "arational"—and therefore to be avoided or controlled. This explains, in part, the recurring difficulties in managing creative processes and group decision making, the illegitimacy of intuition

*Table 1* Rationality and emotionality: thick descriptions

| Domains | Rationality | Emotionality |
|---|---|---|
| Orientation to organization | Mechanistic<br>Technical<br>Pragmatism<br>Objectivity | Organic<br>Social<br>Vision<br>Subjectivity |
| Orientation to means/ends | Outcomes<br>Instrumentality<br>Predictability<br>Consistency<br>Specialization<br>Stability<br>Reliability<br>Quantitative<br>Analysis<br>Efficiency<br>Control | Processes<br>Phenomenology<br>Spontaneity<br>Variety<br>Holistic<br>Creativity<br>Authenticity<br>Qualitative<br>Intuition<br>Indulgence<br>Exploration |
| Intrapersonal orientation | Role<br>Performance<br>Understanding<br>Cognition<br>Beliefs<br>Compliance | Person<br>Satisfaction<br>Experiencing<br>Affect<br>Values<br>Commitment |
| Interpersonal orientation | Roles<br>Hierarchies<br>Impersonalized<br>Obedience<br>Orders<br>Direction<br>Contracts<br>Utility<br>Dispensability of individual | Relationships<br>Networks<br>Personalized<br>Individuality<br>Inspiration<br>Support<br>Community<br>Empathy<br>Indispensability of individual |

and hunches, the relatively low status of many occupations requiring frequent emotional labor (e.g., counseling, nursing), the low tolerance of emotional displays, the greater ease organizations have defending their performance rather than their values, and the historical emphasis in business schools and organizational training programs on technical skills rather than social skills. Further, activities ostensibly conforming to the norms of rationality usually take precedence over those that do not. James (1989) describes how hospice workers—though explicitly hired to provide emotional support as well as more traditional nursing—found that the relatively predictable and routinized physical work often squeezed out the more spontaneous and open-ended (and thus "disruptive") emotional work. Similarly, organizations often lack a vocabulary and a culture for even discussing emotive activities and subjective experience (Sandelands, 1988). Meyerson (1990) reports that hospital social workers found it very difficult to articulate their experience of ambiguity to her because the culture of the hospital encouraged only the use of precise language in the service of the norms of rationality.

## How emotion is regulated

Given the somewhat pejorative view of emotion in organizations, only a limited range of emotional expression tends to be socially acceptable. Expressions of *negative* emotion, such as fear, anxiety, and anger, tend to be unacceptable except under fairly circumscribed conditions (e.g., a high status task group member conveying impatience with a low status member). Flett, Blankstein, Pliner, and Bator (1988) found that individuals who tended to engage in impression management generally reported that their negative emotions were less frequent, less intense, and shorter in duration than did other individuals. Further, expressions of *intense* emotion, whether negative or positive, tend also to be unacceptable except under certain conditions (e.g., celebrating a record year) since they are believed to impair routine task performance (Thoits, 1985).

Accordingly, at least four somewhat overlapping means have evolved for regulating the experience and expression of emotion in work settings. As argued below, "neutralizing" is used to prevent the emergence of socially unacceptable emotions, while the remaining means are used to regulate emotions that are either unavoidable or inherent in role performance: "buffering" is used to encapsulate and segregate potentially disruptive emotions from ongoing activities, "prescribing" is used to specify socially acceptable means of experiencing and expressing emotions, and "normalizing" is used to diffuse or reframe unacceptable emotions to preserve the status quo. These four means are essentially substitutes. However, as one descends the list, potentially unacceptable emotions are more directly implicated in ongoing task activities. It should be noted that we are *not* arguing that organizations assume a universal stance toward emotion: we recognize that the general tendency to regulate emotion may be affected by local norms (e.g., Plas & Hoover-Dempsey, 1988).

### *Neutralizing emotion*

Norms of rationality may be invoked and institutionalized to *prevent* the emergence of emotion. Citing the psychodynamic notions of Freud, Jung, Denhardt, and others, Morgan (1986, p. 229) suggests that "rationality is often irrationality in disguise," that is, that formal organizational structures and processes may exist to preclude or compensate for strong emotions, such as insecurity and compulsiveness. Similarly, Diamond (1984) and Hummel (1987) argue that by rigorously structuring roles, relationships, and language, organizations provide a substitute for interpersonal relations. The emphasis on role obligations inhibits the development and expression of an emotional connection between role occupants.

Indeed, some have argued that the norms of rationality often seduce ordinary men and women into committing profoundly antisocial acts on behalf of the organization: the division of labor and the repetitiveness of task performance distance one from the effects of one's behavior, the division of authority fragments responsibility, organizational ideologies justify otherwise repugnant acts, and so forth, such that role occupants may remain emotionally disaffected from their acts (e.g., Gioia, 1992; Kelman & Hamilton, 1989; Silver & Geller, 1978). This phenomenon led Arendt (1965) to subtitle her book on Adolph Eichmann, a senior Nazi administrator of the Final Solution, "A report on the banality of evil."

The upshot is that an emphasis on rationality often displaces an emphasis on emotionality. This is perhaps most evident in service industries where clients interact with service agents in face-to-face encounters and have relatively complex and pressing needs (e.g., social work, medicine, policing, education) (Ashforth & Humphrey, 1993). Service encounters in such industries tend to be emotionally taxing for both service agents and clients. Accordingly, an array of "rational" institutionalized tactics are often used to neutralize emergent emotions. A good example is provided by Millman (1987). She notes that the anger and mistrust commonly experienced by hospital patients is potentially disruptive of efficient operations. Thus, hospitals have developed various means of precluding the experience and expression of these emotions: consent forms minimize the perceived risk of surgery, doctors and medical staff present a united front in support of the recommended procedures and one anothers' expertise, doctors act as if they assume that patients are thoroughly trusting and they largely ignore all but direct queries from patients, bedside visits are kept brief and hurried, and patients are encouraged to view their doubts as natural nervousness and to dismiss them.

Most of the research implicating strong emotions in organizational settings has focused on relatively dramatic occupations—such as health care employee, police officer, and rescue worker—that frequently involve life or death decisions or other intense emotional factors. As a result, researchers have generally overlooked the applicability of emotions and emotional regulation to a wide range of organizational settings. Numerous norms and bureaucratic practices have emerged in a variety of settings to preclude the emergence of strong emotions. For example, a boundary-spanner may be forbidden to accept gifts above a certain value from clients, a newly promoted person is transferred to a new department to avoid confounding her leadership role with her former collegial role, a supervisor is counseled to allow a cooling down period before confronting wayward subordinates, soldiers are punished for fraternizing with the enemy, a person is prohibited from working in the same department as his spouse, and sales agents and company representatives are rigorously trained so that combative clients do not provoke debilitating anxiety. The very absence of strong emotions in many similar situations attests to the effectiveness of such neutralization tactics.

## Buffering emotion

Not all emotion, however, can be prevented. The remaining means of regulating emotion tend to be utilized when emotions are an unavoidable by-product of role performance or when emotional experience or expression are inherent or desired in the role.

Buffering consists of procedures that attempt to *compartmentalize* emotionality and rationality. Thompson (1967) argues that, under norms of rationality, organizations seek to buffer or insulate their technical cores from sources of uncertainty. Given that emotion is often viewed as the antithesis of rationality, organizations frequently seek to buffer their regular operations from potential sources of emotion.

Buffering is evident in roles that normatively require dispassionate performance. Customer service representatives, receptionists, public relations experts, and other "frontstage" personnel (Goffman, 1959) manage the often affectively-charged demands of the public, enabling the "backstage" personnel to perform the routine tasks necessary to fulfill the public's demands. Lief and Fox (1963) and Katz (1963) describe how medical students train for "detached concern," oscillating between the human concern necessary for establishing a rapport with patients and the professional detachment necessary for hard, rational analysis. Van Maanen and Kunda (1989) describe the use of "time-outs," such as office parties and retreats, where everyday norms are temporarily suspended so that emotion may be more freely experienced and expressed.

Buffering is also evident in roles that normatively require the appearance of authentic concern for the welfare of others. Doctors provide care for patients while receptionists collect the fees, individuals dressed as Santa Claus or the Easter Bunny act warmly toward children while photographers sell pictures, and ministers speak of God's love while ushers collect the offering (Hickey, Thompson, & Foster, 1988). Buffering preserves the image of personal concern, untainted by commercial motives.

## Prescribing emotion

Where emotional expression is an inherent or desired component of role performance, the manner in which emotions are expressed tends to be more or less prescribed. Hochschild (1983) argues that common expectations exist concerning the appropriate emotional stance of service providers. These expectations give rise to "feeling rules" or norms that specify the range, intensity, duration, and object of private emotions that should be experienced. These norms are often institutionalized in organizationally-sanctioned scripts (Humphrey & Ashforth, 1994). Thus, flight attendants are trained to appear cheerful and bill collectors are trained to convey a sense of urgency. By regulating the experience and expression of emotion, scripts help ensure that these seemingly "irrational" impulses at least appear to conform to rational task requirements.

We recently extended this argument, speculating that such norms may apply to *any* organizational role involving interpersonal interaction (Ashforth & Humphrey, 1993). Thus, the prescription of emotion may well be a pervasive practice in organizations. A manufacturing executive states:

> Your degree of happiness is important. If someone is always pissing and moaning then that affects your evaluation of them. ... If you're not happy in what you do, you can generate a synergism of apathy. ... Happy people are nicer to be around. It's important to be an up person.
> (Jackall, 1988, p. 55)

Such opinions give rise to and reflect feeling rules. Note that while expressive norms frequently apply to *occupations* (e.g., the courteous and helpful salesperson), and thus cut across organizations, they tend to be subject to local variation (e.g., the *very* courteous and helpful Nordstrom salesperson) and are often learned through socialization within the context of a specific organization. Through observation and imitation, instruction, trial and error, feedback, and reinforcement and punishment, role occupants are taught to feel and display socially desired emotions. Thus, emotional prescriptions typically reflect a meld of organizational and extra-organizational influences.

### *Suppressing emotion*

A critical subset of prescribed emotion involves the socialization of role occupants to *mask* felt emotions that may disrupt role performance. For example, executives were taught to appear calm and rational by peers who would discourage emotional outbursts by instructing one another to "get back to facts" or to "keep personalities out of this" (Argyris, 1966), patients were taught to be "good" by nurses who would reprimand and then avoid patients who created emotional scenes (Glaser & Strauss, 1965), and high steel ironworkers learned from peers that expressions of fear were unacceptable (Haas, 1977). Socialization practices typically reinforce what Maccoby (1976) calls "qualities of the head," while "qualities of the heart" remain underdeveloped.

### *Normalizing emotion*

Finally, no matter how extensive the controls, disruptive or socially unacceptable emotions inevitably arise. Accordingly, organizations have evolved numerous means of maintaining or restoring the status quo by: (1) diffusing or lessening unacceptable emotions, or (2) reframing the meaning of the emotions.

Unacceptable emotion is often diffused by the more or less reflexive use of normalizing and face-saving rituals. For example, given their counter-normative quality, emotional outbursts are frequently followed by an apology, that is, an acknowledgment of at least partial responsibility and an expression of remorse (Ashforth & Lee, 1990). Humor, too, is often used reflexively to diffuse emotion. Pogrebin and Poole (1988) describe how police officers used jokes and sarcasm to dispel their fear and disgust in the face of danger and tragedy. Finally, individuals who frequently display emotion in an unacceptable manner are apt to be assigned a pejorative label (e.g., "bleeding heart," "petty tyrant"). By categorizing an individual as a certain kind of person, such labels serve to *stigmatize* them, reducing their social status such that their behavior can be effectively ignored (Goffman, 1963).

A common means of reframing emotion is to express it in the guise of rationality. Thus, a manager states that she has rejected a major reform because of the high cost, not because of her personal fear about coping with the change, and a second manager states that he has hired a person because of her excellent qualifications, not because he is sexually attracted to her. Indeed, the literature on self-affirmation suggests that the managers themselves may be unaware of the role that emotion plays in their ostensibly rational decisions (Steele, 1988). Another common means of reframing the meaning of emotion is the use of accounts, that is, explanations that either lessen one's responsibility for an event or lessen the apparent severity of the consequences (Ashforth & Lee, 1990). Dilorio and Nusbaumer (1993) describe how client escorts at an abortion clinic collectively worked to interpret their occasional emotional outbursts at antiabortion protesters and the police as a humanistic and justified response to the provocations of these parties. Like apologies, accounts often have a ritualistic cast, involving stock phrases ("I've been under a lot of stress") that tend to be accepted at face value—provided the unacceptable emotions are not expressed too frequently.

An intriguing combination of diffusing and reframing emotion is offered by Plutchik (1984). He argues that certain social institutions have arisen to enable people to express or redirect emotions associated with common life events. Thus, religion enables individuals to cope with the fear and sadness of death, warfare and sports allow individuals to vent the anger caused by daily frustrations and inhibitions, medicine enables people to deal with the disgust associated with disease, and science permits the indulgence of curiosity. This argument implies that certain institutions (i.e., military, organized sports, and scientific establishments) essentially appropriate emotion as instruments of social objectives, thus harnessing emotionality in the service of rationality.

In summary, through the avenues of neutralizing, buffering, prescribing, and normalizing, the experience and expression of emotion is constrained to conform to the norms of rationality.

## The importance of everyday emotion

The overrationalized view of organizations, and the consequent attempts to regulate emotion, have made it difficult to recognize the pervasiveness and utility of emotion in organizational life and how qualities of the heart give value and meaning to qualities of the head. The ubiquitous role of emotion can be illustrated by applications to motivation, leadership, and group dynamics.

## *Motivation*

The literature on motivation also reflects an overrationalized view of individuals. Two of the most influential process theories of motivation are expectancy theory (Vroom, 1964) and reinforcement theory or organizational behavior modification (e.g., Luthans & Kreitner, 1975). These theories basically hold that individuals are motivated to the extent that their behavior is expected to lead to desired outcomes. The image is that of rational exchange: the employee essentially trades effort for pay, security, promotions, and so forth.

What is missing in these theories is the emotional connection of the individual to the content and context of the work. Even such concepts as "valence" (i.e., the perceived attractiveness of an outcome) and "intrinsic motivation" (i.e., the drive that results from the perception that the task *per se* is rewarding) are implicitly couched as cognitive abstractions, as cool perceptions and rational calculations (cf. Shamir, 1991). They are devoid of the emergent joy, excitement, surprise, and frustration that are the *sine qua non* of involving work.

The great potential for emotion to revitalize our perspectives on motivation has only begun to be tapped. Two recent examples will suffice. Kahn (1990, 1992) suggests that the greater the investment of oneself in work, the greater one's motivation. Following Kelman (1958), the lowest investment is *solely* physical (i.e., devoid of cognitive or emotional involvement); the next level is cognitive, the traditional focus of rational theories of motivation; and the highest level is emotional, typified by the individual who forgets to have dinner and works late into the night, lost in the thrill of her work. Individuals experiencing high "personal engagement" (Kahn, 1990, 1992) and "flow" (Csikszentmihalyi, 1990), become physically, cognitively, *and* emotionally immersed in the experience of activity, in the pursuit of a goal. In a real sense they may forget themselves and their context, and rational calculations of inducements and contributions cease to be salient. Fine (1988, p. 125) quotes a cook discussing the "high" that characterizes smooth performance: "I just love the activity. ... I concentrate totally, so I don't know how I feel. ... It's like another sense takes over."

Second, research on organizational citizenship behaviors indicates that people perform numerous tasks that are vital to the smooth functioning of the organization and yet are not explicitly recognized by the reward system, such as assisting others, bending rules to accomplish a task, suggesting improvements, and volunteering for unpopular assignments (Brief & Motowidlo, 1986; Organ, 1990). Such behavior presents an obvious puzzle for a rational exchange perspective. Ashforth (1993) and Organ (1990) argue that the individual-organizational relationship often becomes suffused with affect over time so that a narrow, contractual perspective ("economic exchange") gives way to a sense of trust, concern for the others' needs, and a more open-ended and diffuse commitment ("social exchange").

The *calculative commitment* inherent in traditional motivational models tends to give way to *affective commitment.* Indeed, to presage the discussion of group dynamics below, some would argue that social interaction could not be sustained without this sense of trust and affective commitment (e.g., Barber, 1983; Lewis & Weigert, 1985).

The common theme underlying these perspectives is that strong motivation and psychological involvement are not possible without an *emotional* connection to the work or work context. The traditional focus on effort (behavior) and expectations (cognition) addresses the hands and the head of the individual, but not the heart.

## *Leadership*

According to the enactment perspective, a major task of senior management is to create and maintain a system of shared meanings to provide a basis for coordinated behavior (Daft & Weick, 1984; Smircich & Stubbart, 1985). Managers bracket and punctuate experience, suggesting patterns of events, causal sequences, and meanings. Through action and interaction, they help organizational members triangulate on common interpretations. The enactment perspective further suggests that the system of meanings is disseminated and maintained through the techniques of *symbolic management* (Griffin, Skivington, & Moorhead, 1987; Pfeffer, 1981). Through the use of metaphors, stories, myths, language and acts, rituals, and so forth, management communicates a set of beliefs and guiding values.

We contend that *the success of symbolic management is largely dependent upon the evocation of emotion.* Consistent with our interpretive approach to emotion, the growing literature on organizational culture suggests that managers employ symbols to both foster and shape arousal (e.g., Schneider, 1990; Van Maanen & Kunda, 1989). This literature, however, remains unclear regarding the mechanisms through which symbols affect arousal. We can extend this literature by considering the work of Ortner (1973).

Drawing on anthropological research, Ortner (1973) distinguishes between *summarizing* and *elaborating* symbols. The former represent bundles of experience, evoking affectively-charged memories, values, and beliefs. Images of a role model or company logo may provoke an immediate, visceral reaction and thus act as "catalysts of emotion" (p. 1340). Elaborating symbols, such as metaphors and myths, provide vehicles for understanding experience and ordering thoughts, feelings, and events. While summarizing symbols appear to be associated chiefly with emotion, and elaborating symbols with cognition, Ortner notes that both often play a dual role. Tommerup (1990), for example, describes how subordinates' stories about their charismatic manager served as both a catalyst for "rapture" and as a means of communicating values and desired behaviors.

From this perspective, the practice of symbolic management involves orchestrating summarizing and elaborating symbols to evoke emotion which can be generalized to organizational ends, and to articulate frameworks for understanding organizational experience. Symbolic management is effective because it draws on the qualities of the heart and of the head—and, at times, it entirely bypasses the latter for the former. The medium and the message of much symbolic management is not easily translated into the precise words and classifications of rational discourse (Klapp, 1969). The evoked emotions and meanings are often subtle and ineffable. Thus, one may feel moved without being able to articulate precisely how or why. Indeed, if a given symbolic message *was* stated baldly and directly (e.g., "We are like a family," "We are all winners"), it would often seem sterile and manipulative, and lose much of its motivational force.

A good example of the evocative role of symbols is Rosen's (1988) description of an advertising agency's annual Christmas party. The party, sponsored by the agency, involved Christmas decorations, casual dress (although only top management chose this mode), the sharing of a meal, consuming alcohol, dancing, and skits which spoofed management and the agency's mission and culture. These festive and communal trappings symbolized a family setting furnished by a benevolent and tolerant parent. The resulting sense of fun, excitement, and intimacy presumably helped foster a stronger sense of organizational identity and community.

As this example illustrates, organizational ceremonies and rites in particular function as "strong situations" (Mischel, 1977). The explicit purpose, the designated roles, the setting and props, and the more or less scripted events serve to elicit a succession of rich emotions—such as the moments of goodwill, joy, and melancholy during a retirement dinner. It is as much the *process* of the ritual as the *content* that evokes this shared emotion, and the variety and intensity of the emotion helps engender and affirm the desired values and beliefs (Trice & Beyer, 1984; Van Maanen & Kunda, 1989).

## *Group dynamics*

To this point, emotion has been largely discussed as an individual-level or interpersonal phenomenon. Here, emotion is discussed as a group-level phenomenon. The role of emotion in group dynamics has been a constant though often only implicit theme in the social psychological and organizational behavior literatures. For example, "cohesiveness" is typically defined as the attractiveness of a group to its members, highlighting the affective bond between individuals. Conceptual and empirical work regularly notes the central role of cohesion in the formation, maintenance, and effectiveness of various groups. Thus, armies typically rely on a soldier's loyalty to his or her platoon rather than to the army as an institution (Dyer, 1985), and many business organizations rely on collective socialization in part because a newcomer's peers can often induce him or her to do things that no rulebook or supervisor ever could (Van Maanen & Schein, 1979).

A second example of the role of emotion in groups is found in the literature on intra- and intergroup conflict. Tensions are often fuelled by affective or expressive concerns that have little to do with instrumental or task-focused concerns, and minor disagreements can quickly escalate into major conflicts with groups polarized into rival camps. Smith (1982) describes how intergroup conflict—whether over ends, means, resources, etc.—may generate distrust and hostility such that the conflict *itself* becomes the focal point and the initial causes become forgotten. Smith and Berg (1987) discuss the tensions that groups experience from several inherent paradoxes, such as the need for trust to exist before trust can develop, and the need to affirm one's individual identity as well as one's collective identity. And Hirschhorn (1988) describes how individuals may cope with anxiety by externalizing it, often precipitating conflict with co-workers and superiors.

## *Emotional contagion*

The impact of emotion on group dynamics, however, goes beyond these frequently examined ways. For one, the interpretive approach to emotion highlights how the social context may induce and shape physiological arousal and its interpretation. This is evident in the literature on *emotional contagion.* Hatfield, Cacioppo, and Rapson (1992) define contagion as "A tendency to mimic another person's emotional experience/expression ... and thus to experience/express the same emotions oneself." People "catch" emotions through conscious information processing (e.g., feeling sad upon reading about a tragedy) and/or nonconscious or automatic imitation (via facial, postural, and vocal cues, e.g., a person sensing and feeling his co-worker's distress). Emotional contagion underlies such phrases as "team spirit," "electricity in the air," and "esprit de corps," and has been documented in a variety of organizational settings, including between college roommates (Howes, Hokanson, & Loewenstein, 1985), clients and clinicians (Hatfield *et al.,* 1992), teammates in a sporting event (Zurcher, 1982), and women at a Tupperware sales rally (Peven, 1968). For example, two gymnasts commented on why they applauded teammates: "when everyone yells, it helps you to get psyched up and go harder for it"; "During a floor exercise the team will clap and cheer rhythmically, to 'go, go, go'; it helps us to get through the routine" (Snyder, 1990, p. 265).

Research on factors influencing emotional contagion is relatively scarce. However, it seems reasonable that contagion would emerge or become stronger when: (1) interaction and cohesion are high, (2) an emotion is clearly expressed by a high status or well-liked member, (3) an emotion is congruent with feeling rules, (4) strong contrary emotions are not already extant, and (5)—at least for conscious processing—there is ambiguity about the meaning of an event and the appropriate emotional stance, and a common interpretation begins to coalesce. These conditions may often converge in organizational subunits, given members' interdependencies, proximity, and shared social identity (Ashforth & Mael, 1989; George & Brief, 1992), Further, the earlier discussion of symbolic management complements this perspective, suggesting that emotional contagion may at times be deliberately cued by leaders (Lofland, 1982).

Emotional contagion may be a very strong constructive *or* destructive force in organizations. On the positive side, contagion may increase empathy and solidarity, creating a cohesive group, and increase psychological involvement, creating a motivated work force. This contagion can be mobilized in the pursuit of organizational goals. Indeed, Zurcher (1982, p. 14) maintains that "One of the key elements in the evolution of a group from liminality to communitas [i.e., from anonymity and confusion to cohesiveness and common purpose] is that along the way the members share intense emotional experiences." Shared emotions help connect individuals phenomenologically, perhaps to the extent that the individuals become—at least temporarily—submerged in a kind of "group mind." For example, in a discussion of momentum in sport, Adler and Adler (1978) discuss how a big play, a coach berating an umpire, the entry of a charismatic player, or a cheering audience can galvanize players to think, feel, and act as a *team,* creating a collective aura of energy and invincibility that propels them to victory.

On the negative side, contagion can also impair performance. Otherwise positive emotions may become so overwhelming that individuals cannot continue to perform their tasks. Contagion may cause negative emotions such as fear and anxiety to quickly pervade the organization, inhibiting needed problem-solving. Further, negative emotions may galvanize individuals to collectively attack others or resist otherwise advantageous change, and may provide an "emotional climate" that legitimates such behavior. Stein (1990) studied a medical subsidiary that the parent company had allowed to atrophy and found a collective sense of despondency, apprehension, anger, and impotence. These emotions were associated with apathy and withdrawal, infighting and factionalism, and a decrease in reality testing, punctuated by manic episodes of hope and energy. Contagion, then, can foster social momentum or inertia. This may be one reason for Horwitz and Rabbie's (1982, p. 269) conclusion that, "Both experimental and naturalistic observations suggest that hostility erupts more readily between [groups] than between individuals."

Thus, the notion of emotional contagion may play a critical role in a variety of group-level phenomena, including group synergy, organizational momentum or inertia, morale, groupthink, and organizational neuroses and other bureaupathologies, as well as intergroup conflict.

*Play and humor*

A second example of the pervasiveness of emotion in group life is the growing literature on play and humor in organizational settings. Consistent with the perceived bifurcation of rationality and emotionality, work and play are generally seen as dichotomous (Dandridge, 1986; Fine, 1988). The perception of work in Western society is based largely on the Protestant work ethic. Work is stereotypically seen as serious, structured activity in pursuit of productive goals. The focus is on outcomes. In contrast, play is seen as "fun"—lighthearted, frequently emergent activity pursued for personal enjoyment. The focus is on process. While play is seen as voluntary and sustained by intrinsic rewards, work is seen as necessary and sustained by extrinsic rewards. The right to play is "earned" through work.

In reality, work activities and the work context are typically laced with elements of play and humor. This is most evident in ethnographic studies of work, such as Roy's (1959–60) classic discussion of "banana time," Fine's (1988) description of playful activities in restaurant kitchens, and Collinson's (1988) discussion of informal shop-floor behavior. For example, Fine notes how cooks would relieve the boredom of a slow night by playing pranks on one another (e.g., spiking a soda with Tabasco sauce), initiate new workers by requesting something impossible (e.g., a can of steam), sing together while preparing meals, and call one another nicknames, and Collinson describes how teasing and pranks were used to gauge whether an individual could "take a joke" and thus fit in to the shop-floor culture.

Such activities have two major benefits. First, they provide a rich sense of community and social identity. Mutual production of an intrinsically enjoyable activity fosters a shared memory of a rewarding experience, creates and affirms a sense of "groupness," and facilitates a richer appreciation of one's peers as whole *persons* rather than as stereotypical *role occupants.* These qualities in turn facilitate cooperation, communication, and the affective commitment that underlies prosocial behavior.

The second benefit of play and humor is that they frequently facilitate task effectiveness. Some forms of play have much in common with our discussion of motivational flow or personal engagement. Abramis (1990) found that tasks high in autonomy, skill variety, task identity and significance, and feedback, were associated with a sense of work as a game, sport, or puzzle, and this sense of "work as play" was in turn associated with a sense of learning, excitement, and involvement, though not performance *per se.* The impact of other forms of play may be more problematic. For example, although Abramis (1990) found that fooling around at work undermines performance, other analyses suggest that such activities may enhance performance by relieving boredom and tension (Fine, 1988) and by fostering creativity (Csikszentmihalyi, 1990).

### *A composite illustration: transformational leadership*

By way of summary, a good illustration of the relevance of emotion to motivation, leadership, and group dynamics is provided by the growing literature on transformational leadership. Transformational leadership refers to the process of fostering dramatic changes in an organization by building commitment to the organization and its mission (Seltzer & Bass, 1990). The literature suggests that this process is largely dependent upon the evocation, framing, and mobilization of *emotions,* whereas conventional "transactional leadership" depends more upon subordinates' *cognitions.* Transactional leaders follow a rational exchange model of motivation: they show subordinates how effort is instrumental to the attainment of extrinsic rewards, such as pay and security.

Transformational leaders, in contrast, appear to deemphasize narrow self-interest and rationality. Specifically, Shamir, House, and Arthur (1993) argue that they engage in several practices. First, they tend to increase the intrinsic value of effort by emphasizing: (1) the symbolic and expressive aspects of effort—by making effort "a moral statement," and (2) one's membership in the collective, thus transforming effort into both a contribution to the collective and a statement that affirms a valued social identity. Further, transformational leaders seem to enhance the value of the social identity by emphasizing the uniqueness and superiority of the collective (cf. Ashforth & Mael, 1989).

Second, transformational leaders tend to increase the intrinsic value of goal accomplishment by representing organizational goals in terms of the values they represent—by articulating a compelling vision. These values are ones that are difficult to justify on pragmatic or narrowly rational grounds: they represent transcendental or transrational ideals. Indeed, extrinsic rewards may be downplayed so that followers will attribute their behavior to internalized ideals. Additionally, transformational leaders often stress the importance of the goal to the maintenance and superiority of the social identity, further connecting the individual to a larger entity and to concerns that transcend self-interests.

Third, transformational leaders appear to instill faith in a better future by emphasizing Utopian goals. Again, such goals are difficult to justify on rational grounds since they are distant and vague. Nevertheless, having faith may be emotionally satisfying in itself. Thus, work may be transformed from a rational instrument for attaining extrinsic rewards into a sort of moral calling. Additionally, transformational leaders often act as "living symbols," modeling and thus defining the appropriate interpretation of the new order and the emotional stance toward it (Wasielewski, 1985).

By arousing emotion and harnessing it to the pursuit of lofty goals, transformational leadership represents a potentially potent force for change. Field and laboratory research suggests that transformational leadership is associated with higher effort and performance among subordinates, and higher effectiveness ratings from superiors (House, Woycke, & Fodor, 1988). Evidence of the impact of transformational leadership on organizational change, however, tends to be more anecdotal—though voluminous (e.g., Nadler & Tushman, 1990; Tichy & Devanna, 1986). Recent examples appear to include General Electric under Jack Welch, Walt Disney under Michael Eisner, Drake Business School under Mary Ann Lawlor, and Nucor Corporation under Ken Iverson.

However, the literature on transformational leadership also raises a cautionary flag regarding the potency of aroused emotion in organizational settings. As Yukl (1989) notes, history is replete with examples of political, business, and religious leaders who became corrupted by the adulation of others and the power it conferred, or simply used the adulation for self-serving purposes. As suggested earlier, a leader may cue an emotional contagion and this can be mobilized toward a prosocial or antisocial vision, depending on the leader's motives. Further, transformational leadership can foster an unhealthy emotional dependence on the leader and the abnegation of autonomy and independent selfhood (Howell, 1988).

## Research directions

This broad-brushed discussion of emotion in the workplace suggests a variety of issues for future research. For one, the emphasis in the paper on the experiencing of emotions and on organizational processes suggests the utility of studying the dynamics of emotion and how emotions change over time. Thus, researchers could focus on the experience and expression of emotion during discrete episodes, such as staff meetings and task performance. How do roles, objectives, interpersonal relationships, relative power, and so forth, affect the emergence of feeling rules and the range and intensity of felt emotion, and how does emotion affect these variables? Researchers could pursue the issue of emotional change at the individual level (e.g., as a function of role transitions and tenure), group level (e.g., as a function of group stability and relative success), and organizational level (e.g., as a function of life cycle stage). For example, regarding the latter Perkins, Nieva, and Lawler (1983) discuss the passion and excitement surrounding the start-up of a new organization. This likely gives way to a more stable and abiding sense of commitment, which may be periodically interrupted by fluctuations in performance, mergers and acquisitions, changes in leadership, and so forth. Studies of the emotions generated by major structural transitions (Pettigrew, 1985) and bankruptcy (Sutton & Callahan, 1987) provide instructive examples.

Perhaps the most promising research questions concern the specific links between the content and context of work and the emergence of emotions. Sample issues include: what mix of task characteristics promotes personal involvement? How are emotion and organizational citizenship behaviors connected (cf. George & Brief, 1992)? What is the link between specific symbols, their manner of presentation, and the evocation of specific emotions? To what extent is emotion a necessary catalyst for various group-level phenomena? Under what conditions are play and humor functional and dysfunctional for the group and organization? How can emotions be mobilized to increase receptiveness to organizational change? In what respects are transactional leadership and transformational leadership antagonistic and complementary? What factors affect whether the emotions aroused by transformational leadership are used constructively or destructively vis-à-vis followers, organizations, and society?

We argued that the emphasis on rationality has led to a pervasive neglect of emotionality in organizational life. This artificial bifurcation raises several intriguing questions about the management of emotion-laden issues. For example, how do organizations such as crisis centers and service-intensive retailers recognize and respond to the emotional needs of their clients, and how do organizations recognize and respond to the emotional problems of their own members, such as frustration and burnout? To what extent and through what processes is objectivity maintained by professionals and quasi-professionals (e.g., journalists, doctors, counsellors, scientists), or by managers vis-à-vis their subordinates? Similarly, the neglect of emotionality raises the question of how organizations that essentially sell emotional arousal tend to function. How do organizations that produce entertainment (e.g., sports, movies), religious worship, or the arts (e.g., drama, music, dance) choreograph emotional arousal? How do advertising agencies and public relations firms create and disseminate emotionally evocative images of products, causes, and organizations? How do news organizations select and frame stories to elicit desired emotional reactions (e.g., sympathy for the victims of a tragedy)?

We also argued that norms of rationality are invoked to regulate emotionality. However, the psychodynamic theories of Freud, Jung, and others suggest that emotions cannot be eliminated and will break through the veneer of rationality in myriad, disruptive ways. This begs the question of how and to what extent neutralized, buffered, and prescribed emotions manifest themselves both on and off the job. For example, Morgan (1986) suggests that politicking, stress, lying, depression, and sabotage may be manifestations of suppressed impulses, and Ashforth (1991) argues that vicious circles and other seemingly irrational behaviors in organizations are partially sustained by emotional needs.

Finally, the four tactics for regulating emotion were derived inductively from a review of a fairly eclectic organizational literature. As one reviewer noted, these tactics may also be utilized in other social domains such as marriages, families, peer groups, and various public settings. For example, Stearns and Stearns (1986) discuss the gradual emergence of normative constraints on the expression of anger in both the workplace and the home. An intriguing issue for future research is the extent to which our typology of emotional control tactics does in fact generalize to other social domains.

## Conclusion

It was argued that the role of everyday emotion in mundane organizational life has been neglected. Further, organizational researchers and practitioners often seem to assume that emotionality is the antithesis of rationality and, consequently, that emotion is potentially problematic. Accordingly, at least four institutionalized mechanisms have evolved for regulating the experience and expression of emotion in organizations: neutralizing, buffering, prescribing, and normalizing emotion.

In contrast to this perspective, we argued that the experience of work is saturated with emotion and that emotionality and rationality are interpenetrated. This argument was illustrated by applications to three domains:

1   The traditional focus of process theories of motivation on effort (behavior) and instrumentalities and expectancies (cognition) has neglected the crucial role of personal engagement (emotion). While rational computation may induce one to join an organization and put forth at least minimal effort, true dedication is only possible if there is an emotional connection to the work or the work context.
2   A major task of leadership is to create and maintain a system of shared meanings. This is accomplished through symbolic management, which is based largely on the evocation of emotion. Many symbols evoke affectively-charged memories, values, and beliefs which can be generalized to organizational ends. In contrast, more direct appeals to rationality are apt to be perceived as sterile and manipulative.

3   As a group-level phenomenon, emotion has typically been discussed under the rubric of cohesion and intra- and intergroup conflict. More recently, the notion of emotional contagion suggests that emotion may act as a catalyst for a variety of group phenomena such as groupthink and organizational momentum, and the notion of play and humor suggests that the positive emotions stimulated by fun at work can promote social identity, a sense of community, and task effectiveness.

In summary, management research and practice have emphasized rationality at the expense of emotionality. Rather than view emotion as the dysfunctional antithesis of rationality, we argue that scholars and practitioners need to recognize the functional complementarity of emotionality and rationality.

## Acknowledgments

We are indebted to an anonymous reviewer and to the participants in Gary Johns' doctoral seminar in Organizational Behavior at Concordia University for their helpful comments. Portions of the paper were presented at the 1993 meeting of the British Academy of Management in Milton Keynes, England.

## Notes

1 Several recent exceptions include Albrow (1992), Hosking and Fineman (1990), Isen and Baron (1991), and Van Maanen and Kunda (1989).
2 See Frijda (1986) and Thoits (1989) for discussions of how these constructs differ.

## References

Abramis, D. J. Play in work: Childish hedonism or adult enthusiasm? *American Behavioral Scientist,* 1990, *33,* 353–373.
Adler, P., & Adler, P. A. The role of momentum in sport. *Urban Life,* 1978, *7,* 153–176.
Albrow, M. Sine ira et studio—or do organizations have feelings? *Organization Studies,* 1992, *13,* 313–329.
Arendt, H. *Eichmann in Jerusalem: A report on the banality of evil* (revised and enlarged ed.). New York: Penguin, 1965.
Argyris, C. Interpersonal barriers to decision making. *Harvard Business Review,* 1966, *44*(2), 84–97.
Argyris, C. *Strategy, change and defensive routines.* Boston: Pitman, 1985.
Ashforth, B. E. The whys and wherefores of organizational Catch-22s: Common types and their implications for organization development. *Public Administration Quarterly,* 1991, *14,* 457–482.
Ashforth, B. E. Political and apolitical action: Toward a reconciliation of discrepant models of organizational behavior. *International Journal of Organizational Analysis,* 1993, *1,* 363–384.

Ashforth, B. E., & Gibbs, B. W. The double-edge of organizational legitimation. *Organization Science,* 1990, *1*, 177–194.

Ashforth, B. E., & Humphrey, R. H. Emotional labor in service roles: The influence of identity. *Academy of Management Review,* 1993, *18*, 88–115.

Ashforth, B. E., & Lee, R. T. Defensive behavior in organizations: A preliminary model. *Human Relations,* 1990, *43*, 621–648.

Ashforth, B. E., & Mael, F. Social identity theory and the organization. *Academy of Management Review,* 1989, *14*, 20–39.

Barber, B. *The logic and limits of trust.* New Brunswick, NJ: Rutgers University Press, 1983.

Brenner, M. *House of dreams: The Bingham family of Louisville.* New York: Random House, 1988.

Brief, A. P., & Motowidlo, S. J. Prosocial organizational behaviors. *Academy of Management Review,* 1986, *11*, 710–725.

Burrough, B., & Helyar, J. *Barbarians at the gate: The fall of RJR Nabisco.* New York: Harper & Row, 1990.

Chatman, J. A. Improving interactional organizational research: A model of person-organization fit. *Academy of Management Review,* 1989, *14*, 333–349.

Collinson, D. L. "Engineering humour": Masculinity, joking and conflict in shop-floor relations. *Organization Studies,* 1988, *9*, 181–199.

Csikszentmihalyi, M. *Flow: The psychology of optimal experience.* New York: Harper & Row, 1990.

Daft, R. L., & Weick, K. E. Toward a model of organizations as interpretation systems. *Academy of Management Review,* 1984, *9*, 284–295.

Dandridge, T. C. Ceremony as an integration of work and play. *Organization Studies,* 1986, *7*, 159–170.

Diamond, M. A. Bureaucracy as externalized self-system: A view from the psychological interior. *Administration & Society,* 1984, *16*, 195–214.

Dilorio, J. A., & Nusbaumer, M. R. Securing our sanity: Anger management among abortion escorts. *Journal of Contemporary Ethnography,* 1993, *21*, 411–438.

Dyer, G. *War.* Toronto: Stoddart, 1985.

Fine, G. A. Letting off steam? Redefining a restaurant's work environment. In M. D. Moore and R. C. Snyder (Eds.), *Inside organizations: Understanding the human dimension.* Newbury Park, CA: Sage, 1988, pp. 119–128.

Flett, G. L., Blankstein, K. R., Pliner, P., & Bator, C. Impression-management and self-deception components of appraised emotional experience. *British Journal of Social Psychology,* 1988, *27*, 67–77.

Frijda, N. H. *The emotions.* Cambridge: Cambridge University Press, 1986.

Garson, B. *All the livelong day: The meaning and demeaning of routine work.* New York: Penguin, 1977.

Geertz, C. *The interpretation of cultures: Selected essays.* New York: Basic Books, 1973.

George, J. M., & Brief, A. P. Feeling good—doing good: A conceptual analysis of the mood at work—organizational spontaneity relationship. *Psychological Bulletin,* 1992, *112*, 310–329.

Gerhards, J. The changing culture of emotions in modern society. *Social Science Information,* 1989, *28*, 737–754.

Gioia, D. Pinto fires and personal ethics: A script analysis of missed opportunities. *Journal of Business Ethics,* 1992, *11*, 379–389.

Glaser, B. G., & Strauss, A. L. *Awareness of dying.* Chicago: Aldine, 1965.

Goffman, E. *The presentation of self in everyday life.* Garden City, NY: Doubleday, 1959.

Goffman, E. *Stigma: Notes on the management of spoiled identity.* Englewood Cliffs, NJ: Prentice-Hall, 1963.

Gordon, S. L. Social structural effects on emotions. In T. D. Kemper (Ed.), *Research agendas in the sociology of emotions.* Albany: State University of New York Press, 1990, pp. 145–179.

Griffin, R. W., Skivington, K. D., & Moorhead, G. Symbolic and international [sic] perspectives on leadership: An integrative framework. *Human Relations,* 1987, *40*, 199–218.

Haas, J. Learning real feelings: A study of high steel ironworkers' reactions to fear and danger. *Sociology of Work and Occupations,* 1977, *4*, 147–170.

Hatfield, E., Cacioppo, J., & Rapson, R. L. Primitive emotional contagion. In M. S. Clark (Ed.), *Review of personality and social psychology* (Vol. 14). Newbury Park, CA: Sage, 1992, pp. 151–177.

Hickey, J. V., Thompson, W. E., & Foster, D. L. Becoming the Easter Bunny: Socialization into a fantasy role. *Journal of Contemporary Ethnography,* 1988, *17*, 67–95.

Hirschhorn, L. *The workplace within: The psychodynamics of organizational life.* Cambridge, MA: MIT Press, 1988.

Hochschild, A. R. *The managed heart: Commercialization of human feeling.* Berkeley, CA: University of California Press, 1983.

Horwitz, M., & Rabbie, J. M., Individuality and membership in the intergroup system. In H. Tajfel (Ed.), *Social identity and intergroup relations.* Cambridge: Cambridge University Press, 1982, pp. 241–274.

Hosking, D., & Fineman, S. Organizing processes. *Journal of Management Studies,* 1990, *27*, 583–604.

House, R. J., Woycke, J., & Fodor, E. M. Charismatic and noncharismatic leaders: Differences in behavior and effectiveness. In J. A. Conger, R. N. Kanungo, and Associates (Eds.), *Charismatic leadership: The elusive factor in organizational effectiveness.* San Francisco: Jossey-Bass, 1988, pp. 98–121.

Howell, J. M. Two faces of charisma: Socialized and personalized leadership in organizations. In J. A. Conger, R. N. Kanungo, and Associates (Eds.), *Charismatic leadership: The elusive factor in organizational effectiveness.* San Francisco: Jossey-Bass, 1988, pp. 213–236.

Howes, M. J., Hokanson, J. E., & Loewenstein, D. A. Induction of depressive affect after prolonged exposure to a mildly depressed individual. *Journal of Personality and Social Psychology,* 1985, *49*, 1110–1113.

Hummel, R. P. *The bureaucratic experience* (3rd ed). New York: St. Martin's Press, 1987.

Humphrey, R. H., & Ashforth, B. E. Cognitive scripts and prototypes in service encounters. In T. A. Swartz, D. E. Bowen, and S. W. Brown (Eds.), *Advances in services marketing and management: Research and practice* (Vol. 3). Greenwich, CT: JAI Press, 1994.

Isen, A. M., & Baron, R. A. Positive affect as a factor in organizational behavior. In L. L. Cummings and B. M. Staw (Eds.), *Research in organizational behavior* (Vol. 13). Greenwich, CT: JAI Press, 1991, pp. 1–53.

Jackall, R. *Moral mazes: The world of corporate managers.* New York: Oxford University Press, 1988.

James, N. Emotional labour: Skill and work in the social regulation of feelings. *Sociological Review,* 1989, *37*, 15–42.

James, W. What is an emotion? *Mind,* 1884, *9,* 188–205.

Kahn, W. A. Psychological conditions of personal engagement and disengagement at work. *Academy of Management Journal,* 1990, *33,* 692–724.

Kahn, W. A. To be fully there: Psychological presence at work. *Human Relations,* 1992, *45,* 321–349.

Katz, R. L. *Empathy: Its nature and uses.* New York: Free Press, 1963.

Kelman, H. C. Compliance, identification, and internalization: Three processes of attitude change. *Journal of Conflict Resolution,* 1958, *2,* 51–60.

Kelman, H. C, & Hamilton, V. L. *Crimes of obedience: Toward a social psychology of authority and responsibility.* New Haven, CT: Yale University Press, 1989.

Kemper, T. D. How many emotions are there? Wedding the social and the autonomic components. *American Journal of Sociology,* 1987, *93,* 263–289.

Klapp, O. E. *Collective search for identity.* New York: Holt, Rinehart and Winston, 1969.

Levy, R. I. *Tahitians: Mind and experience in the Society Islands.* Chicago: University of Chicago Press, 1973.

Lewis, J. D., & Weigert, A. J. Social atomism, holism, and trust. *Sociological Quarterly,* 1985, *26,* 455–471.

Lief, H. I., & Fox, R. C. Training for "detached concern" in medical students. In H. I. Lief, V. F. Lief, and N. R. Lief (Eds.), *The psychological bases of medical practice.* New York: Harper & Row, 1963, pp. 12–35.

Likert, R. *The human organization: Its management and value.* New York: McGraw-Hill, 1967.

Lofland, J. Crowd joys. *Urban Life,* 1982, *10,* 355–381.

Luthans, F., & Kreitner, R. *Organizational behavior modification.* Glenview, IL: Scott, Foresman, 1975.

Maccoby, M. *The gamesman.* Toronto: Bantam Books, 1976.

Mainiero, L. A. A review and analysis of power dynamics in organizational romances. *Academy of Management Review,* 1986, *11,* 750–762.

Matsumoto, D., & Sanders, M. Emotional experiences during engagement in intrinsically and extrinsically motivated tasks. *Motivation and Emotion,* 1988, *12,* 353–369.

Mayo, E. *The social problems of an industrial civilization.* Boston: Harvard University, 1945.

Meyerson, D. E. Uncovering socially undesirable emotions: Experiences of ambiguity in organizations. *American Behavioral Scientist,* 1990, *33,* 296–307.

Millman, M. The enactment of trust: The case of cardiac patients. In H. D. Schwartz (Ed.), *Dominant issues in medical sociology* (2nd ed.). New York: Random House, 1987, pp. 182–190.

Mischel, W. The interaction of person and situation. In D. Magnusson and N. S. Endler (Eds.), *Personality at the crossroads: Current issues in interactional psychology.* Hillsdale, NJ: Erlbaum, 1977, pp. 333–352.

Morgan, G. *Images of organization.* Beverly Hills, CA: Sage, 1986.

Mumby, D. K., & Putnam, L. L. The politics of emotion: A feminist reading of bounded rationality. *Academy of Management Review,* 1992, *17,* 465–486.

Nadler, D. A., & Tushman, M. L. Beyond the charismatic leader: Leadership and organizational change. *California Management Review,* 1990, *32*(2), 77–97.

Organ, D. W. The motivational basis of organizational citizenship behavior. In B. M. Staw and L. L. Cummings (Eds.), *Research in organizational behavior* (Vol. 12). Greenwich, CT: JAI Press, 1990, pp. 43–72.

Ortner, S. B. On key symbols. *American Anthropologist,* 1973, *75,* 1338–1346.

Perkins, D. N. T., Nieva, V. F., & Lawler, E. E., III. *Managing creation: The challenge of building a new organization.* New York: Wiley, 1983.

Pettigrew, A. M. *The awakening giant: Continuity and change in Imperial Chemical Industries.* Oxford: Blackwell, 1985.

Peven, D. E. The use of religious revival techniques to indoctrinate personnel: The home-party sales organization. *Sociological Quarterly,* 1968, *9,* 97–106.

Pfeffer, J. Management as symbolic action: The creation and maintenance of organizational paradigms. In L. L. Cummings and B. M. Staw (Eds.), *Research in organizational behavior* (Vol. 3). Greenwich, CT: JAI Press, 1981, pp. 1–52.

Plas, J. M., & Hoover-Dempsey, K. V. *Working up a storm: Anger, anxiety, joy, and tears on the job.* New York: Norton, 1988.

Plutchik, R. Emotions: A general psychoevolutionary theory. In K. R. Scherer and P. Ekman (Eds.), *Approaches to emotion.* Hillsdale, NJ: Erlbaum, 1984, pp. 197–219.

Pogrebin, M. R., & Poole, E. D. Humor in the briefing room: A study of the strategic uses of humor among police. *Journal of Contemporary Ethnography,* 1988, *17,* 183–210.

Ratner, C. A social constructionist critique of the naturalistic theory of emotion. *Journal of Mind and Behavior,* 1989, *10,* 211–230.

Roethlisberger, F. J., & Dickson, W. J. *Management and the worker: An account of a research program conducted by the Western Electric Company, Hawthorne Works, Chicago.* Cambridge, MA: Harvard University Press, 1943.

Rosen, M. You asked for it: Christmas at the bosses' expense. *Journal of Management Studies,* 1988, *25,* 463–480.

Roy, D. F. "Banana time": Job satisfaction and informal interaction. *Human Organization,* 1959–1960, *18,* 158–168.

Salancik, G. R., & Pfeffer, J. A social information processing approach to job attitudes and task design. *Administrative Science Quarterly,* 1978, *23,* 224–253.

Sandelands, L. E. The concept of work feeling. *Journal for the Theory of Social Behavior,* 1988, *18,* 437–457.

Sandelands, L. E., & Buckner, G. C. Of art and work: Aesthetic experience and the psychology of work feelings. In L. L. Cummings and B. M. Staw (Eds.), *Research in organizational behavior* (Vol. 11). Greenwich, CT: JAI Press, 1989, pp. 105–131.

Schneider, B. (Ed.) *Organizational climate and culture.* San Francisco: Jossey-Bass, 1990.

Seltzer, J., & Bass, B. M. Transformational leadership: Beyond initiation and consideration. *Journal of Management,* 1990, *16,* 693–703.

Shamir, B. Meaning, self and motivation in organizations. *Organization Studies,* 1991, *12,* 405–424.

Shamir, B., House, R. J., & Arthur, M. B. The motivational effects of charismatic leadership: A self-concept based theory. *Organizational Science,* 1993, *4,* 577–594.

Shrivastava, P., & Schneider, S. Organizational frames of reference. *Human Relations,* 1984, *37,* 795–809.

Silver, M., & Geller, D. On the irrelevance of evil: The organization and individual action. *Journal of Social Issues,* 1978, *34*(4), 125–136.

Smircich, L., & Stubbart, C. Strategic management in an enacted world. *Academy of Management Review,* 1985, *10,* 724–736.

Smith, K. K. *Groups in conflict: Prisons in disguise.* Dubuque, IA: Kendall/Hunt, 1982.

Smith, K. K., & Berg, D. N. *Paradoxes of group life: Understanding conflict, paralysis, and movement in group dynamics.* San Francisco: Jossey-Bass, 1987.

Snyder, E. E. Emotion and sport: A case study of collegiate women gymnasts. *Sociology of Sport Journal,* 1990, *7,* 254–270.

Stearns, C. Z., & Stearns, P. N. *Anger: The struggle for emotional control in America's history.* Chicago: University of Chicago Press, 1986.

Steele, C. M. The psychology of self-affirmation: Sustaining the integrity of the self. In L. Berkowitz (Ed.), *Advances in experimental social psychology* (Vol. 21). San Diego: Academic Press, 1988, pp. 261–302.

Stein, H. F. Adapting to doom: The group psychology of an organization threatened with cultural extinction. *Political Psychology,* 1990, *11,* 113–145.

Sutton, R. I., & Callahan, A. L. The stigma of bankruptcy: Spoiled organizational image and its management. *Academy of Management Journal,* 1987, *30,* 405–436.

Terkel, S. *Working.* New York: Avon, 1975.

Thoits, P. A. Self-labeling processes in mental illness: The role of emotional deviance. *American Journal of Sociology,* 1985, *91,* 221–249.

Thoits, P. A. The sociology of emotions. In W. R. Scott and J. Blake (Eds.), *Annual review of sociology* (Vol. 15). Palo Alto, CA: Annual Reviews, 1989, pp. 317–342.

Thompson, J. D. *Organizations in action: Social science bases of administrative theory.* New York: McGraw-Hill, 1967.

Tichy, N. M., & Devanna, M. A. *The transformational leader.* New York: Wiley, 1986.

Tommerup, P. Stories about an inspiring leader: "Rapture," and the symbolics of employee fulfillment. *American Behavioral Scientist,* 1990, *33,* 374–385.

Trice, H. M., & Beyer, J. M. Studying organizational cultures through rites and ceremonials. *Academy of Management Review,* 1984, *9,* 653–669.

Van Maanen, J., & Kunda, G. "Real feelings": Emotional expression and organizational culture. In L. L. Cummings and B. M. Staw (Eds.), *Research in organizational behavior* (Vol. 11). Greenwich, CT: JAI Press, 1989, pp. 43–103.

Van Maanen, J., & Schein, E. H. Toward a theory of organizational socialization. In B. M. Staw (Ed.), *Research in organizational behavior* (Vol. 1). Greenwich, CT: JAI Press, 1979, pp. 209–264.

Vroom, V. H. *Work and motivation.* New York: Wiley, 1964.

Wall, J. A. *Bosses.* Lexington, MA: Lexington, 1986.

Wasielewski, P. L. The emotional basis of charisma. *Symbolic Interaction,* 1985, *8,* 207–222.

Weber, M. *Economy and society: An outline of interpretive sociology* (3 Vols., translated by E. Fischoff et al.). G. Roth and C. Wittich (Eds.). New York: Bedminster Press, 1968.

Yager, R. R. (Ed.) *Fuzzy set and possibility theory: Recent developments.* New York: Pergamon Press, 1982.

Yukl, G. A. *Leadership in organizations* (2nd ed.). Englewood Cliffs, NJ: Prentice Hall, 1989.

Zurcher, L. A. The staging of emotion: A dramaturgical analysis. *Symbolic Interaction,* 1982, *5,* 1–22.

# 14

# THE MEASUREMENT OF WELL-BEING AND OTHER ASPECTS OF MENTAL HEALTH

*Peter Warr*

Source: *Journal of Occupational psychology* 63 (1990): 193–210.

### Abstract

New instruments are described for the measurement of both job-related and non-job mental health. These cover two axes of affective well-being, based upon dimensions of pleasure and arousal, and also reported competence, aspiration and negative job carry-over. Baseline data are presented from a sample of 1686 job-holders, and earlier uses of the well-being scales are summarized. The instruments appear to be psychometrically acceptable, and are associated with demographic and occupational features in expected ways. For example, older employees report greater job-related well-being; occupational level is positively correlated with job depression–enthusiasm but negatively associated with job anxiety–contentment; depression–enthusiasm is more predictable from low-to-medium opportunity for skill use and task variety, whereas anxiety–contentment is more a function of workload or uncertainty.

Many studies have examined the impact of work and careers on job-related and non-job mental health. Nevertheless, there is still a shortage of instruments whose psychometric properties have been determined through data from large samples of employees of both genders and several occupational levels. In particular, there is a need for measures which can provide information about affective well-being, subjective competence and aspiration, through scores which can be compared with known means and standard deviations from appropriate demographic groups.

This paper aims to address those deficiencies, by describing new instruments and summarizing values obtained from a large sample of British job-holders. The approach to affective well-being is through two principal axes ('anxiety–contentment' and 'depression–enthusiasm') which have emerged as important in non-occupational research, and which will be examined through parallel measures in both job-related and non-job settings. No other instruments are currently available which cover the full range of those axes in both types of setting.

The approach taken is one which emphasizes practicality as well as psychometric acceptability. Many occupational researchers are deterred by the length and cumbersome language of some previous instruments, and are tempted to introduce their own modifications or create new scales for one-off application. Such developments prevent the accumulation of comparative data and encourage an over-extensive range of instruments which all purport to tap the same construct. It is hoped that the straightforward nature of the scales introduced in this paper will be of value in many occupational settings.

## Affective well-being

A large number of measures of job-related affective well-being has already been developed. These cover specific facets of satisfaction, alienation from work, job attachment, job tension, depression, burnout, involvement and job morale (e.g. Cook, Hepworth, Wall & Warr, 1981). Context-free measures are available to tap life satisfaction, happiness, positive affect, negative affect, anxiety, depression, general dysphoria, self-esteem and other types of feeling (e.g. Diener, 1984; Goldberg, 1972).

Research into these aspects of well-being has been valuable and productive, but there is merit also in drawing upon findings from investigations into the structure of emotions and moods. Research has demonstrated the existence of two orthogonal dimensions, which account for the majority of observed variance (e.g. Russell, 1979, 1980; Watson & Tellegen, 1985; Watson, Clark & Tellegen, 1988; Zevon & Tellegen, 1982). These are summarized in Fig. 1, using the labels of 'pleasure' and 'arousal', with illustrative affective states ordered around the perimeter.

We may describe any form of affective well-being in terms of its location in relation to those separate dimensions and its distance from the mid-point of the figure. A particular level of pleasure may be accompanied by high or low levels of arousal, and a particular level of arousal may be either pleasurable or unpleasurable. In devising primary measures of well-being, decisions have thus to be taken about the location of key vectors in that two-dimensional space.

Warr (1987) has suggested that three main axes should be considered. Two of these take account of arousal as well as pleasure, by running diagonally between opposite quadrants through the mid-point of Fig. 1. In addition, in view of the central importance of low or high pleasure, it is helpful to take measures along that horizontal dimension alone, without regard to variations in arousal.

That possibility is illustrated in Fig. 2. Pleasure and arousal are retained as the horizontal and vertical dimensions, with two diagonal axes running between opposite quadrants. The latter, and that representing pleasure alone, are labelled as the three key indicators of affective well-being: (a) displeased–pleased,

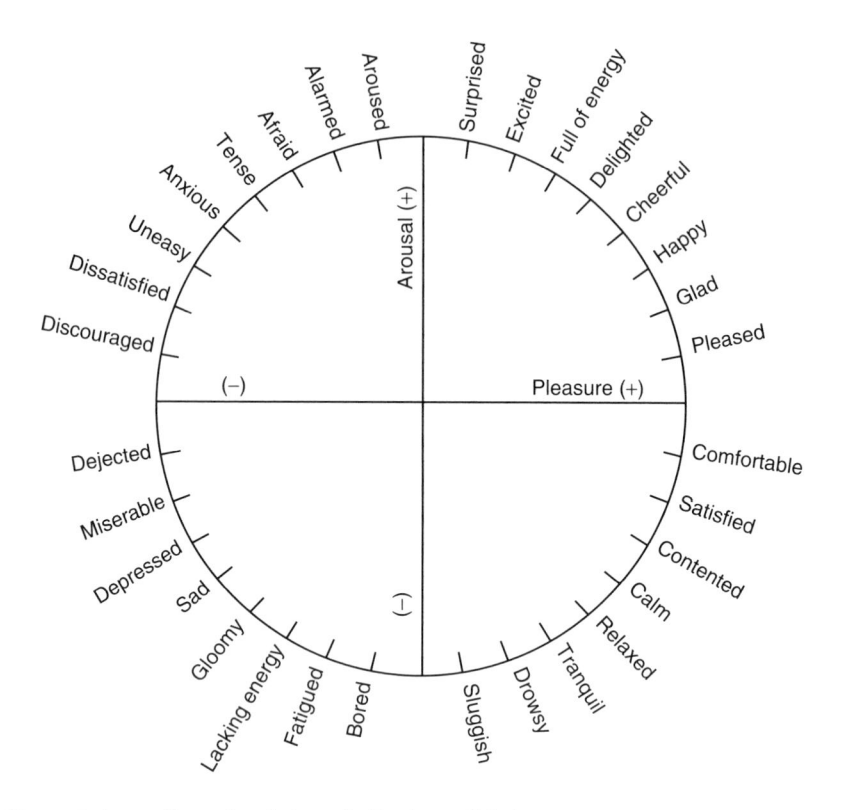

*Figure 1* A two-dimensional view of affective well-being.

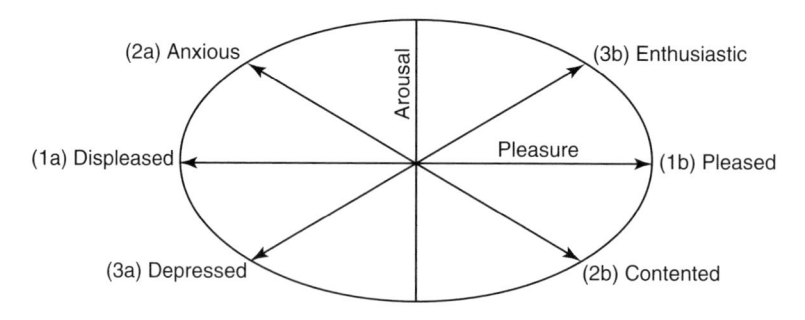

*Figure 2* Three principal axes for the measurement of affective well-being.

(2) anxious–contented, and (3) depressed–enthusiastic. Principal types of affect may be located anywhere along those axes. The arousal dimension on its own is not considered to reflect well-being, and its poles are therefore left unlabelled.

The diagram is presented as an elongated (rather than circular) shape to indicate that pleasure is empirically accorded greater weight than arousal. Experienced pleasure may differ substantially across situations, and these differences are more likely to be reflected in well-being than variations in arousal. Scores on axes two and three are thus likely to be positively intercorrelated in practice, rather than being independent, as suggested by the ideal conceptualization of Fig. 1.

Within this framework, the precise location of the diagonal axes may be varied according to research needs. For example, studies of cognitive performance in complex tasks may be particularly concerned with possible changes in arousal, to examine the degree to which job conditions lead to feelings of lethargy and fatigue. The third axis may in those cases be defined towards the vertical dimension. Measurements then would be more concerned with tiredness–vigour than with depression–enthusiasm. In some cases, both forms of the third axis may be studied; this possibility is considered later.

As outlined in the research literature cited above, it is not possible to reduce all emotional experiences to these principal dimensions. The structure shown in Fig. 1 is viewed as complementary to more differentiated accounts, particular types of which might be more appropriate in certain settings. For example, detailed examination of aspects of well-being associated with specific pharmaceutical agents may benefit from measures which cover a wider set of feelings. However, assessment of these three forms of well-being can provide basic information, permitting addition of other measures when that is desired.

The pleasure axis, shown horizontally in the figures, has often been measured through scales of reported job or life satisfaction. Many instruments are available for job-specific or context-free application (e.g. Cook *et al.*, 1981), and the present paper will focus on well-being axes two and three. These deserve particular attention in occupational research, to examine feelings of arousal as well as pleasure.

Relevant 10-item scales have been devised by Watson, Clark & Tellegen (1988), with respondents indicating the degree to which they are distressed, hostile, jittery, attentive, interested, alert, etc. Impressive data about reliability and concurrent validity are available, and links with the pleasure/arousal perspective have been emphasized. However, the scales are limited in that all items fall into the top half of Figs 1 and 2, rather than covering the full length of the axes. Furthermore, their focus is intentionally very broad, also asking, for example, whether respondents felt ashamed, guilty, proud and strong. These context-free instruments do not lend themselves easily to occupational research.

Axes two and three have also been tapped through the context-free checklist described by Mackay, Cox, Burrows & Lazzerini (1978); (see also Cox & Mackay, 1985; and Cruickshank, 1984). This contains 34 adjectives, 19 of which fall on axis two as shown in Fig. 2. The others range from tiredness to vigour, covering a more vertical form of axis three than the one shown in the figure. A 20-item derivative of this context-free measure has been examined by Fischer & Donatelli (1987), Fischer, Hansen & Zemore (1988), King, Burrows & Stanley (1983), and King, Stanley & Burrows (1987), in studies which provide encouraging evidence about internal reliability and psychometric adequacy.

These and other authors have demonstrated the robustness of the diagonal axes shown in Fig. 2. However, the emphasis has been on context-free mental health, and many items are unsuitable for occupational application. The present study examines the two diagonal axes through scales which use familiar adjectives, and cover equally the four quadrants of Fig. 2; axis three is represented by depression–enthusiasm rather than tiredness–vigour; and the focus is upon job-related as well as non-job well-being.

## Other aspects of mental health

In addition to affective well-being, high or low mental health is also exhibited through behaviour in transactions with the environment. Such behaviours are conceptually quite distinct from the feelings involved in well-being, although associations between behaviour and well-being are likely to be observed in practice. Two major behavioural components are competence and aspiration (Warr, 1987).

Competence (e.g. Smith, 1968) has been widely discussed in the psychological literature. For example, Jahoda (1958) wrote in terms of 'environmental mastery', Bradburn (1969) examined people's ability to cope with and transcend their 'difficulties in living', and Bandura (e.g. 1977) investigated beliefs about 'self-efficacy' or 'expectations of personal mastery'. A competent person is one who has adequate psychological resources to deal with experienced difficulties. As with other aspects of mental health, a distinction should be drawn between context-free competence and domain-specific competence, and separate measurement of the two forms can be made. In both cases, it is necessary to distinguish between subjective and independent assessments, with subjective competence being measured through self-reports, and independent assessments being made by a relevant observer. The present study examines two scales of subjective competence, covering separately job and non-job experiences.

A similar approach is taken to the measurement of aspiration. A mentally healthy person is often viewed as having an interest in, and engaging with, the environment. He or she establishes goals and makes active efforts to attain them, through motivated behaviour, alertness to new opportunities, and efforts to meet challenges that are personally significant. Conversely, low levels of aspiration are exhibited in reduced involvement and activity, and in an acceptance of present conditions even when they are unsatisfactory. This aspect of mental health has been emphasized in occupational research by Herzberg (1966), who examined the impact of job features on workers' 'psychological growth'. Maslow (e.g. 1973) developed a similar perspective in terms of 'self-actualization', and parallel themes have been explored by Csikszentmihalyi (1975) and Kornhauser (1965). Two measures of reported aspiration, job and non-job, will be investigated here.

There appear to be no instruments available to tap reported job-related competence and aspiration in a manner appropriate for both shop-floor and managerial employees. Baseline data about non-job as well as job-related components of those kinds would be useful for comparison with subsequent investigations.

There has also been interest in the carry-over of job experiences into other activities and feelings. For example, Evans & Bartolome (1980), Piotrkowski (1978) and others have documented negative influences on family and leisure life. Reports of such carry-over have been examined in the present study, for comparison with other findings, and in relation to scores on the measures summarized above.

## Aims of this paper

This paper will describe new measures of these aspects of mental health, and present baseline information from a large sample of male and female workers. Two axes of affective well-being, and reported competence and aspiration, will be studied through parallel sets of questionnaire items to assess both job-related and non-job mental health. The aims are to characterize these instruments, and to make available comparative data from men and women of different ages and occupational levels.

Scale validity will be examined in terms of demographic features, other aspects of mental health, and through correlations with reported job characteristics. For example, it is expected from research with other measures that older people will exhibit greater job-related well-being than younger people, and that employees in high-level jobs will report more job enthusiasm and aspiration than those at lower levels. Positive correlations with intrinsic job characteristics are expected, but the measures described here permit us to go beyond most earlier research in investigating a differential pattern of associations, with varied relationships with job features expected according to which aspect of mental health is under investigation; this point will be developed later.

Evidence about axes two and three of job-related well-being will also be provided through results from two separate samples, shop-floor workers in a manufacturing company and professional staff attending a clinic for assistance in the management of personal job stress.

## Method

### *Respondents and data-gathering*

Data were obtained from 1686 employed men and women, all of whom were in jobs for more than 30 hours a week. A sample was drawn with approximately equal numbers of men and women (839 and 847), in which gender was balanced within occupational level and age.

Three occupational levels were specified, in terms defined by the Registrar-General as grades A and B, C1 and C2, and D. Grades A and B include professional and managerial workers in relatively senior positions; grades C1 and C2 cover lower professional and supervisory jobs and skilled non-supervisory positions; and grade D jobs are those manual positions requiring little or no skill. Within these three levels, the numbers of male and female respondents respectively were: AB, 269 and 247; C1C2, 307 and 342; D, 263 and 258.

Three age levels were specified in drawing up the sample: 18 to 34 years, 35 to 49, and 50 years or above. Within each age group, the numbers of men and women were: 18 to 34, 279 and 299; 35 to 49, 287 and 289; 50 and above, 273 and 259.

Respondents were interviewed at home by survey research company staff in 75 locations throughout the United Kingdom. Initial and final groups of questions were asked orally, covering a range of job and personality issues, and respondents themselves completed two questionnaires during the middle part of the meeting. The first of these was headed 'Questions about your job', and instructions asked for responses in terms of 'how things have been going in the past few weeks'. The second questionnaire was labelled 'Questions about your life outside your job', and asked respondents to 'turn your attention away from your job and think about other parts of your life, your family and spare-time activities'. As before, the focus was on 'the past few weeks'.

Both questionnaires contained items in the sequence of well-being axes two and three followed by reported competence and aspiration. Within the job-related questionnaire, subsequent items, not reported in detail here, concerned perceptions of job features such as workload and opportunity for personal control.

## *The measures*

Axes two and three of affective well-being were examined in the terms described earlier, through six-item scales derived from pre-tests carried out in a range of settings. The job-related items were preceded by the question, 'Thinking of the past few weeks, how much of the time has your job made you feel each of the following?' Responses were: never, occasionally, some of the time, much of the time, most of the time, all of the time; and answers were scored from 1 to 6 respectively. Items covering the two axes were intermingled in the questionnaire.

Axis two, job-related anxiety–contentment, was assessed through the adjectives tense, uneasy, worried, calm, contented and relaxed. Responses to the first three items were reverse-scored, so that high scores indicated positive well-being, and coefficient alpha was found to be .76.

Axis three, job-related depression–enthusiasm, was tapped by depressed, gloomy, miserable, cheerful, enthusiastic, optimistic. The first three items were again reverse-scored, and coefficient alpha was .80.

For non-job well-being these two axes were measured in the same way, but with the question, 'In the past few weeks, how much of the time in your life outside your job have you felt each of the following?' Alpha coefficients were .81 for each of the axes.

Reported job competence and job aspiration were each measured through responses scored 1 to 5 along the continuum: strongly disagree, disagree, neither disagree nor agree, agree, strongly agree. Six statements were used in each case, interspersed in the first questionnaire, and coefficients alpha were .68 and .62 respectively. These scales, and those for non-job competence and non-job aspiration (intermixed in the second questionnaire), are presented in Appendix 1. Coefficients alpha for the non-job measures were .71 and .64 respectively. Both sets of measures were based upon concepts and more wide-ranging questionnaires developed by Pearlin, Menaghan, Lieberman & Mullan (1981), Rotter (1966) and Wagner & Morse (1975). Note that they cover reported competence or aspiration which is relative to a person's own circumstances. For example, the job competence items tap ability to cope with a current job rather than absolute levels of occupational ability.

Within the first questionnaire were four items to cover negative job carry-over. Responses were again in terms of the five-point agree–disagree scale, and coefficient alpha was found to be .78. These items are also in Appendix 1.

## Results

### *Affective well-being: Principal components analyses*

The 12 adjectives to tap well-being were chosen on the basis of the earlier studies described above, which have pointed to the existence of two bipolar axes running diagonally through the midpoint of Figs 1 and 2. Can these axes be identified empirically, through principal components analyses of the present data? Previous analyses in other settings (for example, of the Multiple Affect Adjective Check List and the Profile of Mood States) have pointed to the need to control for generalized response set. It is typically found that, without such control, the two major components in this kind of data are separate groups of positive and negative items, to the right and left of the vertical axis in Figs 1 and 2.

Such a separation appears likely to reflect the operation of acquiescent response set. Gotlib & Meyer (1986) and others have pointed out that this feature may be of differential impact, for example, between respondents, or with variations in acquiescence greater for negative than for positive adjectives. These effects would reduce correlations between negative and positive scale items and increase correlations within negative and positive groups, giving rise to factors made up entirely of either negative or positive items.

Several investigators have therefore controlled for acquiescent response set in examining the factor structure of adjectives in context-free self-report scales. For example, Lorr, Shi & Youniss (1989) found in a 60-item list the two bipolar components which are expected here. Response set was estimated as the total score across all items, without any reverse-scoring, and this was controlled in

*Table 1* Varimax-rotated factor loadings greater than .40, from partial correlations between affective well-being items, controlling for response set ($N = 1686$)

|  | Job-related affect |  | Non-job affect |  |
|---|---|---|---|---|
| Tense | .70 |  | .71 |  |
| Uneasy | .43 | .52 | .58 |  |
| Worried | .66 |  | .66 |  |
| Calm | .78 |  | .76 |  |
| Contented | .41 | .62 | .65 |  |
| Relaxed | .79 |  | .81 |  |
| Depressed |  | .68 | .47 | .67 |
| Gloomy |  | .75 | .44 | .61 |
| Miserable |  | .71 | .47 | .63 |
| Cheerful |  | .56 |  | .47 |
| Enthusiastic |  | .79 |  | .72 |
| Optimistic |  | .65 |  | .79 |

*Note*: Scoring of the six negative items has been reversed.

partial correlations between each item; factor analysis was carried out on the matrix of these partial correlations. Applying this procedure to the 12 adjectives in the present well-being measure revealed the structure shown in Table 1. For both job-related and non-job affect two factors were present (eigenvalues greater than 1.00), and it can be seen that these correspond to axes two and three of well-being as defined above.

There is another way to examine the structure of the well-being items without possible interference from differential acquiescence response set for positive and negative items. This involves separate analyses for the six positive and the six negative items making up the two scales. Four principal component analyses of those kinds have been carried out separately for positive and negative items in the job-related and the non-job scales. Each varimax-rotated two-factor solution contained distinct three-item components representing quadrants above and below the horizontal axis of Figs 1 and 2, supporting the structure assumed in the pleasure/arousal model.

### *Intercorrelations between measures*

The correlations observed between these measures of affective well-being and other aspects of mental health are shown in Table 2. Recall that higher scores indicate greater contentment or enthusiasm (and thus lower anxiety or depression), as well as greater competence, aspiration and negative carry-over.

Consistent with the location of axes in Fig. 2 (at less than 90 degrees to each other), the two well-being scores in each domain (job and non-job) are strongly intercorrelated (.66 and .73). Correlations of job-related depression–enthusiasm are significantly greater with job aspiration than with job competence (.46 and

*Table 2* Intercorrelations between aspects of mental health ($N = 1686$)

|  | 2 | 3 | 4 | 5 | 6 | 7 | 8 | 9 |
|---|---|---|---|---|---|---|---|---|
| *Affective well-being* | | | | | | | | |
| 1. Job anxiety–contentment | .66 | .34 | .48 | .36 | .24 | −.54 | .28 | .13 |
| 2. Job depression–enthusiasm | | .27 | .58 | .26 | .46 | −.30 | .27 | .21 |
| 3. Non-job anxiety–contentment | | | .73 | .30 | .17 | −.46 | .48 | .25 |
| 4. Non-job depression–enthusiasm | | | | .28 | .30 | −.32 | .49 | .40 |
| *Other aspects of mental health* | | | | | | | | |
| 5. Reported job competence | | | | | .36 | −.37 | .44 | .21 |
| 6. Reported job aspiration | | | | | | −.10 | .29 | .38 |
| 7. Negative carry-over | | | | | | | −.30 | −.13 |
| 8. Reported non-job competence | | | | | | | | .49 |
| 9. Reported non-job aspiration | | | | | | | | |

*Note*: As described in the text, high scores on variables 1 and 3 reflect contentment, and high scores on variables 2 and 4 reflect enthusiasm. Values greater than .07 are significant at the $p < .001$ level.

.26, $p < .001$). This appears to reflect the impact of the arousal dimension, with reports of enthusiasm and aspiration both deriving from high arousal as well as high pleasure (the top right-hand quadrant in the well-being figures).

Conversely, negative carry-over from the job is significantly more strongly correlated with job anxiety–contentment than with depression–enthusiasm (−.54 and −.30), and inverse carry-over correlations are significantly greater with reported competence than reported aspiration (both job and non-job). Anxiety–contentment is also significantly more predictable from reported competence than from aspiration. (The $p < .001$ criterion has been used in all cases.)

## *Mean scores and demographic variations*

Mean scores are set out in Table 3, with the overall pattern summarized in the first column. Because of the large number of cases, these values may be used in comparison with subsequently gathered data, but it should be noted that the sample was not intended to be entirely representative of the population. In order to permit reliable analyses of sub-group data, the design sought disproportionately more people in occupational levels either higher or lower than the average. In the present sample, 31, 38 and 31 per cent of respondents are in occupational levels AB, C1C2 and D respectively; comparable figures for the employed population as a whole are around 17, 58 and 25 per cent.

Comparisons between male and female responses (in columns two and three) reflect job and other environmental variations as well as possible gender effects on their own. In the present case, women exhibit significantly greater job enthusiasm than men, and report significantly greater difficulty in coping with their paid work (in terms of the job competence scale).

Table 3  Mean mental health scores (standard deviations in parentheses)

| | Full sample | Gender | | Occupational level | | | | Age | | |
|---|---|---|---|---|---|---|---|---|---|---|
| | | Men | Women | AB | C1C2 | D | | 18 to 34 | 35 to 49 | 50 and above |
| *Affective well-being* | | | | | | | | | | |
| 1. Job anxiety–contentment | 4.17(.81) | 4.12 (.82) | 4.22 (.80) | 3.96*(.77) | 4.20*(.82) | 4.35*(.80) | | 4.06*(.80) | 4.12*(.82) | 4.34*(.82) |
| 2. Job depression–enthusiasm | 4.55(.79) | 4.48*(.81) | 4.62*(.76) | 4.61*(.70) | 4.58*(.82) | 4.46*(.83) | | 4.48*(.78) | 4.51*(.81) | 4.68*(.76) |
| 3. Non-job anxiety–contentment | 4.41(.76) | 4.43 (.75) | 4.39 (.78) | 4.31*(.74) | 4.43*(.77) | 4.48*(.77) | | 4.36*(.75) | 4.36*(.79) | 4.52*(.73) |
| 4. Non-job depression–enthusiasm | 4.62(.72) | 4.63 (.70) | 4.62 (.73) | 4.66 (.69) | 4.65 (.70) | 4.56 (.75) | | 4.60 (.67) | 4.57 (.76) | 4.71 (.71) |
| *Other aspects of mental health* | | | | | | | | | | |
| 5. Reported job competence | 3.88(.54) | 3.94*(.54) | 3.82*(.53) | 3.78*(.56) | 3.93*(.53) | 3.93*(.50) | | 3.77*(.53) | 3.91*(.53) | 3.98*(.54) |
| 6. Reported job aspiration | 4.06(.50) | 4.03 (.53) | 4.09 (.48) | 4.22*(.42) | 4.07*(.50) | 3.90*(.53) | | 4.04 (.50) | 4.07 (.52) | 4.09 (.49) |
| 7. Negative carry-over | 2.73(.91) | 2.68 (.91) | 2.77 (.92) | 3.03*(.95) | 2.65*(.90) | 2.53*(.82) | | 2.75 (.88) | 2.77 (.91) | 2.65 (.95) |
| 8. Reported non-job competence | 3.76(.53) | 3.79 (.50) | 3.74 (.56) | 3.78 (.54) | 3.79 (.53) | 3.72 (.53) | | 3.75 (.52) | 3.76 (.55) | 3.79 (.53) |
| 9. Reported non-job aspiration | 3.92(.48) | 3.90 (.48) | 3.95 (.50) | 3.99*(.47) | 3.93*(.48) | 3.84*(.50) | | 3.97 (.46) | 3.91 (.51) | 3.88 (.49) |
| Number of cases | 1686 | 839 | 847 | 516 | 649 | 521 | | 578 | 576 | 532 |

*Note:* Significant differences between means in each group have been confirmed in more controlled analyses through multiple regressions of each mental health variable on gender, occupational level and age together.
* $p < .001$, in comparisons between groups.

Occupational-level scores present a coherent pattern of differences, with the direction of trends varying between specific aspects of mental health. As would be expected, people in high-level jobs report significantly more job-related enthusiasm; but their scores are also significantly lower on job anxiety–contentment (that is, they report more anxiety). Higher-level employment is thus associated with greater arousal levels of both kinds identified by axes two and three.

Reported job aspiration and negative carry-over are also greater at higher job levels, but the reverse pattern is found for reported job competence. This latter finding reflects the fact that the subjective job competence scale taps reported ability to cope with one's own job; it is not an absolute index of competence of the kind that would be expected to correlate positively with job level.

Significant age differences are found in respect of job-related anxiety–contentment, depression–enthusiasm and reported job competence, with older people exhibiting higher scores. This pattern is widely found (e.g. Rhodes, 1983), and is likely in part to reflect variations in job content. Observed greater non-job contentment in older respondents is also likely to derive from environmental differences associated with increasing age within this range; note, however, that reported non-job competence and aspiration remain constant across the age groups.

Two-way analyses of variance were carried out on all combinations of gender, occupational level and age; no interactions were statistically significant. Additional examination was made in order to identify the pattern of associations with the number of weekly hours worked (mean = 44.67; SD = 10.83). Correlations with all the mental health variables were insignificant ($p > .001$), except for negative carry-over ($r = .19$). Controlling for gender, occupational level, age, marital status and educational qualifications left that correlation unchanged (partial $r = .19$).

## *Associations with job content*

It is of interest to examine the associations of mental health scores with variations in perceived job characteristics. Table 4 summarizes correlations with reports on three-item scales of perceived skill use, personal control and workload. These scales were designed to cover low-to-medium values of each characteristic, with items worded consistently in terms of very little skill use, control or workload (for further details, see Warr, 1990).

Low levels of intrinsic job characteristics, such as skill use and personal control, might be expected to be primarily associated with reduced arousal, reflected in low depression–enthusiasm and low job aspiration, rather than in terms of anxiety–contentment and ability to cope as tapped by the job competence scale. That pattern is found in the table. For skill use, correlations are significantly greater with job and non-job depression–enthusiasm (.26 and .14) than with anxiety–contentment (.01 and .04) ($p < .001$), and differences between correlations with job aspiration and job competence mirror that contrast (.45 and .02 respectively; $p < .001$). These differences are also significant for personal control ($p < .001$ for the two axes of job well-being and for job competence and aspiration). In general, variations in those

Table 4 Correlations between perceived job characteristics and nine indices of mental health ($N = 1686$)

|  | Low-to-medium levels |  |  |
|---|---|---|---|
|  | Skill use | Personal control | Work-load |
| *Affective well-being* |  |  |  |
| 1. Job anxiety–contentment | .01 | .25 | −.10 |
| 2. Job depression–enthusiasm | .26 | .37 | .17 |
| 3. Non-job anxiety–contentment | .04 | .17 | −.01 |
| 4. Non-job depression–enthusiasm | .14 | .22 | .11 |
| *Other aspects of mental health* |  |  |  |
| 5. Reported job competence | .02 | .13 | .00 |
| 6. Reported job aspiration | .45 | .40 | .39 |
| 7. Negative carry-over | .10 | −.14 | .23 |
| 8. Reported non-job competence | .09 | .17 | .13 |
| 9. Reported non-job aspiration | .13 | .20 | .18 |

*Note*: Values greater than .07 are significant at the $p < .001$ level.

two job characteristics are accompanied by variations in low-arousal pleasure, in the terms of Fig. 2.

Conversely, perceived workload is significantly more negatively associated with anxiety–contentment than with depression–enthusiasm (−.10 vs. .17, and −.01 vs. .11 for job and non-job affect respectively; $p < .001$), as expected from the fact that raised workload is likely to be associated with both greater arousal and negative feelings: the top-left quadrant of the figures. The scales for well-being dimensions two and three are in these ways differentially associated with job characteristics in a manner which parallels the common belief, in clinical psychology, that depressed feelings are more associated with loss or deprivation whereas anxious feelings are more likely to reflect a response to threat or danger.

The correlations in Table 4 remain almost unchanged after controls are introduced for occupational level, educational qualifications, age, gender and marital status. However, the exact values are of less concern here than the finding that associations with job features vary between the separate instruments under examination.

## Additional data

Earlier versions of the scales to tap axes two and three of job-related affective well-being have been used in research with several other groups. Two examples will be cited here: from 246 shop-floor assembly workers in a micro-electronics factory (both male and female), and 96 professional and managerial workers (male and female) who were taking part in psychotherapy to reduce their high levels of job strain. Data were gathered by Wall, Clegg, Davies, Kemp & Mueller (1987) and Shapiro, Barkham, Hardy & Morrison (1990) respectively.

Well-being axes two and three were each examined through six adjectives. Seven of the 12 were the same as in the study described above; and anxious, frustrated, comfortable, keen and lively were used in place of the later selection of worried, uneasy, contented, cheerful and optimistic respectively. Controlling for acquiescent response set again revealed the expected two-factor structure in both sets of data.

The two forms of job-related affective well-being were significantly intercorrelated (.54 and .58 in the two studies), but their validity is again supported through a differentiated pattern of associations with other variables. For example, Table 5 shows that job depression–enthusiasm is significantly more closely related to intrinsic job satisfaction than is anxiety–contentment ($r = .40$ and .21 respectively, measuring satisfaction through the scale described by Warr, Cook & Wall, 1979). This significant difference is also present in relation to reported job motivation, measured through items similar to those in the scale of job aspiration described above.

In terms of job characteristics, the pattern is similar to that in Table 4. Strong associations are found between depression–enthusiasm and aspects of intrinsic job features: reported skill use, job complexity, attentional control and the absence of repetition; correlations of these variables with the anxiety–contentment axis are significantly lower. Conversely, work overload is associated with greater job anxiety ($r = -.40$), but there is no such association with job enthusiasm–contentment ($r = -.09$).

Finally, it can be seen in Table 5 that both aspects of job-related well-being are significantly correlated with scores on the 12-item General Health Questionnaire (Goldberg, 1972). That questionnaire is an indicator of context-free well-being

Table 5 Affective well-being dimensions two and three among shop-floor workers in a micro-electronics assembly department: Correlations with other variables ($N = 248$)

|  | Job anxiety–contentment | Job depression–enthusiasm |
|---|---|---|
| Intrinsic job satisfaction | .21* | .40* |
| Extrinsic job satisfaction | .31 | .33 |
| Reported job motivation | .20* | .40* |
| Reported skill use | .15* | .46* |
| Reported job complexity | .18* | .47* |
| Reported attentional control | .12* | .31* |
| Reported task repetition | .05* | −.22* |
| Reported work overload | −.40* | −.09* |
| Context-free distress (GHQ) | −.46 | −.39 |

*$p < .001$ between a pair of correlations.

Table 6 Affective well-being dimensions two and three among professional and managerial workers attending a job stress clinic: Correlations with other variables before commencement of therapy ($N = 96$)

|  | Job anxiety–contentment | Job depression–enthusiasm |
|---|---|---|
| Intrinsic job satisfaction | .34* | .52* |
| Extrinsic job satisfaction | .40 | .45 |
| Negative carry-over | −.46* | −.30* |
| Reported skill use | .30* | .51* |
| Reported control opportunity | .29 | .34 |
| Reported task variety | .02 | .19 |
| Reported social support | .31* | .48* |
| Reported job clarity | .32 | .19 |
| Reported work overload | −.39** | −.10** |
| Context-free depression | −.09 | −.24 |
| Self-esteem | .33 | .30 |

$*p < .05$; $**p = .01$ between a pair of correlations.

along the left-hand side of the horizontal axis of Fig. 2. The new scales described here provide additional data to those derived from the GHQ, in that they cover separate diagonal axes and permit measurement of both job-related and non-job affect.

A third set of data is illustrated in Table 6, which presents intercorrelations between variables measured before the commencement of therapy. The job characteristic measures were different from those described above, but the scale of job satisfaction was the same as in the manufacturing study. The findings provide similar support for the new well-being scales.

As expected from the previous results, job depression–enthusiasm is significantly more closely associated with intrinsic job satisfaction and reported skill use than is anxiety–contentment. On the other hand, anxiety–contentment is more predictable from job clarity (about standards and future prospects) and (negatively) from reported overload than is the other dimension. Table 6 also reports associations with two context-free measures of mental health, the Beck Depression Inventory (BDI) (Beck, Ward, Mendelson, Mock & Erbaugh, 1961) and an eight-item self-esteem measure based on that devised by Rosenberg (1965). As would be predicted, job-related depression–enthusiasm is more related than anxiety–contentment to the (context-free) BDI (−.24 vs. −.09), but no differences are found for the more general self-esteem measure. However, for this size of sample the difference between correlations with the BDI is not significant.

This study also permitted measurements of changes as a result of psychotherapy. Significant improvements were recorded in several standard clinical indicators, assessing context-free mental health. Since the focus of the therapy was on job-related as well as more general problems, scores on both axes two and three of job-related well-being would also be expected to improve significantly. This was in fact observed ($p < .001$ in both cases).

## Discussion

These questionnaire measures of affective well-being and other aspects of mental health appear to be psychometrically acceptable, easy for job-holders at all levels to complete, and associated with demographic and occupational features in predicted ways. The approach to well-being is based upon an externally supported two-dimensional framework, and, although the well-being instruments yield scores which are (as expected) intercorrelated, they exhibit different associations with other factors which provide evidence of their validity.

For example, higher occupational level was found to be positively associated with job depression–enthusiasm but negatively associated with anxiety–contentment, reflecting raised arousal of both kinds in higher-level jobs. Age differences paralleled those found in earlier research, but provided additional information through the comparison of job-related competence and aspiration; the former was significantly positively correlated with age, but the latter was not. The length of a person's working week was unrelated to all aspects of mental health examined here, except for negative carry-over ($r = .19$).

Intrinsic job satisfaction tended to covary more with depression–enthusiasm than with anxiety–contentment, but no difference was observed for extrinsic satisfaction; this pattern is consistent with the meanings of the constructs. So is the observed overlap between negative carry-over, job anxiety–contentment and reported competence. Across the studies, with different measures of job features, depression–enthusiasm was more predictable from variables such as low-to-medium opportunity for skill use and task variety, whereas anxiety–contentment was more a function of high workload or uncertainty. The former characteristics can be viewed as illustrating aspects of deprivation, whereas the latter reflect possible threats; the pattern is consistent with nonoccupational thinking about depression and anxiety.

Context-free constructs of those kinds have been investigated in clinical and community research. Measures of anxiety and depression are consistently found to be highly intercorrelated (Dobson, 1985, reports an average correlation of .61), but there is usually agreed to be merit in retaining both concepts when examining context-free mental health and ill-health. By the same token, the present domain-specific measures of axes two and three of affective well-being are empirically associated (between .54 and .73 with the samples used above), but they are differentially correlated with other factors. It is important to consider them both.

The third axis of well-being was identified in Fig. 2 as running from depression to enthusiasm, and items to tap those aspects of the opposed quadrants of the figures have been described here. However, it was suggested in the introduction to this paper that in some investigations there might be particular interest in a more vertical axis within those quadrants, closer to the arousal dimension and ranging from tiredness to vigour. Such an axis has also been examined in the present study, but for clarity of presentation full results have not been included in this paper. Summary details are provided in Appendix 2.

The new scales of reported competence and aspiration in job and non-job settings were found to yield coherent results along plausible lines. Significant associations with occupational level, age, job characteristics and affective well-being have been described above. However, those measures are so far primarily supported by other forms of self-report data. This also applies to the instruments for measuring axes two and three of affective well-being, and there is now a general need to test the validity and usefulness of all these scales against behavioural and other objective criteria.

## Acknowledgement

I am very grateful to Jan Jackson, for extensive help with data-processing.

## References

Bandura, A. (1977). Self-efficacy: Toward a unifying theory of behavioral change. *Psychological Review*, 84, 191–215.

Beck, A. T., Ward, C. H., Mendelson, M., Mock, J. & Erbaugh, J. (1961). An inventory for measuring depression. *Archives of General Psychiatry*, 4, 561–571.

Bradburn, N. M. (1969). *The Structure of Psychological Well-being*. Chicago: Aldine.

Cook, J. D., Hepworth, S. J., Wall, T. D. & Warr, P. B. (1981). *The Experience of Work*. London: Academic Press.

Cox, T. & Mackay, C. (1985). The measurement of self-reported stress and arousal. *British Journal of Psychology*, 76, 183–186.

Cruickshank, P. J. (1984). A stress and arousal mood scale for low vocabulary subjects: A reworking of Mackay *et al.* (1978). *British Journal of Psychology*, 75, 89–94.

Csikszentmihalyi, M. (1975). *Beyond Boredom and Anxiety*. San Francisco: Jossey Bass.

Diener, E. (1984). Subjective well-being. *Psychological Bulletin*, 95, 542–575.

Dobson, K. S. (1985). The relationship between anxiety and depression. *Clinical Psychology Review*, 5, 307–324.

Evans, P. & Bartolome, F. (1980). *Must Success Cost So Much?* London: Grant McIntyre.

Fischer, D. G. & Donatelli, M. J. (1987). A measure of stress and arousal: Factor structure of the Stress Adjective Checklist. *Educational and Psychological Measurement*, 47, 425–435.

Fischer, D. G., Hansen, R. J. & Zemore, R. W. (1988). Factor structure of the Stress Adjective Checklist: Replicated. *Educational and Psychological Measurement*, 48, 127–136.

Goldberg, D. P. (1972). *The Detection of Psychiatric Illness by Questionnaire*. Oxford: Oxford University Press.

Gotlib, I. H. & Meyer, J. P. (1986). Factor analysis of the Multiple Affect Adjective Check List: A separation of positive and negative affect. *Journal of Personality and Social Psychology*, 50, 1161–1165.

Herzberg, F. (1966). *Work and the Nature of Man*. Chicago: World Publishing Company.
Jahoda, M. (1958). *Current Concepts of Positive Mental Health*. New York: Basic Books.
King, M. C., Burrows, G. D. & Stanley, G. V. (1983). Measurement of stress and arousal: Validation of the stress/arousal adjective checklist. *British Journal of Psychology*, 74, 473–479.
King, M. C., Stanley, G. V. & Burrows, G. D. (1987). *Stress: Theory and Practice*. Sydney: Grune and Stratton.
Kornhauser, A. W. (1965). *Mental Health of the Industrial Worker*. New York: Wiley.
Lorr, M., Shi, A. Q. & Youniss, R. P. (1989). A bipolar multifactor conception of mood states. *Personality and Individual Differences*, 10, 155–159.
Mackay, C., Cox, T., Burrows, G. & Lazzerini, T. (1978). An inventory for the measurement of self-reported stress and arousal. *British Journal of Social and Clinical Psychology*, 17, 283–284.
Maslow, A. H. (1973). *The Farther Reaches of Human Nature*. London: Penguin.
Pearlin, L. I., Menaghan, E. G., Lieberman, M. A. & Mullan, J. T. (1981). The stress process. *Journal of Health and Social Behavior*, 22, 337–356.
Piotrkowski, C. S. (1978). *Work and the Family System*. New York: Free Press.
Rhodes, S. R. (1983). Age-related differences in work attitudes and behavior. *Psychological Bulletin*, 93, 328–367.
Rosenberg, M. (1965). *Society and the Adolescent Self-image*. Princeton: Princeton University Press.
Rotter, J. B. (1966). Generalized expectancies for internal versus external control of reinforcement. *Psychological Monographs*, 80, 1–28.
Russell, J. A. (1979). Affective space is bipolar. *Journal of Personality and Social Psychology*, 37, 345–356.
Russell, J. A. (1980). A circumplex model of affect. *Journal of Personality and Social Psychology*, 39, 1161–1178.
Shapiro, D. A., Barkham, M. J., Hardy, G. E. & Morrison, L. A. (1990). The Second Sheffield Psychotherapy Project: Rationale, design and preliminary outcome data. *British Journal of Medical Psychology*, 63, 97–108.
Smith, M. B. (1968). Competence and 'mental health'. In S. B. Sells (Ed.), *The Definition and Measurement of Mental Health*. Washington: Department of Health, Education and Welfare.
Wagner, F. R. & Morse, J. J. (1975). A measure of individual sense of competence. *Psychological Reports*, 36, 451–459.
Wall, T. D., Clegg, C. W., Davies, R, T., Kemp, N. J. & Mueller, W. S. (1987). Advanced manufacturing technology and work simplification: An empirical study. *Journal of Occupational Behaviour*, 8, 233–250.
Warr, P. B. (1987). *Work, Unemployment, and Mental Health*. Oxford: Oxford University Press.
Warr, P. B. (1990). Decision latitude, job demands and employee well-being. In preparation.
Warr, P. B., Cook, J. & Wall, T. D. (1979). Scales for the measurement of some work attitudes and aspects of psychological well-being. *Journal of Occupational Psychology*, 52, 129–148.
Watson, D. & Tellegen, A. (1985). Toward a consensual structure of mood. *Psychological Bulletin*, 98, 219–235.

Watson, D., Clark, L. A. & Tellegen, A. (1988). Development and validation of brief measures of positive and negative affect: The PANAS scales. *Journal of Personality and Social Psychology*, 54, 1063–1070.

Zevon, M. A. & Tellegen, A. (1982). The structure of mood change: An idiographic/nomothetic analysis. *Journal of Personality and Social Psychology*, 43, 111–122.

# Appendix 1

The items used to measure reported competence, aspiration and negative job carry-over are given below. Those marked '(R)' were reverse-scored.

*Reported job competence*
I can do my job well
I sometimes think I am not very competent at my job (R)
I can deal with just about any problem in my job
I find my job quite difficult (R)
I feel I am better than most people at tackling job difficulties
In my job I often have trouble coping (R)

*Reported job aspiration*
In my job I like to set myself challenging targets
I am not very interested in my job (R)
I enjoy doing new things in my job
I prefer to avoid difficult activities in my job (R)
In my job, I make a special effort to keep trying when things seem difficult
I am not very concerned how things turn out in my job (R)

*Negative job carry-over*
After I leave my work, I keep worrying about job problems
I find it difficult to unwind at the end of a work-day
I feel used up at the end of the work-day
My job makes me feel quite exhausted by the end of a work-day

*Reported non-job competence*
I can deal with just about any problem in my non-job life
I sometimes think I am not very competent in my non-job life (R)
Most things I do, I do well
I find my non-job life quite difficult (R)
I feel I am better than most people at tackling difficulties
I often have trouble coping in my non-job life (R)

*Reported non-job aspiration*
I enjoy doing new things in my non-job life
I am not very interested in the world around me (R)
I like to set myself challenging targets in my non-job life
I prefer to avoid difficult activities in my non-job life (R)
I make a special effort to keep trying when things seem difficult
I am not very concerned how things turn out in my non-job life (R)

## Appendix 2

As indicated in the Discussion section, this study also obtained information about an alternative indicator of the third axis of affective well-being, ranging from tiredness to vigour. The items used to measure this set of feelings in both the job and non-job questionnaires were: fatigued, lifeless, tired, alert, full of energy and lively; and as with the other scales the first three were reverse-scored. These items were additionally presented with the 12 items of the two primary scales, described above.

Principal component analyses of these axis three items with the previously described axis two items revealed the separate factors specified by the model. Using the partial correlation procedure described earlier, the expected two-component structure was apparent in both job and non-job responses after varimax rotation.

In order to assist comparison with future studies using the tiredness–vigour scale, the following mean values and standard deviations (in parentheses) are cited. Job-related responses: full sample, 4.20 (.76); men, 4.18 (.75), women 4.22 (.77); level AB, 4.16 (.69), level C1C2, 4.23 (.75), level D, 4.22 (.82); age 18 to 34, 4.14 (.75), age 15 to 49, 4.17 (.77), age 50 and above, 4.31 (.74) ($p < .001$). For non-job responses, corresponding values were: 4.22 (.74); 4.22 (.72) and 4.22 (.75); 4.12 (.71), 4.24 (.72) and 4.29 (.77) ($p < .001$); 4.24 (.72), 4.16 (.75) and 4.26 (.74). Samples sizes are shown in Table 3.

# 15

# WELL-BEING AND OCCUPATIONAL HEALTH IN THE 21ST CENTURY WORKPLACE

*Kate Sparks, Brian Faragher and Cary L. Cooper*

Source: *Journal of Occupational and Organizational Psychology* 74 (2001): 489–509.

## Abstract

Over the last 40 years, major changes have taken place in the workplace. The growth in the use of information technology at work, the globalization of many industries, organizational restructuring, changes in work contracts and worktime scheduling have radically transformed the nature of work in many organizations. The workforce itself is also diversifying, with an increase in female participation, a growing number of dual-earner couples and older workers. The present paper discusses the impact of these workplace transitions on employee well-being. We focus on four issues that are current concerns for organizations and the workforce; job insecurity, work hours, control at work, and managerial style. For each topic, recent research is presented, with suggestions for future research and recommendations for practitioners working in the organizations of today. The paper concludes with some final considerations for researchers and practitioners that may benefit both employee well-being and organizational effectiveness.

Over the last four decades of the 20th century, the nature of work has changed dramatically for some people. The 1960s and 1970s saw the introduction of new technology, particularly the use of computers, into the workplace. This was followed in the 1980s by a huge shift towards globalization, with many organizations undergoing mergers, acquisitions, strategic alliances and privatizations. This entrepreneurial period resulted in increased economic competitiveness in international markets for those countries that embraced it (Cooper & Jackson, 1997). In the 1990s, a major restructuring of work started to take place. Organizations in countries hit by recession were downsizing or delayering in an effort, to survive. During the last decade, this trend for restructurig and downsizing has continued in many organizations, together with an increase in sub-contracting and outsourcing, in order to compete successfully in the increasingly competitive global market. There has been a rise in short-term contracts, as a result, possibly, of the deregulation of fixed-term contracts and the limited requirements on permanent employment in many countries (OECD, 1999). Other changes include new patterns of working, such as teleworking, self-regulated work and team work, an increased reliance on computerized technology and a move towards a more flexible workforce, both in number of employees and in their skills and functions (Cox, Griffiths, & Rial-Gonzalez, 2000). Many countries have seen a growth in female participation in the workforce, resulting in more part-time work, an increase in dual-earner couples, and a general growth in the number of older workers.

As the workplace has slowly transformed, research in organizational psychology has followed these trends. Studies have looked at the consequences of workplace changes, particularly their impact at both the individual employee level and the organizational level. The present paper focuses on research addressing occupational health and employee well-being, concentrating on four major areas in organizational psychology; job insecurity, work hours, control at work, and managerial style. Each of these issues has become a major concern as a result of the recent radical organizational changes. There are now fewer people at work, doing more and feeling less security and control in their jobs. Management in particular have increased pressures trying to keep pace and manage their workforce against a background of rapid change. This heightened pressure can impact on their behaviour towards employees.

For each of the four topics, research investigating the impact on employee health and well-being will be summarized, further research suggested, and the implications and recommendations that can be made for practitioners working in the rapidly changing workplace of the 21st century discussed.

## Job insecurity

Researchers have found that the trend for restructuring and downsizing in many organizations has led to an increase in perceived job insecurity, particularly for white-collar workers (e.g. Pahl, 1993; Worrall & Cooper, 1998). Worrall and Cooper (1998), for example, found that over 60% of a national sample of 5000 British managers had undergone a major restructuring during the previous 12 months involving downsizing and outsourcing. The consequences of this change, even among an occupational group (middle and senior managers) supposedly in control of events, were that nearly two out of three experienced increased job insecurity, lowered morale, and an erosion in motivation and loyalty.

The growth in non-permanent employment contracts in many countries has also increased job insecurity (Bureau of Labor Statistics, 1995). Organizations are increasingly utilizing contingent workers as an alternative to conventional full-time employees. 'Contingent work' includes temporary and occasional part-time employment, often contracted from outside agencies or independents. In many developed industrial economies, such workers usually have fewer entitlements and protections within the organization compared to full-time employees. Hence, contingent workers have less job security as the organization considers this workforce to be on a contract basis selling their services as opposed to actually being an intrinsic part of the organization.

However, despite the increase in the use of a flexible workforce and contingent workers, objective data taken from OECD surveys show little change in job security levels over the past decade (OECD, 1999). Whilst this may conflict with other findings (e.g. Bureau of Labor Statistics, 1995), a breakdown of the statistics indicates that tenure and retention rates in certain OECD member countries declined over this period, in certain occupations. Hence, job security may differ according to occupation. Furthermore, another survey in the UK indicated only a slight increase in temporary contracts over a 10-year period (1987–1997; Eurostat, 1997).

None the less, survey findings from several OECD member countries indicate that the *perception* of job insecurity has increased over the last decade (OECD, 1999), a finding replicated in other national surveys (e.g. Burchell *et al.*, 1999). This perception may be due to a greater spread across industries and occupations of temporary work and the associated longer spells of unemployment between contracts (Burke, 1998). Smithson and Lewis (2000) further argue that the perception of high levels of job insecurity may be fuelled by the fact that not only blue-collar occupations, but also professional and graduate jobs that were once deemed secure, are at risk now. Perceived job insecurity also seems to be more prominent amongst the youngest and oldest members of the workforce (Burchell *et al.*, 1999). Whilst objective data may suggest that job insecurity should not be a major concern for employees, research indicates that it is this *perception* of job insecurity that is the most important correlate with employee health and well-being. Recent studies have found that perceived job insecurity impacts negatively on employee well-being (e.g. Ferrie *et al.*, 1995). McDonough (2000), for example, found perceived job insecurity to be associated with lower scores in self-rated general health and increases in both distress and the use of medications among a national sample of Canadian workers. Borg, Kristensen, and Burr (2000) analysed data from 5001 Danish employees over a 5-year period and found that high levels of perceived job insecurity were significantly related to lowered self-rated general health. A study of over 2000 Swiss employees by Domenighetti, D'Avanzo, and Bisig (2000) found that psychosocial stress induced by perceived job insecurity had negative effects on 10 different self-reported indicators of health and health-related behaviours.

Organizations may suffer financially from heightened employee perceptions of job insecurity due to the associated costs of increased absenteeism and sickness resulting from lowered employee well-being. For example, a longitudinal study of Finnish government workers found a significant relationship between the degree of organizational downsizing and medically certified, long-term (i.e. greater than 3 days) sickness absence (Vahtera, Kivimaki, & Pentti, 1997). Other studies indicate that perceived job insecurity may impact on organizations in terms of less employee organizational commitment and lowered morale and motivation (e.g. Worrall & Cooper, 1998). King (2000) found that white-collar workers who reported a high job insecurity were less supportive of organizational goals, gave less effort to produce quality work and were more actively seeking alternative employment. However, an important factor for organizations to consider is whether employees voluntarily take up work that is perceived to be insecure. Pearce (1998) reports no differences in employee attitudes (job satisfaction, intention to leave, and organizational commitment) between a sample of contract workers and more secure employees and argues that choosing contingent work status (e.g. contracted consultancy work) is more important than the actual status itself for employee attitudes.

The available research clearly suggests that perceived job insecurity is bad for employee well-being. This, in turn, can impact on organizations through increased sickness absence (Vahtera *et al.*, 1997). Given the reported increase in perceived job insecurity (e.g. Burchell *et al.*, 1999), organizations need to consider the financial costs associated with those employees who are reluctant to be working in jobs which they perceive to be insecure.

The long-term costs to both employee health and organizational performance of heightened perceptions of job insecurity are not known. If the present trend towards non-permanent work continues, researchers in organizational psychology will need to explore the impact of this through longitudinal studies. Methods for helping employees cope in their unstable work environments must be identified if negative health effects are to be minimized. Research also needs to identify the internal effects on organizations if they move to employing increased numbers of non-permanent staff. More secure employees may resent non-permanent staff who occupy positions that were once assumed by permanent staff (Pearce, 1998). Organizations should ensure that temporary staff are not isolated or alienated by permanent workers, as this would obviously affect the well-being and attitudes for both types of employees.

Employers must take measures not only for the health of their employees but also to reduce any financial costs in terms of employee performance and commitment associated with perceived job insecurity. Smithson and Lewis (2000) suggest that employers can, to some extent, compensate for high job insecurity by providing other benefits such as training and self-development opportunities, greater respect and adequate pay. Employees should be encouraged to learn transferable skills to improve their employment prospects. Open communication needs to be encouraged between managers and employees during periods of employment uncertainty in order to ameliorate any negative consequences (Cameron, Freeman, & Mishra, 1991). Organizations should develop and maintain trust and a good rapport with employees so that any assurances are seen as credible. Furthermore, HR managers need to be aware of how job insecurity can impact on an individual's life outside work. In a sample of young workers (aged 18–30), Smithson and Lewis

(2000) found these individuals more accepting of insecure work compared to older workers, but only in the short-term. Long-term insecurity was seen to be more problematic, especially in combination with major non-work activities such as buying a house or starting a family. These life stages were often postponed or even avoided due to the lack of financial stability and parental leave rights associated with non-permanent work. Hence, if non-permanent work is to continue, employers need to consider ways of providing such entitlements to non-permanent staff, not least for the well-being of their employees but also to attract younger workers.

## Work hours

In recent decades, the reorganization of working time arrangements has been a key feature of economic restructuring in many nations (Bosch, 1999). This is partly due to advances in technology and industry but is mainly driven by employers' demands for greater flexibility in work schedules to cover extended operating or opening hours, predictable peaks in labour demand at different parts of the day, week, or year as well as less predictable requirements for additional cover due to market uncertainty (OECD, 1999). There has been an increase, for example, in the use of work days or work shifts longer than 8 h (Rosa, 1995). Some schedules compress the work week so that 36–48 h of work are completed in 3–4 days instead of 5. Other situations require frequent overtime work due to tight deadlines, understaffing or emergency contingencies. Industries such as mining, shipping, and oil-drilling, routinely schedule long work periods, followed by long rest periods. This is because frequent staff change-overs would be impractical due to the difficulties with travel to often remote work sites.

The use of other types of alternative work schedules is also increasing. For example, flexible worktime systems, based on weekly, monthly or yearly work hours, are now used subtantially in organizations across Europe (Brewster, Mayne, Tregaskis, Parsons, & Atterbury, 1996).

In terms of actual weekly work hours, some countries have reduced worktime, whilst in others, it has been extended. The OECD (1999) report a gradual decline over the last few decades in annual working hours across all member countries as a result of voluntary agreements between employers and employees and in part, government regulations, for example the EU legislation on working hours (EC Working Time Directive, 1990). However, in some countries, work hours have been rising slowly, particularly in those nations where labour markets have been deregulated and income inequalities have widened (e.g. New Zealand, United Kingdom, and United States) (Bosch, 1999). In many developing countries, also, annual worktimes are increasing, often exceeding 2000 h or even 3000 h with overtime (compared with an average annual rate of 1500 h in industrialized countries) (Maddison, 1995).

The increase in work hours in some countries is in part due to the trend for restructuring and downsizing in many organizations. Reduced staffing can result in employees remaining in a downsized organization taking on increased workloads and having to work longer hours to cope with the extra demands (e.g. Worrall & Cooper, 1997). The heightened perception of job insecurity inherent with downsizing also makes many employees reluctant to refuse increases in their workload, enabling employers to set hours constraints above employees' preferences (e.g. Beatson, 1995). The huge expansion of the use of information technology has further resulted in information overload and accelerated the pace of work (Cooper & Jackson, 1997).

Working time has increased in some countries due to the stagnation or decline in real income levels, particularly among low wage earners (e.g. state countries) (Bosch, 1999). Furthermore, the minimum wage in many countries has fallen relative to the average wage in the last 10 years (OECD, 1999), widening income inequalities. Hence, many workers have to compensate for the drop in earnings by working more hours or taking on more than one job (Bosch, 1999).

The recent changes in the organization of working time have been investigated by organizational psychologists to assess the impact on employee well-being and work performance. Numerous studies have addressed the effects of the compressed work week, particularly the change to an extended 10–12-h shift. Within an extended shift, Rosa, Colligan, and Lewis (1989) found a decreased reaction time and grammatical reasoning performance, with increased subjective fatigue after 7 months of 12-h shifts relative to the previous 8-h shift schedule. Performance, however, did not deteriorate overall across the work week, suggesting that the shorter work week compensated somewhat for the longer work shift. Rosa (1995) also found excess fatigue, sleepiness, and significant loss of sleep for workers on extended work shift schedules. Poissonnet and Veron (2000) reviewed studies on new forms of shift schedules for effects on health. They found that no particular work system was favourable, but evidence indicated that extended work days (9–12 h) should be avoided as much as possible to minimize fatigue.

None the less, compressed worktime schedules are often popular among shiftworkers, not only because of the reduction in commuting, but also because the extra non-work days allow larger blocks of time for recuperation from night work, for family and friends and for other leisure pursuits (Rosa *et al.*, 1989).

Research investigating the impact of flexible work hours has found advantages and disadvantages to its implementation (e.g. Christensen & Staines, 1990; Pierce & Newstrom, 1983). Major advantages claimed include lower stress levels, increased job enrichment, morale and autonomy, reduced absenteeism and tardiness, and improved job satisfaction and productivity. The major disadvantages identified include increased costs, problems with scheduling and work co-ordination, difficulties in supervising all employees due to differing work hours, and changes in the organizational culture. Flexible hours appear to have a positive impact on work–family balance and employee stress (e.g. Dunham, Pierce, & Castaneda, 1987), although these findings may be attributable to a reduction in work hours rather than alternative methods of work scheduling (Gottlieb, Kelloway, & Barham, 1998). There is little evidence to suggest that overall job satisfaction differs between employees working flexible systems and those with a more traditional schedule (McGuire & Liro, 1987). However, flexible work hours do appear to increase satisfaction with the work environment and the work schedule itself (McGuire & Liro, 1987).

One reason for these inconsistent findings may be a failure to account for whether employees have any choice or control over their flexible work schedules. Employees assigned to a particular schedule may find that its flexibility does not meet with their own needs and lifestyle. In contrast, other employees may have the opportunity to customize their flexible work schedules to match their own requirements.

Evidence for this comes from research investigating flexible work hour systems in Canada. A Canadian research group (e.g. CARNET, 1995; Work Family Directions, 1993) investigated the impact of flexible work arrangements on productivity and employee well-being. At first, they found inconsistent effects for performance, work–family balance, stress, and attitudinal outcomes. However, when accounting for choice over flexible work schedules, they found a compelling case for employees choosing their work hours. Employees who reported choosing their worktime schedules had higher performance ratings, reported less stress, greater overall well-being and reduced work interference with family life, compared with employees assigned to their work schedule. Employee choice is clearly an important factor in the implementation of a successful flexible work schedule.

Given the increase in the actual number of work hours in some countries, researchers have also investigated the impact of prolonged work hours on employee health. Sparks, Cooper, Fried, and Shirom (1997), for example, conducted a meta-analytic review of the long work hours literature and found a relationship between prolonged work hours and employee mental and physical ill-health. The long duty hours of trainee doctors have also received attention, with a number of studies reporting both health and performance impairments (e.g. Scott, 1992). Leonard, Fanning, Attwood, and Buckley (1998) assessed the effects of a 32-h on-call shift on pre-registration house doctors in an Irish hospital; they found that prolonged periods of duty without sleep adversely affected psychological well-being and the junior doctors' ability to carry out simple tasks on alertness and concentration. Numerous studies have been conducted in Japan where employees work excessively long hours, with many workers not taking their full holiday entitlement (Blyton, 1989). These investigations indicate that prolonged hours of work are linked to ill health, including heart problems such as acute myocardial infarction (Sokejima & kagamimori, 1998) and, more seriously, 'karoshi' or 'death due to overwork' (e.g. Uehata, 1991).

Worryingly, employees who work long hours have been found to be more prone to poor lifestyle habits, such as heavy smoking, inadequate diet, lack of exercise (e.g. Maruyama, Kohno, & Monmoto, 1995), behaviours that can lead to health problems. Another growing concern is the effect of prolonged exposure to the increasing number of chemicals used in industry for employees working prolonged hours. Emmet (1991) reported that approximately 65 000 chemicals, in the US alone, are used in businesses with around 700 new chemicals being introduced into the workplace each year. Baker and Landrigan (1990) cite 35 different workplace illnesses with their causal agents and the industries where they are used.

There have been few longitudinal studies of the effects of prolonged work hours. However, recent research from the British Household Panel Survey (1998) involving 5000 households found that health problems were particularly manifest in employees who had worked persistently long hours over a 5-year period. Such individuals reported higher blood pressure, more problems with their limbs, more chronic headaches and sleepiness than those working shorter hours. Moreover, these health problems persisted even after a reduction in prolonged work hours, suggesting that some health impairments may be irreversible. Perhaps not surprisingly, this study also found that family relationships between parents and children were negatively affected by long working hours. Another longitudinal study on the after-effects of prolonged work hours (Falk, Hanson, Isacsson, & Oestergen, 1992) investigated whether job strain affected mortality in a sample of elderly retired Swedish men. Exposure to job strain (demanding and hectic work) was found to be related to an increased risk of mortality after retirement. Thus, whilst individuals may not experience health problems during their working life, undue job strain (including long work hours) may present problems later in life.

The British Household Panel Survey (1998) found that long work hours can impact on homelife. Work stress can affect the psychological health, physical health, life expectancy and the marital satisfaction of employees' partners (Fletcher, 1988). Morrison and Clements (1997) found that the work overload of naval officers had a negative effect on the well-being of their partners. Galambos and Walters (1992) found that husbands in dual-earner couples, whose wives worked longer hours, were more prone to depression and anxiety compared with husbands whose wives worked fewer hours. The authors suggest that wives often play an emotional supportive role for the husband, so if they work long hours, they may be unavailable to provide a buffer against the stresses of work for the husband. This, in turn, may result in the husband experiencing more stress. The findings from such studies warrant concern in those countries with prolonged work hours, especially as the number of households with dual-earner couples is increasing (Bosch, 1999).

Overall, recent research on the changes in worktime schedules shows that prolonged work hours and work shifts have detrimental effects on employee well-being. However, most research has focused on only certain health outcomes, in particular mental health and cardiovascular disorders (Sparks *et al.*, 1997). Further studies are required to assess the effects of the different worktime schedules on other aspects of health, especially those associated with occupational stress (e.g. gastrointestinal disorders, musculo-skeletal disorders, etc.) and the longitudinal effects on poor lifestyle habits. The long-term effects of increased exposure to hazardous chemicals also need to be addressed. Investigations must encompass Third World and developing economies, given the often extreme number of work hours found in these nations. With the increase in dual-earner couples and the number of women entering the workforce, further study is required on the impact of domestic work hours on employee well-being. A high domestic workload can exacerbate any negative effects from work hours (Tierney, Romito, & Messing, 1990). The dual role of worker and carer can also lead to significant levels of anxiety (Field & Bramwell, 1998). This is a further research consideration given the aging population and the increase in employees caring for elderly relatives (Berry-Lound, 1993).

More studies are required on the effects of the different flexible worktime schedules. Annualized hour systems have received particularly little research attention (Gall, 1996). In a meta-analytic review of the literature, Baltes, Briggs, Huff, Wright, and Neuman (1999) found an overall waning effect with time, for flexible worktime schedules. Any positive outcomes decreased over time, at least for work-related criteria such as job satisfaction, productivity and performance. Further research needs to explore the effects of time on such schedules for employee well-being and also to clarify the influence of employee choice over schedules.

The current research on worktime schedules provides some recommendations for practitioners. The literature on compressed worktime systems suggests that prolonged work shifts (9–12 h) should be avoided to minimize risk to safety and health for employees. Where extended work shift schedules are to be implemented, these must be carefully evaluated and appropriate precautions made to reduce work overload and environmental exposure to chemicals and other hazards (Rosa, 1995).

Given the reported benefits in both work-related criteria and employee well-being, flexible worktime schedules are a worthwhile option in many organizations and industries. Some precautions are required, however. Flexible worktime schedules need to be economically viable to meet the interests of the employer but also need to take into account the home and family responsibilities of employees. Research has emphasized the importance of employee choice over worktime schedules for both performance and well-being (e.g. CARNET, 1995). Allowing employees to be involved in the design and implementation of a new flexible worktime schedule will benefit both the employee and the organization.

Flexible work schedules can be incorporated into 'Family Friendly' policies designed to help employees balance work and family demands. These policies reduce the strain of multiple roles and work–family conflict (e.g. Thomas & Ganster, 1995), can solve other organizational problems such as skill shortages, the need to recruit and retain women with family commitments (to meet equal opportunity requirements in some countries), and can also reduce absenteeism (Lewis, Watts, & Camp, 1996). Practitioners need to ensure, however, that the prevailing organizational culture does not prevent the full utilization of such schemes. For example, many employees may feel that owning up to having family responsibilities or commitments may be interpreted by their employer as a lack of job commitment, engendering a reluctance to use these schemes (Lewis, 1997). With the increase in dual earner couples and their family responsibilities, and the rise in elderly dependents, organizational cultures need to change to adapt to the changing needs of their employees.

With so many studies highlighting the ill effects of prolonged work hours, organizations need to consider the costs of the associated raised sickness/absenteeism rates and the lower performance/productivity levels. Furthermore, employers may find themselves facing legal costs as more employees turn to litigation to seek compensation for stress-related injury (Earnshaw & Cooper, 1996). HR managers must encourage a reduction in working hours in organizations with a prolonged worktime culture. Senior managers, themselves, should set standards by reducing their own work hours and also enforce a lower expectation of employee work hours and availability. From an organizational perspective, this at first may seem rash given the widely held perception that such actions will be followed by economic losses. However, reductions in worktime do not always lead to financial losses for the organization concerned. Indeed, Thomas and Raynar (1997) found that prolonged work hours of 50–60 h a week resulted in a loss of efficiency in the construction industry. Other research has shown that a reduction in work hours has no effect on productivity (e.g. Richardson, 1993).

A further consideration for practitioners, particularly in organizations where employees have to cope with periods of very heavy workloads, is the provision of training in self-efficacy. A recent study by Jex and Bliese (1999) found that individuals with a strong self-efficacy (defined as 'an individual's beliefs regarding the likelihood that a particular course of action or behaviour can be carried out') reported less psychological and physical strain with long work hours and work overload compared with those with lower self-efficacy. In those situations where long work hours are unavoidable, training in self-efficacy for the employees concerned may help to reduce any negative consequences from the work schedule.

Employers should consider the long-term costs and benefits of recruiting more staff to spread the workload, and improving standards of pay, both causes of long work hours. Such actions would benefit both employee performance and their health and safety. This is, of course, exactly the opposite of the downsizing trends discussed earlier. Organizations, therefore, need to question the policy of downsizing to improve efficiency.

## Control at work

Over the past few years, many employees have perceived a gradual loss of control over their work lives and careers. Even those in managerial positions that are usually associated with some degree of control at work have been affected (e.g. Worrall & Cooper, 1998). This is a consequence of the heightened perception of job insecurity, the increased pace of work and the constant advances in technology in the workplace that many individuals have had to adapt to.

The concept of perceived autonomy or control has been extensively investigated in research. 'Perceived control' concerns the amount of control that an individual believes they have over their environment, whether direct or indirect, to make it less threatening or more rewarding (Ganster & Fusilier, 1989). A great deal of evidence from animal and human research indicates that the presence or absence of control has profound effects on health and well-being (e.g. Averill, 1973; Miller, 1979). Degree of control has also occupied a central position in theories of job design and organizational behaviour. Within the work setting, this concept concerns the extent to which an individual is free to decide how to accomplish a task or goals of the job. Considered a basic human need, it is also a motivational characteristic of work. Employees who perceive themselves as choosing to perform an activity, as opposed to being directed to do so, are intrinsically motivated and accept more personal responsibility for the consequences of their work (e.g. Hackman & Oldham, 1975). Very low levels of personal control have been found to be psychologically harmful, whereas greater control has been associated with better mental health (e.g. Evans & Carrére, 1991; Ganster & Fusilier, 1989). High levels of perceived control are associated with increases in job satisfaction, commitment, involvement, performance and motivation, and with low levels of physical symptoms, emotional distress, and absenteeism (e.g. Spector, 1986).

Much of the research in organizational psychology has stemmed from Karasek's (1979) job demands–job control model. This model proposes that the effects of job demands (psychological stressors in the work environment) on employee well-being are influenced by job decision latitude (the degree to which the employee has the potential to control their work). The model predicts that job decision latitude attenuates any negative effects of job demands on employee well-being. Early studies, using large heterogeneous samples, showed moderate support for Karasek's model (e.g. Karasek, 1979; Karasek, Baker, Marxer, Ahlbom, & Theorell, 1981). More recent investigations using Karasek's measure of job decision latitude and other measures of work control have demonstrated that high levels of control are directly related to a range of positive health and work-related outcomes; for example, decreased anxiety and depression (e.g. Mullarkey, Jackson, Wall, Wilson, & Grey-Taylor, 1997), psychosomatic health complaints (e.g. Carayon, 1993), life satisfaction (e.g. Fletcher & Jones, 1993) and job performance (e.g. Greenberger, Strasser, Cummings, & Dunham, 1989).

The formulation of Karasek's model and other research on control provided the impetus for job redesign, with an emphasis on employee work control. One method used to increase perceived control for employees in many organizations is the introduction of participative decision-making, whereby those employees involved in carrying out any decisions also have some input into the actual formulation of the decision (Lowin, 1968). The rationale behind this method is that valuable insight often can be gained by the participation of employees who are involved in implementing a decision. Other methods of increasing perceived control include greater freedom over start and finish times, more discretion over how tasks are performed, and autononous or self-regulated work teams. This last method involves groups of employees with overlapping skills who work together on a relatively discrete task (e.g. producing a particular product) whilst having a high degree of discretion over the way in which they work.

Whilst there are a plethora of studies providing evidence on the benefits of increased control for employee well-being and job-related criteria, there are also studies with conflicting findings. For example, recent research has failed to replicate the hypothesized interaction effect of high job demands and low job control on measures of strain in Karasek's demand-control model (e.g. Fletcher & Jones, 1993). Studies of autonomous work groups have found positive effects on productivity and other work criteria but a lack of improvement in well-being, motivation and absenteeism (e.g. Goodman, Devada, & Hughson, 1988). The mixed findings for Karasek's model may be due in part to specificity of the control measure used (Wall, Jackson, Mullarkey, & Parker, 1996). Individual differences between employees may further explain the discrepant findings. For example, studies have found considerable variation in the desire for control in the workplace (e.g. Hackman & Oldham, 1980). Hence, a perceived lack of control may be stressful to some employees but not to others. Some employees may want minimum control in their jobs, perhaps not warning the increased responsibility that is often connected with greater job autonomy. In such situations, a greater degree of job control would not necessarily be associated with any positive effects on well-being or work-related criteria. De Jonge, Landeweerd, and van Breukelen (1994; cited in de Rijk, Le Blanc, Schaufeli, & de Jonge, 1998) found a negative relationship between job autonomy and both emotional exhaustion and health complaints only for those individuals with a high need for autonomy.

Another difference between individuals is their actual use of the control that they have in their job to cope with stressful situations. Some individuals may cope with a stressful situation by cognitively analysing or using concrete actions to reduce or solve the situation. In a study of Dutch nurses, de Rijk *et al.* (1998) found that overall job control was positively related to employees' well-being, but for nurses who used active (or control) coping, high job control reduced the increase in emotional exhaustion due to job demands. In contrast, for nurses with low active coping, high job control overtaxed such individuals when faced with high job demands, resulting in a lowered well-being; having high levels of control acted as a stressor for these individuals.

In sum, the above research has highlighted the importance of perceived work control for employee well-being. However, further clarification is required on the impact of perceived control in the workplace. Most researchers have viewed work control as a unidimensional construct; it is, however, multi-dimensional, with employees perceiving different levels of control over different aspects of their work environment. Ganster (1988), for example, proposes several different types of work control, including task control, pacing control and scheduling control. Some types may be more important for well-being than others. Task control, for example, appears to act as a stress buffer, particularly when the stressor is task-related (Terry & Jimmieson, 1999). Future investigations need to identify which aspects of work control are the most beneficial to employee well-being. As the majority of work control studies to date are cross-sectional (Terry & Jimmieson, 1999), longitudinal research is also required. The influence of individual differences (e.g. desire for control) also warrants further attention. Several studies have identified social support as an important factor in the stress-buffering effects of work control (e.g. van der Doef, Maes, & Diekstra, 2000). This dimension must be considered in future investigations. Multiple methods and data sources (e.g. both objective and subjective measures) are also important when assessing work control (Jick, 1979). Overall, research needs to consider other factors in the workplace, such as individual and work-environment characteristics, to provide a clearer picture of the relationship between perceived control and employee well-being.

The above research emphasizes the importance for practitioners to be aware of the complexities of the relationship between perceived control and employee well-being. Increasing control in the workplace is not a pre-cursor to improved well-being. Individual differences, for example, in the desire or need for control, as well as in coping skills, must be taken into account when making changes in job autonomy or decision-making responsibilities. This ideally should be conducted with employee consultation and relevant training support. Where appropriate, problem-solving sessions should be held between supervisors and employees to identify job demands or stressors. Strategies should then be instigated that will increase the employees' perceived control so that they can cope more effectively (Spector, 2000). Although the recent major changes in the workplace have left many employees feeling that they have less control, at the same time, some individuals have found that they have increased work control due to the deregulation of the work force. Aside from whether this extra job control is wanted or not, this increase in autonomy is often not enough to meet the demands of the job, leaving such individuals vulnerable to stress (Houtman, 1999). Organizations need to address this issue, whereby any planned increases in employee control need to be adequate enough to meet the psychological demands placed on the worker.

## Managerial style

There is evidence that the managerial job is a demanding one (Burke, 1988). Managers are usually at the forefront of any changes in an organization, actively involved in the decision-making process and responsible for the consequences of any changes made. In the present global economy, competition between industries across countries is increasing (Thurow, 1993), making the management of organizations especially challenging (Whetten & Cameron, 1995). This, together with the constant changes taking place in many workplaces, has resulted in managers being particularly prone to high levels of occupational stress. For example, Cartwright and Cooper (1993) found that 6 months after a merger in a UK building society, more than one-third of 157 middle managers reported mental-health levels comparable to, or worse than, psychoneurotic outpatients.

Increased managerial pressure can also impact on employee well-being. By virtue of their superior position in an organization, managers and supervisors, intentionally or unintentionally, can cause stress for their subordinates. For example, Ganster, Schaubroeck, Sime, and Mayes (1990) found that Type A behaviour patterns exhibited by supervisors were positively related to subordinates' physical health symptoms. When under pressure, many managers may react by exhibiting a negative managerial style. Managers who display an 'inconsiderate' management style may contribute to workers' reports of increased job pressure (Buck, 1972). In an investigation of organizational management style, Beehr and Gupta (1987) found greater levels of perceived stressors (under-utilization of skills and job overload) for employees in a traditional organization compared to those working under a more democratic management style. Managerial support, such as effective communication and feedback, also appears to be an important factor for employee well-being. Poor supervisor support has been linked with increased stress levels (e.g. Balshem, 1988; Kirmeyer & Dougherty, 1988) and symptoms of depression (Repetti, 1993). Lobban, Husted, and Farewell (1998) investigated supervisory style, job demands, decision latitude, and role conflict and ambiguity on self-reported job satisfaction. Their results indicated that good communication and direction from supervisors had a significant additional influence on job satisfaction, suggesting that supervisory style may, in fact, be a precursor of other job characteristics that have been associated with increased stress levels.

Some individuals may display a bullying management style with subordinates when under pressure. A recent survey of over 5000 employees in 70 UK organizations found managers to be the perpetrators for 74.7% of employees who reported being victims of bullying (Hoel & Cooper, 2000). Bullying at work has been linked with employee ill health, including psychosomatic stress symptoms, musculo-skeletal symptoms, anxiety, and depression (Hoel, Rayner, & Cooper, 1999).

The relationship between manager and subordinate is of course a two-way process. A negative management style can exacerbate stress levels for managers if their behaviour results in a deterioration in an employee's work performance or attitude towards them. Unfortunately, there are relatively few studies addressing the impact of negative management styles, with most research focusing on effective management behaviour (Yukl, 1994). Few studies have assessed the effects of managerial stress on the manager–subordinate relationship and the consequences for employee well-being. Further investigations are needed to identify the consequences of a negative management style, for both the manager and the employee. The impact of managerial stress on the manager–subordinate relationship deserves attention. Researchers need to explore the efficacy of training in different managerial styles, which is aimed at increasing managers' awareness of their behaviour and the consequences when dealing with subordinates.

Until then, however, various studies have pinpointed possible ways forward for practitioners to combat or minimize the effects of a negative management style. Existing research has identified two types of leadership style that can benefit employee well-being and work performance, namely transformational and transactional leadership (Bass, 1985; Burns, 1978). Leaders using transformational skills promote inspiration, intellectual stimulation, individual consideration, participative decision-making and elective delegation among their subordinates. Such leaders encourage their employees to view their work from a higher perspective and develop innovative methods of dealing with work-related problems. Transactional leadership skills, however, encompass goal-setting, feedback, and reinforcement strategies that help employees to work effectively. Numerous studies have highlighted the efficacy of transformational leadership in developing employees (e.g. Bass, 1998; Yukl, 1994) and reducing employee stress (e.g. Seltzer, Numeroff, & Bass, 1989; Sosik & Godshalk, 2000). Transactional skills can also aid employee well-being by clarifying performance expectations, reducing uncertainty, and raising efficacy expectations (Sims & Lorenzi, 1992).

Practitioners therefore should encourage managerial training in transactional and transformational skills to enhance employee performance and well-being. The correct combination of these skills will vary according to the organization and the actual tasks being performed. The above research on managerial support provides further training recommendations for practitioners. Organizations should raise awareness amongst their managers of the importance of providing support for their employees. Jex (1998), for example, proposes that interpersonal skills training could benefit many managers and may be a more practical and effective option than attempting to change any personality traits (e.g. Type A behaviour) that may be deleterious in the manager–subordinate relationship. By being trained in different skills, and raising their awareness of their behaviour in the workplace, managers will benefit themselves. The resulting improved relations with their employees may help to allay managers' stress levels, in turn, by providing them with the support and co-operation of their workforce, an important outcome given the pressures many managers face in the workplace today.

An additional consideration for practitioners concerns the growing number of older workers in the workforce. This trend will increase competition for younger workers, and many employees may find themselves working for managers younger than themselves (Jamieson & O'Mara, 1991). Jex (1998) suggests that this may cause resentment in the older, more experienced, subordinate worker and at the same time increase pressures on the younger manager, who may not have sufficient experience to cope with managerial responsibilities and demands.

## Conclusions

In this paper, we have attempted to present a brief overview of research and recommendations for employee well-being on four issues, job insecurity, working hours, work control, and managerial style, which are topical and pertinent to the present-day workplace. To conclude, there are a few final considerations that are relevant to both researchers and practitioners.

Firstly, a greater focus is required on the impact of the changing workplace for employees at the lower end of the organizational hierarchy. Many research investigations and workplace interventions for employee well-being are conducted at the managerial level, frequently excluding more subordinate employees (e.g. Neck & Cooper, 2000; Worrall & Cooper, 1998). Subordinate employees are often from lower social classes, which in turn are associated with poorer health (e.g. Chandola & Jenkinson, 2000). These individuals are often the most affected by changes such as organizational or work restructuring. Hence, there is a definite need for both researchers and practitioners to redress this neglect of subordinate workers.

Secondly, there are obviously other important workplace issues not discussed in this paper that increasingly may present problems for employee well-being in the future. The growing dependence on information technology in the workplace, for example, has resulted in many employees spending long periods at a computer terminal. Numerous studies have found that prolonged work at visual display terminals (VDTs) can impact negatively on employee health, in terms of musculoskeletal problems, visual discomfort and other eye problems, general fatigue, and psychological stress (e.g. Aaras, Horgen, & Ro, 2000; Dillon & Emurian, 1996; Ekberg *et al.*, 1995). More research is required to investigate the long-term health effects of VDTs. However, organizations need to be aware of what hazards or stressors may be present in the workplace of the future and to take preventive measures not only to protect employee well-being but also to cover themselves against any potential legal action from injured employees.

Thirdly, when investigating potential stressors in the workplace both researchers and practitioners must consider employee perceptions. Some researchers have distinguished between positive and negative work experiences or stressors (e.g. Hart, Wearing, & Headey, 1995). Cavanaugh, Boswell, Roehling, and Boudreau (2000) found that work demands perceived as a challenge had positive outcomes for employee well-being, whereas those perceived as a hindrance had produced lower job satisfaction and increased turnover/job searching. Thus, distinguishing between perceived positive and negative stressors in the workplace is an important consideration for both practical interventions and research investigations.

As already mentioned in this paper, there have been major shifts in the demographic composition of the workforce, with an increase in older workers, women, and dual-earners. Another significant trend is the growth in cultural diversity (Kandola & Fullerton, 1996). This has important implications for practitioners. Organizations need to be fully aware of cultural differences in work values, dress code and religion, together with potential problems in communications due to differing proficiencies in the native language used in the organization. Many individuals may require extra training to raise their competencies in skills required for their job. Managers may require further training also to raise their awareness of how cultural differences may impact on the workplace and on employee well-being. Individuals from ethnic-minority groups may be more prone to stress, given the problems they may have with a range of issues spanning the experience of racism and discrimination (e.g. Jones, 1993), potential language difficulties and cultural attitudes to aspects of work such as job control (Jamieson & O'Mara, 1991).

To cope with the increasingly diverse workforce, organizations need to become more flexible, not only in their worktime schedules, but in their procedures and practices as a whole (Kandola & Fullerton, 1996). Employers need to become responsive to individual needs to maximize employee well-being and also their commitment (Herriot, 1989). There is much evidence in support of such adaptable organizations. For example, the benefits of introducing flexible work hours have already been discussed. However, other research has shown that the provision of child-care and the introduction of flexible working options in organizations can help to reduce absenteeism, raise retention rates, and increase employee return after maternity leave (Hammond & Holton, 1991; New Ways to Work, 1993; Young-Blood & Chambers-Cook, 1984). A strategy for increasing flexibility is required, based on an assessment of needs within an organization. This assessment should involve employee participation and communication to address the real issues of the workforce and not just those envisaged by management.

A final consideration concerns the development of a healthy workforce in the 21st century through properly managed health-promotion schemes within the workplace. By offering such schemes, organizations may enhance not only employee well-being but also employee commitment and performance. Previous research has indicated favourable results for employees from the instigation of these programmes, such as improved diet, increased exercise, weight loss, smoking cessation, and the acquisition of stress-reduction techniques (e.g. Demmer, 1995; Dugdill & Springett, 1994). In turn, organizations have also benefited, with reductions in medical and disability costs, absenteeism and turnover, and raised levels of employee mental alertness, job satisfaction, morale, productivity, and an enhanced corporate image (e.g. Conrad, 1988; Daley & Parfitt, 1996; Neck & Cooper, 2000). Whilst these health-promotion schemes have produced positive results for both employees and organizations, a proper needs assessment, involving employee participation, is required to maximize the benefits of any intervention (Springett & Dugdill, 1999).

The issues discussed in this paper have repeatedly highlighted the importance for practitioners of good communications between employees and management. In today's constantly changing work environment, it is particularly important to develop and nurture the confidence of employees from all levels of the organizational hierarchy so that they are prepared to experiment with new working methods. In turn, an improvement in communications between managers and employees will enhance the success of any interventions planned that are aimed at improving employee well-being and ultimately improve organizational effectiveness.

## References

Aaras, A., Horgen, G., & Ro, O. (2000). Work with the visual display unit: Health consequences. *International Journal of Human–Computer interaction, 12*, 107–134.

Averill, J. R. (1973). Personal control over aversive stimuli and its relationship to stress. *Psychological Bulletin, 80*, 286–303.

Baker, D. B., & Landrigan, P. J. (1990). Occupational related disorders. *Environmental Medicine, 74*, 441–460.

Balshem, M. (1988). The clerical workers' boss: An agent of job stress. *Human Organization, 47*, 361–367.

Baltes, B. B., Briggs, T. E., Huff, J. W., Wright, J. A., & Neumann, G. A. (1999). Flexible and compressed work week schedules: A meta-analysis of their effects on work-related criteria. *Journal of Applied Psychology, 84*, 496–513.

Bass, B. M. (1985). *Leadership and performance beyond expectations.* New York: Free Press.

Bass, B. M. (1998). *Transformational leadership: Industry, military, and educational impact.* Mahwah, NJ: Erlbaum.

Beatson, M. (1995). *Labour market flexibility.* Series No. 48. London: Employment Department Research.

Beehr, T. A., & Gupta, N. (1987). Organizational management style, employee supervisory status, and employee responses. *Human Relations, 40,* 45–58.

Berry Lound, D. J. (1993). *A carer's guide to eldercare.* Horsham, UK: The Host Consultancy.

Blyton, P. (1989). Hours of work. In R. Bean (Ed.), *International labour statistics.* London: Routledge.

Borg, V., Kristensen, T. S., & Burr, H. (2000). Work environment and changes in self-rated health: A five year follow up study. *Stress Medicine, 16,* 37–47.

Bosch, G. (1999). Working time: Tendencies and emerging issues. *International Labour Review, 138,* 131–150.

Brewster, C., Mayne, L., Tregaskis, O., Parsons, D., & Atterbury, S. (1996). *Working time and contract flexibility in Europe.* Cranfieid, UK: Cranfield School of Management.

British Household Panel Survey (1998). In BBC News Release (1998). *BBC V's Panorama reveals nation of willing workabolics.* BBC News Media Relations, 28th September. 1998.

Buck, V. (1972). *Working under pressure.* London: Staples Press.

Burchell, B. J., Day, D., Hudson, M., Lapido, D., Mankelew, R., Nolan, J. P., Reed, H., Wichert, C. I., & Wilkinson, F. (1999). *Job insecurity and work intensifiction: Flexibility and the changing boundaries of work.* York: York Publishing Services.

Bureau of Labor Statistics (1995). *Contingent and alternative employment arrangements.* Report 900, Washington, DC: United States Department of Labor.

Burke, R. J. (1988). Sources of managerial and professional stress in large organizations. In C. L. Cooper & R. Payne (Eds.), *Causes, coping and consequences of stress at work.* New York: Wiley.

Burke, R. J. (1998). Correlations of job insecurity among recent business school graduates, *Employee Relations, 20,* 92–100.

Burns, J. M. (1978). *Leadership.* New York: Harper & Row.

Cameron, K., Freeman, S., & Mishra, A. (1991). Best practices in white-collar downsizing: Managing contradictions. *Academy of Management Executive, 5,* 57–63.

Carayon, P. (1993). A longitudinal test of Karasck's job strain model among office workers. *Work and Stress, 7,* 299–314.

CARNET: The Canadian Aging Research Network (1995). *Flexible work arrangements: A user's guide.* Guelph, Ontario: University of Guelph, Psychology Department.

Cartwright, S., & Cooper, C. L. (1993). The psychological impact of merger and acquisitions on the individual: A study or building society managers. *Human Relations, 46,* 327–347.

Cavanaugh, M. A., Boswell, W. R., Roehling, M. V., & Boudreau, J. W. (2000). An empirical examination of self reported work stress among U.S. managers. *Journal of Applied Psychology, 85,* 65–74.

Chandola, T., & Jenkinson, C. (2000). The new UK statistics Socio-economic Classification (NS-SEC); investigating social class differences in self-reported health status, *Journal of Public Health Medicine, 22*, 182–190.

Christensen, K. E., & Staines, G. L. (1990). Flextime. A viable solution to work/family conflict? *Journal of Family Issues, 4*, 455–477.

Conrad, P. (1988). Worksite health promotion: The social context. *Social Science Medicine, 26*, 485–489.

Cooper, C. L., & Jackson, S. (1997). *Creating tomorrow's organizations: A handbook for future research in organizational behavior*. Chichester, UK: Wiley.

Cox, T., Griffiths, A., & Rial-Gonzalez, E. (2000). *Research on work-related stress*. Luxembourg: European Agency for Safety and Health at Work.

Daley, A. J., & Parfitt, G. (1996). Good health—is it worth it? Mood states, physical well-being, job satisfaction and absenteeism in members and non-members of British corpotate health and fitness clubs. *Journal of Occupational and Organizational Psychology, 69*, 121–134.

Demmer, H. (1995). *Work site health promotion: How to go about it. European health promotion series (4)*. Copenhagen: WHO/Europe.

de Rijk, A. E., Le Blanc, P. M., Schaufeli, W. B., & de Jonge, J. (1998). Active coping and need for control as moderators of the job demand–control model: Effects of burnout. *Journal of Occupational and Organizational Psychology, 71*, 1–18.

Dillon, T. W., & Emurian, H. H. (1996). Some factors affecting reports of visual fatigue resulting from use of a VDU. *Computers in Human Behavior, 12*, 49–59.

Domenighetti, G., D'Avanzo, B., & Bisig, B. (2000). Health effects of job insecurity among employees in the Swiss general population. *International Journal of Health Services, 30*, 477–490.

Dugdill, L., & Springett, J. (1994). Evaluation of workplace health promotion: A review. *Health Education Journal, 53*, 337–347.

Dunham, R. B., Pierce, J. L., & Castaneda, M. B. (1987). Alternative work schedules: Two field quasi-experiments. *Personnel Psychology, 40*, 215–242.

Earnshaw, J., & Cooper, C. L. (1996). *Stress and employer liability, lan and employment series*. London: Institute of Personnel and Development.

EC Working Time Directive (1990). Council Directive concerning certain aspects of the organization of working time. *Official Journal of the European Communities, No. C254/4*, 1990.

Ekberg, K., Eklund, J., Tuvesson, M., Oertengren, R., Odenrick, P., & Ericson, M. (1995). Psychological stress and muscle activity during data entry at visual display units. *Work and Stress, 9*, 475–490.

Emmet, E. A. (1991). Physical and chemical agents at the workplace. In G. M. Green & F. Baker (Eds.), *Work, health and productivity*. New York: Oxford University Press.

Eurostat (1997). *Labour force survey*. Brussels, Belgium: European Commission.

Evans, G. W., & Carrére, S. (1991). Traffic congestion, perceived control, and psychophysiological stress among urban bus drivers, *Journal of Applied Psychology, 76*, 658–663.

Falk, A., Hanson, B., Isacsson, S., & Oestergen, P. (1992). Job strain and mortality in elderly men: Social network, support and influence as buffers, *American Journal of Public Health, 82*, 1136–1139.

Ferrie, J. E., Shipley, M. J., Marmot, M. G. et al. (1995). Health effects of anticipation of job change and non-employment: Longitudinal data from the Whitehall II study. *British Medical Journal, 311*, 1264–1269.

Field, S., & Bramwell, R. (1998). An investigation into the relationship between caring responsibilities and the levels of perceived pressure reported by female employees. *Journal of Occupational and Organizational Psychology, 71*, 165–170.

Fletcher, B. C. (1988). Occupation, marriage and disease-specific mortality. *Social Science and Medicine, 77*, 615–622.

Fletcher, B. C., & Jones, F. (1993). A refutation of Karasek's demand-discretion model of occupational stress with a range of dependent measures. *Journal of Organizational Behavior, 14*, 319–330.

Galambos, N. L., & Walters, B. J. (1992). Work hours, schedule inflexibility, and stress in dual-earner spouses. *Canadian Journal of Behavioural Science, 24*, 290–302.

Gall, G. (1996). All year round: The growth of annual hours in Britain. *Personnel Review, 25*, 35–52.

Ganster, D. C. (1988). Improving measures of work control in occupational stress research. In J. J. Hurrell, L. R. Murphy, S. L. Sauter, & C. L. Cooper (Eds.), *Occupational stress: Issues and developments in research*. New York: Taylor & Francis.

Ganster, D. C., & Fusilier, M. R. (1989). Control in the workplace. In C. L. Cooper & I. T. Robertson (Eds.), *International review of industrial and organizational psychology*. Chichester, UK: Wiley.

Ganster, D. C., Schaubroeck, J., Sime, W. E., & Mayes, B. T. (1990). Unhealthy leader dispositions, work group strain and performance. *Best papers. Proceedings of the Academy of Management*, 191–195.

Goodman, P. S., Devada, R., & Hughson, T. G. (1988). Groups and productivity: Analyzing the effectiveness of self-managing teams. In J. P. Campbell, R. J. Campbell & Associates (Eds.), *Productivity in organizations*. San Francisco, CA: Jossey-Bass.

Gottlieb, B. H., Kelloway, E. K., & Barham, E. (1998). *Flexible work arrangements: Managing the work–family boundary*. Chichester, UK: Wiley.

Greenberger, D. B., Strasser, S., Cummings, L. L., & Dunham, R. B. (1989). The impact of personal control on performance and satisfaction. *Organizational Behavior and Human Decision Processes, 43*, 29–51.

Hackman, J. R., & Oldham, G. R. (1975). Development of the Job Diagnostic Survey. *Journal of Applied Psychology, 60*, 159–170.

Hackman, J. R., & Oldham, G. R. (1980). *Work redesign*. Reading, MA: Addison-Wesley.

Hammond, V., & Holton, V. (1991). *A balanced workforce*. Ashridge: Management Research Group.

Hart, P., Wearing, A., & Headey, B. (1995). Police stress :and well-being: Integrating personality, coping and daily work experiences. *Journal of Occupational and Organizational Psychology, 68*, 133–156.

Herriot, P. (1989). *Recruitment in the 90s*. London: Institute of Personnel Management.

Hoel, H., & Cooper, C. L. (2000). *Destructive conflict and bullying at work*. Manchester School of Management, UMIST. Unpublished report.

Hoel, H., Rayner, C., & Cooper, C. L. (1999). Workplace bullying. In C. L. Cooper & I. T. Robertson (Eds.), *International review of industrial and organizational psychology* (Vol. 14). Chichester, UK: Wiley.

Houtman, I. L. D. (1999). The changing workplace. In *Work, stress, and health 1999: organization of work in a global economy. Conference Proceedings. March*, 1999. APA & NIOSH.

Jamieson, D., & O'Mara, J. (1991). *Managing workforce 2000.* San Francisco, CA: Jossey-Bass.

Jex, S. M. (1998). *Stress and job performance: Theory, research, and implications for managerial practice.* Thousand Oaks, CA: Sage Publications.

Jex, S. M., & Bliese, P. D. (1999). Efficacy beliefs as a moderator of the impact of work-related stressors: A multi-level study. *Journal of Applied Psychology. 84,* 349–361.

Jick, T. D. (1979). Mixing qualitative and quantitative methods: Triangulation in action. *Administrative Science Quarterly, 24,* 602–611.

Jones, T. (1993). *Britain's ethnic minorities.* London: Policy Studies Institute.

Kandola, R., & Fullerton, J. (1996). *Managing the mosaic: Diversity in action.* London: Institute of Personnel Management.

Karasek, R. A. (1979). Job demands, job decision latitude and mental strain: Implications for job redesign. *Administrative Science Quarterly, 24,* 285–308.

Karasek, R. A., Baker, D., Marxer, F., Ahlbom, A., & Theorell, T. (1981). Job decision latitude, job demands and cardiovascular disease: A prospective study among Swedish men. *American Journal of Public Health, 71,* 694–705.

King, J. E. (2000). White-collar reactions to job insecurity and the role of the psychological contract: Implications for human resource management. *Human Resource Management, 39,* 79–91.

Kirmeyer, S. L., & Dougherty, T. W. (1988). Work load, tension and coping: Moderating effects of supervisor support. *Personnel Psychology, 41,* 125–139.

Leonard, C., Fanning, N., Attwood, J., & Buckley, M. (1998). The effect of fatigue, sleep deprivation and onerous working hours on the physical and mental well-being of pre-registration house officers. *Irish Journal of Medical Science, 167,* 22–25.

Lewis, S. (1997). 'Family Friendly' employment policies: A route to changing organizational culture or playing about at the margins? *Gender, Work and Organization, 4,* 13–23.

Lewis, S., Watts, A., & Camp, C. (1996). In S. Lewis (1997). 'Family Friendly' employment policies: A route to changing organizational culture or playing about at the margins? *Gender, Work and Organization, 4,* 13–23.

Lobban, R. K., Husted, J., & Farewell, V. T. (1998). A comparison of the effect of job demand, decision latitude, role and supervisory style on self-reported job satisfaction. *Work and Stress, 12,* 337–350.

Lowin, A. (1968). Participative decision making: A model, literature critique, and prescriptions for research. *Organizational Behavior and Human Performance, 3,* 68–106.

McDonough, P. (2000). Job insecurity and health. *International journal of Health Services, 10,* 453–476.

McGuire, J. B., & Liro, J. R. (1987). Absenteeism and flexible work schedules. *Public Personnel Management, 16,* 47–59.

Maddison, A. (1995). *Monitoring the world economy 1820–1992. Development Centre of Organisation for Economic Development and Cooperation.* Paris: OECD.

Maruyama, S., Kohno, K., & Morimoto, K. (1995). A study of preventive medicine in relation to mental health among middle-management employees (Part 2)—Effects of long working hours on lifestyles, perceived stress and working-life satisfaction among white-collar middle-management employees. *Japanese Journal of Hygiene, 50,* 849–860.

Miller, S. M. (1979). Controllability and human stress: Method, evidence and theory. *Behavior Research and Therapy, 17,* 287–304.

Morrison, D. L., & Clements, R. (1997). The effect of one partner's job characteristics on the other partner's distress: A serendipitous, but naturalistic, experiment. *Journal of Occupational and Organizational Psychology, 70,* 307–324.

Mullarkey, S., Jackson, P. R., Wall, T. D., Wilson, J. R., & Grey-Taylor, S. M. (1997). The impact of technology characteristics and job control on worker mental health, *Journal of Organizational Behavior, 18,* 471–489.

Neck, C. P., & Cooper, K. H. (2000). The fit executive: Exercise and diet guidelines for enhancing performance. *Academy of Management Executive, 14,* 72–83.

New Ways to Work (1993). *Change at the top: Working flexibly at senior and managerial levels in organizations.* London: New Ways to Work.

OECD (1999). *Implementing the OECD job strategy: Assessing performance and policy.* Paris: OECD.

Pahl, R. (1993). Rigid flexibilities? Work between men and women. *Work Employment and Society, 7,* 636–642.

Pearce, J. L. (1998). Job insecurity is important, but not the reasons you might think: The example of contingent workers. In C. L. Cooper & D. M. Rousseau (Eds.), *Trends in organizational behavior* (Vol. 5). Chichester, UK: Wiley.

Pierce, J. L., & Newstrom, J. W. (1983). The design of flexible work schedules and employee responses: Relations and process. *Journal of Occupational Behavior, 4,* 247–262.

Poissonnet, C. M., & Veron, M. (2000). Health effects of work schedules in health care professions. *Journal of Clinical Nursing, 9,* 13–23.

Repetti, R. L. (1993). The effects of workload and the social environment at work on health. In L. Goldberger & S. Breznitz (Eds.), *Handbook of stress: Theoretical and clinical aspects.* New York: Free Press.

Richardson, R. (1993). *The economic effects of reductions in working hours: The UK engineering industry: 1989–1993.* Seminar presented at the TUC/Friedrich Ebert Foundation Seminar on Working Time.

Rosa, R. R. (1995). Extended work shifts and excessive fatigue. *Journal of Sleep Research, 4,* 51–56.

Rosa, R. R., Colligan, M. J., & Lewis, P. (1989). Extended work days: Effects of 8 hour and 12 hour rotating schedules on performance, subjective, alertness, sleep patterns and psychosocial variables. *Work and Stress, 3,* 21–32.

Scott, A. J. (1992). Editorial: House staff = shift workers? *Journal of Occupational Medicine, 34,* 1161–1163.

Seltzer, J., Numeroff, R. E., & Bass, B. M. (1989). Transformational leadership: Is it a source of more or less burnout or stress? *Journal of Health and Human Resource Administration, 12,* 174–185.

Sims, H., & Lorenzi, P., (1992). *The new leadership paradigm.* Newbury Park, CA: Sage Publications.

Smithson, J., & Lewis, S. (2000). Is job insecurity changing the psychological contract? *Personnel Review, 29,* 680–698.

Sokejima, S., & Kagamimori, S. (1998). Working hours as a risk factor for acute myocardiol infarction in Japan: Case-control study. *British Medical Journal, 317/7161,* 775–780.

Sosik, J. J., & Godshalf, V. M. (2000). Leadership styles, mentoring functions received, and job-related stress: A conceptual model and preliminary study. *Journal of Organizational Behavior, 21*, 365–390.

Sparks, K., Cooper, C., Fried, Y., & Shirom, A. (1997). The effects of hours of work on health: A meta-analytic review. *Journal of Occupational and Organizational Psychology, 70*, 391–408.

Spector, P. E. (1986). Perceived control by employees: A meta-analysis of studies concerning autonomy and participation at work. *Human Relations, 39*, 1005–1016.

Spector, P. E. (2000). A control theory of the job stress process. In C. L. Cooper (Ed.), *Theories of organizational stress*. New York: Oxford University Press,

Springett, J., & Dugdill, L. (1999). *Health promotion programmes and policies in the workplace: A new challenge for evaluation. European health promotion series (7)*. Copenhagen: WHO/Europe.

Terry, D. J., & Jimmieson, N. L. (1999). Work control and employee well-being: A decade review. In C. L. Cooper & I. T. Robertson (Eds.), *International review of industrial and organizational psychology, 1999* (Vol. 14). Chichester, UK: Wiley.

Thomas, H. & Raynar, K. (1997). Scheduled overtime and labor productivity: Quantitative analysis. *Journal of Construction Engineering and Management—ASCE, 123*, 181–188.

Thomas, L. T., & Ganster, D. C. (1995). Impact of family-supportive work variables on work–family conflict and strain: A control perspective, *Journal of Applied Psychology, 80*, 6–15.

Thurow, L. (1993). *Head to head the coming economic battle among Japan, Europe and America*, New York: Warner Books.

Tierney, D., Romito, P., & Messing, K. (1990). She ate not the bread of idleness: Exhaustion is related to domestic and salaried working conditions among 539 Quebec hospital workers. *Women and Health, 16*, 21–42.

Uehata, T. (1991). Karoshi due to occupational stress-related cardiovascular injuries among middle-aged workers in Japan. *Journal of Science Labour, 67*, 20–28.

Vahtera, J., Kivimaki, M., & Pentti, J. (1997). Effect of organisational downsizing on health of employees. *Lancet, 350*, 1124–1128.

van der Doef, M., Maes, S., & Diekstra, R. (2000). An examination of the job-demand-control-support model with various occupational strain indicators. *Anxiety Stress and Coping, 13*, 165–185.

Wall, T. D., Jackson, P. R., Mullarkey, S., & Parker, S. K. (1996). The demands-control model of job strain: A more specific test. *Journal of Occupational and Organizational Psychology, 69*, 153–166.

Whetten, D. A., & Cameron, K. S. (1995). *Developing management skills*. New York: HarperCollins.

Work Family Directions (1993). *Workplace flexibility: A strategy for doing business*. Boston, MA: Work Family Directions.

Worrall, L., & Cooper, C. L. (1997). *IM-UMIST, quality of working life survey*. London: Institute of Management.

Worrall, L., & Cooper, C L. (1998). *Quality of working life 1998 survey of managers' changing experiences*. London: Institute of Management.

Young-Blood, S. A., & Chambers-Cook, K. (1984). Child care assistance can improve employee attitudes and behaviour. *Personnel Administrator, February*, 93–95.

Yukl, G. (1994). *Leadership in organizations*. Englewood Cliffs, NJ: Prentice-Hall.

# 16

# WORKING HOURS AND HEALTH (EDITORIAL)

*Cary L. Cooper*

Source: *Work and Stress* 10(1) (1996): 1–4.

There is a growing debate and concern throughout Europe about the increasing trend in both public- and private-sector organizations toward longer working hours, and their impact on the health and well-being of workers (Paoli 1992, Harrington 1994). This development stems partly from the European recession of the late 1980s and its aftermath in the early 1990s, as many companies massively downsized to reduce their labour costs for short-term competitive advantage. This has meant inevitably that there are fewer and fewer workers, doing more and more work, and inevitably feeling more job insecure as they see increasing job losses and the re-structuring of the nature of work in terms of short-term contracts (Rousseau, 1995). This has had the effect of forcing people to work longer hours to deal with the increased workloads, with new technology creating the added burden of information overload as well as accelerating the pace and flow of work, as a greater immediacy of response (e.g. faxes, email) becomes the normative business expectation.

While fewer people at work certainly means heavier workloads, it also creates palpable job insecurity, with its accompanying insidious competitive corporate climate of long working hours, as individuals vie to demonstrate 'organisational commitment' in an effort to avoid the second or third tranche of job losses/redundancies. Whether it is out of fear or an intrinsic organizational norm, senior executives in many companies in a number of countries are creating 'workaholic cultures', where hours of work equate in their minds to productivity—'the longer the better'—and in some curious but unproven way, 'the longer the more efficient'.

In a recent national UK survey carried out by Austin Knight (1995) of a sample of employees from 22 large UK organizations representing over 1 million white collar workers, it was found that (1) although three-quarters of employees sampled have contracted hours of between 35 and 37 hours per week, two-thirds regularly work more than 40 hours and 25% more than 50 hours per week (2) 76% said that continually working long hours had adversely affected their physical health; (3) 47% admitted that their families suffered from their absence, but fewer than one-third would 'stand up to their boss in order to improve their family time'; (4) 57% acknowledged that their 'personal life suffered because of long hours'; and finally, but ironically, (5) 90% of employers surveyed see long hours as a corporate problem in terms of reduced performance and lowered morale.

European employers are being bombarded not only by the results of such national surveys but also by their own employee attitude surveys which are indicating increasing levels of stress at work due to work overload and extended working hours (Cooper and Bramwell 1992, Bogg and Cooper 1995). But even more significant for them is the trend in Europe for employees to litigate against their employers for stress at work in general (Earnshaw and Cooper 1994), and for long working hours and work overload in particular. An example of this can be seen in the Johnstone v Bloomsbury Health Authority case in the UK, as described by Eamshaw and Cooper (1996).

Chris Johnstone was a junior hospital doctor whose contract of employment required him to work a basic 40-hour week and to be available on call for up to a further 48 hours overtime. He alleged that as a result of working excessively long hours he suffered symptoms of stress and depression which were manifested through difficulty in eating and sleeping, by occasionally being physically sick from exhaustion, and by frequently experiencing suicidal feelings. In addition to claiming damages, he sought a declaration that he could not be required to work 'for so many hours in excess of his standard working week as would foreseeably injure his health' even if this was less than the 48 hours availability stipulated in his contract. In essence, the issue was whether the 'implied term' of his contract, that his employer would take reasonable care for his health and safety, took precedence over the 'express provision' to work up to 88 hours in total.

Whilst the judges were at variance over the issue of the supremacy of the express terms (88 hours), they were nevertheless in agreement that if the express terms of the contract were to prevail, they would arguably be rendered ineffective by the Unfair Contract Terms Act 1977. This provides that 'a person cannot by reference to any contract term ... exclude or restrict his liability for ... personal injury resulting from negligence'.

This hearing in the UK Court of Appeal in 1991 was merely an unsuccessful application by the employer to have the claim thrown out without its proceeding to trial. Much interest centred not only on what would be the final legal outcome, but also on the potential implications for the working conditions of hospital doctors and other occupational groups throughout the UK. Some 4 years later, very shortly before the trial of the main action was due to begin, the claim was settled out of court for £5600 and payment of costs. No doubt Johnstone regarded this as a moral victory, but the lack of a ruling leaves the law in a state of uncertainty on what is clearly an important issue for cases involving working hours. More cases, however, are in the pipeline on long working hours and other more wide ranging stress-related issues (e.g. bullying at work) (Earnshaw and Cooper 1996).

In addition to the employee litigation cases, there is also the very important recent European Council Directive on working time (93/104/EC). This Directive highlights a range of restrictions on night work, minimum rest periods (11 hours of rest in every 24-hour period), rest days, annual leave entitlements, and the like, but the most controversial element is the maximum 48-hour working week provision. Under this provision, many employees (with some exceptions such as hospitals) would have the right to refuse work that forced them to work over 48 hours. This issue has divided Employers Federations and Trade Union organizations in a number of European countries, and has led to a European Court of Justice challenge to this provision, to be held in 1996. This has come to a head because the British government refutes the European claim that working hours should be considered as a 'health and safety' issue as opposed to a 'working conditions' issue (Harrington 1994). The implication is that if it is considered a 'health and safety' issue, the work hours limitations can be approved by a qualified majority vote of EU member states, whereas if it is a 'working conditions' one, it has to be approved by a unanimous vote, thereby allowing the UK, or any other country, to veto the 48-hour working week provision.

These European developments have focused research attention on the link between working hours and health. The problem is that although some research evidence does exist to indicate that long working hours may adversely affect health, most of it is either not very recent or is not systematically or broadly based research (in terms of different occupational groups), or is too US orientated. As early as the 1940s, Fraser (1947) identified eight factors responsible for increased incidence of stress at work or what he termed 'work neurosis'. Although the study was undertaken during the Second World War, it involved interviewing over 3000 workers in a number of engineering firms during a 6-month period. One of the major factors predictive of increased work-related stress was 'more than 75 hours of industrial work each week' (Cox 1978). There were also studies carried out in the 1950s and 1960s showing links between hours of work and heart disease. In a study of 100 young coronary patients, for example, Russek and Zohman (1958) found that 25% had been working at two jobs and an additional 45% had worked at jobs which required (due to work overload) 60 or more hours per week. They added that although prolonged emotional strain preceded the attack in 91% of the cases, similar stress was only observed in 20% of the controls. Breslow and Buell (1960) also reported findings that support a relationship between hours of work and death from coronary disease in a sample of 22 176 over 3 years. In an investigation of mortality rates of men in California, they observed that workers in light industry under the age of 45, who were on the job more than 48 hours a week, had twice the risk of death from coronary heart disease compared with similar workers working 40 or under hours a week.

Harrington (1994a) reviewed a number of studies assessing the link between working hours and ill-health affects (from shift work to extended working time to long working hours). He concluded 'astonishingly, 100 years after the first experiments on shorter working hours and performance (McIvor 1987), we are still unable to decide whether working long hours is bad for health'. However, he goes on to say in another paper (Harrington 1994b) that 'it does appear that working weeks in excess of perhaps 48–56 hours are harmful'.

The systematic exploration of the relationship between working hours and health, therefore, is a major research challenge, if we are rationally to alter occupational and public health policy. It is important that social scientists engage in more controlled and wide-ranging research which assesses the impact of working hours and different 'working time' practices, not only on health but also on family life and corporate performance. In terms of the latter, occupational psychology's influence in the workplace will only be realised if it can be demonstrated to senior executives in the public and private sectors that long working hours is not only a health issue, but also one of productivity.

John Ruskin summed up our empirical challenge, as long ago as 1851, when he asserted: 'In order that people may be happy in their work, these three things are needed: they must be fit for it; they must not do too much of it; and they must have a sense of success in it'.

## References

Bogg, J. and Cooper, C.L., 1995, Job satisfaction, mental health, and occupational stress among senior civil servants, *Human Relations*, **48**(3), 327–341.

Buell, P. and Breslow, L., 1960, Mortality from CHD in California men who work long hours. *Journal of Chronic Disease*, **11**(b), 615–626.

Cooper, C.L. and Bramwell, R.S., 1992, A comparative analysis of occupational stress in managerial and shopfloor workers in the brewing industry: mental health, job satisfaction and sickness. *Work and Stress*, **6**(2), 127–138.

Cox, T., 1978, *Stress* (Macmillan, London).

Earnshaw, J. and Cooper, C.L., 1994, Employee stress litigation. *Work and Stress*, **8**(4), 287–295.

Earnshaw, J. and Cooper, C.L., 1996, *Stress and Employer Liability* (IPD, London).

Fraser, R., 1947, The incidence of neurosis among factory workers. Industrial Health Research Board of the Medical Research Council Report, **90** (HMSO, London).

Harrington, J.M., 1994a, Working long hours and health, *British Medical Journal*, **308**, 1581–82.

Harrington, J.M., 1994b, Shift work and health—a critical review of the literature on working hours, *Annals of Academic Medicine (Singapore)*, **23**(5), 699–705.

Knight, A., 1995, *Long Hours Culture* (Austin Knight, London).

Mcivor, A.J., 1987, Employers, the government and industrial fatigue in Britain: 1890–1918, *British Journal of Industrial Medicine*, **44**, 724–732.

Paoli, P., 1992, *The First European Survey on the Work Environment* (European Foundation for Living and Working Conditions, Dublin).

Rousseau, D., 1995, *Psychological Contracts in Organizations* (Sage, Beverly Hills).

Russek, H.I. and Zohman, B.L., 1958, Relative significance of heredity, diet, and occupational stress in CHD of young adults, *American Journal of Medical Science*, **235**, 266–275.

# 17

# ORGANIZATIONAL JUSTICE

## A fair assessment of the state of the literature

*Jason A. Colquitt and Jerald Greenberg*

Source: J. Greenberg (ed.), *Organizational Behavior: The State of the Science*, Mahwah, NJ: Erlbaum, 2003, pp. 165–210.

Social scientists long have noted that feelings of justice and injustice are experienced commonly in everyday life (Cohen, 1986). This is especially so on the job, where employees are sensitive to matters such as how much they are paid relative to others, how openly and consistently decisions are made, and how thoroughly and sensitively these decisions are explained to them (Greenberg, 1996). Such experiences reflect the domain of *organizational justice*—a term coined by Greenberg (1987) to refer to the extent to which people perceive organizational events as being fair. Specifically, organizational justice is widely regarded to take three major forms.

- *Distributive justice*: The perceived fairness of decision outcomes, such as pay. Distributive justice is promoted by following appropriate norms (e.g., equity, equality, or need) for allocating resources (Adams, 1965; Deutsch, 1975; Homans, 1961; Leventhal, 1976).
- *Procedural justice*: The perceived fairness of the procedures used to make decisions. Procedural justice is fostered by the use of certain procedural rules, such as granting voice in the decision-making processes (i.e., *process control*), and making decisions in a manner that is consistent, accurate, correctable, and that suppresses bias (Leventhal, 1980; Leventhal, Karuza, & Fry, 1980; Thibaut & Walker, 1975).
- *Interactional justice*: The perceived fairness of how decisions are enacted by authority figures. Interactional justice has an interpersonal component that is fostered by dignified and respectful treatment, and an informational component that is fostered by adequate and honest explanations (Bies, 2001; Bies & Moag, 1986).

These types of justice have received considerable attention over the years, and have been the subject of detailed historical analyses (Byrne & Cropanzano, 2001; Cohen & Greenberg, 1982).

The organizational justice literature has grown dramatically during the 1990s. In fact, organizational justice was cited as the most popular topic of papers submitted to the Organizational Behavior Division of the Academy of Management for several years during the mid- to late 1990s (Cropanzano & Greenberg, 1997). A search of 20 psychology and management journals in the *Web of Science* database using the key terms "justice" or "fairness" further confirms this boom in popularity. From 1989 through 1992, there were only 15 publications using these key terms. From 1993 through 1996, there were 53; and from 1997 through 2000, the figure grew to 100. Clearly, the literature grew dramatically in the 1990s.

In part, this growth was fueled by the publication of a literature review by Greenberg (1990), that bookmarked the field's progress to that date. In that article, Greenberg delineated what already was established about organizational justice, what work was underway at the time, and what challenges he believed lay ahead. In this chapter, we examine the current state of the literature by updating the conceptual and empirical developments in organizational justice in the decade following Greenberg's (1990) review. In so doing, we follow Greenberg's lead by applying Reichers and Schneider's (1990) construct life cycle to the development of organizational justice. Our adaptation of their life cycle is summarized in Fig. 5.1.

As Fig. 5.1 reveals, three stages are evident during the life of a construct or content area: evaluation, augmentation, and consolidation and accommodation. In the *evaluation stage* critical reviews of the literature question the conceptualization and operationalization of key constructs and point out equivocal empirical results. In the *augmentation stage* these weaknesses are addressed, as new conceptualizations appear and mediating and moderating variables are added. Finally, in the *consolidation and augmentation stage* controversies wane as definitions, antecedents, and consequences become well accepted. The end of this stage is signaled by the integration of the concept into mainstream literature and textbooks.

In his 1990 review, Greenberg argued that certain topics in the justice literature—distributive justice, for example—had reached the consolidation and accommodation stage. However, research on procedural justice was still in the evaluation or augmentation stage. Accordingly, he characterized the justice literature as being in its "intellectual adolescence" (Greenberg, 1993a, p. 135). We now

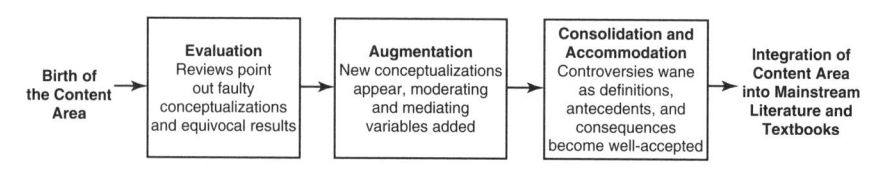

*Figure 5.1* An adaptation of Reichers and Schneider's (1990) construct life cycle.

ask: How far has the literature come in these intervening years? As we reveal, some questions now have been answered, consequently reaching the consolidation and accommodation stage. In contrast, other questions remain the subject of much debate. Our analysis of the development of the field of organizational justice will focus on four specific questions that have dominated the literature. These are as follows:

- How distinct are the various types of justice?
- How are justice judgments formed?
- What outcomes are associated with justice judgments?
- What are the boundary conditions for justice effects?

We detail the various stages through which each question has progressed, using Greenberg's (1990) review as our starting point. Finally, we conclude this chapter by offering observations about the field's current maturity and, acting as meddlesome caretakers, imposing our ideas about how to develop that maturity further.

## How distinct are the various types of justice?

In studying justice in organizations, the question most commonly posed is, "How fair is X?" When X is defined as the outcome of an allocation decision, the subject of study is distributive justice. When X is defined as the procedures that led to that outcome, procedural justice is the phenomenon of interest. When X is defined as the enactment of a procedure by an authority figure, we are examining interactional justice. Although such distinctions are logical and convenient for social scientists, it is useful to determine whether this same trichotomy is acknowledged in common use (Greenberg, 1990). As such, the first question we examine concerns the distinctions among the various types of justice.

### *Evaluation stage*

The evaluation stage is marked by several key criteria, most notably, the publication of critical reviews of the literature and the existence of equivocal empirical findings. Each of these criteria characterized the literature as the "how distinct" question entered the evaluation stage.

#### *Literature reviews*

As the 1990s began, a variety of literature reviews were published, many of which discussed the distinctions among the various justice types. For example, Greenberg's (1990) review discussed support for the distributive–procedural distinction, including the results of open-ended content coding studies and the demonstration of different antecedents and consequences. However, Greenberg did not endorse the distinction between procedural and interactional justice proposed by Bies and Moag (1986). Instead, he conceived of interpersonal treatment and adequate explanations as "interpersonal aspects of procedural justice" (p. 411).

The combining of procedural and interactional justice is consistent with another review published that same year by Tyler and Bies (1990), which referred to interactional justice as the "interpersonal context of procedural justice" (p. 77). In so doing, they argued that the enactment of a procedure was not psychologically distinct from the formal qualities of the procedure itself. These sentiments echoed a prior review by Folger and Bies (1989), which had identified the interpersonal treatment and adequate explanations facets of interactional justice as "managerial responsibilities in procedural justice" (p. 82). Importantly, both of these reviews argued that the interactional form of justice included managers' consideration of subordinates' viewpoints, suppression of biases, and consistent application of criteria, in addition to the interpersonal treatment and adequate explanations facets introduced by Bies and Moag (1986). These additions, which overlap with Leventhal's (1980) criteria for procedural justice, further blurred the distinction between procedural and interactional justice.

*Equivocal empirical findings*

A second key characteristic of the evaluation stage is the existence of equivocal empirical findings. Equivocal results were found in efforts to distinguish the various types of justice empirically. For example, with respect to the distinction between distributive and procedural justice, some studies yielded weak to moderate correlations between these forms of justice (e.g., Daly & Geyer, 1994; Greenberg, 1994; White, Tansky, & Baik, 1995), whereas others reported correlations that were very high (e.g., Ball, Trevino, & Sims, 1993; Conlon & Ross, 1993; Gilliland, 1994). Similar inconsistencies were evident with respect to the procedural–interactional relationship: Some studies reported only modest relationships (e.g., White et al., 1995) whereas others found very high correlations (e.g., Kidwell & Bennett, 1994; Niehoff & Moorman, 1993). Still other studies made no effort to separate procedural and interactional justice at all (e.g., Brockner, Wiesenfeld, & Martin, 1995; Folger & Konovsky, 1989; Konovsky & Folger, 1991).

**Augmentation stage**

In the augmentation stage, we begin to find clarification of the conflicting results and conceptualizations evident in the evaluation stage. In the early-to-mid 1990s, this clarification began to occur for the distributive–procedural justice distinction.

*Confirmatory factor-analytic studies*

One of the first sources of clarification was Moorman's (1991) confirmatory factor analysis of distributive and procedural justice in his study of organizational citizenship behavior. The best-fitting model was one in which the two justice types remained distinct. Sweeney and McFarlin (1993) also used confirmatory factor analysis to compare multiple models: one in which distributive and procedural justice were independent, and two that posited a causal connection between them. The models' fit statistics supported separation of distributive and procedural justice, and also showed that the addition of a causal connection did not enhance fit.

*Evidence of outcome × process interactions*

A second source of clarification regarding the distributive–procedural distinction came by recognizing that these two forms of justice often interacted statistically in affecting outcomes. Brockner and Wiesenfeld (1996) reviewed studies using 45 independent samples published between 1983 and 1996 and noted that procedural justice was more strongly related to work attitudes when outcomes were low rather than high. Conversely, outcomes were more strongly related to work attitudes when procedures were unfair than when they were fair. Scientists have characterized this interaction in various ways, such as, "it is not only what you do, but how you do it" (Brockner & Wiesenfeld, 1996, p. 206) or "the means justify the ends" (Greenberg, 1987, p. 55). Regardless of how it is expressed, the robustness of the interaction demonstrates the importance of treating distributive and procedural justice as distinct concepts.

*New conceptualizations*

The distinction between procedural justice and interactional justice also received a great deal of attention throughout the 1990s. The augmentation stage is marked by the appearance of new conceptualizations of existing constructs. Greenberg (1993b) offered a new conceptualization of interactional justice by arguing that interactional justice should be broken down into two components: interpersonal justice, which captures the dignity and respect aspects of Bies and Moag's (1986) conceptualization, and informational justice, which captures the adequacy and honesty of explanations. It is noteworthy that Greenberg excluded such factors as consideration of others' viewpoints, suppression of biases, or consistent application of criteria—facets that were included in the conceptualizations by Folger and Bies (1989) and by Tyler and Bies (1990). This bit of reductionism began to clarify the construct boundaries of procedural and interactional justice.

*Distinguishing justice content from justice source*

The procedural–interactional boundary was clarified further as researchers began distinguishing justice content (e.g., consistency vs. interpersonal treatment) from justice source (e.g., formal system vs. human agent). Although previous studies comparing procedural and interactional justice usually confounded these factors, recent studies have crossed them intentionally (Byrne & Cropanzano, 2000;

Masterson, Bartol, & Moye, 2000; Tyler & Blader, 2000). For example, Byrne and Cropanzano (2000) used confirmatory factor analysis to separate four distinct justice dimensions: supervisor-originating procedural justice, supervisor-originating interactional justice, organization-originating procedural justice, and organization-originating interactional justice.

### Consolidation and accommodation stage

In the consolidation and accommodation stage we see a waning of controversies and a consensus regarding the definitions and correlates of key constructs. Such consensus currently is evident regarding the distributive–procedural justice distinction and the procedural–interactional justice distinction.

#### Meta-analytic evidence of consensus

One source of that consensus is provided by the first meta-analytic review of the justice literature (Colquitt, Conlon, Wesson, Porter, & Ng, 2001). Colquitt et al.'s review encompassed 183 articles with 242 independent samples, published between 1975 and 2001. Ninety-two of those samples included the correlation between distributive justice and procedural justice, which ranged from 0.34 to 0.57 depending on how procedural justice was captured (e.g., with respect to process control; Leventhal's [1980] criteria; or direct "how fair" measures). These results clearly show that distributive justice and procedural justice are unique, though highly intercorrelated.

The procedural–interactional distinction also has received clarification from meta-analytic findings. Notably, Colquitt et al. (2001) examined the validity of separating not just procedural and interactional justice, but also the interpersonal and informational aspects of Bies and Moag's (1986) construct. They found a correlation of .66 between interpersonal justice and informational justice (after correcting for unreliability). Because this correlation was not significantly different than the procedural-distributive correlation, the authors lent support to Greenberg's (1993b) four-dimensional conceptualization of organizational justice. The correlations between the two interactional facets and procedural justice also supported keeping those dimensions separate (.63 for procedural and interpersonal justice; .58 for procedural and informational justice). Colquitt's (2001) confirmatory factor analytic support for Greenberg's conceptualization provides further evidence for the four-dimensional view.

#### Conceptual reviews

A second source of consolidation can be found in the theoretical review of the distributive–procedural distinction by Cropanzano and Ambrose (2001). These authors noted that, in an effort to separate the two constructs, justice scholars had perpetuated some artificial distinctions. For example, scholars generally examined distributive justice using some relative standard, whereas procedural justice was studied using more absolute rules or criteria. In fact, like distributive justice, procedural justice can be judged relative to social comparisons or individual expectations (Grienberger, Rutte, & Van Knippenberg, 1997). Another artificial distinction lies in the different sets of criteria used to foster the two types of justice. Equity, equality, and need—allocation norms used to promote distributive justice (Deutsch, 1975)—can be applied just as easily to procedural justice. For example, equal amounts of process control can be provided to all, or greater opportunities for correctability can be provided to those most in need of it. By separating true differences from artificial differences, Cropanzano and Ambrose provided consolidation and accommodation to the distributive–procedural distinction.

Bies (2001) provided another source of theoretical consolidation and accommodation in his review of the debate about whether to separate interactional justice from procedural justice. His conclusion, that "it makes theoretical and analytical sense to maintain the distinction between interactional justice and procedural justice" (p. 99) was identical to that reached by Bobocel and Holmvall (2001). Specifically, these theorists reached this conclusion by illustrating that procedural justice and interactional justice: (a) have different causal effects on outcomes, (b) have different antecedents, and (c) correlate with organizational outcomes to different degrees.

### *Conclusion: how distinct are the various types of justice?*

The answer to the question "How distinct are the various types of justice?" has changed as the justice literature has developed (see Table 5.1). The equivocal results that characterized the evaluation stage called into question the existence of more than two types of justice. However, the new conceptualizations that appeared in the augmentation stage illustrated the independence of interactional justice, and even argued for its separation into interpersonal and informational facets. Furthermore, recent meta-analytic and narrative reviews have brought consolidation and accommodation to this critical question. This suggests that at least one key question in the justice literature has reached the final stage of Reichers and Schneider's (1990) life cycle.

## How are justice judgments formed?

Once they clarified the types of justice that exist, scientists considered a more sophisticated question: How are justice judgments formed? Fig. 5.2 presents a model of this process around which we organize our discussion.

### *Evaluation stage*

In the evaluation stage, the literature regarding the formation of justice judgments was based, in part, on a debate between *relational* and *instrumental*

Table 5.1 The evolution of key questions in the organizational justice literature

| Stage of development | | | |
|---|---|---|---|
| Key question | Evaluation | Augmentation | Consolidation and accommodation |
| How distinct are the various types of justice? | • Reviews support DJ–PJ distinction, but blur PJ–IJ boundary<br>• Inconsistent (and often high) correlations among justice types | • Use of confirmatory factor analysis to support distinctions<br>• Process x Outcome interaction supports DJ–PJ separation<br>• Greenberg (1993b) presented reconceptualization of IJ<br>• Justice source and content begin to be separated | • Colquitt et al. (2001) provided meta-analytic support for four-dimensional taxonomy<br>• Cropanzano and Ambrose (2001) reviewed artificial DJ–PJ differences<br>• Bies (2001) and Bobocel and Holmvall (2001) cemented PJ–IJ differences |
| How are justice judgments formed? | • Tyler and Lind (1992) distinguished between instrumental and relational models of justice<br>• Folger (1986a, 1986b, 1987, 1993) introduce and update RCT | • Lind et al. (1993) developed fairness heuristic theory, based on the relational model<br>• Van den Bos, Lind, and colleagues conducted series of experiments testing fairness heuristic theory<br>• Folger and Cropanzano (1998) developed fairness theory, based on RCT | • Not yet attained |

| | | |
|---|---|---|
| What outcomes are associated with justice judgments? | • Reviews begin to distinguish distributive and procedural justice according to effects on system and person-referenced variables<br>• Reviews speculate on the relative effects of procedural and interactional justice | • Masterson et al. (2000) identified differences in mediators of justice effects<br>• Colquitt et al. (2001) conducted meta-analytic tests of two-factor and agent–system models<br>• New conceptualizations build on two-factor and agent-system models | • Not yet attained |
| What are the boundary conditions for justice effects? | • Reviews begin to make general extensions of justice effects (e.g., to dispute resolution, political, organizational, and interpersonal contexts)<br>• Empirical studies widen the bounds of justice applications to many specific contexts (e.g., performance evaluation, selection, compensation, organizational change) | • Researchers focus on explicit contextual moderators of justice effects (e.g., culture, uncertainty)<br>• Researchers focus on explicit individual moderators of justice effects (e.g., gender, personality) | • Not yet attained |

*Note.* DJ = distributive justice; PJ = procedural justice; IJ = interactional justice.

THE MEANING AND IMPACT OF WORK

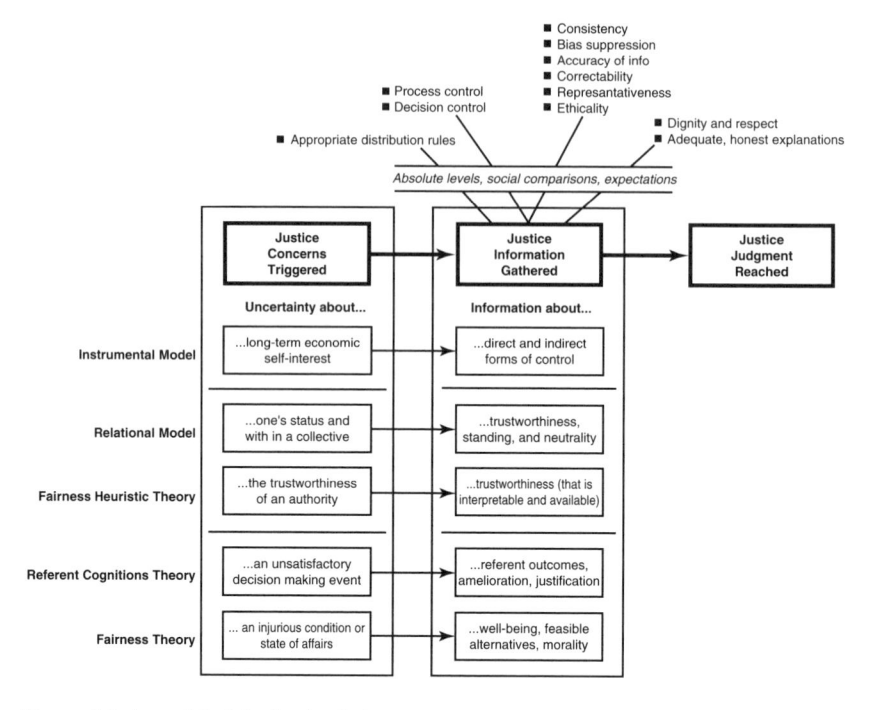

*Figure 5.2* A model of the justice judgment process.

models of justice. These models had implications for the reasons that justice concerns were triggered, and the way that justice information was gathered once concerns had become salient. The evaluation stage also was marked by the development of referent cognitions theory (Folger, 1986a, 1986b, 1987), which offered a distinct but complementary view of the judgment process.

### *Relational versus instrumental models*

At the beginning of the last decade, questions about the motives underlying people's judgments of fairness were a central topic of critical reviews. For example, Greenberg (1990) provided an overview of the *self–interest model* and the *group value model* proposed by Lind and Tyler (1988). These models, which later were recast as the *instrumental model* and the *relational model* respectively (Tyler & Lind, 1992), proposed different triggers of the justice judgment process (see Fig. 5.2). The instrumental model argued that people attend to matters of justice in keeping with their long-term interest in control over economic outcomes (Lind & Tyler, 1988; Thibaut & Walker, 1975). For example, process control is valued as a fair procedure insofar as it helps protect one's self-interest, making the future appear more predictable. The relational model, by contrast, argues that people attend to justice because fair procedures are "symbols of group values" (Tyler & Lind, 1992, p. 140), which signal that they are valued by others with whom they associate. Process control is valued in this case because it reinforces feelings of self-worth and acceptance by one's group.

These models also differ with respect to how individuals gather and organize information when forming justice judgments (see Fig. 5.2). From the instrumental perspective, the guiding question is, "Does this procedure enhance my control over desired outcomes?" In this regard, assessments of process control and decision control are critical pieces of information (Thibaut & Walker, 1975). However, they are not the *only* considerations. Leventhal's (1980) criteria, such as bias suppression, correctability, and representativeness, also make outcomes more controllable (or at least predictable). And, as Cropanzano and Ambrose (2001) noted, information relevant to the justice judgment process may be gathered in either absolute or relative terms (i.e., compared to some external standard or compared to one's own expectations).

According to the relational perspective (Tyler & Lind, 1992), three guiding questions organize information gathering: (a) What is my standing in this group? (b) Are the authorities trustworthy? and (c) Are the authorities neutral? Standing is based primarily on the dignity and respect criteria of interpersonal justice. Trustworthiness is concerned with the ethicality and benevolence of authorities and their actions, and therefore can depend on a number of criteria, including process control, representativeness, and adequate and honest explanations (Tyler, 1990). Finally, neutrality depends on bias suppression, as well as consistency and honesty (Tyler, 1990).

## *Referent cognitions theory*

Greenberg's (1990) review also discussed one other theory relevant to the justice judgment process: Folger's (1986a, 1986b, 1987) referent cognitions theory (RCT). This approach argues that people react to decisions by comparing what actually happened to their assessments of what might have been. These *referent cognitions,* as they are termed, come in three forms: *referent outcomes* (which compare the decision event to other easily imagined outcomes), the *likelihood of amelioration* (which considers whether a negative outcome eventually will be rectified), and *justification* (which compares the sequence of events that led to the outcome to other—perhaps, more justifiable—sequences). The first two cognitions concern distributive justice, whereas the third is concerned with procedural justice (Folger, 1986a, 1986b, 1987).

RCT assumes that a discrete event triggers the justice judgment process (see Fig. 5.2). Once the referent cognitions process begins, justice information is gathered and organized around the three RCT elements. Referent outcomes draw on distributive information. In contrast, the likelihood of amelioration draws on explanations (which could shed light on future outcomes) or on consistency and correctability (which could signal whether future outcomes will differ). Justification draws on any information conveying the fairness of the decision-making process, from process control to bias suppression to ethicality. Finally, we note that subsequent work has expanded the scope of the justification cognition. Folger (1993) argued that procedures have value beyond their "means to an end" function, because they signal whether certain moral obligations have been met. Thus, in assessing fairness, information on ethicality or dignity and respect could be considered, even if it has no bearing on any material outcomes.

### *Augmentation stage*

As we described previously, the augmentation stage is marked by the introduction of new conceptualizations that clarify debates in the literature. In the mid-1990s, new conceptualizations of the justice judgment process began to appear that were based on the approaches offered by the relational model (Tyler & Lind, 1992) and RCT (Folger, 1987). Subsequently, these developed into the formal conceptualizations known as fairness heuristic theory (see Lind, 2001a; Van den Bos, 2001a; Van den Bos, Lind, & Wilke, 2001) and fairness theory (see Folger & Cropanzano, 1998, 2001).

#### *Fairness heuristic theory*

Fairness heuristic theory originated as an extension of Tyler and Lind's (1992) relational model (Lind, Kulik, Ambrose, & de Vera Park, 1993). The relational model argues that fair treatment signals that authorities are legitimate—and therefore, that compliance with their directives will result in beneficial consequences (Tyler & Lind, 1992). Accordingly, fairness can be used as a *heuristic* that alleviates the need to fully explore all consequences of all responses to an authority figure's decisions (Lind et al., 1993).

Because it is useful and efficient, people are motivated to form this heuristic during the early stages of interaction with potentially untrustworthy authorities or other organizational parries (see Fig. 5.2). Importantly, this means that procedural issues play a larger role than distributive justice in forming justice judgments because procedural information typically is more readily available than distributive information. Van den Bos, Vermunt, and Wilke (1997) tested this notion in an experiment in which the order of presentation of procedural and distributive information was manipulated. They showed that individuals' justice judgments were driven more by the accuracy of the procedure when that information was presented first. However, when information on outcome favorability was presented first, that information proved to be the primary driver of justice judgments.

Subsequent research has shed further light on the development of fairness heuristics. In addition to the order and timing of information (Lind, Kray, & Thompson, 2001; Van den Bos, Vermunt, et al., 1997), the interpretability of information also is critical (Van den Bos, Lind, Vermunt, & Wilke, 1997; Van den Bos, Wilke, Lind, & Vermunt, 1998). Specifically, when distributive justice is difficult to judge (e.g., when social comparisons are impossible) procedural issues have a greater impact on fairness heuristics than distributive issues. Likewise, procedural issues also are more important when the trustworthiness of authorities is difficult to determine (Van den Bos, Wilke, & Lind, 1998).

*Fairness theory*

The augmentation stage also has seen the introduction of a second reconceptualized theory relevant to the justice judgment process. Fairness theory (Folger & Cropanzano, 1998, 2001) builds on RCT by examining people's reactions to negative decisions. Like RCT, fairness theory is built on cognitive representations of what might have been. In RCT, these are called referent cognitions, whereas in fairness theory they are referred to as *counterfactuals* (i.e., simulated events contrary to the facts). Three counterfactuals determine reactions to decisions: (a) the *would* counterfactual, which compares the current state of well-being with other potential states; (b) the *could* counterfactual, which assesses whether other feasible behaviors were available to the authority; and (c) the *should* counterfactual, which compares an authority figure's actions with prevailing moral standards.

Although the three counterfactuals can be constructed in any order, the logical trigger is some negative decision outcome—what Folger and Cropanzano (2001) called "an injurious condition or state of affairs" (p. 3; see Fig. 5.2). The impact of this negative outcome, procedure, or interpersonal interaction then is gauged by means of the would counterfactual, which takes into account relevant social comparisons, expectations, and referent standards. Attention then turns to issues of accountability. Could the authority have acted differently, or were the actions the result of some external influence? Should the authority have acted differently: Were his or her actions justified on moral or ethical grounds? All three counterfactuals are necessary for inferring injustice. As the authors noted, "If the chain is broken in any place, then a social injustice has not occurred ... injury, conduct, and standards are the constituent elements from which blame is built" (Folger & Cropanzano, 2001, p. 5).

Despite its newness, predictions based on fairness theory have been supported by two recent studies. Gilliland, Groth, Baker, and Dew (2001) applied fairness theory to job applicants' reactions to rejection letters by creating explanations based on each of the counterfactuals. For example, an explanation based on the could counterfactual attributed the rejection to a hiring freeze, and an explanation based on the should counterfactual attributed the rejection to an ethically appropriate selection process. They found that the perceived fairness of the negative outcomes was enhanced when they were explained by the counterfactuals. Similar results were obtained by Colquitt and Chertkoff (2002), who manipulated whether or not participants in their laboratory study received desired outcomes (a requested partner on a group task). Explanations geared toward the should counterfactual had especially strong effects when the outcome was unexpectedly negative (thereby maximizing the would counterfactual).

### Consolidation and accommodation stage

As noted previously, the consolidation and accommodation stage is marked by a waning of controversies and a consensus regarding key questions and concepts. However, given that the differences between fairness heuristic theory and fairness theory have spurred debate among some proponents of the theories (Cropanzano, Byrne, Bobocel, & Rupp, 2001a, 2001b; Lind, 2001b), it appears that this stage has not yet been reached with respect to the justice judgment process. This manifests itself in terms of the theories' different claims regarding the cognitive loads placed on the people making justice judgments. Specifically, whereas fairness theory requires some controlled processing, fairness heuristic theory relies more on automatic processing (on this distinction, see Bargh & Ferguson, 2000). In this connection, several points are particularly critical to our discussion.

#### Differences in triggers of justice judgments

The two theories differ with respect to the triggers of the justice judgment process. Fairness theory, for example, suggests that the process is triggered whenever an injurious condition or state of affairs arises. However, according to fairness heuristic theory, an injurious state might *not* trigger the justice judgment process because it would force individuals to revisit a heuristic they already have been using comfortably (Lind, 2001a; Van den Bos et al., 2001). The theory argues that individuals are motivated to avoid revisiting the heuristics formed during early stages of interaction.

However, this apparent difference can be reconciled by considering the *magnitude* of an injurious event. If an event is only slightly injurious, then the would counterfactual would not be fully activated and no search for blame and accountability occurs. In such a case, neither theory would predict a full iteration of the judgment process. On the other hand, if an event is highly injurious, then the would counterfactual is activated and the search for blame and accountability moves forward. In the case of fairness heuristic theory, Lind (2001a) argued that certain events are "phase shifting"—that is, they are able to end the use of the heuristic and prompt a fresh judgment. For example, events may be phase shifting because they signal a change in an organizational relationship or because they lie significantly outside one's expectations. Thus, assuming that the injurious event is of sufficient magnitude to trigger phase shifting, both theories would predict a full iteration of the justice judgment process.

#### Differences in central concerns

Other differences between the theories cannot be as easily reconciled. For example, whereas trust is the central concern of fairness heuristic theory, blame is the central concern of fairness theory. To illustrate this point, consider a case in which a trusted authority figure fails to provide the expected level of process control during a decision, when he or she could have (and should have) done so. The trust felt for the authority will likely deter a dysfunctional response by the employee, but it will not necessarily prevent the assessment of blame and accountability. Instead, employees are likely to conclude that although the authority figure is to blame, they owe that individual another chance. Thus, fairness theory does not put much importance on trust because it offers no mechanism to account for its effects on blame.

Analogously, fairness heuristic theory does not place much importance on blame. In fact, the theory argues that the injury (would), conduct (could), and standards (should) elements never would be processed fully by the person forming the judgment. Instead, whatever information was available first, or was most easily interpreted, would determine the selection of a fairness heuristic. Not only would blame not be an outcome of the process, but the information purportedly needed to assess it would not be completely considered. Thus, the two theories differ with respect to both the triggers of the justice judgment process and the manner in which the information on which those judgments are based is used.

If the consolidation and accommodation stage is to be reached, the importance of the blame and trustworthiness components of the theories must be reconciled. To do so requires a more comprehensive research design than typically is used in justice research. In addition to measuring the distributive, procedural, informational, and interpersonal inputs into the judgment process, researchers also must measure explicitly the motives, goals, and mechanisms underlying those judgments. If repeated investigations failed to yield significant main, moderating, or mediating effects of trust and blame, then revisions to the theories would have to be made. However, to fully assess the mechanics of the judgment process such research would have to rely on more detailed measurement methods than typically are used (e.g., interviews or verbal protocol analysis).

### *Conclusion: How are justice judgments formed?*

The answer to the question "How are justice judgments formed?" has changed as the literature has developed (see Table 5.1). The initial conceptualizations that were introduced in the evaluation stage provided preliminary views of the triggering and organizing steps of the judgment process. However, the new conceptualizations that appeared in the augmentation stage have proposed more complete and integrative processes. Two such theories—fairness theory and fairness heuristic theory—have important differences that must be reconciled if the consolidation and accommodation stage is to be reached.

## What outcomes are associated with justice judgments?

Although our model in Fig. 5.2 ends with a justice judgment, practicing managers and applied researchers generally are more concerned with the next step—the effects of those judgments. Do decisions perceived to be fair promote beneficial reactions (e.g., commitment) and discourage counter-productive behavior (e.g., aggressive behavior and stealing)? In an attempt to answer this question, justice researchers have examined the practical impact of justice judgments.

## *Evaluation stage*

Critical reviews published during the evaluation stage revealed patterns in the relationships between justice judgments and certain key outcomes. Initially, these patterns concerned the relative predictive power of distributive and procedural justice, but more current reviews considered the relative predictive power of procedural justice and interactional justice.

### *The two-factor model*

Three studies at the close of the 1980s examined distributive and procedural justice as predictors of key organizational outcomes, such as organizational commitment, pay satisfaction, trust in management, and leader evaluation (Alexander & Ruderman, 1987; Folger & Konovsky, 1989; Konovsky, Folger, & Cropanzano, 1987). These studies supported conclusions by Lind and Tyler (1988) that procedural justice was a stronger predictor than distributive justice of system-referenced evaluations (e.g., organizational commitment, trust in management), and that distributive justice was a stronger predictor than procedural justice of person-referenced outcomes (e.g., pay satisfaction). In reviewing this research, Greenberg (1990) concluded, "Whereas procedural justice perceptions tend to be associated with organizational system evaluations ... distributive justice perceptions tend to be associated with the outcomes received" (p. 407).

Two studies by McFarlin and Sweeney further support this pattern. McFarlin and Sweeney (1992) regressed pay satisfaction, job satisfaction, leader evaluation, and organizational commitment on procedural and distributive justice in a sample of bank employees. They found that distributive justice was the best predictor of satisfaction, but that procedural justice was the best predictor of leader evaluation and organizational commitment. In a follow-up study, Sweeney and McFarlin (1993) verified this pattern of effects using structural equation modeling. Specifically, they contrasted four structural equation models containing distributive and procedural justice, pay satisfaction, and organizational commitment. The best fitting model was the one in which procedural justice had a direct effect on commitment only and distributive justice had a direct effect on satisfaction only. This model, which Sweeney and McFarlin (1993) dubbed the "two-factor model," fit the data better than alternative models containing multiple effects for the justice variables.

### *The agent-system model*

Examinations of the two-factor model focused only on distributive and procedural justice, ignoring the predictive effects of interactional justice—a factor that some theorists considered the key determinant of reactions to authorities (Bies & Moag, 1986; Folger & Bies, 1989; Tyler & Bies, 1990). For example, Tyler and Bies (1990) suggested that "Evidence that procedures are being inappropriately implemented should be particularly important in undermining people's support for the authorities with whom they are dealing" (p. 93). The idea that interactional justice is a stronger predictor of agent-referenced outcomes whereas procedural justice is a stronger predictor of system-referenced outcomes has recently been termed the "agent–system model" (Colquitt et al., 2001).

The agent–system model received little testing at the beginning of the 1990s because the belief prevailed that interactional justice was a subset of procedural justice. As we noted earlier, many researchers combined the two dimensions into a single variable, precluding assessment of their relative effects (e.g., Brockner, Wiesenfeld, & Martin, 1995; Folger & Konovsky, 1989; Konovsky & Folger, 1991). Importantly, this practice had a critical side effect on many of the tests of the two-factor model. For example, Folger and Konovsky's findings that procedural justice predicted organizational commitment and trust in one's supervisor, but that distributive justice predicted pay satisfaction, must be interpreted in light of the fact that their procedural measure included criteria of an interactional nature (e.g., honesty, explanations). Similarly, given the nature of their measure, Brockner et al.'s (1995) significant correlation between a procedural–interactional composite and trust could be taken as support for either the two-factor model or the agent–system model.

## *Augmentation stage*

As exemplified by the first two focal questions identified in this review, the augmentation stage clarifies some of the controversies in the literature by introducing new conceptualizations and adding moderating and mediating variables. At the end of the 1990s, although such clarification began to occur for the two-factor model and the agent–system model, other developments increased confusion associated with justice effects.

### *Addition of mediating variables*

Hagedoorn, Buunk, and Van de Vliert (1998) described the relationship between justice and outcome variables as a "black box" (p. 41), suggesting that the intervening mechanisms linking justice with various reactions are not well understood. One way of opening that "black box" is by measuring the mediators that link justice dimensions to certain outcomes. Masterson, Lewis, Goldman, and Taylor (2000) provided a good example of such an approach in two field studies. Their first study demonstrated that interactional justice predicted an agent-referenced outcome (supervisor legitimacy), whereas procedural justice predicted two system-referenced outcomes (organizational commitment and turnover intentions).

In their second study, Masterson et al. (2000) added mediators for their predicted effects, and found that interactional justice predicted agent-referenced outcomes (e.g., supervisor-directed citizenship behaviors) through the intervening mechanism of leader–member exchange (LMX; Graen & Uhl-Bien, 1995). In contrast, procedural justice predicted system-referenced outcomes (e.g., organizational citizenship behavior, OCB) through the mechanism of perceived organizational support (Eisenberger, Huntington, Hutchinson, and Sowa, 1986). Cropanzano, Prehar, and Chen (2002) found similar results in their study of LMX as a mediator of procedural and interactional justice effects. Like Masterson et al. (2000), they found that although LMX mediated the effects of interactional justice on agent-referenced outcomes, it did not mediate the effects of procedural justice.

## *New conceptualizations*

Colquitt et al.'s (2001) meta-analytic review provided a powerful test of both the two-factor model and the agent–system model. It is important to note, however, that their review was based on Greenberg's (1993) four-dimensional conceptualization of justice, with interactional justice decomposed into its interpersonal and informational components. In assessing the two-factor and agent–system models, Colquitt et al. regressed 11 different outcome variables onto the four justice dimensions. Importantly, any study that used a procedural–interactional composite index was omitted from this analysis, allowing for a "confound-free" test of the two models.

The two-factor model received support for the most commonly examined attitudinal outcomes. Specifically, procedural justice was the strongest predictor of job satisfaction and organizational commitment, but distributive justice was the strongest predictor of outcome satisfaction. However, the model did not accurately capture behavioral effects. Although the two-factor model predicts that procedural justice would be the most significant antecedent of OCB, withdrawal, job performance, and counterproductive behavior, this prediction was not supported. Apparently, the two-factor model is more accurate for attitudes, which by definition have focal objects that can be classified as person versus system-referenced. However, because behavior generally lacks such a classifiable referent, it is not as readily predictable.

Mixed results were also found for the agent–system model. Using this model, one *would not* expect strong relationships between interpersonal or informational justice and system-referenced variables like job satisfaction and organizational commitment. However, one *would* expect strong relationships with agent-referenced variables like agent-referenced evaluation of authority and OCB. Colquitt et al.'s (2001) meta-analytic evidence supported each of these predictions. However, the agent–system model underestimated the effects of interpersonal and informational justice on behavioral outcomes. Specifically, systemic outcomes like withdrawal, organization-directed citizenship, and counterproductive behaviors were strongly predicted by interpersonal and informational justice, even though such effects are inconsistent with the agent–system model.

A new conceptualization of the two-factor model could potentially clarify these equivocal results. Ambrose and Hess (2001) presented a new version of the two-factor model that encompasses all four dimensions of organizational justice. Drawing on Greenberg's (1993b) taxonomy, they suggested that the informational–interpersonal distinction mimics the procedural–distributive distinction. Specifically, they claimed that both procedural and informational justice capture aspects of a long-standing decision-making system, particularly when informational justice provides important details about that system. Similarly, both distributive and interpersonal justice can capture aspects of a discrete decision event, particularly when interpersonal justice provides sincere and respectful treatment to ameliorate the effects of an unfavorable outcome. Accordingly, the Ambrose and Hess (2001) model predicts that procedural and informational justice will predict system- referenced outcomes, whereas distributive and interpersonal justice will predict person-referenced outcomes. This new conceptualization adequately captures Colquitt et al.'s (2001) results for system-referenced evaluations of authority, which were predicted strongly by procedural and informational justice but not by interpersonal and distributive justice. Much like the original two-factor model and the agent–system model, the Ambrose and Hess model fails to predict behavioral effects. Still, as more researchers employ a four-dimensional view of justice, this revised two-factor model could potentially become a more accurate gauge of the impact of various justice judgments.

Another new conceptualization is offered by Byrne and Cropanzano (2000) in their research distinguishing justice content from justice source. As we noted earlier, 'these investigators used confirmatory factor analysis to distinguish four distinct justice dimensions: supervisor-originating procedural justice, supervisor-originating interactional justice, organization-originating procedural justice, and organization-originating interactional justice. They also used structural equation modeling to determine the degree to which each type of justice is associated with specific supervisor and organization-referenced outcomes (e.g., citizenship, commitment, job performance). This conceptualization offers a new spin on both the two-factor and the agent–system model by suggesting that *source* (rather than *content*) may be the critical factor driving justice effects.

## *Consolidation and accommodation stage*

Two key characteristics of the consolidation and accommodation stage are the waning of controversies and the reaching of consensus regarding key questions and concepts. Certainly it is not controversial to state that justice judgments exhibit significant zero-order correlations with a variety of important organizational outcomes. Indeed, of the 82 justice-outcome correlations included in Colquitt et al.'s (2001) meta-analytic review, only 5 failed to reach statistical significance. However, important controversies remain when the question is which of the four dimensions of justice have the *strongest unique effects* on certain outcomes.

We believe that the question regarding outcomes associated with justice judgments has not yet reached the consolidation and accommodation stage. Rather, it lies at the same point as the question regarding justice judgment processes. Unfortunately, the two questions differ with respect to the level of theory building geared toward each. We believe it may be easier to reach consensus about the nature of the justice judgment process insofar as the relative merits of fairness theory and fairness heuristic theory can be assessed. These theories have provided the necessary frame-works for reconciling the remaining disagreements. However, no such framework exists that provides insights into the matter of justice effects. We see two possible ways to reconcile this controversy.

*Should there be a moratorium on comparative research?*

One way of eliminating controversies about the relative effects of different types of justice is to stop doing this type of research altogether. After all, fairness heuristic theory would suggest that there is little value in considering all four dimensions of justice given that only the information encountered first would be fully considered. Consider a case in which informational justice is a stronger predictor of supervisor-referenced evaluations than distributive justice. This would be consistent with both the two-factor model and the agent–system model. It also could be interpreted as showing stronger effects for supervisor-originating justice than for organization-originating justice. However, it may be that the information needed to gauge informational justice was simply available first (Van den Bos, Vermunt et al., 1997) or that it was easier to judge (Van den Bos, Wilke et al., 1998). In contrast, if distributive information were available first, or if it were easier to judge, then distributive justice might have had the stronger effect. In this case, any inferences supporting the two-factor model, the agent–system model, or the justice source model would be misleading.

Minimally, this suggests that the testing of the models cannot occur absent the context in which justice judgments are formed. At most, this suggests that a more effective way to connect justice judgments to various outcomes is by involving a "general justice" or "organizational justice" variable (Lind, 2001b). For example, a second-order structural equation model could be created with "organizational justice" as a latent variable, using distributive, procedural, interpersonal, and informational justice as latent indicators of it. Any difference in factor loadings across the four latent indicators would be a function of mechanisms such as availability of information or ease of interpretation, as proposed by fairness heuristic theory. The latent organizational justice variable could then be connected to the outcomes of interest. Researchers still would have an incentive to measure all four types of justice—not to compare their regression weights, but to maximize the construct and predictive validity of the organizational justice factor.

On the other hand, to design justice interventions effectively, we must understand the unique effects of justice dimensions on key outcomes (Greenberg & Lind, 2000). In practice, limited time and resources necessarily restrict the scope of such interventions. Should an organization devote its time and resources to improving the consistency and accuracy of formal procedures (thereby promoting procedural justice), or to publicizing and explaining the elements of procedures (thereby promoting informational justice)? Likewise, if supervisors are to be trained in justice principles (e.g., Skarlicki & Latham, 1996, 1997), would it be more effective to invest limited time in improving the way procedures are designed or the manner they are enacted? The answers to such questions can only be derived from comparative research.

## Building better theory

If we accept that making comparative inferences is important, then it is clear that better theory will be needed to support such inferences. Whetten (1989) suggested that a good theory explains when and how a relationship occurs. The issue of *when* concerns the boundary conditions, or moderators of the theory (an issue we discuss in the next section). The issue of *how* concerns the intervening mechanisms, or mediators of the theory. As we noted, however, very few studies have included mediators when linking justice judgments to outcome variables. Rather, the mechanisms tend to remain obscured in a "black box" (Hagedoorn et al., 1998, p. 41). In the absence of such mediators, it is difficult to explain, for example, why informational justice is strongly related to evaluation of authority, but weakly related to organizational commitment (Colquitt et al., 2001).

Some justice theories specify mediators of outcome linkages. For example, the relational model suggests that justice judgments influence outcomes through the mechanism of *legitimacy* (Tyler, 1990; Tyler & Lind, 1992). The belief that authorities are legitimate fosters voluntary compliance, stemming not from external rewards or punishments, but from internal beliefs and expectations. Illustrating this, Tyler (1990) assessed the legitimacy of the police and the court system using items such as "The basic rights of citizens are well protected in the courts" and "I feel that I should support the courts." He found that these perceptions were more strongly predicted by procedural justice than by distributive justice. This is consistent with Colquitt et al.'s (2001) finding that procedural justice effects were strongly predicted by three outcomes that are conceptually related to legitimacy—organizational commitment, system-referenced evaluation of authority, and trust.

Subsequent work by (Tyler, 1999; Tyler & Blader, 2000) offers a second potentially useful mediator of justice judgment effects—*identification*, the extent to which individuals define themselves in terms of their membership in a group or organization. Measuring identification with items such as "The organization in which I work says a lot about who I am as a person" and "When I talk about where I work, I usually say 'we' rather than 'they,'" Tyler and Blader (2000) found that procedural justice increases identification. Presumably, this is because individuals feel respected by the group, enhancing their pride in membership (Tyler, 1999; Tyler & Blader, 2000) when that group uses procedures perceived to be fair. Not surprisingly, Tyler and Blader (2000) also found identification to be an important antecedent of compliance, in-role behavior, and extra-role behavior. This is in keeping with the strong procedural justice effects Colquitt et al. (2001) found for job performance and OCB—two variables that seem to be driven by identification.

A third potential mediator is *blame*, which may mediate justice effects on counterproductive behaviors, such as theft (Greenberg, 1998), aggression (Greenberg & Alge, 1998), or organizational retaliation (Skarlicki & Folger, 1997). According to fairness theory, blame is placed whenever an authority could have and should have acted differently, and when one's well-being would have been better as a result (Folger & Cropanzano, 1998, 2001). Mikula (1993) argued similarly, claiming that blame results when an actor is intentionally responsible for some violation of an entitlement in the absence of a sufficient explanation. Thus, it appears that several types of injustice are relevant to blame. Low distributive justice provides the violation, low informational justice satisfies the absence of an explanation, and low procedural justice supplies the intent. With this in mind, it is not surprising that the "negative reactions" and withdrawal variables in Colquitt et al.'s (2001) review were driven by all four forms of justice.

### *Conclusion: what outcomes are associated with justice judgments?*

The answer to the question "What outcomes are associated with justice judgments?" has changed as the literature has developed (see Table 5.1). Initial conceptualizations sought to predict the relative effects of different types of justice according to the referent of the dependent variable. New conceptualizations updated this practice while adding critical mediators to explain why certain effects occur. To reconcile the remaining controversies surrounding the effects of distributive, procedural, interpersonal, and informational justice, it would be useful to identify and explicitly measure additional intervening mechanisms.

## What are the boundary conditions for justice effects?

To this point, we have discussed the processes through which justice judgments are formed and the outcomes associated with those judgments. Now, we address the next logical question: What are the boundary conditions of justice effects? In other words, are there certain individual or contextual variables that qualify the nature of the justice judgment process or the strength of justice–outcome relationships? The existence of such boundary conditions has important implications not only for theory development, but also for enhancing justice in organizations (Greenberg & Lind, 2000).

## Evaluation stage

Many of the critical reviews that marked the beginning of the decade were concerned with illustrating the wide applicability of organizational justice. In other words, rather than illustrating when justice *was not* important, the reviews focused on when it *was* important. Such efforts were understandable given that the justice literature was still in its infancy. Some reviews focused on laying out more general extensions of justice phenomena; others focused on specific contexts.

### General extensions

Lind and Tyler's (1988) landmark review described a variety of contexts in which justice principles apply. For example, justice principles long have been considered critical in legal and dispute-resolution contexts. This is evident in Thibaut and Walker's (1975) original conceptualization of procedural justice and in Tyler's (1990) work linking procedural justice to evaluations of judges, police officers, and court systems. Likewise, the importance of justice principles has also been established in the political arena, such as in investigations of people's reactions to political figures and systems (Lind & Tyler, 1988).

A key extension has come in recognizing that procedural justice accounts for behavior in organizations (Folger & Greenberg, 1985; Greenberg & Folger, 1983). These authors argued that justice principles might be even more important in organizations than in legal or political settings insofar as there is generally more variation in organizational procedures. Typically, organizational procedures are not constrained by institutional precedents, and the variety of decisions made by the procedures creates even more variation. Even within a single organization, for example, the procedures governing selection, training, performance evaluation, and compensation decisions may offer different levels of such key procedural variables as process control, consistency, and correctability.

Other reviews also discussed general extensions of justice principles and effects. For example, Tyler and Bies (1990) argued that justice effects are not bounded by the characteristics of formalized legal, political, or organizational procedures. Instead, they claimed, these effects extend to how decision makers conduct themselves interpersonally while implementing formal procedures. Moreover, Tyler and Lind (1992) suggested that justice principles are relevant in any context in which an authority figure seeks compliance from others.

### Specific extensions

Aside from these more general extensions, other reviews focused on the specific organizational contexts in which justice effects have been observed. For example, Greenberg (1986a, 1986b, 1990) detailed the application of justice principles to performance evaluation contexts. Allowing employees to have a voice in the process and ensuring that justice judgments are based on accurate and consistent information improves the acceptance of the evaluation (regardless of its favorability). Analogously, Greenberg (1990) reviewed the applicability of justice to managerial dispute resolutions. In this context as well, fair procedures enhanced acceptance of dispute decisions.

Several other specific extensions widened the bounds of justice applications during the early to mid-1990s. For example, Gilliland (1993) applied justice principles to a selection context by detailing the criteria for a fair selection process. In an empirical test, he showed that the fairness of the selection process was related to intentions to recommend a job to others, as well as to efficacy and performance on the job (Gilliland, 1994). Similarly, Konovsky and Cropanzano (1991) showed that the perceived fairness of employee drug testing procedures was related to trust in management, organizational commitment, and job performance.

The boundaries of justice applications have also been extended to other areas of human resource management. Quinones (1995), for example, examined the perceived fairness of being assigned to remedial training rather than advanced training. He found that trainees' perceptions of fairness were correlated with their motivation to learn and job performance. Welbourne, Balkin, and Gomez-Mejia (1995) applied justice principles to compensation by examining the perceived fairness of a gainsharing system. They found that the system was more effective when employees believed that the formulas used to establish payouts were fair. Others have applied justice concepts to areas such as mentoring (Scandura, 1997), comparable worth (Greenberg & McCarty, 1990), and affirmative action (Parker, Baltes, & Christiansen, 1997).

Justice principles have also been applied in cases of wide-scale organizational change. For example, many have examined the perceived fairness of layoff decisions (e.g., Brockner et al., 1995; Brockner, Wiesenfeld, Reed, Grover, & Martin, 1993). In general, the more fairly layoffs are handled, the more committed layoff survivors are to their organization (Brockner & Greenberg, 1990), and the less likely layoff victims are to sue on the grounds of wrongful termination (Lind, Greenberg, Scott, & Welchans, 2000). Daly and Geyer (1994) examined organizational justice in the context of job relocations. They found that the perceived fairness of the relocation was correlated with intention to remain. Others have applied justice concepts to the implementation of corporate strategies (Kim & Mauborgne, 1993).

### *Augmentation stage*

Many of the studies performed during the evaluation stage sought to widen the boundaries of justice applications—to show when and where justice is important. However, other work has focused on determining when and where justice *is not* important. Specifically, researchers have focused on explicit moderators of justice effects, including both contextual variables (e.g., culture, uncertainty) and individual variables (e.g., gender, personality). Here, we describe some of these key variables.

### Voluntariness of association

Tyler (1986) was one of the first to discuss moderators of justice effects in a review that asked, "When does procedural justice matter in organizational settings?" (p. 7), One moderator suggested by Tyler was voluntariness of association, with justice effects purported to be stronger when association was involuntary. Gordon and Fryxell (1989) later tested this proposition by assessing the relationship between justice judgments and satisfaction with union and management. They found that these relationships were stronger when union membership was mandatory rather than voluntary. It may be that the imposition of an association reinforces a lack of control, triggering control-based justice concerns.

### National culture

Another contextual variable that has been examined as a moderator of justice effects is national culture. Lind, Tyler, and Huo (1997) tested the relational model of justice in two studies using samples from the United States, Germany, Hong Kong, and Japan. Specifically, they examined the relationships between relational justice information (i.e., trustworthiness, standing, and neutrality) and procedural justice judgments. In the second study, standing was more strongly related to procedural justice in the United States than in Japan, suggesting that American and Japanese people have different expectations regarding standing. Brockner et al. (2001) also found that national culture moderated justice effects. Specifically, in four independent studies they found that people responded less favorably to low levels of voice in low-power distance countries (the United States and Germany) than in high-power distance countries (the People's Republic of China, Mexico, and Hong Kong). Taken together, these studies suggest that national culture is an important moderator of justice effects.

### Contextual moderators inspired by fairness heuristic theory

Additional moderators have been identified in research designed to test fairness heuristic theory. As shown in Fig. 5.2, this theory suggests that justice concerns are triggered by uncertainty about trustworthiness, and that justice information is gathered to serve as indirect evidence of trustworthiness. In support of fairness heuristic theory, Van den Bos, Wilke, et al. (1998) showed that the relationship between process control and reactions was stronger when participants lacked information on trustworthiness than when they had such information. In a recent extension, Van den Bos (2001b) showed that uncertainty also moderates the effects of justice. Specifically, when individuals were asked questions that aroused feelings of uncertainty, process control had a stronger effect on reactions than when no such questions were asked.

More recent work by Van den Bos and his colleagues has examined inclusion as a moderator of justice effects (Van Prooijen, Van den Bos, & Wilke, 2001). In a lab study, individuals who were included in a group reacted more strongly to variations in process control than those who were excluded. A lack of inclusion weakened the effects of justice-relevant information. A similar effect was observed by Holbrook and Kulik (2001) among bank customers applying for loans. The longer they did business with the bank, the more strongly they reacted to the level of process control granted during the loan process.

### Norms as contextual moderators

Norms also are likely to moderate justice effects. Leung and Tong (2001) recently proposed a "normative model of justice" that articulates the roles of norms in making and responding to justice judgments. Specifically, their model suggests that injustice creates feelings of resentment among those who were treated unfairly. This resentment occurs not only because of its effects on outcomes, status, or trustworthiness, but because it often violates important norms regarding the treatment of others. These norms may arise from codes of ethics, cultures, or moral obligations (Greenberg, in press) or from violated expectations of prevailing practices (Greenberg, Eskew, & Miles, 1991). Importantly, Leung and Tong (2001) noted that norms are dependent on context. In other words, they claim that differences in socialization and experiences can cause norms to differ across certain subgroups, which may alter people's expectations for justice and their responses to injustice.

### Gender effects

Just as context can amplify certain justice effects, so too can various characteristics of individuals. Gender, for example, has been found to moderate the effects of an equity allocation norm; males tend to value equity whereas females tend to value equality (e.g., Brockner & Adsit, 1986; Major & Deaux, 1982). This effect is consistent with the finding that women have lower outcome expectations than men (McFarlin, Frone, Major, & Konar, 1989). More recent research has focused on gender as a moderator of procedural justice effects. Sweeney and McFarlin (1997) speculated that women are more sensitive to characteristics of formal procedures because of past discrimination and lack of access to informal advancement mechanisms. Not surprisingly, they found that procedural justice exerted stronger effects on intention to remain employed by an organization among females than among males.

### Traditional personality variables

Personality is another moderator of procedural justice effects. For example, Sweeney, McFarlin, and Cotton (1991) found that the relationship between process control and procedural justice was stronger for internal locus of control individuals. This is in keeping with earlier research showing that reactions to procedural violations were more extreme among people who highly endorsed the Protestant work ethic (Greenberg, 1979), a correlate of internal locus of control. Additional research has shown that people who are predisposed to delay gratification are highly sensitive to the nature of organizational procedures (Joy & Witt, 1992). After all, such individuals are inclined to take a long-term view on their organizations. In addition, Skarlicki, Folger, and Tesluk (1999) examined the moderating effects of affectivity and agreeableness. Specifically, individuals high in negative affectivity (NA) and low in agreeableness were more likely to react to unfair treatment by retaliating against the organization than those who scored in an opposite manner on these dimensions.

*Justice-related personality variables*

In contrast to these studies, which investigated traditional personality variables, others have focused on aspects of personality specifically geared to justice concerns. Notably, equity sensitivity moderates individuals' reactions to departures from an equity allocation norm (e.g., Huseman, Hatfield, & Miles, 1987; King, Miles, & Day, 1993). Individuals showing an "entitled" pattern react weakly to overpayment inequity whereas individuals with a "benevolent" pattern react weakly to underpayment inequity. Between these extremes are "equity sensitives," who react to either type of inequity.

Another justice-based personality variable, known as sensitivity to befallen injustice (SBI), has been studied by Schmitt (1996). This construct assesses the intensity of anger following injustice, the intrusiveness of thoughts about unjust events, and people's inclination to punish the agent of the injustice. Schmitt (1996) treated people unfairly in the course of a laboratory experiment. He found that participants who scored most highly on SBI believed that the injustice was more extreme, leaving them angrier, more resentful, and more inclined to redress that injustice.

## Consolidation and accommodation stage

With respect to boundary conditions, we do not believe that the organizational justice literature has reached the consolidation and accommodation stage because consensus has not been reached regarding key questions and because controversies remain. Despite the broad scope of the justice literature, research on explicit moderators has been extremely limited. Such work is not only relatively uncommon, but also "scattershot" in nature when conducted. With the exception of culture and gender, most of the moderators have been examined in single investigations. Many of the moderators also are so narrow in scope that they are based on little or no specific literatures. As a result, our knowledge of justice moderation remains limited.

*A framework for justice moderation*

To facilitate explanations of justice moderation, we propose the integrative framework shown in Fig. 5.3. This model expands Fig. 5.2 by including reactions to

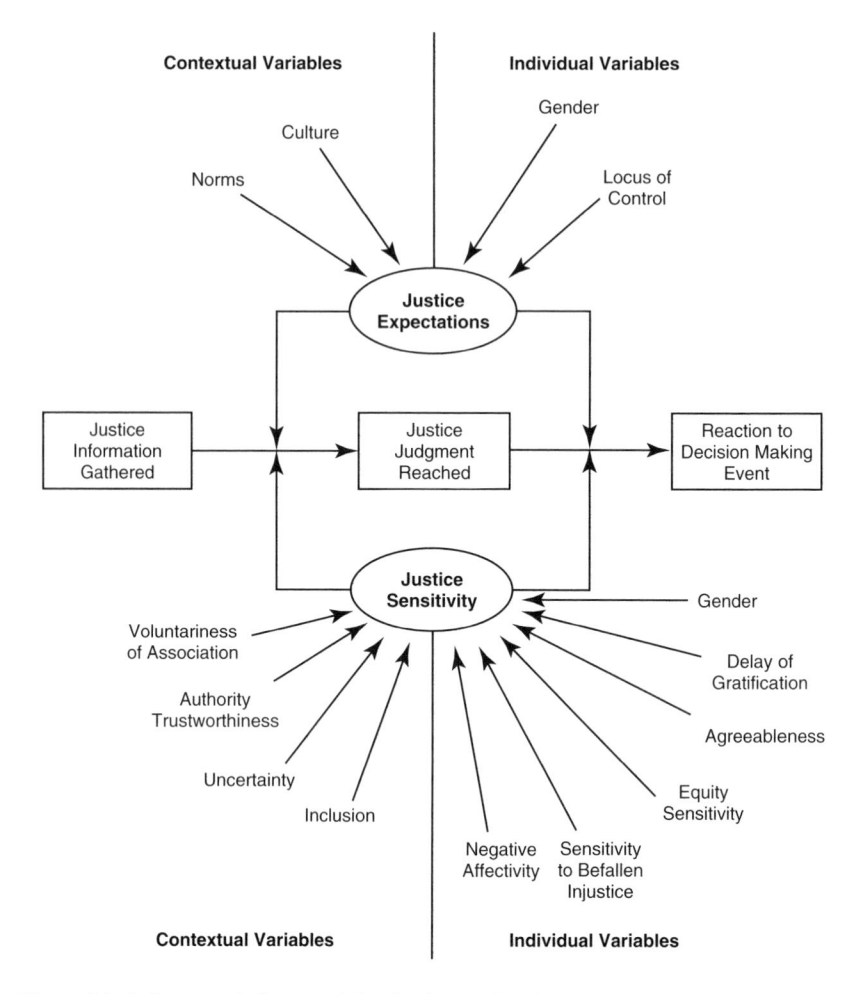

*Figure 5.3* A framework for examining justice moderation.

decision-making events. Existing research has focused on both linkages proposed in this model. Specifically, some studies have identified amplifiers or neutralizers of the relationship between such variables as equity and voice on justice judgments, whereas others have identified variables that strengthen or weaken the effects of justice judgments on subsequent attitudes (e.g., satisfaction, anger) or behaviors (e.g., retaliation, withdrawal; for a review, see Greenberg, 2000).

As Fig. 5.3 illustrates, these moderators include both characteristics of the context (e.g., norms or uncertainty) and characteristics of the individual (e.g., gender or personality). The figure further classifies moderators into two types—justice expectation moderators and justice sensitivity moderators. *Justice expectation moderators* are variables affecting expectations of what justice means and the degree of justice expected. For example, an individual's native culture may influence his or her expectations regarding the qualities that characterize a "fair procedure." Indeed, it has been argued that culture's justice effects are moderated primarily by expectations (Kidder & Miller, 1991; Steiner, 2001). For example, people from cultures considered low with respect to Hofstede's (1980) power distance dimension (e.g., the United States and Germany) were found to express lower levels of organizational commitment in response to limited opportunities for voice than people from countries that are high in power distance (e.g., the People's Republic of China, Mexico, and Hong Kong; Brockner et al., 2001). Apparently, differing cultural expectations about the appropriateness of acknowledging status differences led to different reactions among people from those cultures when expectations with respect to this were violated.

*Justice sensitivity moderators* are variables that make concerns about justice more salient and reactions to justice more severe. The two most obvious examples of this kind of moderator are equity sensitivity and SBI, both of which were conceived to assess this type of effect. However, other individual variables also capture a sensitivity to justice issues, albeit more indirectly. For example, Skarlicki et al.'s (1999) results suggest that individuals scoring high in negative affectivity or low in agreeableness are especially sensitive to injustice, promoting stronger attitudinal and behavioral reactions. The same can be said for contextual variables like uncertainty and inclusion. This is illustrated by Van den Bos's (2001b) finding that uncertainty heightens concerns over predictability, increasing sensitivity to variations in process control.

In Fig. 5.3 we represent justice expectations and justice sensitivity as unmeasured, latent variables to acknowledge that these variables have not been measured explicitly in past research. Instead, more narrow variables have been used as indirect indicators of justice expectations and sensitivity. For example, Sweeney et al. (1991) speculated that people scoring high on internal locus of control expected higher levels of process control, but failed to measure such expectations directly. We also should caution that the indicators of justice expectations and sensitivity shown in Fig. 5.3 are not meant to be an exhaustive list. Rather, they reflect the variables that researchers have examined in at least one study during the past decade.

## *Conclusion: what are the boundary conditions for justice effects?*

As in the case of the other questions we have examined, the answer to the question "What are the boundary conditions for justice effects?" has changed as the organizational justice literature has developed. Early reviews focused primarily on illustrating the contexts in which justice was relevant. Shortly thereafter, researchers began to examine individual and contextual moderators in an effort to determine when justice was and was not important. At present, the matter of boundary conditions has received less research attention than the three other questions we have identified. However, by offering a framework for understanding boundary conditions (see Fig. 5.3), we hope that future researchers will pay closer attention to them, further moving this area toward the consolidation and accommodation stage.

## How does the future of fairness fare?

Three of the four focal issues that currently dominate the organizational justice literature have failed to reach Reichers and Schneider's (1990) final stage of construct development, consolidation, and accommodation (see Table 5.1). As a whole, therefore, the field may be characterized as falling between the augmentation stage and the consolidation and accommodation stage. However, to the extent that we can refine answers to the four focal questions we have been addressing, full maturity will have been attained. With this, our understanding of organizational justice will have advanced to the state in which it provides a useful reservoir of valid knowledge that can be drawn on as the basis for promoting fairness in organizations (Greenberg & Lind, 2000). For this to occur it will be necessary to more throughly integrate knowledge of organizational justice within the overarching discipline of organizational behavior. We believe that such linkages may be most fruitfully developed in three key areas: leadership, climate, and motivation.

### *Justice and leadership*

Perhaps the most natural connection can be made between justice and leadership. After all, many of the practices advocated in the popular management literature offer recipes for effective leadership that bear a striking resemblance to the established practices for maintaining justice (e.g., Kouzes, Posner, & Peters, 1996). These include: give employees a voice, treat people in an unbiased and consistent fashion, be respectful of people, and explain decisions fully and sincerely. Likewise, many of the specific dimensions on which taxonomies of leader behavior are based parallel those from the justice literature. For example, Yukl's taxonomy of leader behaviors includes rewarding, consulting, supporting, and informing (Yukl & Van Fleet, 1992)—behaviors that echo distributive justice, process control, interpersonal justice, and informational justice, respectively. Similarly, Bass's (1985) transactional and transformational leadership behaviors include contingent rewards (reflecting distributive justice), intellectual stimulation (reflecting, in part, process control), and individual consideration (reflecting interpersonal justice). Finally, according to LMX theory (Graen & Uhl-Bien, 1995), high-quality leader-member relationships are founded on high levels of respect, trust, and mutual discretion—dimensions that correspond to high levels of interpersonal justice, informational justice, and process control.

Several leadership researchers have developed more explicit linkages between leadership and justice. For example, Vecchio, Griffeth, and Horn (1986) linked LMX to distributive justice perceptions, and Keller and Dansereau (1995) showed that the practice of empowering others promoted their perceptions of procedural justice. Justice scholars have also used evaluations by leaders as a dependent variable and have examined justice issues in the context of leader behavior. For example, Skarlicki and Latham (1996, 1997) trained leaders on various justice principles, which led to increased OCB among followers. Although such efforts are a good beginning, we believe that both literatures would benefit by more deeply integrating their theories and concepts.

This may be accomplished in several ways. For example, leadership theories have long been interested in predicting leader behaviors using characteristics of the leader, the situation, and followers (House & Aditya, 1997; Yukl & Van Fleet, 1992). In contrast, the justice literature has all but ignored what causes leaders to act fairly. Specifically, we know little about personality differences between fair and unfair leaders and how characteristics such as gender or age impact a leader's fairness. Likewise, we do not know the specific contexts that trigger fair or unfair treatment. Perhaps injustice is more common in complex, stressful, or novel contexts. Finally, we know little about the characteristics of followers that prompt leaders to employ fair treatment (for a notable exception, see Korsgaard, Roberson, & Rymph, 1998, who linked followers' assertiveness to leaders' use of inter-personal and informational justice). Perhaps diligent, hard–working subordinates engender fair treatment on the part of leaders. Examining such questions would bring more balance to a literature that has virtually ignored the *actor* who creates fairness, in favor of the *observer* who reacts to it.

Another potential source of theoretical integration can be drawn from contingency theories of leadership, which examine critical moderators that make some behaviors more appropriate under certain circumstances (House & Aditya, 1997; Yukl & Van Fleet, 1992). Following from this tradition, it is likely that various characteristics of the situation and of the followers might alter the appropriateness of high levels of process control or informational justice. For example, new employees may be too inexperienced for process control, and may remain on a "need to know basis" until they prove themselves. Also, situations in which team-based rewards are used may alter the appropriateness of an equity norm, possibly in favor of an equality norm. In this connection, the literature on "substitutes for leadership" (Kerr & Jermier, 1978) might be used to predict conditions under which the effects of perceived injustices are likely to be most damaging.

## *Justice and climate*

Forehand and Gilmer (1964) defined organizational climate as a set of enduring characteristics that describe an organization, distinguish it from other organizations, and influence its members' attitudes and behaviors. Although the conceptualizations and methods used to study climate vary widely, most scholars assume that certain organizational attributes (e.g., size, structure, practices, procedures, routines, symbols, jargon, ceremonies) create shared perceptions of "the way things are around here" (Ostroff, Kinicki, & Tamkins, in press;

Reichers & Schneider, 1990). The content of those shared perceptions also varies widely, with some scholars assessing one global form of climate, others assessing climate with multiple general dimensions (e.g., reward, risk, warmth, support), and still others referencing climate to very specific issues (e.g., safety, service, transfer of training).

This last form of climate represents the clearest bridge to the justice literature. If scholars can examine a "climate for safety" or a "climate for service," why not also consider a "climate for justice"? Naumann and Bennett (2000) did precisely this. Building on work by Mossholder, Bennett, and Martin (1998), Naumann and Bennett showed that bank employees converged on perceptions of procedural justice, particularly in branches in which work groups were highly cohesive and in which leaders were highly visible. This "procedural justice climate" explained variance in individuals' helping behavior, even after controlling for individuals' own justice perceptions. Colquitt, Noe, and Jackson (2002) extended this work in two ways. First, they identified group characteristics that lead to "strong climates," characterized by high levels of perceptual convergence. Second, they showed that justice climates in work groups had stronger effects on performance and absenteeism when climate strength was high rather than low.

The notion of justice climate fills a void in the justice literature by acknowledging the multilevel influences and effects of justice. Specifically, because formal procedures and practices exist at the group level, their effects should go beyond individual perceptions. As such, justice climate may be used to link justice to various team-, department-, and organization-level variables (e.g., retention, goal achievement, profitability). Justice climate also is important insofar as it acknowledges that justice perceptions are socially constructed, derived from a complex process of social comparison and normative influences. Although the social construction of justice perceptions has been acknowledged in the case of distributive justice, it has received little attention with respect to procedural justice (Cropanzano & Ambrose, 2001). However, by virtue of its focus on social information processing, future research on justice climate is destined to direct justice researchers to the processes underlying the social construction of procedural justice perceptions.

To strengthen the connection between justice and climate, it would be helpful to know the specific organizational characteristics that comprise the most important drivers of climate. Representing a step in this direction, Schminke, Ambrose, and Cropanzano (2000) examined the relationships between individual justice judgments and organizational size, centralization, and formalization—three attributes often linked to climate. They found that size hindered interpersonal justice whereas centralization hindered procedural justice. It also would be important to know what factors differentiate strong climates from weak climates. For example, it may be that procedural justice climates, which are based in part of long-standing formalized practices, are stronger than interpersonal justice climates, and therefore have greater impact. This represents a potentially fruitful direction for future research.

## *Justice and motivation*

Another path for integrating organizational justice into mainstream OB may be taken through the literature on motivation. In several respects, the justice literature and the motivation literature already are closely tied. For example, equity theory routinely is described in the motivation chapter of OB textbooks, and a discussion of justice is featured prominently in Kanfer's (1991) motivation chapter in the *Handbook of Industrial and Organizational Psychology*. In other ways, however, the linkage is less well developed. Making this point, Colquitt and Chertkoff (2002) noted that few, if any, justice scholars have measured motivation explicitly.

Why is it that job satisfaction and organizational commitment are popular dependent variables in justice research, but motivation is virtually ignored? Is it that justice scholars do not believe that unjust treatment will result in a decrease in the intensity or persistence of task-related effort (apart from the predicted effects of underpayment inequity)? Or, is it that justice scholars simply view motivation as an intervening mechanism whose influence is so obvious that it can remain unmeasured? In our opinion, neither view holds much merit. To the contrary, we believe that by more closely considering motivation it would be possible to clarify the inconsistent effect of procedural justice on job performance that has been reported in the literature. For example, Colquitt et al. (2001) found that procedural justice had a meta-analytic correlation of .36 with performance, but that relationship varied widely across studies and across procedural justice conceptualizations. Given that motivation is often cited as a determinant of task performance (e.g., Porter & Lawler, 1968), it makes sense to pay closer attention to motivation as a variable in future studies of organizational justice.

Drawing on Kanfer's (1991) taxonomy, various motivational theories suggest different ways in which this may be done. For example, *need-motive-value* theories (e.g., Alderfer, 1972; Maslow, 1954) are founded on the notion that meeting one's needs triggers task effort. To the extent that maintaining fairness is a universal need, as Kanfer argued, it follows from the instrumental model of justice that people will be motivated to engage in behavior designed to satisfy it. Likewise, the idea that people are motivated to satisfy needs for affiliation and recognition is in keeping with relational models of justice.

*Cognitive choice* theories (e.g., Bandura, 1991; Carver & Scheier, 1981; Vroom, 1964) emphasize the cognitive reasoning required when deciding to initiate a given level of effort. As such, they are relevant to justice in two key ways. First, justice judgments affect (and are affected by) many of the same ingredients found in cognitive choice theories. For example, perceptions of distributive justice and procedural justice affect performance-outcome contingencies, thereby altering instrumentality (Vroom, 1964). Second, the status and self-worth signals that accompany fair treatment (Tyler & Lind, 1992) could affect effort-performance contingencies, thereby altering expectancy.

*Self-regulation* theories (e.g., social cognitive theory, Bandura, 1991; control theory, Carver & Scheier, 1981) emphasize the self-governed allocation of cognitive resources that control the persistence of effort. These regulatory processes may be used to explain the counterfactual and phase shifting mechanisms described by fairness theory (e.g., Folger & Cropanzano, 2001) and the development of heuristics described by fairness heuristic theory (Lind, 2001a). Efforts to juxtapose these underlying mechanisms promise to benefit both literatures.

Given these kinds of linkages, it should be possible to build a theory of motivation built primarily on justice needs, justice concerns, and justice judgment processes. Such a theory would clarify many of the inconsistencies that currently exist in the literature. For example, it could be used to ground predictions about which types of justice are most influential for various forms of outcomes. This would be responsive to our earlier plea to develop mediators that support comparative predictions. A justice-based theory of motivation also would integrate justice with other variables relevant to motivation, such as goals, job characteristics, and individual difference variables. This broader view of motivated behavior could then be used to combine justice interventions with other kinds of performance improvement strategies.

## Conclusion

Clearly, the field of organizational justice has grown out of its "intellectual adolescence" (Greenberg, 1993a, p. 135). Its "stumbling awkwardness" (p. 136) now has given way to a fairly linear progression of better theory, more refined conceptualizations, and research characterized by more rigorous methodology. This is not to say, however, that the field has reached the consolidation and accommodation stage, signaling full maturity. Witness the compelling nature of the issues that remain, as chronicled in our analyses of the state of the field's most rudimentary research questions. Given this state of affairs, we conclude that the field of organizational justice has blossomed into a "promising young adult"—and a very popular one, at that.

We acknowledge that this popularity may be both a blessing and a curse. Although the arrival of new theories and research directions promises to move the field forward, this may come at the expense of jeopardizing the field's current structure and coherence. However, by revisiting where the field has been and by offering suggestions as to where it should be going, we hope that other theorists will be inspired to preserve the field's integrity while improving its coherence. To the extent that future work can bring closure to the four key questions identified here, we will be well on our way to reaching that elusive final stage of maturity. Then, by building stronger connections to other areas of OB research, the concept of organizational justice will stand a good chance of being not only one of OB's most popular topics, but among its most important ones as well. When this occurs, the field of organizational justice promises to have a fruitful, mature life without ever having to face retirement. It is hoped that our remarks have paved the way for this to occur.

## References

Adams, J. S. (1965). Inequity in social exchange. In L. Berkowitz (Ed.), *Advances in experimental social psychology* (Vol. 2, pp. 267–299). New York: Academic.

Alderfer, C. P. (1972). *Existence, relatedness, and growth*. New York: The Free Press.

Alexander, S., & Ruderman, M. (1987). The role of procedural and distributive justice in organizational behavior. *Social Justice Research, 1*, 177–198.

Ambrose, M. L., & Hess, R. L., Jr. (2001, September). *Individuals' responses to fairness: A consideration of management and marketing models*. Paper presented at the International Roundtable on Innovations in Organizational Justice Research, Vancouver, British Columbia, Canada.

Ball, G. A., Trevino, L. K., & Sims, H. P., Jr. (1993). Justice and organizational punishment: Attitudinal outcomes of disciplinary events. *Social Justice Research, 6*, 39–67.

Bandura, A. (1991). Social cognitive theory of self-regulation. *Organizational Behavior and Human Decision Processes, 50*, 248–287.

Bargh, J. A., & Ferguson, M. J. (2000). Beyond behaviorism: On the automaticity of higher mental processes. *Psychological Bulletin, 126*, 925–945.

Bass, B. M. (1985). *Leadership and performance beyond expectations*. New York: The Free Press.

Bies, R. J. (2001). Interactional (in)justice: The sacred and the profane. In J. Greenberg & R. Cropanzano (Eds.), *Advances in organizational justice* (pp. 89–118). Stanford, CA: Stanford University Press.

Bies, R. J., & Moag, J. F. (1986). Interactional justice: Communication criteria of fairness. In R. J. Lewicki, B. H. Sheppard, & M. H. Bazerman (Eds.), *Research on negotiations in organizations* (Vol. 1, pp. 43–55). Greenwich, CT: JAI.

Bobocel, D. R., & Holmvall, C. M. (2001). Are interactional justice and procedural justice different? Framing the debate. In S. Gilliland, D. Steiner, & D. Skarlicki (Eds.), *Theoretical and cultural perspectives on organizational justice* (pp. 85–110). Greenwich, CT: Information Age.

Brockner, J., Ackerman, G., Greenberg, J., Gelfand, M. J., Francesco, A. M., Chen, Z. X., Leung, K., Bierbauer, G., Gomez, C., Kirkman, B. L., & Shapiro, D. (2001). *Journal of Experimental Social Psychology, 37*, 300–315.

Brockner, J., & Adsit, L. (1986). The moderating impact of sex on the equity-satisfaction relationship: A field study. *Journal of Applied Psychology, 71*, 585–590.

Brockner, J., & Greenberg, J. (1990). The impact of layoffs on survivors: An organizational justice perspective. In J. Carroll (Ed.), *Advances in applied social psychology: Business settings* (pp. 45–75). Hillsdale, NJ: Lawrence Erlbaum Associates.

Brockner, J., & Wiesenfeld, B. M. (1986). An integrative framework for explaining reactions to decisions: Interactive effects of outcomes and procedures. *Psychological Bulletin, 120*, 189–208.

Brockner, J., Wiesenfeld, B. M., & Martin, C. L. (1995). Decision frame, procedural justice, and survivors' reactions to job layoffs. *Organizational Behavior and Human Decision Processes, 63*, 59–68.

Brockner, J., Wiesenfeld, B. M., Reed, T., Grover, S., & Martin, C. (1993). Interactive effect of job content and context on reactions of layoff survivors. *Journal of Personality and Social Psychology, 64*, 187–197.

Byrne, Z. S., & Cropanzano, R. (2000, April). *To which source do I attribute this fairness? Differential effects of multi-foci justice on organizational work behaviors*.

Paper presented at the meeting of the Society for Industrial and Organizational Psychology, New Orleans, LA.

Byrne, Z. S., & Cropanzano, R. (2001). The history of organizational justice: The founders speak. In R. Cropanzano (Ed.), *Justice in the workplace: Vol. 2. From theory to practice* (pp. 3–26). Mahwah, NJ: Lawrence Erlbaum Associates.

Carver, C. S., & Scheier, M. F. (1981). *Attention and self-regulation: A control theory approach to human behavior.* New York: Springer-Verlag.

Cohen, R. L. (1986). *Justice: Views from the social sciences.* New York: Plenum.

Cohen, R. L., & Greenberg, J. (1982). The justice concept in social psychology. In J. Greenberg & R. L. Cohen (Eds.), *Equity and justice in social behavior* (pp. 1–41). New York: Academic.

Colquitt, J. A. (2001). On the dimensionality of organizational justice: A construct validation of a measure. *Journal of Applied Psychology, 86,* 386–400.

Colquitt, J. A., & Chertkoff, J. (2002). Explaining injustice: The interactive effect of explanation and outcome on fairness perceptions and task motivation. *Journal of Management, 28,* 591–610.

Colquitt, J. A., Conlon, D. E., Wesson, M J., Porter, C. O. L. H., & Ng, K. Y. (2001). Justice at the millennium: A meta-analysis of 25 years of organizational justice research. *Journal of Applied Psychology, 86,* 425–445.

Colquitt, J. A., Noe, R, A., & Jackson, C. L. (2002). Justice in teams: Antecedents and consequences in procedural justice climate. *Personnel Psychology, 55,* 83–109.

Conlon, D. E., & Ross, W. H. (1993). The effects of partisan third parties on negotiator behavior and outcome perceptions. *Journal of Applied Psychology, 78,* 280–290.

Cropanzano, R., & Ambrose, M. L. (2001). Procedural and distributive justice are more similar than you think: A monistic perspective and a research agenda. In J. Greenberg & R. Cropanzano (Eds.), *Advances in organizational justice* (pp. 119–151). Stanford, CA: Stanford University Press.

Cropanzano, R., Byrne, Z. S., Bobocel, D. R., & Rupp, D. E. (2001a). Moral virtues, fairness heuristics, social entities, and other denizens of organizational justice. *Journal of Vocational Behavior, 58,* 164–209.

Cropanzano, R., Byrne, Z. S., Bobocel, D. R., & Rupp, D. E. (2001b). Self-enhancement biases, laboratory experiments, George Wilhelm Friedrich Hegel, and the increasingly crowded world of organizational justice. *Journal of Vocational Behavior, 58,* 260–272.

Cropanzano, R., & Greenberg, J. (1997). Progress in organizational justice: Tunneling through the maze. In C. L. Cooper & I. T. Roberson (Eds.), *International review of industrial and organizational psychology* (Vol. 12, pp. 317–372). Chichester, England: Wiley.

Cropanzano, R., Prehar, C. A., & Chen, P. Y. (2002). Using social exchange theory to distinguish procedural from interactional justice. *Group Organization Managment, 27,* 324–351.

Daly, J. P., & Geyer, P. D. (1994). The role of fairness in implementing large-scale change: Employee evaluations of process and outcome in seven facility relocations. *Journal of Organizational Behavior, 15,* 623–638.

Deutsch, M. (1975). Equity, equality, and need: What determines which value will be used as the basis for distributive justice? *Journal of Social Issues, 31,* 137–149.

Eisenberger, R., Huntington, R., Hutchinson, S., & Sowa, D. (1986). Perceived organizational support. *Journal of Applied Psychology, 71,* 500–507.

Folger, R. (1986a). A referent cognitions theory of relative deprivation. In J. M. Olson, C. P. Herman, & M. P. Zanna (Eds.), *Relative deprivation and social comparison: The Ontario symposium* (Vol. 4, pp. 33–55). Hillsdale, NJ: Lawrence Erlbaum Associates.

Folger, R. (1986b). Rethinking equity theory: A referent cognitions model. In H. W. Bierhoff, R. L. Cohen, & J. Greenberg (Eds.), *Justice in social relations* (pp. 145–162). New York: Plenum.

Folger, R. (1987). Reformulating the preconditions of resentment: A referent cognitions model. In J. C. Masters & W. P. Smith (Eds.), *Social comparison, justice, and relative deprivation: Theoretical, empirical, and policy perspectives* (pp. 183–215). Hillsdale, NJ: Lawrence Erlbaum Associates.

Folger, R. (1993). Reactions to mistreatment at work. In K. Murnighan (Ed.), *Social psychology in organizations: Advances in theory and research* (pp. 161–183). Englewood Cliffs, NJ: Prentice-Hall.

Folger, R., & Bies, R. J. (1989). Managerial responsibilities and procedural justice. *Employee Responsibilities and Rights Journal, 2*, 79–89.

Folger, R., & Cropanzano, R. (1998). *Organizational justice and human resource management*. Thousand Oaks, CA: Sage.

Folger, R., & Cropanzano, R. (2001). Fairness theory: Justice as accountability. In J. Greenberg & R. Cropanzano (Eds.), *Advances in organizational justice* (pp. 89–118). Stanford, CA: Stanford University Press.

Folger, R., & Greenberg, J. (1985). Procedural justice: An interpretive analysis of personnel systems. In K. Rowland & G. Ferris (Eds.), *Research in personnel and human resources management* (Vol. 3, pp. 141–183). Greenwich, CT: JAI.

Folger, R., & Konovsky, M. A. (1989). Effects of procedural and distributive justice on reactions to pay raise decisions. *Academy of Management Journal, 32*, 115–130.

Forehand, B., & Gilmer, B. V. (1964). Environmental variation in studies of organizational behavior. *Psychological Bulletin, 62*, 361–382.

Gilliland, S. W. (1993). The perceived fairness of selection systems: An organizational justice perspective. *Academy of Management Review, 18*, 694–734.

Gilliland, S. W. (1994). Effects of procedural and distributive justice on reactions to a selection system. *Journal of Applied Psychology, 79*, 691–701.

Gilliland, S. W., Groth, M., Baker, R. C., & Dew, A. F. (2001). Improving applicants' reactions to rejection letters: An application of fairness theory. *Personnel Psychology, 54*, 669–703.

Gordon, M. E., & Fryxell, G. E. (1989). Voluntariness of association as a moderator of the importance of procedural and distributive justice. *Journal of Applied Social Psychology, 19*, 993–1009.

Graen, G. B., & Uhl-Bien, M. (1995). Relationship-based approach to leadership: Development of leader–member exchange (LMX) theory of leadership over 25 years: Applying a multi-level multi-domain perspective. *Leadership Quarterly, 6*, 219–247.

Greenberg, J. (1979). Protestant ethic endorsement and the fairness of equity inputs. *Journal of Research in Personality, 13*, 81–90.

Greenberg, J. (1986a). The distributive justice of organizational performance evaluations. In H. W. Bierhoff, R. L. Cohen, & J. Greenberg (Eds.), *Justice in social relations* (pp. 337–351). New York: Plenum.

Greenberg, J. (1986b). Organizational performance appraisal procedures: What makes them fair? In R. J. Lewicki, B. H. Sheppard, & M. H. Bazerman (Eds.), *Research on negotiation in organizations* (Vol. 1, pp. 25–41). Greenwich, CT: JAI.

Greenberg, J. (1987). A taxonomy of organizational justice theories. *Academy of Management Review, 12*, 9–22.

Greenberg, J. (1990). Organizational justice: Yesterday, today, and tomorrow. *Journal of Management, 16*, 399–432.

Greenberg, J. (1993a). The intellectual adolescence of organizational justice: You've come a long way, maybe. *Social Justice Research, 6*, 135–148.

Greenberg, J. (1993b). The social side of fairness: Interpersonal and informational classes of organizational justice. In R. Cropanzano (Ed.), *Justice in the workplace: Approaching fairness in human resource management* (pp. 79–103). Hillsdale, NJ: Lawrence Erlbaum Associates.

Greenberg, J. (1994). Using socially fair treatment to promote acceptance of a work site smoking ban. *Journal of Applied Psychology, 79*, 288–297.

Greenberg, J. (1996). *The quest for justice on the job.* Thousand Oaks, CA: Sage.

Greenberg, J. (1998). The cognitive geometry of employee theft: Negotiating "the line" between taking and theft. In R. W. Griffin, A. O'Leary-Kelly, & J. Collins (Eds.), *Dysfunctional behavior in organizations: Vol. 2. Nonviolent behaviors in organizations* (pp. 147–193). Greenwich, CT: JAI.

Greenberg, J. (2000). Promote procedural justice to enhance acceptance of work outcomes. In E. A. Locke (Ed.), *A handbook of principles of organizational behavior* (pp. 191–195). Oxford, England: Blackwell.

Greenberg, J. (in press). Who stole what, and when? Individual and situational determinants of employee theft. *Organizational Behavior and Human Decision Processes.*

Greenberg, J., & Alge, B. (1998). Aggressive reactions to workplace injustice. In R. W. Griffin, A. O'Leary-Kelly, & J. Collins (Eds.), *Dysfunctional behavior in organizations: Vol. 1. Violent behavior in organizations* (pp. 119–145). Greenwich, CT: JAI.

Greenberg, J., Eskew, D., & Miles, J. A. (1991, August). *Adherence to participatory norms as a moderator of the fair process effect: When voice does not enhance procedural justice.* Paper presented at the meeting of the Academy of Management, Miami Beach, FL.

Greenberg, J., & Folger, R. (1983). Procedural justice, participation, and the fair process effect in groups and organizations. In P. Paulus (Ed.), *Basic group processes* (pp. 235–256). New York: Springer-Verlag.

Greenberg, J., & Lind, E. A. (2000). The pursuit of organizational justice: From conceptualization to implication to application. In C. L. Cooper & E. A. Locke (Eds.), *I/O psychology: What we know about theory and practice* (pp. 72–108). Oxford, England: Blackwell.

Greenberg, J., & McCarty, C. (1990). Comparable worth: A matter of justice. In G. R. Ferris & K. M. Rowland (Eds.), *Research in personnel and human resources management* (Vol. 8, pp. 265–301). Greenwich, CT: JAI.

Grienberger, I. V., Rutte, C. G., & Van Knippenberg, A. F. M. (1997). Influence of social comparisons of outcomes and procedures on fairness judgments. *Journal of Applied Psychology, 82*, 913–919.

Hagedoorn, M., Buunk, B. P., & Van de Vliert (1998). Opening the black box between justice and reactions to unfavorable outcomes in the workplace. *Social Justice Research, 11*, 41–57.

Holbrook, R. L., & Kulik, C. T. (2001). Customer perceptions of justice in service transactions: The effects of strong and weak ties. *Journal of Organizational Behavior, 22*, 743–757.

Homans, G. C. (1961). *Social behaviour: Its elementary forms*. London: Routledge & Kegan Paul.

House, R. J., & Aditya, R. N. (1997). The social scientific study of leadership: Quo vadis? *journal of Management, 23*, 409–473.

Huseman, R. C., Hatfield, J. D., & Miles, E. W. (1987). A new perspective on equity theory: The equity sensitivity construct. *Academy of Management Review, 12*, 222–234.

Joy, V. L., & Witt, L. A. (1992). Delay of gratification as a moderator of the procedural justice–distributive justice relationship. *Group and Organization Management, 17*, 297–308.

Kanfer, R. (1991). Motivation theory and industrial and organizational psychology. In M. D. Dunnette & L. M. Hough (Eds.), *Handbook of industrial and organizational psychology* (Vol. 1, pp. 75–170). Palo Alto, CA: Consulting Psychologists Press.

Keller, T., & Dansereau, F. (1995). Leadership and empowerment: A social exchange perspective. *Human Relations, 48*, 127–146.

Kerr, S., & Jermier, J. M. (1978). Substitutes for leadership: Their meaning and measurement. *Organizational Behavior and Human Performance, 22*, 375–403.

Kidder, L. H., & Miller, S. (1991). What is "fair" in Japan? In H. Steensma & R. Vermunt (Eds.), *Social justice in human relations: Vol. 2. Societal and psychological consequences of justice and injustice* (pp. 139–154). New York: Plenum.

Kidwell, R. E., & Bennett, N. (1994). Employee reactions to electronic control systems: The role of procedural fairness. *Group and Organization Management, 19*, 203–218.

Kim, W. C., & Mauborgne, R. A. (1993). Procedural justice, attitudes, and subsidiary top management compliance with multinationals' corporate strategy decisions. *Academy of Management Journal, 36*, 502–526.

King, W. C., Jr., Miles, E. W., & Day, D. D. (1993). A test and refinement of the equity sensitivity construct. *Journal of Organizational Behavior, 14*, 301–317.

Konovsky, M. A., & Cropanzano, R. (1991). Perceived fairness of employee drug testing as a predictor of employee attitudes and job performance. *Journal of Applied Psychology, 76*, 698–707.

Konovsky, M. A., & Folger, R. (1991). The effects of procedures, social accounts, and benefits level on victims' layoff reactions. *Journal of Applied Social Psychology, 21*, 630–650.

Konovsky, M. A., Folger, R., & Cropanzano, R. (1987). Relative effects of procedural and distributive justice on employee attitudes. *Representative Research in Social Psychology, 17*, 15–24.

Korsgaard, M. A., Roberson, L., & Rymph, R. D. (1998). What motivates fairness? The role of subordinate assertive behavior on managers' interactional fairness. *Journal of Applied Psychology, 83*, 731–744.

Kouzes, J. M., Posner, B. Z., & Peters, T. (1996). *The leadership challenge*. San Francisco: Jossey-Bass.

Leung, K., & Tong, K. K. (2001, September). *Toward a normative model of justice*. Paper presented at the International Roundtable on Innovations in Organizational Justice Research, Vancouver, British Columbia, Canada.

Leventhal, G. S. (1976). The distribution of rewards and resources in groups and organizations. In L. Berkowitz & W. Walster (Eds.), *Advances in experimental social psychology* (Vol. 9, pp. 91–131). New York: Academic.

Leventhal, G. S. (1980). What should be done with equity theory? New approaches to the study of fairness in social relationships. In K. Gergen, M. Greenberg, & R. Willis (Eds.), *Social exchange: Advances in theory and research* (pp. 27–55). New York: Plenum.

Leventhal, G. S., Karuza, J., & Fry, W. R. (1980). Beyond fairness: A theory of allocation preferences. In G. Mikula (Ed.), *Justice and social interaction* (pp. 167–218). New York: Springer-Verlag.

Lind, E. A. (2001a). Fairness heuristic theory: Justice judgments as pivotal cognitions in organizational relations. In J. Greenberg & R. Cropanzano (Eds.), *Advances in organizational justice* (pp. 56–88). Stanford, CA: Stanford University Press.

Lind, E. A. (2001b). Thinking critically about justice judgments. *Journal of Vocational Behavior, 58*, 220–226.

Lind, E. A., Greenberg, J., Scott, K. S., & Welchans, D. (2000). The winding road from employee to complainant: Situational and psychological determinants of wrongful termination claims. *Administrative Science Quarterly, 45*, 557–590.

Lind, E. A., Kray, L., & Thompson, L. (2001). Primacy effects in justice judgments: Testing predictions for fairness heuristic theory. *Organizational Behavior and Human Decision Processes, 85*, 189–210.

Lind, E. A., Kulik, C., Ambrose, M., & de Vera Park, M. (1993). Individual and corporate dispute resolution: Using procedural fairness as a decision heuristic. *Administrative Science Quarterly, 38*, 224–251.

Lind, E. A., & Tyler, T. R. (1988). *The social psychology of procedural justice*. New York: Plenum.

Lind, E. A., Tyler, T. R., & Huo, Y. J. (1997). Procedural context and culture: Variation in antecedents of procedural justice judgments. *Journal of Personality and Social Psychology, 73*, 767–780.

Major, B., & Deaux, K. (1982). Individual differences in justice behavior. In J. Greenberg & R. L. Cohen (Eds.), *Equity and justice in social behavior* (pp. 43–76). New York: Academic.

Maslow, A. H. (1954). *Motivation and personality*. New York: Harper & Row.

Masterson, S. S., Bartol, K. M., & Moye, N. (2000, April). *Interactional and procedural justice: Type versus source of fairness*. Paper presented at the meeting of the Society for Industrial and Organizational Psychology, New Orleans, LA.

Masterson, S. S., Lewis, K., Goldman, B. M., & Taylor, M. S. (2000). Integrating justice and social exchange: The differing effects of fair procedures and treatment on work relationships. *Academy of Management Journal, 43*, 738–748.

McFarlin, D. B., Frone, M., Major, D. B., & Konar, E. (1989). Predicting career-entry pay expectations: The role of gender-based comparisons. *Journal of Business and Psychology, 3*, 331–340.

McFarlin, D. B., & Sweeney, P. D. (1992). Distributive and procedural justice as predictors of satisfaction with personal and organizational outcomes. *Academy of Management Journal, 35*, 626–637.

Mikula, G. (1993). Exploring the experience of injustice. *European Journal of Social Psychology, 4*, 223–244.

Moorman, R. H. (1991). Relationship between organizational justice and organizational citizenship behaviors: Do fairness perceptions influence employee citizenship? *Journal of Applied Psychology, 76*, 845–855.

Mossholder, K. W., Bennett, N., & Martin, C. L. (1998). A multilevel analysis of procedural justice context. *Journal of Organizational Behavior, 19*, 131–141.

Naumann, S. E., & Bennett, N. (2000). A case for procedural justice climate: Development and test of a multilevel model. *Academy of Management Journal, 43*, 881–889.

Niehoff, B. P., & Moorman, R. H. (1993). Justice as a mediator of the relationship between methods of monitoring and organizational citizenship behaviors. *Academy of Management Journal, 36*, 527–556.

Ostroff, C., Kinicki, A. J., & Tamkins, M. M. (in press). Organizational culture and climate. In W. C. Borman, D. R. Ilgen, & R. J. Klimoski (Eds.), *Comprehensive handbook of psychology: Vol. 12. Industrial and organizational psychology*. New York: Wiley.

Parker, C. P., Baltes, B. B., & Christiansen, N. D. (1997). Support for affirmative action, justice perceptions, and work attitudes: A study of gender and racial–ethnic group differences. *Journal of Applied Psychology, 82*, 376–389.

Porter, L. W., & Lawler, E. E., III. (1968). *Managerial attitudes and performance*. Home-wood, IL: Irwin.

Quinones, M. A. (1995). Pretraining context effects: Training assignment as feedback. *Journal of Applied Psychology, 80*, 226–238.

Reichers, A. E., & Schneider, B. (1990). Climate and culture: Life cycles of constructs. In B. Schneider (Ed.), *Organizational climate and culture* (pp. 5–39). San Francisco: Jossey-Bass.

Scandura, T. A. (1997). Mentoring and organizational justice: An empirical investigation. *Journal of Vocational Behavior, 51*, 58–69.

Schminke, M., Ambrose, M. L., & Cropanzano, R. S. (2000). The effect of organizational structure on perceptions of procedural justice. *Journal of Applied Psychology, 85*, 294–304.

Schmitt, M. (1996). Individual differences in sensitivity to befallen injustice (SBI). *Personality and Individual Differences, 21*, 3–20.

Skarlicki, D. P., & Folger, R. (1997). Retaliation in the workplace: The roles of distributive, procedural, and interactional justice. *Journal of Applied Psychology, 82*, 434–443.

Skarlicki, D. P., Folger, R., & Tesluk, P. (1999). Personality as a moderator in the relationship between fairness and retaliation. *Academy of Management Journal, 42*, 100–108.

Skarlicki, D. P., & Latham, G. P. (1996). Increasing citizenship behavior within a labor union: A test of organizational justice theory. *Journal of Applied Psychology, 81*, 161–169.

Skarlicki, D. P., & Latham, G. P. (1997). Leadership training in organizational justice to increase citizenship behavior within a labor union: A replication. *Personnel Psychology, 50*, 617–633.

Steiner, D. D. (2001). Cultural influences on perceptions of distributive and procedural justice. In S. Gilliland, D. Steiner, & D. Skarlicki (Eds.), *Theoretical and cultural perspectives on organizational justice* (pp. 111–138). Greenwich, CT: Information Age.

Sweeney, P. D., & McFarlin, D. B. (1993). Workers' evaluations of the "ends" and "means": An examination of four models of distributive and procedural justice. *Organizational Behavior and Human Decision Processes, 55*, 23–40.

Sweeney, P. D., & McFarlin, D. B. (1997). Process and outcome: Gender differences in the assessment of justice. *Journal of Organizational Behavior, 18*, 83–98.

Sweeney, P. D., McFarlin, D. B., & Cotton, J. L. (1991). Locus of control as a moderator of the relationship between perceived influence and procedural justice. *Human Relations, 44*, 333–342.

Thibaut, J., & Walker, L. (1975). *Procedural justice: A psychological analysis*, Hillsdale, NJ: Lawrence Erlbaum Associates.

Tyler, T. R. (1986). When does procedural justice matter in organizational settings? In R. J. Lewicki, B. H. Sheppard, & M. H. Bazerman (Eds.), *Research on negotiations in organizations* (Vol. 1, pp. 7–23). Greenwich, CT: JAI.

Tyler, T. R. (1990). *Why people obey the law: Procedural justice, legitimacy, and compliance*. New Haven, CT: Yale University Press.

Tyler, T. R. (1999). Why people cooperate with organizations: An identity-based perspective. In B. M. Staw & R. Sutton (Eds.), *Research in organizational behavior* (Vol. 21, pp. 201–246). Greenwich, CT: JAI.

Tyler, T., & Bies, R. J. (1990). Beyond formal procedures: The interpersonal context of procedural justice. In J. Carroll (Ed.), *Applied social psychology and organizational settings* (pp. 77–98). Hillsdale, NJ: Lawrence Erlbaum Associates.

Tyler, T. R., & Blader, S. L. (2000). *Cooperation in groups: Procedural justice, social identity, and behavioral engagement*. Philadelphia: Psychology Press.

Tyler, T. R., & Lind, E. A. (1992). A relational model of authority in groups. In M. P. Zanna (Ed.), *Advances in experimental social psychology* (Vol. 25, pp. 115–191). San Diego, CA: Academic.

Van den Bos, K. (2001a). Fairness heuristic theory: Assessing the information to which people are reacting has a pivotal role in understanding organizational justice. In S. Gilliland, D. Steiner, & D. Skarlicki (Eds.), *Theoretical and cultural perspectives on organizational justice* (pp. 63–84). Greenwich, CT: Information Age.

Van den Bos, K, (2001b). Uncertainty management: The influence of uncertainty salience on reactions to perceived procedural fairness. *Journal of Personality and Social Psychology, 80*, 931–941.

Van den Bos, K., Lind, E. A., Vermunt, R., & Wilke, H. A. M. (1997). How do I judge my outcome when I do not know the outcome of others? The psychology of the fair process effect. *Journal of Personality and Social Psychology, 72*, 1034–1046.

Van den Bos, K., Lind, E. A., & Wilke, H. A. M. (2001). The psychology of procedural and distributive justice viewed from the perspective of fairness heuristic theory. In R. Cropanzano (Ed.), *justice in the workplace: Vol. 2. From theory to practice* (pp. 49–66). Mahwah, NJ: Lawrence Erlbaum Associates.

Van den Bos, K., Vermunt, R., & Wilke, H. A. M. (1997). Procedural and distributive justice: What is fair depends more on what comes first than on what comes next. *Journal of Personality and Social Psychology, 72*, 95–104.

Van den Bos, K., Wilke, H. A. M., & Lind, E, A. (1998). When do we need procedural fairness? The role of trust in authority. *Journal of Personality and Social Psychology, 75*, 1449–1458.

Van den Bos, K., Wilke, H. A. M., Lind, E. A., & Vermunt, R. (1998). Evaluating outcomes by means of the fair process effect: Evidence for different processes in fairness and satisfaction judgments. *Journal of Personality and Social Psychology, 74*, 1493–1503.

Van Prooijen, J. W., Van den Bos, K., & Wilke, H. A. M. (2001, September). *A group dynamics focus model of procedural justice*. Presented at the International Roundtable on Organizational Justice, Vancouver, British Columbia, Canada.

Vecchio, R. P., Griffeth, R. W., & Horn, P. W. (1986). The predictive utility of the vertical dyad linkage approach. *Journal of Social Psychology, 126*, 617–625.

Vroom, V. H. (1964). *Work and motivation*. New York: Wiley.

Welbourne, T. M., Balkin, D. B., & Gomez-Mejia, L. R. (1995). Gainsharing and mutual monitoring: A combined agency-organizational justice interpretation. *Academy of Management Journal, 38*, 881–899.

Whetten, D. A. (1989). What constitutes a theoretical contribution? *Academy of Management Review, 14*, 490–495.

White, M. M., Tansky, J. A., & Baik, K. (1995). Linking culture and perceptions of justice: A comparison of students in Virginia and South Korea, *Psychological Reports, 77*, 1103–1112.

Yukl, G., & Van Fleet, D. D. (1992). Theory and research on leadership in organizations. In M. D. Dunnette & L. M. Hough (Eds.), *Handbook of industrial and organizational psychology* (Vol. 3, pp. 147–197). Palo Alto, CA: Consulting Psychologists Press.